Entered
1 Feb '89

S0-CBZ-323

JUL 21 1987

LAW DEPARTMENT
NOT TO BE REMOVED

ECONOMIC ANALYSIS OF LAW

EDITORIAL ADVISORY BOARD

Little, Brown and Company
Law Book Division

A. James Casner, Chairman
Austin Wakeman Scott Professor of Law, Emeritus
Harvard University

Francis A. Allen
Edson R. Sunderland Professor of Law
University of Michigan

Clark Byse
Byrne Professor of Administrative Law, Emeritus
Harvard University

Thomas Ehrlich
Provost and Professor of Law
University of Pennsylvania

Richard A. Epstein
James Parker Hall Professor of Law
University of Chicago

E. Allan Farnsworth
Alfred McCormack Professor of Law
Columbia University

Geoffrey C. Hazard, Jr.
Nathan Baker Professor of Law
Yale University

Bernard Wolfman
Fessenden Professor of Law
Harvard University

ECONOMIC ANALYSIS OF LAW

THIRD EDITION

RICHARD A. POSNER

Judge, U.S. Court of Appeals for the Seventh Circuit; Senior Lecturer, University of Chicago Law School

LITTLE, BROWN AND COMPANY   BOSTON AND TORONTO

Copyright © 1986 by Richard A. Posner

All rights reserved. No part of this book may be reproduced in any form or by any electronic or mechanical means including information storage and retrieval systems without permission in writing from the publisher, except by a reviewer who may quote brief passages in a review.

Library of Congress catalog card no. 85-80152

ISBN 0-316-71438-0

Second Printing

MV

Published simultaneously in Canada by Little, Brown & Company (Canada) Limited

Printed in the United States of America

SUMMARY OF CONTENTS

TABLE OF CONTENTS

PREFACE

Perhaps the most important development in legal thought in the last quarter century has been the application of economics to an ever-increasing range of legal fields, including those at once so fundamental and apparently noneconomic as torts, criminal law, family law, procedure, and constitutional law. Beset as it has been by controversy wholly expectable concerning a movement that challenges not only the methodological but also the political predispositions of many traditional legal scholars as well as many law students, lawyers, and judges — derided as it has often been both as obvious and as obviously wrong — the economic analysis of law has nevertheless managed to attract steadily growing interest, both academic and practical, and to generate an expanding and improving literature.[1]

When the first edition of this book was published in 1973, there was neither textbook nor treatise on the application of economics to law. This book was, and is, both. Although still the only treatise, it is no longer the only textbook. There are now on the market a number of edited books of readings, mainly by lawyers, designed particularly for students;[2] two textbooks by economists;[3] and a law-and-economics casebook, also by an economist.[4] None of these books, however, attempts the breadth and depth of coverage of this one.

The basic choice in doing a textbook about the economics of law is structural: whether to use economic principles or legal principles to organize the book. If economic principles are used, legal principles are then appended as examples. Such an approach, whatever its other

1. For recent, though already somewhat outdated, surveys of the field, see C.G. Veljanovski, The New Law-and-Economics: A Research Review (1982); The Place of Economics in Legal Education, 33 J. Leg. Educ. 183 (1983).
2. See, e.g., Economic Foundations of Property Law (Bruce A. Ackerman, ed. 1975); The Economics of Contract Law (Anthony T. Kronman & Richard A. Posner, eds. 1979); Economics of Corporation Law and Securities Regulation (Richard A. Posner & Kenneth E. Scott, eds. 1980); Readings in the Economics of Law and Regulation (A.I. Ogus & C.G. Veljanovski, eds. 1984).
3. Werner Z. Hirsch, Law and Economics: An Introductory Analysis (1979); A. Mitchell Polinsky, An Introduction to Law and Economics (1983).
4. Charles J. Goetz, Cases and Materials on Law and Economics (1984).

merits, cannot convey an adequate sense of the integrated structure of legal principles and institutions. The law is a system; it has a unity that economic analysis can illuminate; but to see the unity you must study the system. This book tries to make the economic principles emerge from a systematic (although necessarily incomplete) survey of legal principles. A glance at the index will show that most topics in microeconomics (price theory)[5] are discussed in the book, although not in the same order as in an economics textbook. Since so much of the legal system is concerned with nonmarket behavior — with the family, crime, accidents, litigation, and much else that is remote from the conventional marketplace of economic theory — this book emphasizes the economics of nonmarket behavior more than is customary in a microeconomics text. In contrast to the heavily normative emphasis of most writing, both legal and economic, on law, the book emphasizes positive analysis: the use of economics to shed light on the principles of the legal system rather than to change the system.

The book presupposes no previous acquaintance by the reader with economics.[6] Law students with math block need not fear this book. The book presupposes no previous acquaintance with law, either; and although it will mean more to people who have studied at least some law than to those who have studied none, it can serve as an introduction to law for economists and other social scientists who would like to learn something about the legal system and perhaps do research on it.[7] Finally, the book is as I have said a treatise on the economic analysis of law, but of course a shorter and less thorough treatise than it would be if it had not been written primarily for students. Although for the most part a summary of ideas contained in previously published scholarship, my own and many others' (cited in the reference section at the end of each chapter), the present edition, like its predecessors, contains a significant amount of original analysis.

Those familiar with the previous editions may be surprised how extensive are the revisions that I have made for this one. But not only has a great deal of law-and-economics scholarship been produced since 1977 (the date of the second edition); my experience as a federal court of appeals judge since 1981 has stimulated me to explore applications of economics in fields I had not gone deeply into as a law professor or consultant, and has caused me to modify some of my ideas about other

5. The principles of economics, excluding special principles used to analyze aggregate economic phenomena such as inflation, unemployment, economic growth, and business cycles; those phenomena are the subject of macroeconomics.

6. Those wishing to develop an acquaintance would be well-advised to begin with Jack Hirshleifer, Price Theory and Applications (3d ed. 1984); also very worthwhile, but more difficult, are Gary S. Becker, Economic Theory (1971), and George J. Stigler, The Theory of Price (3d ed. 1966).

7. Where there is a good text, accessible to nonlawyers, on the law discussed in a chapter, I cite it (occasionally them) in the first footnote of the chapter.

fields. I hope the result is a better book; I know it is a longer one, and this leads me to make a suggestion about teaching and learning. The book is too long to be taught in a quarter or semester course. For such a course, which in a law school is best offered either in the second half of the first year or the first half of the second year, I suggest trying to cover only Parts I through III (basic economic principles, the common law, and the regulation of monopolies) plus VI (the legal process, including procedure). I hope, however, that the student who takes such a course will read the rest of the book on his own time, for he (or she) will find the other parts both an aid to understanding the fields of law that they discuss and a reinforcement of his understanding of the parts covered in the course.

A number of friends and colleagues were kind enough to read and comment on various chapters: Douglas Baird, Mary Becker, Walter Blum, Christopher DeMuth, Frank Easterbrook, Robert Ellickson, Daniel Fischel, Walter Hellerstein, James Krier, William Landes, Saul Levmore, Michael Lindsay, Sam Peltzman, Carol Rose, Andrew Rosenfield, Steven Shavell, George Stigler, Geoffrey Stone, Cass Sunstein, and Robert Willis. I am most grateful to them; to Dwight Miller, Keith Crow, and Richard Cordray for research assistance; to the Law and Economics Program of the University of Chicago Law School for defraying the cost of that assistance; to Robert Mrofka, for the idea behind Figures 13.2 and 13.3 in Chapter 13; to my wife, Charlene, for editorial assistance; and to the economists who have most shaped my thinking about economics — Gary Becker, Ronald Coase, Aaron Director, William Landes, and George Stigler.

Richard A. Posner

October 1985

ECONOMIC ANALYSIS OF LAW

PART I

LAW AND ECONOMICS:
AN INTRODUCTION

CHAPTER 1

THE NATURE OF ECONOMIC REASONING

This book is written in the conviction that economics is a powerful tool for analyzing a vast range of legal questions but that most lawyers and law students — even very bright ones — have difficulty connecting economic principles to concrete legal problems. A student takes a course in price theory and learns what happens to the price of wheat when the price of corn falls and to the price of grazing land when the price of beef rises, but he does not understand what these things have to do with free speech or accidents or crime or the Rule Against Perpetuities or corporate indentures. This book's design is to anchor discussion of economic theory in concrete, numerous, and varied legal questions; the discussion of economic theory in the abstract is confined to this chapter.

§1.1 Fundamental Concepts

Many lawyers think that economics is the study of inflation, unemployment, business cycles, and other mysterious macroeconomic phenomena remote from the day-to-day concerns of the legal system. Actually the domain of economics is much broader. As conceived in this book, economics is the science of rational choice in a world — our world — in which resources are limited in relation to human wants.[1] The task of economics, so defined, is to explore the implications of assuming that man is a rational maximizer of his ends in life, his satisfactions — what we shall call his "self-interest." Rational maximization should not be confused with conscious calculation. Economics is not a theory about consciousness. Behavior is rational when it conforms to the model of

§1.1 1. See Gary S. Becker, The Economic Approach to Human Behavior (1976), and for criticism of so broad a definition of economics, Ronald H. Coase, Economics and Contiguous Disciplines, 7 J. Leg. Stud. 201 (1978).

rational choice, whatever the state of mind of the chooser. And self-interest should not be confused with selfishness; the happiness (or for that matter the misery) of other people may be a part of one's satisfactions.

The concept of man as a rational maximizer of his self-interest implies that people respond to incentives — that if a person's surroundings change in such a way that he could increase his satisfactions by altering his behavior, he will do so. From this proposition derive the three fundamental principles of economics:

1. The first is the inverse relation between price charged and quantity demanded (the Law of Demand). If the price of steak rises by 10¢ a pound, and if other prices remain unchanged, a steak will now cost the consumer more, relatively, than it did before. Being rational and self-interested he will react by investigating the possibility of substituting goods that he preferred less when steak was at its old price but that are more attractive now because they are cheaper relative to steak. Many consumers will continue to buy as much steak as before; for them, other goods are not good substitutes even at somewhat lower relative prices. But some purchasers will reduce their purchases of steak and substitute other meats (or other foods, or different products altogether), with the result that the total quantity demanded by purchasers, and hence the amount produced, will decline. This is shown in Figure 1.1. Dollars are plotted on the vertical axis, units of output on the horizontal. A rise in price from p_1 to p_2 results in a reduction in the quantity demanded from q_1 to q_2. Equally, we could imagine quantity supplied falling from

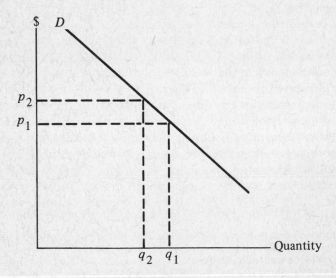

Figure 1.1

q_1 to q_2 and observe that the effect was to raise the price of the good from p_1 to p_2. Can you see why the causality runs in both directions?

This analysis assumes that the only change occurring in the system is the change in relative[2] price, or in quantity. Yet if, for example, demand were increasing at the same time that price was rising, the quantity demanded and supplied might not fall; it might even rise. (Can you graph an increase in demand? If not see Figure 9.5 in Chapter 9.) The analysis also assumes away the possible impact of a change in relative price on incomes. Such a change might have a feedback effect on the quantity demanded. Suppose that a reduction in a person's income will cause him to buy more of some good.[3] Then an increase in the price of the good will have two immediate effects on consumers of the good: (1) substitutes will become more attractive and (2) consumers' wealth will be reduced because the same income now buys fewer goods. The first effect reduces demand but the second (under the assumption of an inferior good) increases it and might conceivably, but improbably, outweigh the first.[4] The wealth effects of a change in the price of a single good are likely to be so slight as to have only a negligible feedback effect on demand; in other words, the substitution effects of a price change ordinarily exceed the income or wealth effects. So the latter can usually be ignored.

The Law of Demand doesn't operate just on goods with explicit prices. Unpopular teachers sometimes try to increase class enrollment by raising the average grade of the students in their classes; for, other things being equal, hard graders have smaller class enrollments than easy graders. The convicted criminal who has served his sentence is said to have "paid his debt to society," and an economist would find the metaphor apt. Punishment is, at least from the criminal's standpoint (why not from society's?), the price that society charges for a criminal offense. The economist is led to predict that an increase in either the severity of the punishment or the likelihood of its imposition will raise the price of crime and therefore reduce its incidence. The criminal will be encouraged to substitute other activity.

2. The consumers in our steak example — and the criminal — were assumed to be trying to maximize their utility (happiness, pleasure, satisfactions).[5] The same is presumably true of the producers of beef, though in the case of sellers one usually speaks of profit maximization rather than utility maximization. Sellers seek to maximize the difference between their costs and their sales revenues; but for the moment we

2. If the price *level* is rising for all goods (i.e., if there is inflation), there is no quantity effect (why not?).

3. Such a good is called by economists an "inferior" good. A good is a "superior" good if people buy more of it when their incomes rise. Otherwise it is a "normal" good.

4. This is the Giffin paradox; no well-authenticated real-world example of a "Giffin good" has been found.

5. We shall examine the concept of utility more critically in a moment.

are interested only in the lowest price that a rational self-interested seller would charge. That minimum is the price that the resources consumed in making (and selling) the seller's product would command in their next best use — the alternative price. It is what the economist means by the cost of a good, and suggests why (subject to some exceptions that need not trouble us here) a rational seller would not sell below cost. For example, the *cost* of making a lawn mower is the *price* the manufacturer must pay for the capital, labor, materials, and other resources consumed in making it. That price must exceed the price at which the resources could have been sold to the next highest bidder for them, for if the lawnmower manufacturer had not been willing to beat that price he would not have been the high bidder and would not have obtained the resources. We postpone the complication that is introduced when the sellers of a resource price it higher than *its* alternative price.

A corollary of the notion of cost as alternative price is that a cost is incurred only when someone is denied the use of a resource. Since I can breathe as much air as I want without depriving anyone of any of the air he wants, no one will pay me to relinquish my air to him; therefore air is costless.[6] So is a good with only one use. (Can you see why?) Cost to the economist is "opportunity cost" — the benefit forgone by employing a resource in a way that denies its use to someone else. Here are two more examples of opportunity cost: (1) The major cost of higher education is the forgone earnings that the student would make if he were working rather than attending school; this cost exceeds the tuition cost. (2) Suppose the labor, capital, and materials costs of a barrel of oil total only $2, but because low-cost oil is being rapidly depleted, a barrel of oil is expected to cost $20 to produce in 10 years. The producer who holds on to his oil for that long will be able to sell it for $20 then. That $20 is an opportunity cost of selling the oil now — although not a net opportunity cost, because if the producer waits to sell his oil, he will lose the interest he would have earned by selling now and investing the proceeds.

This discussion of cost may help dispel one of the most tenacious fallacies about economics — that it is about money. On the contrary, it is about resource use, money being merely a claim on resources.[7] The economist distinguishes between transactions that affect the use of resources, whether or not money changes hands, and purely pecuniary transactions — transfer payments. Housework is an economic activity, even if the houseworker is a spouse who does not receive pecuniary

6. That is not to say that *clean* air is costless. Cf. §3.7 *infra*.

7. Noneconomists attach more significance to money than economists. One of Adam Smith's great achievements in The Wealth of Nations was to demonstrate that mercantilism, the policy of trying to maximize a country's gold reserves, would impoverish rather than enrich the country that followed it.

compensation; it involves cost — primarily the opportunity cost of the houseworker's time. In contrast, the transfer by taxation of $1,000 from me to a poor (or to a rich) person would be, in itself, and regardless of its effects on his and my incentives, the (other) costs of implementing it, or any possible differences in the value of a dollar to us, costless; it would consume no resources. It would diminish my purchasing power, but it would increase the recipient's by the same amount. Put differently, it would be a private cost but not a social cost. A social cost diminishes the wealth of society; a private cost merely rearranges that wealth.

The distinction between opportunity costs and transfer payments, or in other words between economic and accounting costs, shows that cost to an economist is a forward-looking concept. "Sunk" (incurred) costs do not affect decisions on price and quantity. Suppose a plastic white elephant cost $1,000 to build ($1,000 being the alternative price of the inputs that went into making it) but that the most anyone will pay for it now that it is built is $10. Then the opportunity cost of the plastic white elephant is $10. The fact that $1,000 was sunk in making it will not affect the price at which it is sold, for if the seller takes the position that he will not sell the white elephant for less than it cost him to make it, the only result will be that instead of losing $990 he will lose $1,000.

The most celebrated application of the concept of opportunity cost in the economic analysis of law is the Coase Theorem.[8] The theorem (explored more fully in the next chapter) is that, if transactions are costless, the initial assignment of a property right will not determine the ultimate use of the property. Suppose that a farmer has a right not to have his crop destroyed by sparks from railroad locomotives; that the value of the crops to him is $100, based on the difference between revenue of $330 and labor and capital costs of $230, but the cost to the railroad of installing spark arresters is $110; and that transactions between railroads and farmers are costless. The real cost of the crops to the farmer is not $230; it is between $330 and $340, for it includes the price that the farmer could get by agreeing with the railroad not to use his property in a fire-sensitive way. Since the true cost of exercising his right to grow crops exceeds his revenues, he will sell that right, and the use of his land will be the same as if the railroad had had the right to emit sparks freely. In this example the initial assignment of the property right really does not dictate the use of the affected property.

The forces of competition tend to make opportunity cost the maximum as well as minimum price. (Can you see why our farmer-railroad example is an exception to this generalization?) A price above opportunity cost is a magnet drawing resources into the production of the good

8. See Ronald H. Coase, The Problem of Social Cost, 3 J. Law & Econ. 1 (1960).

until the increase in output drives price, by the Law of Demand, down
to the level of cost (why will competition not drive price below opportunity cost?). This process is illustrated in Figure 1.2. *D* represents the
demand schedule for the good in question and *S* the opportunity cost
of supplying a unit of output at various levels of output. Another name
for *S* is the industry marginal-cost curve. Marginal cost is the change
in total costs brought about by a one-unit change in output; in other
words, it is the cost of the last unit of output — the cost that would
be avoided by producing one unit less. (Marginal cost is considered
further in Chapters 9 and 10.) This definition should help you see why
the intersection of *D* and *S* represents the equilibrium price and output
under competition. "Equilibrium" means a stable point where unless
the conditions of demand or supply change there is no incentive for
sellers to alter price or output. Why would any point to either the left
or the right of the intersection represent an unstable, disequilibrium
price-output level?

Even in long-run competitive equilibrium, there is no assurance that
all sales will take place at prices equal to the opportunity costs of the
goods sold. This is implicit in the upward slope of the supply curve in
Figure 1.2. The fact that the cost of producing the good rises with
the quantity produced implies that its production requires some resource
that is inherently very scarce in relation to the demand, such as fertile
or well-located land. Suppose, for example, that the very best corn land
can produce corn at a cost of $1 a bushel, with the cost consisting
both of the direct costs of producing corn (labor, fertilizer, etc.) and
the value of the land in its next best use, and that the market price of

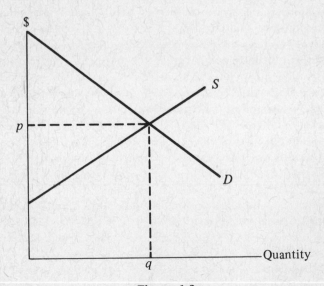

Figure 1.2

the corn produced on such land would be $10 a bushel if no other corn were produced. Clearly, there are incentives to expand production. Other, albeit inferior, land will be shifted into corn production, and this process will continue until price and marginal cost are equalized as in Figure 1.2. At this point the market price will equal the cost of the marginal producer. Suppose that cost is $2.50. All corn farmers will be selling corn at $2.50 a bushel, but those with the best land will be incurring a (social) opportunity cost of only $1.

The difference between the total revenues of the industry depicted in Figure 1.2 (that is, $p \times q$) and the total opportunity costs of production (the area under S) is called economic rent (not to be confused with rental). Rent for our purposes is simply a (positive) difference between total revenues and total opportunity costs. Who gets the rents in Figure 1.2? The owners of the good land. Competition between producers will eliminate any producer rents, leaving all the rents to be captured by the owners of the resource that generates them. If the owners of the land, or others, could increase the quantity of ideal land costlessly, competition among them would eliminate the scarcity that generates the rents, and with it the rents themselves. Thus under competition rents are earned only by the owners of resources that cannot be augmented rapidly and at low cost to meet an increased demand for the goods they are used to produce.

The very high incomes earned by a few singers, athletes, and lawyers contain economic rents that are due to the inherent scarcity of the resources that they control — a fine singing voice, athletic skill and determination, the analytical and forensic skills of the successful lawyer. Their earnings may greatly exceed their highest potential earnings in an alternative occupation even though they sell their services in a competitive market. A different kind of economic rent, discussed in Chapter 9, is earned by the monopolist, who creates an *artificial* scarcity of his product.

3. The third basic economic principle is that resources tend to gravitate toward their most valuable uses if voluntary exchange — a market — is permitted. Why did the manufacturer of lawn mowers in an earlier example pay more for labor and materials than competing users of these resources? The answer is that he thought he could use them to obtain a higher price for his finished good than could competing demanders; they were worth more to him. Why does farmer A offer to buy farmer B's farm at a price higher than B's minimum price for the property? It is because the property is worth more to A than to B, meaning that A can use it to produce a more valuable output as measured by the prices consumers are willing to pay. By a process of voluntary exchange, resources are shifted to those uses in which the value to consumers, as measured by their willingness to pay, is highest. When resources are being used where their value is highest, we may say that they are being employed efficiently.

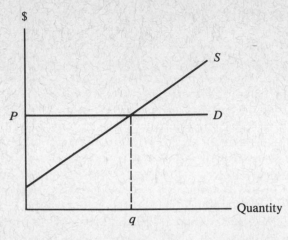

Figure 1.3

A methodologically useful although unrealistic assumption is that there are no unexploited profit (in the sense of rent, not cost of equity capital) opportunities. A profit opportunity is a magnet drawing resources into an activity. If the magnet doesn't work, the economist takes this as a sign not that people are dumb or have weird tastes or have ceased to be rational maximizers but that there are barriers to the free flow of resources. The barrier could be high information costs, externalities, inherent scarcities as in our rent-of-land example, or other economic conditions discussed in this book. If there are no such barriers, then in the market depicted in Figure 1.2 each seller will (as shown in Figure 1.3) confront a horizontal demand curve equal to *p,* even though the market as a whole faces a downward-sloping demand curve (which can be viewed as the sum of a very large number of individual-firm demand curves, each of which is only trivially downward-sloping, i.e., approximately horizontal).[9] The significance of a horizontal demand curve is that if the seller raises, however slightly, his price above the market price, his sales will go to zero; this is because, by raising his price and thereby opening a gap between price and marginal cost, he will create a profit opportunity that another seller will immediately snatch away from him.

9. It is not necessary to assume, however, that there is an infinitely large number of sellers in the market — only that entry is instantaneous. This is discussed more fully in Chapter 9. Notice that the firm's marginal cost curve is shown upward-sloping just like the industry's curve in Figure 1.2. The same things that cause the industry's curve to rise will cause the individual firm's curve to rise; and an additional factor is the increasing cost of information and control as a firm grows larger and more complex. See §14.1 *infra.* Notice that if a firm did not encounter rising marginal costs at some point, its output would be indeterminate. The relationship between costs and demand is discussed more fully in Chapter 12.

10

§1.2   Value, Utility, Efficiency

The previous section bandied about some pretty highly charged words —
value, utility, efficiency — about which we need to be more precise.
The economic value of something is how much someone is willing to
pay for it or, if he has it already, how much money he demands to
part with it. (These are not always the same amounts and that can cause
difficulties which we shall consider later.) "Utility" is used in two quite
different senses in economics, and it is essential to distinguish them.

First, it is used to mean the value of an expected cost or benefit as
distinct from a certain one. Suppose you were asked whether you would
prefer to be given $1 million, or a 10 percent chance of getting $10
million. Probably you would prefer the former, even though the expected
value of the two choices is the same: $1 million (= .10 × $10 million).
Probably, then, you are risk averse. Risk aversion is a corollary of the
principle of diminishing marginal utility of money, which just means
that the more money you have, the less additional happiness you would
get from another dollar. Diminishing marginal utility is more dramatically
illustrated by less versatile commodities than money — it is easy to picture in the context, say, of chairs, or lamps, or pet gerbils. Nevertheless
it should be apparent on reflection that another dollar means less to a
person as his wealth increases. Risk aversion is not a universal phenomenon; gambling illustrates its opposite, risk preference (can you see why?).
But economists believe, with some evidence (notably the popularity of
insurance), that most people are risk averse most of the time, though
we shall see that institutional responses to risk aversion such as insurance
and the corporation may make people effectively risk neutral in many
situations.

The use of the words "value" and "utility" to distinguish between
(1) an *expected* cost or benefit (i.e., the cost or benefit, in dollars, multiplied by the probability that it will actually materialize) and (2) what
that expected cost or benefit is worth to someone who is *not* risk neutral
obscures a more dramatic distinction between (1) value in a broad economic sense, which includes the idea that a risk-averse person "values"
$1 more than a 10 percent chance of getting $10, and (2) utility in
the sense used by philosophers of utilitarianism, meaning happiness.

Suppose that pituitary extract is in very scarce supply relative to the
demand and is therefore very expensive. A poor family has a child who
will be a dwarf if he does not get some of the extract, but the family
cannot afford the price and could not even if they could borrow against
the child's future earnings as a person of normal height; for the present
value of those earnings net of consumption is less than the price of
the extract. A rich family has a child who will grow to normal height,
but the extract will add a few inches more, and his parents decide to

buy it for him. In the sense of value used in this book, the pituitary extract is more valuable to the rich than to the poor family, because value is measured by willingness to pay; but the extract would confer greater happiness in the hands of the poor family than in the hands of the rich one.

As this example shows, the term efficiency, when used as in this book to denote that allocation of resources in which value is maximized, has limitations as an ethical criterion of social decisionmaking — although perhaps not serious ones, as such examples are very rare.[1] Utility in the utilitarian sense also has grave limitations, and not only because it is difficult to measure when willingness to pay is jettisoned as a metric. The fact that one person has a greater capacity for pleasure than another is not a very good reason for a forced transfer of wealth from the second to the first. Other familiar ethical criteria have their own serious problems. Although no effort will be made in this book to defend efficiency as the only worthwhile criterion of social choice, the book does assume, and most people probably would agree, that it is an important criterion. In many areas of interest to the economic analyst of law, such as antitrust, it is, as we shall see, the main thing that students of public policy worry about.

Some economists use a less controversial definition of efficiency that confines the term to purely voluntary transactions. Suppose A sells a wood carving to B for $10, both parties have full information, and the transaction has no effect on anyone else. Then the allocation of resources that is brought about by the transaction is said to be Pareto superior to the allocation of resources before the transaction. A Pareto-superior transaction is one that makes at least one person in the world better off and no one worse off. (In our example, it presumably made both A and B better off, and by assumption it made no one worse off.) In other words, the criterion of Pareto superiority is unanimity of all affected persons. Now this is a very austere conception of efficiency, with rather few applications to the real world, because most transactions (and if not a single transaction, then a series of like transactions) have effects on third parties, if no more than by changing the prices of other goods (how?). In the less austere concept of efficiency used in this book — the Kaldor-Hicks concept — if A values the wood carving at $5 and B at $12, so that at a sale price of $10 (indeed at any price between $5 and $12) the transaction creates a total benefit of $7 (at a price of $10, for example, A considers himself $5 better off and B considers himself $2 better off), then it is an efficient transaction, provided that the harm (if any) done to third parties (minus any benefit to them) does not exceed $7. The transaction would not be Pareto superior unless A and B actually compensated the third parties for any harm suffered

§1.2   1. See, for a further reference to the example, §5.4 infra.

by them. The Kaldor-Hicks concept is also and suggestively called potential Pareto superiority: The winners could compensate the losers, but need not (not always, anyway).

Because the conditions for Pareto superiority are almost never satisfied in the real world, yet economists talk quite a bit about efficiency, it is pretty clear that the operating definition of efficiency in economics is not Pareto superiority. When an economist says that free trade or competition or the control of pollution or some other policy or state of the world is efficient, nine times out of ten he means Kaldor-Hicks efficient, as shall this book.

The dependence of even the Pareto-superiority concept of efficiency on the distribution of wealth — willingness to pay, and hence value, being a function of that distribution — suggests a serious limitation of efficiency as an ultimate criterion of the social good. If income and wealth were distributed differently, the pattern of demands might also be different and efficiency would require a different deployment of our economic resources. Since economics yields no answer to the question of whether the existing distribution of income and wealth is good or bad, just or unjust[2] (although it may be able to tell us a great deal about the costs of altering the existing distribution, as well as about the distributive consequences of various policies), neither does it answer the ultimate question of whether an efficient allocation of resources would be socially or ethically desirable. Nor can the economist tell us. assuming the existing distribution of income and wealth is just, whether consumer satisfaction should be the dominant value of society. Thus, the economist's competence in a discussion of the legal system is limited. He can predict the effect of legal rules and arrangements on value and efficiency, in their strict technical senses, and on the existing distribution of income and wealth, but he cannot issue mandatory prescriptions for social change.

An important question, already alluded to, in the economic analysis of law is whether and in what circumstances an *involuntary* exchange may be said to increase efficiency. Even if efficiency is not defined as something that only a voluntary transaction can create — even if the Kaldor-Hicks concept is used instead — there is the evidentiary point that willingness to pay can be determined with great confidence only by actually observing a voluntary transaction. Where resources are shifted pursuant to a voluntary transaction, we can be reasonably sure that the shift involves an increase in efficiency.[3] The transaction would not have occurred if both parties had not expected it to make them better off. This implies that the resources transferred are more valuable in their new owner's hands. But many of the transactions either affected

2. A question we reconsider, however, in Chapter 16.
3. We cannot be completely sure because that would require that everyone affected by the transaction be a party to it, and this requirement is almost never satisfied.

or effected by the legal system are involuntary. Most crimes and accidents are involuntary transactions, and so is a legal judgment to pay damages or a fine. How is one to know when such transactions increase, and when they reduce, efficiency?

The answer is that one cannot know with anywhere near the same confidence with which one can judge voluntary transactions to be efficiency enhancing. But if we insist that a transaction be truly voluntary before it can be said to be efficient — truly voluntary in the sense that all potential losers have been fully compensated — we shall have very few occasions to make judgments of efficiency, for very few transactions are voluntary in that sense; we shall be back with Pareto superiority. An alternative approach, which is in the spirit of Kaldor-Hicks and is used very heavily in this book, is to try to guess whether, if a voluntary transaction had been feasible, it would have occurred. If, for example, the question were whether clean water was more valuable as an input into paper production than into boating, we might try to determine, using whatever quantitative or other data might be available to help us, whether in a world of zero transaction costs the paper industry would purchase from the boaters the right to use the water in question.

This approach attempts to reconstruct the likely terms of a market transaction in circumstances where instead a forced exchange took place — to mimic or simulate the market, in other words. Granted, a coerced exchange with the legal system later trying to guess whether the exchange increased or reduced efficiency is a less efficient method of allocating resources than a market transaction — where market transactions are feasible. But often they are not, and then the choice is between a necessarily rather crude system of legally regulated forced exchanges and the even greater inefficiencies of forbidding all forced exchanges, which could mean all exchanges, as all have some third-party effects.

Besides the evidentiary problem involved in applying the Kaldor-Hicks concept, there is a philosophical problem. In an explicit market, both parties to a transaction are compensated for entering into it; if one were not, the transaction would not be voluntary in even a loose sense. But when, for example, the legal system abates a nuisance on the ground that the value of the defendant's activity is less than the decline in the value of surrounding land caused by the nuisance, the defendant is not compensated. A legally coerced transaction is less likely to promote happiness than a market transaction, because the misery of the (uncompensated) losers may exceed the joy of the winners. And if legal efforts to simulate market results do not promote happiness, how can they be defended? What, in short, is the philosophical basis of the Kaldor-Hicks concept, corresponding to the utilitarian basis of Pareto superiority? One answer is that the things that wealth makes possible — not only luxury goods but also leisure and modern medicine, and even departments of philosophy — are major ingredients of most people's happiness, so that wealth maximization is an important — conceivably the only effective — social instrument of utility maximization. This answer ties efficiency to utilitarianism; answers that relate it to other ethical concepts will be considered in Chapters 8 and 16.

A somewhat more technical problem in the use of willingness to pay as the criterion of efficiency arises in cases where the subject matter of the transaction is a large part of one of the parties' wealth. Suppose I refuse a $100,000 offer for my house but then the government condemns it, paying me $50,000, which is its market value. Suppose further that the government would happily sell the house back to me for $100,000 — it is worth less than that to the government, though more than $50,000 — but I neither have nor can borrow $100,000. In whose hands is the house worth more — mine or the government's? In considering this conundrum, bear in mind that the term wealth as used by economists is not an accounting concept; it is measured by what people would pay for things (or demand in exchange for giving up things they possess), not by what they do pay for them. Thus leisure has value, and is a part of wealth, even though it is not bought and sold. We can speak of leisure as having an implicit or shadow price (computed how?). Even explicit markets create value over and above the price of the goods sold in them. Go back to Figure 1.2, and notice that if the quantity sold were smaller, price would be higher; evidently consumers would be willing to pay more for some units of the product, and so they obtain value from being able to buy them at the competitive price. This value, called consumer surplus (see §9.3 *infra*), too, is part of the wealth of society.

§1.3   The Realism of the Economist's Assumptions

To the reader having no previous acquaintance with economics or any other science, much of the discussion in the previous sections of this chapter may seem weird. In particular, he may be troubled by what appear to be the severely unrealistic assumptions that underlie economic theory. The basic economic assumption that human behavior is rational seems contradicted by the experiences and observations of everyday life, though the contradiction is less acute once one understands that the term rationality as used by the economist is objective rather than subjective, so that it would not be a solecism to speak of a rational frog. But it is true that the assumptions of economic theory are one-dimensional and pallid when viewed as *descriptions* of human behavior — especially the behavior of such unconventional economic "actors" as the judge, the litigant, the parent, the rapist, and others whom we shall encounter in the economic analysis of law. However, abstraction — reductionism, if you like — is of the essence of scientific inquiry. A scientific theory [1] must select from the welter of experience that it is trying to explain, and it is therefore necessarily unrealistic when compared directly to actual conditions. Newton's law of falling bodies, for example, is unrealistic in its basic assumption that bodies fall in a vacuum, but it is still a useful theory because it predicts with reasonable accuracy the behavior of a wide variety of falling bodies in the real world. Similarly, an economic theory of law will not capture the full complexity, richness, and confusion of the phenomena — criminal or judicial or marital or whatever — that it seeks to illuminate. But its lack of realism, far from invalidating the theory, is the essential precondition of theory. A theory that sought faithfully to reproduce the complexity of the empirical world in its assumptions would not be a theory — an explanation — but a description.

The real danger for positive economics in general, and the positive economic theory of law expounded in many places in this book (especially in Part II) in particular, is the opposite of reductionism: call it complicationism. When the economic analyst seeks to make a very simple economic model more complex, for example by bringing in (as we shall do many times in this book) risk aversion and information costs, he runs the risk of finding himself with too many degrees of freedom: that is, with a model so rich that no empirical observation can refute it — which means that no observation can support it, either.

All this is not to suggest that the analyst has a free choice of assumptions. An important test of a theory is its ability to explain reality. If it does a lousy job, the reason may be that its assumptions are insufficiently realistic; but we need not try to evaluate the assumptions directly in order to evaluate it. Judged by the test of explanatory power, economic theory must be judged a significant, although only partial, success (implying that the assumption of rational maximizing, properly understood, is not so unrealistic as the noneconomist might at first think). Many examples can be given of the ability of economic theory to predict correctly how people will behave in response to changes in their environment.[2] The examples are not limited to explicit markets, the conventional domain of economics. They involve education and the family,[3] and the law itself, where, as we shall see, economic theory has

§1.3   1. And positive economics *is* a scientific discipline. See Alexander Rosenberg, Microeconomic Laws: A Philosophical Analysis (1976).

2. Two examples discussed in this book are the response of the demand for labor to increases in the minimum wage and the behavior of investors. See §11.6 and Chapter 15 *infra.*

3. See, e.g., Education, Income, and Human Behavior (F. Thomas Juster ed. 1976); Household Production and Consumption (Nestor E. Terleckyj ed. 1975); Michael Grossman, The Demand for Health (Natl. Bureau Econ. Res. 1972); Gary S. Becker, Introduction, in The Economic Approach to Human Behavior 3 (1976).

been shown to have surprising explanatory power with respect to the behavior of criminals, prosecutors, common law judges, and other participants in the legal system.

Suggested Readings

1. Bruce J. Caldwell, Beyond Positivism: Economic Methodology in the Twentieth Century (1982).
2. Jules L. Coleman, The Economic Analysis of Law, 24 Nomos 83 (1982).
3. Milton Friedman, The Methodology of Positive Economics, in his Essays in Positive Economics 3 (1953).
4. Jack Hirshleifer, Price Theory and Applications (3d ed. 1984).
5. Frank H. Knight, The Economic Organization (1933).
6. Thomas C. Schelling, Choice and Consequence, ch. 1 (1984).
7. George J. Stigler, The Theory of Price, ch. 2 (3d ed. 1966).
8. The Philosophy of Economics: An Anthology (Daniel M. Hausman ed. 1984).

Problems

1. Would economics be worth studying if resources were not scarce? Can contemporary U.S. society be described as one of scarcity? It is said from time to time that there is a scarcity of doctors, or gasoline, or something else. How do these episodes differ from the scarcity of all valuable goods?
2. What determines human wants? Is that an economic question? Are human wants insatiable? How is this question relevant to economics?
3. Suppose all people were unselfish, benevolent, and altruistic. Would economics be less relevant to social ordering? How does the benevolent individual allocate resources? Might he use the market — that is, sell to the highest bidder — rather than give goods away? Why?
4. The market is only one method of directing the allocation of resources to various uses. Another might be administrative decisions by a governmental body. How would you expect these methods to differ?
5. One of the costs of punishing bribery is higher wages for government employees. Explain.
6. Explain how a buffet meal in a restaurant illustrates the concept of marginal cost.
7. It is often said both that litigation costs too much and that there is too much of it. Under what assumptions can both propositions be true without violating economic logic?

CHAPTER 2

THE ECONOMIC APPROACH TO LAW

§2.1 Its History

Until 25 years ago economic analysis of law was almost synonymous with economic analysis of antitrust law, though there was also important economic work on taxation (e.g., by Henry Simons), corporations (e.g., by Henry Manne), and public utility and common carrier regulation (e.g., by Ronald Coase). The records in antitrust cases provided a rich mine of information about business practices, and economists set about to discover the economic rationales and consequences of such practices. Their discoveries had implications for legal policy, of course, but basically what they were doing was no different from what economists traditionally have done — trying to explain the behavior of explicit economic markets.

The economic analysis of antitrust and related problems of explicitly economic regulation remains a thriving field, and the important recent advances in our knowledge in these areas receive considerable attention in this book. However, the hallmark of the "new" law and economics — the law and economics that is new within the last 25 years — is the application of the theories and empirical methods of economics to the legal system across the board — to common law fields such as torts, contracts, restitution, admiralty, and property; the theory and practice of punishment; civil, criminal, and administrative procedure; the theory of legislation and regulation; law enforcement and judicial administration; and even constitutional law, primitive law, and jurisprudence.

The new law and economics may be dated somewhat arbitrarily from the beginning of the 1960s, when Guido Calabresi's first article on torts and Ronald Coase's article on social cost were published.[1] These were

§2.1   1. Guido Calabresi, Some Thoughts on Risk Distribution and the Law of Torts, 70 Yale L.J. 499 (1961); Ronald H. Coase, The Problem of Social Cost, 3 J. Law & Econ. 1 (1960).

the first modern[2] attempts to apply economic analysis *systematically* to areas of law that do not avowedly regulate economic relationships. One can find earlier glimmerings of an economic approach to the problems of accident and nuisance law that Calabresi and Coase discussed,[3] especially in the work of Pigou,[4] which provided a foil for Coase's analysis; but the earlier work had made no impact on scholarship related to law.

Coase's article introduced the Coase Theorem, which we met in Chapter 1, and, more broadly, established a framework for analyzing the assignment of property rights and liability in economic terms. This opened a vast field of legal doctrine to fruitful economic analysis.[5] An important although for a time neglected feature of Coase's article was its implications for the positive economic analysis of legal doctrine. Coase suggested that the English law of nuisance had an implicit economic logic. Later writers have generalized this insight and argued that many of the doctrines and institutions of the legal system are best understood and explained as efforts to promote the efficient allocation of resources — a major theme of this book.

A list of the founders of the "new" law and economics would be seriously incomplete without the name of Gary Becker. Becker's insistence on the relevance of economics to a surprising range of nonmarket behavior (including charity and love), as well as his specific contributions to the economic analysis of crime, racial discrimination, and marriage and divorce, opened to economic analysis large areas of the legal system not reached by Calabresi's and Coase's studies of property rights and liability rules.[6]

§2.2   Normative and Positive Economic Analysis of Law

Subsequent chapters will show how the insights of Coase, Calabresi, Becker, and other pioneers have been generalized, empirically tested,

---

2. Important work on the economics of criminal law was done in the eighteenth and early nineteenth centuries by Beccaria and Bentham — and remains well worth reading today. See Cesare Beccaria, On Crimes and Punishments (Henry Paolucci trans. 1963 [1764]); Jeremy Bentham, An Introduction to the Principles of Morals and Legislation, in 1 Works of Jeremy Bentham 1, 81-154 (John Bowring ed. 1843); Jeremy Bentham, Principles of Penal Law, in 1 id. at 365.

3. See William M. Landes & Richard A. Posner, The Positive Economic Theory of Tort Law, 15 Ga. L. Rev. 851, 852-854 (1981), for examples.

4. See A.C. Pigou, The Economics of Welfare, ch. 9 (4th ed. 1932).

5. The modern literature on property rights also reflects, however, the influence of Frank Knight's important early work, Some Fallacies in the Interpretation of Social Cost, 38 Q.J. Econ. 582 (1924); see §3.1 *infra*.

6. For the character of Becker's contributions to economics, see Gary S. Becker, The Economic Approach to Human Behavior (1976).

and integrated with the insights of the "old" (and also rapidly evolving) law and economics to create an economic theory of law with growing explanative power and empirical support. The theory has normative as well as positive aspects. For example, although as noted in Chapter 1 the economist cannot tell society whether it should seek to limit theft, the economist can show that it would be inefficient to allow unlimited theft and can thus clarify a value conflict by showing how much of one value — efficiency — must be sacrificed to achieve another. Or, taking a goal of limiting theft as a given, the economist may be able to show that the means by which society has attempted to attain that goal are inefficient — that society could obtain more prevention, at lower cost, by using different methods. If the more efficient methods did not impair any other values, they would be socially desirable even if efficiency were low on the totem pole of social values.

As for the positive role, which explains legal rules and outcomes as they are rather than changing them to make them better, we shall see in subsequent chapters that many areas of the law, especially but by no means only the great common law fields of property, torts, crimes, and contracts, bear the stamp of economic reasoning. Although few judicial opinions contain explicit references to economic concepts, often the true grounds of legal decision are concealed rather than illuminated by the characteristic rhetoric of opinions. Indeed, legal education consists primarily of learning to dig beneath the rhetorical surface to find those grounds, many of which may turn out to have an economic character. Remember how broadly economics was defined in Chapter 1. It would not be surprising to find that legal doctrines rest on inarticulate gropings toward efficiency, especially when we bear in mind that many of those doctrines date back to the late eighteenth and the nineteenth century, when a *laissez faire* ideology based on classical economics was the dominant ideology of the educated classes in society.

The efficiency theory of the common law is not that *every* common law doctrine and decision is efficient. That would be completely unlikely, given the difficulty of the questions that the law wrestles with and the nature of judges' incentives. The theory is that the common law is best (not perfectly) explained as a system for maximizing the wealth of society. Statutory or constitutional as distinct from common law fields are less likely to promote efficiency, yet even they as we shall see are permeated by economic concerns and illuminated by economic analysis.

But, it may be asked, do not the lawyer and the economist approach the same case in such different ways as to suggest a basic incompatibility between law and economics? X is shot by a careless hunter, Y. The only question in which the parties and their lawyers are interested and the only question decided by the judge and jury is whether the cost of the injury should be shifted from X to Y, whether it is "just" or "fair" that X should receive compensation. X's lawyer will argue that it is just that X be compensated since Y was at fault and X blameless. Y's lawyer may argue that X was also careless and hence that it would be just for the loss to remain on X. Not only are justice and fairness not economic terms, but the economist is not (one might think) interested in the one question that concerns the victim and his lawyer: Who should bear the costs of *this* accident? To the economist, the accident is a closed chapter. The costs that it inflicted are sunk. The economist is interested in methods of preventing future accidents (that are not cost-justified) and thus reducing the sum of accident and accident-prevention costs, but the parties to the litigation have no interest in the future. Their concern is limited to the financial consequences of a past accident.

This dichotomy, however, is overstated. The decision in the case will affect the future and so it should interest the economist, because it will establish or confirm a rule for the guidance of people engaged in dangerous activities. The decision is a warning that if one behaves in a certain way and an accident results, he will have to pay a judgment (or will be unable to obtain a judgment, if the victim). By thus altering the prices that confront people, the warning may affect their behavior and therefore accident costs.

Conversely, the judge (and hence the lawyers) cannot ignore the future. Since any ruling of law will constitute a precedent, the judge must consider the probable impact of alternative rulings on the future behavior of people engaged in activities that give rise to the kind of accident involved in the case before him.[1] If, for example, judgment is awarded to the defendant on the ground that he is a "deserving," albeit careless, fellow, the decision will encourage similar people to be careless, a type of costly behavior.

Once the frame of reference is thus expanded beyond the immediate parties to the case, justice and fairness assume broader meanings than what is just or fair as between this plaintiff and this defendant. The issue becomes what is a just and fair result for a *class* of activities, and it cannot be sensibly resolved without consideration of the impact of alternative rulings on the frequency of accidents and the cost of accident precautions. The legal and economic approaches are not so divergent after all.

§2.3   Criticisms of the Economic Approach

The economic approach to law, both in its normative and in its positive aspects, has aroused considerable antagonism, especially, but not only,

§2.2   1. For a study of the U.S. Supreme Court's growing receptivity to this and other aspects of the economic approach, see Frank H. Easterbrook, The Supreme Court, 1983 Term, Foreword: The Court and the Economic System, 98 Harv. L. Rev. 4 (1984).

among academic lawyers who dislike the thought that the logic of the law might be economics. The major criticisms of the approach, as distinct from particular applications, will be discussed briefly here and should be kept in mind by the reader throughout the rest of this book.[1]

The most frequent criticism is that the normative underpinnings of the economic approach are so repulsive that it is inconceivable that the legal system would (let alone should) embrace them. This criticism may appear to confound positive and normative analysis, but it does not. Law embodies and enforces fundamental social norms, and it would be surprising to find that those norms were inconsistent with the society's ethical system. But is the Kaldor-Hicks concept of efficiency really so at variance with that system? Besides what we said in the first chapter, we shall see in Chapter 8 that, provided only that this concept is a component, though not necessarily the only or most important one, of our ethical system, it may be the one that dominates the law as administered by the courts because of the courts' inability to promote other goals effectively. And so long as efficiency is any sort of value in our ethical system, two normative uses of economics mentioned earlier — to clarify value conflicts and to point the way toward reaching given social ends by the most efficient path — are untouched by the philosophical debate.

Even more clearly, the ability of economic analysis to enlarge our understanding of how the legal system actually operates is not undermined by philosophical attacks on efficiency,[2] as distinct from attacks that deny that efficiency is a significant goal in fact in our society. If the participants in the legal process act as rational maximizers of their satisfactions — if the legal process itself has been shaped by a concern with maximizing economic efficiency — the economist has a rich field of study whether or not a society in which people behave in such a way, or institutions are shaped by such concerns, is a good society.

Another criticism of the economic approach to law, this one limited to the positive use of the approach, is that it doesn't explain every important rule, doctrine, institution, and outcome of the legal system. This criticism actually attacks a caricature of one component of the positive approach, the component being the hypothesis that the dominant — not exclusive — explanatory variable of the common law is wealth maximization. In any event, excessive emphasis on puzzles, anomalies, and contradictions is misplaced when speaking of so recent and yet so fruitful a field of scholarship. Bearing in mind the considerable explanatory

§2.3   1. For a lively attack on the economic approach to law as embodied in the first edition of this book, see Arthur Allen Leff, Economic Analysis of Law: Some Realism About Nominalism, 60 Va. L. Rev. 451 (1974). Other criticisms will be found in the works referenced at the end of this chapter. The criticism that the approach is reductionist was discussed in the first chapter.

2. As pointed out in C. Edwin Baker's review of the first edition of this book, The Ideology of the Economic Analysis of Law, 5 Philo. & Pub. Affairs 3, 47-48 (1975).

power that the economic approach to law has managed to achieve by the efforts of a small number of scholars in a short space of years, it is too soon to write off the endeavor as a failure. The attempt to do so also ignores an important lesson from the history of scientific progress: A theory, unless quite hopeless, is overturned not by pointing out its defects or limitations but by proposing a more inclusive, more powerful, and above all more useful theory.[3]

The economic theory of law is the most promising positive theory of law extant. While anthropologists, sociologists, psychologists, political scientists, and other social scientists besides economists also make positive analyses of the legal system, their work is thus far insufficiently rich in theoretical or empirical content to afford serious competition to the economists.[4] (The reader is challenged to adduce evidence contradicting this presumptuous, sweeping, and perhaps uninformed judgment.)

A related but more powerful criticism of positive economic analysis of law is that it ought to give an economic reason why judges might be led to use efficiency to guide decision. Efforts to meet this criticism are made in Chapters 8 and 19. We shall also see that the idea of the common law as efficiency-promoting is just one aspect of a broader positive economic theory that says that law has been shaped by economic forces, not always in the direction of greater efficiency. For example, Chapter 11 will argue that modern labor law, although explicable in economic terms, is not a system for maximizing efficiency; its goal, which is an economic although not efficient one, is to increase the incomes of union members by cartelizing the labor supply.

Another common criticism of the "new" law and economics — although it is perhaps better described as a reason for the distaste with which the subject is regarded in some quarters — is that it manifests a conservative political bias.[5] We shall see that its practitioners have found, for example, that capital punishment has a deterrent effect, legislation designed to protect consumers frequently ends up hurting them, no-fault automobile insurance is probably inefficient, and securities regulation may be a waste of time. Findings such as these indeed provide ammunition to the supporters of capital punishment and the opponents

3. This is one implication of Thomas S. Kuhn, The Structure of Scientific Revolutions (2d ed. 1970), and The Copernican Revolution: Planetary Astronomy in the Development of Western Thought (1959). On scientific methodology generally, see Ian Hocking, Representing and Intervening: Introductory Topics in the Philosophy of Natural Science (1983).

4. For some evidence, see Donald J. Black, The Mobilization of Law, 2 J. Leg. Stud. 125 (1973); Alan Hyde, The Concept of Legitimation in the Sociology of Law, 1983 Wis. L. Rev. 379; Robert Martinson, What Works? — Questions and Answers About Prison Reform, Public Interest 22 (Spring 1974).

5. Although not enough for some tastes. See, e.g., James M. Buchanan, Good Economics — Bad Law, 60 Va. L. Rev. 483 (1974); Richard A. Epstein, A Theory of Strict Liability, 2 J. Leg. Stud. 151, 189-204 (1973).

of the other policies mentioned. Yet economic research that provides support for liberal positions is rarely said to exhibit political bias. For example, the theory of public goods (see §16.4 *infra*) could be viewed as one of the ideological underpinnings of the welfare state but is not so viewed; once a viewpoint becomes dominant, it ceases to be perceived as having an ideological character. The criticism also overlooks a number of findings of economic analysts of law, discussed in subsequent chapters of this book — concerning right to counsel and standard of proof in criminal cases, bail, products liability, application of the First Amendment to broadcasting, social costs of monopoly, damages in personal-injury cases, and many others — that support liberal positions.

The economic approach to law is also criticized for ignoring "justice." In evaluating this criticism, one must distinguish between different meanings of the word. Sometimes it means distributive justice, which is the proper degree of economic equality. Although economists cannot tell society what that degree is, they have much to say that is highly relevant to the debate over inequality — about the actual amounts of inequality in different societies and in different periods, about the difference between real economic inequality and inequalities in pecuniary income that merely offset cost differences or reflect different positions in the life cycle, and about the costs of achieving greater equality. These matters are discussed in Chapter 16.

A second meaning of justice, perhaps the most common, is efficiency. We shall see, among many other examples, that when people describe as unjust convicting a person without a trial, taking property without just compensation, or failing to make a negligent automobile driver answer in damages to the victim of his negligence, this means nothing more pretentious than that the conduct wastes resources (see further §8.3 *infra*). Even the principle of unjust enrichment can be derived from the concept of efficiency (see §4.14 *infra*). And with a little reflection, it will come as no surprise that in a world of scarce resources waste should be regarded as immoral.

But there is more to notions of justice than a concern with efficiency. It is not obviously inefficient to allow suicide pacts; to allow private discrimination on racial, religious, or sexual grounds; to permit killing and eating the weakest passenger in the lifeboat in circumstances of genuine desperation; to force people to give self-incriminating testimony; to flog prisoners; to allow babies to be sold for adoption; to allow the use of deadly force in defense of a purely property interest; to legalize blackmail; or to give convicted felons a choice between imprisonment and participation in dangerous medical experiments. Yet all of these things offend the sense of justice of many (some almost all) modern Americans, and all are to a greater or lesser (usually greater) extent illegal. An effort will be made in this book to explain some of these prohibitions in economic terms, but most cannot be; there is more to justice than economics, a point the reader should keep in mind in evaluating normative statements in this book. There may well be definite although wide boundaries on both the explanative and reformative power of economic analysis of law. Always, however, economics can provide value clarification by showing the society what it must give up to achieve a noneconomic ideal of justice. The demand for justice is not independent of its price.

Suggested Readings

1. Ronald H. Coase, The Problem of Social Cost, 3 J. Law & Econ. 1 (1960).

2. Jules L. Coleman, Economics and the Law: A Critical Review of the Foundations of the Economic Approach to Law, 94 Ethics 649 (1984).

3. Duncan Kennedy, Cost-Benefit Analysis of Entitlement Problems: A Critique, 33 Stan. L. Rev. 387 (1981).

4. William M. Landes & Richard A. Posner, The Positive Economic Theory of Tort Law, 15 Ga. L. Rev. 851 (1984).

5. Arthur Allen Leff, Economic Analysis of Law: Some Realism About Nominalism, 60 Va. L. Rev. 451 (1974).

6. Richard A. Posner, A Reply to Some Recent Criticisms of the Efficiency Theory of the Common Law, 9 Hofstra L. Rev. 775 (1981).

7. Ethics, Economics, and the Law, 24 Nomos (1982).

8. Law, Economics, and Philosophy: A Critical Introduction with Applications to the Law of Torts, pt. 1 (Mark Kuperberg & Charles Beitz eds. 1983).

9. Symposium on Efficiency as a Legal Concern, 8 Hofstra L. Rev. 485, 811 (1980).

PART II

THE COMMON LAW

CHAPTER 3

PROPERTY[1]

This chapter begins our examination of the common law — a term that like many legal terms is ambiguous. It is used to mean the body of principles applied by the royal law courts of England in the eighteenth century (thus excluding equity and admiralty law but including some statutory law); the fields of law that have been created largely by judges as the by-product of deciding cases, rather than by legislatures; or any field of law shaped largely by judicial precedents. This part of the book concerns the common law mainly in its second sense, but excludes two important areas, procedure and conflict of laws, both of which are discussed later, in Chapter 21. Also discussed later are fields that could be considered common law in the third and broadest sense of the word, including important areas of constitutional law.

Common law in the second sense, in its substantive aspect, can be conceived in economic terms as having three parts:

(1) the law of property, concerned with creating and defining property rights, which are rights to the exclusive use of valuable resources;

(2) the law of contracts, concerned with facilitating the voluntary movement of property rights into the hands of those who value them the most; and

(3) the law of torts, concerned with protecting property rights, including the right to bodily integrity.

Fields such as admiralty, restitution, and commercial law, and even criminal law and family law, can be conceived as specialized subcategories of one or more of the fundamental fields. Although the law is much less neat than this typology suggests (and even in principle, as we shall see in §3.5 *infra*, property and tort overlap), it is useful in organizing thought and in bringing out the principal theme in this part of the book: the remarkable if imperfect congruence between the rules of

---

1. On the law of property, see Jesse Dukeminier & James E. Krier, Property (1981); Robert C. Ellickson & A. Dan Tarlock, Land-Use Controls: Cases and Materials, chs. 2-3, 6 (1981); Charles J. Meyers & A. Dan Tarlock, Water Resource Management (2d ed. 1980).

the common law and the principle of economic efficiency sketched in Chapter 1.

§3.1 The Economic Theory of Property Rights: Static and Dynamic Aspects

To understand the economics of property rights, it is first necessary to grasp the economist's distinction between *static* and *dynamic* analysis. Static analysis suppresses the time dimension of economic activity: All adjustments to change are assumed to occur instantaneously. The assumption is unrealistic but often fruitful; the attentive reader of Chapter 1 will not be too disturbed by a lack of realism in assumptions.

Dynamic analysis, in which the assumption of instantaneous adjustment to change is relaxed, is usually considered more complex and advanced than static analysis. So it is surprising that the economic basis of property rights was first perceived in dynamic terms. Imagine a society in which all property rights have been abolished. A farmer plants corn, fertilizes it, and erects scarecrows, but when the corn is ripe his neighbor reaps it and takes it away for his own use. The farmer has no legal remedy against his neighbor's conduct since he owns neither the land that he sowed nor the crop. Unless defensive measures are feasible (and let us assume for the moment that they are not), after a few such incidents the cultivation of land will be abandoned and society will shift to methods of subsistence (such as hunting) that involve less preparatory investment.

As this example suggests, legal protection of property rights creates incentives to use resources efficiently. Although the value of the crop in our example, as measured by consumers' willingness to pay, may have greatly exceeded its cost in labor, materials, and forgone alternative uses of the land, without property rights there is no incentive to incur these costs because there is no reasonably assured reward for incurring them. The proper incentives are created by parceling out mutually exclusive rights to the use of particular resources among the members of society. If every piece of land is owned by someone — if there is always someone who can exclude all others from access to any given area — then individuals will endeavor by cultivation or other improvements to maximize the value of land. Of course, land is just an example. The principle applies to all valuable resources.

All this has been well known for hundreds of years.[1] In contrast,

§3.1   1. See, e.g., 2 William Blackstone, Commentaries on the Laws of England 4, 7 (1766). And property-rights systems are prehistoric in their origins. See Vernon L. Smith, The Primitive Hunter Culture, Pleistocene Extinction, and the Rise of Agriculture, 83 J. Pol. Econ. 727 (1975).

The proposition that enforcing property rights will lead to a greater output is questioned by Frank I. Michelman in Ethics, Economics, and the Law of Property, 24 Nomos

the static analysis of property rights is little more than 50 years old.[2] Imagine that a number of farmers own a pasture in common; that is, none has the right to exclude any of the others and hence none can charge the others for the use of the pasture. We can abstract from the dynamic aspects of the problem by assuming that the pasture is a natural (uncultivated) one. Even so, pasturing additional cows will impose a cost on all of the farmers: The cows will have to graze more in order to eat the same amount of grass, and this will reduce their weight. But because none of the farmers pays for the use of the pasture, none will take this cost into account in deciding how many additional cows to pasture, with the result that more cows will be pastured than would be efficient. (Can you see an analogy to highway congestion?)

The problem would disappear if someone owned the pasture and charged each farmer for its use (for purposes of this analysis, disregard the cost of levying such a charge). The charge to each farmer would include the cost he imposes on the other farmers by pasturing additional cows, because that cost reduces the value of the pasture to the other farmers and hence the price they are willing to pay the owner for the use of the pasture.

The creation of exclusive rights is a necessary rather than sufficient condition for efficient use of resources: The rights must be transferable. Suppose the farmer in our first example owns the land that he sows but is a bad farmer; his land would be more productive in someone else's hands. Efficiency requires a mechanism by which the farmer can be induced to transfer the property to someone who can work it more productively; a transferable property right is such a mechanism. Suppose Farmer A owns a piece of land that he anticipates will yield him $100 a year above his labor and other costs, indefinitely. Just as the price of a share of common stock is equal to the present value of the anticipated earnings to which the shareholder will be entitled, so the present value of a parcel of land that is expected to yield an annual net income of $100 can be calculated and is the minimum price that A will accept in exchange for his property right.[3] Suppose Farmer B believes that he can use A's land more productively than A. The present value of B's

---

3, 25 (1982). He suggests that the farmer who knows that half his crop will be stolen may just plant twice as much. But this suggestion overlooks

  (1) the added incentive to theft that will be created by planting a larger crop, and the resulting likelihood that more than one-half of the larger crop will be stolen;

  (2) the unlikelihood that farming would be so much more profitable than substitute activities not entailing preparatory investment as to keep people in farming; and

  (3) the likelihood that the farmer, if he remained in farming, would divert some of his resources from growing crops to protecting them with walls, guards, etc.

    2. See Frank H. Knight, Some Fallacies in the Interpretation of Social Cost, 38 Q.J. Econ. 582 (1924).

    3. Discounting to present value is discussed in greater detail in §6.13 *infra*.

    The certainty with which A anticipates continuing to receive this return, the prevailing interest rate, his preference for or aversion to risk, and other factors will enter into his valuation of the property. Cf. §4.5 *infra*. We can ignore these refinements for now.

expected earnings stream will therefore exceed the present value calculated by A. Suppose the present value calculated by A is $1,000 and by B $1,500. Then at any price for the land between $1,000 and $1,500 both A and B will be made better off by a sale. Thus there are strong incentives for a voluntary exchange of A's land for B's money.

This discussion implies that if every valuable (meaning scarce as well as desired) resource were owned by someone (universality), ownership connoted the unqualified power to exclude everybody else from using the resource (exclusivity) as well as to use it oneself, and ownership rights were freely transferable, or as lawyers say alienable (transferability), value would be maximized. This leaves out of account, however, the costs of a property-rights system, both the obvious and the subtle ones.

An example will illustrate a subtle cost of exclusivity. Suppose our farmer estimates that he can raise a hog with a market value of $100 at a cost of only $50 in labor and materials and that no alternative use of the land would yield a greater net value — in the next best use, his income from the land would be only $20. He will want to raise the hog. But now suppose his property right is qualified in two respects: He has no right to prevent an adjacent railroad from accidentally emitting engine sparks that may set fire to the hog's pen, killing the hog prematurely; and a court may decide that his raising a hog on this land is a nuisance, in which event he will have to sell the hog at disadvantageous (why disadvantageous?) terms before it is grown. In light of these contingencies, he must reevaluate the yield of his land: He must discount the $100 to reflect the probability that the yield may be much less, perhaps zero. Suppose that, after discounting, the expected revenue from raising the hog (market value times the probability that it will reach the market) is only $60. He will not raise the hog. He will put the land to another use, which we said was less valuable;[4] the value of the land will fall.

But the analysis is incomplete. Removing the hog may increase the value of surrounding residential land by more than the fall in value of the farmer's parcel; or the cost of preventing the emission of engine sparks may be larger than the reduction in the value of the farmer's land when he switches from raising hogs to growing, say, fireproof radishes. But, the alert reader may wish to interject, if the increase in value to others from a different use of the farmer's land exceeds the decrease to him, let them buy his right: The railroad can purchase an easement to emit sparks; the surrounding homeowners can purchase a covenant from the farmer not to raise hogs; there is no need to limit the farmer's property right. But as we shall see (in §3.7 *infra*), the costs of effecting

---

4. The anticipated profit from raising the hog is now only $10 (the farmer's costs are $50). The next best use, we said, will yield a profit of $20.

a transfer of rights — transaction costs — are often prohibitive, and when this is so, giving someone the exclusive right to a resource may reduce rather than increase efficiency.

We could, of course, preserve exclusivity in a purely notional sense by regarding the property right in a given thing as a bundle of distinct rights, each exclusive; that is in fact the legal position. The economic point however is that the nominal property owner will rarely have exclusive power over his property.

§3.2   Problems in the Creation and Enforcement of Property Rights; Herein of Wild Animals, Treasure Trove, Intellectual Property, Privacy, and Other Exotica

Property rights are not only less exclusive but less universal than they would be if they were not costly to enforce. Imagine a primitive society in which the principal use of land is for grazing. The population of the society is small relative to the amount of land, and its flocks are small too. No technology exists for increasing the value of the land by fertilizer, irrigation, or other techniques. The cost of wood or other materials for fencing is very high, and, the society being illiterate, a system for publicly recording land ownership is out of the question. In these circumstances, the costs of enforcing property rights might well exceed the benefits. The costs would be the costs of fencing to keep out other people's grazing animals, and would be substantial. The benefits might be zero. Since there is no crowding problem, property rights would confer no static benefits, and since there is no way of improving the land, there would be no dynamic benefits either. It is therefore not surprising that property rights are less extensive in primitive than in advanced societies and that the pattern by which property rights emerge and grow in a society is related to increases in the ratio of the benefits of property rights to their costs.[1]

§3.2   1. There is a surprisingly extensive economic literature on the historical development of property-rights systems: for example, in the prehistoric, primitive, and ancient world (see Smith article in §3.1 *supra*, note 1, and discussion and references in Richard A. Posner, The Economics of Justice 179-182 (1981)); in the middle ages (see, e.g., Carl J. Dahlman, The Open Field System and Beyond: A Property Rights Analysis of an Economic Institution (1980)); and in the nineteenth-century American West (see, e.g., Terry L. Anderson & P.J. Hill, The Evolution of Property Rights: A Study of the American West, 18 J. Law & Econ. 163 (1975); Gary D. Libecap, The Evolution of Private Mineral Rights: Nevada's Comstock Lode (1978); John R. Umbeck, A Theory of Property Rights, With Application to the California Gold Rush (1981)). Though not a work of economics, William Cronon, Changes in the Land: Indians, Colonists, and the Ecology of New England (1983), contains a fascinating discussion of the development of property rights in colonial New England.

The common law distinction between domestic and wild animals illustrates the general point. Domestic animals are owned like any other personal property; wild animals are not owned until killed or put under actual restraint (as in a zoo). Thus, if your cow wanders off your land, it is still your cow; but if a gopher whose burrow is on your land wanders off, he is not your property, and anyone who wants can capture or kill him, unless he is tame — unless he has an *animus revertendi* (the habit of returning to your land). (Can you think of an economic argument for the doctrine of *animus revertendi*?)

The reason for the difference in legal treatment between domestic and wild animals is that it would be both difficult to enforce a property right in a wild animal and pretty useless; most wild animals, as in our gopher illustration, are not valuable, so there is nothing to be gained from creating incentives to invest in them. But suppose the animals are valuable. If there are no property rights in valuable fur-bearing animals such as sable and beaver, hunters will hunt them down to extinction, even though the present value of the resource will be diminished by doing so. The hunter who spares a mother beaver so that it can reproduce knows that the beavers born to her will almost certainly be caught by someone other than him (so long as there are many hunters), and he will not forgo a present gain to confer a future gain on someone else. Property rights would be desirable in these circumstances, but it is hard to see how a feasible scheme could be devised for enabling the hunter who decided to spare the mother beaver to establish a property right in her unborn litter; the costs of (effective) property rights would still exceed the benefits, though the benefits would now be substantial.

There are two possible solutions. One, which is the more common, is to use the regulatory powers of the state to reduce hunting to the approximate level it would be at if the animals were hunted at an optimal rate; this is an example of how regulation can be a substitute for property rights in correcting a divergence between private and social costs or benefits. The other solution is for one person to buy up the entire habitat of the animals; he will then regulate hunting on his property optimally because he will obtain all the gains from doing so.[2]

Another example of the correlation between property rights and scarcity is the difference in the water law systems of the eastern and western states of the United States. In the eastern states, where water is plentiful, water rights are communalized to a significant extent, the basic rule being that riparian owners (i.e., the owners of the shore of a body of water) are each entitled to make reasonable use of the water — a use that does not interfere unduly with the uses of the other riparians. In

2. On the economics of the fur trade, see Harold Demsetz, Toward a Theory of Property Rights, 57 Am. Econ. Rev. Papers & Proceedings 347, 351-353 (1967), one of the path-breaking articles in the "new" law and economics.

the western states, where water is scarce, exclusive rights can be obtained, by appropriation (use).

Now consider the example of things, often very valuable things such as the treasure in a shipwreck, which were once owned but have been abandoned. Here the general rule is finders keepers. In a sense this is the same rule as for wild animals. Ownership of the thing is obtained by reducing it to actual possession. Until then the thing is unowned (the unborn beavers, the abandoned ship), and it is this gap in owner-ship — this interval when no one has a property right — that is the source of the economic problem.

But the problem is slightly different in the two cases. In the case of wild animals the main problem is too rapid exploitation; in the case of abandoned property it is too costly exploitation. Suppose the treasure in the shipwreck is worth $1 million, and it will cost $250,000 to hire a team of divers to salvage it. Because the expected profit of the venture is so high, someone else may decide to hire his own team and try to beat the first team to it. A third and even a fourth may try, too, for if each one has the same chance (25 percent) of reaching the treasure first, then the expected value of the venture to each one ($1 million × .25) will still cover each one's expected cost. If four try, however, the cost of obtaining the treasure, $1 million, will be four times what it would have been if only one had tried.[3] Actually the net social loss from this competition will be less than $750,000, because the competition probably will result in the treasure's being found faster than if only one were trying, but the gain in time may be modest and not worth the additional expenditures that accelerated the search.

There would be no problem if the treasure had not been abandoned; for then the owner would simply have hired one of the four salvagers for $250,000. But when we call property abandoned in the legal sense, we mean that the cost of revesting the property in the original owner is prohibitive, either because he cannot be found at reasonable cost or he considers the property (perhaps incorrectly) to be worth less than the cost of finding or using it. The problem of too costly exploitation of a valuable resource, like the problem of too rapid exploitation, is rooted ultimately in the sometimes prohibitive costs of enforcing prop-erty rights.

The law can do something about the abandonment problem and to some extent has done so. The common law sometimes gives the first committed searcher for abandoned property a right to prevent others from searching so long as his search is conscientiously pursued. Another common law rule makes abandoned treasure trove (currency and bul-

3. The tendency of an expected gain to be translated into costs through competitive efforts is called rent-seeking, recurs many times in this book, and is the subject of a growing literature. See essays collected in Toward a Theory of the Rent-Seeking Society (James Buchanan, Robert Tollison & Gordon Tullock eds. 1980).

lion), if found, escheat to the government rather than becoming the property of the finder. This rule reduces the investment in finding to whatever level the government thinks proper; the government determines that level by determining how much reward to give the finder. In the case of currency, the optimal level is very low, perhaps zero. Finding money does not increase the wealth of society; it just enables the finder to have more of society's goods than someone else. The optimal reward may therefore be very low — maybe zero. The trend in the common law is to expand the escheat principle of treasure trove into other areas of found property and thus give the finder a reward rather than the property itself; this makes good economic sense.[4]

It might appear that nothing could be more remote from sunken treasure than patented inventions; and yet the economic problem created by patents is remarkably like that of abandoned property. Ideas are in a sense created but in another sense found. Suppose that whoever invents the widget will, if allowed to exclude others from its use by being granted a patent, be able to sell the patent to a manufacturer for $1 million. And suppose that the cost of invention is $250,000. We are in the same fix as with the sunken treasure. Others will try to be first to invent the widget. This competition will cause it to be invented sooner. But suppose it is invented only one day sooner; the value of having the widget a day earlier will be less than the cost of duplicating the entire investment in invention.

The law could decide not to recognize property rights in ideas, but then too few ideas would be discovered. The person who invented widgets might not be able to recoup his investment, since others who had not borne the costs of invention could underprice him without going broke. Also, inventive activity would be heavily biased toward inventions that could be kept secret, in just the same way that a complete absence of property rights would (as we saw in §3.1 *supra*) bias production toward things that involve minimum preparatory investment. So we have patents; but the law uses several devices to try to minimize the costs of duplicating inventive activity that a patent system invites. Here are four of them:

1. A patent expires after 17 years, rather than being perpetual. This reduces the value of the patent to the owner and hence the amount of resources that will be devoted to obtaining patents.

2. Inventions are not patentable if they are "obvious." The functional meaning of obviousness is, discoverable at low cost.[5] The lower the cost of discovery, the less necessary is patent protection to induce the discovery to be made, and the greater is the danger of overinvestment

4. There is a brief economic discussion of other types of finding in Werner Z. Hirsch, Law and Economics: An Introductory Analysis 21-23 (1979).

5. See Edmund W. Kitch, Graham v. John Deere Co.: New Standards for Patents, 1966 S. Ct. Rev. 293; Roberts v. Sears, Roebuck & Co., 723 F.2d 1324, 1344 (7th Cir. 1983) (*en banc*) (concurring and dissenting opinion).

if patent protection is allowed. If an idea worth $1 million costs $1 rather than $250,000 to discover, the amount of wasteful duplication from granting a patent will be greater, perhaps $249,999 greater.

3. Patents are granted early — before an invention has been carried to the point of commercial feasibility — in order to head off costly duplication of expensive development work.[6]

4. Fundamental ideas (the laws of physics, for example) are not patentable, despite their great value. Until the advent of costly atomic-particle accelerators, basic research generally did not require substantial expenditures, and patent protection might therefore have led to too much basic research. By confining patentability to "useful" inventions in rather a narrow sense, the patent law identifies (though only in a very crude fashion) inventions likely to require costly development before they can be brought to market. But the nonpatentability of basic discoveries, like the limited term of patents, probably reflects more than just a concern with costs of acquiring patents; there are also serious identification problems, as in the case of wild animals. An idea does not have a stable physical locus, like a piece of land. With the passage of time it becomes increasingly difficult to identify the products in which a particular idea is embodied; and it is also difficult to identify the products in which a basic idea, having many and varied applications, is embodied.

The costs of the patent system include, besides inducing potentially excessive investment in inventing, driving a wedge between price and marginal cost, with results explored in Part III of this book. Once an invention is made, its costs are sunk; in economic terms, they are zero. Hence a price that includes a royalty to the inventor will exceed the opportunity cost of the product in which the invention is embodied. This wedge, however, is analytically the same as the cost of a fence to demarcate a property right in land; it is an indispensable cost of using the property rights system to allocate resources.

The field of intellectual property, of which patent law is a part, provides many other interesting examples of the economics of property law. Take trademarks. It would make no economic sense to allow a person to take a word that is already part of the language and assert an exclusive right over it (why not?). But suppose a person invents a new word, such as "aspirin," to denote his product. He ought to be able to use the word exclusively as a product identifier. Otherwise he would have no incentive to develop a distinctive mark, yet such a mark is a form of valuable information to consumers. But should the right be absolute? Suppose that (as happened in the case of "aspirin," which was once a trademark of a German company named Bayer, "bandaid,"

---

6. See Edmund W. Kitch, The Nature and Function of the Patent System, 20 J. Law & Econ. 265 (1977). Notice analogy to the "Committed Searcher" principle mentioned earlier.

and many other common words) in time consumers come to use the word to denote the product generically, rather than a particular manufacturer's brand. Competitors will find it hard to tell the consumer what they are making unless they can use the word too. The trademark will now serve not just to identify a brand but to confer monopoly power on the owner of the mark. The total reward he will thus obtain from his invention will exceed the (normally modest) cost of thinking up a distinctive mark. The law's solution to this problem is to terminate the property right in a trademark when the mark becomes generic.

Consider now the fair use doctrine of the law of copyright, which, for example, allows a book reviewer to quote passages from the book without getting the permission of the copyright holder.[7] The value of the copyright is actually enhanced by this application of the doctrine, because the use the reviewer makes of the copyrighted material will usually result in more sales of the book than if the copyright owner tried to charge the reviewer. A related insight seems to lie behind the Supreme Court's recent decision in the video-recorder case,[8] where the fair use doctrine was applied to allow the sale of video recorders for use in recording television programs, even though no royalty was paid to the copyright owners for the privilege of recording.[9] Many people use their video recorders to record programs that are being shown at an inconvenient time or that they want to watch more than once. Such uses, like more conventional fair uses, benefit the copyright owner even though no royalty is paid. Most programs are bought by advertisers, and they pay more the more viewers they reach; by enlarging the effective audience for a program, a video recorder enables the copyright owner to charge more to the advertisers. However, since the evidence was compiled on which the Supreme Court based its decision, devices have come on the market that make it very easy for the owner of a video recorder to erase the commercials in a program he records before he watches it. What does this imply about the current economic validity of the Court's decision?

An interesting example of a property right in intangibles is the right of privacy, usually discussed as a branch of tort law, but functionally a branch of property law.[10] The earliest judicial recognition of an explicit right of privacy came in a case where the defendant had used the plain-

7. This and several other aspects of copyright law are discussed from an economic standpoint in Wendy J. Gordon, Fair Use as Market Failure: A Structural and Economic Analysis of the Betamax Case and Its Procedure, 82 Colum. L. Rev. 1600 (1982). Question: Why is the term of a copyright longer than that of a patent?

8. Sony Corp. of America v. Universal City Studios, Inc., 464 U.S. 417 (1984).

9. The defendants were the companies who made the recorders; they were sued as "contributory infringers." The people who bought the recorders at retail would have been "direct infringers." What is the economic rationale of the doctrine of contributory infringement?

10. See Posner, note 1 *supra*, chs. 9-10.

tiff's name and picture in an advertisement without the plaintiff's consent. Paradoxically, this branch of the right of privacy is most often invoked by celebrities avid for publicity; they just want to make sure they get the highest possible price for the use of their name and picture in advertising. It might seem that creating a property right in such use would not lead to any socially worthwhile investment but would simply enrich already wealthy celebrities. But this ignores the congestion (or static) rationale for property rights. Whatever information value a celebrity's endorsement has to consumers will be lost if every producer can use the celebrity's name and picture in his advertising.

The most interesting question in privacy law is whether a person should have a right to conceal embarrassing facts about himself — for example that he is an ex-convict. There is some, but not much, judicial support for such a right. The economist sees a parallel to the efforts of sellers to conceal hidden defects in their products. A person "sells" himself by trying to persuade potential transacting partners — an employer, a fiancée, even a casual acquaintance — that he has good qualities. Should he be encouraged to deceive these people, by being given a right to sue anyone who unmasks his hidden "defects"? At least on economic grounds, the answer seems to be no. It would be different if what was "unmasked" was not an embarrassing fact but a superb dinner recipe. We would then be in the realm of the trade secret, broadly defined, and the case would be no different in principle from the theft of a secret formula by a commercial rival. Here secrecy is a method of enforcing an informal property right and encourages an investment in a socially valuable idea. Concealing discreditable facts about a private individual, a firm, or a product does not.

§3.3 Property Rights in Law and Economics: The Case of Broadcast Frequencies

Thus far our focus has been tied pretty closely to the lawyer's idea of a property right (except regarding privacy), analyzed in economic terms. But often the legal and economic conceptions of property rights diverge. Here is an example from broadcasting.[1]

In the early days of radio, before comprehensive federal regulation, there was some judicial support for the proposition that the right to broadcast on a particular frequency in a particular area without interference from other users was a property right that could be protected by

§3.3   1. See Ronald H. Coase, The Federal Communications Commission, 2 J. Law & Econ. 1 (1959); Jora R. Minasian, Property Rights in Radiation: An Alternative Approach to Radio Frequency Allocation, 18 J. Law & Econ. 221 (1975).

injunction. With the creation in 1928 of the Federal Radio Commission (forerunner of the Federal Communications Commission), Congress took a different tack. Licenses authorizing the use of particular frequencies in particular areas were to be granted at nominal charge for renewable three-year terms to applicants who persuaded the commission that licensing them would promote the public interest. Congress expressly provided that licensees were to have no property rights in the use of the frequencies assigned them; the purpose of this provision was to foreclose any claim to compensation by a licensee whose license was withdrawn at the end of the three-year term.

Some of the objections that were advanced to the recognition of private property rights in the use of radio frequencies have an odd ring in an economist's ear. For example, it was said that if broadcasting rights could be bought and sold like other property, the broadcast media would come under the control of the wealthy. This confuses willingness to pay with ability to pay. The possession of money does not dictate the objects that will be purchased. The poor frequently bid goods away from the rich by being willing to pay more in the aggregate.

In the actual administration of the federal regulatory scheme for broadcasting, willingness to pay has played a decisive role and a system of *de facto* property rights has emerged. The desirable radio and television licenses have been awarded in comparative proceedings in which, much as in a system of property rights, willingness to pay — not for the license as such but for the legal representation and political influence that may determine the outcome — has decided in many cases who would control the resource at stake. But this method of initially assigning broadcast rights is less efficient than an auction or other sale. There is a good deal of uncertainty in the political regulatory process, so the applicant who pays his lawyers, lobbyists, etc., the most money — thereby indicating that he attaches the greatest value to obtaining the right — will often not receive it. Moreover, the social costs of this method of allocation are much greater than the costs of allocation through the market (how about the private costs?). Competition to obtain a license could dissipate the expected value of the license in legal, lobbying, and related expenses. (Where have we seen this problem before?) Participation in an auction of broadcast frequencies would not require costly legal and lobbying services, at least if rigging the auction can be prevented at low cost.

The failure to assign the right to the applicant who values it the most is only a transitory inefficiency. Once broadcast rights have been obtained in a licensing proceeding, they can be sold as an incident to the sale of the physical assets of the radio or television station. When a television station having a transmitter and other physical properties worth only a few hundred thousand dollars is sold for $30 million, one can be confident that the major part of the purchase price is payment for the right to use the frequency. Thus broadcast rights usually end up in the hands of those who are willing to pay the most money for them, even if the initial "auction" may not have allocated the rights efficiently.

The willingness of broadcasters to pay tens of millions of dollars for a right terminable after three years may seem peculiar. But broadcast licenses have been terminated only for serious misconduct, in much the same way that one can lose one's land for nonpayment of real estate taxes.

So in economic, although not in formal legal, terms there are property rights in broadcast frequencies. The right is obtained initially in a competition in which willingness to pay plays an influential, and quite possibly decisive, role. Once obtained, the right is transferable, though imperfectly, as we shall see in §3.10 *infra.* It is exclusive (interference with a licensee's use of his frequency will be enjoined). And it is for all practical purposes perpetual. The holder of the right is subject to various regulatory constraints but less so than a public utility, the principal assets of which are private property in the formal legal sense.

The concept of a *de facto* property right is of broad applicability. Some economists, indeed, use the term property right to describe virtually every device — public or private, common law or regulatory, contractual or governmental, formal or informal — by which divergences between private and social costs or benefits are reduced.[2] In a book on law, this usage can be confusing, so we shall generally confine our use of the term to formal property rights, recognizing however that they are just a subset of property rights in a broader economic sense.

§3.4   Future Rights

The rights system in broadcasting is not only costly and *sub rosa* but also incomplete in important respects. One is the difficulty of obtaining rights for future use, a problem we have already encountered in connection with shipwrecks and wild animals. To purchase vacant land with the intention of holding it for future development is a common type of transaction, while to disclose in an application for a broadcast license an intention to indefinitely defer starting to broadcast would guarantee denial. The same thing is true of water rights under the appropriation system that prevails in the western states: One acquires property rights in water by the actual diversion and use of a stream, and the right embraces only the amount of water actually used; a right may not be

---

2. For illustrations, see Armen A. Alchian & Harold Demsetz, The Property Right Paradigm, 33 J. Econ. Hist. 16 (1973), and essays in The Economics of Property Rights (Eirik G. Furubotn & Svetozar Pejovich eds. 1974).

obtained for exercise at a later date. But both the broadcast and water
limitations are circumvented to some extent, in the case of broadcasting
by deferring actual construction after the license has been obtained,
in the case of water by obtaining a preliminary permit that establishes
the applicant's prior right even though the construction of diversion
works and the use of the diverted water are postponed.

The hostility to recognizing rights for future use may be related to
the apparent "windfall" element that is present in both the broadcasting
and water contexts. In both cases the right is awarded without charge,
although the applicant may have gone to great expense to obtain it,
and often can be resold immediately at a considerable profit. This need
not be evidence of a true windfall; applicants as a group may just break
even. The windfall, however, would appear even larger if the profit
were obtained by someone who appeared not to be providing any service.

A related hostility, reflected in many corners of the law, is to speculation, the purchase of a good not to use but to hold in the hope that it
will appreciate in value.[1] Speculation performs a valuable economic function (as we shall see in §4.9 *infra*) by helping make prices reflect accurately the conditions of supply and demand. In the case of land, water,
and broadcast frequencies — or fur-bearing animals — the speculator
can (if permitted) perform the additional function of optimizing the
use of resources over time. But in any event purchases for future use
need not be speculative; they can be the opposite of speculative — hedging. A farmer may know that he will need more water for irrigation in
a few years, and rather than take the risk of changes in the price of
water he signs a contract now, at a fixed price, for future delivery of a
specified quantity of the water. (Hence the seller will be speculating
on future changes in the price of water — speculation facilitates hedging!) If such sales are forbidden, the farmer may decide to use more
water now than he really needs, just to be sure of having a right to
the water in the future when he will need it. The main effect of forbidding
purchases of water or broadcast frequencies or oyster beds for future
use is to encourage uneconomical uses, uses not to meet a demand
but to stake a claim.

§3.5   Incompatible Uses

As suggested in our hog hypothetical, and developed here at greater
length, property rights aren't really exclusive, in the sense of giving

§3.4   1. Or the sale of a good in the expectation that its value will decline, as in
short selling of stocks. An example is given in this paragraph.

the owner of a resource the absolute right to do with it what he will and exclude the whole world from any participation or say in the use of the resource. Absolute rights would conflict. If a railroad is to enjoy the exclusive use of its right of way, it must be permitted to emit engine sparks without legal limitation. The value of its property will be impaired otherwise. But if it is permitted to do that, the value of adjacent farmland will be reduced because of the fire hazard from the sparks. Is the emission of sparks an incident of the railroad's property right (i.e., part of his bundle of rights) or an invasion of the farmer's property right (or bundle)?

Before answering this question, we must ask whether anything turns on the answer, which in turn will require us to consider more closely the Coase Theorem of Chapter 1. Suppose that the right to emit sparks, by enabling the railroad to dispense with costly spark-arresting equipment, would increase the value of the railroad's right of way by $100 but reduce the value of the farm by $50, by preventing the farmer from growing crops close to the tracks. If the farmer has a legal right to be free from engine sparks, the railroad will offer to pay, and the farmer will accept, compensation for the surrender of his right; since the right to prevent spark emissions is worth only $50 to the farmer but imposes costs of $100 on the railroad, a sale of the farmer's right at any price between $50 and $100 will make both parties better off. If instead of the farmer's having a right to be free from sparks the railroad has a right to emit sparks, no transaction will occur. The farmer will not pay more than $50 for the railroad's right and the railroad will not accept less than $100. Thus, whichever way the legal right is assigned initially, the result is the same: The railroad emits sparks and the farmer moves his crops.

The principle is not affected by reversing the numbers. Assume that the right to emit sparks would increase the value of the railroad's property by only $50 but would reduce the value of the farmer's property by $100. If the railroad has a right to emit sparks, the farmer will offer to pay and the railroad will accept some price between $50 and $100 for the surrender of the railroad's right. If instead the farmer has a right to be free from emissions, there will be no transaction, since the farmer will insist on a minimum payment of $100 while the railroad will pay no more than $50. So, as Coase showed, whatever the relative values of the competing uses, the initial assignment of legal rights will not determine which use ultimately prevails.[1]

§3.5 1. See Ronald H. Coase, The Problem of Social Cost, 3 J. Law & Econ. 1 (1960). Coase's article makes three other important points, which are sometimes overlooked, relating to the case in which the costs of transferring the property right are so high that a voluntary transfer is not feasible:

(1) Placing liability on the party who in some crude sense "causes" the damage, i.e., the active party (the railroad in our example), may not produce the efficient solution to the conflict. The reader can verify this by referring to our first example and

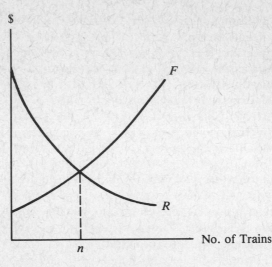

Figure 3.1

The operation of the Coase Theorem is depicted graphically in Figure 3.1. The curve labeled R shows the railroad's marginal revenue as a function of the number of trains it runs each day. The curve is declining

---

assuming that the farmer has the property right and, because of heavy transaction costs, cannot transfer it to the railroad.

(2) The common law of nuisance can be understood as an attempt to increase the value of resource use by assigning the property right to the party to a conflicting land use in whose hands the right would be most valuable.

(3) In deciding whether government intervention in the economic system is appropriate, it is not enough to demonstrate that the market would operate imperfectly without intervention; government also operates imperfectly. What is necessary is a comparison between the actual workings of the market and of government in the particular setting.

Two refinements of the Coase Theorem should be mentioned here:

(1) The initial assignment of rights, even where transaction costs are zero so that efficiency is not affected, may affect the relative wealth of the parties, and this may affect the use of resources in two ways: (a) If the parties do not spend their money in identical ways, a shift of wealth between them will alter demand, however slightly, for the various goods and services that they buy. Cf. §1.1 *supra.* (b) If the value of the right is a large fraction of the wealth of either party, where the right ends up may depend on how the initial assignment is made. The extreme example of this problem (which was mentioned in §1.2 *supra*) is the right to a barrel of water in a desert. See E.J. Mishan, Pareto Optimality and the Law, 19 Oxford Econ. Papers (n.s.) 255 (1967). Neither point, however, undermines Coase's conclusion that efficiency is unaffected by the rule of liability if transaction costs are zero.

(2) Transaction costs are never zero. In fact they may be quite high in two-party transactions, as we shall see many times in this book, although generally the costs of a transaction rise with the number of parties to the transaction — perhaps exponentially. The formula for the number of links required to join all members of a set of n members is suggestive in this connection: $n(n-1)/2$. Although transaction costs are never zero, the Coase Theorem should describe reality whenever the transaction cost is less than the value of the transaction to the parties.

because each additional train is assumed to contribute less net revenue to the railroad than the train before. The curve labeled F shows the farmer's marginal cost of crop damage, also as a function of the number of trains. It rises as the number of trains rises, on the assumption that the farmer can adjust to some spark damage but that each additional train is more destructive. (Must F and R be assumed to be falling and rising, respectively?) Changing the number of trains is assumed to be the only way of changing the amount of crop damage. Whether or not the railroad is liable for crop damage, the number of trains operated each day will be n, if transaction costs are zero. To the left of n the railroad can add more to its revenues by running additional trains than the farmer is hurt, so of course the railroad will increase the number of trains. To the right of n, where reducing the number of trains would add more to the farmer's net revenues than it would subtract from the railroad's, the farmer will pay the railroad to reduce the number of trains to n. The number will be the same if the farmer has the legal right to be free from crop damages, rather than the railroad the right to emit sparks. To the right of n, the farmer will sue the railroad to reduce the number of trains; to the left of n the railroad will pay the farmer to surrender a portion of his right to be free from damage.

It does not follow, however, that the initial assignment of rights is completely immaterial from an efficiency standpoint. Since transactions are not costless, efficiency is promoted by assigning the legal right to the party who would buy it — the railroad in our first hypothetical situation and the farmer in the second — if it were assigned initially to the other party. Moreover, as we shall see, the cost of transacting is sometimes so high relative to the value of the transaction as to make transacting uneconomical. In such a case the initial assignment of rights is final.

Unfortunately, assigning the property right to the party to whom it is more valuable is incomplete as an economic solution. It ignores the costs of administering the property rights system, which might be lower under a simpler criterion for assigning rights (a matter taken up in §§20.4 and 21.5 *infra*); and it is difficult to apply in practice. The engine-spark example was grossly oversimplified in that it permitted only two property right assignments, a right to emit sparks and a right to be free from sparks. If administrative (mainly information) costs are disregarded, the combined value of the farmer's and the railroad's property might be maximized by a more complex definition of property rights, such as one that permitted the farmer to grow one kind of crop but not another, to plant nothing within 200 feet of the tracks, and to have no wooden buildings within 250 feet of the tracks, while permitting the railroad to emit sparks only up to a specified level. The possible combinations are endless, and it is unrealistic to expect courts to discover the optimum one — and uneconomical to make them search too hard for it! But in most cases, and without excessive cost, they may be able to approximate the optimum definition of property rights, and these approximations may guide resource use more efficiently than would an economically random assignment of property rights.

Some examples may help to clarify this fundamental point. Under English common law, a landowner who built in such a way as to so block his neighbor's window that the neighbor would need artificial light to be able to read in the half of the room nearest the window was considered to have infringed the neighbor's property rights, provided that the neighbor had had unobstructed access to light for 20 years (why this qualification?). Consider the consequences if the property right had instead been given to the building party. Ordinarily the cost to the person whose windows were blocked would exceed the cost to the other person of setting back his wall slightly (all that would be necessary, given how limited the right was), so the former would buy the right. The assignment of the right to him in the first instance avoids the transaction and its attendant costs.[2] But the courts did not extend the rule to protect distant views. If A had a house on a hill with a beautiful prospect, and B built a house that ruined the prospect, A could not claim an invasion of his property rights even if the value of his property had fallen. Here the presumption of relative values is reversed. A house with a view commands a large land area. The values that would be created by developing such an area are likely to exceed the loss of value to the one landowner whose view is impaired.

Another common law rule (conventionally a rule of tort law, but as it defines a property owner's rights it can equally be viewed as a rule of property law) was that a railroad owed no duty of care to people using the tracks as paths (except at crossings). The cost to these "trespassers" of using alternative paths would generally be small in comparison to the cost to the railroad of making the tracks safe for them. The railroad's right, however, was a qualified one: The railroad was required to keep a careful lookout for cattle.[3] It would be very costly for farmers to erect fences that absolutely prevented cattle from straying, so, if transactions between farmers and railroads were feasible, farmers would frequently pay railroads to keep a careful lookout for animals on the track.

As with cattle, the burden of preventing accidents to child trespassers would, in the absence of a duty in the landowner, fall on an adult custodian and be costly to discharge: Children are difficult to pen. Even young children, however, have more sense than cattle or sheep. The doctrine of attractive nuisance provides an ingenious solution to the conflicting interests of parents and landowners: The landowner must fence or otherwise secure against child trespassers those artificial land conditions (clas-

2. This common law rule ("ancient lights") was rejected in the United States. Can you think of an economic reason why?
3. See 3 Byron K. Elliott & William F. Elliott, A Treatise on the Law of Railroads §1205 (1897).

sically, railroad turntables) that young children mistake for harmless playthings. It would be impracticable for the child or his parents to protect effectively against this type of hazard, while the landowner can do so at relatively small cost, smaller, anyway, than the cost of fencing an entire railroad right of way. And this is another area in which the initial assignment of rights is also the final assignment; it would be impracticable for landowners to negotiate in advance with all of the parents whose children might stray onto their property.[4]

The economic theory of property rights implies that rights will be redefined from time to time as the relative values of different uses of land change. The fencing of cattle again provides an illustration. Suppose cattle wander off the land where they are grazing and onto a neighbor's land, where they damage his crops. Should the cost be borne by the neighbor on the theory that he should have fenced the cattle out, or by the owner of the cattle on the theory that *he* should have fenced them in? The answer would seem to depend (and a comparison of rules over time and between different common law jurisdictions suggests it does depend[5]) on the ratio of cattle to crops. If there are more cattle than crops (more precisely, if more land is devoted to grazing than to crop growing), it will be cheaper for the farmers to fence their land than for the ranchers to fence theirs, and the law will place the burden of fencing on the farmers; but the burden will be reversed when the ratio of land uses reverses.

Are you concerned that continually redefining property rights to se- cure efficiency under changing conditions might create instability and discourage investment? X buys a farm long before there is a railroad in his area. The price he pays is not discounted to reflect future crop damage from sparks, because the construction of a railroad line is not foreseen. But eventually a line is built and is near enough to X's farm to inflict spark damage on his crops. He sues the railroad but the court holds that the level of spark emission is reasonable because it would be more costly for the railroad than for the farmer to prevent the crop loss. With property values thus exposed to uncompensated depreciation by unforeseen changes in neighboring land uses, the incentive to invest in farming will be reduced.[6] But as with our earlier example of raising hogs, a reduced level of investment in farming may be an efficient adjust- ment to the possibility that some day the highest value of the farmer's land may be as a dumping ground for railroad sparks.

4. For criticism of the analysis in this and the preceding paragraph, and rejoinder to the criticism, see Gordon Tullock, Two Kinds of Legal Efficiency, 8 Hofstra L. Rev. 659, 666-668 (1980); Richard A. Posner, A Reply to Some Recent Criticisms of the Efficiency Theory of the Common Law, 9 Hofstra L. Rev. 775, 781-784 (1981).

5. See Richard A. Posner, Tort Law: Cases and Economic Analysis 492-493 (1982).

6. But the example in the text is not a realistic one, since the coming of the railroad usually increased the agricultural value of nearby land.

A more serious problem when property rights are subject to being redefined as values change is that, for people who are averse to risk, uncertainty is a source of disutility. Whether any of the methods of eliminating the risks created by uncertainty would be feasible in the situation under discussion may be doubted.[7] However, the amount and consequences of the uncertainty are easily exaggerated. If a harmful neighboring land use is foreseen at the time of sale, the price of land will be reduced accordingly, and the buyer will have no disappointed expectations. If the use is unforeseen, chances are that it lies well in the future, and a cost to be incurred in the far future will (unless astronomical) have little impact on present decisions (cf. §6.7 *infra*). The alternative — always to assign the property right to the prior of two conflicting land uses — would be highly inefficient, for the later use will often be the more valuable.[8]

§3.6   Trespass and Eminent Domain

The landowner's right to repel a physical intrusion in the form of engine sparks is only a qualified right. The intruder can defeat it by showing that his land use, which is incompatible with the injured landowner's, is more valuable. But if your neighbor parks his car in your garage, you have a right to eject him as a trespasser no matter how convincingly he can demonstrate to a court that the use of your garage to park his car is more valuable than your use of it.

The difference between the cases is, at least on a first pass at the problem, the difference between conflicting claims and conflicting uses. In general the proper (because cheaper and more accurate) method of resolving conflicting claims is the market. If your neighbor thinks your garage is worth more to him than to you, he can pay you to rent it to him. But if he merely *claims* that he can use your garage more productively, he thrusts on the courts a difficult evidentiary question: Which of you would really be willing to pay more for the use of the garage? In the spark case, negotiation in advance may be infeasible because of the number of landowners potentially affected, so if courts

7. The farmer might not be in a position to eliminate the risk either by diversifying (e.g., by owning large amounts of railroad common stock) or by buying insurance. Insurance against a decline in land values that is due to changes in the definition of property rights would be difficult to buy because the appropriate premium, which depends on both the probability and the magnitude of the loss if the risk materializes, would be so difficult to compute (see §4.5 *infra*).

8. Another problem with a first-in-time, first-in-right rule, already examined, is that it can lead to a premature, or an excessive, commitment of resources.

want to encourage the most productive use of land they cannot avoid comparing the values of the competing uses.

If the *government* wants my garage, however, it can seize it under the eminent domain power; it need not negotiate with me at all. This result is inconsistent with the distinction just suggested, because it is a case of competing claims rather than competing uses. The familiar argument that the eminent domain power is necessary to overcome the stubbornness of people who refuse to sell at a "reasonable" (that is, the market) price is bad economics. If I refuse to sell for less than $250,000 a house that no one else would pay more than $100,000 for, it does not follow that I am irrational, even if no "objective" factors such as moving expenses justify my insisting on such a premium. It follows only that I value the house more than other people. The extra value I place on the property has the same status in economic analysis as any other value.

A good economic argument for eminent domain, although one with greater application to railroads and other right-of-way companies than to the government, is that it is necessary to prevent monopoly. Once the railroad or pipeline has begun to build its line, the cost of abandoning it for an alternative route becomes very high. Knowing this, people owning land in the path of the advancing line will be tempted to hold out for a very high price — a price in excess of the opportunity cost of the land. (This is a problem of bilateral monopoly; see §3.7 *infra.*) Transaction costs will be high, land-acquisition costs will be high, and for both reasons the right-of-way company will have to raise the price of its services. The higher price will induce some consumers to shift to substitute services. Right-of-way companies will therefore have a smaller output; as a result they will need, and buy, less land than they would have purchased at prices equal to the opportunity costs of the land. Higher land prices will also give the companies an incentive to substitute other inputs for some of the land they would have bought. As a result of all this, land that would have been more valuable to a right-of-way company than to its present owners will remain in its existing, less valuable uses, and this is inefficient. (What other inefficiency is created?)

This analysis shows that the distinction between conflicting claims to a resource and conflicting or incompatible uses of resources is not fundamental. What is fundamental is the distinction between low-transaction-cost settings and high-transaction-cost settings. In the former, the law should require the parties to transact in the market; it can do this by making the present owner's property right absolute (or nearly so), so that anyone who thinks the property is worth more has to negotiate with the owner. But in settings of high transaction cost people must be allowed to use the courts to shift resources to a more valuable use, because the market is by definition unable to perform this function in those settings. This distinction is only imperfectly reflected in the law. While some government takings of land do occur in high-transaction-cost settings — taking land for a highway, or for an airport or military base that requires the assembly of a large number of contiguous parcels (does this mean that private developers should be given eminent domain powers to assemble land for shopping centers and resort communities?) — many others do not (public schools, post offices, government office buildings).

In low-transaction-cost settings, the exercise of the eminent domain power is really just a form of taxation; it taxes away subjective values. Is this an efficient form of taxation? Surprisingly enough, it may be. As we shall see in Chapter 17, the best tax is a tax that does not change the behavior of the people taxed; and since the incidence of eminent domain is hard to predict, the eminent domain "tax" may be pretty good from this standpoint.

"Just compensation," in the words of the Fifth Amendment, must be paid to an owner whose property is taken from him under the eminent domain power. Why? The answer may seem transparent: otherwise there would be a hideous loss to the owner of the property that was taken. But people insure against the destruction of their homes by fire, why not by government taking? Then the only uncompensated taking, besides the subjective or nonmarket values that just compensation excludes, would be the cost of the insurance premium. The existence of well-developed insurance markets casts doubt on a recent effort to explain the requirement of just compensation by reference to risk aversion,[1] and on the slightly older view that failure to compensate would "demoralize" condemnees and lead them to use resources less efficiently in the future, for example by always renting rather than buying property that might be condemned.[2] As long as a rule of not paying compensation was well known, no one would be surprised or demoralized. Indeed, people who bought property after the rule was announced would not be hurt at all, for the risk of a government taking (a risk measured by the cost of insurance against such a taking) would be reflected in a lower price for the property; the buyer would be fully compensated. If the point is that the risk of a government taking would be less readily insurable than that of a natural disaster, because it would be less predictable, one is entitled to be skeptical. The government's eminent domain takings probably do not vary more from year to year than the losses from, say, earthquakes; and insurance can be bought against expropriation of property by foreign governments. If the concern is that the gov-

§3.6   1. See Lawrence Blume & Daniel L. Rubinfeld, Compensation for Takings: An Economic Analysis, 72 Calif. L. Rev. 569 (1984).

2. See Frank I. Michelman, Property, Utility, and Fairness: Comments on the Ethical Foundations of "Just Compensation" Law, 80 Harv. L. Rev. 1165 (1967).

ernment might use the power of eminent domain to oppress its political enemies or vulnerable minority groups, a partial answer at least is that such conduct would violate such constitutional guarantees as free speech and equal protection of the laws.

A straightforward economic explanation for the requirement of just compensation is that it prevents the government from overusing the taking power. If there were no such requirement, the government would have an incentive to substitute land for other inputs that were socially cheaper but more costly to the government. Suppose the government has a choice between putting up a tall but narrow building on a small lot and a short but wide building on a large one. The market value of the small lot is $1 million, and of the large lot $3 million. The tall narrow building would cost $10 million to build and the short wide one $9 million. Obviously the cheaper alternative from the standpoint of society as a whole is to build the tall building on the small lot (total cost: $11 million) rather than the short building on the large lot ($12 million). But if the land is free to the government, it will build the short building on the large lot, for then the net cost to it will be $1 million less. Of course, this assumes that the government makes its procurement decisions approximately as a private enterpreneur would do, that is, on the basis of private rather than social costs unless forced to take social costs into account. Although government procurement decisions cannot be assumed to be made on the same profit-maximizing basis as private procurement decisions (for reasons explored later in this book), there is little doubt that private costs influence government procurement decisions heavily; the use of manpower by the military when there is a draft (a good example of the taking power exercised without just compensation) is evidence of this point.

The calculation of just compensation presents many interesting questions. We have already remarked the exclusion of subjective values; although illogical in pure theory, it may well be justified by the difficulty (cost) of measuring those values. There is one good lower-bound measure of these values that would occasionally be usable, though — the owner's recent rejection of a bona fide offer at a price above the market price. And it is hard to see why out-of-pocket costs of relocation aren't considered a component of constitutionally required just compensation.

An exclusion that may make some practical sense is the refusal to compensate for goodwill when business premises are taken. Here the problem is not measurement (although that is what the courts say it is) as much as uncertainty about whether the goodwill is really tied to the premises; if it can be transferred intact to other premises, it has not been taken with the land.

Difficult questions arise when the market value of the property is due in some sense to the government itself and the question is whether its contribution should be credited against the price it must pay the owner. Suppose that in time of war the government requisitions a large fraction of the nation's privately owned boats, and the tremendous reduction in the supply of the boats to the private market causes the market price to rise.[3] Should the government have to pay the new market price for any further requisitions? If the answer is yes, the result is a pretty capricious wealth distribution from taxpayers to boat owners. But a no is problematic, too; it will result in the government's taking too many boats, because it will not consider the competing needs of the remaining private customers for boats.

Should it make a difference whether the government requisitioned the boat from someone who owned it before the market price began to rise, or from someone who bought it from the previous owner at the current high price? This question brings out the administrative complexity of trying to base just-compensation law on an aversion to windfalls. Much, maybe most, of the property the government takes has benefited from government expenditures. A conspicuous example is land reclaimed from a lake or river by the Corps of Engineers — but there is a sense in which all privately owned land benefits from public expenditures on maintaining law and order, a title-recording system, etc. However, the benefits may long ago have been impounded in the price of the land, so that payment of full compensation will confer no windfall on anyone. Maybe the best rule therefore would be to ignore the government's possible contribution to the current market price of the land that is being taken.

Thus far, the assumption has been that taking is well defined. But it is not. Pennsylvania once passed a law forbidding subsurface mining of anthracite coal if the mining would cause the surface of the land above the mine to subside, with possible damage to houses and other buildings above the mine. The Supreme Court held that the statute was unconstitutional because it made the property rights of the coal-mining companies (whose mineral rights before the law was passed allowed mining coal without regard for subsidence) much less valuable.[4] Despite this precedent, most regulatory measures that reduce the value of property without the government's taking possession of it are held not to require payment of compensation. Is this economically correct? It has been argued that if the just-compensation principle were really founded on considerations of efficiency, then if the market value of my home fell by $10,000 as a result of some government regulation I would be entitled to the same compensation as if the government had taken a corner of my property worth $10,000.[5] But there are economic

3. See United States v. Cors, 337 U.S. 325, 333 (1949).
4. Pennsylvania Coal Co. v. Mahon, 260 U.S. 393 (1922).
5. See Bruce A. Ackerman, Private Property and the Constitution, ch. 6 (1977).

differences between these cases. When the government regulation affecting property values is general in its application, as will normally be the case, the costs of effecting compensation would be very high, especially if efforts were made, as in economic logic they should be (why?), to take account of people benefited by the regulation, by awarding them negative compensation (i.e., taxing away their windfalls). Imagine the difficulties involved in identifying, and then transacting with, everyone whose property values were raised or lowered by government regulation of the price of natural gas or heating oil.

An additional consideration comes into play when the regulation affects interactive land uses. An example would be a zoning ordinance forbidding the development of land other than for residential use. Suppose such an ordinance is invoked to prevent a landowner from creating a pigsty on his land, the neighbors' land being used exclusively for residential purposes. We cannot regard the ordinance as an infringement of the first landowner's property rights until we first decide that those rights include the right to inflict aesthetic damage on one's neighbors by means of a pigsty. And we cannot decide this prior question without evaluating the competing uses affected by the ordinance. Once that evaluation is made, however, and the property right assigned accordingly, no further economic function is served by forcing the gainers from the ordinance to compensate the losers.[6]

How well does compensation work in practice? An empirical study of Chicago's urban renewal program found that, under eminent domain, high value parcels systematically receive more than fair market value and low value parcels less.[7] There are three reasons for this pattern.

First, the government's ability to vary its input of legal services in a case according to the value of the parcel to be taken is severely limited by the regulations governing the prosecution of a condemnation case: The result is a tendency for the government to spend too much on the trial of a case involving a low-value parcel and too little on the trial of a case involving a high-value parcel.

Second, while the fixed or threshold costs of going to trial are significant for both parties (and they are more significant, the less valuable the parcel), the government may be able to spread these costs over a number of parcels that it is seeking to acquire simultaneously.

Third, there may be additional economies of scale for the government when the parcels that it is simultaneously acquiring are homogeneous, as this permits effective consolidation of the government's legal efforts; and, empirically, low value parcels tend to be more homogeneous than high ones.

6. Even if the pigsty was there before the neighbors' used their land for residential purposes. See preceding section of this chapter.
7. See Patricia Munch, An Economic Analysis of Eminent Domain, 84 J. Pol. Econ. 473 (1976).

§3.7 Pollution: Nuisance and Easement Approaches

A factory belches smoke from its smokestacks that blackens laundry and drapes in a nearby residential area and increases the incidence of respiratory diseases. Analytically the problem is the same as in our spark example: to allocate rights and liabilities in such a way as to minimize the sum of the costs of smoke damage and of avoiding smoke damage. Among the possible adjustments, the factory could install smoke-sup-pression equipment, it could shut down, or the affected homeowners could install air-cleaning equipment or move away from the vicinity of the factory. The question which of these or other methods of resolving the conflict in land uses is cheapest is more difficult than in the engine-spark case, primarily because the effects of pollution on human health are not as yet clearly understood and because the aesthetic costs of pollution are difficult to measure.[1] And the choice of the correct initial assignment of rights is critical; high transaction costs probably will make it impossible to correct a mistaken initial assignment through subsequent market transactions.

It is time that we inquired more closely into the sources of high transaction costs. The factor usually stressed by economists, and men-tioned earlier in this chapter, is a large number of parties to a transaction. Other factors, such as mental incapacity, figure importantly in particular legal settings (see §4.7 *infra*). And fewness of parties is not a sufficient condition of low transaction costs. If there are significant elements of bilateral monopoly in a two-party transaction, that is, if neither party has good alternatives to dealing with the other, transaction costs may be quite high. Negotiations to settle a lawsuit are an example.[2] Because the plaintiff can settle only with the defendant, and the defendant only with the plaintiff, there is a range of prices within which each party will prefer settlement to the more costly alternative of litigation. Ascer-taining this range may be costly, and the parties may consume much time and resources in bargaining within the range. Indeed, each party may be so determined to engross the greater part of the potential profits from the transaction that they never succeed in coming to terms.[3]

---

§3.7   1. In principle, where the level of pollution varies geographically the costs of pollution can be estimated by comparing property values, holding other factors that might affect those values constant. See, e.g., Timothy A. Deyak & V. Kerry Smith, Residential Property Values and Air Pollution: Some New Evidence, 14 Q. Rev. Econ. & Bus. 93 (1974); K.F. Wizard, Air Pollution and Property Values: A Study of the St. Louis Area, 13 J. Regional Sci. 91 (1973). See also Ronald G. Ridker, Economic Costs of Air Pollution: Studies in Measurement (1967). Are there any objections, besides difficulty of estimation to this approach?

2. Discussed in detail in §21.4 *infra*.

3. This is especially likely to happen if one (or both) desires to establish a reputation as a hard bargainer in order to be able to strike better bargains in future transactions. An example is discussed in §10.7 *infra*.

Although the frustration of a potentially value-maximizing exchange is the most dramatic consequence of bilateral monopoly, it is not the usual consequence. Usually the parties will bargain to a mutually satisfactory price, as we shall see in Chapter 21. But it doesn't follow that bilateral monopoly is not a serious social problem. It is, because the transaction costs incurred by the parties in an effort by each to engross as much of the profit of the transaction as possible are a social waste. They alter the relative wealth of the parties but do not increase the aggregate wealth of society. A major thrust of common law, as we shall see, is to mitigate bilateral-monopoly problems.

If transaction costs are high enough (higher than they usually are in a simple bilateral monopoly) — specifically, if they are higher than the value of the transaction — then they won't be incurred; the parties will be better off forgoing the transaction. In such a case the social loss is equal not to the transaction costs but to the value of the forgone transaction.

The costs of transacting are highest where elements of bilateral monopoly coincide with a large number of parties to the transaction — a quite possible conjunction. For example, if homeowners have a right to be free from pollution, the factory that wants to have a right to pollute must acquire it from every homeowner. If only 1 out of 1,000 refuses to come to terms, the rights that the factory has purchased from the other 999 are worth nothing (why?). Because the holdout can extract an exorbitant price, just as in our right-of-way example in the previous section, each homeowner has an incentive to delay coming to terms with the factory; the process of negotiation may therefore be endlessly protracted.[4]

If instead of the homeowners' having the right to be free from pollution, the factory has the right to pollute, the homeowners must get together and buy the factory's right if they wish to be free from pollution. Transaction costs will again be high. Each homeowner will again have an incentive to drag his feet in negotiations with the factory — to "hold out" or "free ride." He will think: "If I refuse to contribute my fair share of the purchase price, others, who care more deeply about pollution than I do, will make up the difference. The factory will be induced to stop polluting. I will benefit along with the others, but at zero cost." The costs of overcoming this foot-dragging by negotiations among the affected homeowners will be high if there are many of them, so again a transaction may be infeasible.

In the presence of high transaction costs, absolute rights, whether to pollute or to be free from pollution, are likely to promote inefficiency. If the factory has the absolute right to pollute and transaction costs are prohibitive, the factory will have no incentive to stop (or reduce)

4. Why would this be less likely in the right-of-way case even without eminent domain?

pollution even if the cost of stopping would be much less than the cost of pollution to the homeowners. Conversely, if homeowners have an absolute right to be free from pollution and transaction costs are again prohibitive, the homeowners will have no incentive to take steps of their own to reduce the effects of pollution even if the cost to them of doing so (perhaps by moving away) is less than the cost to the factory of not polluting or of polluting less.

The common law recognized (although somewhat fitfully) the danger of assigning exclusive rights, whether to polluters or to their victims. Under the doctrine of nuisance[5] and cognate doctrines applicable to special areas such as water rights, courts followed a standard of reasonable use in many though not all cases. Pollution was lawful if reasonable in the circumstances, which meant (at least approximately) if the benefit from continuing to pollute exceeded the cost to the victims of pollution of either tolerating or eliminating it, whichever was cheaper. This is the same standard suggested earlier for resolving conflicts in land use, as in the engine-spark example. But while correct in principle, the approach seems to have had little bite in practice,[6] because of the difficulty of tracing pollution to a particular source[7] and the lack of a procedural device for aggregating small claims. If no single victim of a polluter suffered damage as great as the cost of bringing a lawsuit, no suit would be brought even if the harm to all of the victims greatly exceeded the benefits of continued pollution. Recent developments in the class action, discussed in Chapter 21, are helping to overcome this procedural shortcoming.

Another possible common law solution to the problem of pollution[8] is suggested by the legal treatment of airplane noise. Owners of airplanes that fly at very low altitudes are liable to the subjacent property owner for the diminution in the market level of his property brought about by the airplane's noise, whether or not the costs to that owner exceed the benefits of flight. The property owner cannot enjoin the invasion as a trespass. He cannot, therefore, compel the airline to negotiate with him. But he can compel the airline to condemn an easement to continue its overflights. If the cost of noise-abatement procedures is greater than the noise damage suffered by the subjacent property owners, presumably

5. For an introduction to the law and economics of nuisance, see Richard A. Posner, Tort Law: Cases and Economic Analysis, ch. 10 (1982).

6. Although it is very difficult to be sure of this without knowing how much pollution was (and is) cost-justified.

7. Two problems must be distinguished: that of multiple polluters (for which the joint-tortfeasor doctrine, discussed in Chapter 6, provides at least a partial solution); and that of the polluting source that is only one of many causes of the pollution, the others not being tortfeasors (for example, weather or a cost-justified polluter). On the latter problem cf. the discussion of liability for radiation damage in §6.7 *infra*.

8. Direct regulation of pollution is discussed in Chapter 13.

the airline will condemn the easements. If the noise damage is greater than the cost of the noise-abatement procedures, the airline will adopt the procedures. Conceivably, if the cheapest method of noise abatement happens to be soundproofing the subjacent houses, the airline will pay the subjacent owners to soundproof, since by hypothesis the payment will be less than the airline's liability; but high transaction costs may preclude this result, and if so the eminent domain approach may produce less efficient consequences than a nuisance approach (why?). But it is better than a trespass approach. If the subjacent owners had property rights against airplane noise that they could not be forced to sell — if, in other words, they could enjoin overflights — then in cases where the efficient solution was for the airline to continue to make noise and for the subjacent owners either to suffer the noise or to soundproof their houses, the market would not work. Each owner in the path of flight would have an incentive to act the holdout; and the airline, unable to purchase at a reasonable price all of the rights of subjacent owners to be free from noise, would have either to discontinue its flights or to adopt noise-abatement procedures — both, by hypothesis, inefficient solutions.

A problem with the eminent domain approach is that once the airline concludes that the costs of noise-abatement procedures are greater than the benefits to it in reduced liability to the subjacent owners, and therefore acquires easements from them that authorize a high level of noise, it will have no incentive to reconsider the adoption of such procedures when and if their cost falls or their effectiveness increases; for the benefit of a lower noise level in the future would enure entirely to the subjacent owners. This problem could be solved by creating time-limited noise easements[9] but the solution would create a fresh problem. Property owners who grant perpetual noise easements have thereafter every incentive to adopt any noise-reduction measure that costs less than it raises the value of their property, but they do not have this incentive under a system of time-limited easements, because any measure taken by a property owner that reduces noise damage will reduce by an equal amount the price that he will receive in the next period for a noise easement.

---

9. As proposed in William F. Baxter & Lillian R. Altree, Legal Aspects of Airport Noise, 15 J. Law & Econ. 1 (1972). If the easement is limited (say) to 10 years, the airline will periodically review the state of the art in noise abatement in order to determine whether the adoption of noise-abatement procedures would save it more money by reducing its expected easement costs than the procedures would add to its capital and operating costs.

§3.8 Other Solutions to the Problem of Incompatible Land Uses Herein of the Difference Between Property and Contract Rights and Between Injunctive and Damage Remedies

Attaining the efficient solution in the spark case, the factory smoke case, and our other examples of conflicting land uses would have been much simpler if a single individual or firm had owned all of the affected land. A single owner of both the factory and the residential property affected by its smoke would want to maximize the combined value of both properties. This is the correct economic goal and the effort to reach it would not be burdened by the costs of obtaining the agreement of many separate owners.

So why are such mergers so infrequent? First, buying all of the affected property would be administratively costly because it would require transacting with many individual rights holders. Second, a single firm may not be able to operate efficiently in unrelated markets — factory production and residential real estate, railroading and farming, airport management and real estate. The firm may have higher costs in both markets than firms specializing in either one would have. Sheer size may be a source of cost too, in a loss of control over subordinate managers. The extra costs may offset the savings from solving the incompatible-uses problem.[1]

The single-ownership solution to the problem of conflicting land uses is approximated by those oil and gas states — the majority — that allow compulsory unitization, by which the vote of a substantial majority (usually two-thirds) of the owners of an oil or gas field to operate the field as under common ownership will bind the minority. (Why would a requirement of unanimity be inefficient?) The problem to which compulsory unitization is the solution is that the owners of the oil and gas rights will be pumping from an underground pool that in effect they own in common, and each will have an incentive to drill many wells in order to pump as much oil or gas as fast as possible, even though the total cost of production for the field as a whole could be reduced, and the total yield of oil or gas increased, by drilling fewer wells and depleting the resource more slowly.

Another method that has some of the strengths of the single-ownership approach but avoids the problem of underspecialization is the restrictive covenant. The developer of a tract will want to maximize the

§3.8   1. It may be possible to offset some of the costs of underspecialization by leasing, but the coordination of the lessees may be almost as costly as the market — as we shall see shortly. Loss of control in organizations is discussed in the next section of this chapter and also in §14.1 *infra*.

value of the entire property but may not want to administer it. One possibility is to include in each deed of sale restrictions against land uses that would reduce the net value of the property as a whole. Such restrictions run with the land, which means that they are enforceable against any future owner of the land, as well as the present owner, and enforceable by successors to the original buyers. A mere contractual obligation on the buyer and his successors *to the developer,* who having developed the tract would have no further interest in enforcing the obligation, would not be good enough. Anyway such a contract would not bind a buyer from the original buyer unless the second buyer knew or had reason to know about the contract that his predecessor had entered into with the neighbors. The second buyer can't be counted on to observe the restriction voluntarily, moreover; for although by assumption the restriction increases the value of the entire tract, if everyone else observes the restriction then the land of the owner who does not will be even more valuable (why?). So the buyer will observe the restriction only if he is paid to do so. But he will not be paid — not much, anyway. The other property owners, if numerous, will have difficulty overcoming the problem of holdouts in their ranks. And they will gain little if they do, since, if the present owner sells, the other owners may have to transact all over again with the buyer (why "may"?).

This discussion highlights the economic difference between property and contract rights. Whereas a property right excludes (in the limit) the whole rest of the world from the use of a thing except on the owner's terms, a contract right excludes only the other party to the contract. Freedom to contract but not to create property rights would not optimize resource use. If A buys from B the right to work B's land, but B has no right to exclude others from working it, A (like B before him) will not have an incentive to exploit the land optimally. Similarly, without property rights, the problem of excessive grazing in our common pasture example would not be solved even if the farmers using the pasture sold their rights to a single individual or firm. After the new owner had reduced congestion by charging the farmers who had sold him their rights an appropriate fee for continuing to use the pasture, other farmers would begin to graze *their* cows on the pasture; they would have no obligation to pay a fee. Congestion would return.

Restrictive covenants have two limitations. First, they generally are feasible only in the rather special setting of initial single ownership of a large area. They provide no solution to the typical pollution problem, for it is rare that an area large enough to encompass a factory and all or most of the residences affected by its smoke will be under common ownership. (Why not force the factory to condemn those residences?)

Second, a system of restrictive covenants is inflexible in the face of changes that may alter the relative values of conflicting land uses. The owner who wants to put his land to a use forbidden by a restrictive covenant must get the consent of all the property owners in whose favor the covenant runs; if there are many of them, the costs of transacting may be prohibitive. Some covenants provide therefore that they will expire after a certain number of years unless renewed by majority vote of the affected landowners. And courts may refuse to enforce a restrictive covenant on the ground that it is obsolete, that the forbidden land use is now clearly more valuable than the use protected by the covenant.

The problem of the obsolete covenant would be less serious if courts refused to enjoin breaches of restrictive covenants and instead limited victorious plaintiffs to damages. Damage liability would not deter a breach that increased the value of the defendant's property by more than it diminished the value of the other properties in the tract, since, by hypothesis, his damage liability would be smaller than his gain from the breach. In contrast, an injunction places the prospective violator in the same position as the airline that is enjoinable by subjacent property owners or the railroad that is enjoinable from trespassing on property that it requires to complete its right-of-way: To get the injunction lifted the prospective violator will have to negotiate with every right holder, may have to pay an exorbitant price to a few holdouts, and may even fail to complete the transaction.

The inflexibility of restrictive covenants has led increasing numbers of developers to establish homeowners' associations empowered to modify the restrictions on the uses to which they may put their property. This method of coping with the problem of high transaction costs resembles another method, the business firm, which we discuss in a later chapter.[2] Besides these private solutions to the problem of conflicting land uses, there is, of course, a public solution: zoning. Two types of zoning should be distinguished. Separation-of-uses zoning divides a city or other local governmental unit into zones and permits only certain land uses in each zone, so that there are separate zones for high-rise apartment houses, for single family homes, for businesses, for factories, and so on. Exclusionary zoning (a term often used pejoratively, but here neutrally), ordinarily adopted by smaller units than a city or county, tries to exclude certain land uses altogether; a suburb that requires minimum lot sizes would be engaged in exclusionary zoning. The main question about separation-of-uses zoning is whether it makes much difference.[3] One is unlikely to find a house and a factory cheek-by-jowl even if there is no zoning. Residential real estate usually commands a higher price than real estate used for industrial purposes (why?), and

---

2. See Chapter 14. Still another solution is taxation. See §13.5 *infra.*
3. For a negative answer, see Bernard H. Siegan, Land Use Without Zoning 75 (1972); for other economic analysis of zoning, see Werner Z. Hirsch, Law and Economics: An Introductory Analysis, ch. IV (1979).

therefore a factory owner would not want to build his factory in a residential area unless his purpose were extortion, which nuisance law should be able to deal with effectively.

Exclusionary zoning is more likely than separation-of-uses zoning to affect the use of land. A large lot might be worth more if used for a high-rise apartment building than if used for a single house — at least if the effects on other homeowners in the community are neglected, as the developer often would do (why?). These effects may include highway and parking congestion and burdens on municipal services such as public schools. Notice, however, that:

(1) If the residents of the high-rise are charged for the extra costs they impose through use of public schools and of the streets, there will be no externality justifying exclusionary zoning.

(2) Even though exclusionary zoning may be efficient in principle, the practice may be quite different. The incentives of public officials — the people who draft zoning ordinances and enforce them — may lead them away from the goal of efficiency, as we shall see in Chapters 19 and 23.

(3) Exclusionary zoning is apt to redistribute wealth from poor to rich (why?).

We discussed restrictive covenants as a device for internalizing the costs of using land, but this is not a logically necessary characteristic of promises (often called easements or servitudes) that run with the land (that is, are enforceable as property rights). Suppose the seller of a piece of land promises the buyer that he will not sell goods or services in competition with the buyer, or that he will sell the buyer firewood at a low fixed price every year for 20 years. Should these promises run with the land? The common law answers no, because they do not "touch and concern" the land. But if the seller (who in this example retains a neighboring lot) promised not to build a fence that would cut off the buyer's view, this promise would run with the land — that is, would be enforceable against the seller's successors in interest even if they do not know about the promise — because the promise involves an actual land use.

Why the distinction? One problem is that having too many sticks in the bundle of rights that is property increases the cost of transferring property. Another is that promises that do not deal with the use of the land itself are hard to keep track of in the absence of a recording system, which England did not have. The seller in our first two examples might have moved away from the buyer's neighborhood. It would be difficult for people negotiating to buy the seller's property to determine whether he had obligations that would bind them, despite their lack of knowledge or reason to know of those obligations, because the obligations were the property right of another owner of real estate, which that owner could enforce against the whole world. Can you see an analogy to the discussion of why property rights are not recognized in basic research? Might we say that efficiency requires that property rights be in some sense open and notorious? How can this suggestion be reconciled with the protection of trade secrets? And does the "touch and concern" requirement make any sense in a system where property rights must be publicly recorded in order to be enforceable?[4]

We have several times seen property rights distinguished from other sorts of legal interest in terms of remedies, and the point has now to be generalized: In conflicting-use situations in which transaction costs are high, the allocation of resources to their most valuable uses is facilitated by denying owners of property an injunctive remedy against invasions of their rights and instead limiting them to a remedy in damages (why?).[5] But where transaction costs are low, injunctive relief should normally be allowed as a matter of course (why?); for a possible exception see §4.12 *infra.*

The problem of incompatible land uses, which we have been discussing in terms of the definition and transfer of property rights, is frequently discussed (as we have begun to do in this section) in terms of externalities. The damage to the farmer's crops caused by engine sparks is a cost of railroading that the railroad, unless forced by law to do so or unless it is the owner of the farmland, will not take into account in making its decisions; the cost is external to its decisionmaking process. (What is an "external benefit"?) The term is useful, but potentially misleading. It suggests that the correct solution in the spark case is to impose liability on the railroad, although there is no presumption in economic theory that the railroad rather than the farmer should be made to bear the cost of spark damage. If the joint value of railroading and farming would be maximized by discontinuing crop production, substituting a more fire-resistant crop, or removing the crop to some distance from the railroad right-of-way, then placing liability on the railroad would be inappropriate. Even if "externality" is defined as external to market processes of decision rather than to the injurer, it is still a potentially misleading usage since if transaction costs are low the market may operate efficiently despite the presence of externalities.

4. For criticism of the "touch and concern" requirement, see Richard A. Epstein, Notice and Freedom of Contract in the Law of Servitudes, 55 So. Calif. L. Rev. 1353 (1982).

5. See Frank I. Michelman, Book Review, 80 Yale L.J. 647, 670-672 (1971); Guido Calabresi & A. Douglas Melamed, Property Rules, Liability Rules, and Inalienability: One View of the Cathedral, 85 Harv. L. Rev. 1089 (1972). But this assumes that damages can be computed with reasonable accuracy. If they cannot, there is an argument for injunctive relief. The law of equity, which is among other things the body of doctrine governing equitable (which means, in essence, other than damage) remedies, provides a flexible test for when an injunction can be obtained. One requirement is that the plaintiff have no adequate remedy at law (i.e., no adequate damage remedy). Cf. §21.4 *infra.*

§3.9 Divided Ownership — Estates in Land

More than one person may have a property right in the same thing. Our common-pool resource was an example of this; a more traditional example is the different "estates" in land. Property rights in real estate may be divided between a life tenant and a remainderman, between joint tenants (a special type of co-ownership), between a tenant and a landlord, and in other ways. Such divisions (whether concurrent but nonexclusive, or exclusive but time-limited) create incentives for inefficient use similar to those created by the separate ownership of the railroad right-of-way and the adjacent farmland, or the airport and the adjacent residential community. The problem has been discussed extensively in connection with the poverty of Ireland in the nineteenth century.[1] Most farmers were tenants; and it might seem that a tenant would have little incentive to improve the land because any improvement that outlasted the period of the lease would confer an uncompensated benefit on the landlord under the doctrine of fixtures (anything affixed to the property by the tenant becomes the property of the landlord on the expiration of the lease — can you think of an economic reason for this doctrine?). Yet this suggestion seems on its face to violate the Coase Theorem. Why didn't the landlords agree in the leases to compensate their tenants for improvements, for example by giving the tenant a percentage of the net revenues from the land after the lease expires? Much can be done along these lines, but the problem is not entirely solvable by careful drafting.

Suppose the landlord does enter into some sort of sharing agreement with the tenant (in fact, sharecropping is common where tenant farming is common). Suppose he agrees to provide the land, seeds, and fertilizer, and the farmer agrees to provide the labor, with the revenues from the sale of the crops to be split 50-50. The results will not be optimal, as a simple example will show. Suppose that if the farmer worked an extra hour every week on improving the land he would increase the dollar value of the farm's output by $2 (net of any extra cost besides his time), and that the opportunity cost — or shadow price[2] — of his time in forgone leisure is only $1.50. Efficiency requires that he work the extra hour, but he will not, because he will receive only $1 for that work. A more complicated sharing agreement will be required for optimal results, and the more complicated it is the more costly it will be to negotiate and enforce.

The problem of the tenant's incentive to improve the land will be

§3.9   1. See, e.g., A.C. Pigou, The Economics of Welfare 174-175, 178-183 (4th ed. 1932); Barbara Lewis Solow, The Land Question and the Irish Economy, 1870-1903 (1971).
    2. The price a person would charge for something that is not sold in a market.

less serious the longer the lease; so it is perhaps not surprising that a
system of tenant customary rights evolved in Ireland that made it difficult
for the landlord to evict the tenant, either directly or indirectly (the
latter by jacking up rents until the tenant was forced to abandon the
lease). There would still have been a problem of tenant incentives (as
we are about to see) if optimal tenant improvements were likely to outlast
the tenants' lives; but major capital improvements, the kind most likely
to outlast the current tenant, had to be made by the landlords rather
than the tenants anyway, because the landlords had the capital. If anything, the problem was not that tenants lacked incentives to improve
the land but that customary tenant rights made it difficult for landlords
to recoup the cost of their own improvements by charging higher rents,
since the tenant might complain that the rate increase violated his customary rights.

All this suggests that there is no simple solution to the problem of
divided ownership except single ownership, but it is not so simple either.
If the tenant is demoted to an employee of the landlord, the problem
of divided ownership disappears but is replaced by a quite analogous
problem of agent shirking due to the employee's not getting to keep
every dollar in added output from working—just like the tenant. And
the tenant may be unwilling to buy the farm from the landlord (although
this would eliminate the problem of shirking), even if he were able to
do so (what would determine whether or not he was able to do so?),
because of the additional risk he would incur — illustrating the important
point that leasing is a form of risk-spreading.[3]

So there is an important role for law to play in regulating divided
ownership. We might expect the courts to interpret leases as if the parties' intent had been that the property would be managed by the lessee
as if he were the owner;[4] for that presumably *was* the parties' intent,
if they are rational profit-maximizers. And, as a matter of fact, an interesting common law doctrine, the law of waste, emerged to reconcile the
often competing interests of life tenants and remaindermen. A life tenant
will have an incentive to maximize not the value of the property, that
is, the present value of the entire stream of future earnings obtainable
from it, but only the present value of the earnings stream obtainable
during his expected lifetime. He will therefore want to cut timber before
it has attained its mature growth — even though the present value of
the timber would be greater if the cutting of some or all of it were
postponed — if the added value will enure to the remainderman. The
law of waste forbade this. There might seem to be no need for a law
of waste, because the life tenant and the remainderman would negotiate
an optimal plan for exploiting the property. But since the tenant and

3. See Steven N.S. Cheung, The Theory of Share Tenancy (1969).
4. For an excellent example, see Suydam v. Jackson, 54 N.Y. 450 (1873).

remainderman have only each other to contract with, the situation is again one of bilateral monopoly, and transaction costs may be high. Also, the remaindermen may be children, who do not have the legal capacity to make binding contracts; they may even be unborn children. The problem of bilateral monopoly is less acute in the landlord-tenant case, because the terms of a lease are set before the landlord and tenant become locked into a relationship with each other, whereas very often a life tenancy is created by will, and the testator (for whom estate planning may be a once-in-a-lifetime experience) may not be alert to the potential conflicts between life tenants and remaindermen.

The law of waste has largely been supplanted by a more efficient method of administering property that resembles unitization: the trust. By placing property in trust, the grantor can split the beneficial interest as many ways as he pleases without worrying about divided ownership. The trustee will manage the property as a unit, maximizing its value and allocating that value among the trust's beneficiaries in the proportions desired by the grantor.[5]

The tenant does not always have a shorter time horizon than the owner of the fee simple (in the case of a landlord) or the remainderman (in the case of a life tenancy). Take the case of an oil lease (gas, or oil and gas, would do just as well), where the deal is that the lessor will receive a fixed royalty per barrel of oil. Unless the lessor expects the price of oil to rise faster than the interest rate, he will want the oil pumped as fast as possible, whether or not the field is unitized. That will mean drilling a lot of wells. But the lessee, who has to pay for those wells, will want to pump the oil more slowly so that he can economize on the number of wells. He may indeed drill too few wells, since in deciding how much a new well is worth he will disregard the part of its revenues that will go to the lessor as royalty. Therefore, most oil and gas leases contain a "development" clause that requires the lessee to drill a reasonable number of wells — reasonable meaning cost-justified.

An interesting question has arisen in the interpretation of such clauses: whether the lessee, in figuring the costs of a new well, may include not only his drilling and other direct costs but the reduced revenue from the old wells, since the new well will deplete the pool from which the old wells as well as the new draw. The answer, for which there is some judicial support, is yes, because that depletion is a genuine opportunity cost of the new well.[6]

5. On the problem of appropriately compensating the trustee, see W. Bishop & D.D. Prentice, Some Legal and Economic Aspects of Fiduciary Remuneration, 46 Mod. L. Rev. 289 (1983).

6. For an interesting law and economics analysis of these problems, see Stephen F. Williams, Implied Covenants in Oil and Gas Leases: Some General Principles, 29 U. Kan. L. Rev. 153 (1981).

We have thus far been discussing vertical or temporal division of a property right. There is also horizontal division. The extreme example is the communal right, as in the pasture that is shared by a number of farmers. Communal rights differ only in degree from no rights, and thus are inefficient unless the costs of enforcing individual rights are disproportionate to the benefits.[7] Odd as it may sound, communal rights are frequently created by individuals, although in circumstances where the problem of inefficiency is minimized. For example, A may leave a plot of land to B and C, his children, in undivided joint ownership (a tenancy in common or a joint tenancy). B and C are formally in much the same position as the inhabitants of a society that does not recognize property rights. If B spends money to repair structures on the property, C will share equally in the value of the repairs, and vice versa. Although there are only two parties, there is the familiar bilateral-monopoly problem. But it is mitigated by the familial relationship; we expect more cooperation between persons united by bonds of affection (more on this in Chapter 5). In addition, the law credits the joint tenant with the value of any improvements he makes to the property, up to the amount by which the improvements increase the value of the property (why this qualification?). The law also, and wisely, allows any joint tenant to obtain a partition of the property into separate, individually owned parcels; this power eliminates every vestige of bilateral monopoly and communal rights.

Suppose adjacent owners of row houses, who share a party wall, are unable to agree on how to split the cost of replacing the wall, which is in imminent danger of collapse. One of the owners goes ahead and replaces it at his own expense, and then sues the other for half the cost. There is a fair amount of judicial authority for allowing the suit, as a way around the bilateral-monopoly problem. Cf. §4.14 *infra*.

The law's ingenuity is not limitless, and we end this section with a homely example of a case of divided ownership about which the law can do nothing: automobile rentals. As everyone who has ever rented a car well knows, people do not treat the cars they rent with as much care as the cars they own; they are much rougher on them, reflecting the enormously foreshortened time horizon of their use. But because the rental company cannot supervise or monitor that use, there is no way in which it can induce the renter to take the right amount of care of the car. Here, then, is a case where transaction costs are high despite fewness of parties and no problem of bilateral monopoly. The problem is that the cost of enforcing the transaction agreed on is prohibitive. This is the problem of Irish tenant farming and of property rights in primitive societies (see §3.2 *supra*), writ small.

---

7. A good example is a supermarket's parking lot: It doesn't pay to charge each customer for his use of a space, although doing so would enable the supermarket to have a slightly smaller lot.

§3.10   Problems in the Transfer of Property Rights

In order to facilitate the transfer of resources from less to more valuable uses, property rights, in principle, should be freely transferable. The principle must be qualified; but before doing so, we must notice how divided ownership makes transfer difficult in practice even if there is no formal limitation. If 50 different people are joint tenants in a piece of property, a sale of the property will require them to agree both on the price and on the division of the proceeds among them; there will be holdout problems. The elaborate kinship networks of primitive societies is another reason why property rights are slow to emerge in such societies.[1] Efficiency requires that property rights be transferable; but if many people have a claim on each piece of property, transfers will be difficult to arrange.

The history of English land law is largely a history of efforts to make land more readily transferable, and hence to make the market in land more efficient. Two doctrines will illustrate this point. One, the Rule in Shelley's Case, provided that if a grantor gave a life estate to A with the remainder to A's heirs, A had a fee simple; the heirs were cut out. If the remainder in A's heirs were recognized, it would be very difficult for A to transfer the property, because his heirs would not be ascertained until his death. The other doctrine, the Doctrine of Worthier Title, provided that if the grantor gave property to A for life, with the remainder to the grantor's heirs, the grantor — not his heirs — owned the remainder, and thus could sell it, as his heirs apparent might well not be able to do. The only economic problem with these doctrines (besides their immense complexity, not hinted at in the above very simplified descriptions) is that they imply that the grantor is not able to trade off the costs of reduced transferability against whatever benefits he derives from dividing ownership in the way that the doctrines prevent; and this assumption seems paternalistic and hence questionable from an efficiency standpoint. People ought to know their own best interests better than courts. But maybe the explanation is, as suggested earlier, that many of these grants are once-in-a-lifetime transactions for the grantor, and he may not have good information about the problems they create. We shall come back to this problem in Chapter 18.

Now let us turn to the case where, although ownership is not divided, the transfer affects more than the immediate parties to the transaction. Water rights provide a good example.[2]

§3.10   1. See Richard A. Posner, The Economics of Justice 180-181 (1981).
2. See Charles J. Meyers & Richard A. Posner, Market Transfers of Water Rights: Toward an Improved Market in Water Resources (National Water Commission report, July 1, 1971, published by the National Technical Information Service); Stephen F. Williams, The Requirement of Beneficial Use as a Cause of Waste in Water Resource Develop-

As mentioned earlier, in the western states a property right in water is obtained by diverting water from a natural stream and using it for irrigation or other purposes. In time, a stream will become completely appropriated in the sense that the total volume of the stream is owned in varying amounts by various users. For example, A might have a right to take 10 cubic feet per second during the months of July to December from a ditch at a specified location, B a right to take 8 cubic feet per second at another location during a specified period, and so forth. In addition, water rights are labeled by the date acquired (the date of the first diversion, or appropriation). In times of drought, the available supply is rationed in accordance with priority of appropriation.

If A wants to sell his right to X, and X plans to use the water in the same place and manner as A, the transfer has no impact on the water rights of the other users of the stream. But suppose that A and all of the other present users are farmers who use the water they divert for irrigation, while X, the prospective purchaser of A's right, is a municipality. Then the transfer will affect right holders downstream from the point of diversion. On average, about half the water that a farmer diverts for irrigation seeps back into the stream, and this return flow can be and is appropriated by other farmers. A municipality may consume a much higher percentage of the water it diverts, and what it does not consume may be returned to the stream at a different point — or may flow into a different stream altogether, if the municipality is located in a different watershed from the farmer whose water right it has bought.

If the return-flow problem were ignored, water transfers would frequently reduce overall value. Suppose A's water right is worth $100 to him and $125 to X, the municipality; but whereas A returns one-half of the water he diverted to the stream, where it is used by B, X will return only one-fourth of the water it obtains from A, and at a point far below B, where it will be appropriated by D. And suppose B would not sell his right to A's return flow for less than $50, while D would sell his right in the municipality's return flow for $10. Given these facts, to let A sell his water right to X because it is worth more to X than to A would be inefficient, for the total value of the water would be less in its new uses (X's and D's) — $135 — than in its present uses (A and B's) — $150.

The law deals with this problem by requiring the parties to show that the transfer will not injure other users. In practice this means that A and X in our example, in order to complete their transaction, would have to compensate B for the loss of A's return flow; they would not do so; and the transaction would fall through, as under our assumptions

ment, 23 Natural Resources J. 7 (1983); Ronald N. Johnson, Micha Gisser & Michael Werner, The Definition of a Surface Water Right and Transferability, 24 J. Law & Econ. 273 (1981).

it should. But there is a weakness in this solution: Any new return flow that the purchaser generates will not be his property. Let the values to A, X, and B remain $100, $125, and $50 respectively but now let the value of X's return flow to D be $60. The value of the water if sold ($185) will now exceed its value in its present uses ($150), but the law would require X to pay a minimum of $150 ($100 to A — his reservation price — plus $50 to B) for water that is worth only $125 to it. X will not be compensated for the $60 in new value that its use will create, so it will refuse to complete the sale unless it can induce D to ante up the difference between $125 and what it owes to A and B. To do this it must convince D that it will not complete the purchase without such a contribution, for D knows that it will be able to appropriate X's return flow, should it materialize, without having to pay anything. So we have a bilateral-monopoly problem once again. A more efficient solution, especially where more than one user may be benefited by the newly created return flow, would be to deem the transferee (X) the owner of any new return flow that the transfer creates.

The absence of explicit property rights in broadcast frequencies — a resource that has some of the same economic characteristics as water — may be responsible for the lack of any mechanism for permitting the sale of a frequency for a different use. The broadcaster can sell to another broadcaster (see §3.3 *supra*), and this is like the sale by one farmer to another. But he cannot sell to a nonbroadcast user, for example a municipal police department that wants another frequency for its patrol cars. Such a sale would create the same problems as in our example of the sale of water by a farmer to a municipality. The mobile radio user, unlike the broadcaster with his fixed transmitter, will be transmitting part of the time from the former periphery of the broadcaster's broadcast radius. This will interfere with stations broadcasting on the same frequency in adjacent areas. The problem could be solved by procedures similar to those used in the transfer of water rights, but this has not been the approach followed. The only machinery that the law provides for the transfer of a frequency to a new use is a petition to the Federal Communications Commission requesting a change in the allocation of frequencies between classes of use. Willingness to pay for the expenses involved in influencing the commission is substituted for willingness to pay a present owner of the resource.[3]

Problems in transferring property rights are part of a larger problem, that of deciding who owns what property. Much of this chapter has been devoted to problems of whether to recognize property rights in a particular resource and if so how to define them. But even if it is

---

3. The feasibility of instituting an explicit property rights system in frequencies is explored in Arthur S. De Vany et al., A Property System for Market Allocation of the Electromagnetic Spectrum: A Legal-Economic-Engineering Study, 21 Stan. L. Rev. 1499 (1969), and in the Minasian article cite in §3.3 *supra*.

clear that someone owns Blackacre, it may be quite unclear who that someone is. (We met this problem in connection with gifts to unborn remaindermen.) A system of recorded titles is a great help; and one of the problems in the transfer of water rights is the absence of an adequate such system. Not only can water rights not be acquired except by actually using the amount of water claimed, but disuse will lead after a period of years to a forfeiture of the rights and a vesting of them in the actual user. A "deed" to water rights, stating that A has the right to take a specific number of cubic feet per second during a specific period at a specific point, is only evidence of what A's legal right is, and of what, therefore, he has the power to sell. An on-the-site investigation is necessary to verify that A in fact owns (i.e., uses) what the paper record shows him to own. And in order to determine the significance of A's priority for times of drought, the actual uses of other appropriators must also be investigated. It would improve efficiency to institute a system of paper water titles analogous to the systems used to record land titles.[4]

But a recording system is not a panacea, as is shown by the doctrine of adverse possession. If for a given period of years (which is different in different states, but seven is a common number) you hold property adversely to the real owner (i.e., not as tenant, agent, etc.), claiming it as your own, and he does not bring suit to assert his right, the property becomes yours. Oliver Wendell Holmes long ago suggested an interesting economic explanation for adverse possession. Over time, a person becomes attached to property that he regards as his own, and the deprivation of the property would be wrenching. Over the same time, a person loses attachment to property that he regards as no longer his own, and the restoration of the property would cause only moderate pleasure.[5] This is a point about diminishing marginal utility of income. The adverse possessor would experience the deprivation of the property as a diminution in his wealth; the original owner would experience the restoration of the property as an increase in *his* wealth. If they have the same wealth, then probably their combined utility will be greater if the adverse possessor is allowed to keep the property.

This is a nice point, with general application to statutes of limitations (indeed, adverse possession is a transfer effected by the statute of limitations), though adverse possession also has the more mundane function

4. See Joseph T. Janczyk, An Economic Analysis of the Land Title Systems for Transferring Real Property, 6 J. Leg. Stud. 213 (1977), for an analysis of land title recording systems. What are the economic benefits of a system of paper titles besides making it easier to identify the owner of the property right?

5. See Oliver Wendell Holmes, The Path of the Law, 10 Harv. L. Rev. 457, 477 (1897). This explanation of adverse possession implies, does it not, that the adverse possessor believes himself to be the real owner. There is strong support for this requirement in the case law, as shown in R.H. Helmholz, Adverse Possession and Subjective Intent, 61 Wash. U.L.Q. 331 (1983).

of correcting titles, since most adverse possessions are mistakes caused by uncertainty over boundary lines. And statutes of limitations also serve a procedural function discussed in Chapter 21: They reduce the error costs that are caused by using stale evidence to decide a dispute.

Another illustration of a forced transfer is the doctrine of bona fide purchasers. A entrusts his diamond to his agent B with directions to pawn it, and B, misunderstanding, sells it to C. Provided C does not know or have reason to know that B was not authorized to sell the diamond to him, C will acquire a good title to it. This is a simple case of A's being the lower-cost avoider of the mistake than C. But now suppose that B was not A's agent, but stole the diamond from A and sold it to C without giving C any reason to suspect he was buying stolen merchandise. C will not acquire a good title; a thief cannot pass good title to his purchaser. Although A could prevent the erroneous transfer at lower cost than C by taking greater precautions against theft, allowing C to obtain a good title would encourage theft. Thieves would get higher prices from their "fences," because the fences could (provided they took steps to throw the buyer off the scent) get higher prices in the resale market; people will pay more for an assured than a clouded title. We do not want an efficient market in stolen goods.[6]

§3.11 The Distributive Effects of Property Right Assignments

The economist can assist the policymaker not only by explaining the effects of a policy on the efficiency with which resources are used but also by tracing its effects on the distribution of income and wealth. Consider, for example, a proposal to make a factory liable for the damage that its smoke causes to residential property owners. On a superficial analysis the only wealth effect is to make the homeowners better off and the factory owner — surely a rich man — worse off. But the matter is more complicated. If the amount of smoke damage (and the cost of various measures to reduce it) increases as output increases, the new liability will increase the factory's production costs. If the firm was previously selling its product at a price just equal to its cost, either it will have to raise its price to cover the new cost or it will have to reduce

---

6. Some property rights are nontransferable (inalienable). For example, people aren't allowed to sell themselves into slavery, to sell their vital organs, or (in England) their blood to blood banks. Some of these restrictions (e.g., on selling babies for adoption) are discussed in later chapters. For a recent review essay by an economist see Susan Rose-Ackerman, Inalienability and the Theory of Property Rights, 85 Col. L. Rev. 931 (1985).

its output, perhaps to zero. But suppose the firm has competitors who also sell at a price equal to their cost, which is identical to its cost except that they are not liable for smoke damage (or perhaps have newer machinery that does not produce smoke as a by-product). Then the firm cannot raise its price; i.e., consumers would immediately switch to its competitors, which sell the identical product at a price equal to the firm's old price. If the firm's cost of production would be lower with a smaller output (why might it be?), it may be able to cover the additional cost by reducing its output; otherwise it must close down. In either case there will be a reduction not only in profits but in the number of people the factory employs, in the amount of supplies it purchases, and in the amount of rent that it can afford to pay for land and other scarce resources.

Now suppose that all of the competing factories are made subject to liability for smoke damage, and as a result all experience an increase in their costs of production. A price increase is now feasible. Sales will not drop to zero. The product is identical for all of the firms but it is not identical to other products, so consumers may pay more rather than do without. But we know from Chapter 1 that there will be *some* substitution, and therefore the output of the industry will decline. The only difference between this and the previous case is that the consumers now share the burden of the liability,[1] for some of them substitute other products when they would have preferred to continue to buy the industry's product at its former price, while others continue to buy and pay higher prices for the product.

Figure 3.2 graphs these two cases. The left-hand side presents the case of the firm subjected to a cost increase not experienced by its competitors; i.e., it faces a horizontal demand curve because the slightest increase in its price would cause its sales to fall to zero as consumers switched to its competitors.[2] The right-hand side depicts a cost increase that affects all competitors equally; here the industry's demand curve rather than the firm's demand curve is relevant.[3]

The analysis, however, is incomplete because it ignores the effects elsewhere in the economy of a reduction in the output of one product. The output of substitute products will increase, and this may benefit the workers in the industries that manufacture those substitutes. (Consumers may be helped or hurt, depending on whether costs in those industries rise or fall with increases in output.) Attention to effects in other markets distinguishes "general equilibrium" analysis from the more common "partial equilibrium" analysis of changes in the economic environment.

§3.11   1. How might consumers bear a part of the burden in our previous example?
2. Is the existence of competitors a sufficient condition for the demand curve faced by each firm to be horizontal? Why not? What difference does it make to the analysis in the text?
3. Subscript F in Figure 3.2 stands for firm, subscript I for industry.

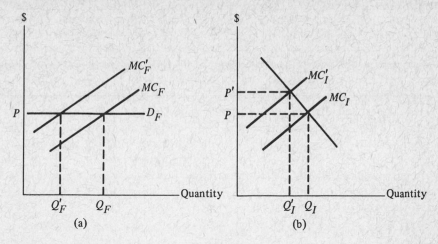

Figure 3.2

With regard to the distributive consequences of pollution control, evaluated in a partial-equilibrium framework, it should be noted that the workers and (in our second case) consumers who pay a part of the cost of compliance may be a less affluent group than those who benefit from the reduction in pollution. Some costs of pollution are matters of aesthetics rather than health and are incurred primarily by well-educated, leisured, and well-to-do people. Furthermore, if the properties the value of which is enhanced by a reduction in pollution are rental properties, the primary beneficiaries will be not the tenants but the owners (who may be wealthy): They will demand a higher rent for what is now more valuable property.[4]

So far we have assumed that a change in property rights is bound to have *some* distributive effect, but this is correct only if the resources affected by the change are specialized — that is, cannot command so high a price in an alternative use. If the land on which the factory is located is as valuable for some other, and smokeless, use, imposing liability will not affect its value. Similarly, if the workers have as good employment opportunities elsewhere, they will suffer only to the extent of moving costs from the reduction in the factory's demand for their services. Only if the land and their skills are more valuable in their present use than in any other use will the contraction or disappearance of the factory affect the landowner's and the workers' wealth.

The distributive effects may also depend on contract. If the employees have long-term employment contracts with the factory owner, he will be forced to absorb a portion of the costs that otherwise would have

4. For some empirical evidence of the regressive incidence of pollution control, see Nancy S. Dorfman & Arthur Snow, Who Will Pay for Pollution Control?, 28 Nat. Tax J. 101 (1975).

fallen on them. If the renters have long-term leases, a part of the benefit of reduced pollution will enure to them rather than to the owners. Although it is thus possible to protect by contract against the wealth effects of a change in property rights, the party desiring protection will have to compensate the other party for assuming the risk of the change.

When high transaction costs make contracting infeasible, wealth effects may still be cushioned by anticipation. Suppose the traditional rule is that farmers have the right to be free from spark damage, but there is some expectation that the rule might be changed. Then purchasers of farmland will pay less, and if the change materializes their loss will be smaller. In sum, a change in law will alter the distribution of wealth only to the extent that the change is unanticipated and affects the demand for specialized resources.

§3.12   Public Lands

Much of the land in the western United States is owned and managed by the federal government. The original impetus for retention of extensive public lands came from the conservation movement, which feared that private development would result in the premature depletion of natural resources, notably timber. There is no economic basis for such a concern. The exploitation of forests for timber, unlike the exploitation of the seas for fish, involves no externalities. In deciding whether to cut down a tree, the private owner of the land on which the tree is growing will consider not only the revenue from the sale of the timber and the cost of cutting down and sawing the tree but also the opportunity cost of not waiting till the tree has grown to its full height.

Government management of the resource has been perverse. The government limits cutting on each tract of government land to the number of trees that have been added by new growth since the last cutting, to prevent a net reduction in the number of trees on the tract. Very old forests tend to have little new growth, because the trees are crowded together. Therefore few trees are allowed to be cut from such tracts — even though greater cutting might, by enabling faster growth, maximize the yield from the forest in the long run. Conversely, the "rule of increase" may lead to excessive cutting of young forests.

The main justification for the government's extensive land ownership is aesthetic: preserving wilderness areas for the enjoyment of campers. The economic rationale is the difficulty of charging for access, and it is weak. Few roads lead into these areas, and toll booths could easily be set up at the entry points. National parks similarly could be privatized; the case for urban public parks is stronger (why?). If for some reason it is desired to subsidize the use of such facilities (though very few of the users are poor), this can be done by a grant of money to the private owner; there is no economic case for government ownership.[1]

Suggested Readings

1. Louis De Alessi, The Economics of Property Rights: A Review of the Evidence, 2 J. Res. L. & Econ. 1 (1980).

2. William F. Baxter, People or Penguins: The Case for Optimal Pollution (1974).

3. Guido Calabresi & A. Douglas Melamed, Property Rules, Liability Rules, and Inalienability: One View of the Cathedral, 85 Harv. L. Rev. 1089 (1972).

4. Marion Clawson, The Economics of National Forest Management (1976).

5. Ronald H. Coase, The Problem of Social Cost, 3 J. Law & Econ. 1 (1960).

6. Harold Demsetz, Toward a Theory of Property Rights, 57 Am. Econ. Rev. Papers & Proceedings 347 (1967).

7. ———, When Does the Rule of Liability Matter?, 1 J. Leg. Stud. 13 (1972).

8. Ross D. Eckert, The Enclosure of Ocean Resources: Economics and the Law of the Sea (1979).

9. Robert C. Ellickson, Alternatives to Zoning: Covenants, Nuisance Rules, and Fines as Land Use Controls, 40 U. Chi. L. Rev. 681 (1973).

10. Thomas W. Merrill, Trespass, Nuisance, and the Costs of Determining Property Rights, 14 J. Leg. Stud. 13 (1985).

11. A.I. Ogus & G.M. Richardson, Economics and the Environment: A Study of Private Nuisance, 36 Camb. L.J. 284 (1977).

12. Bernard H. Siegan, Land Use Without Zoning (1972).

13. John R. Umbeck, A Theory of Property Rights, With Application to the California Gold Rush (1981).

14. Stephen F. Williams, Implied Covenants in Oil and Gas Leases: Some General Principles, 29 U. Kan. L. Rev. 153 (1981).

15. Economic Foundations of Property Law (Bruce A. Ackerman ed. 1975).

Problems

1. Suppose you can find out whether there is a deposit of oil under someone's land by directing a radio wave under the surface of his land.

---

§**3.12** 1. Several topics discussed in property law courses appear later in this book. See §§16.6 (enforcement of housing codes), 17.4 (real estate taxes), 18.2-18.6 (inheritance). See also the discussion of the *Boomer* case in §4.12 *infra*.

You need not be directly over the deposit, i.e., within his boundary lines; the beam can be directed obliquely. Should the owner of the land have the right to enjoin such electronic penetration as a trespass? Is the owner's possible aversion to risk relevant?

2. If the government auctioned off rights to use broadcast frequencies, would the amount bid by the high bidder be equal to the expected social value of the use? Why might it not be?

3. Should the government be required to pay for the information that it collects from individuals and firms for census purposes?

4. Suppose the government condemns a property on which the tenant has made improvements that will outlast the lease. Should the value of the improvement be included in the amount of compensation that the government is required to pay the lessee of the property for the taking? See Almota Farms Elevator Warehouse Co. v. United States, 409 U.S. 470 (1973).

5. A beautiful waterfall runs by A's house. Should A be permitted to appropriate a right to the waterfall as against other users of the stream (assuming he is the prior claimant)? Are there any technical difficulties in recognizing such a right?

6. If there were no right to prevent a man from building so as to block a neighbor's windows, would extortion be encouraged?

7. Are the following formulations of the economic test for which party to assign the property right to equivalent? If not, which is the best one?

(a) Assign the right so as to minimize transaction costs.
(b) Assign the right so as to maximize the probability that, if the right is more valuable to someone else than to the right holder, a transaction will occur.
(c) Assign the right so as to make a transaction unnecessary to achieve efficiency.
(d) Assign the right so as to minimize the sum of transaction costs and the losses resulting from failures to make value-maximizing exchanges.

8. A man finds the entrance to a large scenic cave on his property. The cave runs under other people's land as well. Should he be given the property right to the cave, or should the superjacent owners each own the portion of the cave directly below their land, or should they be deemed joint and undivided owners of the cave? See Edwards v. Sims, 232 Ky. 791, 24 S.W.2d 619 (1929).

9. A tuberculosis sanatorium is built in a residential area. Property values decline because the residents of the area fear contagion from the patients in the sanatorium. Their fear has no scientific basis. Should the sanatorium nonetheless be deemed a nuisance if the fall in residential property values is greater than the increase in the value of the parcel used for the sanatorium? See Everett v. Paschall, 61 Wash. 47, 111 P. 879 (1910); cf. §28.2 infra.

10. Suppose you buy an expensive solar collector and put it on your roof. Later the owner of a neighboring tract puts up a building that blocks your collector. What legal recourse would you have in an efficient system of property law? See Stephen F. Williams, Solar Access and Property Rights: A Maverick Analysis, 11 Conn. L. Rev. 430 (1979); Prah v. Moretti, 108 Wis. 2d 223, 321 N.W.2d 182 (1982).

11. Looking at the question from the standpoint of economics, do you approve or disapprove of the recent efforts of coastal nations to extend their national boundaries to 200 miles from shore? Should a distinction be made between the assertion of national authority over shipping and over mineral exploitation?

12. Discuss the economic effects of inclusionary zoning, whereby a developer of housing for middle-class people is required to set aside a portion of the housing for poor people. See Robert C. Ellickson, The Irony of "Inclusionary Zoning," 54 So. Calif. L. Rev. 1167 (1981).

13. If you were an author and received a flat percentage royalty from your publisher, would you want the publisher to charge a higher or a lower price for the book than the publisher would want to charge? Relate to issues of divided ownership.

CHAPTER 4

CONTRACT RIGHTS AND REMEDIES[1]

§4.1 The Process of Exchange and the Economic Roles of Contract Law

The last chapter emphasized the importance of voluntary exchange (normally of goods or services for money) — market transactions — in moving resources from less to more valuable uses, and it noted various obstacles to value-maximizing exchanges; but the *process* of exchange, once terms are agreed on, was assumed to operate reliably without legal intervention. This is strictly true, however, only where both parties perform their obligations under the contract simultaneously; and that is very rare. Where the simultaneity condition does not hold, two dangers to the process of exchange arise — opportunism and unforeseen contingencies — for which the law offers remedies.

A hires B to build a house, payment due on completion. While the house is being built and before any payment has been made, B is at A's mercy, for he would find it difficult (especially if A owns the land that the house is being built on!) to sell the house to anyone else if A decided not to pay for it. So A could, in principle, force B to reduce his price after construction was under way. (Since contract law, like every other social institution, does not work perfectly, one is not surprised to find that builders insist on progress payments — and not because their customers are their lowest-cost lenders.) After the house is constructed and A pays B, their roles are reversed. A is now at B's mercy. For the construction of the house is not really the end of B's performance but the beginning. A is counting on receiving a stream of services from the house for many years. If B has built the house

---

1. On the law of contracts, see E. Allen Farnsworth, Contracts (1982), and Alan Schwartz & Robert E. Scott, Commercial Transactions: Principles and Policies (1982); the latter is a casebook with many economic notes.

shoddily, and it disintegrates after a few months of use, A's expectations will be bitterly disappointed.

Notice the parallel to the discussion in the last chapter of the disincentive to cultivate land in a world without property rights. Both that problem and the problem of contract opportunism arise from the sequential character of economic activity. If sowing and reaping were simultaneous, the need for recognition of property rights in land (as distinct from harvested crops) would be less urgent; and if contractual exchanges were really simultaneous (as they are not), the need for legal protection of contract rights would be less urgent.[1]

In both areas the absence of legally enforceable rights would, among other consequences, bias investment toward economic activities that could be completed in a short time; and this would reduce efficiency. Suppose A wants to sell his cow. There are two bidders, B and C. The cow is worth $50 to B and $100 to C (and only $30 to A), so efficiency requires that the cow be sold to C rather than B. But B has $50 cash in hand while C cannot obtain any cash for a week. C promises to pay $75 to A in a week, and let us assume that this $25 premium would fully compensate A for the costs, in the event of default, of bringing suit for damages or for return of the cow, discounted by the risk of default — if the law made C's promise to A enforceable. But if the law does not enforce such promises, A may decide that, since C may fail to raise the money and B in the interim lose interest in the transaction, he is better off selling the cow to B now. If he does, it means that the failure of the law to provide a remedy if C breaks his promise will have induced a misallocation of resources, by discouraging an exchange in which the performance of one party is deferred. B might of course resell the cow to C later, but this would involve an additional transaction cost.

Now suppose that A offers to sell a shirt for $5, and B offers one for $6 which he claims (truthfully) will last three times as long as A's shirt and is therefore a better value, but the difference is not apparent on casual inspection or handling. B may be willing to guarantee the superior durability of his shirt, but, if his promise is not legally enforceable, consumers may doubt the honesty of his claim and buy A's shirt instead, again a suboptimum result.

It does not follow that without a law of contracts the system of voluntary exchange would break down completely. There are contracts in societies that have no formal law-enforcement machinery and contracts between nations that recognize no legal constraints on their sovereignty.

§4.1   1. This implies, and we find, that in primitive societies, where contractual exchanges tend to be simultaneous, the law of contracts, in contrast to many other areas of primitive law, is rudimentary; in particular, executory contracts — contracts where neither party has yet begun to perform his contractual undertaking — are not enforced. See Richard A. Posner, The Economics of Justice 182-184 (1981).

Someone who is known not to perform his side of bargains will find it difficult to find anyone willing to make exchanges with him in the future, which is a costly penalty for taking advantage of the vulnerability of the other party to a contract, the vulnerability that is due to the sequential character of performance. There might even be more explicit definition, either in writing or by reference to custom, of the undertakings of the parties to an exchange than there would be under a regime of enforceable contracts. Transacting parties would be particularly eager to minimize misunderstandings that might give rise to charges of bad faith, since someone against whom such charges were lodged would find it more difficult to get people to make exchanges with him in the future than would be true if contract rights were legally enforceable.

A purely voluntary system would not be efficient, though. Apart from the costs involved in maintaining credit bureaus and administering security deposits (especially in a world where the return of the deposit could not be legally compelled), self-protection would not always work. Although someone contemplating breaking his contract would consider the costs to him of thereby reducing the willingness of other people to contract with him in the future, the benefits from breach might exceed those costs. He might be very old; or (a related point) the particular contract might dwarf all future contracts that he expected to make; or he might not be dependent on contracts but be able to function quite nicely in the future on a cash-and-carry basis.

Thus the fundamental function of contract law (and recognized as such at least since Hobbes's day[2]) is to deter people from behaving opportunistically toward their contracting parties, in order to encourage the optimal timing of economic activity and make costly self-protective measures unnecessary. But it is not always obvious when a party is behaving opportunistically. Suppose A hires B to paint his portrait "to A's satisfaction." B paints a portrait that connoisseurs of portraiture admire, although not enough to buy it themselves at the contract price. A rejects the portrait and refuses to give any reason for the rejection. If the rejection is not made in good faith, A will be held to have broken the contract. Good faith — which means in this context not trying to take advantage of the vulnerabilities created by the sequential character of performance under a contract — is an implied term of every contract. No one would voluntarily place himself at the mercy of the other party to a contract; it is therefore reasonable to assume that if the parties had thought about the possibility of bad faith they would have forbidden it expressly.

Should the law go further, and read into the contract an implied duty of reasonableness on A's part? It should not (and does not). The parties probably meant A to be the sole judge of the adequacy of B's performance. The language of the contract so suggests, though not

2. See Thomas Hobbes, Leviathan 70-71 (1914 [1651]).

conclusively; and the suggestion is reinforced by reflecting on the incompetence of a judge or jury to determine whether A, though in fact (by assumption that he is acting in good faith) dissatisfied with the portrait, ought to have liked it. On the other hand, if the contract, although containing the same language, were for the painting of the outside walls of a factory, the court might decide that the parties had not intended to make the buyer's whimsy the measure of the seller's compliance, as judge or jury could determine without great difficulty whether the paint job was adequate to its workaday purpose.[3]

In speaking of an implied contractual term we identify another important function of contract law besides preventing opportunistic behavior, and that is filling out the parties' agreement. This function too is related to the sequential character of contractual performance. The longer the performance will take — and bear in mind that in performance we must include the entire stream of future services that the exchange contemplates — the harder it will be for the parties to foresee the various contingencies that might affect performance. Moreover, some contingencies, although foreseeable in the sense that both parties well know that they could occur, are so unlikely to occur that the costs of careful drafting to deal with them might exceed the benefits, when those benefits are discounted by the (low) probability that the contingency will actually occur. It may be cheaper for the court to "draft" the contractual term necessary to deal with the contingency if and when it occurs. The two types of contingency are closely related: The less frequent an event is, the less likely it is that the parties thought about it, their neglect to do so being a rational response to the costs of information relative to the benefits.

The task for a court asked to apply a contract to a contingency that the parties did not foresee is to imagine how the parties would have provided for the contingency if it had occurred to them to do so. Often there will be clues in the language of the contract; but often there will not be, and then the court may have to engage in economic thinking — may have to decide what is the most efficient way of dealing with the contingency. For this is the best way of deciding how the parties would have provided for it. Each party, it is true, is interested just in his own profit, and not in the joint profit; but the larger the joint profit is, the bigger the "take" of each party is likely to be. So they have a mutual interest in minimizing the cost of performance, and the court can use this interest to fill out a contract along lines that the parties would have approved at the time of making the contract. (Can you see a parallel here to the analysis in the last chapter?)

Suppose A buys goods from B, with delivery to take place in a month,

3. See Morin Building Products Co. v. Baystone Construction, Inc., 717 F.2d 413 (7th Cir. 1983).

and during the month B's warehouse burns down and the goods are destroyed. The contract is silent on the allocation of the risk of loss before delivery. But since A can prevent (or insure against) a fire in his own warehouse at lower cost than B can, the parties, if they had thought about the matter, would have assigned the risk to A, even though he no longer "owns" the goods; and that is the assignment the court should make in the absence of any other evidence of the parties' intentions.

This approach suggests a general rule for deciding what warranties (legally enforceable promises) should be held to be implied in a sale of goods. The manufacturer warrants those and only those dimensions of performance that are primarily within his control rather than the buyer's. Thus he is held to impliedly warrant that the goods are fit for their intended use — but not that they will last indefinitely; their durability may depend to a significant degree on how the buyer uses them, a matter within the latter's control.

Here is a more difficult problem of using economics to interpret a contract. The State of Wisconsin once hired a man named Bentley to build wings on the state capitol under the direction of the state's architect. Bentley followed the architect's plans faithfully, but they were no good, and the wings collapsed shortly after being completed. The state sued Bentley, alleging that he had guaranteed his work against such a calamity. The contract said nothing germane on the subject; obviously neither party had thought it likely that the wings would collapse because the architect's plans were no good. The state lost its suit.[4] This seems the right economic result. The state could have prevented the calamity at lower cost than Bentley, by more careful selection or supervision of the architect. Even so, it is possible to argue that one purpose of the contract was to insure the state against the collapse of the wings from any cause; for insurance is one way of dealing with unforeseen contingencies, and contracts are often a method of insurance (see §4.5 *infra*). But it is unlikely that Bentley was a better insurer than the state. Bentley would probably have to go out and buy an insurance policy; the state could self-insure against the particular risk. (We shall come back to the insurance function of contracts.)

We have thus far hewed very closely to the notion of contract law as a handmaiden of exchange (of transfer of property rights, in the terminology of the last chapter). But this takes too narrow a view of the subject, as some examples will illustrate.

(1) A wealthy man in an expansive moment promises to pay my way through college. I give up my part-time job, but he then breaks his promise, and I am unable to get a new job.

(2) A promises to deliver goods to B "on the twelfth." B thinks he

4. Bentley v. State, 73 Wis. 416, 41 N.W. 338 (1889).

means the twelfth of this month, but in fact A means the twelfth
of next month — he could not possibly deliver so soon as B (un-
beknownst to him) expects.

(3) The A steel company agrees to deliver steel to the B bridge-
building company within 60 days, but A experiences a wildcat
strike and cannot make delivery.

In none of these cases is the issue whether a party to an exchange
has *refused* to carry out his end of the bargain. There is no exchange
in the first case; giving up my part-time job confers no advantage on
the wealthy promisor. He may not even have known that I gave it up.
In the second case, there is no exchange, in fact or in intent; the parties
intended different transactions. In the third case, performance was prevented by circumstances beyond the promisor's control. Yet in all three
cases there is an economic argument for imposing sanctions on the
party who fails to perform.

In the first case, the wealthy man's idle promise induced reliance
that cost the promisee heavily when it was broken. Such a cost can be
avoided for the future by holding such a promisor liable for the promisee's reliance costs. We must distinguish, however, between the sort
of donative promise that is likely to induce reliance and the sort that
is not. I promise you a trivial gift and the next day withdraw my promise.
I had no reason to expect you to rely — your reliance was precipitate,
imprudent — so whether or not you do rely the law will not hold me
to my promise.

Suppose, in the case where the buyer and seller confuse the date,
that the custom of the industry is that a delivery date without specification
of the month refers to the current month. A is new to the industry
and ignorant of the custom. Nevertheless, to hold A to the promise
understood by B will have the salutary effect of inducing newcomers
to master the language of the trade promptly — although to be confident
that this would be the optimal result we would have to consider (1)
whether existing firms might not be the cheapest source of newcomers'
information about the custom and (2) the possible anticompetitive effects
of placing the burden of acquiring this information on new entrants
into the market.[5]

As for the third case, the steel company is probably in a better position
to anticipate and take appropriate safeguards against an interruption
of production due to a wildcat strike. If so, placing the risk of such an
interruption on the steel company, by making it liable for damages to
the purchaser from delay, may be the cheapest way of minimizing the
costs of such delays in the future.

In these examples, the question of whether to treat a failure to carry

---

5. See Elizabeth Warren, Trade Usage and Parties in the Trade: An Economic Rationale
for an Inflexible Rule, 42 U. Pitt. L. Rev. 515 (1981).

through an undertaking as a breach of contract is in economic analysis similar to the question of whether to treat an interference with a neighbor's land use as an invasion of the neighbor's property rights. We ask: Will imposing liability create incentives for value-maximizing conduct in the future? Another example may help fix this point. I sell wool to a garment manufacturer, neither of us inspects, the wool turns out to have a latent defect, and the dresses he makes out of the wool are ruined. Assume that the cost of inspection by either of us would be lower than the cost of the damage discounted by the probability that the wool would have a defect. The manufacturer sues me for breach of contract. The central legal issue in the case is which of us had a duty to inspect. The answer depends, as to an economist it should depend, on the relative costs of inspection. If it is cheaper for the other fellow to inspect, his suit will fail in order to encourage him in his future dealings and others in similar situations to inspect; that is the solution that minimizes the sum of inspection and damage costs.

If it really is cheaper for me to inspect, but the court nevertheless holds that I did not break the contract, in the future the buyer will pay me to include a clause in which I promise to compensate him for any latent defects. A corrective transaction is more likely than in a pollution case, where transaction costs often are prohibitive. But this point only underscores the futility of a contract-law ruling that ignores the economics of the case. The ruling will not affect future conduct; it will be reversed by the parties in their subsequent dealings. But it will impose additional (and avoidable) transaction costs.

§4.2 Consideration

The doctrine that a promise, to be legally enforceable, must be supported by consideration may seem at first glance a logical corollary to the idea that the role of contract law is to facilitate the movement of resources, by voluntary exchange, into their most valuable uses. If the promise is entirely one-sided, it cannot be part of the exchange process. But it is not true that the only promises worth enforcing are those incidental to an exchange. Recall the case where a young man gives up a part-time job on the basis of a wealthy man's promise to pay his way through college. There is no exchange in any realistic sense, yet the law treats the breach of promise as the breach of a contract. It does this through the fiction that "detrimental reliance" (giving up the part-time job) is a form of consideration — but it does it nevertheless.

Here is a more difficult case: A rescues B from some peril, and B promises A an annuity for the rest of his life. Enforceable? Yes, on the theory (if one can call it that) that there is "moral consideration," even though the rescue was complete before any promise was made. The result makes sense, provided B intends a legally binding promise. Making B's promise binding will in these circumstances actually enhance B's welfare, ex ante (that is, at the time of the promise). B wants to make a generous gift; but if he cannot make a binding assurance to A that the gift will be rendered according to its terms (that is, throughout A's entire life), the gift will be worth less to A, and hence it will yield less satisfaction (utility) to B as well. Thus, making the promise legally enforceable makes everyone better off — most clearly in the case, presumably the most common, where A never has to seek legal enforcement of B's promise.

If the law is so willing to fictionalize the requirement of consideration, what possible function could the doctrine serve?

1. It reduces the number of phony contract suits, by requiring the plaintiff to prove more than just that someone promised him something; he must show there was a deal of some sort — which is a little harder to make up out of whole cloth. This evidentiary function is important in a system like ours that enforces oral contracts (a virtual necessity in the age of the telephone).

2. It reduces the likelihood of inadvertent contractual commitments due to careless or casual use of promissory language. (Is the doctrine of moral consideration consistent with points 1 and 2?)

3. A function perhaps better discussed when, much later in this book, we consider systematically the costs of administering the judicial system is that of sparing the courts (the costs of which, as we shall see, are not borne entirely by the parties to litigation) from having to enforce a lot of trivial gratuitous promises arising in social and family settings. The concept of detrimental reliance (or promissory estoppel) confines enforcement to those gratuitous promises likely to induce substantial costs on the part of the promisee.

4. A related function is to keep out of the courts cases where, although the context is one of exchange, the undertaking of one or both of the parties is left entirely vague. For example, the parties may not have specified a price, or any method or formula for computing a price. To enforce the parties' agreement in such a case a court would have to determine a reasonable price. But courts have no comparative advantage in determining at what price goods should be sold. On the contrary, in all but very exceptional cases negotiation between buyer and seller is the more reliable method of determining a reasonable price, i.e., one at which exchange is mutually beneficial. The parties should not be allowed to shift the costs of negotiating price to the taxpayers who pay for the judicial system,[1] although as noted in the last section, courts

---

§4.2   1. The Uniform Commercial Code (in force in all states) liberalizes the common law in this area. Among other things, it permits the parties to omit price in circumstances

may have a comparative advantage over the parties in supplying some of the other terms of the contract.

5. The doctrine of consideration plays a role in preventing opportunistic behavior. In *Alaska Packers' Assn. v. Domenico*,[2] the defendant hired seamen in San Francisco for a voyage to Alaska to fish for salmon. When the defendant's boat arrived in Alaskan waters, the seamen announced they would do no work unless the defendant raised the wages that had been agreed on before the voyage began. Unable to procure substitute help during the short Alaskan fishing season, the defendant yielded and promised to pay the seamen the higher wages they demanded when the boat returned to San Francisco. (Did he have to yield? How would his situation vis-à-vis the seamen be described in economic terms?) He reneged when the boat returned to San Francisco, and they sued. They lost, on the ground that the modification of the contract was unenforceable because it was not supported by fresh consideration. This is the correct economic result, as once it is well known that such modifications are unenforceable workers in the position of the seamen in the *Domenico* case will know that it will do them no good to take advantage of their employers' vulnerability.[3] An opposite result had been reached, but in critically different circumstances, in *Goebel v. Linn*.[4] The plaintiff had promised to supply the defendant with ice, but the ice "crop" failed because of unseasonably warm weather, and the plaintiff demanded and obtained the defendant's promise to pay a higher price. The defendant reneged, and the plaintiff's suit for breach of contract was met with the defense that the modification had not been supported by consideration. But the evidence showed that the plaintiff (quite unlike the seamen in *Domenico*) would have gone broke if the defendant had tried to enforce the contract as written, and if that had happened the defendant might not have gotten any ice. The modification was not opportunistic (in bad faith) on the plaintiff's part (there was no suggestion that the plaintiff had deliberately courted the risk of bankruptcy), but a reasonable adjustment to an unintended and unprovided for change of circumstances.

The difference between the two cases can be generalized as follows. In the opportunistic case (*Domenico*), nothing has happened to raise the cost of the promisor's performance; all that has changed is that the promisee has put himself in the promisor's power. (This assumes, it should be noted, that the promisee does not have adequate contract remedies against the promisor's threat not to perform. If he did, the threat would not be credible even if the law allowed modification without fresh consideration.) In the nonopportunistic case (*Goebel*), the promi-

where there is a published spot price. Not only is the ascertainment of price mechanical in these circumstances, but specifying the price would defeat the purpose of the contract, which is to transact at a changing market price.

2. 117 F. 99 (9th Cir. 1902).

3. Issues similar to those in *Domenico* are discussed in Chapter 11 (labor law).

4. 47 Mich. 489, 11 N.W. 284 (1882).

sor's cost of performance has risen unexpectedly since the contract was signed. This implies that he is not bluffing; if the contract is not modified, he really will not perform. In the opportunistic case, since the promisor could perform at a profit by complying with the original terms of the contract, he probably (why just probably?) will perform if the law deprives his threat of efficacy.

Goebel shows that there are, and on economic grounds must be, exceptions to the principle that contract modifications are unenforceable without fresh consideration. The tendency in the modern law is to jettison the requirement of fresh consideration and simply refuse to enforce modifications procured by duress — a term that can be given a precise economic meaning by reference to the facts of *Domenico*. See §4.7 *infra*.

Consistent with the economic interpretation of the doctrine of consideration, courts inquire only as to the existence, not as to the adequacy, of the consideration for a promise. To ask whether there is consideration is simply to inquire whether the situation is one of exchange and a bargain has been struck. To go further and ask whether the consideration is adequate would require the court to do what we have said it is less well equipped to do than the parties — decide whether the price (and other essential terms) specified in the contract are reasonable.

§4.3   Mutual Assent and Unilateral Contracts

The presumption that a contemplated exchange is value-maximizing is valid only when the parties actually agree on the terms of the exchange. If you offer to buy my watch for $10, but the telegraph company makes a mistake in transmission and the telegram as I receive it says "$20," the fact that I accept the offer as I understand it is no evidence that the sale will increase value; the watch might be worth $14 to me, and only $12 to you. The "subjective" theory of contract, which holds that there must be an actual meeting of the minds of the contracting parties for an enforceable contract to arise, thus makes economic sense. But it does not follow that damages should never be assessed against one who refuses to carry out a promise that he would not have made but for a failure of communication — the objective theory of contract, too, has a core of economic justification, although in economic analysis such a refusal is more like a tort than a breach of contract.

In the telegraph case, the question that principally interests the economist is which party is in a better position to prevent misunderstandings as a result of garbled transmission.[1] Possibly it is the party who selects

§4.3   1. In what circumstances might the telegraph company itself be the least-cost avoider?

the method of communication; he could send a confirmatory letter or use the telephone or a messenger. If he could have avoided the misunderstanding at lower cost than the other party, then placing liability on him will make future mishaps less likely. But when liability is imposed on this ground it is somewhat misleading to speak of the defective communication as having created an enforceable contract; the defect makes it impossible to say whether an exchange was intended.

An interesting problem of mutual assent is presented by the unilateral contract. I offer $10 for the return of my lost cat. There is no negotiation with potential finders, no acceptance of my offer in the conventional sense. Yet someone who hears of the reward and returns my cat has a legally enforceable claim to the reward; his compliance with the terms of the offer is treated as acceptance. This result is correct because it promotes a value-maximizing transaction: The cat is worth more than $10 to me and less than $10 to the finder, so the exchange of money for cat increases social welfare yet would not be so likely to occur if the finder did not have a legally enforceable claim to the reward.[2]

A more difficult question is whether, as most courts hold, the finder must have actual knowledge of the offer in order to have a legal claim to the reward. The legal reason, casuistic rather than practical, is that acceptance requires knowledge of the offer. The economic issue is whether the return of lost property would be encouraged or discouraged by a rule requiring actual knowledge of the offer.

One must distinguish between the two types of finder: the finder who is induced to search for lost property by the knowledge that there is a reward for its return, and the casual finder, who will not invest in search but who may return lost property if he happens to find it, knowing that there *may* be a reward. A rule requiring actual knowledge discourages the casual finder (if — a big if — he knows about the rule and if he is not altruistic), but by the same token encourages the active searcher by reducing the likelihood that his competitor, the casual finder, will return the property if he finds it first.

The question then becomes whether the increase in returns by active searchers is likely to be greater or less than the decrease in returns by casual finders. Although active searchers are less common than casual finders, it seems quite unlikely that many casual finders, who by definition do not know whether or not there is a reward — only that there may be a reward — will actually bother to return what they find. Giving them a legal entitlement to any reward that is offered, therefore, is unlikely to increase significantly the number of returns by casual finders. But by the same token it will not discourage active searchers much either. Maybe neither rule will lead to more returns, in which event the rule

---

2. The unilateral contract is a device for overcoming high transaction costs; can you see why?

that requires actual knowledge, by cutting down on the number of legal claims, is preferable as being cheaper.[3]

§4.4   Mutual Mistake

In the famous case of the sale of the cow Rose 2d of Aberlone,[1] both seller and buyer believed that the cow was barren, and the price was set accordingly. In fact, the cow was pregnant and worth about 10 times as much as the selling price. The mistake was discovered before the cow was delivered to the buyer, and the seller canceled the sale. The court upheld the cancellation. If we accept the version of the facts presented in the majority opinion, the result may appear consistent with efficiency. There was no basis for presuming the cow more valuable in the buyer's possession than in the seller's — its true worth being an order of magnitude different from what the parties had thought — and the seller had not been careless in thinking the cow barren; he made a reasonable — indeed, an unavoidable (at reasonable cost) — mistake.

But the case can be approached differently and more fruitfully by observing that it was a case where an unforeseen contingency occurred and by asking how the parties would have allocated the risk of this occurrence had they foreseen it. There was some evidence that Rose's sale price included her value if pregnant, discounted (very drastically of course) by the probability of that happy eventuality.[2] This evidence suggested that the parties had intended to transfer the risk of the cow's turning out to be pregnant to the buyer, in which event the contract clearly should have been enforced. But even without such evidence there is an argument for placing the risk that the cow is not what it seems on the seller. In general, if not in every particular case, the owner will have access at lower cost than the buyer to information about the characteristics of his property and can therefore avoid mistakes about these characteristics more cheaply than prospective buyers can. This is why the seller of a house is liable to the buyer for latent (as distinct from obvious) defects; a similar principle could be used to decide cases of mutual mistake.

Where a contingency affecting performance occurs *after* the contract has been signed (Rose had been pregnant when the contract was signed), the courts have less difficulty in recognizing that the issue is how the

---

3. This assumes that the reduction in the number of claims is not offset by the increased complexity of processing each one. The increase in complexity is due to the presence of an additional issue: whether the finder knew of the reward.

§4.4   1. Sherwood v. Walker, 66 Mich. 568, 33 N.W. 919 (1887).

2. See id. at 580, 33 N.W. at 924-925 (dissenting opinion).

parties (implicitly) allocated the risk of an unexpected event. At the most elementary level, if a contract calls for the delivery of wheat on a fixed date at $3 a bushel, the fact that on that date the market price is $6 will not operate to discharge the contract; the parties plainly intended to assign the risk of price changes to the supplier. But sometimes the intended assignment of risks is unclear. This is the domain of the doctrines of impossibility, impracticability, and frustration, discussed next.

§4.5 Contracts as Insurance — Impossibility and Related Doctrines and the Interpretation of Insurance Contracts

We have noted the possible confusion that is created by stating the issue in a contract case as whether to enforce the contract rather than whether to impose liability. Suppose I agree to supply someone with 1,000 widgets by July 1; my factory burns to the ground; and I cannot procure widgets from anyone else in time to fulfill the contract. Suppose, further, that there was no way in which I could have anticipated or prevented the fire, so that fulfillment of the contract was genuinely impossible. It does not follow that I should not be liable for the buyer's losses that resulted from my failure to perform. My undertaking may have implicitly included a promise to insure him in the event of my inability to deliver the promised goods on time. And if such a contract of insurance was implicit in the transaction, it should be enforced.

The distinction between *prevention* and *insurance* as methods of minimizing loss is fundamental to the analysis of contract law. A loss that can be averted by an expenditure smaller than the expected loss is preventable, but not all losses are preventable in this sense; the fire that destroyed the factory in the preceding example was assumed not to be. It may be possible through insurance, however, to reduce the costs created by the risk of loss. The insured exchanges the possibility of a loss for a smaller, but certain, cost (the insurance premium).

Suppose there is a 1 percent probability of a fire that will cause $10,000 in damage. As noted in Chapter 1, to someone who was risk averse this risk would be more costly than a certain loss of its actuarial equivalent, $100. Shifting the risk to an insurance company may eliminate the extra cost. By pooling the insured's fire risk with many other risks with which the insured's is uncorrelated (i.e., the probabilities are independent), the insurance company transforms a risk into a (nearly) certain cost and thus eliminates the disutility of risk. This is why the company can charge an insurance premium that covers all of its own costs yet is still attractive to the insured because it is lower than his costs, including the disutility he attaches to risk.

For example, the insurance company might insure 1,000 buildings, each with a 1 percent probability of experiencing a $10,000 fire loss.[1] If these probabilities are independent (can you guess the meaning and significance of this qualification?), the insurance company can be reasonably certain that it will have to pay out very close to $100,000 in insurance claims; the probability that it will have to make good the total loss insured against — $10,000,000 — is infinitesimal. In contrast, the probability that if uninsured the individual building owner would sustain his maximum loss is as we know a nonnegligible 1 percent.

The purchase of an explicit insurance policy is referred to as market insurance. In some cases, self-insurance is possible. A real estate company may own the 1,000 buildings in the previous example; if so, its "risk" of fire loss is a nearly certain prospect of incurring a $100,000 cost. We shall see in Chapter 15 that an investor can reduce the risks associated with a particular security by holding a diversified portfolio — a set of securities whose risks are (at least partially) uncorrelated with one another. The principle is the same as in the fire example. And ordinary commercial contracts also shift risks and thus provide a form of insurance. The risk-shifting or insurance function of contracts is related to the fact that a contract (other than the truly simultaneous exchange, which is not problematic) by its nature commits the parties to a future course of action; and the future is uncertain.

A nice example of how contracts allocate risk is "demurrage," the charge that carriers levy on shippers who (in the case of carriage by rail, for example) keep the railroad's boxcars for loading or unloading longer than their contract with the carrier provides for. The shipper can choose between two forms of demurrage agreement. Under the first, called straight demurrage, the shipper pays a fixed charge for every day he keeps the cars after a two-day grace period. (The charge is $10 per car per day for the third day, rising to $30 after six days.) But the charge is forgiven if the delay in returning the cars is due to severe weather or other circumstances beyond the shipper's control. Under the second agreement, called the average agreement, there are no excuses for delay; but on the other hand the shipper gets $10 for each car he returns within the first day of the car's arrival at his loading dock. Thus straight demurrage allocates the risk of bad weather to the railroad, while the average agreement allocates it to the shipper and compensates him for bearing it by entitling him to charge the railroad for early delivery. The shipper's attitude toward risk as well as any comparative advantage he may have in coping with unexpectedly severe

---

§4.5   1. Intermediate loss possibilities are ignored for the sake of simplicity.

weather or other surprises will determine which form of demurrage he chooses.[2]

Thus, even if an event rendering the contract uneconomical (such as unexpectedly severe weather) is not preventable — that is, not preventable at a cost less than the expected value of the loss caused by nonperformance — one of the contracting parties may be the cheaper insurer. If so, this furnishes a reason, independent of ability to prevent the event from occurring, for assuming that the parties, if they had adverted to the issue, would have assigned that party the risk of the particular event. If the promisee is the intended risk bearer, the promisor should be discharged if the risk materializes and prevents him from completing performance under the contract.

To determine the cheaper insurer, it is convenient to divide the costs of insurance into two categories: (1) measurement costs and (2) transaction costs. The first consists of the costs of estimating (a) the probability that the risk will materialize and (b) the magnitude of the loss if the risk does materialize. The product of the two is the expected value of the loss and is the basis for computing the appropriate insurance premium that will be built into the contract price (sometimes in odd ways, as in the demurrage example). The main transaction cost is that of pooling the risk with other risks to reduce or eliminate it; where self-insurance is feasible, this cost may be lower than if market insurance has to be purchased.

This analysis provides a way of understanding the doctrine of impossibility and related grounds for discharging a contract. It explains, for example, why physical impossibility as such is not a ground for discharge. If the promisor is the cheaper insurer, the fact that he could not have prevented the occurrence of the event that prevented him from performing should not discharge him.[3] Conversely, the fact that performance remains physically possible, but is uneconomical, should not *ipso facto* defeat discharge. If the promisor could not have prevented at reasonable cost the event that has prevented him from fulfilling his promise and the promisee was the cheaper insurer of the resulting loss, the promisor has a good argument that he did not break the contract.

It is therefore not surprising that discharge is routinely allowed in personal service contracts where the death of the promisor prevents performance, unless the promisor had reason to believe (and failed to warn the promisee) that his life expectancy was less than normal for someone of his age. The event, death, is probably not preventable at reasonable cost by either party,[4] but the promisee is the cheaper insurer;

2. See Field Container Corp. v. ICC, 712 F.2d 250, 255-256 (7th Cir. 1983).

3. This was recognized by Holmes long ago. See Oliver Wendell Holmes, Jr., The Common Law 300 (1881).

4. To put it differently, the prospect of liability for breach of contract is not likely to induce the promisor to take additional precautions against dying.

although both parties are in an equally good position to estimate the probability of the promisor's death, the promisee is in a better position to estimate the cost to him if the promisor is unable to provide the agreed-upon services.

Another example is a contract to drill for water. The contractor who, because of unexpectedly difficult soil conditions, is unable to complete performance at the cost he projected is not excused. He probably is the superior insurer, even if he could not have anticipated the soil conditions. He will know better than the promisee both the likelihood, and the consequences for the costs of drilling, of encountering subsoil conditions that make drilling difficult. He may also be able to self-insure at low cost because he does a lot of drilling in different areas and the risks of encountering unexpectedly difficult conditions are independent.

These examples could be multiplied,[5] but instead of doing this let us examine the related case where completion of performance by one of the parties is prevented, again by circumstances beyond his control, and that party wants to be excused from further performance or even wants to be paid for what he has done although it is not what the contract called for him to do. I hire a contractor to build a house and midway through construction the building burns down. The contractor demands to be paid for the material and labor that he expended on the construction or, alternatively, refuses to rebuild the house without a new contract. The fact that he was prevented through no fault of his own from performing as contemplated by the contract should not automatically entitle him to cancel it or to be paid as if the burned-down building had been what I contracted for. The issue should be which of us was intended to bear the risk of fire.

In the absence of evidence of the parties' actual intentions, the question can be answered by comparing the relative costs to the parties of preventing or insuring against fire. The contractor is probably the cheaper insurer since he is in a better position than the owner to estimate the likelihood and consequences of fire at various stages in the construction. An additional consideration is that even if the particular fire was not preventable in an economic sense, the contractor (like a manufacturer whose goods are destroyed by fire before delivery) is generally better situated than the owner for fire prevention because he has custody of the premises and knowledge about the fire hazards of buildings under construction.

Issues closely related to those discussed in this and the preceding section arise under other contract doctrines. We gave an example in

5. See Richard A. Posner & Andrew M. Rosenfield, Impossibility and Related Doctrines in Contract Law: An Economic Analysis, 6 J. Leg. Stud. 83 (1977); Jeffrey M. Perloff, The Effects of Breaches of Forward Contracts Due to Unanticipated Price Changes, 10 J. Leg. Stud. 221 (1981); cf. Paul L. Joskow, Commercial Impossibility, the Uranium Market, and the Westinghouse Case, 6 J. Leg. Stud. 119 (1977).

discussing contract modification in a previous section. Here is another example: War is declared while a ship is in port en route to its ultimate destination, and the crew refuses to continue the voyage unless the master of the ship promises a higher wage. He does so, but later refuses to honor the promise on the ground that it was unsupported by consideration, the crew having been contractually obligated to complete the voyage. The question is how the original employment contract allocated the risk of war. If it was allocated to the crew they were presumably compensated for assuming it, and hence a promise to pay them additional wages would not be supported by consideration. Probably, however, the master is better able to estimate both the probability and magnitude of the risk of war. Hence we may assume that the employment contract implicitly assigned the risk to him, in which event the crew's agreement to continue the voyage under wartime conditions would be consideration for the promise of higher wages.

Understanding the insurance function of contracts makes it easier to understand the interpretation of contracts with insurance companies. Take the principle that insurance contracts are to be construed against the insurer. This may seem paternalistic or sentimental, but there is an economic argument for it. One's insurance coverage will turn out to be less extensive than it appeared to be, if ambiguities in the insurance policy are resolved against the insured. The insurance company is the superior bearer of this risk, too. Of course, if all interpretive doubts are resolved against the insurance company, its costs, and hence premium rates, will be higher. But all this means is that the insured is buying some additional insurance.

In the infancy of formal insurance, insurance contracts were construed strictly against the insured, not the insurer; anything that the insured did that increased the insurer's risk was apt to be viewed as a deviation that excused the insurer from performing his side of the bargain.[6] Naturally the insurer doesn't want the insured to increase the risk on which the insurance premium was based; but at the same time the insured does not have perfect control over the conditions (including the conduct of his own employees) that may affect that risk.[7] As insurance markets expanded, insurers had less need to impose the risk of change on the insured; the risk pool was large enough to enable insurers to offset the increase in the risk of one insured during the policy period against a decline in the risk of another insured during the same period. Hence the doctrine of deviations was progressively liberalized — a trend consistent with the changing market conditions.

An interesting question in the interpretation of insurance contracts

6. For an interesting discussion of the evolution of insurance law, see Morton J. Horwitz, The Transformation of American Law, 1780-1860, at 226-237 (1977).

7. A parallel problem in the financing of business ventures is discussed in §§14.2 and 14.4 *infra*.

has arisen recently in suits by asbestos manufacturers against their insurers.[8] Asbestos sold many years ago has turned out to have devastating consequences for the health of workers who inhaled the asbestos fibers. The workers have sued Manville and the other asbestos manufacturers on grounds of products liability (discussed in Chapter 6), and they in turn have tried to collect from their products liability insurers. The insurance policies, however, insured the manufacturers against losses due to "occurrences" during the term of the policies, which lapsed many years ago, and the insurance companies argue that the inhalation of the fibers was not the occurrence against which they insured the manufacturers; the actual illnesses on which products liability suits against the manufacturers might be based are the occurrences, and they did not occur till years after the inhalation, when as a delayed consequence the workers began to manifest the symptoms of asbestosis and other lung diseases.

The problem with the insurance companies' argument is that once the symptoms are manifest, it is no longer possible for the manufacturers to buy insurance; suits for products liability are now a certainty, not a risk. The only way to insure against a long-delayed consequence of a liability-creating act is to buy insurance before the act occurs or is known to be hazardous, and that is a possible interpretation of what the asbestos manufacturers did.

§4.6   Fraud

Even when nothing has happened since the signing of the contract to make performance uneconomical, discharge may be permitted where the presumption that performance would produce a value-increasing exchange is rebutted, as when it is shown that the promisee induced the promise by a lie. But suppose the promisee does not lie but also does not disclose information, known to him, which if communicated to the promisor would have made the deal fall through. In *Laidlaw v. Organ*,[1] a merchant in New Orleans named Organ, learning of the Treaty of Ghent (which ended the War of 1812) before news of it had been made public, ordered a large quantity of tobacco from the Laidlaw firm at a specified price. When the public learned of the treaty, which ended the British naval blockade of New Orleans, the price of tobacco rose

8. See, e.g., Keene Corp. v. Insurance Co. of North America, 667 F.2d 1034 (D.C. Cir. 1981); Insurance Co. of North America v. Forty-Eight Insulations, Inc., 633 F.2d 1212 (6th Cir. 1980); Eagle-Picher Indus., Inc. v. Liberty Mut. Ins. Co., 628 F.2d 12 (1st Cir. 1982).

§4.6.   1. 15 U.S. (2 Wheat.) 178 (1817), discussed in Anthony T. Kronman, Mistake, Disclosure, Information, and the Law of Contracts, 7 J. Leg. Stud. 1, 9-18 (1978).

rapidly by 30 to 50 percent, and Laidlaw tried to back out. The Supreme Court held it could not. If Organ when he placed his order had told Laidlaw, as he easily could have done, that the treaty had been signed, Laidlaw would have insisted on a higher price; and since it would have been costless for Organ to communicate information he already had, it might seem that the Supreme Court's result simply handed him an outrageous windfall. But this is not correct. Although information once obtained may be cheap to convey to another person, it often is not cheap to obtain; and if we do not allow people to profit from information by keeping it to themselves, they will have less or no incentive to obtain it in the first place, and society often will be the loser. (Can you see a parallel between the result in *Laidlaw v. Organ* and the discussion of patent law in Chapter 3?) Of course this is a very poor argument if the information is kept secret forever; and indeed there may seem a paradox in defending secrecy by its effect in promoting information. But Organ didn't keep his information completely secret. By placing his order with Laidlaw, thereby adding to the demand for tobacco, he caused the price to rise, albeit not so far as it did when the information was fully disclosed. The process of price adjustment to the information that the war had ended began sooner because of Organ's transaction. He would not have had any incentive to begin it if he could not have profited from concealing some of the information he had — the rest, though, got impounded in the market price.

The lie is different. The liar makes a positive investment in misinformation. This investment is completely wasted from a social standpoint, so naturally we do not reward him for his lie. Here is an intermediate case: A, knowing his house is infested by termites, fails to reveal this fact to B. It can be argued (judicial authority is divided on the question) that A has a duty to disclose, or in legal language that his failure to do so is an actionable omission. Probably A has not invested (much) in discovering that the house has termites, but acquired the information just as a by-product of living there. Also, this information benefits fewer people (why?) than information about the value of tobacco. So the benefit of the information is less, and the need to provide legal protection in order to induce its production is also less. Now apply this analysis to the case of the pregnant cow.

With the termite example we pass into the realm of consumer fraud, often thought a more serious problem than fraud in commercial contracts because of the disparity of resources and expertise between seller and buyer in the consumer product setting. But if the business purchaser is deemed particularly competent because he specializes in the purchase of goods that he uses in his business, the consumer is a specialist in the purchase of consumer goods. A better reason for believing that fraud is a graver problem in consumer than in commercial transactions is the difficulty of devising effective legal remedies where the stakes are small. The efforts of the legal system to cope with this problem are discussed later in this book.[2] The reader should note, however, that many consumer frauds — for example, in the sale of a house or an automobile — involve sufficiently large stakes to make the prosecution of a lawsuit worthwhile.

It might seem that the availability of legal remedies would be unimportant; that the market remedies against misrepresentations would be adequate in consumer and all other markets. If a firm is gaining sales away from its rivals by making false claims about its (or about their) products, they have an incentive to expose the false claims to the consumer. The efforts of firms to correct misleading advertising by rivals are commonly centralized in trade associations, which establish standards of quality and quantity upon which consumers can rely. And with the increasing complexity of products and services, businesses have sprung up whose function is to inform consumers about the merits of particular goods. The department store is an important example. An expert purchaser of the goods of many competing manufacturers, it helps the consumer choose sensibly among competing products.

But there are counters to these arguments. The process by which competitors correct misleading impressions created by one of their number does not work instantaneously, and the interim profits obtainable by the fraudulent seller may exceed any long-term costs in loss of reputation, especially if the seller can leave the market at low cost. Moreover, if a fraudulent seller is diverting only a small amount of business from each of his rivals, none of them will have an incentive to take costly measures to correct his misrepresentations, even though the aggregate sales diverted by him may be very large. The trade association is only a partial answer. Members of an industry do not have strong incentives to support trade association activity, because the seller who contributes nothing to the trade association's campaign against fraud will derive (under what conditions?) virtually the same benefits from the campaign as the other sellers, and at no cost. This is the familiar free-rider problem.

Also, not all industries are competitive. A monopolist (or cartel) may have a greater incentive than a firm in a competitive industry to misrepresent the qualities of its product, as the effect of the larger output will be spread across a large number of substitute goods, none of which will be greatly affected; so there is even less likelihood than in the competitive case that any seller will have a strong incentive to combat the misrepresentation. A related but more general point is that where a fact about a product pertains equally to all brands of the product, no

---

2. See §21.8 *infra.* Notice that the remedial problem may not be acute when the consumer's performance follows the seller's, as in the typical installment contract. In such a case the defrauded consumer does not have to start a lawsuit: He can rescind. The effectiveness of this remedy depends, of course, on when he discovers the fraud and also on the applicability of the holder-in-due-course doctrine, which is discussed in the next section.

producer may have a strong incentive to disclose it, even if the industry is competitive. If one cigarette manufacturer advertises that smoking is good for your health, other cigarette manufacturers will have no incentive to disparage his claim. And since there are no close nontobacco substitutes whose producers could anticipate a big increase in sales by persuading consumers not to smoke, no other manufacturer has a strong incentive to disparage cigarettes either.

This example invites attention to the question of whether there should be a general legal duty on a seller of consumer goods to disclose material information to consumers. Although there is no *Laidlaw v. Organ* type of objection to such a duty (why not?), imposing it across the board would be inefficient. The question of liability for nondisclosure should turn on which of the parties to the transaction, seller or consumer, can produce or obtain information at lower cost. If the relevant product characteristic is one that the purchaser can determine by casual inspection or handling at the time of purchase — the softness of a cashmere sweater, for example — then it would be redundant to require the seller to disclose the characteristic. Often, however, determining a product characteristic requires actual use rather than just presale inspection or handling (the whitening effect of a household bleach is an illustration). But if the product is an inexpensive one that is purchased repeatedly, the cost to the consumer of ascertaining the characteristic will still be very low — the cost of the first purchase.

If the seller lies about his product, as distinct from merely failing to disclose negative information about it, his conduct is unlawful even if the buyer could unmask the lie at very low cost. This makes economic sense. A offers to sell B a box of candy. B asks A whether it is necessary to open the box to see whether there is candy and A replies that it is not necessary, that B can take his word for it. So B buys the box without inspecting it, and when he gets home discovers that it contains dry cat food rather than candy. If the lie is not actionable, on the theory that B could easily have avoided its consequences by inspection, then the B's of the world will have to inspect, and the aggregate costs of inspection could be substantial. In contrast, the costs to A of not lying are zero and maybe even, as suggested earlier, negative (cf. §6.15 *infra*).

The case for making nondisclosure actionable is strongest where a product characteristic is not ascertainable by the consumer at low cost, as where:

(1) the product is infrequently purchased, and the characteristic is not discoverable by inspection or handling at the time of purchase;
(2) although the product is more frequently purchased, it is very expensive, like an automobile; and
(3) the characteristic may not be discoverable even through repeated or long use (an example is the quality of the advice in a book on how to make a million dollars in the real estate market).

But it does not follow that the government should intervene by requiring sellers to make elaborate disclosures. Competitive pressures make sellers offer warranties (enforceable guarantees) of particular characteristics of their products. A warranty is not a disclosure. It is better than that: It is a guarantee of results, and so makes the disclosure of information unnecessary. A manufacturer of television sets who warrants that the tube will last three years need not disclose what the useful life of the tube is. If it wears out after only one year, the consumer is no worse off; he gets the tube replaced free of charge.

If it is clear that the parties intend the seller to bear the risk of the consumer's ignorance about a particular attribute of the product, there is no need even for an explicit warranty; contract law will perform its familiar function of economizing on transaction costs by reading a warranty into the contract of sale. An implied warranty that a can of sardines is untainted is a cheap alternative both to an express warranty of fitness for human consumption and to a legal requirement that the seller disclose the health characteristics of the product.[3]

Another approach to the problem of consumer information would be to recognize property rights in such information. It would then no longer be produced simply as a by-product of selling products. There would be firms that investigated and tested products and sold the results of their investigations to consumers. Although there are some firms of this sort today — publishers of stock market news letters are an example — they are relatively few in number because they have such difficulty in appropriating the fruits of their efforts; anyone can use the information they produce. Libraries complicate the problem. The problem would disappear if product information were protected from appropriation by laws akin to the patent laws, although the difficulties of enforcement would be considerable and probably disabling.[4]

Thus far, our attention has been confined to fraud in contracts of sale between strangers. In the type of relationship that the law calls fiduciary or confidential, the duty to disclose material information is much greater. Most agents (lawyers, accountants, brokers, trustees, etc.) are fiduciaries toward their principals (fiduciary duties within the corporation are the subject of a separate discussion in §14.8 infra). The agent is paid to treat the principal as he would treat himself; to be his alter

---

3. See further §6.6 infra (liability for injuries from defective or unreasonably dangerous products).

4. Useful discussions of the problems of consumer information and fraud may be found in Howard Beales, Richard Craswell & Steven C. Salop, The Efficient Regulation of Consumer Information, 24 J. Leg. Stud. 491 (1981); Michael R. Darby & Edi Karni, Free Competition and the Optimal Amount of Fraud, 16 J. Law & Econ. 67 (1973); Phillip Nelson, Information and Consumer Behavior, 78 J. Pol. Econ. 311 (1970); Paul H. Rubin, Business Firms and the Common Law: The Evolution of Efficient Rules, ch. 6 (1983); and George J. Stigler, The Economics of Information, in The Organization of Industry 171 (1968).

ego. The fiduciary principle is the law's answer to the problem of unequal costs of information. It allows you to hire someone with superior information to deal on your behalf with others having superior information. It is thus a device for lowering transaction costs. So why isn't every seller deemed a fiduciary of his buyer, at least where the buyer is a consumer? The answer may be that with regard to most product attributes the consumer has enough knowledge to be able to make intelligent decisions, and so he doesn't want to pay the seller for the additional information that a fiduciary would be required to disclose to his principal; he can protect himself at lower cost.

§4.7   Duress, Bargaining Power, and Unconscionability

There is a well-recognized defense of duress to an action for breach of contract. But unfortunately the term does not have a well-defined meaning — being used, in fact, in four distinct senses.

(1) Duress in its original sense implies a threat of violence. B gives a promissory note to A because A is holding a knife at B's throat. The courts will not compel B to make good on his note to A. This is not because B did not act of his own free will — on the contrary, he was probably extremely eager to exchange the note for A's forbearance to kill him — but because A's behavior retards rather than advances the movement of resources to their most valuable uses and creates deadweight losses akin to those of lying (A's investment in making threats and prospective victims' investments in warding them off).[1]

(2) By a modest extension of meaning, the word can be used to describe the use of a threat of nonperformance to induce a modification of contract terms in cases such as *Alaska Packers' Assn. v. Domenico,* discussed in §4.2 *supra,* where the promisee lacks adequate legal remedies.

(3) The word is frequently a synonym for fraud, as where an illiterate is induced to sign a contract that contains unfavorable terms that are not explained to him. Most cases involving the abuse of a confidential or fiduciary relationship, although grouped with duress cases, are at bottom (as should be clear from the previous section) cases of fraud.

(4) Duress is also used as a synonym for monopoly. A finds B wandering lost in a snowstorm and refuses to help him until B promises

§4.7   1. A "deadweight loss" is a cost that produces no benefit: a totally unproductive consumption of valuable resources.

to give A all his wealth. Perhaps here too B should be excused from having to make good on the promise; if we permit monopoly profits in rescue operations, an excessive amount of resources may be attracted to the rescue business. We shall come back to this example.

Where a transaction is between a large corporation and an ordinary individual, it is tempting to invoke the analogy of duress and compare the individual to the helpless fellow forced to sign a promissory note with a knife at his throat — especially if his contract with the corporation is a standard contract or the consumer is a poor person — and conclude that the terms of the deal are coercive. Many contracts (insurance contracts are a good example) are offered on a take-it-or-leave-it basis. The seller hands the purchaser a standard printed contract that sets forth, sometimes in numbing detail, the respective obligations of the parties. The purchaser can sign it or not as he pleases but there is no negotiation over terms. It is an easy step from the observation that there is no negotiation to the conclusion that the purchaser lacked a free choice and therefore should not be bound by onerous terms. But there is an innocent explanation: The seller is just trying to avoid the costs of negotiating and drafting a separate agreement with each purchaser. These costs, of which the largest probably is supervising the employees and agents who engage in the actual contract negotiations on the company's behalf, are likely to be very high for a large company that has many contracts. Consistent with the innocent explanation, large and sophisticated buyers, as well as individual consumers, often make purchases pursuant to printed form contracts.

The sinister explanation is that the seller refuses to dicker separately with each purchaser because the buyer has no choice but to accept his terms. This assumes an absence of competition. If one seller offers unattractive terms, a competing seller, wanting sales for himself, will offer more attractive terms. The process will continue until the terms are optimal. All the firms in the industry may find it economical to use standard contracts and refuse to negotiate with purchasers. But what is important is not whether there is haggling in every transaction; it is whether competition forces sellers to incorporate in their standard contracts terms that protect the purchasers.

Under monopoly, by definition, the buyer has no good alternatives to dealing with the seller, who is therefore in a position, within limits, to compel the buyer to agree to terms that in a competitive market would be bettered by another seller. But there is no reason to expect the terms (such as the seller's warranties or the consequences of the buyer's default) to be different under monopoly from what they would be under competition; the only difference that is likely is that the monopolist's price will be higher. The problem is monopoly, not bargaining power — unless, unhelpfully, these are treated as synonyms.

An objectionable feature of some printed contracts is the use of fine print or obscure terminology to slip an onerous provision past an unwary customer; and such conduct is more likely in a monopolized than in a competitive market (see §4.6 *supra* and §13.2 *infra*). But to thus impose excessive search costs on buyers is, analytically, a species of fraud (though one rarely actionable) rather than an exercise of bargaining power.

Contracts are sometimes said to involve duress if the terms seem disadvantageous to buyers, and the buyers are poor. An example is a sale on credit where the buyer agrees that the seller may discount the buyer's promissory note to a finance company. At common law the finance company, as a holder in due course, could enforce the note free from any defense that the buyer might have raised in a collection suit by the seller. So if you bought a chest of drawers from a furniture store and the chest turned out to be defective, but the store had discounted your note to a finance company, you would have to pay the full amount of the note and would be left with a right to sue the store for breach of warranty.

But it does not follow that the purchaser must have been coerced into agreeing to so unfavorable a contractual provision. The holder-in-due-course provision reduces the cost of financing installment purchases by making collection suits cheaper and more certain.[2] In its absence, this cost — which is borne at least in major part by the consumer since it is a marginal cost (cf. §3.12 *supra*) — would be higher. It is not obviously wiser for the consumer to decide to pay more for a product than to decide to give up one of his legal remedies against the seller.

Suppose that an installment contract provides that default entitles the seller to repossess the good no matter how small the remaining unpaid balance of the buyer's note and to keep the full proceeds from reselling the good to someone else.[3] If default occurs toward the end of the term of the note, repossession will confer a windfall gain on the seller since he has already received almost the full price for the good, including interest. But if default occurs early, the seller sustains a windfall loss; he has received only a small part of the price, too little to cover both the depreciation of the good and the costs of repossession. Assuming that competition among sellers of consumer goods is sufficiently vigorous to eliminate supracompetitive profits,[4] limiting the wind-

2. Suppose that in the absence of such provisions finance companies would extract from sellers promises to indemnify them for any losses suffered as a result of the finance company's being unable to collect its note because the purchaser has a good defense against the seller. Would this alter the conclusion that banning such provisions causes higher financing costs to consumers?

3. Cf. Williams v. Walker-Thomas Furniture Co., 350 F.2d 445 (D.C. Cir. 1965). The example is extreme; to deny the buyer any share of the proceeds of the resale of the repossessed merchandise would be considered a penalty and therefore forbidden. See §4.13 *infra* for further discussion of repossession.

4. A plausible assumption; most retail markets are highly competitive. And it might not make much difference if the market were monopolistic. See §9.2 *infra*.

fall gains of late defaults would lead sellers to require either larger down payments or higher initial installment payments, or charge higher prices, in order to protect themselves against windfall losses from early defaults. Consumers unable to make large down payments or high initial installment payments would be harmed by the change in the contractual form.

The foregoing discussion raises the general question whether the concept of unequal bargaining power is fruitful, or even meaningful. Similar doubts are raised by the vague term "unconscionability," a ground of contract discharge in the Uniform Commercial Code. If unconscionability means that a court may nullify a contract if it considers the consideration inadequate or the terms otherwise one-sided, the basic principle of encouraging market rather than surrogate legal transactions where (market) transaction costs are low is badly compromised. Economic analysis reveals no grounds other than fraud, incapacity, and duress (the last narrowly defined) for allowing a party to repudiate the bargain that he made in entering into the contract.

After this long excursus into some dubious extensions of the concept of duress, let us return to a real case of duress (economically conceived). A ship becomes disabled, and the crew flees, leaving on board only the master, who, we shall assume to simplify the example, is also the shipowner's authorized representative to deal with any salvors who may chance by. A tug operated by a salvage company comes alongside, and the captain of the tug offers the master a contract to save the ship for a price equal to 99 percent of the value of the ship and its cargo. If the master signs, should the owner of the ship be held to the contract? The law of admiralty answers no, and this seems the correct economic result. The situation is one of bilateral monopoly, with the added complication that transaction costs are even higher than in other bilateral-monopoly contexts, since if the master of the ship tries to hold out for a better deal, the ship and all its cargo may sink beneath him. These transaction costs can be avoided by a rule — the cornerstone of the admiralty rules of salvage — that the salvor is entitled to a reasonable fee for saving the ship, but that a contract made after the ship gets into trouble will only be evidentiary of what that reasonable fee is.[5]

This solution is necessary to avoid high transaction costs, but, perhaps surprisingly, may not be necessary to avoid attracting too many resources into the salvage business. For there is no reason to think that if contracts such as the one illustrated above were enforced, salvors really would get anything like 99 percent of the value of the ships and cargoes they saved. The salvor has as much to lose if the deal falls through as the

5. See William M. Landes & Richard A. Posner, Salvors, Finders, Good Samaritans, and Other Rescuers: An Economic Study of Law and Altruism, 7 J. Leg. Stud. 83, 100-104 (1978).

shipowner does (put aside any risk to the master's life, in our example). This is not true in the example in the last section of the man lost in the snowstorm. He has his wealth and his life to lose; his rescuer has only the man's wealth to lose. The man may therefore not be able to make a credible threat to walk away from a deal unless the rescuer relaxes his terms. And yet the law does not impose a duty to rescue, or entitle the rescuer to a reasonable fee as under salvage law. A possible reason for this result is considered in §6.9 *infra*.

§4.8   Fundamental Principles of Contract Damages

When a breach of contract is established, the issue becomes one of the proper remedy. There are, in theory anyway, a bewildering variety of possibilities, which in very rough order of increasing severity can be arrayed as follows:

(1) the promisee's reliance loss (the costs he incurred in reasonable reliance on the promisor's performing the contract);

(2) the expectation loss (loss of the anticipated profit of the contract);

(3) liquidated damages (damages actually specified in the contract as the money remedy for a breach);

(4) consequential damages (ripple effects on the promisee's business from the breach);

(5) restitution (to the promisee of the promisor's profits from the breach);

(6) specific performance (ordering the promisor to perform on penalty of being found in contempt of court);

(7) a money penalty specified in the contract, or other punitive damages; and

(8) criminal sanctions.

We shall examine all of these possible sanctions — plus self-help — in this and succeeding sections.

It will help to frame the discussion to come back to the fundamental distinction between opportunistic and other breaches of contract. If a promisor breaks his promise merely to take advantage of the vulnerability of the promisee in a setting (the normal contract setting) where performance is sequential rather than simultaneous, then we might as well "throw the book" at the promisor. An example would be where A pays B in advance for goods and instead of delivering them B simply pockets A's money. Such conduct has no economic justification and ought to be heavily punished to deter such conduct in the future. However, as we shall see in Chapter 7, severe sanctions are costly to impose, so that, in general anyway, the lightest sanction that will do the trick is the most efficient. In the case of the opportunistic breach, that sanction is restitution. The promisor broke his promise in order to make money — there can be no other reason in the case of such a breach. We can deter this kind of behavior by making it worthless to the promisor, which we do by making him hand over all his profits from the breach to the promisee; no lighter sanction would deter.

Most breaches of contract, however, are not opportunistic. Many are involuntary (performance is impossible at a reasonable cost); others are voluntary but (as we are about to see) efficient — which from an economic standpoint is the same case as that of an involuntary breach. These observations both explain the centrality of remedies to the law of contracts (can you see why?) and give point to Holmes's dictum, overbroad though it is, as we shall see, that it is not the policy of the law to compel adherence to contracts but only to require each party to choose between performing in accordance with the contract and compensating the other party for any injury resulting from a failure to perform.[1] This view contains an important economic insight. In many cases it is uneconomical to induce completion of performance of a contract after it has been broken. I agree to purchase 100,000 widgets custom-ground for use as components in a machine that I manufacture. After I have taken delivery of 10,000, the market for my machine collapses. I promptly notify my supplier that I am terminating the contract, and admit that my termination is a breach of the contract. When notified of the termination he has not yet begun the custom grinding of the other 90,000 widgets, but he informs me that he intends to complete his performance under the contract and bill me accordingly. The custom-ground widgets have no use other than in my machine, and a negligible scrap value. To give the supplier any remedy that induced him to complete the contract after the breach would result in a waste of resources. The law is alert to this danger and, under the doctrine of mitigation of damages, would not give the supplier damages for any costs he incurred in continuing production after my notice of termination.

But isn't the danger unreal, if the Coase Theorem is true? There are only two parties, and there is a price for the supplier's forbearing to enforce his contract rights — indeed a range of prices — that will make both parties better off. But of course this is just another example of bilateral monopoly; transaction costs will be high even though (in a sense, because) there are only two parties.

Now suppose the contract is broken by the seller rather than the buyer. I need 100,000 custom-ground widgets for my machine but the supplier, after producing 50,000, is forced to suspend production because of a mechanical failure. Other suppliers are in a position to supply

§4.8   1. See Oliver Wendell Holmes, The Path of the Law, 10 Harv. L. Rev. 457, 462 (1897) ("The duty to keep a contract at common law means a prediction that you must pay damages if you do not keep it, — and nothing else.")

the remaining widgets that I need but I insist that the original supplier complete his performance of the contract. If the law compels completion (specific performance), the supplier will have to make arrangements with other producers to complete his contract with me. Not only *may* it be more costly for him to procure an alternative supplier than for me to do so directly (after all, I know my own needs best); it probably *is* more costly; otherwise the original supplier would have done it voluntarily, to minimize his liability for the breach of contract. To compel completion of the contract (or costly negotiations to discharge the promisor) would again result in a waste of resources, and again the law does not compel completion but confines the victim to simple damages.

But what are simple contract damages? Usually the objective of giving the promisor an incentive to fulfill his promise unless the result would be an inefficient use of resources (the production of the unwanted widgets in the first example, the roundabout procurement of a substitute supplier in the second) can be achieved by giving the promisee his expected profit on the transaction. If the supplier in the first example receives his expected profit from making 10,000 widgets, he will have no incentive to make the unwanted 90,000. We do not want him to make them; no one wants them. In the second example, if I receive my expected profit from dealing with the original supplier, I become indifferent to whether he completes his performance.

In these examples the breach was in a sense involuntary. It was committed only to avert a larger loss. The promisor would have been happier had there been no occasion to commit a breach. But in some cases a party would be tempted to break the contract simply because his profit from breach would exceed his expected profit from completion of the contract. If his profit from breach would also exceed the expected profit to the other party from completion of the contract, and if damages are limited to the loss of that expected profit, there will be an incentive to commit a breach. But there should be, as an example will show. I sign a contract to deliver 100,000 custom-ground widgets at 10¢ apiece to A, for use in his boiler factory. After I have delivered 10,000, B comes to me, explains that he desperately needs 25,000 custom-ground widgets at once since otherwise he will be forced to close his pianola factory at great cost, and offers me 15¢ apiece for 25,000 widgets. I sell him the widgets and as a result do not complete timely delivery to A, causing him to lose $1,000 in profits. Having obtained an additional profit of $1,250 on the sale to B, I am better off even after reimbursing A for his loss, and B is no worse off. The breach is Pareto superior, assuming that A is fully compensated and no one else is hurt by the breach. True, if I had refused to sell to B, he could have gone to A and negotiated an assignment to him of part of A's contract with me. But this would have introduced an additional step, with additional transaction costs.

Notice how careful the law must be not to exceed compensatory damages if it doesn't want to deter efficient breaches. This raises the question of whether the problem of overdeterring breaches of contract by heavy penalties could not be solved more easily by redefining the legal concept of breach of contract so that only inefficient terminations count as breaches. It could not be. Remember that an important function of contracts is to assign risks to superior risk bearers. If the risk materializes, the party to whom it was assigned must pay. It is no more important that he could not have prevented the risk from occurring at a reasonable, perhaps at any, cost than it is important that an insurance company could not have prevented the fire that destroyed the building it insured. The breach of contract corresponds to the occurrence of the event that is insured against.

Is the expectation loss, the loss of the expected profit of the contract, always the correct measure of compensatory damages for breach of contract? What if it exceeds the reliance loss? Suppose a manufacturer agrees to sell a machine for $100,000, delivery to be made in six months; and the day after the contract is signed the manufacturer defaults, realizing that he will lose $5,000 at the agreed-on price. The buyer's reliance loss — the sum of the costs he has irretrievably incurred as a result of the contract — is, let us say, zero, but it would cost him $112,000 to obtain a substitute machine. Why should he be allowed to use a measure of damages that gives him more (by $12,000) than he has actually lost? Isn't the $12,000, the money he would have saved if the contract had not been broken, a windfall? Whether it is or not, the reliance measure would encourage inefficient breaches. In the example, the net gain to the buyer from contractual performance is greater (by $7,000, the difference between $12,000 and $5,000) than the net loss ($5,000) to the seller, and we make that net gain a cost of breach to the seller, by giving the buyer his profit on the deal if the seller breaks the contract, in order to discourage an inefficient breach.[2]

What if the reliance loss exceeds the expectation loss? In *Groves v. John Wunder Co.*,[3] the defendant, as part of a larger deal, had agreed to level some land owned by the plaintiff but willfully failed to carry out his agreement. The cost of leveling would have been $60,000 and the value of the land, after leveling, no more than $12,000 — the Depression of the 1930s having supervened after the contract was signed. The court awarded the plaintiff $60,000, reasoning that he was entitled to get the performance he had contracted for and that it was no business of the defendant whether, or how much, his performance would have made the plaintiff's property more valuable. This was not a case, familiar to us from our discussion of just compensation in the last chapter, where

---

2. What will the parties do then?
3. 205 Minn. 163, 286 N.W. 235 (1939).

value and market price were different. The land in question was a commercial parcel. If the plaintiff had wanted the performance rather than the $60,000, he probably would have brought an action for specific performance (routinely ordered in cases involving land). He did not bring such an action and, even more telling, did not use the money he won from the defendant to level the land.[4] The measure of damages was incorrect from an economic standpoint because, had it been known to the defendant from the start, it would have made him indifferent between breaking his promise to level the land and performing it, whereas efficiency dictated breach; the $60,000 worth of labor and materials that would have been consumed in leveling the land would have bought a less than $12,000 increase in value.[5]

True, the result of not enforcing the contract would have been to confer a windfall on the defendant. But enforcing the contract gave the plaintiff an equal and opposite windfall: a cushion, which almost certainly the parties had not contemplated, against the impact of the Depression on land values. Since the plaintiff, as the owner of the land, rather than the defendant, a contractor, would have enjoyed the benefit of any unexpected increase in the value of the land, probably the parties, if they had thought about the matter, would have wanted the plaintiff to bear the burden of any unexpected fall in that value, as well.

The expectation or lost-profit measure of damages focuses on the gain that the victim of the breach anticipated from performance of the contract. The reliance measure focuses on the victim's loss from the breach. If the victim "relied" by forgoing an equally profitable contract, the two measures merge. If not, the expectation measure may actually be a better approximation of the victim's real economic loss than the reliance measure, as well as producing better incentives. In long-run competitive equilibrium, the total revenues of the sellers in a market are just equal to their total costs; there is no "profit" in an economic sense but rather reimbursement of the costs of capital, of entrepreneurial effort, and of other inputs, including the marketing efforts that led up to the contract. All these items of cost are excluded by the reliance measure of damages, which will therefore tend to understate the true social costs of breach. Even if the breach occurs before the victim has begun to perform, the victim may have incurred costs (especially precontractual search costs). And although it is true that the costs that the reliance measure leaves out mount up as performance proceeds, to hold

4. See John P. Dawson, William Burnett Harvey & Stanley D. Henderson, Cases and Comment on Contracts 17-18 (4th ed. 1982).

5. Would the defendant in fact have leveled the land pursuant to the contract had he known in advance what the measure of damages would be if he did not? Why not? Does it follow that the economist should be indifferent to the measure of damages in the case?

A result opposite to *Groves* was reached in Peevyhouse v. Garland Coal Mining Co., 382 P.2d 109 (Okla. 1963).

on this account that the only allowable measure of damages is the reliance measure until performance begins is to say — since until then the reliance cost will usually be zero — that parties should be allowed to walk away from their contracts while the contracts are still purely executory. Except in special situations, it is unclear what the social gain is from having this "cooling off" period. The cost is uncertainty of legal obligation and having to make additional transactions.[6] Moreover, reliance costs during the executory period are very difficult to compute. Having signed a contract, a party will immediately begin to make plans both for performing the contract and for making whatever adjustments in the rest of his business are necessary to accommodate the new obligation; but the costs of this planning, and the costs resulting from the change of plans when he finds out that the contract will not be performed, will be difficult to estimate.

There are, however, some cases where the expectation measure, mechanically applied, would yield economically unsound results. Compare the following cases: (1) A tenant defaults, and the landlord promptly rents the property to another tenant at a rental only slightly below that of the defaulting tenant. In a suit against the defaulting tenant for the rental due on the balance of the tenant's lease, should the landlord be required to deduct the rental of the substitute tenant? (2) A manufacturer of widgets receives an order for 1,000 widgets from X, but X refuses to accept delivery and the manufacturer resells the widgets to Y at a price only slightly lower than what X had agreed to pay. In a suit against X for the profits that were lost on the sale, should the manufacturer be required to deduct the profits he received on the substitute sale to Y?

The law answers yes in the first case and no in the second, and these answers are correct from an economic standpoint. The good supplied by the landlord is fixed in the short run; he cannot add a room because one more family wants to lease from him. The rental that he receives from the substitute tenant in our first case is thus a gain *enabled* by the breach of contract by the first tenant,[7] and his true loss is therefore the difference between the two rentals.[8] But a manufacturer can usually vary his output even in the short run. X's default did not enable the manufacturer to obtain a profit from selling to Y; for if X had not defaulted, the manufacturer could still have supplied Y with 1,000 widgets. The profit on the sale to Y is a gain that the manufacturer would have obtained regardless of the default, so his true loss is the entire expected profit from the sale to X.

---

6. Why is there not also a cost in discouraging value-maximizing exchanges? Will the exchange go through if the contract is broken? Cf. hint in note 2 *supra*.

7. Must mitigation of damages be required for this damage rule to be efficient?

8. Does this depend on whether all of the other apartments are occupied? And what about the first tenant's deposit? Should it be returned? See discussion of forfeitures in §4.11 *infra*.

That profit may be difficult to estimate. It is the difference between the contract price and the cost of performance to the seller, but what is that cost? At least two components must be distinguished: fixed and variable costs. Fixed costs are those that do not vary with the amount produced; variable are those that do. Virtually all costs are variable in the long run, but in the case of a contract to be performed over a relatively brief period of time the long run can be ignored. And in the short run such costs as rent, insurance, (some) taxes, officers' salaries, and interest on long-term debt are fixed. As they will not be saved if the seller does not make this particular sale, they are not a cost to be subtracted from the contract price in deciding how much worse off the seller is as a result of the breach. Concretely, suppose the contract price is $11 per widget, the seller's variable costs are $6, and his fixed costs are $4. The breach will cost the seller $5, not $1, for the $4 in fixed costs that he allocated to the sale for accounting purposes he will, by definition, still have to pay even though the sale has fallen through. The loss of the sale saves $6 in costs, but causes an $11 loss of revenues.

To measure the variable costs of performing a contract (say to produce 1,000 widgets), it is tempting simply to divide the company's total costs (after subtracting its fixed costs) by its total output to get an average variable cost, and to assume that that is the cost the seller would have incurred in making another 1,000 widgets. But it probably will cost the seller more to make these additional widgets. Ask yourself why the seller doesn't produce more widgets than he does. One possible answer is that producing more will bring him into a region where he encounters net diseconomies of scale, forcing up his unit costs. He may have to hire additional workers, and if so he may have to pay higher wages to bid them away from other producers; this is an implication of the law of demand discussed in Chapter 1. Or he may have to buy additional materials, and by adding his demand to that of other buyers in the market bid up the price of those materials. Moreover, he may incur these higher costs not only on his incremental output but on his entire output. For example, if he offers higher wages to new workers to attract them away from their present employers, he may have to offer the same higher wages to his existing workers (why?). The higher costs of the firm's intramarginal output are the consequence of the additional output called for by the contract and are thus costs assignable in an economic sense to that contract — they would be avoided if the contract fell through. Hence an apparently lucrative contract may in fact give the seller only a modest profit, although a positive one (why?).

This is shown in Figure 4.1. The seller is assumed to have only variable costs, so that AC is its schedule both of average variable and of average total costs. MC is the seller's schedule of marginal costs (the cost of the last unit produced, at the various possible levels of output). If as in Figure 4.1 marginal cost is rising, average variable cost will be rising too, but more slowly, because the increase in total costs from moving

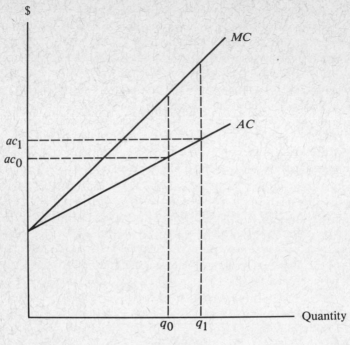

Figure 4.1

to successively higher outputs is being averaged over the firm's entire output. The lost sale would have expanded the firm's output from q_0 to q_1, causing its average costs to rise from ac_0 to ac_1. If damages for the lost sale are determined by subtracting from the contract price $(q_1 - q_0) \times ac_0$ (a known figure), rather than $(q_1 - q_0) \times ac_1$ (a hypothetical figure, based on a sale that was not made), the firm will be overcompensated for the breach. (Marginal cost and other cost concepts are discussed more fully in Chapters 9 and 11.) But the change in cost brought about by a new contract is apt to be small when the contract contemplates a proportionately small increase in the firm's output (in Figure 4.1 the proportion is large). As to such contracts the firm's average variable cost before the contract is performed is probably a good approximation to the actual cost of performing the contract.

Here now is a problem in buyers' damages. A contracts with B to sell 1,000 widgets for delivery on January 11, 1986, at a price of $1 per widget. On July 11, 1985, A tells B that he is not going to be able to sell him the widgets. This anticipatory repudiation is a breach of contract, and it entitles B to look elsewhere for the widgets. (Where have we seen anticipatory repudiation before?) On that day, the price of widgets is $2. B could go into the market and "cover" by signing another forward contract (i.e., a contract for future delivery — on January

112

11, 1986) for 1,000 widgets, and then his damages would be $1,000, assuming the current and forward prices are the same, $2, on the date of cover. Suppose that instead B waits till January 11 and on that day buys 1,000 widgets for immediate delivery at the then price of $3 per widget, thereby losing $2,000. Should he be able to collect the larger loss? He should not (the answer in economics and also in law).[9] For suppose the market price had fallen between July and January below the contract price, say to 50¢. Then B would have had a gain from waiting that would not be credited to A. Allowing B to wait enables him to gamble at no risk to himself. No matter how high the price of widgets shoots, he is protected because the contract places a ceiling on his expense. But if it falls below the contract price, he gets to keep the difference. Presumably this was not intended by the parties when by the form of contract they chose they shifted the whole risk of price changes, not just the risk of a price increase, from B to A by fixing the price of widgets for future delivery.

A forward contract is a good example of the risk-shifting function of contracts, but an even better example is the futures contract.[10] A futures contract has the same general form as a forward contract but differs in that normally delivery is not contemplated (only 1 or 2 percent of all futures contracts result in an actual delivery). Futures contracts are generally used in connection with agricultural commodities and metals, whose prices are volatile and thus risky.[11] Suppose a grain elevator has a large stock of grain that its customers will not need for another six months. If the grain elevator does not want to bear the risk of price fluctuations over this period, it can sell a futures contract that promises delivery at a fixed price in six months (say $3 a bushel). When the six months roll around, the grain elevator will sell the grain at the market price, which let us say is now only $1 a bushel, and at the same time it will cancel its futures contract by buying an identical contract for immediate delivery at $1. This transaction will net it $2 a bushel (the profit on its futures contract), which will exactly offset its loss from having to sell its grain for only $1 a bushel (what loss?). The advantage of the futures contract over the forward contract is that the seller need not, in order to hedge against a price drop, go out and find someone who actually wants to commit to taking delivery in six months. He just has to find someone who thinks the price will rise. Futures contracts

9. See Thomas H. Jackson, "Anticipatory Repudiation" and the Temporal Element in Contract Law: An Economic Inquiry Into Contract Damages in Cases of Prospective Nonperformance, 31 Stan. L. Rev. 69 (1978); but see Alan Schwartz & Robert E. Scott, Commercial Transactions: Principles and Policies 323-325 (1982).

10. See Dennis W. Carlton, Futures Markets: Their Purpose, Their History, Their Growth, Their Successes and Failures, 4 J. Futures Mkts. 237 (1984); Lester G. Telser, Why There Are Organized Future Markets, 24 J. Law & Econ. 1 (1983).

11. Financial futures are of increasing importance, but they raise distinct problems of the sort discussed in Chapter 15.

thus increase the scope for speculation, which both facilitates hedging and, by giving people (speculators) a stake in forecasting prices correctly even though they are not involved in producing or consuming the commodity traded in the market, increases the amount of price information in the market.

§4.9 Consequential Damages

An important issue of buyers' damages is whether the buyer can get consequential damages for the seller's breach. (Why are buyers much more likely than sellers to incur consequential harm?) The common law's traditional hostility to consequential damages in contract cases is epitomized by the famous case of *Hadley v. Baxendale*.[1] Consider the following variant of the facts in that case. A commercial photographer purchases a roll of film to take pictures of the Himalayas for a magazine. The cost of developing the film is included in the purchase price. The photographer incurs heavy expenses (including the hire of an airplane) to complete the assignment. He mails the film to the manufacturer but it is mislaid in the developing room and never found.

Compare the incentive effects of allowing the photographer to recover his full losses and limiting him to recovery of the price of the film. The first alternative creates few — maybe no — incentives to avoid similar losses in the future. The photographer will take no precautions; he will be indifferent between the successful completion of his assignment and the receipt of full compensation for its failure. The manufacturer of the film will probably take no additional precautions either, because he cannot identify the films whose loss would be extremely costly, and unless there are many of them it may not pay to take additional precautions on *all* the films he develops. The second alternative, in contrast, should induce the photographer to take precautions that turn out to be at once inexpensive and effective: Using two rolls of film or requesting special handling when he sends the roll in to be developed.

The general principle illustrated by this example is that if a risk of loss is known to only one party to the contract, the other party is not liable for the loss if it occurs. This principle induces the party with knowledge of the risk either to take appropriate precautions himself or, if he believes that the other party might be the more efficient preventer or spreader (insurer) of the loss, to reveal the risk to that party and pay him to assume it. Incentives are thus created to allocate the risk in the most efficient manner.[2]

§4.9   1. 9 Ex. 341, 156 Eng. Rep. 145 (1854).
2. What is the relationship between the rule of *Hadley v. Baxendale* and the rule governing discharge of a contract on the ground of impossibility (§4.5 *supra*)?

Often the principle is stated in terms of the foreseeability of the risk. But this word, much favored in the law though it is, is maddeningly vague. In our tale of the commercial photographer, although the developer does not know the consequences of losing or spoiling the film he knows that such losses can occur. It is just that the buyer is in a better position than he to avoid the consequences of the breach, though the buyer cannot avoid the breach itself. The rule of *Hadley v. Baxendale* thus resembles the rule of tort law (not universally adopted) that an accident victim will not be allowed to recover damages that he could have avoided by fastening his seat belt. Since he could not have avoided the accident by doing so, the injurer's liability is not affected; but the amount of damages is.[3]

The rule of *Hadley v. Baxendale* is not applied, it should be noted, where what is unforeseeable is the other party's lost profit. Suppose I offer you $140,000 for a house that has a market value of $150,000, you accept the offer but later breach, and I sue you for $10,000, my lost profit. You would not be permitted to defend on the ground that you had no reason to think the transaction was such a profitable one for me. Any other rule would make it difficult for a good bargainer to collect damages unless before the contract was signed he had made disclosures that would reduce the advantage of being a good bargainer — disclosures that would prevent the buyer from appropriating the gains from his efforts to identify a resource that was undervalued in its present use. This is just the application of the principle of *Laidlaw v. Organ* in a damage setting.

§4.10   Penalties, Liquidated Damages, and Forfeitures

Sometimes a contract will specify the damage to be awarded if there is a breach (as with demurrage); and if the specification is a reasonable ex ante estimate of the likely damages from breach, it will be enforced under the rubric of liquidated damages even if the actual damages turn out to be much less (or more). But if it is plain from the beginning that the specification is designed to give the victim of the breach much more than he could expect actually to lose as a result of the breach, or the contract breaker to gain, then it is a penalty clause and is unenforceable. The name is well chosen; the imposition on a violator of a cost in excess of the actual damage caused by the violation is, as we shall see in Chapter 7, the essence of a penal sanction.

3. Cf. *EVRA Corp. v. Swiss Bank Corp.*, 673 F.2d 951 (7th Cir. 1982), for an application of this principle ("avoidable consequences") to the question of whether a bank should be liable for consequential damages resulting from a negligent failure to make an electronic funds transfer.

It might seem obvious that the law would not — and in fact it does not — enforce penalty clauses in contracts. A penalty would deter efficient as well as inefficient breaches, by making the cost of the breach to the contract breaker greater than the cost of the breach to the victim; would create bilateral-monopoly problems (how so?); and might induce the prospective victim to provoke a breach, since he would profit from it. These are good reasons for not awarding punitive damages for nonopportunistic breaches of contract (precisely the line that the law draws — punitive damages increasingly are available as a sanction for opportunistic breaches), but not for refusing to enforce voluntarily negotiated penalty clauses, which would not be put into contracts — not often, anyway — unless the parties expected the gains to outweigh the costs we have just identified. And they might. Suppose I know that I will honor my contracts but I find it difficult to convince others of this fact. By signing a penalty clause I communicate credible information about my own estimate of my reliability — information useful in determining on what terms to do business with me. A closely related point is that a penalty clause may simply compensate the seller for a high risk of default. As we saw in discussing installment contracts (see §4.7 *supra*), if the seller cannot recover his full price when default occurs early (because depreciation will have exceeded the buyer's payments), there is an argument for letting him keep the buyer's payments when default occurs late; the apparent windfall may (in a competitive market will) merely compensate him for the losses from early defaults. Interest rates will be lower if the seller is allowed to obtain what amounts to a penalty on a late default.

The common law, at the same time that it was forbidding penalty clauses, allowed sellers to keep deposits and installment payments even if the result was to give the seller more money than any reasonable estimate of his damages. The Uniform Commercial Code has changed the rule with regard to sales of goods, but the older rule persists in other cases, particularly cases involving land, although with an important limitation: A mortgagee who forecloses does not thereby become the owner of the property; if the property is sold at a foreclosure sale, the mortgagor is entitled to the excess (if any) of the sale price over the amount due on the mortgage.

There are three differences between penalties and forfeitures.

(1) Enforcing a forfeiture doesn't require a lawsuit; hence it is a cheaper remedy for the legal system to administer.

(2) The party subject to a forfeiture is normally the payor; and the paying party is less likely to commit an involuntary breach than the performing party (why is that relevant?).

(3) A forfeiture is unlikely to be ruinous, since it is limited to money already paid over by the party against whom the forfeiture is sought.

Points 2 and 3 suggest that forfeitures are less likely to be the result of fraud or duress than penalties.

These differences may explain the law's preference for forfeitures over penalties but not the absolute prohibition of the former or the trend against the latter (see also §4.13 *infra*). One possibility is that since forfeitures and penalties — especially the latter — increase the risk of bankruptcy consequent on contractual default, they increase the number and hence total cost of bankruptcies (resource costs, not just pecuniary transfers); and some of that cost is external to the parties, as we shall see when we discuss bankruptcy in Chapter 14. There is a related, macroeconomic argument against penalties and forfeitures clauses: If they were common, it would increase the amplitude of the business cycle, because the number of bankruptcies would be greater in depressions and recessions.[1]

Should the law require that every contract contain a liquidated damages clause on the theory that the parties know better than the courts what the damages are likely to be? It should not. The costs of estimating damages may be lower when the damages arise than much earlier, when the contract is signed. And under a regime of compulsory liquidated damages clauses those costs would be incurred in every case rather than just in the small fraction of cases in which the contract is broken and a suit ensues.

§4.11   Specific Performance[1]

Generally, specific performance (ordering the party who breaks his contract to perform, on penalty of being held in contempt of court if he does not) will not be ordered as a remedy for breach of contract; the promisee will have to make do with damages, as suggested in the Holmes dictum quoted earlier. But there is an exception for cases where damages are difficult to compute because of the lack of good market substitutes for the performance of the contract breaker. The exception has swallowed the rule in the case of contracts for the sale of real estate, and rightly so, it would seem.

Suppose I have a contract to buy a house and the seller defaults.

§4.10   1. See Daniel A. Farber, Contract Law and Modern Economic Theory, 78 Nw. U.L. Rev. 303, 335 (1983).

§4.11   1. There is an extensive literature on the economics of specific performance. For some examples see Anthony T. Kronman, Specific Performance, 45 U. Chi. L. Rev. 351 (1978); Alan Schwartz, The Case for Specific Performance, 89 Yale L.J. 271 (1979); Thomas S. Ulen, The Efficiency of Specific Performance: Toward a Unified Theory of Contract Remedies, 83 Mich. L. Rev. 341 (1984); William Bishop, the Choice of Remedy for Breach of Contract, 14 J. Leg. Stud. 299 (1985).

The estimation of damages may be very difficult, since, as we have seen (in §3.5 *supra*), I may value the house a good deal more than the market does. To remit a purchaser to damages in such cases might result in a systematic undervaluation of the costs of breach, since a court will perforce be guided by market price and be skeptical of a buyer's claim that the house is worth more to him.[2]

Although this problem is solved by decreeing specific performance, another economic problem is created. The fact that the seller defaulted may indicate that there is another transaction that increases value by even more than would completion of the sale to me; if so, we want to encourage the breach. The results of decreeing specific performance are not catastrophic, since the seller can always pay me to surrender my right of specific performance and presumably will do so if a substitute transfer would yield a higher price. But to require the seller to conduct this additional negotiation imposes additional transaction costs. This is particularly clear in a case of physical impossibility where discharge is unwarranted because the promisor was an insurer of the risk of impossibility. Suppose the promisee could obtain a decree ordering the promisor to complete the performance due under the contract. Although the promisor could pay the promisee to remove the injunction (as an alternative to suffering the penalties, sometimes quite severe, for disobeying an injunction), the amount of the payment would bear little or no relation to the costs to the promisee of the promisor's failure to perform. Indeed, since an injunction could require the promisor to incur possibly unlimited costs (infinite, in a case of true physical impossibility) to comply with the contract, the promisor might, depending on the costs of defying an injunction, have to yield his entire wealth to the promisee in order to obtain a release from his obligation, even though nonperformance might have imposed only trivial costs on the promisee. In fact, the promisor is unlikely to have to pay *that* much; the lesser of his wealth and of the cost of defying the injunction would merely be the upper limit of the range within which bargaining would occur between the parties to the contract (what would be the lower limit?). But this just means that the availability of injunctive relief in this case creates a bilateral monopoly, which is a source of high transaction costs. Although this is no problem in the case of an opportunistic breach — by definition, completion of performance by the contract breaker is not impossible or even uneconomical — specific performance is not necessary in this case; restitution will do just as well, and will require less supervision by the court.

This suggests another reason for preferring damage remedies to specific performance. The damage remedy is, for the court, a one-shot deal; the court enters judgment, and the sheriff goes and sells some

2. Can you reconcile the rule allowing specific performance in land cases with the rule giving eminent domain powers to the government?

of the defendant's assets if the defendant refuses to pay the judgment voluntarily. But specific performance, like other equitable remedies, requires the court to keep the case on its docket till performance is complete, so that if necessary it can respond to the plaintiff's argument that the defendant is failing to perform in good faith. Since the costs of the court system are not borne fully by the parties (as we shall see in due course), the costs of specific performance are to some extent externalized by the parties to the contract. Since specific performance is thus more costly to administer than damage remedies and since injunctive remedies[3] create bilateral-monopoly problems that damage remedies do not, it is not surprising that a basic principle of equity is that the applicant for an equitable remedy must show that his remedy at law (almost always an order to pay damages or some other lump sum) is inadequate, for example, because the estimation problems are insuperable (see further §21.4).

The problem of bilateral monopoly created by injunctive remedies is not limited to specific performance in contract cases and provides another economic reason for the equity principle just mentioned. For example, in *Boomer v. Atlantic Cement Co.*,[4] the plaintiffs were seeking an injunction against pollution from the defendant's plant. Although the plaintiffs succeeded in demonstrating an invasion of their legal rights, injunctive relief was denied, and the plaintiffs remitted to damages, because the cost to the defendant of compliance (which would have involved closing the plant) would have been grossly disproportionate to the damage sustained by the plaintiffs. The tremendous difference between the harm to the plaintiffs and the cost to the defendant of avoiding that harm created an enormous range of possible prices at which the plaintiffs would have sold their injunctive right to the defendant, had an injunction been issued.[5] And the larger the bargaining range under bilateral monopoly, the greater the potential dissipation of scarce resources in the bargaining process.

§4.12   Self-Help — Contract Conditions

Often the most effective remedy for breach of contract involves no suit or even threat of suit. Suppose a consumer buys an automobile on the

---

3. A decree of specific performance is a form of mandatory injunction.
4. 26 N.Y.2d 219, 257 N.E.2d 870 (1970).
5. Is it possible to square the result in *Boomer* with the principle noted in the last chapter that injunctive remedies should be allowed as a matter of course in conflicting-use situations where transaction costs are low? What is the proper domain of that principle as applied to two-party transactions? Should even damages have been allowed in the *Boomer* case?

installment plan, takes possession, but fails to complete his payments. The automobile dealer may decide not to sue for the balance of the purchase price. The amount in default may be too small to warrant the costs of suit, although small claims courts — used more by sellers than by buyers, be it noted — facilitate the collection of small contract claims. Instead the dealer may repossess the car, sell it, and remit the proceeds of the sale to the buyer minus the costs of sale and the amount due the dealer on the contract. If the dealer were allowed to keep the entire proceeds, this would be a forfeiture, and it is no longer allowed.

Should it matter whether the dealer resells the car at retail or at wholesale? It might seem that since retail prices are higher than wholesale prices, the dealer should, for the buyer's sake, be required to sell at retail. But the law does not require this, and it is right not to. Assuming that retailing and wholesaling are competitive rather than monopolistic industries — and they are — both the retail and the wholesale price of a good should be equal to the cost of selling the good. The retail price will be higher only because the costs of retailing are greater than the costs of wholesaling. The net proceeds to the owner of the good sold should be the same.

The right of repossession can be restated in the language of conditions, an important doctrine in the law of contracts, as follows. The buyer's right to force the seller to perform by supplying him with the car is conditional on the buyer's paying the seller in full for the car. If the buyer breaks his part of the contract, the seller is entitled to retract his performance and thus retake the car. Suppose the buyer had defaulted before the car was delivered. Then the seller could explicitly have invoked the doctrine of conditions as a ground for refusing delivery. But could he have kept the money that the buyer had already paid him on the contract of sale? He could not have. The payments might greatly exceed the seller's damages from the breach. The seller would have to offset the damages against the payments and return the excess to the buyer.

Similarly, the doctrine of substantial performance prevents one who has hired a contractor to build a house from refusing payment because of a minor breach of contract. The breach need not be forgiven; the promisee can sue for his damages. But minor, immaterial breaches will not excuse the other party from carrying out his part of the bargain (in the last example, paying for the house).

These examples illustrate the important point that self-help could be, but for the rule against penalties and (some) forfeitures, and doctrines such as substantial performance and material breach, an excessively severe remedy for a breach of contract — a remedy that like an explicit penalty could deter efficient breaches and should therefore be forbidden, unless, perhaps, the parties agree to it when they make their contract. Maybe in the last example a change in circumstances has made the car worth only $5,000 to the buyer. The purchase price was $7,000, and the seller's damages from breach are $1,000 (because the market price of the car is now only $6,000), but the buyer has already paid $4,000. Since the buyer cannot get this money back (assuming that in the event of a breach the seller could keep any money already collected), the buyer will go ahead and complete payment ($3,000 allows him to keep a car worth $5,000 to him), even though the car is worth more to the dealer. Presumably the buyer can resell, but less efficiently than the dealer.

Buyers' self-help[1] is a commonplace and normally unproblematic remedy in sales cases. B orders widgets from A, but when they arrive and are inspected B realizes right away that they are defective and sends them back. This is a cheaper remedy, socially as well as privately, than B's keeping the widgets and suing A for damages, or even selling them on A's account — A presumably has a better sense of what do with the defective widgets than B (repair them, scrap them, sell them to someone else as "seconds," etc.).

If B fails to inspect and as a result doesn't discover the defects until much later, he may be deemed to have accepted the goods, and will have to pay for them. This may seem a pointless requirement, since the law allows B to sue for A's breach of warranty in supplying defective goods, notwithstanding acceptance. But the longer B delays in returning the goods, the more the goods will have depreciated — the more costly, in other words, the buyer's self-help remedy will be to the seller. Assuming that the added costs could have been avoided by the buyer at a lower cost in careful inspection of the goods on arrival, the parties presumably would have wanted the buyer to forfeit his self-help remedy of rejection, as an inducement to the buyer to use due care.

What makes self-help a cheap remedy in the sale-of-goods case if promptly invoked is that the seller can often resell the goods at little or no loss after they are returned to him and normally he is better at reselling them than the buyer would be. But what if you contract for the construction of a house, and when the day comes for the builder to turn over the completed house to you, you notice that the house does not comply with all the specifications in the contract. Should you be allowed to refuse the tender, although you have not yet paid anything toward the price of the house?

Again the key issue is the relation between the cost of your self-help to the builder and the damages to which you would be entitled if you had sued instead. Suppose that because the house was custom designed to your idiosyncratic tastes its resale value is very low; the builder will incur a $50,000 loss if you are allowed to walk away from the contract,

§4.12 1. See George L. Priest, Breach and Remedy for the Tender of Nonconforming Goods Under the Uniform Commercial Code: An Economic Approach, 91 Harv. L. Rev. 960 (1978).

whereas the damages that you would be able to collect for his minor breaches of the contract if you sued would come to only $1,000. Self-help is not an efficient remedy in this instance. Hence we predict (and find) that the law does not allow the promisee to excuse his performance because of a minor breach by the promisor. The law implicitly compares the cost of the promisee's self-help to the promisor with the promisee's damages, and refuses to allow self-help when the former cost substantially exceeds the latter. Thus we expect self-help to be allowed more frequently in cases of fungible goods than in cases of customized goods.

§4.13   Implied Contracts

A doctor chances on a stranger lying unconscious on the street, treats him, and later demands a fee. Has he a legal claim? The law's answer is yes. The older legal terminology spoke of an implied contract between the physician and the stranger for medical assistance. This idea has been attacked as a fiction, and modern writers prefer to base the physician's legal right on the principle of unjust enrichment. This term suggests a moral basis for law (perhaps) divorced from the economic. In fact, the principal case outcomes are better explained in economic than moral terms. The concept of an implied contract is a useful shorthand for an economic approach, for that approach suggests that there is a considerable continuity between express contracts and the questions nowadays treated under the rubric of unjust enrichment.[1]

In the first case, that of the doctor, the costs of a voluntary transaction would be prohibitive. The source of the high transaction costs in that case was incapacity; in other cases it might be time (e.g., the stranger is conscious but bleeding profusely and there is no time to discuss terms). In such cases we must consider whether, had transaction costs not been prohibitive, the parties would have come to terms and if so what (approximately) the terms would have been. If a court can be reasonably confident both that there would have been a transaction and what its essential terms would have been (that the doctor use his best efforts and that the patient pay the doctor's normal fee for treatment of the sort rendered), it does not hesitate to write a contract between the parties after the fact.[2]

§4.13   1. For fuller discussions, see William M. Landes & Richard A. Posner, Salvors, Finders, Good Samaritans, and Other Rescuers: An Economic Study of Law and Altruism, 7 J. Leg. Stud. 83 (1978); Saul Levmore, Explaining Restitution, 71 Va. L. Rev. 65 (1985); Note, A Theory of Hypothetical Contract, 94 Yale L.J. 415 (1984).

2. As was the situation in the party-wall case, discussed in §3.9 *supra*, where the source of the high transaction costs was bilateral monopoly.

Should it make a difference whether the defendant can prove that he was a Christian Scientist and would not, if conscious, have contracted for the doctor's services? It should not — unless in the other cases of treating unconscious people doctors are given premiums to compensate them for the risk that the unconscious person doesn't really want (and hence won't be made to pay for) their services. But now suppose that a man stands under my window, playing the violin beautifully, and when he has finished knocks on my door and demands a fee for his efforts. Though I enjoyed his playing I nonetheless refuse to pay anything for it. The court would deny the violinist's claim for a fee — however reasonable the fee might appear to be — on the ground that, although the violinist conferred a benefit on me (and not with the intent that it be gratuitous), he did so officiously. Translated from legal into economic terminology, this means he conferred an unbargained-for benefit in circumstances where the costs of a voluntary bargain would have been low. In such cases the law insists that the voluntary route be followed — and is on firm economic grounds in doing so.[3]

Should it make a difference if the violinist had been hired by my neighbor and by mistake played under my window instead? If the violinist, instead of playing his violin, mistakenly paid an installment of my mortage?[4]

Suggested Readings

1. John H. Barton, The Economic Basis of Damages for Breach of Contract, 1 J. Leg. Stud. 277 (1972).

2. Charles J. Goetz & Robert E. Scott, The Mitigation Principle: Toward a General Theory of Contractual Obligation, 69 Va. L. Rev. 967 (1983).

3. Anthony T. Kronman, Mistake, Disclosure, Information, and the Law of Contracts, 7 J. Leg. Stud. 1 (1978).

4. ———— & Richard A. Posner, The Economics of Contract Law (1979).

5. Timothy J. Muris, Opportunistic Behavior and the Law of Contracts, 65 Minn. L. Rev. 521 (1981).

6. Jeffrey M. Perloff, Breach of Contract and the Foreseeability Doctrine of *Hadley v. Baxendale*, 10 J. Leg. Stud. 39 (1981).

7. A. Mitchell Polinsky, Risk Sharing Through Breach of Contract Remedies, 12 J. Leg. Stud. 427 (1983).

8. Richard A. Posner, Gratuitous Promises in Economics and Law, 6 J. Leg. Stud. 411 (1977).

---

3. There is no bilateral-monopoly problem; why not?
4. For further discussion of unjust enrichment, see §§6.9, 8.4 *infra*.

9. ——— & Andrew M. Rosenfield, Impossibility and Related Doctrines in Contract Law: An Economic Analysis, 6 J. Leg. Stud. 83 (1977).

10. Samuel A. Rea, Jr., Efficiency Implications of Penalties and Liquidated Damages, 13 J. Leg. Stud. 147 (1984).

11. Steven Shavell, Damage Measures for Breach of Contract, 11 Bell J. Econ. 466 (1980).

12. Thomas S. Ulen, The Efficiency of Specific Performance: Toward a Unified Theory of Contract Remedies, 83 Mich. L. Rev. 341 (1984).

Problems

1. Suppose courts, in determining the rights and duties of parties to contracts, do not use the criterion of efficiency to guide their decision, but use instead some noneconomic criterion of fairness. What effect would their decisions have on the process of exchange? Why is contract law in general an inappropriate area in which to enforce moral (insofar as they may be distinct from economic) principles?

2. Paradine v. Jane, Alleyn 26, 82 Eng. Rep. 897 (K.B. 1647), was an action for rent by a landlord. The lessee's defense was that he had been dispossessed by the army of Prince Rupert, a foreign invader. As a matter of economics, should the court have accepted this defense?

3. Discuss the following propositions:

(a) Reliance rather than expectation damages are the proper measure of damages for breach of contract in cases (e.g., mistake) where there was no actual meeting of minds.

(b) Reliance loss corresponds in general to short-run variable cost, expectation loss to long-run variable cost (cf. §10.6 *infra*).

4. Why isn't it rational never to pay one's debts, and instead always put the creditor to the cost of collection proceedings, on the theory that he will compromise the debt rather than incur those costs? See Arthur Allen Leff, Injury, Ignorance, and Spite — The Dynamics of Coercive Collection, 80 Yale L.J. 1 (1970).

5. "I believe that there is value as well as an element of real nobility in the judicial decision to throw out, every time the opportunity arises, consumer contracts designed to perpetuate the exploitation of the poorest class of buyers on credit." Duncan Kennedy, Form and Substance in Private Law Adjudication, 89 Harv. L. Rev. 1685, 1777 (1976). The author apparently has reference to the type of installment contract discussed in §4.7 *supra*. See 89 Harv. L. Rev. at 1777 n.160. In what sense are such contracts in fact exploitive of the poorest class of buyers? Would those buyers be better off if the courts rewrote their contracts to give increased protection to the defaulting buyer? Does your answer depend on whether the poorest class of buyers is defined as all poor buyers or as poor buyers who are especially likely to default?

6. Can you think of an economic reason why bilateral promises within the family (e.g., husband promises wife to buy her a piano if she will walk the dog every night for a year, and she agrees but later reneges) should not be judicially enforced?

7. If insurance is an important function of contracts, which contract remedies carry out this function best (and worst), and should the winning party be entitled to have his legal fees paid by the loser?

8. A pays $100 for a ticket to a Super Bowl game. Through some mix-up caused by the ticket broker, the ticket is never delivered to A, and he misses the game. He would have paid $10,000 for the ticket. Assume that the mix-up was not avoidable at reasonable cost by the broker but that he has broken his contract. What should A's damages be? See Samuel A. Rea, Jr., Nonpecuniary Loss and Breach of Contract, 11 J. Leg. Stud. 35 (1982).

9. Section 3 of the Harter Act, 46 U.S.C. §192, provides:

If the owner of any vessel transporting merchandise or property to or from any port in the United States of America shall exercise due diligence to make the said vessel in all respects seaworthy and properly manned, equipped, and supplied, neither the vessel, her owner or owners, agents, or charterers, shall become or be held responsible for damage or loss resulting from faults or errors in navigation or in the management of said vessel.

Can you think of any possible economic function of this law?

10. Usually, illegality (e.g., a violation of antitrust law) is a defense to enforcement of an executory contract, but not to enforcement of a partially executed contract. Why the difference?

CHAPTER 5

FAMILY LAW[1]

The marital relationship is fundamentally contractual in character, and an analysis of family law therefore follows naturally that of contract law. This chapter, though, is just an introduction to the economics and law of the family; inheritance (which is largely intrafamilial) and sex discrimination (a topic inseparable from the family) will be discussed later in the book.

§5.1   The Theory of Household Production

The economic analysis of the family is founded on the perception that the household is not merely a consuming, but more importantly a producing, unit in society. The food, clothing, furniture, medicines, and other market commodities that the household purchases are really inputs into the production of nourishment, warmth, affection, children, and the other tangible and intangible goods that constitute the output of the household. A most important input into this productive process is not a market commodity at all; it is the time of the household members, in particular — in the traditional family — of the wife.

The persistence of the family as a social institution suggests to an economist that the institution must have important economizing properties. What might these be? Economies of scale (for instance, from sharing a kitchen)? But these could be, and often are, achieved outside of marriage, and in any event are often smaller than the costs of having to adapt one's tastes, schedule, etc., to another person's. A more important factor is that the family facilitates the division of labor, resulting in

1. See Homer H. Clark, Jr., Cases and Problems on Domestic Relations (3d ed. 1980); Caleb Foote, Robert J. Levy & Frank E.A. Sander, Cases and Materials on Family Law (3d ed. 1985).

gains from specialization. In the traditional family the husband specializes in some market employment (for example, engineering) that yields
income that can be used to purchase the market commodities needed
as inputs into the final production of the household, while the wife
devotes her time to processing market commodities (for example, grocer-
ies) into household output (for example, dinner). By specializing in production for the market, the husband maximizes the family's money
income with which to buy the market commodities that the family needs.
By specializing in household production the wife maximizes the value
of her time as an input into the production of the household's output.
The division of labor — the husband working full-time in the job market,
the wife full-time in the household — operates to maximize the total
real income of the household by enabling husband and wife to specialize
in complementary activities. It is the same principle by which we expect
a person who works half-time as a doctor and half-time as a lawyer to
produce less than one-half the total output of medical and legal services
of two people of equal ability to his, one of whom is a full-time doctor
and the other a full-time lawyer. People who do the same thing all the
time tend to do it better than people who divide their time between
unrelated tasks.

But of course it is an exaggeration to speak of husband and wife
each devoting full time to their respective roles as market and household
producer respectively, for if their roles were totally separate it would
be a puzzle why marriage, rather than a business partnership, was the
institution for organizing the home. The key to the puzzle lies in the
nature of the major "commodity" that marriage produces: children. Although many marriages are childless, only a few are childless by choice;
and it is hard to believe that marriage would be a common institution
if most people didn't want children. Raising children requires, especially
in their early years, an enormous amount of parental (traditionally mater-
nal) time, and a woman who is busy raising a child will not have the
time to work in the market for the money she needs for complementary
inputs (food, clothing, shelter, etc.). So she "trades" her work in the
home for the husband's work in the market; he "buys" her care of children that are his as well as hers.

Nothing in this theory requires that the market producer be the man
and the household producer the woman; but neither is this traditional
division of functions completely arbitrary, or the result solely of discrimination. Until this century, a woman, in order to be reasonably confident
of producing even a modest number of children surviving to adulthood,
had to be more or less continuously pregnant or nursing during her
childbearing years. If anyone was to specialize in market production,
it had to be the husband. Even today, most women who have children
take more time off from work than their husbands do, at least while
the children are babies, and this leaves the women with less time to

specialize in the market. But we shall see that it is quite important for modern women to hedge their bets on marriage by working in the market as well, notwithstanding the resulting sacrifice of specialization (both the woman's and her husband's).

While marriage can be likened to a partnership, and the household to a small factory, there are important differences between business and familial organization. For example, the division of the marital income may not be determined by the relative value of each spouse's contribution, as it would be in a business partnership. A related point (can you see why?) is that specific tasks within the household are not directed and monitored in a hierarchical, bureaucratic, or even contractual manner. There is a substitute in marriage for the control mechanisms within a business firm. Economists naturally do not call this factor "love," but describe it as a form of altruism. Altruism is the condition in which the welfare of one person is a positive function of (i.e., increases with) the welfare of another. If H loves W, then an increase in W's happiness or utility or welfare (synonyms) will be felt by H as an increase in his own happiness or utility or welfare. Altruism facilitates cooperation; it is a cheap and efficacious substitute for (formal) contracting.

Declining marriage and birth rates, and rising divorce rates, suggest that the traditional family is in decline. Economic theory provides an explanation. Advances in contraception, the advent of cheap household labor-saving devices, the great reduction in child mortality, and the increasing fraction of jobs that do not require much physical strength or stamina have reduced the cost to women of working in the market and increased the demand for their services by employers. The net income that women can earn in the market (wages minus costs of work, those costs including loss of time for household production) has soared, which has greatly increased the opportunity cost of being a housewife, for that cost is the net market income forgone by staying home.

The household commodity that places the greatest demands on the wife's time is rearing children, so an increase in the opportunity cost of that time is immediately translated into an increase in the shadow price of children to the household. A rise in the price of children can be expected to reduce the quantity of children demanded; and since rearing children is not only one of the most important activities of the household but also the one most difficult to conduct at comparable cost outside of the household, a decline in the demand for children should result — and evidently has resulted — in a decline in the demand for marriage. But even without any increase in women's net market income, there would be a reduction in the number of children per household, for with dramatically reduced child mortality a couple needs fewer children in order to be reasonably confident of having as many (grown) children as desired.

We have treated children as an ultimate "commodity," but it is possible to treat them instead as an input into other commodities. The economist speculates that children are produced

(1) as an unintended by-product of sexual activity,

(2) as an income-producing investment,

(3) as a source of other services to the parents, and

(4) (really a subset of (3)) out of an instinct or desire to preserve the species or perpetuate the genetic characteristics, the name, or the memory of the parents.

In an age of widely available contraception and abortion, (1) has become relatively unimportant (it was never very important, except where law or custom confined sexual activity to marriage — no doubt in order to encourage the production of children, for reasons explored at the end of this chapter). (2) was once important in our society (as it is in very poor societies today); at common law, the parents owned the child's market earnings until his majority and were entitled to support from the child in their old age. The outlawing of child labor, and the prevalence of public and private pension schemes, have obsoleted (2) and prompted a search for less tangible services that parents might derive from a child (for example, respect). (3) and (4) are the most plausible explanations for the desire to have children in contemporary society. Liking children is a subset of (3): The pleasure we get from our children's presence is the result of "consuming" the intangible "services" that they render us.

§5.2 Formation and Dissolution of Marriage

Commercial partnerships are voluntary contractual associations, and so, up to a point, are marriages. Even (otherwise) totalitarian states respect freedom of choice in marriage. And the "marriage market" is an apt metaphor for the elaborate process of search by which individuals seek marital partners with whom to form productive households.

The "transactions" made in these markets are in general the value-maximizing transactions. For example, bright men tend to marry bright women; and an agricultural analogy will suggest the economic reason why. Suppose there are two farms, and the soil of one is (untreated) twice as fruitful as the soil of the other (untreated). A chemical that is in very short supply will double the yield of whichever farm it is applied to, but there is only enough of the chemical for one farm. Should it be applied to the farm with the poorer soil, on the theory that that farm needs it more? Should it be divided between the two farms? (Half the chemical will increase the output of a farm by 50 percent.) Or should it all be applied to the farm with the better soil? The last. Suppose the output of the farm with the richer soil is (before treatment with the chemical) 2, and the output of the other farm 1. If the chemical is applied all to the poorer farm, the total output of the two farms will be 4 (2 + 2); if applied half and half, 4½ (3 + 1½); but if applied all to the better farm, 5 (4 + 1). Coming a little closer to home, we would also expect that law firms that had the best partners would hire the best associates to work with them, that law schools with the best students would have the best teachers, and that firms in thriving markets would have better executives on average than firms in declining ones. And so it should be (and seems on the whole to be) in marriage as well, if we assume that the positive qualities of spouses are related multiplicatively as in the farm, law firm, law school, and corporate examples, and not just additively.

Despite the economic resemblance between marriage and business partnership, the marital relationship is not, or at least was not until the advent of no-fault divorce (about which more later), an unalloyed example of free-market principles. Three features in particular, which seem at once odd from the perspective of the last chapter and incompatible with one another, mark off marriage law from contract law.

First, the parties are not free to set the term of the contract or even to terminate the contract by mutual consent; the term is life, subject (in traditional law) to termination for cause — much as in a university tenure contract.

Second, despite the long term of the contract, the sanction for breach is more severe than the sanction for breach of a regular contract. If the husband abandons the wife (or vice versa), he not only must continue to support her (which is analogous to having to pay damages) but may not marry anyone else, unless she consents to a divorce; it is as if a contract breaker could be enjoined from making a substitute contract for the one he had broken — and for the rest of his life.[1]

Third, despite the locked-in nature of their relationship, if spouses have a dispute during the course of the marriage the courts generally will not intervene to settle the dispute; the spouses will have to work it out for themselves. Marriage law seems an odd amalgam of intrusiveness (in regard to the term of the contract and the sanctions for breach) and hands-off-ness.

How is all this to be explained, and if possible reconciled with the efficiency principle that we have seen at work in other areas of common law? The answer may lie in the fact that the marriage "contract" affects nonconsenting third parties, the children of the marriage. Of course, even in a system of consensual divorce, parents who love their children will take the cost of divorce to the children into account in deciding

---

§5.2   1. Breaches of personal services contracts are enjoined only if the promisor's services are unique, which would make the promisee's damage remedy inadequate.

whether to divorce; but unless they are highly altruistic toward the children, the cost to the children may not be fully internalized by the parents, so that when they balance the cost to the children of divorce against the cost to themselves of remaining married they may reckon the cost to the children at less than it really is and thus decide to divorce even though the total costs to all concerned exceed the total benefits. And, of course, not all parents love their children. Now it might seem that to lock parents into a miserable marriage, by making divorce impossible, would condemn the children to misery too. But this ignores the fact that forbidding divorce will induce more careful search for a marriage partner in the first place. The more costly a mistake is, the less likely it is to be committed; and a mistake in choosing a spouse is more costly in a system that forbids divorce (or makes it very difficult) than in one that permits it. So making divorce hard or impossible fosters happy marriages! Moreover, if people know they are locked into a relationship, they create methods of working out their differences, so there is less need for judicial dispute resolution.

This analysis may explain the curious common law rule, so at variance with the corresponding rule of contract law examined in the last chapter, that fraud is rarely a ground for annulling a marriage unless the fraud involves sex (typically, the husband failed to disclose before the marriage that he was impotent). In a system where divorce is very difficult, prospective marriage partners engage in a lengthy search involving not only a careful comparison of prospects but also a careful inquiry into the qualities of the most promising prospect: hence the tradition of the lengthy courtship. The courtship provides an opportunity for each prospective spouse to unmask the deceptions by which people try to represent themselves in personal relationships as having better qualities and prospects than they really do. Legal remedies should not be as necessary as in ordinary contractual relationships. But fraud as to sex goes to the heart of the marriage contract; more important, dissolution of a childless marriage does not involve the potential inefficiency of a divorce where there are children.

A system in which divorce is absolutely forbidden may seem to put the children's interests too far ahead of that of a cruelly mistreated spouse. And yet it can be argued that the refusal of the English common law until well into the nineteenth century to recognize any grounds for divorce actually protected the weaker spouse (invariably the wife) more effectively than allowing divorce for cause would have done. In a system where divorce is allowed for cause, a husband who wants "out" of the marriage will have an incentive to so mistreat his wife that she is driven to sue for divorce, provided that alimony (of which more later) or other remedies would not visit the full costs of the mistreatment on him, as often they would not in a system where litigation was slow, costly, and uncertain. But if the remedial difficulties can be overcome, then allowing divorce for cause makes economic sense, as it enables at least a rough comparison between the costs to the children of divorce and the cost to a severely wronged spouse of remaining married. Moreover, the traditional grounds of divorce, with one partial and very interesting exception (adultery), seem to have been limited to cases where the husband's misconduct was likely to hurt the children as well as the wife: cases of insanity, extreme cruelty, and criminality.

Regarding adultery, one notes with interest that it often used to be the case that a single act of adultery by the wife was grounds for divorce, while the husband had to be a habitual adulterer in order to entitle the wife to a divorce. The economic explanation for this rule is that the wife's adultery is more costly to the husband than the husband's adultery to the wife, even if the purely emotional cost of adultery — the shame or fury that it engenders in the dishonored spouse when he or she discovers the adultery — is the same to both spouses (but will it be?). If the wife is adulterous, she may conceive a child who is not the child of her husband (or a series of such children); and since the capacity of women to bear children is distinctly finite, the benefits of the marriage to the husband will be distinctly impaired, assuming he wants to have children of his blood. But the husband's adultery need not reduce the number of children that his wife will bear or the support he will give each of them, so the benefits of the marriage to her, at least in terms of children, may not be impaired. If, however, the husband is a habitual adulterer, he may be so distracted from his wife's and (legitimate) children's needs as to impose on her a cost as high as a wife's isolated adultery would impose on the husband.

The problem with having *any* grounds for divorce (and another reason in favor of the old English rule, incomprehensible as it nearly is to the modern mind) is that it erodes the principle, designed we have said for the protection of the children of the marriage, against voluntary dissolutions of marriage. An agreement to dissolve a marriage involves only two people; although there is a bilateral-monopoly problem, transaction costs should not be prohibitive. And once the parties have arrived at mutually agreeable terms, they need only manufacture evidence of a breach that provides legal grounds for divorce in order to get around a law against consensual divorce. The manufacture of evidence is not costless, so a stringent divorce law will preserve some marriages by increasing the costs of dissolution. If society were more determined to preserve marriages than it is, it would at least prevent the parties from controlling the evidence; it would allow divorce only when the public prosecutor, or some other third party, had proved the commission of a breach of the marriage contract. The "fault" system is tantamount to confiding the enforcement of laws punishing such "victimless" crimes as bribery and dope peddling to the bribed official and the narcotics purchaser. And as the gains from marriage have declined, the pressure for divorce has risen. This makes enforcing a policy against consensual divorce increasingly costly and suggests another reason for the trend toward more liberal divorce laws.

A distinct economic issue is presented by recent proposals to permit unilateral divorce. If the term connoted no more than that one party could dissolve the marriage subject to the payment of appropriate compensation to the other, it would mean simply that the marriage contract was now to be treated like any other contract, which either party can terminate at will if prepared to pay the other's damages. We have already got beyond this in the systems of no-fault divorce in force in many states. Sometimes the party who initiates the divorce has to pay the other party's damages, in the form of alimony and property settlement, but not always: A wife who initiates the divorce may still be awarded alimony. Some proposals take unilateral divorce even further away from the contractual model of damages for breach. For example, under the Uniform Marriage and Divorce Act, in community property states the spouse who decides unilaterally to breach the marriage contract is automatically entitled to receive one half of any property accumulated during the marriage.[2] This approach creates incentives for divorce and for marriages designed from the outset to end in divorce. A poor young woman marries a rich old man, knowing that every year his income exceeds his expenses and produces substantial savings. At the end of five years, pursuant to her original intention, she dissolves the marriage and claims one half of the savings built up during it.

The unilateral divorce proposals complete a circle from the pre-Victorian era, when upon marriage the wife's property became the property of her husband. That rule, repudiated as part of the movement for women's emancipation in the latter part of the nineteenth century,[3] encouraged "bounders" to marry wealthy women. Unilateral divorce in the form allowed in the Uniform Act resurrects that incentive and fosters the symmetrical incentive for unscrupulous poor women to marry rich men.

§5.3   Consequences of Dissolution

When a conventional partnership is dissolved, the assets of the partnership must be distributed among the partners. Abstracting from the issue

2. National Conference of Commissioners on Uniform State Laws, Uniform Marriage and Divorce Act 35 (1971).

3. See A.V. Dicey, Lectures on the Relation Between Law and Public Opinion in England During the Nineteenth Century 371-395 (2d ed. 1914). Might it have been the efficient rule for its time? Did the existence of the rule weaken or strengthen the argument for forbidding divorce?

of fault, it is the same with marriage. But there is a difficulty in dividing the assets acquired by the household during the marriage. If the wife has had very little market income, all or most of the household's tangible assets will have been bought with the husband's money.[1] And yet his earning capacity may owe much to her efforts. She may have supported him while he was a student in law school or medical school, forgoing her own chance to increase her earning capacity through advanced training. She incurred an opportunity cost to enhance his earning capacity and, having financed his education, is entitled, like any lender, to compensation. The courts understand this, and act accordingly in the division of assets[2] — but now consider a harder case. The couple was married after the man completed his professional training. The wife specialized exclusively in household production, so once again all the tangible assets of the marriage were bought by the husband. Yet it would be quite mistaken to attribute all of those assets to the husband's productive activity. The value of the housewife's nonpecuniary contributions may be as great as or greater than the husband's[3] and is in any event unlikely to be negligible. If the husband had had to devote substantial time to household production, his market income would have been lower and fewer assets would have been accumulated; some of those assets were thus bought by the wife's labor in the household. Although the rule in community property states that 50 percent of the assets accumulated during the marriage are deemed the wife's property upon dissolution is arbitrary — there is no presumption that the partners in a marriage (or in a law firm) are equally productive — and may be too generous,[4] the costs of determining the spouses' relative contributions to the household's wealth, and the manifest inappropriateness of using the ratio of their pecuniary incomes as a proxy for their relative contributions, may make the rule hard to improve on.[5]

Besides prescribing the division of the marital assets, the divorce decree may order the husband to pay the wife (1) a fixed amount periodi-

§5.3 1. Ignore the complications introduced when the wife has property or other income not earned in the job market.

2. See, e.g., In re Marriage of Haugen, 117 Wis. 2d 200, 220, 343 N.W. 2d 796, 806 (1984), and for good general discussions, using economics, E. Raedene Combs, The Human Capital Concept as a Basis for Property Settlement at Divorce: Theory and Implementation, 2 J. Divorce 329 (1979); Joan M. Krauskopf, Recompense for Financing Spouse's Education: Legal Protection for the Marital Investor in Human Capital, 28 U. Kan. L. Rev. 379 (1980); Lenore J. Weitzman, The Economics of Divorce: Social and Economic Consequences of Property, Alimony and Child Support Awards, 28 U.C.L.A. L. Rev. 1181 (1981).

3. It has been estimated that, on average, the value of the wife's household production is equal to more than 70 percent of the household's money (market) income after taxes, which implies that the wife's household production generates 40 percent of the household's full income. See Reuben Gronau, Home Production — A Forgotten Industry, 62 Rev. Econ. & Stat. 408 (1980).

4. See note 3 *supra.*

5. Should the wife's division be reduced, and if so by how much, if the dissolution of the marriage was due to fault on her part?

cally unless and until she remarries (alimony) and (2) a part of the cost of raising the children of the marriage, of whom she will ordinarily have custody (child support).[6] Alimony is analytically quite complex. It appears to serve three distinct economic functions:

1. It is a form of damages for breach of the marital contract. If this were all there was to alimony, however, one would expect it to be paid in a lump sum, like other forms of damages, in order to minimize the costs of judicial supervision; and it would never be awarded to the spouse who was at fault, as it often is.

2. Alimony is a method of repaying the wife (in the traditional marriage) her share of the marital partnership's assets. Often the principal asset to which the wife will have contributed by her labor in the household or in the market — as in our example of the wife who supports her husband while he is in graduate school — is the husband's earning capacity. As this is an asset against which it is difficult to borrow money (why?), it might be infeasible for the husband to raise the money necessary to buy back from the wife, in a lump sum, so much of the asset as she can fairly claim is hers by virtue of her contributions; he must therefore pay her, over time, out of the stream of earnings that the asset generates. But this is not a complete explanation of alimony either, because if it were the law would not terminate alimony when the wife remarries.

3. The last and perhaps most important economic function of alimony is to provide the wife with a form of severance pay or unemployment benefits. In the traditional family, where the wife specializes in household production, any skills that she may have had in market production depreciate and eventually her prime employment possibilities — should the present marriage dissolve — narrow down to the prospect of remarrying and forming a new household where she can ply her trade. Although she could always find *some* kind of work in the market, the skilled household producer forced to work as a waitress or file clerk is like the lawyer who, unable to find a legal job, becomes a process server.

Because the search for a suitable spouse is often protracted, and because age may depreciate a person's ability (especially if a woman) to form a new marriage that will yield her as much real income as the previous marriage did, it makes sense to provide as a standard term in the marriage contract a form of severance pay or unemployment compensation that will maintain the divorced wife at her previous standard of living during the search for a new husband. Consider an analogy to law practice. By agreeing to work for a law firm that specialized exclusively in negotiating oil-tanker mortgages, a lawyer might make it very difficult for himself, in the event he was ever laid off, to find an equally remunerative position (why?). But that is all the more reason why he

6. Joint custody is becoming increasingly common. Can you think of an economic reason why?

might demand, as a condition of working for such a firm, that it agree that should it ever lay him off it will continue his salary until he finds equally remunerative work, even if the search is protracted.

An alternative in both the housewife's and the lawyer's case would be a higher wage to compensate for the risk of prolonged unemployment in the event of layoff. But in the case of marriage, the husband may be incapable of making the necessary transfer payments to the wife, especially during the early years of the marriage, when the household may not have substantial liquid assets. Also, to calculate in advance the appropriate compensation for a risk as difficult to quantify as that of divorce would be costly, especially since the relevant probability is really a schedule of probabilities of divorce in each year of the marriage. This of course is a reason for awarding alimony on a periodic basis even if the rationale is damages.

Just as severance pay is awarded without regard to whether the employer was at fault in laying off the worker — indeed, often without regard to whether the employee quit or was fired — so alimony, viewed as a form of severance pay, is not dependent on notions of fault. But just as an employee might forfeit his entitlement to severance pay by having quit in breach of his employment contract, so alimony should be denied or reduced (and sometimes it is) if the wife was seriously at fault in procuring dissolution of a marriage. Better, any damages she caused the family by walking out on the marriage could be subtracted from her alimony payments if her share of the marital assets was insufficient to cover them.

Alimony payments are taxed as income to the wife, which is consistent with the tax treatment of severance pay but not with that of unemployment insurance or other fringe benefits — or of damages (see §17.8 *infra*).

§5.4 The Legal Protection of Children

In considering the appropriate role of the state in relation to children, we may begin with the assumption congenial to economic analysis that the state desires to maximize the aggregate welfare of all of its citizens, including therefore children. To realize their potential as adults — in economic terms, to achieve a high level of lifetime utility — children require a considerable investment of both parental time and market inputs (food, clothing, tuition, etc.). Since costs as well as benefits must be considered in any investment decision, the optimal level of investment in a particular child is that which is expected to maximize the combined welfare of the child, his parents, and other family members. That level will vary from family to family depending on such factors as the child's aptitudes and the parents' wealth. It will also depend critically on how much the parents love the child; the more they love it, the higher will be the optimal investment, because the costs of the investment will be felt very lightly, even not at all, by the parents (can you see why?). Parents who make great "sacrifices" for their children are not worse off than those (of the same income) who make few or no sacrifices, any more than people who spend a large fraction of their income on housing are worse off than people who spend a smaller fraction of the same income on housing.

Even when parents love their children very much, there is a danger of underinvestment in children; and it is part of the explanation for free public education. Suppose a child is born to very poor parents. The child has enormous potential earning power if properly fed, clothed, housed, and educated, but his parents can't afford these things. This would not matter if the child or parents could borrow against the child's future earning capacity, but the costs of borrowing against a highly uncertain future stream of earnings, and also the difficulty (given the constitutional prohibition of involuntary servitude) of collateralizing a loan against a person's earning capacity (you cannot make him your slave if he defaults), make such loans an infeasible method of financing a promising child.

This problem, plus the fact that some parents love their children little or not at all[1] and the existence of widespread altruism toward children in general (i.e., not just one's own children), may explain why legal duties are imposed on parents to provide care and support, including education, for their children. Child labor laws, as well as the already mentioned provision of free public education (discussed further in Chapter 16 of this book), are other social responses to the problem of underinvestment in children's human capital.[2]

§5.4   1. Even in an age of universal availability of contraceptive methods and a constitutional right to abortion, some children are produced as an undesired by-product of sexual activity, and in addition parents may have second thoughts once they begin coping with a baby. As a matter of fact the ready availability of contraceptive methods may not significantly reduce the number of unwanted children that are born. Contraception reduces the expected costs of sex and hence increases the incidence of sex; the fraction of unwanted births is thus smaller but the number of sexual encounters, by which the fraction must be multiplied to yield the *number* of unwanted births, is larger.

2. There is a rich economic literature on human capital. See, e.g., Gary S. Becker, Human Capital: A Theoretical and Empirical Analysis, With Specific Reference to Education (2d ed. 1975). We return to the subject in Chapters 11, 16, and 17.

Another reason for subsidizing education is that educated people may produce external benefits. An example is an inventor; the patent laws will not enable him to capture the full social benefits of the invention (explain), so he and his family may underinvest in his human capital.

But are these *reasons* for subsidizing education really the *cause*? The provision of free public education, coupled with the requirement of compulsory schooling, benefits (1) teachers, and (2) workers who would otherwise have to compete with children and teenagers. See Linda Nasif Edwards, An Empirical Analysis of Compulsory Schooling Legislation, 1940-1960, 21 J. Law & Econ. 203 (1978).

A serious practical problem with laws forbidding neglect is what to do with the child if the threat of fine or imprisonment fails to deter the parents from neglecting the child. The law's answer has been to place the neglected child either with foster parents or in a foster home. Both solutions are unsatisfactory because of the difficulty of monitoring the custodian's performance. The state can pay foster parents a subsidy sufficient to enable them to invest optimally in the care and upbringing of the child, but who is to know whether they have made that investment? The state cannot *trust* the foster parents: Because they have no property rights in the child's lifetime earnings, they have no incentive to make the investment that will maximize those earnings.

Another solution to the problem of the neglected or unwanted child is, of course, to allow the parents (or mother, if the father is unknown or uninterested) to put up the child for adoption, preferably before they begin to neglect the child. Provided that the adoptive parents are screened to make sure they do not want the child for purposes of abusing it sexually or otherwise, adoption enables the child to be transferred from the custody of people unlikely to invest optimally in its upbringing to people much more likely to do so. But the universal availability of contraception, the decline in the stigma of being an unwed mother (can you think of an economic reason for this decline?), and the creation of a constitutional right to abortion have reduced to a trickle the supply of children for adoption, since most such children are produced as the unintended by-product of sexual intercourse. Recent advances in the treatment of fertility (perhaps spurred in part by the decline in the supply of babies for adoption) have reduced or at least controlled the demand for babies for adoption, but the demand remains high, and is much greater than the supply. The waiting period to obtain a baby from an adoption agency has lengthened to several years and sometimes the agencies have no babies for adoption. The baby shortage would be considered an intolerable example of market failure if the commodity were telephones rather than babies.

In fact the shortage appears to be an artifact of government regulation, in particular the state laws forbidding the sale of babies. The fact that there are many people who are capable of bearing children but who do not want to raise them and many other people who cannot produce their own children but want to raise children, and that the costs of production to natural parents are much lower than the value that many childless people attach to children, suggests the possibility of a market in babies. And as a matter of fact there is a black market in babies, with prices as high as $25,000 said to be common.[3] Its necessarily clan-

3. See Adoption and Foster Care, 1975 Hearings Before the Subcomm. on Children and Youth of the Senate Comm. on Labor and Public Welfare, 94th Cong., 1st Sess. (1975); Sale of Children in Interstate and Foreign Commerce, Hearings Before the Subcomm. on Criminal Justice of the House Comm. on the Judiciary, 95th Cong., 1st Sess. (1977); Nancy C. Baker, Babyselling: The Scandal of Black-Market Adoption (1978).

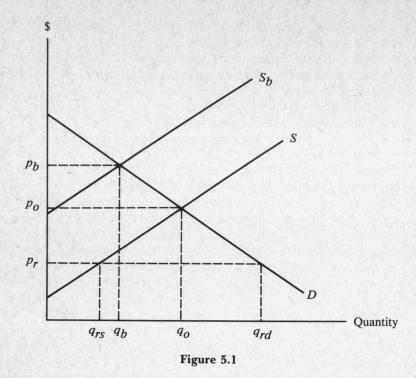

Figure 5.1

destine mode of operation imposes heavy information costs on the market participants as well as expected punishment costs on the middlemen (typically lawyers and obstetricians). The result is higher prices and smaller quantities sold than would be likely in a legal market.

This is shown in Figure 5.1, where p_0 is the free market price of babies and q_0 the free market quantity, and government regulation places a ceiling on price at p_r, well below p_0 (p_r is not shown as zero both because adoption agencies and other legal suppliers do charge fees to adoptive parents and because children are expensive to raise). The result of the price ceiling is a reduction in the quantity supplied to q_{rs}, creating excess demand of $q_{rd} - q_{rs}$. A black market springs up, but such a market is much more costly to operate than a free market would be (because of punishment costs, poor information, and lack of enforceable warranties), and clears at price p_b (where D intersects S_b, the higher, black market supply curve), which is higher than the free market price. So only q_b babies are supplied, compared to q_0 at the free market price.

This analysis is oversimplified in assuming that all babies are adopted through the black market. That of course is not true. Adoption agencies — private, nonprofit organizations licensed by the state — use queuing and various nonmarket criteria (some highly intrusive and constitutionally questionable, such as requiring that the adoptive parents

140

have the same religion as the natural parents) to ration the inadequate supply of babies that they control. The principal objection to the agencies is not, however, the criteria they use to ration the existing supply of babies but their monopoly of adoptions, which ensures (given their profit function) that the supply will remain inadequate.

Most states also permit (subject to various restrictions) independent adoption of babies, wherein the natural parents (normally the mother) arrange for the adoption without using the facilities of an adoption agency. This avoids the sometimes irrelevant and demeaning criteria of the agencies, but since the mother is not permitted to sell the child, independent adoption does not create a real baby market. The lawyer who arranges the adoption, however, is permitted to exact a fee for his services plus payment for the mother's hospital and related childbearing expenses, and since these charges are difficult to police, in practice they will often conceal a payment for the baby itself. And if the mother breaks a contract to give up her child for adoption, the adoptive parents may be able to recover damages measured by the lying-in expenses they had advanced to her.[4] Also close to outright sale is the "family compact," wherein the mother agrees to give up the child to a close relative in exchange for financial consideration running to the child; such contracts have been enforced where the court was satisfied that the arrangement benefited the child.[5]

Should the sale of babies be made legal? The idea strikes most people as bizarre and offensive; the usual proposal for getting rid of the black market in babies is not to decriminalize the sale of babies but to make the criminal penalties more severe. However, economists like to think about the unthinkable, so let us examine in a scientific spirit the objections to permitting the sale of babies for adoption.

There is, it is argued, no assurance that the adoptive parents who are willing to pay the most money for a child will provide it with the best home. But the parents who value a child the most are likely to give it the most care,[6] and at the very least the sacrifice of a substantial sum of money to obtain a child attests to the seriousness of the purchaser's desire to have the child. The reply to this is that the high paying adoptive parents may value the child for the wrong reasons: to subject it to sexual abuse or otherwise to exploit it. But the laws forbidding child neglect and abuse would apply fully to the adoptive parents (as they do under present law, of course). Naturally one would want to screen adoptive parents carefully for possible criminal proclivities — just as is done today.

4. See Gordon v. Cutler, 471 A.2d 449 (Pa. Super. 1983).
5. See Enders v. Enders, 164 Pa. 266, 30 A. 129 (1894); Clark v. Clark, 122 Md. 114, 89 A. 405 (1915); In re Estate of Shirk, 186 Kan. 311, 350 P.2d 1 (1960).
6. The existence of a market in babies would also increase the natural mother's incentive to produce a healthy baby and would reduce the demand for abortion.

A better objection to a market in babies is that the payment of a large sum to buy the child could exhaust the adoptive parents' financial ability to support the child. If so, the equilibrium price of babies would be low, since in deciding how much they are willing to pay for a child the adoptive parents will consider price. But this is not a complete answer to the objection. Few people would pay to adopt a child they could not afford to raise, but the more costly the child is to acquire the less will be the cost-justified investment in the child's upbringing, that investment being as we said a function of the parents' utility as well as the child's.

All this assumes that a free market would raise the price of babies. In fact it is unlikely that the price of babies in such a market would substantially exceed the opportunity costs (mainly the mother's time and medical expenses) that the adoptive parents would have incurred had they produced rather than purchased the child — and that they save by purchasing. For that would be the competitive price. The net cost to the adoptive parents would thus be close to zero, except that the adoptive parents would incur some costs in locating and trying to ascertain the qualities of the child that they would not have incurred had they been its natural parents. The black market price is high because it must cover the sellers' expected punishment costs for breaking the law and because the existence of legal sanctions prevents the use of the most efficient methods of matching up sellers and buyers.[7]

Opponents of the market approach also argue that the rich would end up with all the babies, or at least all the good babies. (Recall the parallel argument against permitting the sale of radio and television frequencies.) Such a result might of course be in the children's best interest, but it is unlikely to materialize. Because people with high incomes tend to have high opportunity costs of time, the wealthy usually have smaller families than the poor. Permitting babies to be sold would not change this situation. Moreover, the total demand for children on the part of wealthy childless couples must be very small in relation to the supply of children, even high-quality children, that would be generated in a system where there were economic incentives to produce children for purchase by childless couples.

The poor may actually do worse under present adoption law than they would in a free baby market. Most adoptions are channeled through adoption agencies, which in screening prospective adoptive parents at-

7. In one respect, however, the black market price is lower than a legal free market price would be. The buyer in the black market does not receive any legally enforceable warranties (of health, genealogy, or whatever), comparable to those that buyers receive in legal markets. The buyer in a legal baby market would receive a more valuable package of rights and it would cost more; the seller would demand compensation for bearing risks formerly borne by the buyer. But the resulting price increase would be nominal rather than real (can you see why?). How might Figure 5.1 be redrawn to reflect this point?

tach great importance to the applicants' income and employment status. People who might flunk the agencies' criteria on economic grounds might, in a free market with low prices, be able to adopt children, just as poor people are able to buy color television sets.[8]

Although the condition of the market for adopting infants is one of chronic excess demand, the condition of the market for adopting children who are no longer infants is one of chronic oversupply (why?). An impediment to their adoption is the fact that foster parents are paid for foster care, but not for adopting a foster child, so that if they do adopt their foster child they incur even higher costs than other adoptive parents, since, as we know, forgone income is a cost. Can you think of any practical measure for overcoming this problem? Cf. §16.5 *infra*.

§5.5 Law and Population

A complete analysis of the issue whether to permit the sale of babies, as of many other actual or proposed public policies relating to the production of children — including laws governing fornication, adultery, contraception, abortion, homosexuality, and marriage itself — would consider the effect of a baby market on the rate of population change and, in turn, the social costs associated with such change.

The production of children can affect other people in the society in ways that the parents may not take into account in deciding whether to have children, just as the production of aluminum may affect third parties by polluting the air. The child may have negative expected lifetime earnings from legitimate activities and may become a charge on the state. He may add to highway and other forms of congestion, imposing costs on other people which neither he nor his parents will ever be asked to defray.[1] Conversely, in a sparsely populated country threatened by external enemies, the production of an additional child may confer a benefit over and above any private gains to the child and his parents, by (eventually) strengthening the country militarily. And maybe external enemies aren't necessary. An increase in population will (up

8. A recent development in reproductive technology should be noted in connection with the discussion in the text: artificial conception. Suppose a woman produces ova but cannot carry a fetus to term. Her fertilized ovum is transplanted to another woman, the surrogate mother, who carries it to term. Should the natural parents or the surrogate mother have the property right in the child? Should a contract between the surrogate mother and the natural parents whereby the latter pay the former to carry the fertilized ovum to term, and the former agrees to give the baby up to the natural parents when it is born, be legally enforceable? In what ways is the economic analysis different from that of baby selling? For background see Walter Wadlington, Artificial Conception: The Challenge for Family Law, 69 Va. L. Rev. 465 (1983).

§5.5 1. What assumption is being made here about the property rights in the highway?

to a point) enable a greater division of labor, causing costs to fall, and enable the fuller exploitation of available economies of scale, causing prices to fall. The result will be an increase in the nation's average as well as total wealth.

The possibility of third-party effects from population change may explain public intervention in sexual and other activities affecting the production of children. Laws forbidding homosexuality may be seen as a response to a social demand for a higher rate of population growth, and the growing opposition to those laws may reflect (1) the growth of the U.S. population to a level at which congestion may have become a serious problem and (2) the declining importance of manpower to national defense.

It has been reported that Japanese civil servants will be fired if they have more than three children. This is clearly the wrong approach to population control. Some people are more efficient at child rearing than others. It may cost them less to produce a fourth child than it does some other couple to produce a first child of the same quality. The same total population growth could be produced, at lowest cost, by giving every couple three child permits and permitting the sale of the permits.

Current public policy in the United States is a confusing mixture of subsidies and penalties for child production. The exemption from income taxation of nonpecuniary income from household production subsidizes the production of children relative to market uses of the woman's time, as does of course the exemption for dependents. The common rule that child-support payments required by a divorce decree will be reduced if the father remarries and produces children of the new marriage reduces the private cost to the father of having more children below the social cost.[2] An example cutting in the opposite direction is easy divorce, which may reduce the incentive to make long-term marital investments, such as child rearing, and hence may reduce the birth rate. But a rule absolutely forbidding divorce — the former rule in England, and still the law in Ireland — may have a similar effect, by increasing the optimal length of the premarital search period and hence increasing the average age of marriage and reducing the number of children produced.

Suggested Readings

1. Gary S. Becker, A Treatise on the Family (1981).
2. ———, Human Capital, Effort, and the Sexual Division of Labor, 3 J. Labor Econ. S33 (1985).

2. Can you distinguish the case where parents reduce the investments in their existing children because a new child is born?

3. ———, Elisabeth M. Landes, & Robert T. Michael, An Economic Analysis of Marital Instability, 85 J. Pol. Econ. 1141 (1977).

4. Elisabeth M. Landes, Economics of Alimony, 7 J. Leg. Stud. 35 (1978).

5. ——— & Richard A. Posner, The Economics of the Baby Shortage, 7 J. Leg. Stud. 323 (1978).

6. John Palmer, The Social Cost of Adoption Agencies (Centre for Economic Analysis of Property Rights, University of Western Ontario, n.d.).

7. Richard A. Posner, The Economics of Justice 184-192 (1981).

8. Yoram Weiss & Robert J. Willis, Children as Collective Goods and Divorce Settlements, 3 J. Labor Econ. 268 (1985).

9. Economics of the Family (Theodore W. Schultz ed. 1974).

Problems

1. Can you think of an economic reason why husbands tend to carry much heavier insurance on their lives than wives? If husband and wife both work (in the market), should they carry more or less total life insurance than if only one does?

2. Might parents ever overinvest in their children's education from the child's standpoint? Why?

3. What are the allocative and distributive effects of forbidding polygamy? What is the source of the demand for the laws against polygamy?

4. We read in Blackstone: "By marriage the husband and wife are one person in law: that is, the very being or legal existence of the woman is suspended during the marriage, or at least is incorporated and consolidated into that of the husband." 1 William Blackstone, Commentaries on the Laws of England 442 (1765) (footnote omitted). Explain the economic basis of this rule and of its abandonment.

5. How does one determine, in normative economic analysis, the community of people whose welfare will be included in the social welfare to be maximized?

6. Is there a parallel between laws against baby selling and usury laws and between the baby black market and loansharking?

7. There are two marital privileges (privileges to withhold evidence) in the law of evidence. The so-called testimonial privilege extends to all communications, whether made before or during the marriage, the public disclosure of which would harm the marriage; but it can be invoked only by the testifying spouse. The marital-communications privilege is limited to communications made during the marriage, but it is absolute: The wife cannot testify to such a communication without her husband's consent, or the husband without the wife's consent. What is the economic rationale of these privileges? Do they make more or less economic sense

in an age of easy divorce? Should either privilege be available if at the time of trial the marriage has been dissolved?

8. There is more and more transplanting of organs (e.g., hearts, kidneys) of dead people into the living. From an economic standpoint, would it be a good idea to allow people to make binding contracts for the sale of their organs after their death? If so, what special regulations might be appropriate that would be unnecessary in a more conventional market? See Simon Rottenberg, The Production and Sale of Used Body Parts, in 2 Toward Liberty: Essays in Honor of Ludwig von Mises 322 (Institute for Human Studies 1971); Marvin Brams, Transplantable Human Organs: Should Their Sale Be Authorized by State Statutes?, 3 Am. J. Law & Med. 183 (1977); Note, The Sale of Human Body Parts, 72 Mich. L. Rev. 1182 (1974).

9. Can you now think of an efficient, nonpaternalistic argument for intervention in the pituitary-extract case hypothesized in Chapter 1 (§1.2 *supra*)?

10. Analyze the following argument: If parents divorce, and one spouse is awarded custody, she (or he) will spend less on the child than she would in the marriage, because the expenditures of one spouse on the child confers a benefit on the other. See Yoram Weiss & Robert J. Willis, Children as Collective Goods and Divorce Settlements, 3 J. Labor Econ. 268 (1985).

CHAPTER 6

TORT LAW[1]

§6.1 The Economics of Accidents and the Learned Hand Formula of Liability for Negligence

Wrongs that subject the wrongdoer to a suit for damages by the victim, other than breaches of contracts, are called torts. There are intentional and unintentional torts, and although as we shall see the line between them is not always clear, especially when they are analyzed in economic terms, we shall follow conventional legal usage and discuss the two classes separately, beginning with unintentional torts: accidents in which the injurer is liable under tort law to his victim.

Everybody takes precautions against accidents; the interesting question is how extensive the precautions taken are. If you were deciding whether to buy an auxiliary generator to make sure that a power failure didn't cut off the oxygen supply to your extremely valuable collection of South American lizards, you would surely balance, at least in a rough and ready way, the benefits of the auxiliary generator in preventing the loss of the lizards against its costs. The benefits can be expressed, at least as a first approximation, as the product of the probability of the lizards' being killed over some interval of time (say a year) by a power failure, and the dollar magnitude of the loss. Assume that the probability and the magnitude — P and L (for loss), call them — are .001 and \$10,000 respectively. Therefore the expected accident cost, PL, will be \$10. Granted, this is a measure of expected disutility as well as expected cost only if you are risk neutral, but put risk aversion to one side by assuming that the insurance that you carry on the lizards' lives will cover death through power failure at an additional premium equal to PL plus some modest loading charge (assumed for the sake

1. See Prosser and Keeton on the Law of Torts (5th ed. 1984); Richard A. Epstein, Modern Products Liability Law (1980); Richard A. Posner, Tort Law: Cases and Economic Materials (1982).

of simplicity to be zero) to cover the insurance company's expenses of administration. Thus the expected benefit of the auxiliary generator to you is $10 a year. Suppose its annualized cost is $8. Then you will buy the generator — assuming no cheaper alternative precaution is available. If the generator cost more than $10, you would not buy it.

Because in this example the person taking precautions and the person who may be injured if they are not taken are the same, the optimal precautions will be achieved without legal intervention. But change the example; suppose the hazard is the loss not of your lizards but of your pinky finger in an automobile accident, and the cheapest way to avoid the accident is for some other driver — a complete stranger — to drive more slowly. Suppose that your expected accident cost is $10, as before (.001 × $10,000) and the cost to the other driver of driving more slowly (and thus taking longer to get to his destination) is $8. Efficiency requires that the driver drive more slowly. But because transaction costs with potential victims such as yourself are prohibitive, he will not do so unless the legal system steps in, as by holding him liable in damages (= $10,000) should an accident occur. Then he has an expected legal judgment cost of $10, and this will induce him to invest $8 in a precaution that will drive his expected judgment cost to zero by preventing the accident. The precaution will yield him a net gain of $2; it is a good investment.

The example we have given would be handled by the law of negligence, as summarized in the negligence formula of Judge Learned Hand.[1] Defining P and L as we have, and denoting by B the cost of the precaution, Hand wrote that a potential injurer is negligent if but only if $B < PL$, which is what our example implied would be the formula for optimal accident avoidance. There is, however, an ambiguity both in Hand's formulation and in ours. Suppose our PL of $10 would be totally eliminated by the driver's reducing his speed by 25 m.p.h., at a cost to him of $9. But suppose further that PL could be reduced to $1 by the driver's reducing his speed by only 5 m.p.h., at a cost to him of only $2. This implies that to get PL down from $1 to zero costs the driver $7 ($9-$2). Clearly we want him just to reduce his speed by 5 m.p.h., which yields a net social gain of $7; reducing his speed by another 20 m.p.h. would yield a net social loss of $6 (it would cost the driver $7 but reduce expected accident costs by only $1). In other words, expected accident costs and accident costs must be compared at the margin, by measuring the costs and benefits of small increments in safety and stopping investing in more safety at the point where another dollar spent would yield a dollar or less in added safety.[2] Fortunately the com-

§6.1   1. See United States v. Carroll Towing Co., 159 F.2d 169, 173 (2d Cir. 1947), and for a contemporary application of the formula United States Fidelity & Guaranty Co. v. Jadranska Slobodna Plovidba, 683 F.2d 1022 (7th Cir. 1982).
    2. The marginal Hand Formula is easily derived by the use of some very simple differential calculus. The problem is to find the level of care ($c*$) that will minimize the social

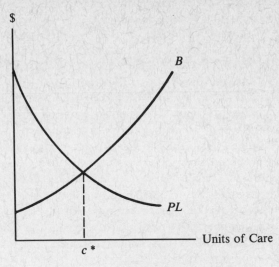

$

B

PL

Units of Care

c*

Figure 6.1

mon law method facilitates a marginal approach; it will usually be difficult for courts to get information on other than small changes in the safety precautions of the injurer. (We shall see that this is sometimes a weakness rather than a strength, but that the law has developed methods of coping with this weakness.)

The Hand Formula (in its correct marginal form) is presented graphically in Figure 6.1. The horizontal axis represents units of care, the vertical axis (as usual) dollars. The curve marked *PL* depicts the marginal change in expected accident costs as a function of care and is shown declining on the assumption that care has a diminishing effect in preventing accidents. The curve marked *B* is the marginal cost of care and is shown rising on the assumption that inputs of care are scarce and therefore their price rises as more and more are bought. The intersection of the two curves represents due care. (Must *PL* be falling and *B* rising?) To the left of this point, *c**, the injurer is negligent; *B* is smaller than *PL*. To the right, where the costs of care are greater than the benefits

costs of accidents, *PL*, plus the costs of accident prevention, *B*. Both *P* and *B* are functions of the potential injurer's care, *c* (we are assuming that potential victims can do nothing to prevent the accidents — their optimal care is zero). Mathematically, the problem is to minimize *A*, the total social costs of accidents, with respect to *c*, where $A(c)$ (total accident costs as a function of amount of care) $= P(c)L + B(c)$, both *P* and *B* being functions of *c* also. Provided certain fairly natural conditions are satisfied, minimization requires taking the first derivative of *A* with respect to *c* and setting the resulting expression equal to zero: $P_cL + B_c = 0$, or $B_c = -P_cL$. In words, care is optimized when a small change in *B*, the expenditures on care, reduces (hence the negative sign) expected accident costs by the same amount. This is the point *c** in Figure 6.1. See William M. Landes & Richard A. Posner, The Positive Economic Theory of Tort Law, 15 Ga. L. Rev. 851, 868-872 (1981), for a fuller discussion.

in reducing expected accident costs, the injurer is not negligent; this is the region of accidents that (subject to various qualifications introduced later) are unavoidable in an economic sense.

A possible objection to the Hand Formula is that it assumes risk neutrality. We waved this point aside before, by pointing out that people can buy insurance, and yet we know from Chapter 4 that the doctrines of contract law do not on similar grounds assume that the people affected by that law are risk neutral. But there is an economic reason for this difference. It is very hard to buy insurance against business losses, because a businessman insured against loss will have little incentive to try to prevent loss and because business losses are potentially so open-ended; an unexpected rise in the price of a key input could cause a large business to go broke. Hence contracts and contract law have a role to play in reducing risk — illustrating the more general point that market insurance is not the only social institution for risk reduction (diversified investment portfolios, discussed in Chapter 15, are another). However, there have long been well-developed markets in insurance against personal injury and death. Although this insurance also involves a "moral hazard" problem (the insured has less incentive to take care — just because he is insured), it is not so severe (why not?), or the losses to be insured against so open-ended, as to prevent the insurance market from working. But what do you think of the argument that the cost of the potential victim's accident insurance premium should be added to *PL* in applying the Hand Formula?

Although the Hand Formula is of relatively recent origin, the method that it capsulizes has been used to determine negligence ever since negligence was first adopted as the standard to govern accident cases.[3] For example, in *Blyth v. Birmingham Water Works*[4] the question was whether a water company had been negligent in failing to bury its water pipes deep enough to prevent them from bursting because of frost and damaging the plaintiff's home. In holding that the water company had not been negligent, the court emphasized that the frost had been of unprecedented severity — i.e., the probability of the loss had been low. The damage was not so great as to make the expected cost of the accident greater than the cost of prevention, which would have involved a heavy expense in burying the pipes deeper.

In *Adams v. Bullock*,[5] a 12-year-old boy, while crossing a bridge over the defendant's trolley tracks, swung an 8-foot-long wire over the bridge. The wire touched the defendant's trolley wire, which ran over the tracks and beneath the bridge, resulting in an electric shock that injured the boy, who sued. The court held for the defendant. *P* was low because

3. See Richard A. Posner, A Theory of Negligence, 1 J. Leg. Stud. 29 (1972); Henry T. Terry, Negligence, 29 Harv. L. Rev. 40 (1915).
4. 11 Exch. 781, 156 Eng. Rep. 1047 (1856).
5. 227 N.Y. 208, 125 N.E. 93 (1919) (Cardozo, J.).

it was unlikely that anyone using the bridge would touch the wire. And
B was high, the court remarking the difference between electric light
and trolley wires in terms strongly suggestive of economic insight:

> The distinction is that the former may be insulated. Chance of harm, though
> remote [low *P*], may betoken negligence, if needless [very low *B*]. Facility
> of protection may impose a duty to protect. With trolley wires, the case is
> different. Insulation is impossible. Guards here and there are of little value.
> To avert the possibility of this accident and others like it at one point or
> another on the route, the defendant must have abandoned the overhead
> system, and put the wires underground [very high *B*].[6]

And here is a case that went the plaintiff's way: *Hendricks v. Peabody
Coal Co.*[7] A 16-year-old boy was seriously injured while swimming in
the defendant's abandoned strip mine, which had become filled with
spring water. The defendant, aware both that the mine was being used
as a swimming hole and that it was dangerous because of a concealed
ledge beneath the surface at the point where the boy had dived and
been hurt, undertook to police the area but did not do so effectively.
"The entire body of water could have been closed off with a steel fence
for between $12,000 and $14,000. The cost was slight compared to
the risk to the children involved."[8]

§6.2   The Reasonable Man Standard

But if the Hand Formula *really* created the proper incentives to avoid
negligent accidents, then no one would be negligent — so how could
there be any negligence cases, at least any such cases won by plaintiffs?
One answer — besides the obvious one that judges and jurors sometimes
make mistakes — is that in deciding whether an accident could have
been avoided by either party at a cost less than the expected accident
cost, the courts do not attempt to measure the actual costs to the parties,
taking account of their individual capacities for avoiding accidents.
Rather, they estimate the accident-avoidance costs of the average (in
legal parlance "reasonable") person in each party's situation. This approach can be justified only by reference to the costs of individualized
measurement. If the average person could at a cost of $120 avoid an
accident the expected cost of which was $100, there would be no legal
duty to avoid, and yet if an exceptional person could avoid the accident

6. Id. at 211, 125 N.E. at 94.
7. 115 Ill. App. 2d 35, 253 N.E.2d 56 (1969).
8. Id. at 45-46, 253 N.E.2d at 61.

at a cost of less than $100, an efficient rule — information costs to one side — would require that he have a legal duty to avoid the accident. Or suppose the average accident-avoidance cost was only $50 but some people could not avoid the accident at a cost of less than $110. They would be liable for failing to avoid the accident, but this liability would not affect their behavior, and the result would be socially wasteful transfer payments.

Where differences in capacity to avoid accidents are ascertainable at low cost, the courts do recognize exceptions to (or subclasses of) the reasonable man standard. For example, blind people are not held to so high a standard of care as sighted, although within the class of blind people a uniform standard of care is imposed.

The above discussion serves as a reminder that administrative costs, and in particular information costs, play an important role in the formulation of efficient legal rules. This point receives its fullest treatment in Chapters 20 and 21. It also shows why there would be some negligence cases even if nobody ever made any mistakes. Some people who are classified as negligent by the legal system cannot in fact avoid the expected cost of a negligence judgment at a lower cost in precautions. So they go ahead and have accidents for which the legal system deems them negligent. They are acting efficiently — and so is the legal system, when administrative costs are taken into account as they must be in a complete economic analysis.

§6.3   Custom as a Defense

A recurrent question is whether the defendant's compliance with the standard of safety that is customary in its industry should be recognized as a defense to a negligence action. If so, only firms that lag behind the average firm in their industry in adopting safety precautions will be held liable. This is a satisfactory result if there is reason to expect the average firm to take all cost-justified precautions without the coercion of law. But a firm will have no incentive to take precautions against accidents dangerous only to people with whom the firm does not, and because of high transaction costs cannot, deal. The potential victims will not pay the firm to take precautions. Nor will its customers. They do not benefit from the precautions, so if the firm tried to pass on the added costs of the precautions to them, in the form of higher prices, it would be undercut by a competitor.

In these circumstances there can be no presumption that the average safety level in the industry is optimum, and the law properly rejects compliance with custom as a defense. Where, however, the type of accident is dangerous only to the industry's customers, the level of precautions taken by sellers is more likely to be efficient. Customers should be willing to pay higher prices for the industry's product or service up to the point where the last dollar spent buys just one dollar in accident cost reduction. It is therefore ironic that the classic statement of the principle that compliance with custom is not a defense to a negligence action should have been made — and by Judge Hand! — in a case in which the plaintiff was the defendant's customer.[1]

In one area of negligence, that of medical malpractice, the courts, consistently with the distinction just suggested, have traditionally allowed a defense of custom. A doctor's duty of care toward his patient is to comply with the customary standards of the medical profession in the area in which the doctor is practicing. Because victim and injurer are in a buyer-seller relationship, the potential injurers (doctors) have an incentive independent of the law to provide the level of care for which potential victims are willing to pay. Observe the overlap here between tort and contract rights. The doctor implicitly promises to treat the patient with the care customary among doctors in the area. If he does not use that much care he is guilty of malpractice, a tort, but he has also and by the identical conduct violated his contract with the patient.

Although this discussion implies that there should be a presumption in favor of allowing a defense of compliance with industry custom in cases where the injurer and the victim have an actual or potential contractual relationship, the presumption is by no means absolute, and its rejection, notably in the field of products liability (liability for injury caused by a defective or unreasonably dangerous product), may be efficient, as we shall see in §6.6 *infra*. Briefly, a product accident that actually injures the user of the product is an extremely low-probability event. It may not pay the consumer to contract with reference to it, even to the extent of reading carefully any disclaimers or warranties of liability; *PL* may be less than his cost of information. This point can be restated in terms of transaction costs. We normally assume that when there are only a few parties to a transaction, a value-maximizing exchange is possible — that we are, in other words, in the domain of contract rather than tort. But we have already seen several times that a two-party transaction, when it occurs under conditions of bilateral monopoly, may involve very high transaction costs, and we now have another example of high transaction costs in a setting of few parties. Although the manufacturer of a consumer product and the consumer are in a two-party relationship (does it matter whether there is an intermediate seller, e.g., a retail dealer?), and there is no problem of bilateral monopoly (why not?), the costs of transacting *over safety* are high. Not absolutely high; but the very low probability of an accident makes the gains from transacting

§6.3   1. The T.J. Hooper, 60 F.2d 737 (2d Cir. 1932).

over safety very low, so that the cost of transacting may exceed the benefits — which is all that matters. The allocation of resources to safety is therefore determined by the courts, just as with remote contingencies in contract performance, examined in Chapter 4.

§6.4 Victim Fault: Contributory and Comparative Negligence, Assumption of Risk, and Duties to Trespassers

That the burden of precaution is less than the probability times magnitude of loss if the precaution is not taken is only a necessary, and not a sufficient, condition for the precaution to be efficient. If another precaution would do the trick at even lower cost, that is the efficient precaution. Since as every pedestrian knows many accidents can be prevented by victims at lower cost than by injurers, the law needs a concept of victim fault in order to give potential victims proper safety incentives. Suppose that an expected accident cost of $1,000 could have been avoided by the defendant at a cost of $100 but by the plaintiff at a cost of only $50. The efficient solution is to make the plaintiff "liable" by refusing to allow him to recover damages from the defendant. If the defendant is liable, the plaintiff will have no incentive to take preventive measures because he will be fully compensated for his injury, and the efficient solution will not be obtained.

No doubt there is some exaggeration here. As we shall see later in this chapter, tort damages are not always fully compensatory, especially where serious personal injuries are concerned; and to the extent they are not, potential victims will have an incentive to take precautions even if their failure to do so will not cut down their entitlement to damages by one cent if they are injured. But the incentive will be less (maybe zero in cases of property damage, as in the railroad spark case discussed in Chapter 3 and below).

How should victim care be worked into the Hand Formula? The traditional common law approach, which goes by the name of "contributory negligence," was, after asking whether the defendant had been negligent and concluding that he was (if he was not, that would be the end of the case), to turn around and ask whether the plaintiff was negligent. If the answer was "yes," the plaintiff lost. This works fine in the example given above, but suppose we reverse the cost-of-precaution figures, so that the cost is $50 for the defendant and $100 for the plaintiff. It seems that the defendant will be deemed negligent but the plaintiff will be contributorily negligent (because $100 is less than $1,000) and so will lose, and that the defendant will have no incentive for the future to take a precaution that by hypothesis is the efficient one. However, the appearance is misleading, provided that the law defines due care — as it does — as the care that is optimal if the other party is exercising due care. Since, in our example, if the defendant is exercising due care the plaintiff's optimal care will be zero, the plaintiff will have no incentive to take care, and knowing this the defendant will spend $50 on care and the accident will be avoided at least cost.

We shall now consider a more elaborate example involving a very important class of accidents known as "joint care" cases. In the previous examples, where the defendant could avoid the accident at a cost of $100 (or $50) and the plaintiff at a cost of $50 (or $100), the implicit assumption was that the case was one of "alternative care," that is, that the efficient solution was for either party, but not both, to take care. The goal therefore was to make sure that the lower-cost avoider was encouraged to take care. In a joint care case, we want each party to take some care rather than one to take care and the other to do nothing. Most collisions are joint care cases.

Table 6.1 illustrates the operation of contributory negligence with an example involving flax and locomotive sparks. *PL* is assumed to be $150. Different levels of care by railroad and by farmer are costed, and the total costs compared on the third line of the table. S.A. means spark arrester, and a super spark arrester is just a better quality (and more expensive) spark arrester. The number of feet is the distance of the flax from the tracks. The farther away the flax is, the safer it is; but there is a cost to the farmer. Thus the three columns represent three different combinations of safety precautions by the railroad and the farmer, all of which have the same benefits ($150, the expected accident cost that the combination averts) but different costs.

The middle combination — an average quality spark arrester and moving the flax 75 feet from the tracks — is the least costly. But will a negligence–contributory negligence rule induce the parties to adopt it? Suppose the railroad, seeking to minimize its cost of accident prevention, does nothing, hoping that the farmer will be deemed negligent because he can prevent the accident at a cost ($110) that is less than the expected accident cost ($150). The farmer, knowing that he will be deemed contributorily negligent only for failing to keep his flax at the distance that will prevent its destruction if the railroad takes the precaution that it

Table 6.1

	Super S.A., 0'	S.A., 75'	No S.A., 200'
Railroad care	$100	$50	$ 0
Farmer care	0	25	110
Total cost	100	75	110

is supposed to take (i.e., installs the average quality spark arrester), will place the flax just 75 feet from the tracks. It will be destroyed, but since the railroad will be held negligent and the farmer will not be held contributorily negligent, the farmer won't care. Knowing all this the railroad will be driven to install the spark arrester. The analysis for the farmer if he starts by placing his flax right next to the tracks is similar. The railroad will not buy the super spark arrester that would prevent the destruction of the flax, for the farmer is contributorily negligent and contributory negligence is a complete defense.

We have thus far taken for granted that contributory negligence should be a defense. But this is not an obvious corollary of the proposition that optimal safety sometimes requires potential victims as well as potential injurers to take care. If the injurer is not negligent, the victim will bear the whole cost of the accident whether negligent or not. The defense of contributory negligence comes into play only when the injurer is negligent too. And if the injurer is negligent, why should he get off scot-free, and the victim be left to bear the whole cost of the accident? The economic answer is that shifting the cost from the victim to the injurer will not do any good as far as creating incentives to take due care in the future is concerned. Both parties already have incentives that in the generality of cases are adequate: The injurer has an incentive to take care to avoid having to pay damages if he is careless, an accident occurs, and the victim was not careless; the victim has an incentive to take care to avoid the cost of the accident if it occurs though the injurer was careful. Since efficiency is not improved by making the negligent injurer pay damages to the negligent victim, the common law traditionally allowed the cost of the accident to lie where it fell, in order to minimize the costs of administering the legal system. A transfer payment from injurer to victim will cost something to make, but will not increase the wealth of society by creating incentives to efficient behavior.

A number of states have, however, replaced contributory negligence with comparative negligence, whereby if both parties (injurer and victim) are negligent the plaintiff's damages are reduced, but not to zero. Comparative negligence has the same effects on safety as contributory negligence. Go back to Table 6.1 and suppose (to make the example dramatic) that even if the farmer takes no precautions at all his damages will be reduced by only 10 percent — not 100 percent as under contributory negligence. It might seem that since he therefore faces an expected accident cost of only $15 (10 percent of the *PL* of $150), he will not spend the $25 that due care requires him to spend on precaution. But this is incorrect. If he does not spend this amount, then the railroad, knowing that it will not be liable whatever happens unless it is negligent, will have every incentive to invest $50 in precautions to avert an expected judgment cost to it of $135 (90 percent of $150); and knowing this, the farmer will have an incentive to incur the $25 cost of moving his flax back 75 feet. Otherwise he will end up bearing the whole accident cost, since if the railroad is not negligent comparative negligence does not come into play and the victim gets nothing.

It does not follow that there is no economic difference between contributory and comparative negligence. Comparative negligence entails a transfer payment that generates no allocative gain, and transfer payments involve administrative costs. Comparative negligence also injects an additional issue into litigation (the relative fault of the parties). This requires the expenditure of additional resources by the parties and the courts, and by making it harder to predict the extent of liability may increase the rate of litigation, resulting in costs explored in Chapter 21.

Comparative negligence makes economic sense only when society wants to use the tort system to provide insurance to accident victims, because it gives the careless victim of a careless injurer something, whereas contributory negligence gives him nothing. It comes as no surprise, therefore, that comparative negligence got its first foothold in admiralty law, where for a long time the rule in collision cases when both vessels were at fault was that each party was liable for one-half of the total damage to both ships. The result was that the less heavily damaged ship picked up part of the damage tab for the other ship. (Recently admiralty has moved toward a relative-fault approach.) Until modern times, ocean transportation was an extraordinarily risky business because of the great value of ships and their cargoes and the significant probability of disaster; market insurance was difficult to come by; and there was therefore a demand for insurance via the tort system, which was met by several doctrines of which divided damages was one.[1] It has the nice property of providing insurance without encouraging the insured to be careless, for if he is careless and the other party to the collision is not, he bears the full accident cost. Of course by the same token this method of insurance is incomplete. The tension between comprehensiveness of insurance coverage and the preservation of incentives for careful conduct is one we shall meet several times in this book.

Comparative negligence has insurance properties similar to divided damages in admiralty. But why in an age of much more widely available market insurance than when contributory negligence held sway in tort

§6.4 1. Another interesting such doctrine, of remarkable antiquity, goes by the uninformative name "general average." If it becomes necessary for the master of the ship to cast cargo overboard, the loss is divided up among the shippers and shipowner according to their relative stakes in the venture (i.e., their fractional shares of the sum of the value of the ship and the value of the cargoes), rather than being left to fall on the shipper whose cargo was actually jettisoned. The rule provides each shipper with a form of insurance without impairing the master's incentive to jettison the cargo that is heaviest in relation to its value. See William M. Landes & Richard A. Posner, Salvors, Finders, Good Samaritans, and Other Rescuers: An Economic Study of Law and Altruism, 7 J. Leg. Stud. 83, 106-108 (1978).

law there should be a desire to provide insurance through the tort system is a mystery to the positive economic theorist of the common law.

Another important doctrine of victim responsibility is assumption of risk. It is like contributory negligence in being a complete bar to recovery of damages but differs in important respects that economics can illuminate. Suppose a man enters a roller-skating derby with full awareness of the risks of falling down, and indeed he does fall down and is hurt. He may have been extremely careful in the sense that, given the decision to enter the derby, he conducted himself as would a reasonable roller-skate racer. And the risk to which he is subjected may seem undue in Hand Formula terms. Suppose that by reducing the speed limit by 2 m.p.h., the owner of the roller-skating rink could have avoided substantial accident costs at a seemingly trivial time cost to the patrons; he will nevertheless be protected by the assumption-of-risk defense from liability to the injured patrons.

To understand the economic function of the defense, we must ask why the patrons do not demand greater safety precautions by the owner. There are several possibilities:

1. The Hand Formula has been misapplied. The cost of the lower speed limit is not a trivial time cost but a substantial diminution in the thrill of racing.

2. The Hand Formula might be applied too narrowly to the victim. It may have been easy for the victim to avoid the accident simply by not going skating. Care in conducting an activity is only one method of precaution; another method is avoiding the activity, or doing less of it. We shall see that the distinction between changes in care level and changes in activity level is fundamental to the understanding of the choice between negligence and strict liability as standards of tort liability.

3. The speed in the rink would be an undue hazard to most people, but this particular rink attracts skaters who are above average in skill. The defense of assumption of risk thus enables people with different capacities for avoiding danger to sort themselves to activities of different dangerousness and thus introduces some play into the joints of the reasonable-man rule.

4. The rink attracts risk preferrers. The Hand Formula assumes risk neutrality and will therefore induce potential injurers to take precautions that are excessive for potential victims who are risk preferrers.

Still another important doctrine of victim fault (a term used loosely, as we have just seen, in regard to assumption of risk), although in decline and subject to many exceptions, is the rule that a landowner is not liable for negligent injuries to trespassers. This may seem to contradict the Hand Formula but can be reconciled with it by noting that in the usual case the accident could have been prevented at lower cost by the trespasser, simply by not trespassing, than by the landowner. If the cost of avoidance by the trespasser is higher, he can purchase the land (or an easement in it) and so cease to be a trespasser. The rule thus serves the function — by now familiar to the reader — of encouraging market rather than legal transactions where feasible.

Occasionally, however, a transaction between landowner and trespasser will not be feasible, as in *Ploof v. Putnam.*[2] The plaintiff, caught in a storm, attempted to moor his boat at the defendant's dock. An employee of the defendant shoved the boat away, and it was later wrecked by the storm. The plaintiff sued for the damage. The value to the plaintiff of being able to trespass on the defendant's property during the storm was great, the cost to the defendant of preventing the wreck of plaintiff's boat was small, and negotiations for landing rights were, in the circumstances, hardly feasible. The court properly held the defendant liable for the wreck. Notice the analogy to excessive self-help in contract cases (§4.13 *supra*).

But the plaintiff would probably have been liable to the defendant for any damage caused to his pier.[3] Such liability is appropriate to assure that the rescue is really cost-justified, to encourage dock owners to cooperate with boats in distress, and to get the right amount of investment in docks (see §6.9 *infra*). But in cases of public necessity, as where the fire department pulls down a house to make a firebreak, compensation is not required. This illustrates a common technique of common law regulation: to encourage the provision of external benefits (saving the rest of the city from the fire) by allowing costs to be externalized (the cost to the person whose house is pulled down).[4]

The defendant in *Ploof v. Putnam* might not have been held to be negligent if there had been no effort to shove off the plaintiff's boat but the pier simply was in bad repair and collapsed when the plaintiff attempted to moor his boat. The probability of a boat's being in distress in the vicinity of the pier may have been so slight that, under the Hand Formula, proper maintenance of the pier would not have been a cost-justified precaution. But at the moment when the plaintiff's boat attempted to land, the probability of a serious accident was high, the expected accident loss great, and the cost of avoidance small. So viewed, *Ploof v. Putnam* is a special application of the last clear chance doctrine. A man is using the railroad track as a path. Since he is a trespasser, the railroad has no duty to keep a careful lookout for him (see §3.5 *supra*). But if the crew happens to see him (and realizes he is oblivious to the train's approach), it must blow the train's whistle and take any

2. 81 Vt. 471, 71 A. 188 (1908).
3. See Vincent v. Lake Erie Transp. Co., 109 Minn. 456, 124 N.W. 221 (1910).
4. During the great London fire of 1666, the mayor refused to order houses taken down in the path of the fire to form a firebreak, stating, "Who will pay for the damage?" See references cited in Richard A. Posner, Tort Law: Cases and Economic Materials 187 (1982).

other feasible precautions to avoid running him down. Even though
the accident might have been prevented at low cost if the trespasser
had simply stayed off the track, at the moment when the train is bearing down upon him it is the engineer who can avoid an accident at
least cost, and this cost is substantially less than the expected accident
cost. Alternatively, the case may be viewed as one where, although
the cost to the victim of preventing the accident is lower than the accident cost, the cost to the injurer of preventing the accident is even lower.

The foregoing analysis, however, leaves out of account the fact that
if there were no doctrine of last clear chance there would be fewer
trespassers (why?) and maybe, therefore, no more accidents (or even
fewer accidents) than with the doctrine. But this point ignores another
complication in the economic analysis of accidents: the probabilistic character of taking care. To stray across the center line in a two way highway
is negligent but everyone does it occasionally because it would be too
costly to adopt a driving strategy that reduced the probability of straying
to (or very close to) zero. Some careful people will occasionally find
themselves trespassers, which implies that we do not want to reduce
the probability of trespassing to zero. And therefore the fact that the
last clear chance doctrine slightly reduces the incentive not to trespass
is not a decisive objection to it.[5]

§6.5   Strict Liability

Strict liability means that someone who causes an accident is liable for
the victim's damages even if the injury could not have been avoided
by the exercise of due care (PL might be $150 and B $300).[1] As a
first approximation, strict liability has the same effects on safety as negligence liability (assuming there is a defense of contributory negligence,
as there usually is in one form or another). If B is smaller than PL,
the strictly liable defendant will take precautions to avoid the accident,
just as the defendant in a negligence system will, in order to reduce
his net costs. But if B is larger than PL, the strictly liable defendant
will not take precautions. True, he will have to pay the victim's damages.
But those damages, discounted by the probability of the accident, are
less than the cost of avoidance; in other words, the expected legal judg-

5. For more detailed analysis of problems of sequential care, see Steven Shavell, Torts
in Which Victim and Injurer Act Sequentially, 26 J. Law & Econ. 589 (1983); Donald
Wittman, Optimal Pricing of Sequential Inputs: Last Clear Chance, Mitigation of Damages,
and Related Doctrines in the Law, 10 J. Leg. Stud. 65 (1981).
   §6.5   1. Notice that this is like liability for breach of contract where the breach is
efficient.

ment cost ($= PL$) is less than the avoidance cost, so avoidance doesn't pay. A defendant in a negligence system also would not take precautions to avoid the accident in these circumstances, since he would not be liable for an accident that could not have been avoided by taking due care (i.e., by $B < PL$).

There are, however, significant economic differences between negligence and strict liability. Think back to our distinction between more care and less activity as methods of reducing the probability of an accident. One way to avoid an auto accident is to drive more slowly; another is to drive less. In general, however, courts do not try to determine the optimal level of the activity that gives rise to an accident; they do not ask, when a driver is in an accident, whether the benefit of the particular trip (maybe he was driving to the grocery store to get some gourmet food for his pet iguana) was equal to or greater than the costs, including the expected accident cost to other users of the road, or whether driving was really cheaper than walking or taking the train when all social costs are reckoned in. Such a judgment is too difficult for a court to make in an ordinary tort case. Only if the benefits of the activity are obviously very slight, as where a man runs into a burning building to retrieve an old hat and does so as carefully as he can in the circumstances but is seriously burned nonetheless, will the court find that engaging in the activity was itself negligence, even though once the decision to engage in the activity was made, the actor (plaintiff or defendant) conducted himself with all possible skill and circumspection.

Judicial inability to determine optimal activity levels except in simple cases is potentially a serious shortcoming of a negligence system. Suppose railroads and canals are good substitutes in transportation but railroads inflict many accidents that cannot be avoided by being careful and canals none. Were it not for these accident costs railroads would be 10 percent cheaper than canals, but when these accident costs are figured in, railroads are actually 5 percent more costly. Under a rule of negligence liability, railroads will displace canals even though they are the socially more costly method of transportation.

In contrast, potential injurers subject to a rule of strict liability will automatically take into account possible changes in activity level, as well as possible changes in expenditures on care, in deciding whether to prevent accidents. Going back to our locomotive spark example, suppose that spark arresters don't work but that the railroad could achieve the same results, at the same costs as in our table, by running fewer trains per day. This is a change in activity level and might well escape notice under a negligence rule — in which event the farmer would be induced to take all the precautions, an inferior solution.

Figure 6.2 shows the effect of strict liability in reducing accident costs by inducing changes in activity level. The industry demand curve is depicted, since the rule of strict liability is presumably imposed on all

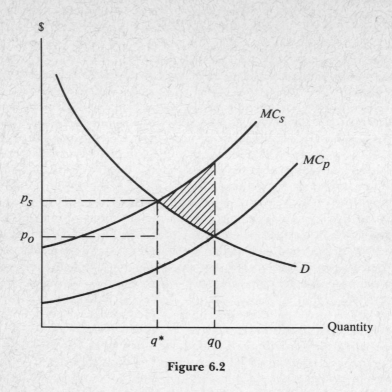

Figure 6.2

members of the industry. Accident costs unavoidable by due care and borne entirely by strangers to the industry (hence external to the industry) are assumed to be proportional to the industry's output. The curve labeled MC_P is the industry's private marginal-cost curve, while the curve labeled MC_s is the industry's social marginal-cost curve, i.e., including the costs of accidents. Under strict liability, MC_s becomes the industry's private-marginal-cost curve, inducing it to reduce output from q_0 to q^*, which results in eliminating socially wasteful accident costs (the shaded area in the diagram).

The problem with using this analysis to support a general rule of strict liability is that changes in activity level by victims are also a method of accident avoidance, and one that is encouraged by negligence liability but discouraged by strict liability. Suppose that the cost to the railroad of preventing damage to the farmer's crops, whether by more care or less activity, is greater than $150, the expected damage cost, so that the railroad will do nothing, but that the farmer could prevent the damage by switching to a fire resistant crop at a cost of $100. Under a rule of strict liability, he will have no incentive to do so, because his failure to change his activity will not be deemed contributory negligence and therefore the railroad will have to pay for the damage. But under a regime of negligence liability, since the railroad will not be liable

162

for the damage, the farmer will switch to the fire resistant crop because he will have an expected gain of $50 from doing so. Thus, strict liability encourages activity-level changes by potential injurers but discourages them by potential victims, while negligence liability encourages activity-level changes by potential victims but discourages them by potential injurers.

If a class of activities can be identified in which activity-level changes by potential injurers appear to be the most efficient method of accident prevention, there is a strong argument for imposing strict liability on the people engaged in those activities. And, conversely, if there is a class of activities in which activity-level changes by potential victims are the most efficient method of accident prevention, there is a strong argument for no liability — a point illustrated by the application of assumption of risk to participation in dangerous sports. Through the concept of ultrahazardous activities, the tort law imposes strict liability on activities that involve a high degree of danger that cannot be prevented just by the actor's being careful or potential victims' altering their behavior. A good example is strict liability for injuries by wild animals. If my neighbor has a pet tiger, there is very little I can do (at reasonable cost) to protect myself. And there is only so much he can do, in the way of being careful, to keep the tiger under control. The most promising precaution may consist simply of his not having a tiger — an activity-level change.[2] But suppose we are speaking not of a neighbor's tiger but of the zoo's. Is it likely that the best way of controlling accidents to visitors at zoos is not to have dangerous animals in zoos — just gentle ones? The cost of this particular activity change would be prohibitive. So it is no surprise that the courts have made an exception to the rule of strict liability for injuries caused by wild animals for zoos, circuses, and other animal parks and shows.

Another area of strict liability for ultrahazardous activities is blasting with explosives. No matter how careful the construction company is, there will be accidents; and since construction goes on everywhere, it is unlikely that the best way to minimize these accidents is for potential victims to alter their activities. The best way may be for the companies to switch to alternative methods of demolition that are less dangerous; and strict liability creates an incentive to consider such alternatives.

The category of ultrahazardous activities is not fixed; rather there is a tendency to affix the label to new activities (often called nonnatural), such as reservoirs in England[3] or ballooning in early nineteenth-century

2. This may seem like a ridiculous example for a resident of Chicago to put in an ostensibly serious book. But as a matter of fact, several years ago the residents of a group of townhouses about a mile from the home of the author of this book put young lions in their fenced back yards to intimidate intruders.

3. See A.W.B. Simpson, Legal Liability for Bursting Reservoirs: The Historical Context of *Rylands v. Fletcher,* 13 J. Leg. Stud. 209 (1984).

America.[4] New activities tend to be dangerous because there is little experience with their safety characteristics. For the same reason, the dangers may not be avoidable simply by taking care — yet the fact that the activities are new implies that there are good substitutes for them. Hence the best method of accident control may be to cut back on the scale of the activity (as in Figure 6.2) — to slow its spread while more is learned about conducting it safely.

The distinction between care and activity is not the only dimension along which negligence and strict liability differ. Another, developed at greater length in Chapter 21, has to do with the costs of administering these different rules. The trial of a strict liability case is simpler than the trial of a negligence case because there is one less issue, negligence. But the saving in information costs is potentially offset by the greater number of claims under a system of strict liability, resulting in greater claims costs.[5] That is why it is important, before deciding in favor of strict liability, to assess the responsiveness of the accident rate to the incentives that strict liability will create. If the accident rate in some activity will fall dramatically if strict liability is imposed, because accident costs exceed the costs of avoiding them through changes in activity level, there may well be fewer claims under strict liability, and the substitution of strict liability for negligence will be an unequivocal economic gain. At the other extreme, if most accidents that occur in some activity are unavoidable in an economic sense either by taking greater care or by reducing the amount of the activity (because the costs of greater care, or less activity, exceed any savings in reduced accident costs), the main effect of switching from negligence to strict liability will be to increase the number of damage claims and hence the costs of the legal system.

Another difference between negligence and strict liability is that the latter operates to insure victims of unavoidable accidents. But this is a gain only if the cost of insurance through the tort system is less than the cost to potential victims of buying accident insurance policies in the insurance market. A related point is that, as shown in Figure 6.2, the size of, and economic rents earned in, an industry subject to strict liability will be smaller than if the industry were subject to negligence. In sum, strict liability differs from negligence in the incentives imparted to injurers and victims to avoid accidents through changes in activity levels; in information and claims costs; in the provision of insurance; and in the size and profitability of the liable activity. Given these many differences we would not expect the tort system to opt all for negligence or all for strict liability, nor would we expect the balance between the

---

4. See Guille v. Swan, 19 Johns (N.Y.) 381, 10 Am. Dec. 234 (1822).
5. In addition, strict liability results in higher information costs within the firm (as distinct from judicial information costs). Can you see why?

two regimes to be the same at all times (we shall come back to the latter point in Chapter 8).

Finally, it should be noted that strict liability looms much larger in contract law than in tort law. The promisee does not have to prove that the costs to him of the breach were greater than the benefits to the promisor in order to collect damages; cases where discharge is allowed on one ground or another (e.g., impossibility, mutual mistake) are exceptional. The heavier reliance on strict liability in contract than in tort cases would seem to rest on two distinctions: the greater importance of market insurance in tort cases (hence lesser value of providing insurance through the legal system), and the fact that contract cases are less likely than tort cases to involve an interactive mishap that either party could have prevented, although possibly at very different costs. Ordinarily one of the contracting parties is performer and the other payor. The former has complete control over performance, the latter complete control over payment. The presumption is therefore strong (although not absolute) that a breach was preventable at lower cost by the promisor than by the promisee, or if not preventable then insurable by the former at lower cost. In contrast, most tort situations are literally collisions between two activities, such as driving and walking, and there is no presumption, such as would warrant a general rule of strict liability, that the injurer was in a better position than the victim to have prevented the collision.

§6.6 Products Liability

The most controversial area of strict liability today is liability, now called strict in most states, for personal injuries (mainly to consumers) caused by defective or unreasonably dangerous products. But the term strict liability is something of a misnomer here, because in deciding whether a product is defective or unreasonably dangerous in design or manufacture the courts often use a Hand Formula approach, balancing expected accident costs against the costs of making the product safer.[1] Thus, if a car is crushed in an accident, the manufacturer is not held strictly liable just because if the car had been built like a tank it would not have been crushed. He is liable only if the design or construction of the car was defective, which in most cases means just about the same thing as negligent. The principal exception is where, although the particular item that the consumer bought was indeed defective — a soft-drink

§6.6 1. See, e.g., Comment, Strict Products Liability and the Risk-Utility Test for Design Defects: An Economic Analysis, 84 Colum. L. Rev. 2045 (1984).

bottle with mouse parts in it, for example — the manufacturer had taken optimal hygienic measures, and the defective item was a one in a million product failure that could not be prevented at a cost less than the (tiny) expected accident cost. The manufacturer would nevertheless be liable. This is genuine strict liability and can be explained by reference to the discussion in the previous section of activity level. There is nothing the consumer can do at reasonable cost to prevent the one in a million product failure. It would not pay for him to inspect every soft drink bottle that he buys for such a minute hazard, or to investigate the possibility that there are safer substitutes; the expected accident cost is just too low to incite him to any self-protective measures. But a slight cost to each consumer, when aggregated over millions of consumers, may be a significant cost to the manufacturer. By hypothesis, it will not lead him to take additional hygienic measures in his factory; otherwise he would be negligent in not having done so already. But it will lead him to increase his price (why?); and although the increase will be small (again by hypothesis), it will lead some consumers to substitute other, and probably safer (why?), products. The activity consisting of the manufacture and sale of this soft drink brand will diminish slightly and with it the number of product accidents.

All this assumes an asymmetry of information between the manufacturer and the consumer. This common assumption was questioned in Chapter 4. But here the situation is different. The kind of product failures against which manufacturers expressly warrant their products are frequent and hence familiar to consumers and therefore enter into their buying decisions. But product failures that cause serious personal injuries are extremely rare, and the cost to the consumer of becoming informed about them is apt to exceed the expected benefit. (If the injury is common and consumer information therefore better, as in the case of the hazards of cigarette smoking, the defense of assumption of risk will bar the injured consumer from obtaining damages — the correct result from an economic standpoint.) Therefore, if the manufacturer is not made liable, the marketplace may fail to discipline him by diverting consumers to safer brands. Strict liability in effect impounds information about product hazards into the price of the product, resulting in a substitution away from hazardous products by consumers who may be completely unaware of the hazards.

This analysis may even explain the law's refusal to enforce disclaimers of liability for personal injuries caused by product accidents. If the hazard is very small, it will not pay the consumer to be attentive to disclaimers; and, for the same reason, the manufacturer will not reap significant ill will when he enforces the disclaimer in those very few cases in which someone is injured. As so often, the solution is not perfect. In particular, if consumers differ in their ability to cope with product hazards, a disclaimer of liability could be a good way of sorting consumers according to that ability. Those best able to avoid the hazards would flock to manufacturers who disclaimed liability and charged lower prices made possible by their lower legal-judgment costs. But there is a better way of sorting customers, and that is by making the hazards of a product obvious, thus bringing the doctrine of assumption of risk into play.

In regard to victim fault, the law of products liability has pioneered an interesting solution to the problem noted earlier of comparing the costs of accident avoidance to the injurer and to the victim in an alternative-care case. This is the doctrine of foreseeable misuse and is related to the point just made about the obvious hazard. A manufacturer sells a machine whose moving parts are not shielded, and a worker is injured when he sticks his hand in them. He was careless in doing so, the danger being apparent, and yet the manufacturer could have shielded the moving parts, and thus prevented the accident, at a trivial cost. In many states, he would be held liable to the worker. Is this an efficient result? Can you see an analogy to the doctrine of last clear chance? Should the doctrine of foreseeable misuse allow every negligent user of a product to recover damages, on the ground that it is well-known that many consumers are negligent?

§6.7   Causation and Foreseeability

It may seem obvious that if the defendant's conduct did not "cause" the plaintiff's injury, in the sense that but for that conduct the plaintiff would not have been injured, the plaintiff ought not recover damages. But it is not obvious, and sometimes it is wrong, from an economic standpoint; and we shall again find the law pretty much in accord with the economics of the situation. Consider first, however, the clear case where the defendant's conduct was causally unrelated to the plaintiff's harm. Suppose that in the *Blyth* case the city had failed to take precautions against a normal frost, but, as we know, the frost that caused damage to the plaintiff's property was abnormal and the precautions would have been unavailing. Therefore it would have made no difference if the defendant had not (in our hypothetical variant of *Blyth*) been negligent. Since the damage caused by abnormal frost is not part of L in the Hand Formula, and L is the damages the defendant must pay if he fails to take the precautions that would have prevented the accident and an accident occurs, the effect of liability would be to make the defendant's expected damages for negligence greater than L. It would be like imposing punitive damages. If punitive damages for simple negligence are a mistake, as we shall see later that they are, so is liability for uncaused harms.

But now change the facts. A and B, out hunting, carelessly mistake C for a deer and shoot. Both hit him, and each shot is fatal. This means that, viewed separately, neither A nor B caused C's death; yet it would be an economic mistake to let both off scot-free (why?). C's estate should be allowed to get damages from A and B — in what proportions we shall discuss later. Oddly to anyone who thinks (contrary to the author of this book) that causal principles ought to play an independent role, unrelated to economic considerations, in tort liability, the analysis is the same as in the case just put even if only one bullet hits C and we do not know whether A or B fired it, provided that both A and B were careless. There is growing judicial support for liability in this situation,[1] as there has long been support for liability in the first (and less common) situation.

The last example involved uncertainty about the injurer's identity. What if there is uncertainty about the victim's identity? Through negligence a nuclear reactor emits a burst of radiation that will cause 10 excess cancer deaths in the neighborhood of the reactor over the next 20 years. During this period 100 people would have died from cancer anyway; so now it will be 110; but we will never know which of the 110 would not have died but for the accident. If a 10 percent increment in the probability of death is deemed causation, then each of the 110 will be able to recover his full damages, and the owner of the nuclear reactor will be forced to pay 11 times the actual damage it caused. But if 10 percent is deemed too little for causation, the owner will pay nothing, and there will be no tort sanction for its negligence. Neither situation is satisfactory, and rather than play with concepts of causation the tort law might be well advised to consider defining the injury as the increased risk of death from cancer, rather than as the cancer itself. Then the whole population exposed to the burst of radiation would be able to sue when the accident occurs, using the class action device (discussed in Chapter 21) to economize on the cost of litigating many small claims. (Notice the symmetry with the previous example, in which the potential injurers were made liable as a group.) If this solution doesn't work, there is a strong argument for direct regulation of safety, as will be explained in Chapter 13.

Here now is a case where causation in a layman's sense is manifestly present but the law properly refuses to award damages. A train breaks down (as a result of the railroad's negligence), and a passenger stays in a hotel and is injured when the hotel burns down. But for the train's breaking down, the passenger would have gone on to his destination and slept in a different hotel that did not burn down that night. So there is negligence, and causation, but there is no liability. The economic

§6.7   1. The leading case is Sindell v. Abbott Laboratories, 26 Cal. 3d 588, 607 P.2d 924 (1980), a DES case.

reason is that the risk of a hotel fire is not a part of *PL*, the expected accident cost that the railroad could have prevented by taking *B* precautions. True, harm to this particular passenger would have been prevented but it was just as likely that the hotel in the next town would have burned down, in which event the railroad's negligence would have conferred a benefit on the passenger for which the railroad would not have been allowed to charge. To hold the railroad liable would thus be to impose (in effect) punitive damages for its negligence, just as in the superficially very different case with which we began this section.

The results in these cases seem to owe little to refined notions of causation, and much to considerations of (economic) policy, yet they are conventionally discussed by lawyers under the rubric of cause in fact. Another group of cases is discussed under the rubric cause in law, but they seem to rest on the same policy considerations as the first group. In *Rickards v. Sun Oil Co.*,[2] the defendant's negligence put the only bridge between an island and the mainland out of commission. Merchants on the island who saw their business dry up as a result of the collision sued the defendant but lost, which was the right result. Although they did lose money, most and perhaps all of their loss was a gain to mainland merchants who picked up their business when customers could no longer reach the island. Since the defendant could not seek restitution from the mainland merchants of the gains he had conferred upon them, it would have been punitive to make him pay the losses of the island merchants. The net social cost was the damage to the bridge.

This suggests a useful tip in analyzing any legal claim from the standpoint of economics: Always consider the gains (by whomever received) as well as the losses caused by an allegedly wrongful act. This will help you see why, for example, competition is not a tort. A is the only merchant in a small town. B opens a shop in competition with A, as a result of which A's profits plummet. Should A be allowed to sue? No; his losses will be smaller than the gains to others. Suppose that before B came along, A's price for some good was $10, his profit $5, and he sold 1,000 units, thus making a total profit of $5,000. After B begins selling the same good, A is forced to cut his price to $6. Total output is now, say, 2,000 units (why greater than before?), and is divided evenly between A and B, who also sells at $6. A's profits are lower by $4,000, but those customers who had bought 1,000 units before and continue to buy them are better off by the same amount, whether they now buy from A or B. Assuming B just breaks even at $6 (let's assume that as a newcomer he has higher costs than A), the only other group whose welfare must be considered consists of those consumers who are buying the good for the first time or buying more than they bought before.

2. 23 N.J. Misc. 89, 41 A.2d 267 (1945).

All of them must be better off or else they would not have switched from whatever good they had been buying instead. So there is a net social gain from the new competition even though A has suffered a loss.

In some cases a defendant escapes liability for the consequences of his negligence on the ground that those consequences are unforeseeable. If this just meant that the accident had been unlikely and therefore unexpected, it would arbitrarily and drastically truncate the defendant's liability, for most accidents are low-probability events. But actually it seems to mean two other things. One is that there is considerable doubt whether there was a causal relationship between the negligence and the injury. A man is told that his pet canary has died through the negligence of a veterinarian, and upon hearing the news drops dead of a heart attack; such a consequence would be deemed unforeseeable, but what this seems to mean is that either we can't believe the shock was enough to kill him or we think that if he was in such a vulnerable state he probably did not have long to live.

The other meaning of unforeseeability in the law of torts is that high costs of information prevented a party from taking any precautions against the particular accident that occurred; put differently, B in the Hand Formula was prohibitive once information about risk is recognized to be a cost of avoiding risk. A trespasser beds down for the night in a newly constructed but unoccupied house in a real estate development and is asphyxiated because the developer had accidentally spliced a gas main and a water pipe to the house. There is an economic basis for refusing to permit the developer to interpose the defense of no duty to trespassers. Sometimes the value of trespassing to the trespasser is greater than the expected accident cost (plus any damage to the owner) and transaction costs are prohibitively high. In these cases trespassing will increase value. Therefore we want prospective trespassers to weigh the relevant values and costs. But they cannot weigh costs that are unforeseeable. A newly constructed residential building is normally a safe place. The trespasser has no reason to foresee being asphyxiated. He may have made a perfectly rational judgment that the value of his trespass exceeded all expected costs, including accident costs.[3]

Observe the symmetry here between torts and contracts. The asphyxiated trespasser is like the contract breaker in *Hadley v. Baxendale* (see §4.11 *supra*): Neither could foresee (i.e., inform himself at reasonable cost about) the consequences of his conduct, and neither was held liable for those consequences. The land developer is like the commercial photographer in our variant of *Hadley v. Baxendale*: Each could foresee the consequences of a failure to take precautions and should either have

---

3. Should the owner in such a case be entitled to deduct fair rental value from any damages awarded the trespasser?

taken precautions himself or, if the other party could do so more cheaply, have communicated the danger to the other party.

An apparent anomaly in the tort treatment of foreseeability is the eggshell skull principle. A tort victim is permitted to recover his damages in full even though the *extent* of his injury was unforeseeable by the defendant because of the victim's unusual vulnerability. A reason for nevertheless imposing liability in such cases is that, in order for total tort damages awarded to equal tort victims' total harm, there must be liability in the eggshell skull case to balance nonliability in the "rock skull" case (i.e., where the victim has above-average resistance to damage). The alternative would be to award in every case the damages an average victim would have incurred; but this approach would distort victim's incentives (why?), as well as create severe measurement problems.[4] (What about the effects on the injurer's incentives?)

§6.8   Joint Torts, Contribution, Indemnity

We have already given some examples of joint torts, and here are two others.
  (1) Two landowners negligently set fires on their properties. The fires spread, join, and roar down on the plaintiff's house, which is consumed. Either fire would have done all the damage. Both landowners are liable.
  (2) An employee is negligent and injures someone. The employer is liable, too, under the doctrine of respondeat superior, which makes an employer liable for the torts of his employees, committed in the furtherance of their employment, even if he was not negligent in hiring, training, supervising, or failing to fire them.

We have discussed the economic rationale for the first type of joint liability (the hunters' case). The rationale for the second rests on the fact that most employees do not have the resources to pay a judgment if they injure someone seriously. They therefore are not very amenable to the incentive effects of tort liability. The employer, however, can induce them to be careful, as by firing or otherwise penalizing them for their carelessness (in what circumstances will firing an employee impose costs on him?); and making the employer liable for his employees' torts will give him an incentive to use such inducements. Notice that his liability is strict; this may be because activity-level changes by the

---

4. Notice, however, an ambiguity in the idea of damages in full in the eggshell skull case. If the eggshell skull made the plaintiff vulnerable to other injuries, any long-term damages (e.g., for lost earnings because of protracted disability) must be discounted by the probability that he would have survived in the long term despite his weakness.

employer (e.g., substituting capital for labor inputs or reducing the scale of the enterprise) are potentially efficient methods of reducing torts by employees. But there is an important qualification to the employer's strict liability to his employees' tort victims: The tort must be committed in the course of employment. This means, for example, that if the employee has an accident while commuting to or from work, the employer will not be liable to the victim. The economic reason for this result (a result that demonstrates, incidentally, the inadequacy of a pure deep pocket explanation for respondeat superior) is that it wouldn't pay for the employer to take steps to reduce his employees' commuting accidents. The probability of such accidents is small, and since they do not occur during work time, the employer lacks good information for taking steps to minimize them. Compare the employee who is a traveling salesman and injures someone while going his rounds.

Another thing to notice is that the employer is not liable for the torts of his independent contractors. The independent contractor is more likely than an employee to be solvent. Also, the employee is paid a wage to do work at the employer's direction, while the independent contractor is paid a price for a contractually specified undertaking. The principal does not supervise the details of the independent contractor's work and is therefore less likely to be able to make him work safely than to make an employee work safely. But there is an exception to the exception, for the case where the independent contractor's work is highly dangerous. This too makes economic sense. The cost-justified level of precaution is by definition higher, making it more likely that the principal can do something to prevent accidents efficiently; in addition, the independent contractor is likelier to have a solvency problem the more dangerous the work is and hence the higher his expected damage bill is.

The examples of the two landowners' liability for fire and the employer's liability for his employees' torts illustrate the two fundamental types of joint tort. (They should be familiar to us from our discussion of victim fault; for an accident in which both injurer and victim are at fault is functionally a joint tort.) Example (1) is a case of joint care, example (2) a case of alternative care. At common law, the rule for liability among joint tortfeasors that was applicable to joint-care joint-tort cases was "no contribution among tortfeasors," and the rule applicable to alternative-care joint-tort cases was indemnity. Does this pattern make economic sense?

No contribution among tortfeasors means that if the plaintiff gets a judgment against one of several tortfeasors, the defendant cannot compel the others to contribute their "fair" share — or any share — of the judgment; and if the plaintiff gets a judgment against a group of tortfeasors he can collect it from them in any proportions he wants even if as a result one or more of them gets off scot-free. It might seem that this rule would lead to underdeterrence, but it does not, the analysis being symmetrical with that of comparative negligence.

Suppose there are just two potential joint tortfeasors, X and Y. B is $10 for X, and $20 for Y, and PL is $80. Since this is a joint care situation, if either X or Y fails to take optimal precautions the accident will occur. Suppose that X estimates that the probability of his being made to pay damages to the victim of such an accident is only 10 percent. Then his expected accident cost is $8. Although this is less than B_x ($10), X must know that if the probability of his having to pay the plaintiff's damages is 10 percent, Y's must be 90 percent, so that Y will face an expected accident cost of $72 and will therefore have an incentive to spend $20 on B_y — in which event Y will not be negligent, and the whole cost of the accident will come to rest on X. So X will have an incentive to spend B_x after all. Both parties will be careful.

Although the rule of no contribution among joint tortfeasors is efficient, it should be obvious that a rule of contribution, which allows a joint tortfeasor made to pay more than his "fair" share of the plaintiff's damages to require contribution from the other joint tortfeasors, will also create the right safety incentives for all joint tortfeasors — and this regardless of how the contribution shares are determined (pro rata, relative fault, etc.). The only difference is that contribution is more costly to administer than no contribution, because it requires the courts to decide another issue and supervise another set of transfer payments.

Under the rule in alternative-care joint-tort cases — indemnity — the joint tortfeasor who would incur the higher cost of preventing the accident can get the other tortfeasor to reimburse him for the whole damage bill. Thus, if Firm X is held liable to the plaintiff for $100,000 in damages as a result of employee Y's negligence, X is entitled (although in practice will rarely be able to obtain) indemnification from Y for the whole $100,000. Similarly, if X was the final assembler of some product and had been held liable to a consumer for injuries caused by a defect in the product, Y was the supplier of the component that had failed, and X could not have discovered the failure by reasonable inspection, X could force Y to indemnify it for the damages.[1]

The economic explanation for the complete shifting of liability from one joint tortfeasor to another that is brought about by indemnity is straightforward. In an alternative care case we do not want both tortfeasors to take precautions; we want the lower cost accident avoider to do so. The liability of the other is a kind of back-up precaution should insolvency prevent the incentives of the tort system from operating on the primary accident avoider. Hence the need for a mechanism that

§6.8   1. Incidentally, this is another example of where strict products liability really is strict. Does this example and that of respondeat superior suggest an additional economic function for strict liability besides those discussed in §6.5 *supra*?

will, where possible, shift the ultimate liability to the most efficient accident avoider — and indemnity does this.

§6.9   Rescue: Liability Versus Restitution

While walking down the street I see a flowerpot fall out of a window,
threatening another pedestrian, and although I could save him simply
by shouting a warning I keep silent. The expected accident cost is high
and the cost of my taking the precaution that would avert it trivial,
yet I am not liable. The result *seems* inconsistent with the Hand Formula,
since if transaction costs had not been prohibitive the endangered pedestrian would surely have paid me enough to overcome my reluctance
to utter a warning cry. To make me liable, therefore, would seem to
increase value. This point holds even if the attempt to warn or rescue
might endanger the rescuer, provided that the danger to the rescuer
(and hence the expected cost of precautions) is less than the danger
to the person in distress (and hence expected accident cost) and that
the victim's life is at least as valuable at the rescuer's. Although the
bystander did not "cause" the accident, causal concepts play only an
incidental role in the economic analysis of torts. But they are relevant
in the following sense. Causation defines the pool of potential defendants: those who in some sense caused the plaintiff's injury. Since the
universe of those who might have prevented the injury is not so circum-
scribed, there would be practical difficulties in limiting good Samaritan
liability to those who really could have prevented the injury at reasonable
cost.

   Another economic objection to good Samaritan liability is that it would
make it more costly to be in a situation where one might be called
upon to attempt a rescue, and the added cost would presumably reduce
the number of potential rescuers — the strong swimmer would avoid
the crowded beach. (Is this point consistent with the result in *Ploof v.
Putnam*, §6.4 *supra*?) It might seem that liability would impose a cost
only on one who, but for the liability, would *not* attempt a rescue —
that altruists would be unaffected. But this is doubtful for two reasons.
First, even the altruist wants to have a choice at the moment of crisis
as to whether or not to attempt a rescue that may be dangerous to
him; he doesn't want to be coerced by the law. Second, one of the
benefits that a person receives from being an altruist is public recognition. (This is suggested by the small fraction of charitable giving that
is anonymous.) Liability would remove this benefit by making it impossible for a rescuer to prove that he was motivated by altruism rather
than by the legal sanctions for failure to rescue.

An alternative to liability or altruism is restitution, an approach followed, as we have seen (in §4.14 *supra*), in the case of physicians and other professionals who render assistance in an emergency, and also widely utilized in admiralty law, where it is known as the law of salvage, which we have also met before. Would it be better to give the whole value of the rescue — the maximum that the rescued person would have been willing to pay in a negotiation with the rescuer — to the rescuer, or give the rescuer nothing?[1] The latter alternative, zero restitution, will produce no nonaltruistic rescues in cases where transaction costs prevent a voluntary negotiation. The former will induce people to take socially excessive precautions to avoid having to be rescued,[2] as well as inducing an excessive investment in resources devoted to rescue (see §3.2 *supra*). The law avoids both extremes. It awards the rescuer an amount roughly equal to what the competitive price for the service would have been — the physician's ordinary fee, or a salvage award based on the salvor's opportunity costs of time, adjusted for peril, skill, risk of failure, and other economically relevant factors.[3]

Despite this example, the common law is much more chary about compensating people for rendering external benefits than it is about making them pay for the external costs they impose.[4] Think back to the defense of public necessity (§6.4 *supra*). A person who saves a city by pulling down a house in the path of a fire will not have to compensate the owner of the house but neither will he be entitled to charge the city's residents for the benefits he has conferred on them. Allowing someone who confers external benefits to externalize some of his costs is a much more common technique of dealing with external benefits than giving him a right of restitution. The reason may be that although external benefits and external costs are symmetrical in economics, they differ with respect to the costs of administering a common law system. Legal sanctions for imposing external costs deter; especially when the legal standard is negligence rather than strict liability, there will be few actual lawsuits. But a right of restitution means a legal claim whenever

§6.9   1. See Peter A. Diamond & James A. Mirrlees, On the Assignment of Liability: The Uniform Case, 6 Bell J. Econ. & Mgmt. Sci. 487, 512 (1975).

2. Suppose that a disaster that would cost the shipowner $1 million if it occurred — the probability of its occurrence being 1 percent — could be avoided either by a rescue that would cost the rescuer $500 or by the shipowner's taking certain safety measures at a cost to him of $5,000. The safety measures are socially inefficient, but if the rescuer would be entitled to the full value of the rescue — $1 million — then it will pay the shipowner to take the safety measures because the cost is less than the discounted rescue expense that he faces.

Does this suggest a possible economic reason why the finder of lost as distinct from abandoned property does not obtain a property right good against the owner?

3. What would be the economic effects of combining liability for failure to rescue with a rescuer's right to restitution?

4. See Note, Efficient Land Use and the Internalization of Beneficial Spillovers: An Economic and Legal Analysis, 31 Stan. L. Rev. 457 (1979).

a benefit is conferred; and the costs of processing the claims can be horrendous. Allowing the benefactor to externalize some of his costs is a much cruder, but also administratively much cheaper, method of encouraging the provision of external benefits.

§6.10   The Function of Tort Damages

Maintaining the credibility of the tort system requires that if a defendant is found liable, he must pay damages at least as great as L in the Hand Formula. Damages equal to L are compensatory damages. But must they be paid to the victim rather than to the state? And should they be limited to L or should punitive damages be awarded as well?

There are two reasons why compensatory damages must indeed be paid to the victim and not the state. The first is to give the victim an incentive to sue, which is essential to the maintenance of the tort system as an effective deterrent to negligence. The second is to prevent victims from taking too many precautions. Think back to our locomotive sparks example, and the table of prevention costs for it (Table 6.1). Recall that the optimal method of prevention was for the railroad to spend $50 on a spark arrester and the farmer $25 on moving his flax back, but that if the railroad did nothing at all the farmer could still prevent the accident, although at a cost of $110, by moving the flax way back. If the farmer will not be compensated for the railroad's negligence, the railroad may decide to go ahead and be negligent, knowing that the farmer will have an incentive to incur a $110 cost to avoid expected damages of $150 and that if he does so the railroad will have saved $50.

The reason for limiting damages to L is obvious when the liability rule is strict liability: Any increase in PL will increase the amount that potential injurers are willing to spend on safety precautions, and it is important therefore that L reflect the actual costs of injury.[1] But if the liability rule is negligence, the potential injurer can always avoid liability by being careful, and so in principle it should not matter how severe the sanction is; he still will just spend B on safety. But we know from our discussion of the reasonable man rule that negligence has an element of strict liability. And there is always the risk of legal error; if by taking more care a potential injurer can reduce the probability of being falsely held to have been negligent, he will do so, and his expenditures will

---

§6.10   1. Suppose $PL = \$100$ and $B = \$150$, so that accident avoidance is uneconomical. If injurers are forced to pay punitive damages equal to actual damages, then PL as viewed by potential injurers becomes $200, and B becomes privately — but not socially — cost justified, resulting in a $50 waste of resources ($150 − $100).

be greater, the greater the potential liability. These are powerful reasons against allowing punitive damages in tort cases as a general rule; we shall consider some exceptions however in a subsequent section.

§6.11 Damages for Loss of Earning Capacity

When an accident disables the victim from working for some period into the future, the court, rather than ordering the defendant to make periodic payments during the period of disability (analogous to alimony payments), will order him to pay the victim a lump sum so calculated as to equal the present value of the expected future stream of earnings that has been lost. This is different from simply multiplying earnings per period of disability by the number of periods. That would overcompensate the victim (assuming no inflation during the period of disability, a matter taken up shortly), because at the end of the disability he would have received not only the sum of the periodic payments but interest on that sum, which he would not have received had payment been made periodically rather than in a lump at the outset. The lump sum should be equal to the price that the victim would have had to pay in order to purchase an annuity calculated to yield the periodic payment for the expected duration of the disability, and no more. This is the present value of the future loss.

The payment of a present-value lump sum is preferable to periodic payments stretching into the future. It both economizes on administrative expenses and avoids the disincentive effects of tying continued receipt of money to continued disability. Having received the lump sum the victim has every incentive to overcome his disability sooner than had been estimated. A system of periodic disability payments, in contrast, would be the equivalent of a 100 percent tax on earned income.[1]

Courts have had difficulty determining damages in cases involving disabled housewives. To value a housewife's services by adding up the amounts that would be required to hire providers of the various components of these services (cleaning, child care, cooking, etc.) has troubled the courts, and rightly so; it would violate the opportunity cost concept. The minimum value of a housewife's services, and hence the cost to the family if those services are eliminated, is the price that her time would have commanded in its next best use. Suppose that she had been trained as a lawyer and could have earned $45,000 working for a law

---

§6.11 1. The tax effect would be exacerbated by the fact that working imposes costs (income tax, commuting, work clothes, etc.) that are avoided by staying home and collecting disability payments. Work might however yield nonpecuniary income that would equal or exceed these expenses — or might yield additional disutility.

firm but chose instead to be a housewife and that the various functions
she performed as a housewife could have been hired in the market for
$10,000. Since she chose to stay at home, presumably her services in
the home were considered by the family to be worth at least $45,000;[2]
if not, the family could have increased its real income by having her
work as a lawyer and by hiring others to perform her household
functions.[3] Therefore, the loss when she was disabled was at least
$45,000. Although it may have been greater, just as the value (discounted
lifetime earnings) of an opera singer may exceed her value in an alternative occupation, the valuation of a housewife's services is difficult because
of the absence of an explicit market in housewives.[4]

The opportunity cost approach may be more feasible, although implementation will not always be easy. Consider the estimation problem
created where, because a woman becomes (and remains) a housewife,
her market earning capacity fails to reach the level it would have reached
had she not become a housewife. Properly applied, the opportunity cost
concept would require estimating what her probable market earnings
would have been (net of any cost of investment, for example in education,
related to her market job) if she had entered the market at the time
when instead she became a housewife. Courts do not yet use the opportunity cost concept in determining damages in such cases, but they approximate it by allowing testimony about the quality of the housewife's
household services. This is an oblique method of avoiding the pitfall
of valuing such services at the cost of domestic servants.[5]

Where the earnings lost as a result of a disabling injury would have
been obtained over a long period of time, both the assumptions made
concerning future changes in the victim's income and the choice of
the interest rate to use to discount those earnings to present value will
greatly affect the size of the award. (The effect of discounting is shown

2. This ignores, for the sake of simplifying the exposition, the incentive that the income
tax system gives a woman to remain at home even if the value of her services outside
of the home would be greater than that of her services as a housewife. See §17.8 *infra*.
An additional possibility is that the woman derives nonpecuniary income, perhaps in
the form of leisure, from remaining at home. This income may or may not (see next
section) be affected by the disability. Suppose the value of the wife's services in the home,
say $45,000, is composed of $40,000 in services rendered and $5,000 in leisure produced.
If the value of her leisure time is unaffected by the disability, the cost of the disability
is $40,000 rather than $45,000 a year. It is also possible, however, that the job outside
the home would have yielded nonpecuniary income on top of the $45,000 salary, in which
event that figure might underestimate the cost of the accident to her.

3. The decision that she remain at home may have been quite rational, for her skills
as a housewife, particularly in child care, may have exceeded what the family could have
obtained in the market at the same price.

4. But see the Gronau study cited in §5.3 *supra*, note 2, which attempted to estimate
the value of the average housewife's output.

Should the tort damage measure include economic rents, i.e., income in excess of
opportunity cost?

5. Suppose a law school professor who has a salary of $75,000 is disabled. He could
earn $200,000 a year practicing law. What are his lost earnings?

Table 6.2
Present Value of Lost Earnings of $25,000 a Year,
for Various Periods and Discount Rates

	Discount Rate			
Period	*2%*	*5%*	*10%*	*12%*
10 years	$224,565	$193,043	$153,615	$141,255
20 years	408,785	311,555	212,840	186,735
30 years	501,603	384,313	235,673	201,138

in Table 6.2.) Let us examine first the problem of estimating future earnings, and then the problem of choosing an appropriate discount (interest) rate.

Setting to one side the problem of determining whether the victim might have changed his occupation at some time, we must determine the wages likely to have been received each year between accident and retirement. The starting point for the inquiry is the wage profile by age for the occupation in question. If for example the victim was a truck driver, age 25, we would need to know the wages not only of 25-year-old truck drivers but, assuming permanent disability and a retirement age of 65, those of 26 to 64-year-old truck drivers. The next step is to determine how the wages in the occupation are likely to change in the future. Many of the factors that might alter the wage level in a particular occupation are very difficult to foresee — such as changes in the demand for the output of the industry in which the worker is employed[6] or in the level of unionization in the industry. These sources of future wage change will generally have to be ignored in estimating damages. The foreseeable sources of wage change are three:

(1) probability of layoff, based on past employment experience in the industry,

(2) rising labor productivity, and

(3) inflation.

Let us consider (2) and (3).

Productivity is the ratio of output to input. An increase in the productivity of labor is an increase in the amount of output per hour of labor. By reducing the employer's production costs, an increase in labor productivity enables him — and competition for workers will compel him — to pay higher wages. Rising labor productivity appears to be responsible for an average annual increase in the real (i.e., inflation adjusted) earnings of workers of about 3 percent.[7]

6. In what circumstances would a change in demand for an industry's product alter the wage rate of the workers employed in the industry?

7. The effect is felt even in industries where productivity is not increasing: Employers in such industries must raise wages to levels competitive with those in other industries or lose their work force.

Having derived an estimate of the real wages[8] that our truck driver would have earned in each year during his working life (by adjusting his current wages for life cycle, unemployment, and productivity growth effects), we must next multiply each year's estimated wages by the actuarial probability that he will still be alive at the end of that year. We could also — although as we shall soon see need not — adjust our estimates of his real wages to reflect the effect on nominal wages of the inflation estimated to occur over his working life. If we did that, we would use investor expectation, as reflected in interest rates on long-term riskless instruments such as U.S. government bonds, to estimate long-term future inflation rates.

An interest rate has three principal components.[9] The first is the real opportunity cost of capital net of any risk of loss and of any expectation of inflation (or deflation). The second is the risk premium necessary to compensate the investor for the possibility that he will never get his capital back, a premium that will be affected by the investor's attitude toward risk.[10] But risk is not a factor in U.S. government securities. The third is the anticipated inflation rate over the period in which the loan will be outstanding. If the loan is for one year and the purchasing power of the dollar is expected to decline by 4 percent during that year, then even if there is no risk of default, the lender will demand the opportunity cost of being without his capital for a year plus 4 percent to compensate him for the loss during the year in the buying power of that capital.

A reasonable estimate of the real, riskless cost of capital is 2 percent;[11] the current interest rate on long-term government bonds is about 10 percent;[12] and this implies an expected long-term inflation rate of 8 percent, which is therefore the relevant figure to use in estimating inflation when the accident victim's disability is expected to last many years. So we should add 8 percent to each year's estimate of the worker's lost earnings.

Having done all this we must discount each year's estimate to present value — a sum that when invested will yield (principal plus interest) the loss in each year. The present-value figure is determined by the

8. Should these be wages before or after income tax? Social security tax?

9. A fourth is the lender's expenses of negotiating and administering the loan. Cf. §14.3 *infra*.

10. Suppose a loan of $100 carries a 1 percent risk of default each year. If the interest rate without risk of default is 5 percent, then a risk-neutral lender will demand 6 percent, because $100 × .99 × 1.06 = $105. (These figures are rounded.) A risk-averse lender will demand more than 6 percent, a risk-preferring lender less.

11. See economic studies cited in Doca v. Marina Mercante Nicaraguense, S.A., 634 F.2d 30, 39 n.2 (2d Cir. 1980). See also O'Shea v. Riverway Towing Co., 677 F.2d 1194 (7th Cir. 1982); Culver v. Slater Boat Co., 688 F.2d 280 (5th Cir. 1982) (en banc).

12. This is a nominal rate; it includes expected inflation as well as the real cost of capital.

interest rate used in discounting. The higher the interest rate, the smaller the present value (see Table 6.2), for a higher rate will make that value grow more rapidly. We could use the nominal interest rate on long-term bonds, that is, an interest rate with an inflation component. This would be a high rate and thus lead to a smaller present value than if a lower present value were used, but the plaintiff would not be hurt. The nominal rate is high because it contains an inflation factor that has already been used to jack up the estimate of the plaintiff's lost future earnings. Inflation is a wash when a present value is calculated correctly. If we figured the plaintiff's lost future earnings in real — inflation-free — terms, each estimate would be 8 percent lower, but we would discount these estimates to a present value using an 8 percent lower interest rate.[13]

But in either case, should the *riskless* interest rate be used (the rate on federally issued or insured securities)? No. The stream of lost earnings of which the damage award is the present-value equivalent is not a riskless stream — death, unemployment, and disability from other causes could have cut it off. If, therefore, the plaintiff is risk averse, he will consider the riskless equivalent of his lost risky stream of earnings to be worth more to him. A risk factor must be added to the discount rate to bring the present value down to a level that confers the same utility as the risky stream of earnings that it is intended to replace.[14]

Here is another complication. The theory of household production discussed in Chapter 5 implies that an individual's real earnings are not limited to the market income that he earns in 40 of the 168 hours in a week.[15] A serious accident that disables a person from working in the market may also impair the productivity of his nonmarket hours, which he would have been using to produce recreation, love, or other ultimate household commodities. Wage rates for second jobs (moonlighting) might be used to estimate the opportunity costs of being disabled from productive use of hours not devoted to earning market income. But if this is done, then the portion of a person's wages that represents compensation for the costs of working (including the forgone nonpecuniary income from leisure, and any hazards or disamenities involved in the job) should be subtracted, in order to determine the worker's net loss from disability.

13. On the general problem of inflation and tort damages, see Keith S. Rosenn, Law and Inflation 220-234 (1982).

14. The cases — including, alas, one written by the author of this book — have missed this point. See, e.g., O'Shea v. Riverway Towing Co., *supra* note 11. In what circumstances might the riskless rate still be correct?

15. See Neil K. Komesar, Toward a General Theory of Personal Injury Loss, 3 J. Leg. Stud. 457 (1974).

§6.12 Damages for Pain and Suffering and the Problem of Valuing Human Life

The layman's confusion, remarked in the first chapter of this book, between pecuniary loss and economic loss is at the bottom of criticisms of awarding damages (frequently quite substantial) for pain, disfigurement, loss of mobility, and other forms of suffering inflicted by accidents, even if earnings are unaffected. Such losses impose opportunity costs. People will pay to avoid them, and demand payment to risk incurring them.

Damage awards for pain and suffering, even when apparently generous, may well undercompensate victims seriously crippled by accidents. Since the loss of vision or limbs reduces the amount of pleasure that can be purchased with a dollar,[1] a very large amount of money will frequently be necessary to place the victim in the same position of relative satisfaction that he occupied before the accident.[2] The problem is most acute in a death case. Most people would not exchange their lives for anything less than an infinite sum of money if the exchange were to take place immediately, since they would have so little time in which to enjoy the proceeds of the sale. Yet it cannot be correct that the proper award of damages in a death case is infinite. This would imply that the optimum rate of fatal accidents was zero, or very close to it (why this qualification?), and it is plain that people are unwilling, individually or collectively, to incur the costs necessary to reduce the rate of fatal accidents so drastically.

The courts have resolved the vexing problem of the proper valuation of life by ignoring it. Damages in a death case are generally limited to compensating the pecuniary loss to survivors (in some states, to the deceased victim's estate), plus medical expenses and any pain and suffering experienced by the victim before death. The pecuniary loss to survivors is the victim's lost earnings minus his living expenses. The test is thus the same as in disability cases except that since the victim's personal expenses (food, etc.) are eliminated by death but not by disability, they are subtracted from the amount awarded in a death case but not in a disability case. The implicit assumption is that the person who has been killed obtained no utility from living!

A frequent loser when a person is killed or disabled, besides his survivors, is his employer. Employers invest money in training their employees that they hope to recoup in the higher productivity that the training will generate. The human capital thus created is as real an asset of

---

§6.12 1. This is an example of how an injury can reduce the nonpecuniary earnings of nonmarket activity. See §6.11 *supra.*

2. Sometimes an infinite amount. What then? See David Friedman, What Is Fair Compensation for Death or Injury?, 2 Intl. Rev. Law & Econ. 81 (1982).

the employer as his machinery, and its destruction is as real a cost, as some foreign courts have (implicitly) recognized in awarding damages to the employer for an injury to an employee.[3] Common law courts used to award such damages but no longer do — erroneously regarding such awards are implying that the employer "owns" the employee.

A particularly difficult problem is the valuation of a child's life. Although there is frequently no basis for estimating lost earnings, a minimum estimate of the parents' loss, which can be used as the basis for awarding damages to them, is their investment of both money and time (the latter monetizable on the basis of market opportunity costs) in the rearing of the child up to the date of his death.[4] This assumes merely that the parents would not have made the investment if the expected value of the child to them had been less than the cost of the investment. Of course the child's value might be much greater but the estimation of the full value would present severe difficulties.

The valuation problem in death cases may be solvable by distinguishing between ex ante and ex post changes in utility brought about by risky activity. If I drive down the street carelessly I will create a risk of injuring many people. From studies of the wage premiums demanded by workers in risky occupations, and even more pertinent studies of people's voluntary trade-offs between safety and cost as revealed by their willingness to buy smoke alarms, use automobile seatbelts, etc., we know something about the costs that people implicitly assign to running risks of injury or death.[5] These studies could be used to estimate the costs of my dangerous driving, for which I could be made liable whether or not my car actually hit anyone. The damages assessed against me would be no greater if my car in fact killed someone, because by hypothesis the victim would have assumed the risk if he had been paid the ex ante cost to him of my dangerous driving; hence his estate, along

3. See Football Club de Metz c. Wiroth, 1956 Recueil Dalloz 723 (Cour d'Appel de Colmar); Camerlo c. Dassary et Demeyere, 1958 Recueil Dalloz 253 (Cour d'Appel de Lyon). Is it relevant whether the employee had a contract of fixed duration with his employer or could quit at any time?

4. See Wycko v. Gnodtke, 361 Mich. 331, 339, 105 N.W.2d 118, 122 (1960); Breckon v. Franklin Fuel Co., 383 Mich. 251, 268, 174 N.W.2d 836, 842 (1970).

5. See, e.g., Richard Thaler & Sherwin Rosen, The Value of Saving a Life: Evidence From the Labor Market, in Household Production and Consumption 265 (Nestor E. Terleckyj ed. 1975); Rachel Dardis, The Value of Life: New Evidence From the Marketplace, 70 Am. Econ. Rev. 1077 (1980); Martin J. Bailey, Reducing Risks to Life: Measurement of the Benefits 28-46 (Am. Enterprise Institute 1980); Craig A. Olson, An Analysis of Wage Differentials Received by Workers on Dangerous Jobs, 16 J. Human Resources 167 (1981); W. Kip Viscusi, Risk by Choice: Regulating Health and Safety in the Workplace, ch. 6 (1983); and for general background M.W. Jones-Lee, The Value of Life: An Economic Analysis (1976); Richard Zeckhauser, Procedures for Valuing Lives, 23 Pub. Policy 419 (1975). Risky occupations will attract people who have an above-average taste for danger. Cf. §6.6 *supra*. In contrast, the taste for danger of people exposed to nonoccupational hazards is presumably average. Of course, there is always the problem that people might, through ignorance, underestimate (or overestimate!) small hazards. See further on this point §13.4 *infra*.

with everyone else my driving had endangered, would be entitled to be paid that cost — and no more — as damages.

Notice that the sum of the ex ante damages thus computed will not equal the common law damages of someone who is actually injured. The fact that my conduct may have subjected each of 100 people to a 1 percent risk of loss of a life that, in a tort case utilizing conventional methods of damage assessment, would have been valued at $500,000 does not imply that each of the 100 would have demanded only $5,000 from me to undergo the risk. Risk aversion aside, since most people obtain nonpecuniary as well as pecuniary income from life they will demand a higher price to assume a risk of death than the purely pecuniary loss from dying, which is all the common law system tries to compensate for.[6]

There are, moreover, seemingly insurmountable practical difficulties to fitting the suggested method of damage valuation into a system in which the initiative in seeking legal redress rests with the victim of injury. Many of the "victims" of dangerous conduct under an ex ante approach would not even be aware of the danger to them, and the estate of someone who happened to be killed would have no special incentive to sue; all it could collect would be his ex ante risk premium — usually a small amount.

A final possibility is to infer the ex post cost from the ex ante cost. Suppose we know that the average person demands $100 in order to assume a .0001 risk of death. Can we infer that he values his life at $1 million? We can — at least for the purpose of setting tort damages for low-probability injuries (i.e., accidents) at the correct level, which is our purpose here. If the potential victim values the elimination of this .0001 risk at $100, then any precaution that would eliminate it at a cost of less than $100 would be efficient. In other words, PL is $100. Since P is .0001, L, which can be calculated by dividing $100 ($PL$) by .0001 ($P$), must be $1 million. If we make this the amount that the injurer who fails to take a precaution that would eliminate the risk at a cost of less than $100 must pay if death ensues as a result of his failure, we shall get the right amount of deterrence — and $1 million is therefore the correct valuation of life for tort purposes.

But this approach will not work when the probability of death is high. The fact that someone demands only $100 to incur a .0001 risk of death does not imply that he will demand only $100,000 to incur a 10 percent risk of death — or $1 million to incur a certainty of death. As we said earlier, most people would not accept any amount of money to give up their life on the spot. But if we infer from this that the value of life is infinite, then PL will also be infinite no matter how

---

6. See Bryan C. Conley, The Value of Human Life in the Demand for Safety, 66 Am. Econ. Rev. 45 (1976).

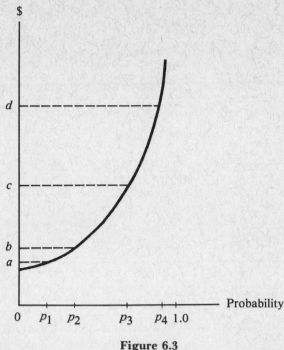

Figure 6.3

small P is, and people would never take any risks — an obviously false
description of human behavior. It would seem, therefore, that the value
of life (the vertical axis in Figure 6.3) rises faster than the risk of death
(the horizontal axis). If every increment of risk produced the same disutility, the function that relates disutility to risk would be a straight line.
The shape of the curve representing the function indicates that people
will demand much more money to take a large risk than the amount
computed by multiplying the money demanded to take a small risk by
the increment in risk. (Thus *cd* in Figure 6.3 is much larger than *ab*,
even though the risk increment compensated by *cd* is the same as that
compensated by *ab*.) This point will become important when we discuss
optimal penalties for murder and other crimes of violence, in the next
chapter.

Why should there be a nonlinear relationship between risk and utility?
Because the greater the risk of death, the less likely it is that the risk
taker will actually get to enjoy the use of the money being paid him
to take the risk. This is clearest of course when the risk is 100 percent:
then no finite amount of money can compensate the risk taker — unless
he is highly altruistic.[7]

7. What would be the shape of the curve in Figure 6.3 if the price were not the
price that the risk taker would demand to take the risk but the price he would pay to
avoid the risk?

§6.13   The Collateral Benefits (Collateral Source) Rule

If an accident insurance policy entitles me to receive $10,000 for a certain kind of accidental injury and I sustain that injury in an accident in which the injurer is negligent, I can both claim the $10,000 from the insurance company and obtain full damages (which, let us assume, are $10,000) from the injurer, provided I did not agree to assign my tort rights to the insurer (subrogation). To permit the defendant to set up my insurance policy as a bar to the action would result in underdeterrence. The economic cost of the accident, however defrayed, is $10,000, and if the judgment against him is zero, his incentive to spend up to $10,000 (discounted by the probability of occurrence) to prevent a similar accident in the future will be reduced. Less obviously, the double recovery is not a windfall to me. I bought the insurance policy at a price presumably equal to the expected cost of my injury plus the cost of writing the policy. The company could if it wished have excepted from the coverage of the policy accidents in which the injurer was liable to me for the cost of the injury, or it could have required me to assign to it any legal rights that I might have arising from an accident. In either case my premium would have been less.

Some courts have had trouble when the collateral benefit was not rendered pursuant to a contract but was "gratuitous." However, most gratuitous benefits turn out to be ones for which the beneficiary has paid indirectly. If an employer gives his injured employees medical treatment free of charge, this means only that the employer pays for their labor partly in money and partly in kind, so that the money wage would be higher if the "gratuitous" benefits were lower. (What about social security disability benefits?)

§6.14   Negligence With Liability Insurance and Accident Insurance; No-Fault Automobile Accident Compensation

The negligence system, whose dominant substantive and remedial features have been described in the previous sections of this chapter, has had a bad press for many years.[1] The principal criticism is that it is an expensive and inadequate compensation system. Attention naturally fo-

§6.14   1. For a forceful if dated attack, primarily economic, on the negligence system, see Guido Calabresi, The Costs of Accidents: A Legal and Economic Analysis (1970), especially pts. 4-5.

cuses on automobile accident cases, the most frequent type of negligence case. Studies show that administrative costs, mainly legal expenses, are a very substantial fraction of the total amounts paid to victims in settlements and lawsuits and that many people injured in automobile accidents receive little or no compensation — sometimes because the victim himself was negligent, sometimes because the defendant was uninsured and insolvent or was a hit-and-run driver and unknown.[2]

If compensation is the only purpose of the negligence system, it is a poor system, being both costly and incomplete. Its economic function, however, is not compensation but the deterrence of inefficient accidents. If the system yields substantial savings in accident costs, its heavy administrative costs, which relate primarily to the determination of liability — the determination whether the accident was uneconomical — may be justified. As for coverage, the deficiencies of the system could be remedied by wider purchase of accident insurance.

The deterrent impact of automobile damage awards is impaired by liability insurance, although, as we shall see, the policy implications of this point are less clear than one might have thought. Automobile liability insurance is now almost universal, although this is partly because states require drivers to buy liability insurance or present equivalent evidence of financial responsibility for accidents. (Requiring proof of financial responsibility is efficient; requiring liability insurance is not. Do you understand why?) But even without compulsion, liability insurance would be common. The prevalence of risk aversion is a necessary but, surprisingly, not sufficient condition for this phenomenon. Theoretically, there is a cheaper way to avoid the risk of being held liable for an automobile injury: Don't be negligent (why is this cheaper even if the insurance involves no administrative expense?). But because courts make mistakes, because negligence contains a strict liability component (the reasonable man rule), and because negligence has a stochastic (probabilistic) element, there is a risk of being adjudged negligent and, hence, a demand for insurance against liability for negligence.

With insurance, the cost of an accident to the negligent injurer is no longer the victim's loss; it is the present value of any premium increase that the injurer may experience as a result of being found negligent. As a result of information costs, regulatory hostility toward "discriminatory" premium rate structures, and governmentally mandated assigned-risk pools that allow even the most dangerous drivers to buy liability insurance at rates only slightly higher than normal, liability insurance premiums are not tailored with precision to the expected accident costs of particular drivers. Although the premiums are not uniform, the differences frequently reflect criteria, such as accident involvement (whether or not the insured was negligent) or what age group the insured belongs

2. See Alfred F. Conard et al., Automobile Accident Costs and Payments (1964).

to, that are only loosely related to negligence. The variance in expected accident costs within the classes is probably very high, so that the method of calculating liability insurance rates overdeters some drivers and underdeters others.

If the liability insurance market were not regulated, insurance companies would charge different premiums to their customers according to differences in the probability that a customer would, through his negligence, injure someone in an accident. The relationship of the insurer to the insured would be similar to that of an employer to an employee under the rule of respondeat superior — a rule generally thought acceptable for controlling negligence by employees. The insurance company, however, would probably have less control over the care of its insureds than an employer would have over the care of his employees, so there would be more accidents than in a system where liability insurance was forbidden. But if victims are fully compensated, liability insurance is efficient even though there are more accidents. The insurer and the insured are better off, and no one else is worse off.[3] The additional premium necessary to pay for the additional accident costs will generate an equal or greater utility in the form of reduced risk to risk-averse drivers (why?). Thus, while liability insurance does blunt the deterrent thrust of tort law somewhat,[4] this need not make it an inefficient system of accident control.

A related criticism of negligence is that it is unrealistic to expect people who are not deterred from careless conduct by fear of bodily injury to be deterred by fear of a money judgment, or, in the case where the negligence of the victim is a bar to recovery, by inability to obtain compensation for the injury from the injurer. Several observations on this point are in order.

1. The argument is inapplicable to injurers not themselves in any personal jeopardy, to employers of injurers (such as a trucking or taxi company), and to accidents where the only significant danger is to property.

2. It ignores the accident-prevention effect of liability insurance premium rates that are so high, reflecting the expected liability of the insured, that they discourage some people from becoming drivers. For example, the high premiums charged young male drivers delay their beginning to drive.[5]

3. See Steven Shavell, On Liability and Insurance, 13 Bell J. Econ. 120 (1982).

4. Though it need not, if insurance companies are efficient monitors of their insureds' safety behavior. For an interesting early discussion of this point see Fleming James, Jr., Accident Liability Reconsidered: The Impact of Liability Insurance, 57 Yale L.J. 549, 559–562 (1948).

5. For evidence of the deterrent effect of liability insurance premiums, see Richard W. Grayston, Deterrence in Automobile Liability Insurance (unpublished Ph.D. thesis, University of Chicago Graduate School of Business 1971), and the comprehensive review of empirical literature in Christopher J. Bruce, The Deterrent Effect of Automobile Insurance and Tort Law: A Survey of the Empirical Literature, 6 Law & Policy 67 (1984).

3. It implies that tort compensation is never full compensation, which if true would reinforce our earlier point that the tendency of tort damages, although so often criticized as excessive, is in fact to undercompensate the victims of serious accidents. If damages compensated the victim fully, he would be indifferent between being injured or not being injured. Notice that if victims are undercompensated by tort damages, liability insurance can create an externality, contrary to the earlier analysis.

4. The experiment with no-fault automobile accident compensation has yielded empirical evidence, discussed below, that tort liability does deter.

5. Although this is not a point about automobile accidents, it shouldn't be forgotten that negligence has a much broader domain. Very few commentators think that medical malpractice or products liability has no effect on the behavior of doctors and manufacturers respectively.

Criticisms of the negligence system as it operates in automobile cases have led to the passage in many states of no-fault automobile accident compensation laws. A surprising feature of these laws from an economic standpoint is that they are not at all concerned with creating better incentives for accident avoidance. They do not seek to make the tort system a better deterrent of unsafe conduct but instead seek to increase the coverage of the system and to reduce the cost of insurance. These goals are inconsistent with each other as well as with the goal of reducing the number of accidents.

The Keeton-O'Connell plan,[6] the model for many of the statutes, illustrates the dilemma. Under the plan, every motorist is required to carry basic protection that entitles him in the event of an accident to recover his medical expenses plus lost earnings, regardless of the injurer's negligence or his own freedom from negligence. Pain and suffering are not compensated, and any collateral benefits are deducted. The victim may waive basic protection and sue in tort in the usual way if he sustains more than $10,000 in damages other than for pain and suffering. Basic protection is first party (accident) rather than third party (liability) insurance. The motorist pays premiums to and collects damages from his own insurer. The injurer and his insurance company are liable only if the victim waives basic protection and sues in tort.

Why exclude damages for pain and suffering and require deduction of collateral benefits? Apparently not because the authors do not consider pain and suffering to be real losses, or consider collateral benefits to be pure windfalls, for they do not exclude these items in serious accidents. But they needed some way of reducing the average damage award in order to prevent the plan from increasing the cost of insurance.

6. Robert E. Keeton & Jeffrey O'Connell, Basic Protection for the Traffic Victim: A Blueprint for Reforming Automobile Insurance (1965).

Because the plan compensates victims of faultless drivers and victims themselves at fault, its coverage is broader than that of the tort system. Hence if the average claim were no smaller under the plan than under the existing tort system, the total amount paid out in claims, and therefore insurance premium costs, would probably be greater (even assuming lower administrative costs) than under the present system. The savings from the deduction of collateral benefits may prove transitory; people may reduce their existing accident insurance to offset the accident insurance that they are forced to buy under basic protection. The strategy of the plan, however, is clear: to increase the number of accident victims who are compensated but to reduce the average compensation.

The plan is inimical to proper safety incentives. Companies writing basic protection insurance would want to charge relatively low premiums to drivers, including careless drivers, of large, heavy automobiles who have no dependents; such drivers are less likely to sustain heavy accident costs than drivers — even careful ones — of small, vulnerable cars who have large families. The result would be to increase the incentive of the second group to take precautions but reduce the incentive of the first group. Yet the cost of accident avoidance may be larger for members of the second group than for members of the first, many of whom could reduce expected accident costs to other people, at relatively low cost to themselves, either by driving more carefully or by substituting a lighter car.

The proponents of no fault argue that deterrence is the province of the criminal law. Since it is unlawful to insure against criminal penalties, the effect of liability insurance in sapping the deterrent efficacy of negligence liability is eliminated. But a greater emphasis on criminal punishment of negligent participants in automobile accidents would undermine the compensatory purpose of the plans. If the negligent victim of an accident is fined, his net compensation is reduced by the amount of the fine, and as a result is no longer equal to his injuries. In addition, the burden and hence costs of proving negligent conduct would be higher in a proceeding to impose a noninsurable penalty, since the court would naturally be sensitive to the quandary of the mistakenly accused defendant unable to protect himself by insurance against the consequences of an erroneous punishment.

A recent study found that states whose no-fault statutes place severe restrictions on tort liability can expect 10-15 percent more automobile accident deaths.[7] This result may seem weird since no-fault statutes leave tort liability intact in death cases. Bear in mind, however, the probabilistic

7. See Elisabeth M. Landes, Insurance, Liability, and Accidents: A Theoretical and Empirical Investigation of the Effect of No-Fault on Accidents, 25 J. Law & Econ. 49 (1982). For criticism, see Jeffrey O'Connell & Saul Levmore, A Reply to Landes: A Faulty Study of No-Fault's Effect on Fault?, 48 Mo. L. Rev. 649 (1983). Bruce's study, *supra* note 5, presents considerable evidence supporting a deterrent theory of tort law.

character of care: If no fault induces more careless driving, there will be more accidents, and some fraction will be fatal.[8]

§6.15 Intentional Torts

This chapter up to now has dealt with accidental, or as they are often called in the law unintentional, torts. We have now to consider the other great category of tort law — intentional torts. As with many legal distinctions, this one is not analytically precise, in part because the term intentional is vague. Most accidental injuries are intentional in the sense that the injurer knew that he could have reduced the probability of the accident by taking additional precautions. The element of intention is unmistakable when the tortfeasor is an enterprise that can predict from past experience that it will inflict a certain number of accidental injuries every year. Conversely, in many intentional torts the element of intention is severely attenuated, as when a surgeon who unwittingly exceeds the limits of the patient's express or implied consent to surgical procedures is held to have committed a battery. In the usual medical battery case, the issue is whether there was a sufficient emergency to justify a procedure to which the patient's consent had not been obtained in advance. This in turn depends on whether the costs of delay (such as the risk that the patient's condition might deteriorate, and the added danger of again subjecting him to a general anesthetic) exceeded the value to the patient of an opportunity to consider whether to undergo the procedure; if so, implied consent to the procedure will be found. The case is much like the property and contract cases discussed in previous chapters — especially the implied contract cases discussed at the end of Chapter 4. It does not isolate a functionally distinct form of conduct.

Another example of how an intentional tort may involve simply a conflict between legitimate activities is provided by the spring gun cases. The defendant in *Bird v. Holbrook*,[1] owned a valuable tulip garden about a mile from his home. Although the garden was walled, some tulips had been stolen, so he rigged a spring gun. A neighbor's peahen escaped and strayed into the garden. A young man, the plaintiff in the case, followed the peahen into the garden in an attempt to recapture it for

8. For other economic analysis of no-fault plans, see Automobile No-Fault Insurance: A Study by the Special Committee on Automobile Insurance Legislation (Am. Bar Assn. 1978).

§6.15 1. 4 Bing. 628, 130 Eng. Rep. 911 (C.P. 1828), discussed in Richard A. Posner, Killing or Wounding to Protect a Property Interest, 14 J. Law & Econ. 201, 209-211 (1971).

its owner, tripped the spring gun, and was injured. The court held that the defendant was liable for the plaintiff's injury because of his failure to post notices that a spring gun had been set. The incident had occurred in the daytime.

The issue in the case, at least as an economist would frame it, was the proper accommodation of two legitimate activities, growing tulips and raising peacocks. The defendant had a substantial investment in the tulip garden; he lived at a distance; and the wall had not proved effective against thieves. In an era of negligible police protection, a spring gun may have been the most cost-effective means of protection for the tulips. But since spring guns do not discriminate between the thief and the innocent trespasser, they deter owners of domestic animals from pursuing their animals onto other people's property and so increase the costs (enclosure costs or straying losses) of keeping animals. The court in the *Bird* case implied an ingenious though perhaps fragile accommodation: One who sets a spring gun must post notices that he has done so. Then owners of animals will not be reluctant to pursue their animals onto property not so posted. A notice will be of no avail at night, but animals are more likely to be secured then and in any event few owners would chase their straying animals after dark. The analysis thus turns out to be the same as in a negligence case — the archetypal unintentional tort case.

There is, however, a set of intentional torts that are economically distinct from unintentional torts. The set consists of such torts as trespass (see §3.6 *supra*), assault,[2] simple battery (for example, mugging, as distinct from medical battery or the technical battery that is committed in an illegal prizefight), fraud, and conversion (the tort counterpart of theft) — torts that resemble, sometimes very closely, such common law crimes as rape, murder, robbery, false pretenses, and larceny. These torts and the corresponding list of crimes involve not a conflict between legitimate (productive) activities but a coerced transfer of wealth to the defendant occurring in a setting of low transaction costs. Such conduct is inefficient because it violates the principle developed in earlier chapters that where market transaction costs are low, people should be required to use the market if they can and to desist from the conduct if they can't. For example, if conversion were freely permitted, property owners would spend a great deal of money on devices for the protection of property and would substitute toward otherwise less valuable goods that happened to be harder to steal, while thieves would spend large sums to neutralize the owners' protective measures. The costs involved in allocating resources by these means would greatly exceed those of

2. Making a threatening gesture that places a person in apprehension of an imminent battery. What economic interest is protected by making assault a tort, given that the victim can recover damages for assault even if he was not actually frightened by the gesture? See Richard A. Posner, The Economics of Justice 285-286 (1981).

voluntary exchange. Conversion would be a little more efficient if the converter, like the railroad when it "takes" the farmer's crops through spark damage, were required to prove that the value to him of the object taken was greater than its value to the previous owner. But it would still be a less efficient method of resource allocation than the market, so it is forbidden too. We tolerate it in the engine spark case only because there the cost of market transactions is higher than the cost of legal transactions.

This analysis shows that theft, or conversion, is not just a costless transfer payment — the objection to which must therefore be sought outside of economics — when the thief values the good stolen at least as highly as the owner of the good does. If such forced transfers are allowed, owners will spend resources on protection, and thieves will spend resources on defeating the owners' efforts. Consider a good worth $100 to both the owner and the thief, and suppose that if the owner spends nothing on protection the thief could steal the good by expending $20 in time and burglar tools. Suppose, too, that knowing this the owner spends $30 on precautions, thereby reducing the probability of theft to 50 percent (the expected benefit of the precaution thus is $50, and is greater than the cost), that the thief can raise the probability to 60 percent by spending another $5 in time and tools (which it will pay him to do), and that there is no other protective measure that the owner could take that would be cost-justified (nevertheless the $30 he has spent already is a good investment). The result is that the owner and the thief will together have invested $55 in trying respectively to prevent and to accomplish the transfer of the good. The sum is totally wasted from a social standpoint; this waste is the economic objection to theft.

The Hand Formula is helpful in illuminating the difference between intentional torts that are qualitatively different from unintentional torts and those that are not. Consider the case where a railroad, because it runs many trains every year, knows with a confidence approaching certainty that it will kill 20 people a year at railroad crossings. Is it therefore an intentional tortfeasor? It is not, either in law or in economics. The same thing that makes PL high — the scale of the railroad's operations — makes B high. The ratio of B to PL is unaffected by the scale of the potential injurer's operation, and it is the ratio that enables us to differentiate between intentional and unintentional torts in an economically relevant sense.

This can be seen by fitting a "real" intentional tort case to the Hand Formula. I want a car, and I decide to save time by stealing your car. B is not only lower than in an accident case; it is actually a negative number, because rather than saving resources by injuring the victim (implying a positive B) I would save resources by not injuring the victim (implying a negative B), since it must cost me something to steal the car. (Of course there is an offsetting gain, or I would not steal it, but that gain does not represent a net social benefit, because it is offset by the loss of the car to the victim.) *P,* furthermore, is very high — much higher than in accident case — because wanting to do someone an injury makes it much more likely that an injury will occur than if the injury if it does occur will simply be an undesired by-product of another activity, such as carrying freight from one point to another. Thus, not only is *B* lower than *PL* in a case of intentional wrongdoing, as it is in a case of negligent wrongdoing; it is dramatically lower.

This has two important implications for legal policy.

1. We would expect, and find, the law to be much more willing to award punitive damages in "real" intentional tort cases than in cases, whether classified as intentional or unintentional, that lack the characteristics of a "real" intentional tort case, that is, that do not involve a pure coercive transfer. We know that in a strict liability case punitive damages would lead to overdeterrence. Less obviously, the same thing is true in a simple negligence case. Because of judicial mistake, the strict liability component in negligence (the reasonable man rule), and the probabilistic nature of care, negligence cannot be avoided just by spending *B* on care. So if *PL* is artificially raised by adding punitive damages to *L,* potential injurers will be induced to spend more than *B* on accident prevention, and that is inefficient. But since the gap between *B* and *PL* is so much larger in the "real" intentional tort case, the danger of deterring socially valuable conduct by making the damage award greater than *L* is minimized and other policies come to the fore, such as making sure that the damage award is an effective deterrent by resolving all doubts as to the plaintiff's actual damages in his favor; this can be done by adding a dollop of punitive damages to the estimate of his actual damages. Moreover, since we want to channel resource allocation through the market as much as possible, we want to make sure that I am not indifferent between stealing and buying my neighbor's car. We do this by making the damage award greater than the value of the car so that I do not consider conversion an acceptable substitute for purchase. Punitive damages are one way of doing this. Another way, also common in intentional tort cases, is to make the tortfeasor pay the victim what the thing taken was worth to the tortfeasor. This is the restitutionary measure of damages mentioned in Chapter 4. It is used in intentional tort cases to try to make the tort worthless to the tortfeasor and thereby channel resource allocation through the market.

2. There is no reason to allow a defense of contributory negligence in what we are calling a "real" intentional tort case (pure coercive transfer), since the cost of avoidance is plainly lower to the injurer than to the victim — is indeed negative to the injurer and positive to the victim. The victim cannot be the lower-cost avoider. Stated otherwise, the victim's optimal care is always zero.

There are intermediate cases between the pure coercive transfer, with its negative B, and the ordinary negligence case, with its B positive though lower than PL, or a strict liability case where B may actually be greater than PL. Take the case of recklessness. I decide to rest my eyes while driving, and plow at high speed into a flock of pedestrians. B is positive but extremely low, while P and L are both extremely high. The "resolve doubts" argument for punitive damages is in play, as is the argument against allowing a defense of contributory negligence. So we are not surprised to find that in such a case the law does allow punitive damages to be awarded and does not allow a defense of contributory negligence.

Thus far in our discussion of intentional torts the emphasis has been on acquisitive torts — conversion, robbing (conversion plus assault, in tort terms), killing for money, etc. But some intentional torts have a different motivation: interdependent utilities. We encountered interdependent positive utilities in Chapter 5. Here we are interested in interdependent negative utilities. A, to humiliate B, his enemy, spits in his face. There is no transfer of wealth. But A's utility is increased by reducing B's utility. If the increase in A's utility is greater than the reduction in B's utility (which is unlikely — especially in a murder case (why?)), the transaction is utility maximizing. But it is not wealth maximizing, and it is not lawful. This is an interesting example of the occasional divergence between efficiency and utility as legal goals.

§6.16   Defamation

The tort of defamation is an interesting mixture of intent, negligence, and strict liability and has other economic properties that make it a suitable capstone to this long chapter. It is usually classified as an intentional tort, because writing or speaking critically about a person is a deliberate act, and yet it has a strong flavor of strict liability, as in the rule that it is no defense that the defendant may have made a reasonable effort not to defame the plaintiff. In the celebrated case of *Jones v. E. Hulton & Co.*,[1] the author of a fictitious newspaper story accidentally gave a character in the story the name of a real person, Artemus Jones, who sued for libel, and won by showing that his neighbors thought the article was about him. Jones was entirely helpless to avoid the injury, and although the newspaper had been careful, the writing of fiction in the guise of truth is not so valuable an activity that the injury could not have been avoided at reasonable cost by a change in that activity. Also, the incident had a flavor of recklessness. Like a man who shoots

§6.16   1. [1909] 2 K.B. 444, *aff'd*, [1910] A.C. 20.

out the windows of a house he thinks is unoccupied and accidentally kills someone, the newspaper was libeling what it thought was a nonexistent person, but someone with the name and some characteristics of the fictitious character would be hit by the blast, and was. Maybe, then, even in a negligence analysis the newspaper would have been found liable. But the newspaper *distributor* would not have been liable to Jones unless negligent in failing to spot the libel; this makes sense because it is hard to see what change in activity level would be optimal for the distributor.

The law of defamation has several exceptions that may seem puzzling, and let us consider two of them that have an interesting economic rationale. The first is the rule that group libels (e.g., "All doctors are quacks") are not actionable. A group libel is not likely to hurt members of the group, because substitution away from an entire trade is so much more costly than substitution away from an individual. If the libel were, "Dr. Jones is a quack," then Jones's patients might and could easily switch to other doctors. But what can they do if all doctors are quacks? They might as well stick with old Jones, whom at least they know. The second, and oddly related, rule is that you cannot defame the dead. The reason is that defamation is injury to reputation; reputation is (as we saw in discussing the tort of invasion of privacy back in Chapter 3) a basis for inducing others to engage in market or nonmarket transactions with one; so if one is dead, and thus has ceased transacting, the injury has ceased. It is a little as if one were disabled from a job that was about to be phased out anyway. Of course, if the libel were that one had an inheritable disease, the adverse consequences would not terminate with death, and the law recognizes an exception for such cases.

The law treats written defamations (libel) more harshly than oral (slander) and this has seemed to many observers anomalous in the age of mass radio and television audiences. But the cost of preventing defamation is much lower in a written than in an oral communication. Writing is a more deliberative activity; there is time to consider the possible impact of one's words, as there often is not in speaking. So there is less danger that liability for defamation will deter socially valuable communications that are written than that it will deter those that are spoken. This implies, incidentally — and there is judicial support for the position — that a radio or television speech read from a script rather than spoken spontaneously should be classified as libel rather than slander. (What if it is spoken from notes?)

A word, now, on defenses in defamation cases. Truth, of course, is one; and this is thoroughly consistent with the analysis of reputation in Chapter 3. There is also the defense of privilege. A good example is the employer's privilege to give a character reference for an employee that may contain defamatory material. The benefit of a candid reference would enure to the prospective rather than current employer, and it would be hard for the former to compensate the latter; although in principle he could promise to indemnify the latter for any damages and costs resulting from a defamation suit, the benefits are too trivial to make such arrangements worthwhile. The law's answer is to externalize some of the costs of giving a character reference in order to encourage the conferral on the prospective employer of an external benefit.[2] The privilege is not absolute; it is forfeited if the employer giving the character reference knew it contained false aspersions on the employee. Here there is no external benefit conferred (why not?), so neither is there any rationale for allowing a cost to be externalized. But truth is an absolute defense, because there is an external benefit even if the defendant thought he was lying.

Suggested Readings

1. Guido Calabresi, The Costs of Accidents: A Legal and Economic Analysis (1970).

2. ———, First Party, Third Party, and Product Liability Systems: Can Economic Analysis Tell Us Anything About Them?, 69 Ia. L. Rev. 833 (1984).

3. Peter A. Diamond, Single Activity Accidents, 3 J. Leg. Stud. 107 (1974).

4. Mark F. Grady, A New Positive Economic Theory of Negligence, 92 Yale L.J. 799 (1983).

5. William M. Landes & Richard A. Posner, Joint and Multiple Tortfeasors: An Economic Analysis, 9 J. Leg. Stud. 517 (1980).

6. ———, An Economic Theory of Intentional Torts, 1 Intl. Rev. Law & Econ. 127 (1981).

7. ———, The Positive Economic Theory of Tort Law, 15 Ga. L. Rev. 851 (1982).

8. ———, Causation in Tort Law: An Economic Approach, 12 J. Leg. Stud. 109 (1983).

9. ———, A Positive Economic Analysis of Products Liability, J. Leg. Stud. (forthcoming 1986).

10. A. Mitchell Polinsky & William P. Rogerson, Products Liability, Consumer Misperceptions, and Market Power, 14 Bell J. Econ. 581 (1983).

11. Samuel A. Rea, Jr., Lump-Sum Versus Periodic Damage Awards, 10 J. Leg. Stud. 131 (1981).

12. Steven Shavell, Strict Liability Versus Negligence, 9 J. Leg. Stud. 1 (1980).

---

2. Cf. discussion of defense of public necessity, §6.4 *supra*.

13. ————, An Analysis of Causation and the Scope of Liability in the Law of Torts, 9 J. Leg. Stud. 463 (1980).

14. The Economics of Medical Malpractice (Simon Rottenberg ed. 1978).

Problems

1. Evaluate the following proposition: The standard measure of damages in tort cases is equivalent to the contract standard of reliance damages, and therefore results in underdeterrence of tortious conduct.

2. Appraise the following statement from the standpoint of economics:

> Indeed one of the major practical concerns created by the increase in malpractice insurance premiums is the inability of young physicians starting out in practice to meet their insurance costs, which are, after all, only one of the many costs to be covered by the gross income from their practice.
>
> In general, it is safe to say that too much has been made of the ability of physicians and insurance companies to pass on the costs of increased malpractice losses. To the extent that these losses arise out of incidents in past years, there is no way for either physicians or insurance companies to recoup these "sunk costs" by charging high rates for future services. . . .

Richard A. Epstein, Medical Malpractice: The Case for Contract, 1 Am. Bar Foun. Res. J. 87, 88 n.3 (1976).

3. Melvin M. Belli, The Use of Demonstrative Evidence 33 (1951), challenges the practice of discounting future earnings to present value. Belli argues that the plaintiff's earnings should be multiplied by the period of the plaintiff's disability and then multiplied again to reflect the estimated increase in the cost of living during the period of disability. Is this the correct economic approach? How would you argue to a judge or jury that it is not?

4. An airplane crashes as the result of a nonnegligent defect in an instrument supplied by A. The airplane was manufactured by B from various components, including the instrument supplied by A, and is operated by C, an airline. What economic difference does it make, if any, whether A is liable for the damages resulting from the crash, or B, or C? Cf. Goldberg v. Kollsman Instrument Corp., 12 N.Y.2d 432, 191 N.E.2d 81 (1963); §4.5 *supra*.

5. Suppose there is a class of automobile accidents in which the injurers are all very wealthy men. The opportunity costs of their time are so great that the expected accident costs are lower than the costs to them of preventing the accidents by driving more slowly, slower driving being the only method by which the accidents could be prevented. In these circumstances, which rule of liability would be more efficient: strict

liability, with no defense of contributory negligence, or no liability at all?

6. Is it arguable that there is a greater economic justification for strict products liability to bystanders than for strict products liability to purchasers of the product?

7. Suppose a doctor chances upon an injured person lying in the street in great pain. The doctor insists as a precondition to treating him that the injured person execute a waiver of the doctor's liability for any malpractice claim arising from the treatment. Should the courts enforce the waiver?

8. Should punitive damages in tort cases be proportioned to
(1) the defendant's wealth;
(2) the amount of the compensatory damages awarded in the case; or
(3) neither?

9. If the tort system were deemed a method of social insurance rather than one of deterrence of uneconomical accidents, would awards in tort cases be on average higher or lower than under the deterrence rationale?

10. It has often been observed that when miners are trapped in a coal mine or a mountaineer is stranded on a mountain top society will devote enormous resources to saving their lives — resources seemingly disproportionate to society's expenditures on preventing people from endangering themselves. Explain the paradox.

11. The chapter points out that ordinarily a potential accident victim is entitled to assume that potential injurers are using due care, and therefore he need not take precautions that would be optimal only if potential injurers were behaving negligently. Yet there is an exception for the case where the danger is palpable, as where a traveler at a crossing, though he sees a speeding train bearing down on him, takes no more precautions than he would take to prevent injury from a safely operated train. Explain the economics of this exception and compare it to the doctrine of last clear chance.

CHAPTER 7

CRIMINAL LAW[1]

§7.1. The Economic Nature and Function of Criminal Law

The types of wrongful conduct examined in previous chapters, mainly torts and breaches of contract, subject the wrongdoer to having to pay money damages to his victim, or sometimes to being prohibited on pain of contempt from continuing or repeating the wrong (i.e., enjoined) — but in either case only if the victim sues. But crimes are prosecuted by the state, and the criminal is forced to pay a fine to the state or to undergo a nonpecuniary sanction such as being imprisoned. Trial procedure is also different in the two kinds of case, but examination of the procedural differences will be deferred to Chapter 21. For now our interest is in why there should be distinctive sanctions, sought by the state, for some types of wrongdoing and what substantive doctrines such sanctions entail.

There are five principal types of wrongful conduct made criminal in our legal system.

1. Intentional torts, examined in the last chapter, that represent a pure coercive transfer either of wealth or utility from victim to wrongdoer. Murder, robbery, burglary, larceny, rape, assault and battery, mayhem, false pretenses, and most other common law crimes (i.e., crimes punishable under the English common law) are essentially instances of such intentional torts as assault, battery, trespass, and conversion, although we shall see that the state-of-mind and injury requirements for the criminal counterpart of the intentional tort sometimes differ. Here, however, are two somewhat more problematic examples of crime-as-pure-coercive-transfer:

1. On the rules and principles, respectively, of the criminal law, see Wayne R. LaFave & Austin W. Scott, Jr., Handbook on Criminal Law (1972), and H.L.A. Hart, Punishment and Responsibility: Essays in the Philosophy of Law (1968).

(1) *Counterfeiting.* This can be viewed as a form of theft by false pretenses, the false pretense being that the payor is paying with legal tender. If the counterfeiting is discovered, the victim is whoever ends up holding the worthless currency. If it is not discovered, the loss is more widely diffused. Since the amount of money in circulation is now larger than it was before the counterfeiting relative to the total stock of goods in society, everyone's money is worth less (inflation); everyone but the counterfeiter is a loser. In addition to this coerced transfer, counterfeiting imposes the usual deadweight costs (such as?).

(2) *Rape.* Suppose a rapist derives extra pleasure from the coercive character of his act. Then there would be no market substitute for rape and it could be argued therefore that rape is not a pure coercive transfer and should not be punished criminally. But the argument would be weak:

(a) Given that there are heavy penalties for rape, the rapes that take place — that have not been deterred — may indeed be weighted toward a form of rape for which there are no consensual substitutes; it does not follow that the rape that is deterred is generally of this character. The prevention of rape is essential to protect the marriage market discussed in Chapter 5 and more generally to secure property rights in women's persons. Allowing rape would be the equivalent of communalizing property rights in women. More generally, crimes of passion bear the same relation to informal markets in human relations as acquisitive crimes such as theft, and murder for gain, bear to explicit markets: They bypass them, which reduces efficiency.

(b) Allowing rape would lead to heavy expenditures on protecting women, as well as expenditures on overcoming those protections. The expenditures would be largely offsetting, and to that extent socially wasted.

(c) Given the economist's definition of value (see Chapter 1), the fact that the rapist cannot find a consensual substitute does not mean that he values the rape more than the victim disvalues it. There is a difference between a coerced transaction that has no consensual substitute and a coerced transaction necessary to overcome the costs of a consensual transaction.

Now back to our typology.

2. Other coerced transfers, such as price fixing (on which see Chapters 9–10) and tax evasion (on which see Chapter 17), the wrongfulness of which may not have been recognized at common law.

3. Voluntary, and therefore presumptively (but only presumptively, as we know from Chapters 3 through 6) value maximizing, exchanges incidental to activities that the state has outlawed. Examples of such exchanges are prostitution, selling pornography, selling babies for adoption, selling regulated transportation services at prices not listed in the carrier's published tariffs, and trafficking in narcotics.

4. Certain menacing but nontortious preparatory acts, such as unsuccessfully attempting or conspiring to murder someone where the victim is not injured and the elements of a tortious attempt are not present (as they would not be if, for example, the victim did not know of the attempt at the time it was made).

5. Conduct that if allowed would complicate other forms of common law regulation. Examples are leaving the scene of an accident and fraudulently concealing assets from a judgment creditor.

Why, though, cannot all five categories be left to the tort law? An answer leaps to mind for categories 3 and 4: No one is hurt. But this is a superficial answer; we could allow whomever the law was intended to protect to sue for punitive damages. A better answer is that detection is difficult where there is no victim to report the wrongdoing and testify against the wrongdoer. This answer is not complete. Punitive damages can be adjusted upward to take account of the difficulty of detection; in principle this device could take care of category 5 crimes as well. But (as we shall see) the higher the optimal level of punitive damages, the less likely it is that they will be a feasible sanction. Another question about categories 3 and 4, however, is, why punish acts that don't hurt anybody? For category 3 the answer lies outside of economics; it is difficult for an economist to understand why, if a crime is truly "victimless," the criminal should be punished. (Of course, ostensibly victimless crimes may, like other contractual exchanges, have third party effects; the sale of liquor to a drunk driver is an example.) For category 4 the answer is bound up with the question — to which we can now turn — why tort law is not adequate to deal with categories 1 and 2 (coerced transfers in violation of common law or statutory principles).

We know from the last chapter that the proper sanction for a pure coercive transfer such as theft is something greater than the law's estimate of the victim's loss — the extra something being designed to confine transfers to the market whenever market transaction costs are not prohibitive. We can be more precise: The extra something should be the difference between the victim's loss and the injurer's gain, and then some.

To illustrate, suppose B has a jewel worth $1,000 to him but $10,000 to A, who steals it ("converts" it, in tort parlance). We want to channel transactions in jewelry into the market, and can do this by making sure that the coerced transfer is a losing proposition to A.[1] Making A liable to pay damages of $10,000 will almost do this, but not quite; A will be indifferent between stealing and buying, so he might just as well steal as buy. (How will attitude toward risk affect his choice?) So let us add something on, and make the damages $11,000. But of course

<hr/>

§7.1 1. Of course, if subjective values were as readily determinable as this example suggests, there would be less reason to force transactions into the market. It is the superiority of the market to the courts in determining subjective values that provides the major reason for the law's seeking to channel resource allocation through the market wherever possible.

the jewel might be worth less to A than to B (A is not planning to pay for it, after all), in which event a smaller fine would do the trick of deterring A. If the jewel were worth only $500 to him, damages of $501 should be enough. But as a court can't determine subjective values, it probably will want to base damages on the market value of the thing in question and then add on a hefty bonus (just how hefty is examined in the next section of this chapter) to take account of the possibility that the thief may place a higher subjective value on the thing.

In the case of crimes that cause death or even just a substantial risk of death, optimal damages will often be astronomical. Turn back to Figure 6.3 in Chapter 6. A normal person will demand an extremely large amount of money to assume a substantial risk of immediate death — an infinite amount, if the probability is one. Even when a person sets out deliberately to kill another, the probability of death is significantly less than one. But it is much higher than in most accident cases. And we know that the relation between risk and compensation is not linear. If A will accept $1 in compensation for a .0001 chance of being accidentally killed by B, it does not follow that he will demand only $10,000 to let B murder him.

In figuring optimal damages for pure coercive transfers, moreover, we have ignored the problem of concealment. Accidents, being a by-product of lawful, public activities, usually are difficult to conceal; breaches of contract usually are impossible to conceal. But when the tortfeasor's entire purpose is to take something of value from someone else, he will naturally try to conceal what he is doing, and will often succeed. The formula for deciding how much to award in damages if the probability that the tortfeasor will actually be caught and forced to pay the damages is less than one is $D = L/p$, where D is the optimal damage award, L is the harm caused by the tortfeasor in the case in which he is caught (including any adjustment to discourage bypassing the market by coercing wealth transfers), and p is the probability of being caught and made to pay the optimal damage award. If $p = 1$, L and D are the same amount. But if, for example, $L = \$10,000$ and $p = .1$, meaning that nine times out of ten the tortfeasor escapes the clutches of the law, then D, the optimal penalty, is $100,000. Only then is the expected penalty cost to the prospective tortfeasor (pD) equal to the harm of his act (L).

Once the damages in the pure coercive transfer case are adjusted upward to discourage efforts to bypass the market, to recognize the nonlinear relationship between risk of death and compensation for bearing the risk, and to correct for concealment, it becomes apparent that the optimal damages will often be very great — greater, in many cases, than the tortfeasor's ability to pay. Three responses are possible, all of which society uses. One is to impose disutility in nonmonetary forms, such as imprisonment or death. Another is to reduce the probability of concealment by maintaining a police force to investigate crimes. A third, which involves both the maintenance of a police force and the punishment of preparatory acts (category 4), is to prevent criminal activity before it occurs. If for reasons discussed in Chapter 22 public policing is more efficient than private, the state is in the enforcement picture and has a claim to any monetary penalties imposed. Hence these penalties are paid to the state as fines, rather than to the victims of crime as damages. The victims can seek damages if the crime is also a tort, whether common law or statutory.

In cases where tort remedies are an adequate deterrent, because optimal tort damages, including any punitive damages, are within the ability to pay of the potential defendant, there is no need to invoke criminal penalties, which, as explained below, are costlier than civil penalties even when just a fine is imposed. The criminal (= tortious) conduct probably will be deterred; and if for reasons explained in the last chapter it is not even though the tort remedy is set at the correct level and there is no solvency problem to interfere with it, there still is no social gain from using the criminal sanction (why not?). Although in some cases, notably antitrust and securities cases, affluent defendants are both prosecuted criminally and sued civilly, criminal sanctions generally are reserved, as theory predicts, for cases where the tort remedy bumps up against a solvency limitation.

This means that the criminal law is primarily designed for the nonaffluent; the affluent are kept in line by tort law. This suggestion is not refuted by the fact that fines are a common criminal penalty. Fines are much lower than the corresponding tort damage judgments, and this for two reasons. The government invests resources in raising the probability of criminal punishment above that of a tort suit, which makes the optimal fine lower than the punitive damages that would be optimal in the absence of such an investment. And a fine is a more severe punishment than its dollar cost. Every criminal punishment imposes some nonpecuniary disutility in the form of a stigma, enhanced by such rules as forbidding a convicted felon to vote. There is no corresponding stigma to a tort judgment.

§7.2 Optimal Criminal Sanctions

In order to design a set of optimal criminal sanctions, we need a model of the criminal's behavior. The model can be very simple: A person commits a crime because the expected benefits of the crime to him exceed the expected costs. The benefits are the various tangible (in the case of crimes of pecuniary gain) or intangible (in the case of so-called crimes of passion) satisfactions from the criminal act. The costs include various out-of-pocket expenses (for guns, burglar tools, masks, etc.), the opportunity costs of the criminal's time, and the expected costs of criminal punishment. The last of these costs will be the focus of our analysis, but it is well to mention the others in order to bring out the possibility of controlling the level of criminal activity other than simply by the amount of law enforcement activity and the severity of punishment. For example, the benefits of theft, and hence its incidence, might be reduced by a redistribution of wealth away from the wealthy. Similarly, the opportunity costs of crime could be increased, and thus the incidence of crime reduced, by reducing unemployment, which would increase the gains from lawful work. The out-of-pocket expenses of crime could also be increased, for example by imposing a heavy tax on handguns.

The notion of the criminal as a rational calculator will strike many readers as highly unrealistic, especially when applied to criminals having little education or to crimes not committed for pecuniary gain. But as emphasized in Chapter 1, the test of a theory is not the realism of its assumptions but its predictive power. A growing empirical literature on crime has shown that criminals respond to changes in opportunity costs, in the probability of apprehension, in the severity of punishment, and in other relevant variables as if they were indeed the rational calculators of the economic model — and this regardless of whether the crime is committed for pecuniary gain or out of passion, or by well educated or poorly educated people.[1]

We saw earlier that the criminal sanction ought to be so contrived that the criminal is made worse off by committing the act. But now a series of qualifications has to be introduced. Suppose I lose my way in the woods and, as an alternative to starving, enter an unoccupied cabin and steal a trivial amount of food which I find there. Do we really want to make the punishment for this theft death, on the theory that the crime saved my life, and therefore no lesser penalty would deter? Of course not. The problem is that while the law of theft generally punishes takings in settings of low transaction costs, in this example the costs of transacting with the absent owner of the cabin are prohibitive. One approach would be to define theft so as to exclude such examples; and there is in fact in the criminal law a defense of necessity that probably could be invoked successfully in this example (see §7.5 *infra*). But as we shall see in Chapter 20, the costs of attempting so detailed a specification of the crime might be very great, and the alternative is to employ a more general, albeit somewhat overinclusive, definition but set the

§7.2   1. A useful but out-of-date summary of this literature is Gordon Tullock, Does Punishment Deter Crime?, Public Interest 103 (summer 1974); a recent but more technical summary is David J. Pyle, The Economics of Crime and Law Enforcement, chs. 3-4 (1983). The leading study remains Isaac Ehrlich, Participation in Illegitimate Activities: An Economic Analysis, in Essays in the Economics of Crime and Punishment 68 (Gary S. Becker & William M. Landes eds. 1974).

expected punishment cost at a level that will not deter the occasional crime that is value maximizing.

There is a related reason for putting a ceiling on criminal punishments such that not all crimes are deterred. If there is a risk either of accidental violation of the criminal law (and there is, for any crime that involves an element of negligence or strict liability) or of legal error, a very severe penalty will induce people to forgo socially desirable activities at the borderline of criminal activity. For example, if the penalty for driving more than 55 m.p.h. were death, people would drive too slowly (or not at all) to avoid an accidental violation or an erroneous conviction. True, if the category of criminal acts is limited through the concept of intentionality and through defenses such as necessity to cases where, in Hand Formula terms, there is a very great disparity between B and PL, the risk of either accident or error will be slight and the legal system can feel freer in setting heavy penalties. But not totally free; if the consequences of error are sufficiently enormous, even a very slight risk of error will generate avoidance measures that may be socially very costly. And as there are costs of underinclusion if the requirements of proof of guilt are set very high, it may make sense to make proof easier but at the same time to make the penalty less severe in order to reduce the costs of avoidance and error.

Once the expected punishment cost for a crime is determined, it becomes necessary to choose a combination of probability and severity of punishment that will impose that cost on the would-be offender. Let us begin with fines. An expected punishment cost of $1,000 can be imposed by combining a fine of $1,000 with a probability of apprehension and conviction of 1, a fine of $10,000 with a probability of .1, a fine of $1 million with a probability of .001, etc. If the costs of collecting fines are assumed to be zero regardless of the size of the fine, the most efficient combination is a probability arbitrarily close to zero and a fine arbitrarily close to infinity. For while the costs of apprehending and convicting criminals rise with the probability of apprehension — higher probabilities imply more police, prosecutors, judges, defense attorneys, etc. (because more criminals are being apprehended and tried) than when the probability of apprehension is very low — the costs of collecting fines are by assumption zero regardless of their size. Thus every increase in the size of the fine is costless, while every corresponding decrease in the probability of apprehension and conviction, designed to offset the increase in the fine and so maintain a constant expected punishment cost, reduces the costs of enforcement — to the vanishing point if the probability of apprehension and conviction is reduced arbitrarily close to zero.

There are, however, several problems with the assumption that the cost of the fine is unrelated to the size of the fine.

1. If criminals (or some of them) are risk averse, an increase in the

fine will not be a costless transfer payment. The reason why, in our model, the only cost of a fine is the cost of collecting it and not the dollar amount of the fine itself is that either the fine is not paid (because the crime is deterred) or, if paid, it simply transfers an equal dollar amount from the criminal to the taxpayer. But for criminals who are risk averse, every reduction in the probability of apprehension and conviction, and corresponding increase in the fine for those who are apprehended and convicted, imposes a disutility not translated into revenue by the state. Thus, the real social cost of fines increases for risk-averse criminals as the fine increases. Nor is this effect offset by the effect on risk-preferring criminals, even if there are as many of them as there are risk-averse criminals. To the extent that a higher fine with lower probability of apprehension and conviction increases the utility of the risk preferrer, the fine has to be put up another notch to make sure that it deters, which makes things even more painful for the risk averse.

2. The stigma effect of a fine (as of any criminal penalty), noted earlier, is not transferred either.

3. The tendency in the model is to punish all crimes by a uniformly severe fine. This, however, eliminates marginal deterrence — the incentive to substitute less for more serious crimes. If robbery is punished as severely as murder, the robber might as well kill his victim to eliminate a witness. Thus, one cost of increasing the severity of punishment of a crime is to reduce the incentive to substitute that crime for a more serious one.[2] If it were not for considerations of marginal deterrence, more serious crimes might not always be punishable by more severe penalties than less serious ones. Of course, marginal deterrence would be uninteresting if all crimes were deterred. And even if all are not (why not, from an economic standpoint?), marginal deterrence involves a tradeoff that may not be worth making. Suppose we want to reduce the number of murders committed in the course of robberies. One way might be to make robbery punishable by death. This would violate the principles of marginal deterrence and would increase the probability that, if a robbery were committed, someone would be murdered in the course of it. But it would reduce the probability that the robbery would be committed in the first place. If the robbery rate was very sensitive to the severity of the punishment, the total number of murders committed during robberies might fall (because there were so many fewer robberies), even though robbers' incentive to kill was greater.[3]

2. Notice, though, that even if all crimes were punished with the same severity, some marginal deterrence could be preserved by varying the probability of punishment with the gravity of the crime — that is, by looking harder for the more serious offenders.

3. Eliminating marginal deterrence of a crime will, however, unequivocally increase the incidence of the crime if the lesser offense that is now to be punished just as severely is a substitute for rather than a complement of the greater (robbery and murder in the course of robbery are complements, for an increase in the former will, other things being equal, lead to an increase in the latter as well). For example, if the punishment for bicycle theft is raised to the same level as auto theft, the incidence of auto theft will rise.

4. Limitations of solvency make the cost of collecting fines rise with the size of the fine — and, for most criminal offenders, to become prohibitive rather quickly. The problem is so acute that the costs of collecting fines would often be prohibitive even if the probability of punishment were one and fines correspondingly much smaller than in the model. This explains the heavy reliance in all criminal justice systems on nonpecuniary sanctions, of which imprisonment is the most common today. Imprisonment imposes pecuniary costs on the violator by reducing his income during the period of confinement and, in many cases, by reducing his earning capacity after release as well (the criminal record effect). It also imposes nonpecuniary costs on people — the vast majority — who prefer living outside of prison.

Since fines and imprisonment are simply different ways of imposing disutility on violators, the Supreme Court is wrong to regard a sentence that imposes a fine but provides for imprisonment if the defendant cannot or will not pay the fine as discriminating against the poor.[4] A rate of exchange can be found that equates, for a given individual, a number of dollars with a number of days in jail. But maybe the Court's real objection is to the fact that most criminal statutes establish a rate of exchange highly favorable to people who have assets. Five hundred dollars is a milder sanction than 100 days in jail (*Williams v. Illinois*), even for people of low income; it is a trivial sanction for other people — those most likely to be able to pay the fine in lieu of serving a jail term.

From an economic standpoint, the use of fines should be encouraged relative to imprisonment. Not only does imprisonment generate no revenue for the state, as fines do, but the social costs of imprisonment exceed those of collecting fines from solvent defendants. There is the expense of constructing, maintaining, and operating prisons (only partly offset by the savings in living expenses on the outside that the criminal would incur if he were not in prison), the loss of the incarcerated individual's lawful production (if any) during the period while he is in prison, the disutility of imprisonment to him (which generates no corresponding benefit to the state, as a fine does), and the impairment of his productivity in legitimate activities after release. Since the forgone income from lawful employment is an opportunity cost of crime, a reduction in the prisoner's lawful earnings prospects reduces the costs of criminal activity to him and thereby increases the likelihood that he will commit crimes after his release. But imprisonment yields one benefit that a fine does not: It prevents the criminal from committing crimes (at least outside of prison!) for as long as he is in prison.

Much can be done to make alternative punishments to imprisonment effective. Fines can be made payable in installments. They can be made proportionate to and payable out of earnings, rather than being a fixed

4. See Tate v. Short, 401 U.S. 395 (1971); Williams v. Illinois, 399 U.S. 235 (1970).

dollar amount. Exclusion from particular occupations can be used as a sanction. Freedom of action can be (and nowadays often is) restricted in ways that permit productive activity, such as by imprisonment at night and on weekends only. But some of these methods are not entirely free from the drawbacks of imprisonment. A fine payable in installments or proportionate to future earnings would reduce the offender's income from lawful activity and therefore also his incentive to choose it over criminal activity, as would exclusion from an occupation.

Nevertheless more white collar crimes — financial, nonviolent crimes committed by middle class people, such as price fixing, tax evasion, securities fraud, and bribery — probably could be punished exclusively by fines. The fact that many of these crimes are less grave than crimes of violence and that many of these criminals are far more solvent than violent criminals suggests that it often would be possible to set a realistic (i.e., a collectable) fine that imposed on the criminal a net disutility equal to that of the normally very short prison sentences that are imposed for these crimes, even when the stigma effect of imprisonment is added to the more tangible deprivations. (Any criminal punishment has some stigma effect.) This might of course require much higher fines than we have been accustomed to — although times are changing.[5] Even so, our analysis of the nonlinear relationship between compensation demanded and risk of death implies that even very large financial crimes are less costly than almost all crimes of violence that create a significant probability of death.

Thus no white collar crime is apt to approach murder in gravity. Moreover, even prolonged incarceration may not impose on the murderer costs equal to those of the victim, which may truly be infinite. This suggests a possible economic justification for capital punishment of murder, which imposes on the convicted murderer a cost roughly commensurate with the cost of his conduct. It might seem that the important thing is not that the punishment for murder equal the cost to the victim but that it be high enough to make murder not pay — and surely imprisonment for the remainder of one's life would cost the murderer more than the murder could possibly have gained him. But this analysis implicitly treats the probability of apprehension and conviction as one. If it is less than one, as of course it is, the murderer will not be comparing the gain from the crime with the cost if he is caught and sentenced; he will be comparing it with the cost of the sentence discounted by the probability that he will be caught and sentenced.

This argument for capital punishment is not conclusive. Because the penalty is so severe, and irreversible, the cost of mistaken imposition

---

5. Recent amendments to the federal criminal code impose very heavy fines on federal criminal offenders, including a maximum fine of $250,000 for individual felony offenders, or twice the offender's gain, or twice the victim's loss, whichever amount is greatest. See 18 U.S.C. §3623.

is very high and therefore substantially greater resources are invested in the litigation of a capital case (see §21.3 *infra*). The additional resources may not be justified if the incremental deterrent effect of capital punishment compared with long prison terms is small. But there is evidence that it is substantial.[6]

Capital punishment is also supported (although equivocally) by considerations of marginal deterrence, which requires as big a spread as possible between the punishments for the least and most serious crimes. If the maximum punishment for murder is life imprisonment, we may not want to make armed robbery also punishable by life imprisonment. But if we therefore step down the maximum punishment for armed robbery from life to 20 years, we shall not be able to punish some lesser crime by 20 years. It does not follow, however, that capital punishment should be the punishment for *simple* murder. For if it is, then we have the problem of marginally deterring the multiple murderer. Maybe capital punishment should be reserved for him, so that murderers have a disincentive to kill witnesses to the murder. An important application of this point is to prison murders. If a prisoner is serving life for murder, he has no disincentive not to kill in prison, unless prison murder is punishable by death.

Problems of this sort vexed medieval thinkers. Because most medieval people believed in an afterlife, capital punishment was not so serious a punishment in those days as it is in our modern, and (it had seemed until recently) increasingly secular, world. In an effort to make capital punishment a more costly punishment, horrible methods of execution (e.g., drawing and quartering[7]) were prescribed for particularly serious crimes, such as treason.[8] Boiling in oil, considered more horrible than hanging or beheading, was used to punish murder by poisoning; since poisoners were especially difficult to apprehend in those times, a heavier punishment than that prescribed for ordinary murderers was (economically) indicated.[9]

---

6. See Isaac Ehrlich, The Deterrent Effect of Capital Punishment: A Matter of Life and Death, 65 Am. Econ. Rev. 397 (1975); Isaac Ehrlich & Joel C. Gibbons, On the Measurement of the Deterrent Effect of Capital Punishment and the Theory of Deterrence, 6 J. Leg. Stud. 35 (1977); David J. Pyle, The Economics of Crime and Law Enforcement, ch. 4 (1983); Stephen Layson, Homicide and Deterrence: A Reexamination of the U.S. Time-Series Evidence (Working Paper in Economics, Center for Applied Research, University of North Carolina at Greensboro, Aug. 1984). The skeptical literature is referenced and discussed in Pyle.

7. Which was still "on the books" in eighteenth-century England. See 4 Blackstone, Commentaries on the Laws of England 92 (1769), for the gruesome details.

8. But is there a realistic method of preserving marginal deterrence for *every* crime?

9. Another example of a penalty whose great severity reflected the low probability of punishment more than the high social cost of the crime was the hanging of horse thieves in the nineteenth-century American West. Still another was the capital punishment of all serious, and many not so serious, crimes in pre–nineteenth-century England, where there was no organized police force and the probability of punishment was therefore very low.

If (coming back to modern times) we must continue to rely heavily on imprisonment as a criminal sanction, there is an argument — subject to caveats that should be familiar by now to the reader, based on risk aversion, overinclusion, avoidance and error costs, and (possibly) marginal deterrence — for combining heavy prison terms for convicted criminals with low probabilities of apprehension and conviction. Consider the choice between combining a .1 probability of apprehension and conviction with a 10 year prison term and a .2 probability of apprehension and conviction with a 5 year term. Under the second approach twice as many individuals are imprisoned but for only half as long, so the total costs of imprisonment will be similar under the two approaches. But the costs of police, court officials, etc. are clearly less under the first approach, since the probability of apprehension and conviction (and hence the number of prosecutions) is only half as great. Although more resources will be devoted to a trial where the possible punishment is greater, these resources will be incurred in fewer trials because fewer people will be punished. And notice that this variant of our earlier model of high fines and trivial probabilities of apprehension and conviction corrects the most serious problem with that model — that of solvency.

But isn't a system under which probabilities of punishment are low unfair because it creates ex post inequality among offenders?[10] Many go scot-free; others serve longer prison sentences than they would if more offenders were caught. To object to this result, however, is like saying that all lotteries are unfair because, ex post, they create wealth differences among the players. In an equally significant sense both the criminal justice system that creates low probabilities of apprehension and conviction and the lottery are fair so long as the ex ante costs and benefits are equalized among the participants. This ignores risk aversion, however, which if prevalent will add to the social costs of the low probability approach. Moreover, a prison term is lengthened, of course, by adding time on to the end of it, and if the criminal has a significant discount rate,[11] the added years may not create a substantial added disutility.[12] At a discount rate of 10 percent, a prison term of 10 years imposes a disutility only 6.1 times the disutility of a one year sentence, and a sentence of 20 years increases this figure to only 8.5 (the corresponding figures for a 5 percent discount rate are 7.7 and 12.5).[13]

10. That is, inequality after the event.
11. What is this? An interest rate?
12. See Michael K. Block & Robert C. Lind, An Economic Analysis of Crimes Punishable by Imprisonment, 4 J. Leg. Stud. 479, 481 (1975).
13. Notice that if criminals' discount rates are very high, capital punishment may be an inescapable method of punishing very serious crimes.

§7.3   Preventing Crime: Multiple-Offender Laws, Attempt and Conspiracy, Aiding and Abetting, Entrapment

The theory of the criminal sanction presented in the preceding section is one of deterrence. The state rations the demand for crime by setting a high price for it in the form of an expected cost of having to pay a fine or go to prison for committing crimes, but people are actually fined or imprisoned only to maintain the credibility of the deterrent. This view, however, leaves many important features of the criminal justice system unexplained.

For example, a convicted criminal who has been convicted of previous crimes will usually be punished more severely than a first offender even if he served in full whatever sentences were imposed for the earlier crimes; also, fines usually are proportioned to wealth. In competitive markets consumers are not charged higher prices just because they are wealthier than other consumers or have bought the same product previously, and they certainly are not required to give back the thing they have bought if they have not consumed it yet, as a thief would be required to do.

A similar puzzle is the punishment of the so-called inchoate crimes, such as attempts and (unsuccessful) conspiracies. If the purpose of the criminal law is to compel the criminal to take fully into account the costs of his acts, why should he be punished when his conduct, because thwarted, imposes no costs? A related point is that imprisonment is often thought to serve the additional value, besides deterrence, of preventing further criminal acts by the imprisoned criminal — the acts he would commit if he were not in prison. Yet if the criminal justice system maintains a proper schedule of prices for unlawful acts, why should anyone care that the criminal, if not imprisoned but punished with equivalent severity by some method that left him at large, might commit further criminal acts? Presumably he would do so only if the acts were socially (as well as privately) cost justified.

To answer these questions, we should begin by noting that the emphasis on preventing, rather than simply pricing, crime falls on the common law crimes — crimes whose essence is a coerced transfer in a setting of low transaction costs.[1] And very little of the criminal activity in this

---

§7.3   1. Bear in mind, in this connection, that where a crime is committed by someone who cannot afford to pay a money judgment equal to the social costs of his crime, the crime cannot be said to be socially cost justified even if the criminal is willing to incur nonpecuniary costs from imprisonment that are greater than those social costs. The economic concept of value is based on willingness to give up something of value to others — to pay — rather than on willingness to suffer a deprivation that confers no benefit on anyone else. Suffering is not a productive act that establishes an economic claim on society's scarce resources.

category is socially cost justified (why?); examples such as the theft from the cabin under conditions of dire necessity are quite rare, and that example may be a noncrime because of the defense of necessity. The high incidence of the common law crimes thus reflects not their social desirability (which is close to zero) but the difficulties, already emphasized, in setting punishment at a high enough level to achieve 100 percent deterrence. If but for the high cost of criminal sanctions the optimum level of criminal activity would be zero — a reasonable approximation to the truth — then these sanctions are not really prices designed to ration the activity; the purpose, so far as possible, is to extirpate it.[2] This explains the emphasis in the criminal law on prevention, which would make no sense in a market setting or even an unintentional tort setting. It also explains why fines should be proportional to the criminal's wealth, quite apart from any notions of a just distribution of wealth,[3] and why a thief who is caught should be required to return what he has stolen on top of whatever other punishment is meted out to him, even if the victim is not seeking restitution (maybe the victim is another thief!).

The practice, systematized in multiple-offender laws, of punishing repeat offenders more severely than first offenders is generally confined to situations where the usual punishment is imprisonment, implying that prevention, and not pricing, is (subject to cost constraints) the appropriate social goal. The practice raises the price of crime to people who, judging from their past behavior, value crime more than other people do. If our object is to minimize the amount of crime, we want to "charge" more to people who value the activity more. We could do this by uniformly increasing the punishment for the particular crime, but punishment is costly; selective increases in the severity of punishment are cheaper. Another point is that the repeat offender has by his behavior demonstrated a propensity for committing crimes. By imprisoning him for a longer time we can therefore expect to prevent more crimes than if we imprisoned a single offender, whose propensities are harder to predict, for the same period. The same prison resources "buy" a greater reduction in crime.[4] Of course, this assumes that the elasticity of supply of offenders is not infinite. If it were — meaning that a small increase in the expected return to criminal activity would result in an enormous

2. A distinction stressed in Robert Cooter, Prices and Sanctions, 84 Colum. L. Rev. 1523 (1984).

3. The principle of diminishing marginal utility of income implies that a heavier fine is necessary to impose the same disutility on a rich as on a poor person, provided that rich and poor people have on average the same marginal utility functions. For the significance of this qualification see §16.2 *infra*.

4. Another reason for heavier punishment of repeat offenders is that the stigma effect of criminal punishment may diminish with successive punishments (why?). And still another is that the fact that the defendant has committed previous crimes makes us more confident that he really is guilty of the crime with which he currently is charged; the risk of error if a heavy sentence is imposed is therefore less.

(literally, an infinite) increase in the supply of offenders, as people in lawful activities flocked into criminal activities now that the latter were more profitable — then putting one offender behind bars would, by creating opportunities for another, simply draw one person from lawful into criminal activity, or cause a part-time criminal to commit more criminal acts. The elasticity of supply of acquisitive crimes may in fact be quite high (why?), but it is not infinite, and presumably the elasticity of supply of crimes of passion is much lower (why?).

Consider now the punishment of attempts. A man enters a bank, intending to rob it, but a guard spots him and seizes him before he can do any harm. The fact that he came so close to robbing it indicates that he is quite likely to try again unless restrained, so by putting him in prison we can probably prevent some robberies. Also, making the attempt punishable increases the expected costs of bank robbery to the robber without making the punishment for bank robbery more severe (which would create the problems discussed earlier). He cannot be certain that his attempt will succeed, and if it fails he will not merely forgo the gains from a successful robbery but will incur additional (punishment) costs. Punishing attempts is thus like maintaining a police force: it raises the expected punishment cost for the completed crime without increasing the severity of the punishment for that crime.

But the attempt will not be punished so severely as the completed crime, and there are two economic reasons for this: (1) to give the offender an incentive to change his mind at the last minute (a form of marginal deterrence) and (2) to minimize the costs of error, since there is a higher probability that the defendant really is harmless than in the case of one punished for the completed crime. Why is the fact that the attempt caused less harm than the completed crime would have done *not* a sufficient economic reason for the lighter punishment of the attempt?

What if the defendant had simply said to a friend (who turned out to be a police informant), "I intend to rob that bank," and had taken no steps toward accomplishing his aim? This would not be deemed an attempt. The probability that he would actually rob a bank is much less than when he is caught on the verge of doing so, so the social benefits from imprisoning him are much less; put differently, the expected costs of error are much higher.

Sometimes attempts fail not because they are interrupted but because the attempter has made a mistake. He may have shot what he thought was a man sleeping in a bed, but it turned out to be a pillow. Or he may have made a voodoo doll of his enemy, and stabbed it repeatedly, in the mistaken belief that this would kill the enemy. The question for the economist is whether the nature of the mistake is such as to make it unlikely that the attempter will ever succeed. If it is, no crime will be prevented by imprisoning him, and then there will be no social benefit, but cost aplenty, from doing so. The second hypothetical case is of this character.

The attempt that fails because of a mistake rather than because it is interrupted provides the strongest case for punishing an attempt more lightly than the completed crime. If the punishment for attempted murder were the same as the punishment for murder, one who shot and missed (and was not caught immediately) might as well try again, for if he succeeds, he will be punished no more heavily than for his unsuccessful attempt. This is a dramatic example of the importance of marginal deterrence.

Conspiracies to commit criminal acts are punished whether or not they succeed. Where the conspiracy succeeds, allowing it to be punished as a separate crime makes the punishment for the crime greater than if only one person had committed it and also confers certain procedural advantages on the prosecutor (making punishment greater in a different sense — can you see why?). The special treatment of conspiracies makes sense because they are more dangerous than one-man crimes.[5] If they were more dangerous only in the sense of committing more serious crimes, there would be no need for extra punishment; the punishment would be more severe anyway. But actually they are more dangerous in being able to commit more crimes (just as a firm can produce more goods or services than an individual), and perhaps do so more efficiently (in a private, not social, sense) by being able to take advantage of the division of labor — e.g., posting one man as a sentinel, another to drive the getaway car, another to fence the goods stolen, etc. Although these advantages are offset to some extent by the fact that a conspiracy is more vulnerable to being detected because of the scale of its activities, that scale may also enable the conspiracy to escape punishment, by corrupting law enforcement officers. And some of the most serious crimes, such as insurrection, can be committed only by conspiracies. All this implies that the optimal punishment of conspiracies is indeed heavier than that of individuals.

A conspiracy that does not succeed is still punished. It is a form of attempt. The principal legal difference is that the conspiracy, which is to say the agreement to commit the crime, is punishable even if the conspirators do not get anywhere near the scene of the crime but are apprehended in the earliest preparatory stage of their endeavor. But again, if conspiracies are more dangerous than one-man crimes, the expected harm may be as great as in the case of the one-man attempt even if the probability of the completed crime is lower because the preparations are interrupted earlier.

5. Does this explain why an illegal sale is not in law a conspiracy between the seller and the buyer, and why a bribe is not a conspiracy between the person paying and the person receiving the bribe?

Related to the concept of conspiracy is the concept of aiding and abetting a crime. Consider the following cases:

(1) A witness fails to report a crime to the police.
(2) A merchant sells a fancy dress to a woman he knows to be a prostitute.
(3) A merchant sells a gun to a man who tells him he is planning to use it in a murder.

In all three cases there is an argument for imposing criminal liability: It will raise the expected costs of the (principal) criminal. In the first case, however, the avoidance costs will be very great; people who have information about crime but don't volunteer it at first will be scared to do so later. In the second case the benefits of criminal liability will be pretty trivial, and only in part is this because the crime is pretty trivial (and victimless); in addition, the prostitute will incur little added cost by shopping at stores that don't know her occupation. In the third case the benefits in criminal liability seem substantial — and it is the only one where the law (occasionally) imposes such liability.

Entrapment is a concept closely related to attempt, even though entrapment is a defense to a criminal prosecution and attempt is a crime. Often the police solicit or assist a person to commit a crime. The commonest form this tactic takes is sending an undercover agent to buy narcotics from a drug dealer, who is then "nabbed" and prosecuted for an illegal sale. It may seem odd that the law should punish such a harmless act, for obviously the sale of narcotics to an undercover agent who then destroys the narcotics does no harm to anyone. The only important thing, it might seem, would be to get the money used for the purchase back from the seller. But the rationale is again prevention. *This* act is harmless, but it is altogether likely that the dealer unless arrested will make illegal sales, and we arrest and convict him now because it is much cheaper to catch him in an arranged crime than in his ordinary criminal activities. The benefits of imprisonment are virtually as great, and yet the costs of apprehension and conviction are much lower.

This sort of entrapment is perfectly lawful. The defense of entrapment comes into play only if the entrapped person lacked a criminal predisposition. This fusty legal term can be given the following economic meaning: The defendant would have committed the same crime, only under circumstances that would have made it harder for the police to catch him, if he had not fallen into the police trap. But suppose that instead of simulating the target's normal criminal opportunities, the police offer him such inducements as would persuade him to commit crimes that he would never commit in his ordinary environment. The police offer a poor man who has no criminal record $1,000 to steal a bicycle, he does so, and is arrested. The resources used to apprehend and convict the man of bicycle theft are socially wasted, because they do not prevent

any crimes. Had it not been for the police offer he would not have
stolen a bicycle (only doing so at a time when they were not looking);
the expected benefits of theft were negative to him; so nothing is achieved
by the police except deflecting scarce resources from genuine crime
prevention. Police inducements that merely affect the timing and not
the level of criminal activity are socially productive; those that induce
a higher level of such activity are not.

§7.4 Criminal Intent

The subjective intentions, or state of mind, of the accused criminal are
a pervasive consideration in the criminal law. This is puzzling to the
economist; one can read dozens of books on economics without encountering a reference to intent. In fact the concept of intent in criminal
law serves three economic functions: identifying the pure coercive transfer, estimating the probability of apprehension and conviction, and determining whether the criminal sanction will be an effective (cost justified)
means of controlling undesirable conduct.

If I foolishly pick up and take home from a restaurant an umbrella
that I think is mine, but it is not, I am not a thief; but if I know the
umbrella is not mine, and take it anyway, I am. The economic difference
is that in the first case, since I would have to expend resources to avoid
taking the umbrella, and the probability of my taking the wrong umbrella
is low, the disparity between B and PL in Hand Formula terms is not
great, and the risk of overdeterrence through a criminal penalty is great;
while in the second case, where I expend resources in order to take
someone else's umbrella (maybe I went to the restaurant for the sole
purpose of stealing an umbrella), B is negative and P is high (see §6.15
supra). The problem is that the external acts involved in these two transactions look alike, and the state of mind with which they are done is a
clue to the difference.[1] Of course we must be careful to distinguish
intent from awareness. Otherwise we could fall into the trap of thinking
that the managers of a railroad are murderers because they know with
an approach to certainty that their trains will run down a certain number
of people at railroad crossings this year. They know, but they derive
no benefit from killing. They only derive a benefit from saving the resources necessary to prevent the killing, and the benefit, social as well
as private, may exceed the cost. The relevant intent is the intent to

---

§7.4   1. But state of mind must (unless the criminal confesses or makes other damaging
admissions) be inferred from external acts too. Is intent therefore simply a laymen's locu-
tion for a high ratio of PL to B?

bring about a certain (forbidden) object by investing resources in its attainment.

Although it would reduce the cost of trying criminal cases not to bother drawing a sharp line between the pure coercive transfer and the accident that it externally resembles, the result would be excessive criminal punishment, leading to all sorts of serious social costs from the avoidance of such lawful activities as checking umbrellas in a restaurant's cloakroom. Yet sometimes the line wavers. A famous example is statutory rape. The girl may look 16 (assume that is the age of consent), but if she is younger, a reasonable mistake will not excuse the male. Another example is felony murder: If death occurs in the course of a dangerous felony through no fault of the felon's, still he is liable as a murderer. In these examples and others that could be given, we do not care about deterring activity in the neighborhood of that at which the basic criminal prohibition is directed; in other words, we do not count the avoidance of that activity as a social cost, and it therefore pays to reduce the costs of prosecution by eliminating the issue of intent. The male can avoid liability for statutory rape by keeping away from young girls and the robber can avoid liability for felony murder by not robbing, or by not carrying a weapon. In effect, we introduce a degree of strict liability into criminal law where, as in tort law, a change in activity levels is an efficient method of avoiding a social cost (see §6.5 *supra*).

To illustrate the second function of intent in the criminal law, consider the fact that premeditated murder is punished more severely than murder committed in a fit of anger. The difference in state of mind serves as a proxy for differences in two important variables determining optimal punishment. The first is the probability of death; it is higher when the murderer acts deliberately rather than in a spasm of rage. Hence L is greater. And p (the probability of apprehension and conviction) in our formula $D = L/p$ is lower. The individual who plans a murder, however briefly, is likely at the same time to plan his escape. A murder committed in the heat of passion is likely to take place in circumstances where concealment neither has been considered nor can be effected.

There might seem to be another reason for punishing the impulsive crime less severely than the deliberated one, and that is that the impulsive crime is less deterrable; punishment is less efficacious, less worthwhile, and therefore society should buy less of it. But this is unclear. To begin with, the fact that a given increment of punishment will deter the impulsive less than the deliberate criminal could actually point to heavier punishment for the former. Suppose that a 20 year sentence is enough to deter virtually all murders for hire, but to achieve the same deterrence of impulse murderers would require a sentence of 30 years. The additional sentence is costly but if the cost is less than the additional deterrence produced it may still be a good investment. And don't forget the incapacitative effect of imprisonment. The fact that certain criminals may not be effectively deterrable argues for greater emphasis on their incapacitation, which implies long prison terms.[2]

The conflict between deterrence and incapacitation as objectives of the criminal sanction is keenest in relation to the defense of insanity. If a person is insane either in the sense that he does not know that what he is doing is criminal (he kills a man who he thinks is actually a giant gerbil) or that he cannot control himself (he hears voices that he believes are divine commanding him to kill people), he will not be deterred by the threat of criminal punishment, so if all there was to the criminal sanction was deterrence, it would be reasonably clear that such people should not be punished as criminals.[3] The resources consumed in punishing them (including the disutility of the punishment to the "criminal" himself) would be socially wasted because they would buy no deterrence. Actually, this is an overstatement; the existence of a defense of insanity will attract resources to proving and disproving it, and deterrence will be impaired to the extent either that criminals succeed in faking insanity or that a reduction (for whatever reason) in the number of people punished reduces the deterrent signal that punishment emits. But all this to one side, once the incapacitative goal is brought into play it is much less clear that there ought to be an insanity defense, which increases the cost of the criminal process without in the least reducing the need to incapacitate the defendant. The stigma effect of criminal punishment, however, would be reduced if a class of complete undeterrables were punishable. (Why? And why is this observation *not* inconsistent with preserving some pockets of strict liability in the criminal law?) This is an argument for using civil rather than criminal law to incapacitate the criminally insane.

Insanity is rarely recognized as a defense in tort law — in general the defendant's state of mind is much less likely to be considered in excuse or mitigation of civil than of criminal liability. This difference makes economic sense. Criminal sanctions are more costly than tort sanctions (why?), and this alters the tradeoff between the costs of fact-finding and the costs of imposing a sanction beyond its intended domain. Thus it is no defense to civil trespass that the trespasser didn't know and could not at reasonable cost have found out that he was on the plaintiff's property, but it is a defense to criminal trespass. Since the sanction for civil trespass is lighter, the costs of a difficult inquiry into the defendant's state of mind are less likely to produce an equal or greater benefit in avoiding the costs of imposing a sanction on conduct

2. Can you see, though, why this means that the relative cost of punishing deliberate compared to impulsive criminals will be even greater than the ratio of the prison sentences of the two types?

3. Is this also true if the defense of insanity requires only that the defendant's crime be the product of his insanity (the *Durham* rule), in the sense that but for his insanity he would not have committed it?

that no one wants to deter (a trespass unavoidable in an economic sense) than where the sanction is a more costly criminal sanction.

Some problems in criminal intent are illuminated by the concept of information costs. For example, it often is unclear whether a buyer of stolen goods knows they are stolen. The test for his criminal liability is whether, suspecting they were stolen, he consciously avoided acquiring the knowledge that would verify or dispel his suspicions. This test in effect places on the buyer a legal duty, enforceable by criminal punishment, of investigating the provenance of the goods when the costs of investigation are extremely low.[4] Something similar may be at work in the hoary maxim, which still however retains much vitality, that ignorance of the law is no defense to criminal liability. Because unclear criminal laws can create substantial avoidance (steering-clear) costs, these laws are generally rather clear, less by being clearly drafted than by being confined to a type of conduct that everyone knows is antisocial. The result is to make the cost of acquiring knowledge of one's duties under criminal law extremely low.

§7.5 Recklessness, Negligence, and Strict Liability Again

We have observed that since criminal sanctions are severe, to attach them to accidental conduct (and *a fortiori* to unavoidable conduct) is to create incentives to steer clear of what may be a very broad zone of perfectly lawful activity in order to avoid the risk of criminal punishment. But there are many exceptions to this generalization; besides the ones already mentioned, here are two more.

1. There is an argument for criminal liability whenever B in the Hand Formula is low relative to PL and where L is high. These are two conditions, not one. If B and PL are close together there is a substantial risk of erroneously imposing liability, and the social costs of that risk are greatly magnified when the liability is criminal. But even if B is much smaller than PL, unless L is huge there is no reason why the matter can't be left to the tort system.

But there is an argument for criminal liability if both conditions are satisfied, as where by driving extremely carelessly you create a substantial risk of killing someone. B will be much smaller than PL and L will be great. True, B will be larger and P smaller than if you are trying to kill someone, but that means only that the case for criminal liability is stronger in the intentional case. The reckless, or grossly negligent, case still fits the basic model for criminal liability, and one is therefore not

4. Cf. Jon Elster, Ulysses and the Sirens: Studies in Rationality and Irrationality 178 (1979).

surprised to find that reckless and grossly negligent life-endangering conduct is criminal.

Another example is killing in the honest but unreasonable belief that it is necessary in self-defense. This is a deliberate killing; hence both P and L are high. B is also high; the killer by definition fears for his own life. Nevertheless the gap between PL and B may well be substantial, which together with the fact that L is large would establish the conditions for criminal punishment of conduct that is in an important sense accidental. In the example the crime would be manslaughter, not murder; the gap between PL and B is smaller than in a case of reckless killing punishable as second degree murder.

Consistently with the above analysis, simple negligence, and non-life-endangering gross negligence, are rarely made criminal.

2. There are, of course, strict liability crimes (meaning that neither intent nor even simple negligence is an element of the crime), of which the most important as a practical matter is driving over the speed limit. But except in extreme cases, where it becomes part of category 1 above, this is not a crime in a functional sense, as it is punished by a small and nonstigmatizing fine, the practical equivalent of tort damages.

The interesting question about speeding and the other strict liability crimes (selling liquor to a minor and selling adulterated foods are two other common examples) is why it is thought necessary to supplement tort remedies for negligent driving with any sort of publicly enforced sanction. Here is an answer that draws on the analysis of ex ante versus ex post sanctions and hence points us ahead to safety regulation in Chapter 13.[1] In the case of life-endangering conduct (a common element in virtually all of the strict liability crimes), the fixing of L in a tort suit (i.e., after the accident has occurred) both is difficult to do because it is hard to estimate the value of a human life, and, more important in the present analysis, may be a futile act because the tortfeasor will lack the money to pay such a large judgment. The alternative to the tort system is to have the government step in and (ideally) make the speeder pay a fine equal to PL[2] in order to induce the taking of the right precautions, approximated by complying with the speed limit. PL will be a much smaller number than L.

Strict liability is a misnomer in this setting; the speed limit is a rough estimation of B, and so with the other regulatory rules the breaking of which establishes strict criminal liability. Because B and PL may be close together, costly criminal sanctions are not optimal even though L is high; small transfer payments to the government may be.

§7.5   1. See Donald Wittman, Prior Regulation Versus Post Liability: The Choice Between Input and Output Monitoring, 6 J. Leg. Stud. 193 (1977); Steven Shavell, Liability for Harm Versus Regulation of Safety, 13 J. Leg. Stud. 357 (1984).
    2. How can PL be determined? See §6.12 *supra*.

§7.6   The Defense of Necessity (Compulsion)

The famous case of *Regina v. Dudley and Stephens*[1] involved a murder trial of several men who, *in extremis* in a lifeboat, killed and ate one of the members of their party. A defense of necessity or compulsion was raised but rejected. In the modern law this defense, although still regarded with disfavor except when it takes the form of self-defense, will usually succeed if there is a very great disparity between the cost of the crime to the victim and the gain to the injurer. Thus in our earlier example of stealing food from a cabin in the woods in order to maintain life, the theft might well be excused. Notice also that unlike the case of insanity — a fundamentally different type of defense — no incapacitative goal would be served by rejecting a defense of necessity; we don't *want* incapacitation in this case.[2]

But change the example slightly: I am starving and beg a crust of bread from a wealthy gourmand, who turns me down. If I go ahead and snatch the bread from his hand, I am guilty of theft and cannot interpose a defense of necessity. The economic rationale for this hardhearted result is that since transaction costs are low, my inability to negotiate a successful purchase of the bread shows that the bread is really worth more to the gourmand. But transaction costs were prohibitive in the cabin example.

Now come back to *Dudley and Stephens*. There was evidence that the crew member who was killed and eaten was near death anyway and that killing and eating him saved the lives of three men (one wasn't charged because he hadn't participated in the killing). Yet for reasons stated earlier, unless the victim knew he was a goner probably he would not have sold his life to the others at any price. Therefore the case seems similar to that of the starving beggar. Yet something must be wrong. Even though transaction costs were not high in the usual sense in *Dudley and Stephens*, most people would think that at some point a sacrifice of one person so that others will live increases social welfare. If it could be shown that in advance of the voyage the members of the crew had agreed to the sacrifice of the weakest if that became necessary to save the others, there would be an economic argument for allowing the defense of necessity if the agreement had to be performed.[3]

§7.6   1. 14 Q.B.D. 273 (1884).
2. What should be the tort liability of the thief to the cabin owner? See §6.4 *supra.*
3. See A.W. Brian Simpson, Cannibalism and the Common Law 140, 145, 233-234 (1984); United States v. Holmes, 26 Fed. Cas. 360 (C.C. Pa. 1842). Would casting lots be a better or worse method of selecting the victim from an economic standpoint? Notice the analogy, weird as it may seem, to the admiralty rule of general average, discussed in §6.4 *supra*, note 2.

§7.7   The Economics of Organized Crime[1]

Much emphasis has been placed in recent years on efforts to control organized crime. The term is used to describe criminals organized into illegal firms linked up in national or even international cartels, operating in such criminal fields as loansharking, prostitution, gambling, and narcotics but also in legitimate fields as well, and employing violence and the corruption of police as key business methods.

From the standpoint of economic analysis some of these alleged characteristics of organized crime seem realistic, others not. The activities associated with organized crime primarily involve willing buyer-seller relationships rather than forced exchanges. Since such relationships ordinarily entail a degree of organization and specialization, we are not surprised to find firms rather than merely individuals engaged in these activities. The relative conspicuousness of an organization in comparison with an individual might seem to make it highly vulnerable. But because the activities of organized crime involve willing victims, the organization is in relatively little danger of apprehension, at least by the usual method of victim complaint. (Hence the importance of undercover agents.) And corruption of the police is facilitated by the continuing nature of the criminal activity (why?).

It is not surprising that organized crime should sometimes employ violence (and more often the threat of violence), since it is forbidden to enforce its contracts by lawful means. And yet there is an argument that organized crime is likely to employ violence less frequently than unorganized crime. Violence frightens the public and therefore leads to greater efforts by the police to prevent the activity that gives rise to it. This consequence of violence is external to the individual criminal but not to a large criminal organization. The organization therefore has an incentive to curb its members' violent propensities.

It is not surprising that criminal organizations should try to enter legitimate businesses; such businesses provide attractive investment opportunities for people with money to invest and with entrepreneurial skills. Should such entry be encouraged or discouraged? On the one hand, a method of reducing the incidence of organized crime is to increase the expected return of alternative, legitimate activities. On the other hand, to the extent that profits earned in organized crime can be safely invested in legitimate activities to yield additional profits, the expected return to organized crime is higher than it would otherwise be.

§7.7   1. See James M. Buchanan, A Defense of Organized Crime?, in The Economics of Crime and Punishment 119 (Am. Enterprise Institute 1973); Thomas C. Schelling, Economic Analysis and Organized Crime, in An Economic Analysis of Crime: Selected Readings 367 (Lawrence J. Kaplan & Dennis Kessler eds. 1976); Thomas C. Schelling, Choice and Consequence, ch. 8 (1984).

The least plausible features in our composite description of organized crime are the alleged national and even international scale of operations and the alleged monopoly profits. Large-scale operations in the usual organized crime fields would encounter substantial diseconomies for two reasons. First, these are mostly fields of wholesale and retail distribution, and most distribution is generally highly decentralized, indicating that there probably are substantial diseconomies of scale. Second, the covert form that organized crime enterprises are constrained to assume probably prevents them from establishing the elaborate control machinery, involving voluminous communication, that is associated with very large firms in other fields.

One area of organized crime where monopoly is important, however, is the well-known protection racket, a form of extortion. To persuade the victim to pay protection, the gang must be able to guarantee the victim that no one else will beat him up or destroy his property; the gang must in other words have a local monopoly of extra-legal violence. Can you see now why public officials are often effective extortionists?

Should public policy be pro or con the monopolizing of criminal markets? Where the criminal activity consists of selling illegal goods or services such as narcotics or prostitution, the effect of monopolization is, by raising the price of the goods or services, to reduce the amount consumed (see §9.3 *infra*). Almost no one thinks that law enforcement activities can actually eliminate these illegal markets; what law enforcement does is increase the price, and hence reduce the consumption, of what is sold in these markets. Making the markets more competitive would thus blunt the edge of law enforcement policy.

It has been suggested that legal sanctions for typical organized crime businesses such as prostitution and gambling have the effect of creating a "tariff" that enables people willing to assume the risk of criminal punishment to obtain monopoly profits by entering those businesses.[2] But since expected punishment cost is a cost of doing illegal business and must be covered like other costs, a price that includes this cost is not a monopoly price but a competitive price, albeit a higher one than would prevail if the activity were legal and involved no punishment costs.[3] Whether the activities of organized crime are cartelized and hence yield monopoly profits is a question that is not answered by observing that they are illegal.[4]

Suggested Readings

1. Gary S. Becker, Crime and Punishment: An Economic Approach, 76 J. Pol. Econ. 169 (1968).

2. Herbert L. Packer, The Limits of the Criminal Sanction 277-282 (1968).
3. Cf. discussion of the baby black market in §5.4 *supra*.
4. The imposition of criminal sanctions on corporations is discussed in Chapter 14, criminal procedure and law enforcement in Chapters 21 and 22.

2. Robert Cooter, Prices and Sanctions, 84 Colum. L. Rev. 1523 (1984).

3. Isaac Erhlich, The Deterrent Effect of Criminal Law Enforcement, 1 J. Leg. Stud. 259 (1972).

4. ———, Participation in Illegitimate Activities: An Economic Analysis, in Essays in the Economics of Crime and Punishment 68 (Gary S. Becker & William M. Landes eds. 1974).

5. ———, On the Usefulness of Controlling Individuals: An Economic Analysis of Rehabilitation, Incapacitation, and Deterrence, 71 Am. Econ. Rev. 307 (1981).

6. A. Mitchell Polinsky & Steven Shavell, The Optimal Tradeoff Between the Probability and Magnitude of Fines, 69 Am. Econ. Rev. 880 (1979).

7. David J. Pyle, The Economics of Crime and Law Enforcement (1983).

8. Richard A. Posner, Optimal Sentences for White-Collar Criminals, 17 Am. Crim. L. Rev. 409 (1980).

9. ———, An Economic Theory of the Criminal Law 85 Colum. L. Rev. 1193 (1985).

10. Thomas C. Schelling, Choice and Consequences, Ch. 8 (1984).

11. Steven Shavell, Criminal Law and the Optimal Use of Nonmonetary Sanctions as a Deterrent, 85 Colum. L. Rev. 1232 (1985).

12. George J. Stigler, The Optimum Enforcement of Laws, 78 J. Pol. Econ. 526 (1970).

13. The Economics of Crime (Ralph Andreano & John J. Siegfried eds. 1980).

Problems

1. Evaluate the following argument from Stephen F. Williams, Book Review, 45 U. Colo. L. Rev. 437, 450, (1974):

> It is hard to believe that a $500 fine has the same deterrent effect on our billionaire as on our postal clerk; yet presumably the social cost of an offense committed by a rich man is no less than that of the same offense committed by a poor man.

2. It is commonly said that people who occupy positions of trust should be well paid in order to reduce the temptation to betray their trust. Can you think of an economic basis for this view?

3. Suppose it costs one dollar in government expenditures on law enforcement to reduce the expected costs of crime by 99 cents. Would such an expenditure be socially cost justifiable?

4. There is a big debate in the economic literature on crime and punishment over whether or not the gains to the criminal from committing the crime should be counted as social gains. (Notice that this question is different from whether the cost to the criminal of his punishment should be counted as a social cost; everyone writing from an economic standpoint assumes it should be.) To help focus the question, assume the law contains a sufficiently expansive defense of necessity to make it impossible for cases like the hypothetical starving man's theft from the cabin, or perhaps even *Regina v. Dudley and Stephens,* to be prosecuted as criminal cases. Now answer the question. (Hint: first explain what difference it makes how the question is answered.)

5. Should potential victims of crime be made to bear some of the costs of crime, for example by being fined for leaving their car doors unlocked or for letting their handguns be stolen?

6. Is the traditional unwillingness of appellate courts to review sentence length consistent with the economic approach to criminal punishment? (If baffled see §21.6 *infra.*)

7. Would statutory rape be committed more or less often if the girl were subject to criminal punishment as well as the man? Cf. *Michael M. v. Sonoma County Superior Court,* 450 U.S. 464 (1981).

8. Discuss the costs and benefits of

(1) giving prisoners job training;

(2) forcing them to work while in prison;

(3) forbidding employers to refuse to hire a person (for a nonsensitive job) because he has a criminal record.

9. If mental incapacity is self-induced, as where a person kills in a drunken fit, should the law excuse the crime? If not, should it punish it less severely?

10. Suppose the defendant would not have committed the crime of which he is accused but for the fact that he was brought up in conditions of severe poverty that prevented him from acquiring any marketable skills. Should the crime be excused? Should the punishment be diminished, increased, or left unchanged?

11. Consent normally is not a defense to a criminal charge. Putting aside the victimless crime, is this principle consistent with economic analysis?

12. Should entrapment by a private individual ever be a defense to a criminal charge?

13. An attempted murderer, even if he does not hurt his intended victim or anyone else, is usually punished more severely than a successful thief. What is the economic logic of this pattern?

14. From an economic standpoint, should the criminal law use the same principles of causation as tort law, or different principles?

CHAPTER 8

THE COMMON LAW, LEGAL HISTORY, AND JURISPRUDENCE[1]

Although our economic study of the common law is not yet complete — in particular, Chapter 21 will examine the common law of civil and criminal procedure, including conflict of laws — we have gone far enough that a consideration of the common law as a whole, bringing together some of the insights developed in the preceding chapters and building from there, may be helpful. This chapter will also consider (though very briefly) some topics normally covered in law school courses in jurisprudence, legal history, and legal anthropology.

§8.1 The Implicit Economic Logic of the Common Law

The common law is to most lawyers a collection of disparate fields, each with its own history, vocabulary, and bewildering profusion of rules and doctrines; indeed, each field may itself seem a collection of only tenuously related doctrines. Yet we have seen that the law of property, of contracts and commercial law, of restitution and unjust enrichment, of criminal and family law, and of admiralty law all can be cast in an economic form that explains the principal doctrines, both substantive and remedial, in these fields of (largely) judge-made law; and more evidence for this conclusion can be found in the many specialized studies on which the previous chapters build.

Those doctrines form a system for inducing people to behave efficiently, not only in explicit markets but across the whole range of social

---

1. See Lawrence M. Friedman, A History of American Law (1973); Jeffrie G. Murphy & Jules L. Coleman, The Philosophy of Law: An Introduction to Jurisprudence (1984); Oliver Wendell Holmes, Jr., The Common Law (1881).

interactions. In settings where the cost of voluntary transactions is low, common law doctrines create incentives for people to channel their transactions through the market (whether implicit — the marriage market for example — or explicit). This is done by creating property rights (broadly defined) and protecting them through such remedies as injunctions, restitution, punitive damages, and criminal punishment. In settings where the cost of allocating resources by voluntary transactions is prohibitively high — where, in other words, market transactions are infeasible — the common law prices behavior in such a way as to mimic the market. For example, the tort system allocates liability for accidents between railroad and farmer, driver and pedestrian, doctor and patient (what is the source of high transaction costs here?) in such a way as to bring about the allocation of resources to safety that the market would bring about if the market could be made to work. The law of contracts does the same thing in regard to unforeseen contingencies that may make it impossible to perform a contract: It places liability on the party better able either to prevent the contingency from occurring or to minimize the disutility of its occurrence by buying insurance or by self-insuring. The law of property does the same thing by limiting property rights in situations where insistence on an absolute right of property would prevent a value-maximizing exchange. An example is allowing right-of-way companies to obtain easements by eminent domain. To reverse the previous order of discussion, the common law establishes property rights, regulates their exchange, and protects them against unreasonable interference — all to the end of facilitating the operation of the free market, and where the free market is unworkable of simulating its results.

Hence the economic analyst can move easily not only within common law fields but between them. Almost any tort problem can be solved as a contract problem, by asking what the people involved in an accident would have agreed on in advance with regard to safety measures if transaction costs had not been prohibitive. A striking example is provided by the old case of *Eckert v. Long Island Railroad.*[1] The defendant's train was going too fast and without adequate signals in a densely populated area. A small child was sitting on the tracks oblivious to the oncoming train. Eckert ran to rescue the child and managed to throw it clear but was himself killed. The court held that Eckert had not been contributorily negligent, and therefore his estate could recover damages for the railroad's negligence. For "it was not wrongful in him to make every effort in his power to rescue the child, compatible with a reasonable regard for his own safety. It was his duty to exercise his judgment as to whether he could probably save the child without serious injury to himself."[2] If (as implied by this passage) the probability that the child

§8.1   1. 43 N.Y. 502 (1870).
2. Id. at 505.

would be killed if the rescue was not attempted was greater than the probability that Eckert would get himself killed saving the child, and if the child's life was at least as valuable as Eckert's life, then the expected benefit of the rescue to the railroad in reducing an expected liability cost to the child's parents was greater than the expected cost of rescue. In that event, but for prohibitive transaction costs, the railroad would have hired Eckert to attempt the rescue, so it should be required to compensate him ex post.[3]

Equally, almost any contract problem can be solved as a tort problem by asking what sanction is necessary to prevent the performing or paying party from engaging in wasteful conduct, such as taking advantage of the vulnerability of a party who performs his side of the bargain first. And both tort and contract problems can be framed as problems in the definition of property rights; for example, the law of negligence could be thought to define the right we have in the safety of our persons against accidental injury. The definition of property rights can itself be viewed as a process of figuring out what measures parties would agree to, if transaction costs weren't prohibitive, in order to create incentives to avoid wasting valuable resources.

The important distinctions in the economic analysis of the common law cut across conventional subject divisions. One is between cases in which compensation is required only if there has been a failure to take some cost-minimizing loss-avoidance measure and cases in which compensation is required regardless. A contract breaker usually is required to pay damages even if the breach of contract leads to a more valuable use of resources; likewise a trespasser. But one who accidentally inflicts a personal injury in circumstances where no cost-justified precaution could have prevented the accident generally is not liable, while intent to do harm is required in most cases of criminal liability. There are economic reasons for these differences. The high costs of criminal sanctions argue for confining them to instances where the risk of legal error is small. The compensation rule in contract cases is simply a corollary of the heavy reliance, which we have seen is economically justifiable, on strict liability for failure to perform one's contractual promises (see §6.5 *supra*), which in turn is a function in part of the insurance function of many contract promises. The rule of strict liability in trespass but not in ordinary accident cases reflects the fundamental distinction between cases in which transaction costs are very high and cases in which, because there is either an actual or a potential buyer-seller relationship between the parties to the interaction and other conditions are satisfied (what other conditions?), transaction costs are relatively low and voluntary transactions should therefore be encouraged (see, e.g., §3.5 *supra*).

The last distinction should not be taken to imply, however, that the

---

3. What if there is a danger of both being killed if the rescue is attempted? How then would you model the issue of contributory negligence in terms of the Hand Formula?

law's assignment of rights or liabilities is economically unimportant in cases where transaction costs are low. Although the most dramatic economic function of the common law is to correct externalities, positive (external benefits) as well as negative, it also has an important function[4] to perform in reducing transaction costs — notably by creating property rights — and thus enabling or facilitating, as distinct from simulating, market processes. These dual roles of the common law are well illustrated by the law's evident concern with problems of bilateral monopoly. Bilateral monopoly increases transaction costs, sometimes to the point where value-maximizing transactions fall through; and then there is an externality. But even when the transaction takes place, it does so at higher cost than if there were no bilateral monopoly; so the law does what it can to reduce bilateral monopoly. The law tries to guess where the parties would want to allocate some burden or benefit, such as responsibility if some happy, or harmful, contingency materializes; if it guesses right, this both minimizes the costs of transacting by making it unnecessary for the parties to transact around the law's allocation, and produces the efficient allocation of resources if transaction costs are prohibitive.

But how is it possible, the reader may ask, for the common law — an ancient body of legal doctrine, which has changed only incrementally in the last century — to make as much economic sense as it seems to do? A complete answer (so far as it is possible to give one) must await Chapters 19-21, where the procedures and institutional environment of the common law are discussed. But here are a few suggestions.

1. Many common law doctrines are economically sensible but not economically subtle. They are commonsensical. Their articulation in economic terms is beyond the capacity of most judges and lawyers but their intuition is not.

2. What Adam Smith referred to as a nation's wealth, what this book refers to as efficiency, and what a layman might call the size of the pie, has always been an important social value — and never more so than in the nineteenth century, the age of *laissez-faire,* when the common law acquired much of its modern shape. It is not surprising that this value is influential in judicial decisions.

3. Perhaps it is especially influential because the competing social goals are both more controversial and difficult to achieve with the limited tools that judges have to work with. The competing goals have mainly to do with ideas about the just distribution of income and wealth — ideas around which no consensus has yet formed. Efficiency is highly controversial when viewed as the only value a society's public institutions should pursue, but it is not very controversial (outside of academic circles) when viewed just as one value. And effective redistributive policies require taxing and spending powers that judges administering doctrines

---

4. Is it really a different function, though?

of or evolved from pre–twentieth-century common law principles just do not have (see, e.g., §16.6 *infra*). As they cannot do much as common law judges to alter the slices of the pie that the various groups in society receive, they might as well concentrate on increasing the size of the pie.

4. Many traditional legal scholars don't think judges should have any truck with social goals; they think judges should apply principles of justice. But on inspection these principles usually turn out to have a functional or instrumentalist character: to be, in fact, a version of efficiency or redistributive policy. More on this later in the chapter.

5. The fact that with few exceptions lawyers and judges are not self-consciously economic in their approach to law is a trivial objection to the positive economic analysis of the common law. The language of economics is a language designed for scholars and students, not for the people whose behavior the economist studies. Poets do not use the vocabulary of literary critics, and judges do not use the vocabulary of economists.

Despite all of the above, not every common law doctrine has an economic rationale. The most important counterexamples that we have discussed to the efficiency theory of the common law are

(1) the law's refusal to enforce penalty clauses,

(2) the method of computing damages in death cases (and the common law's refusal to award any damages for loss of life — such awards are a mid–nineteenth-century statutory innovation), and

(3) the modern movements to substitute comparative for contributory negligence, and contribution for no contribution among joint tort-feasors.

Evidently, then, economic efficiency does not provide a complete positive theory of the common law.

§8.2 The Common Law, Economic Growth, and Legal History

Economic analysis can help clarify the controversial role of the common law in the economic growth of this country. The usual view is that the common law helped promote economic development in the nineteenth century by adopting a permissive, even facilitating, stance toward entrepreneurial activity. A variant is that it subsidized growth by failing to make industry bear all of the costs that a genuine commitment to efficiency would have required it to bear. The permissiveness of the common law in the nineteenth century is contrasted with the many restrictions imposed on economic activity by the law in both the preceding and following periods.[1]

It is necessary to clarify the concepts of growth and of subsidy. The rate of economic growth is the rate at which the output of a society increases. Since growth is fostered by using resources efficiently, there is a sense, but a rather uncontroversial one, in which the common law, insofar as it has been shaped by a concern with efficiency, may be said to have fostered growth. Society can, however, force the pace of growth by compelling people to consume less and save more and by increasing the returns to capital investment. If the common law played any role in accelerating economic growth it must have been by making capital investment more profitable.

In this vein, it has been argued that nineteenth-century contract law consistently favored the performing over the paying party in order to encourage entrepreneurship.[2] But every business firm is simultaneously, and more or less equally, performer and payer. It is the performer with respect to contracts for the sale of its output; it is the payer with respect to contracts for the purchase of its inputs. It derives no clear gain from having the law tilted in favor of performers.

It has been suggested that the common law of industrial accidents favored industry.[3] But we saw in the last chapter that as between parties already in a contractual relationship, the efficient level of safety might be achieved even if the law imposed *no* liability for accidental injury. This would be true even if wages were at the subsistence level — the level at which any further reduction in wages would cause the worker to starve or become so weak that he couldn't work effectively. At a subsistence wage, workers would refuse to trade a reduction in wages for an increase in job safety — but this would be the optimal decision for them to make: better to take some risks than to starve. Even in nineteenth-century America, however, industrial wages were far above subsistence levels. There was in fact an acute labor shortage in the late nineteenth century — that is why there was so much immigration.[4] And one way to compete for workers is by offering safer working condi-

§8.2   1. This is the thesis of Morton J. Horwitz, The Transformation of American Law, 1780-1860 (1977). For criticism from an economic standpoint, see Stephen F. Williams, Book Review, 25 U.C.L.A.L. Rev. 1187 (1978); Herbert Hovenkamp, The Economics of Legal History, 67 Minn. L. Rev. 645, 670-689 (1983).

2. Grant Gilmore, Products Liability: A Commentary, 38 U. Chi. L. Rev. 103 (1970).

3. As by Professor Horwitz, *supra* note 1 at 97-101. For contrasting views on the matter see Richard A. Posner, A Theory of Negligence, 1 J. Leg. Stud. 29, 67-72 (1972); Gary T. Schwartz, Tort Law and the Economy in Nineteenth-Century America: A Reinterpretation, 90 Yale L.J. 1717 (1981). Though critical of industrial accident law, Professor Schwartz rejects the subsidy theory of nineteenth-century tort law.

4. See Jeffrey G. Williamson, Late Nineteenth-Century American Development: A General Equilibrium History 240-243, 249 (1974); Maurice Wilkinson, European Migration to the United States: An Econometric Analysis of Aggregate Labor Supply and Demand, 52 Rev. Econ. & Stat. 272 (1970).

tions. Although the costs of advertising a safer job might be high — especially when many workers do not speak the language — ignorance must have been as or more widespread in eighteenth-century England, yet we know that workers in dangerous or disagreeable jobs did receive significant wage premiums then.[5] Maybe, today, potential workplace hazards are often so subtle that the costs of information about them to the workers would be prohibitive, but this was not true in the nineteenth century; then subtle dangers were likely to escape anyone's notice.

The growing subtlety of those dangers may conceivably explain the movement in this century to a form of strict liability for workplace injuries — workmen's compensation — although not for the limit that workmen's compensation laws place on the amount of damages or for the refusal to make contributory negligence a defense to a workmen's compensation claim.[6] The parallel movement in products liability, from virtually no liability in the nineteenth century to quasi-strict liability today (see §6.6 *supra*), may also be related to rising information costs to potential victims but not potential injurers.[7]

The argument that nineteenth-century common law favored growth is slightly more plausible with regard to accidents to strangers. Consider two alternative rules of law, one that a railroad is liable to travelers injured at railroad crossings only if the railroad was negligent, the other that the railroad is strictly liable to them, unless, perhaps, they were contributorily negligent. The accident rate will be similar under both rules but the railroad's costs will be higher under the second and this will lead to an increase in its prices and a fall in its output and profits, as we saw in Chapter 6. The first rule encourages and the second rule discourages railroading, although perhaps trivially.

It does not follow, however, that the first rule constitutes a subsidy to railroading in any pejorative sense of that term. As we saw in Chapter 6, the choice between negligence and strict liability involves a complex calculus, and it is not clear that the calculus points to strict liability for railroad accidents. And even if it did, so that the choice of negligence could be said to have been a subsidy to railroading, there may have been an economic justification. The construction of a railroad line in the nineteenth century increased the value of land up and down the

5. See Adam Smith, An Enquiry Into the Nature and Causes of the Wealth of Nations 112-113, 116-117 (Edwin Cannan ed. 1976). On the behavior of modern workers in this regard, see W. Kip Viscusi, Wealth Effects and Earning Premiums for Job Hazards, 60 Rev. Econ. & Stat. 408 (1978), and studies cited there; W. Kip Viscusi, Risk by Choice: Regulating Health and Safety in the Workplace, ch. 3 (1983).

6. Except that, given the abolition of contributory negligence, limiting the amount of damages was necessary to preserve the worker's incentive to take care, by denying him full compensation if he did not. This is the same function performed by deductibles in insurance policies. See generally Safety and the Work Force: Incentives and Disincentives in Workers' Compensation (John D. Worrall ed. 1983).

7. This thesis is explored in William M. Landes & Richard A. Posner, A Positive Economic Theory of Products Liability, forthcoming in Journal of Legal Studies.

line by giving the owners better access to markets. Unless the railroad owned the affected land, however, or could negotiate in advance of construction with every landowner, it would not be able to capture the entire increase in value and hence would not invest in new construction up to the point where the last dollar spent increased land values [8] by just one dollar. If the courts chose the less costly (to railroads) of the two efficient liability rules because they sensed that railroad revenues were less than they should be to stimulate the economically correct level of investment in the railroad industry, they may have been nudging the economy a bit closer to the most efficient employment of its resources. We saw in Chapter 6 that externalizing accident costs is one method of stimulating the provision of external benefits.

An even clearer case for externalizing accident costs in order to encourage the provision of external benefits is the traditional immunity of charitable enterprises from tort liability.[9] As we shall see in Chapter 16, a free-rider (external-benefit) problem prevents the market from providing the efficient level of charitable services. One way to reduce the severity of this problem is to allow charities to externalize some of their costs. Notice that the cost externalization was much greater for charities than for railroads since the latter were always liable for their negligently inflicted injuries. But then the external benefits, at least when divided by the number of accidents, were probably greater for charities than for railroads. Notice also that virtually all states have abolished the charitable tort immunity, perhaps because charity is a superior good (see §1.1 *supra*, note 3) (why is that relevant?) and because the charitable deduction from income tax provides a more efficient method of increasing the provision of charitable services (see §17.8 *infra*).

Professor Horwitz offers the following "important example of class bias": In an employment contract for an agreed period (usually one year) with wages to be paid at the end of the period, an employee who broke the contract was not entitled to recover the value of his work done up to the breach (minus any damages caused the employer); yet if a builder broke a building contract without fault, he was entitled to such a recovery.[10] An obvious distinction is overlooked: The deferral of payment in the employment case was a device for assuring that the

8. *Net* values: any reductions in land value due to the construction of the line (the line might, for example, reduce the locational advantage of land closer to markets) would have to be offset against the increases. For estimates of the social benefits from railroading in nineteenth-century America, see Robert William Fogel, Railroads and American Economic Growth, in The Reinterpretation of American History 187 (Robert William Fogel & Stanley L. Engerman eds. 1971); Patrick O'Brien, The New Economic History of the Railways (1977).

9. Termed "outrageous" in Lawrence M. Friedman, A History of American Law 416 (1973).

10. Horwitz, *supra* note 1, at 188.

employee completed the agreed term of work. If he were paid periodically and quit, the employer would have no practical legal remedy. To
make the employer liable for accrued wages subject to having to prove
as an offset the damages that the employee's quitting caused him would
reduce the effectiveness, and increase the cost, of the employer's self-
help remedy.[11] The building cases expressly assume that the builder
has completed the job contracted for but that the completed performance
differs in minor particulars from that agreed upon; in such a case the
owner is properly remitted to his damage remedy against the builder
for reasons explained in Chapter 4 (again see §4.13 *supra*).

Horwitz argues that the rule in the building cases fostered enterprise,
while the rule in the employment cases did not discourage it because:
"Penal provisions in labor contracts, by contrast, have only redistribu-
tional consequences, since they can hardly be expected to deter the
laboring classes from selling their services in a subsistence economy."[12]
No evidence that nineteenth-century America had a subsistence economy
is presented and it seems strange that people living at a subsistence
level could be induced to sign contracts under which they agreed to
receive no wages for a full year! If the workers of the time were living
at a subsistence level, no form of contract could redistribute wealth
from them to employers since they would have no wealth.

Consider the suggestion that the development of impossibility and
related doctrines in the law of contracts demonstrates the decline of
free market principles of law since the nineteenth century.[13] Those principles are indeed less influential than they once were, but the specific
illustration is inapt. As we have seen, impossibility and related excuses
are necessary to make the law of contracts efficient; they are implicit
in the positive economic theory of contract law. This mistake is an especially puzzling one in view of the same author's assertion that nineteenth-
century contract law consistently favored the performing party,[14] who
might be expected to favor a liberal doctrine of excuses.

Economics can be used to illuminate much darker recesses of legal
history than thus far suggested. One of the reasons that negligence
liability for railroad accidents has seemed to legal historians an example
of the law's tilt toward business is that in the eighteenth century, before
the advent of the railroad, accident liability had been to a significant
extent strict liability. The nineteenth century was in fact the culmination
of a long trend away from strict liability in the law — in contract law
and criminal law as well as in tort law. Ancient and primitive societies
were dominated by concepts of strict liability. The trend has an economic

11. See §4.13 *supra*, and notice the analogy to an installment sales contract in which
title does not pass to the buyer until the good is fully paid for.

12. Horwitz, *supra* note 1, at 188.

13. See Grant Gilmore, The Death of Contract 80-82, 94-96 (1974).

14. See note 2 *supra*.

explanation.[15] The spread of literacy and the growth of scientific knowledge have enhanced the factfinding capacities of courts over the centuries, thus reducing the costs of information about the merits of legal disputes. There have also been great advances in the market provision of insurance. As we know from Chapter 6, strict liability both requires less information than negligence liability, because it avoids what is often a difficult factual and analytical inquiry, and provides (in tort and contract, not criminal, law) a form of insurance. Both these advantages were greater in times past than they are today, and since as we know strict liability involves certain costs that negligence liability does not, it is not surprising that as the benefits of strict liability have diminished there has been a movement away from it. What is surprising is the recrudescence of strict liability in the twentieth century, illustrated by the workmen's compensation and strict products liability movements. But as we have suggested, economic factors may explain these movements, too.

This discussion of the economics of legal history is severely incomplete. There are many fascinating studies of the economic history of property rights, some referenced in Chapter 3.[16] The changing role of the family, a changing role illuminated by economics, appears to explain historical changes in family law, as suggested in Chapter 5. Other historical insights have been suggested in other chapters.

§8.3   The Moral Content of the Common Law

The theory that the common law is best understood as a system for promoting economic efficiency will strike many readers as an incomplete — if not severely impoverished — theory, particularly in its apparent disregard of the moral dimension of law. Surely, it will be argued, the true purpose of law, especially of those fundamental principles of law embodied in the common law of England and the United States, is to correct injustices and thereby vindicate the moral sense.

But is there really a fundamental inconsistency between morality and efficiency? The economic value of such moral principles as honesty, truthfulness, frugality, trustworthiness (as by keeping promises), consideration for others, charity, neighborliness, hard work, and avoidance of negligence and of coercion will be apparent to the careful reader of the previous chapters. Honesty, trustworthiness, and love reduce the

15. See Richard A. Posner, The Economics of Justice 199-203 (1981). Part II of The Economics of Justice is an economic study of primitive and ancient social and legal institutions.

16. See, e.g., John R. Umbeck, A Theory of Property Rights, With Application to the California Gold Rush (1981).

costs of transactions. Forswearing coercion promotes the voluntary exchange of goods. Neighborliness and other forms of selflessness reduce external costs and increase external benefits — indeed, economists sometimes call externalities "neighborhood effects." Charity reduces the demand for costly public welfare programs. Care reduces social waste.[1] Granted, adherence to moral principles sometimes reduces the wealth of society — "honor among thieves" illustrates this point. And in Chapter 10 we shall see that cartelization is often thwarted by free-rider problems that would disappear if members of cartels were completely selfless or completely trustworthy. But on balance it would seem that adherence to generally accepted moral principles increases the wealth of society more than it reduces it, especially if the principles are appropriately ordered, so that selflessness, trustworthiness, and other instrumental traits are made instrumental to social rather than private welfare where the two clash.

To the extent that adherence to moral principles enhances an individual's ability to maximize his satisfactions, there is no occasion for attempting to impose them coercively. To some extent they do: The slogan honesty is the best policy was intended as an appeal to self-interest. Failing to honor one's promises is (most of the time) poor business judgment even in the absence of legal sanctions for breach of contract. Empathy with consumers will make it easier to design a product that will sell.

But morality often conflicts with individual self-interest; and the common law may be viewed as an effort to attach costs to the violation of those moral principles that enhance the efficiency of a market economy. True, the law does not seek to enforce any moral principle to the limit. The law of contracts, for example, enforces only a limited subset of promises; many morally objectionable breaches of promise give rise to no cause of action. But this is because the scope of the law is limited by the costs of administering it. The costs of legally enforcing all promises would exceed the gains because many promises do not enhance value significantly, and some that do may be made in circumstances where the costs of legal error outweigh the benefits from enforcing the promise in the form made (for example, a contract rendered unenforceable by the Statute of Frauds because oral rather than written).

Even more fundamentally, the law pays no attention to breaches of the moral code that do not affect other people — for example, the slander uttered in solitude. Here the costs of enforcing morality would be great and the benefits in efficiency small. Yet one can see how a habit of refraining from slander regardless of the circumstances could be viewed (and hence inculcated) as morally desirable, because it reduced the likelihood that an injurious slander would be uttered.

§8.3   1. Does this suggest an economic reason why a person is more likely to feel indignant if struck by a careless driver than if he is the victim of an unavoidable accident?

Further complicating the relationship between law and morals is the fact that the law sometimes attaches sanctions to morally unobjectionable conduct. Many (why not all?) applications of strict liability have this character. But this, an economist may suggest, is because the cost of distinguishing between the moral and the immoral is often disproportionate to the benefits.

Although the above analysis suggests a fairly close congruence between justice and efficiency, here are some examples where the common law seems to deviate from the efficiency ethic:

(1) When I get married I ask my wife to agree, when I die, to fling herself on my funeral pyre. I pay her what she considers fair consideration for this promise, which both of us fully intend to be legally enforceable, knowing that she may want to renege when the time for performance arrives. No court would enforce such a contract or, less dramatically, a suicide pact.

(2) No court would enforce Shylock's contract with Antonio in *The Merchant of Venice*.

(3) No court would enforce a voluntary contract to become another's slave.

(4) A convicted criminal would not be permitted to substitute a lashing that would impose on him pain slightly less than his prison sentence even if he showed that the cost savings to the state would greatly exceed the reduction in the severity of punishment that was his motive for proposing the transaction.

(5) Racially restrictive covenants are not legally enforceable.

Are these really such economic puzzlers? Examples (1) and (3) are not. They are by definition once-in-a-lifetime transactions and the likelihood of a disastrous mistake is very high. Example (2) is a classic contract penalty, made particularly fishy (excuse the pun) by the maritime setting: The probability of default was substantial no matter how much care Antonio exercised. As for example (4), because people have very different and hard to measure thresholds of pain it is difficult (i.e., costly) to impose a desired level of cost or pain by means of afflictive punishment; the differences in the pecuniary costs of imprisonment (due to income differences) and in the nonpecuniary costs of imprisonment (due to social status, standard of living, previous imprisonment, etc.) are somewhat more easily measurable. Finally, example (5) is not a common law example. The legal source of the policy against private racial discrimination, a policy founded on distributive rather than efficiency notions (see Chapter 27), is in the Constitution rather than the common law.

The major ethical problem posed by an efficiency approach to the common law is not the occasional discrepancy between an economically derived ethical scheme and the traditional ethics of everyday life, but the discrepancy between efficiency maximization and notions of the just distribution of wealth. In a market economy where the role of law, and of government generally, is just to control externalities and reduce transaction costs — which is basically all the law and government that economic efficiency requires — differences in people's tastes, abilities, and luck may generate substantial inequalities in the distribution of income and wealth; and in racially or ethnically diverse societies, these inequalities may be correlated with racial and ethnic differences. We shall look at some theories of distributive justice in Part V. The point to be made here is that the common law is, for the most part, distributively neutral. As suggested earlier, there are practical reasons for this, having to do with the incapacity of courts to redistribute wealth systematically; but there is also an ethical reason. Efficiency and redistribution are antithetical (with certain exceptions, as where free-rider problems discourage charitable gifts, and government steps in to correct the problems and bring about the level of poor relief that would exist in their absence).

This surprising point can be made clearer by contrasting efficiency and utility (in the utilitarian sense) as social goods. Although economics, in its normative dimension, can be thought of as a form or variant of applied utilitarianism, there is an important difference in the emphasis that the economist, but not the utilitarian, places on willingness to pay as a criterion of an efficient allocation of resources. It might be that I would get much more pleasure out of an ounce of caviar than a rich man would, and yet the economist would not say that there was a misallocation of resources if (as is the case) the price discourages me, but not him, from consuming caviar. The economist would not say that I should be allowed to steal the caviar from the rich man, merely in order to increase the total human happiness in the universe. But the utilitarian might say that, depending on what he thought would be the overall consequences for happiness of allowing theft. If maximizing happiness requires redistribution, whether on a retail or a wholesale basis, the utilitarian will want redistribution to be part of the idea of justice. But the efficiency ethic takes the existing distribution of income and wealth, and the underlying human qualities that generate that distribution, as given, and within very broad limits (what limits?) is uncritical of the changes in that distribution that are brought about by efficient transactions between persons unequally endowed with the world's tangible and intangible goods.

Even a thoroughgoing utilitarian, however, might approve a division of labor in government whereby the courts in elaborating common law principles confined their attention to efficiency, while the taxing and spending branches of government, with their greater capacity for redistributing wealth cheaply and effectively, concentrated on redistribution. Unless a society is permeated by envy, increasing the size of the pie deserves as much attention as trying to make the slices more equal; at least it deserves some attention. Anyway such a division of labor may explain the emphasis of the common law on efficiency.

§8.4   The Moral Form of Law

The basic theme of this part of the book has been the profound relationship between legal and economic order. If there is such a relationship, it may be possible to deduce the basic formal characteristics of law itself from economic theory.

Law has sometimes been defined simply as a command backed up by the coercive power of the state. By this definition, any order emanating from the sovereign power is law. But that strains the ordinary meaning of the word law and it has been suggested that to be descriptive of the way in which the word is actually used the definition must include the following additional elements:

(1) to count as law, a command must be capable of being complied with by those to whom it is addressed;

(2) it must treat equally those who are similarly situated in all respects relevant to the command;

(3) it must be public;

(4) there must be a procedure by which the truth of any facts necessary to the application of the command according to its terms is ascertained.[1]

These elements are part of the economic theory of law.

The primary (though not exclusive — why?) function of law, in an economic perspective, is to alter incentives. This implies that law does not command the impossible, since a command impossible to fulfill will not alter behavior. The impossible command is to be distinguished from the legal sanction that is unavoidable only because the cost of avoidance is greater than the cost of the sanction, or, as in many contract cases, because the sanction is really just the payment of the proceeds of a kind of insurance policy. There is no incongruity in making the party who breaks his contract liable in damages although the cost of performing the contract would have greatly exceeded the damages from nonperformance, or even though performance would have been literally impossible. The law simply has placed the risk of nonperformance on the party who fails to perform.

The requirement that law must treat equals equally is another way of saying that the law must have a rational structure, for to treat differently things that are the same is irrational. Economic theory is a system of deductive logic: When correctly applied, it yields results that are consistent with one another. Insofar as the law has an implicit economic structure, it must be rational; it must treat like cases alike.

Viewed in an economic perspective as a system for altering incentives

§8.4   1. See John Rawls, A Theory of Justice 237-239 (1971), and references cited therein.

and thus regulating behavior, law must also be public. If the content of a law became known only after the events to which it was applicable occurred, the existence of the law could have no effect on the conduct of the parties subject to it. Stated otherwise, the economic theory of law is a theory of law as deterrence, and a threat that is not communicated cannot deter. The major, but a consistent, exception is the prevention or incapacitation theory behind some doctrines of criminal law.

Finally, the economic theory of law presupposes machinery for ascertaining the existence of the facts necessary to the correct application of a law. The deterrent effect of law is weakened (and in the limit would disappear) if enforced without regard to whether the circumstances are those to which the law was intended to apply. Suppose there is a law against price fixers but no effort is made to ascertain who is fixing prices; instead, one in 10,000 people is selected at random and punished as a price fixer. Then there will be no deterrence of price fixing. The only difference between the price fixer and the person who does not fix prices is that the former has profits from price fixing; the expected liability of the two is the same.

Rawls' formal criteria are awfully austere. Let us go one step further. Ever since Aristotle it has been argued that the basic function of a legal system is to do corrective justice, that is, to rectify wrongful acts; and we must consider whether a legal system animated by economic principles could be said to do corrective justice. If corrective justice is interpreted to mean that the legal system must attempt to compensate for all injuries, then the answer is no.

But Aristotle spoke of rectification rather than compensation and of wrongful rather than merely harmful acts; and in his sense the common law is a system of corrective justice. The common law uses sanctions such as compensatory and punitive damages, injunctions, and fines and prison sentences to correct wrongful (= inefficient, resource wasting) conduct. This is true even where the methods more or less deliberately allow wrongdoers to get off scot-free in particular cases. The rule that contributory negligence is a complete defense to a negligence suit, the rule that there is no right of contribution among joint tortfeasors, and the substitution of heavy criminal penalties for lighter penalties imposed with a probability of one illustrate the common law's apparent willingness to allow wrongs to go uncorrected in many cases. But the appearance is misleading. It results from the common mistake of noneconomists in failing to distinguish ex ante (before the fact) from ex post (after the fact). Ex post, the tortfeasor who has the good fortune to injure a contributorily negligent victim gets off scot-free. But ex ante, as we saw in Chapter 6, a negligence – contributory negligence system imparts correct incentives to potential injurers as well as potential victims. The threat of liability is a kind of price charged in advance that leads the potential injurer (in most instances) to take steps to prevent injury from occurring. And so with the other examples. Of course, if we were very disturbed by the fact that some wrongdoers are lucky and beat the system, we could set up a punishment scheme that would make sure (or more sure than at present) that every wrong was corrected. But nothing in the Aristotelian conception of corrective justice suggests that it is a commodity for which society should be willing to pay an infinite price.

Suggested Readings[2]

1. Gary S. Becker, A Theory of Social Interactions, 82 J. Pol. Econ. 1063 (1974).
2. William Bishop, The Contract-Tort Boundary and the Economics of Insurance, 12 J. Leg. Stud. 241 (1983).
3. Ronald H. Coase, Adam Smith's View of Man, 19 J. Law & Econ. 529 (1976).
4. Herbert Hovenkamp, The Economics of Legal History, 67 Minn. L. Rev. 645 (1983).
5. Nicholas Mercuro & Timothy P. Ryan, Law, Economics and Public Policy 117-137 (1984).
6. Richard A. Posner, The Concept of Corrective Justice in Recent Theories of Tort Law, 10 J. Leg. Stud. 187 (1981).
7. Paul H. Rubin, Business Firms and the Common Law: The Evolution of Efficient Rules (1983).
8. Altruism, Morality, and Economic Theory (Edmund S. Phelps ed. 1975).
9. Law, Economics, and Philosophy: A Critical Introduction with Applications to the Law of Torts (Mark Kuperberg & Charles Beitz eds. 1983).

Problems

1. Assess the argument that employers had such great bargaining power vis-à-vis employees in the nineteenth century that the employees were in no position to bargain for cost-justified safety precautions. Cf. §4.8 *supra.*
2. What would be the effects on the distribution of income and wealth of a judicial ruling that shifted from farmers to railroads the cost of injuries to cattle resulting from failure to keep the cattle off the railroad's right of way?
3. Should accident cases arising out of a contractual relationship (for example, between a railroad and its passengers, or a doctor and his

---

2. See also Suggested Readings for Chapter 2.

patients) be treated as breach of contract rather than tort cases? Is there any utility to maintaining the distinction between tort and contract in such cases?

4. Analyze the moral and economic considerations involved in permitting imprisoned criminals to agree to undergo medical experiments in exchange for a reduction in sentence. For background see National Commission for the Protection of Human Subjects of Biomedical and Behavioral Research, Staff Paper: Prisoners as Research Subjects (Oct. 31, 1975).

5. There is a tort of inducing a breach of contract — committed, for example, by one firm's enticing another's employee to break his contract to come to work for it. Can you think of an economic rationale for this tort? See William M. Landes & Richard A. Posner, Joint and Multiple Tortfeasors: An Economic Analysis, 9 J. Leg. Stud. 517, 552-555 (1980).

6. The Ford Motor Company decides to shut down a plant in South Bend, Indiana, and open a similar plant in Birmingham, Alabama. One effect of the move will be to reduce land values in South Bend and increase them in Birmingham. From the standpoint of efficiency should Ford be required to compensate the adversely affected landowners?

7. Some students of jurisprudence think that legal duties are primary, rights secondary; others reverse the order. Which view is more congenial to economic analysis?

PART III

PUBLIC REGULATION OF THE MARKET

CHAPTER 9

THE THEORY OF MONOPOLY

§9.1 The Monopolist's Price and Output

We observed in Chapter 1 that a seller would not sell at a price lower than his opportunity cost, for that would mean forgoing a higher for a lower price. But what determines the upper bound of his price? Assuming his goal is to maximize profits (the difference between total revenues and total costs), his choice of price is constrained by the demand for his product and by the cost of production.

To relate price to revenue and thence to profit we shall need the concept of marginal revenue, the contribution to total revenue of selling one additional unit. As long as marginal revenue is positive, total revenue is growing. When marginal revenue falls to (or below) zero, it means that an additional sale will not raise (or will decrease) total revenue.

If the demand schedule is known, the marginal revenue schedule can be derived mathematically from it; this has been done in Figure 9.1.[1] The point at which the marginal revenue curve intersects the horizontal axis marks the level of output (q in Figure 9.1) at which total revenue is maximized. The price corresponding to that level of output is p. If the seller sold a smaller quantity, he would be to the left of

§9.1 1. Marginal revenue is simply the rate of change, or in mathematical terms the first derivative, of total revenue. And demand is simply the schedule of average revenue (total revenue divided by quantity), or price, at various levels of output. In the special case where the demand schedule for a product can be approximated by a straight line, as in Figure 9.1, the marginal revenue curve can be plotted very easily by drawing a straight line from the intersection of the demand curve with the vertical axis to a point on the horizontal axis midway between the origin and the intersection of the demand curve with the horizontal axis. For a simple mathematical treatment, see Richard A. Posner, Antitrust Law: An Economic Perspective 237-244 (1976). The important thing to understand is why marginal revenue falls faster than price. The reason is that whenever the seller lowers his price, he lowers it (unless he practices price discrimination, described later in this chapter) on all his output; hence the price he gets on the last unit sold adds less than that price to his total revenues.

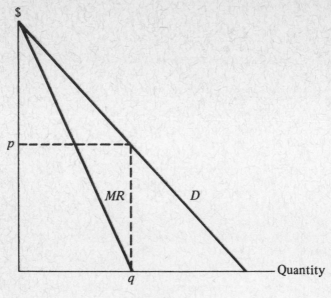

Figure 9.1

that intersection and additional output would increase his total revenues. If he sold a larger quantity, his revenue would be in the negative region of the marginal revenue curve, signifying that a reduction in output would increase his total revenue.

The effect of price on quantity and hence on revenue (which is simply price times quantity) is summarized in the extremely useful concept of *elasticity* — the proportional change in one variable caused by a proportional change in another. Here we are interested in the elasticity of demand with respect to price, i.e., the proportional effect on the quantity demanded of a (very small) proportional change in price. To illustrate, if a 1 percent price increase would cause the quantity demanded to fall by 2 percent, the elasticity of demand with respect to price (or, for brevity, simply the elasticity of demand[2]) is — 2 (why minus?). If the elasticity of demand were — 1, it would mean that a 1 percent increase in price would cause a 1 percent reduction in quantity demanded, and thus that total revenue was unchanged by the price change. This, the point of unitary elasticity, is the point on the demand curve at which the marginal revenue curve intersects the horizontal axis. At all points on the demand curve to the left of this intersection, demand is said to be elastic, because in that region a price increase will lead to a proportionately greater reduction of the quantity demanded and hence to a fall in total revenue. To the right, demand is said to be inelastic because

2. But the price elasticity of demand is not the only type of demand elasticity. See §1.1 *supra,* notes 3, 4 and accompanying text (an implicit discussion of the income elasticity of demand).

250

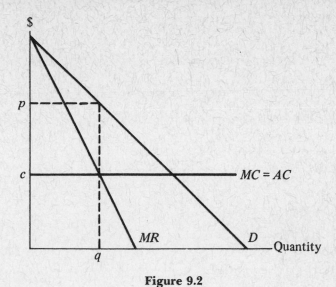

Figure 9.2

in this region a price increase will lead to a proportionately smaller reduction in the quantity demanded and hence to an increase in total revenue.

Since the seller is interested in his net revenue, or profit, rather than in his gross revenue, he needs to consider the effect of his choice of price on his total cost as well as on his total revenue. Price will affect that total by determining the number of units that must be produced and also, if marginal cost varies with the level of output, the cost per unit produced. Marginal cost is the change in total costs brought about by producing one more unit; equivalently, it is the addition to total costs of the last unit produced. There are also fixed costs (the expense of obtaining a patent would be a good example) — costs unaffected by output — but they are irrelevant to the determination of price and output. By definition, they are unaffected by the choice of price and output; they are no greater, and no smaller, whether the monopolist charges a very high price and produces little or a very low price and produces much.

The profit-maximizing seller will expand output so long as an additional unit sold adds more to his total revenue than to his total cost, and stop when the sale of an additional unit would increase his total cost by more than his total revenue. In other words, the profit-maximizing output is the quantity at which marginal revenue and marginal cost are equated, q in Figure 9.2. At this level of output, total revenue equals pq and total cost (average cost times quantity) cq.[3] Notice that if output

3. To make things simple, we assume that marginal costs are constant and that the firm has no fixed costs, i.e., has only variable costs. Under these assumptions, marginal equals average cost.

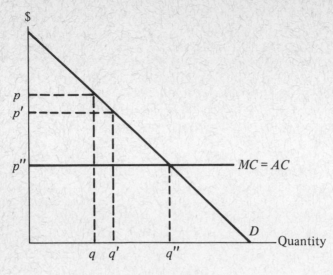

Figure 9.3

were smaller, profit would be smaller too, since the seller would be at the left of the intersection, where additional output would add more to total revenue than to total cost. With a larger quantity, profit would also be smaller. The seller would be to the right of the intersection, in the region where each unit sold adds more to total cost than to total revenue (that is, where marginal cost exceeds marginal revenue).

Another name for p in Figure 9.2 is the monopoly price, because it is the price that a firm having no competition or fear thereof would charge. Competition would make the price untenable. Suppose that A, initially the only seller of the product (widgets of course) whose cost and demand curves are shown in Figures 9.1 and 9.2, establishes a price of p and sells q widgets, and that other sellers can produce and sell widgets at the same cost as A. One of them, B, attracted by A's large profits ($pq - cq$), decides to make and sell widgets, also at price p.

Figure 9.3 shows the result. With B selling one fourth as many widgets as A (B's output is $q' - q$), the total quantity of widgets on the market (q') is one fourth again as large as before. Consumers will not pay p for the larger quantity of widgets, but only p'. Maybe A and B will now cut their outputs — but C, D, E, and others are waiting to enter the market in order to capture a share of the profits that enticed B. Entry will continue until price is bid down to p'', where it is just equal to the opportunity cost of producing additional widgets. Entry is attractive until that point is reached because resources devoted to manufacturing widgets earn more than their opportunity cost, and hence more than they could earn in competitive markets. But the output of widgets will not be expanded beyond q'' (corresponding to p''), because then those resources would be earning less than their opportunity cost.[4]

The possibility of entry may seem to make monopoly an academic concept. But sometimes entry takes a long time, or is forbidden, or the new entrant is not able to produce at so low a cost as the existing firm. An important example of impeded entry is the governmentally protected monopoly — for example, a patent monopoly.

Just as monopoly is not a sufficient condition of monopoly pricing, neither is it a necessary condition. Imagine a market of 100 sellers, each producing 1,000 units, and expansion of production either by existing firms or by the entry of new firms is impossible. Each seller will have monopoly power — the power to raise the market price above the competitive level. For example, if one of the 100 sellers reduced his output from 1,000 to 900 units, the total output of the market would fall from 100,000 to 99,900 units, and the market price would rise, just as if a monopolist of the product had decided to reduce his output by the same amount.

§9.2   Effect of Changes in Cost or Demand on the Monopoly Price

Let's see what happens to the optimum monopoly price and output if the monopolist's costs rise or fall or if demand changes. If costs fall (unless these are fixed costs), the optimum monopoly price will fall and output will rise. Remember that the monopolist stops expanding output at the point where his marginal revenue and marginal cost curves intersect. If the marginal cost curve falls, the marginal revenue curve will now lie above it, and the monopolist will expand his output until that curve again intersects the marginal cost curve. This is shown in Figure 9.4.

Suppose demand declines. That is, at any given price consumers will buy an equal percentage less of the good (in Figure 9.5, about 25 percent less). Assuming constant marginal costs, as in Figure 9.5, the monopolist will not change his price. Marginal cost is unchanged. So is the responsiveness (elasticity) of quantity demanded to a change in price: Although consumers will buy less at any price, the proportional change in quantity demanded brought about by a price change is unaltered. Hence the monopolist will charge the same price as before but will sell less since

---

4. What is each firm's elasticity of demand under perfect competition? Graph the demand curve of the perfectly competitive firm. If stumped, see Figure 3.2 in Chapter 3.

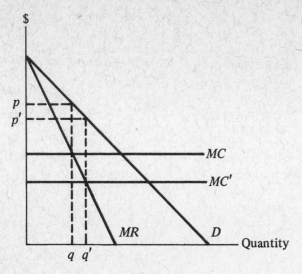

Figure 9.4

demand is lower. This illustrates the important point, to which we shall come back in the next chapter, that the monopoly price depends only on the elasticity of demand and on marginal costs.

If demand falls and the monopolist's marginal costs are not constant, then the optimum monopoly price will change. A nonhorizontal marginal cost curve implies that marginal cost is different at different levels of quantity produced. Since a change in demand will alter the monopolist's optimal output, his marginal cost will change and therefore (from the earlier discussion) his price too.[1]

§9.3 Efficiency Consequences of Monopoly

A glance back at Figure 9.3 will show that output under monopoly is smaller than under competition: q instead of q''. This is because the monopoly price causes some consumers to substitute other products, products that the higher price makes more attractive. The substitution involves a loss in value. This can be seen most clearly by assuming that for each use of the monopolized product there is a substitute product that is identical to the monopolized product but simply costs more to produce, and hence is priced higher than the monopolized product would be priced if it were sold at its competitive price, but lower than

§9.2 1. See Richard A. Posner, Antitrust Law: An Economic Perspective 248-249 (1976), for a slightly more formal treatment of these points.

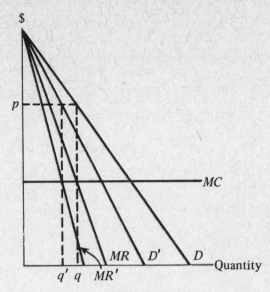

Figure 9.5

the monopoly price. The effect of monopoly is then to make some consumers satisfy their demands by switching to goods that cost society more to produce than the monopolized good. The added cost is a waste to society.

This cost is approximated by the triangle marked *DW* (for deadweight loss) in Figure 9.6. Imagine price rising gradually from P_c to P_m; at each rise consumers are deflected to more costly substitutes and the last consumer deflected buys a product that costs infinitesimally less to produce than the monopoly price.[1]

The concept of deadweight loss nicely illustrates the distinction

§9.3 1. Notice, however, the dependence of this analysis on the assumption that the substitute is sold at a competitive price. If it is not, monopoly may prevent rather than create a deadweight loss. To illustrate, suppose leather buttons are monopolized and sell at a price of 10¢, even though the cost of production is only 6¢. Plastic buttons, the nearest substitute for leather buttons, sell for 8¢ each. As a result of the monopolization of leather buttons, some people substitute plastic buttons, and if the price of a plastic button is equal to its cost this substitution is inefficient. A product that costs 8¢ to produce is being bought in place of one that costs only 6¢ to produce.

But suppose plastic buttons are *not* being sold at a price equal to cost. Their 8¢ price is a monopoly price; they cost only 2¢ to produce, i.e., less than leather buttons. With leather buttons being sold at the monopoly price of 10¢, the consumer will buy more plastic buttons despite *their* monopoly price, and this is efficient since plastic buttons cost less to produce. If the monopoly of leather buttons is now terminated, price will decline to the competitive level, 6¢, and consumers will begin to substitute leather for plastic buttons. This is an inefficient substitution, assuming leather buttons are not worth 4¢ (6¢ − 2¢) more than plastic buttons. The empirical significance of this type of problem (the problem of the "second best") is dubious, however. See Richard Schmalensee, The Control of Natural Monopolies 30-31 (1979).

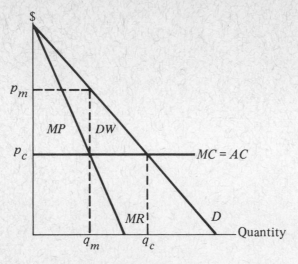

Figure 9.6

stressed in the preceding chapter between economic and utilitarian conceptions of welfare. The conclusion that *DW* in Figure 9.6 is a net social cost rests on the assumption that a dollar is worth the same to consumers and producers, or, stated otherwise, that distributive factors will be ignored in assessing social costs. For *MP*, the transfer of wealth from consumers to producers brought about by increasing the price from the competitive to the monopoly level, is treated as a wash; the consumers' loss is equated to the producers' gain. The social cost of monopoly would be higher than *DW* if a $1 loss to consumers were thought to yield less than a dollar's worth of benefit to producers and would be lower than *DW* if the reverse were assumed.

The transfer of wealth from consumers to producers brought about by monopoly pricing is a conversion of consumer surplus into producer surplus. Consumer surplus is the area under the demand curve above the competitive price; in Figure 9.6 it is the triangle whose base is the line labeled *MC = AC*. *MP* is the part of the triangle that gets transformed into producer surplus. *DW* is the part that gets lost. The remaining area is retained as consumer surplus. Consumer surplus is a measure of the aggregate value that consumers as a group attach to a product over and above the price they pay for it. As price rises, those consumers who do not value the product greatly are deflected to substitutes, while those who stick with the product get less net value from their purchases because they are paying a higher price.

Although *MP*, the part of the consumer surplus that is turned into producer surplus, looks like a pure transfer payment, it can be a source of social costs, even if no distributional weights are assigned to transfers

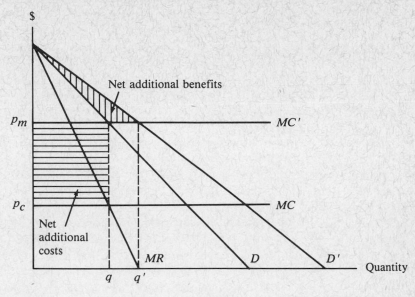

Figure 9.7

from consumers to producers. Assume in Figure 9.7 that the market contains many firms but the government sets price at p_m and forbids new entry into the market.[2] Since each additional sale that a seller can make will yield him a monopoly profit of $p_m - p_c$, each seller will have an incentive to increase his share of the market. He cannot do so by cutting price, because that is forbidden, so he will try to make his product more attractive than his competitors' in other ways — by increasing its quality, providing better service, etc. The process of nonprice competition will continue, in the absence of some agreement to limit such competition, until the sellers' marginal costs rise to the level of the fixed price, so that additional expenditures on product enhancement would yield a loss. Although this competitive process will increase the value of the product to the consumer (i.e., demand will grow), the costs may exceed the consumer benefits, yielding a net social loss as in Figure 9.7.

Until the recent deregulation of the airline industry, the Civil Aeronautics Board prevented both price competition among the airlines that it regulated and the creation of new trunk airlines. As a result, the prices charged by the airlines exceeded competitive levels. Yet the industry had no monopoly profits and indeed was periodically on the verge of bankruptcy. The potential monopoly profits had been transformed into costs by vigorous nonprice competition, especially the scheduling of

2. If the price is fixed but new entry is not prevented, will entry occur and if so with what effects?

excessively frequent flights, resulting in low capacity utilization and therefore high costs per passenger carried.[3]

When price competition and new entry are not prevented by government regulation, the problem of wasteful service competition is less acute. But if a monopoly or cartel has any expected monopoly profits, that expectation will induce firms to expend resources on forming and maintaining monopolies and cartels and, once they are formed (in the case of a cartel), on engrossing as large a portion of the sales of the market as possible through nonprice competition. These resources will be (largely) wasted from a social standpoint.

Notice the close parallel to the analysis of the costs of pure coercive transfers payments, such as theft, in Chapter 6 and especially Chapter 7. Theft is also "just" a transfer payment; the victim's loss is the thief's gain.[4] The economic objection to theft involves not the transfer as such but the effect of the opportunity to obtain such transfers in inducing the expenditure of resources on thieving and on preventing theft. There is an identical economic objection to monopoly that is distinct from the output effect of monopoly pricing — an effect that has no counterpart in theft.

Among other possible economic objections to monopoly, the monopolist may be able to shift the demand curve for his product outward — leading to overproduction rather than underproduction — by misrepresenting the price or quality of his product (see §4.7 *supra*) or by prevailing on government to reduce the supply of competitive products or increase the demand for complementary ones.[5] Some economists also believe that monopoly reduces the incentive of a firm to innovate and to use its inputs efficiently. The theoretical basis for this view is obscure, the evidence mixed.[6] Against monopoly it can be argued:

(1) The monopolist has less to gain from innovation. He already has appropriated much of the available consumer surplus; the competitive firm that might become a monopolist through innovation has not. (Does this argument apply to product innovation or just to process innovation?)

3. See, e.g., George W. Douglas & James C. Miller, III, The CAB's Domestic Passenger Fare Investigation, 5 Bell J. Econ. & Mgmt. Sci. 205 (1974); Airline Deregulation: The Early Experience (John R. Meyer & Clinton V. Oster, Jr., eds. 1981).

4. Is this clearly so when the theft is of a good other than money?

5. Two products are complementary when an increase in the demand for one will lead to an increase in the demand for the other. The ability of firms to obtain governmental assistance in suppressing competition is discussed later. See especially Chapter 19. A competitive industry acting through a trade association may be able to obtain the same kind of governmental protection as a monopolist. This is an instance of the more general proposition that independent firms can often achieve the same results as monopoly by coordination. See §10.1 *infra*.

6. See William D. Nordhaus, Invention, Growth, and Welfare: A Theoretical Treatment of Technological Change, pt. 1 (1969); Morton I. Kamien & Nancy L. Schwartz, Market Structure and Innovation (1982); F.M. Scherer, Industrial Market Structure and Economic Performance, chs. 15-16 (2d ed. 1980).

(2) The monopolist has less to lose than the competitive firm from not innovating. The competitive firm may go broke, and bankruptcy is more costly than just not making handsome profits is, because there are deadweight costs of bankruptcy (more on this subject in Chapter 14). If this point is set aside, however, it can be shown that the penalty for failing to maximize profits, through innovation or otherwise, is the same for the monopolist as for the competitive firm, provided the monopolist's common stock is publicly traded (see §15.4 *infra*).

(3) Firms differ in their ability to innovate. If there is more than one firm in the market, therefore, the market is more likely to contain at least one above-average innovator, and he will cause the rate of innovation to rise.

The principal argument for monopoly as a way of encouraging innovation is that the reward for successful innovation and cost minimization is often greater for the monopolist, since the competitive seller's success may be promptly duplicated by his rivals. It is concern about prompt duplication that has led to the grant of patent protection; but patents, as we know, are limited in time and scope. To put it differently, the monopolist is better able than the competitive firm to internalize externalities (cf. §7.7 *supra*), including information externalities, which is what inventions are.[7]

§9.4 Price Discrimination

The theory of monopoly expounded in the preceding sections assumes that the monopolist sells his product at a single price. Ordinarily the assumption is justified. If he sold at two different prices, purchasers charged the lower price would resell to purchasers charged the higher price. Such reselling (known as arbitrage) would make it impossible for the seller to maintain different prices. But arbitrage is not always feasible. The product may be impossible to store for later resale (as in the case of many services) or there may be contractual restrictions on resale. If the monopolist can prevent arbitrage, he is likely to fix different prices to different purchasers depending not on the costs of selling to them, which are the same, but on the elasticity of their demands for his product. This is price discrimination.

The downward slope of the demand curve implies as we have seen that consumers (or some of them) would be willing to pay prices well in excess of cost for some units of the monopolist's output but prices

7. What do you think would be the effect of monopoly on product quality? Product variety?

only slightly higher than cost for others, and nothing at all for still others. There is no single price that extracts the full value that consumers attach to being able to purchase some units of the good yet does not sacrifice the smaller but still positive profits at which additional units could be sold. Ideally the monopolist would like to negotiate separately with each consumer over each unit. Then he would never turn away a customer willing to pay a price equal to cost; so his output would be identical to that under competition. But the transaction costs of perfect (first degree) price discrimination are prohibitive. Usually the best the discriminating monopolist can do is to divide his customers into a few groups and set a single (although different) price for each group.

The effect on output of imperfect (third degree) price discrimination is indeterminate.[1] Suppose that the single monopoly price is $10 but rather than charging that price the monopolist classifies buyers into two groups and charges $5 to members of one and $20 to members of the other. He gains sales — to those in the first group who will not pay $10 but are willing to pay $5. But he also loses sales — to those in the second group who are willing to pay $10 but refuse to pay $20. The lost sales may outnumber the sales gained. His output may be lower although his profits will be higher.

Even perfect price discrimination would not eliminate the economic objection to monopoly. The competitive output would be attained; but, with the potential profits of monopoly now greater,[2] more resources would be wasted on trying to get, hold, and prevent monopoly. The social costs of monopoly might therefore be higher.

§9.5 Other Impediments to Monopolizing: Competition for the Market, Durability, New Entry

If a buyer agrees to take all his requirements of a particular good from a single seller, the seller will thereby acquire a monopoly — of sorts — over that supply. But the buyer will not pay any more than the competitive price if three conditions are satisfied: that there are several sellers in a position to supply him, that they do not collude, and that the cost of making an effective contract for the period of the monopoly is not prohibitive. For then sellers will vie with one another to offer an attractive

§9.4 1. See F.M. Scherer, Industrial Market Structure and Economic Performance 316, 321 (2d ed. 1980).

2. What would be the total monopoly profits in Figure 9.6 under perfect price discrimination?

contract, and the contract price will be the competitive price.[1] But suppose that once the seller who has gotten the contract begins to perform, it will take a long time for anyone else to step into his place as the buyer's supplier (see §12.1 *infra,* on why this might be so). In such a situation the buyer will need a long-term contract to protect him against monopoly pricing, and long-term contracts may involve costly inflexibilities (see §13.7 *infra*).

There is a special difficulty in monopolizing durable goods,[2] most dramatically illustrated by the case of land. If one person owned all of the land in the United States and wanted to sell at a price that maximized his profits, like any other monopolist he would fix a price at which only a portion of the land would be bought. But once the sale was completed he would have an incentive to begin selling off the remaining portions of the land at a lower price, until eventually all of the land was sold. Knowing this, people would not pay his initial price, and the attempt to monopolize would fail.

Diamonds are a durable good too, yet the production of diamonds has long been controlled by an international cartel that limits output and charges monopoly prices.[3] But unlike land, diamonds are produced continuously. If one year the diamond cartel stepped up production and slashed prices in order to reach a segment of the community that could not ordinarily afford diamonds, the value of every diamond in existence would fall. Having thus demonstrated its unreliability, the cartel would never again be able to charge so high a price as before it went on its spree.

Even the land monopolist could credibly limit his output — if he leased rather than sold land. If after having leased a part of his land, he began leasing or selling additional parcels at lower prices, he could not charge so high a monopoly price when the lease came up for renewal. Knowing that he had an incentive to abide by his initial limitation of output, purchasers would be less afraid to pay the full monopoly price.[4]

The theory of monopoly does not explain how a monopolist maintains a monopoly price, given the attraction of such a price for sellers, in other markets, who are prospective entrants into this one. Since a monopoly return is greater than a competitive return, sellers in competitive markets will gravitate to a market where a monopoly price is being charged. To obtain some of the monopoly profits in that market, the

§9.5 1. See Harold Demsetz, Why Regulate Utilities?, 11 J. Law & Econ. 55 (1968); cf. United States v. El Paso Natural Gas Co., 376 U.S. 651 (1964). Do you see why this is just a special case of the Coase Theorem (§3.4 *supra*)? Why isn't the theorem applicable to *all* monopolization cases? See §10.1 *infra.*

2. See Ronald H. Coase, Durability and Monopoly, 15 J. Law & Econ. 143 (1972).

3. See Godehard Lenzen, The History of Diamond Production and the Diamond Trade 183-196 (F. Bradley trans. 1970).

4. Assurance would be greatest if the monopolist's revenue from the leases were set equal to a percentage of the lessee's revenues. Then any action by the monopolist that reduced the lessee's revenues would reduce his own revenues directly.

new entrant must sell, and his sales will increase the output of the market, causing price to fall. Most monopolies thus contain the seeds of their own destruction. But the rate at which new firms enter a market in which a monopoly price is being charged is critical. If the monopolist has a patent or other legal monopoly, that rate may be zero and the monopoly price will persist until the legal monopoly ends.

Sometimes monopoly will persist without any legal barriers to entry. Maybe the monopolist's costs are so much lower than those of any new entrant that the monopoly price is lower than the price that a new entrant would have to charge in order to cover his costs. Or maybe the monopoly price, although higher than the entrant's costs would be, holds no allure because the prospective entrant knows that if he enters the market the monopolist can easily charge a remunerative price that is below the entrant's costs, the monopolist being the more efficient producer.[5] Monopoly may also be a durable condition of the market because there is room for only one seller (see §12.1 *infra*). But even if the costs of the new entrant are the same as those of the monopolist, it does not follow that the threat of entry will always deter charging a monopoly price. Since cost is negatively related to time (it would cost more to build a steel plant in three months than in three years[6]), *immediate* entry into a monopolized market at costs comparable to the monopolist's will often be impossible. So there will be an interval in which monopoly profits can be obtained, even though there are no barriers to entry in the sense of a cost disadvantage for a new entrant.[7]

Suggested Readings

1. Jack Hirshleifer, Price Theory and Applications, ch. 8 (3d ed. 1984).

2. William M. Landes, Appendix: An Introduction to the Economics of Antitrust, in Richard A. Posner & Frank H. Easterbrook, Antitrust: Cases, Economic Notes, and Other Materials 1055 (2d ed. 1981).

3. Richard A. Posner, Antitrust Law: An Economic Perspective, ch. 2 and appendix (1976).

4. ———, The Social Costs of Monopoly and Regulation, 83 J. Pol. Econ. 807 (1975).

5. F.M. Scherer, Industrial Market Structure and Economic Performance (2d ed. 1980).

---

5. On barriers to entry, see §10.8 *infra*.

6. See Armen A. Alchian, Costs and Outputs, in Readings in Microeconomics 159, 165 (William Breit & Harold M. Hochman eds., 2d ed. 1971).

7. Why won't the monopoly be anticipated and entry timed to coincide with its formation?

Problems

1. Why will the optimum monopoly price always lie in the elastic portion of the monopolist's demand curve?[8]

2. Would a consumer be contributorily negligent in an economic sense if, knowing that the price of some product was a monopoly price, he failed to search assiduously for substitute products?

3. Where have we met consumer surplus before?

8. Unless the monopolist has zero marginal costs (what is the elasticity of demand at the price that such a monopolist will set?) or practices price discrimination.

CHAPTER 10

THE ANTITRUST LAWS[1]

§10.1 Cartels and the Sherman Act

A contract among competing sellers to fix the price of the product they sell (or, what is the same thing, to limit their output) is like any other contract in the sense that the parties would not sign it unless they expected it to make them all better off. But it injures others, consumers, who are not parties to the contract; and as we learned in the last chapter, when substitution effects and the tendency of monopoly profits to be transformed into costs are taken into account, the costs to consumers exceed the cartelists' gains. True, every consumer is in a direct or indirect contractual relationship with the sellers in the cartel, and it might therefore seem that the Coase Theorem would be in play and that consumers would pay the sellers to expand their output to the competitive level. This would imply, however, that the end state of the market would be perfect price discrimination (can you see why?); and even if arbitrage could be prevented, the costs of negotiating separately with each consumer over each unit of output would be prohibitive. This is an example of how transaction costs can be very high even for parties in a contractual relationship (what is another example that we have seen?). So it is not surprising that by the latter part of the nineteenth century courts were refusing to enforce cartel agreements, on the ground that they were against public policy.

It might seem that nonenforcement would be a patently inadequate remedy since even without legal sanctions for breach of contract people would ordinarily be led by considerations of reciprocal advantage to adhere to their contracts (see §4.1 *supra*). But a price-fixing agreement is less stable than most contracts. The party to such an agreement "buys"

---

1. See Richard A. Posner & Frank H. Easterbrook, Antitrust: Cases, Economic Notes, and Other Materials (2d ed. 1981).

the agreement of the other parties not to sell below a certain price, and the "product" — forbearance to compete in price — is difficult to inspect. If one of the parties to the agreement loses sales, there are any number of possible reasons why. One is that a competitor undercut him. But how is he to find out? He could ask the purchasers he has lost but he could not trust their answers. They might tell him that his competitor was underselling him even if it were untrue, in order to induce him to reduce his price. Moreover, the competitor might have adhered to the cartel price but improved his product — a subtle method of cheating.[1]

Although cheating necessarily implies selling at a lower (quality-adjusted) price (why?), if the expansion of the market's output brought about by cheating is small the fall in the cheater's profits resulting from the decline in market price may be less than the increase in his profits from selling additional units each at a monopoly profit. Suppose that the output of the market, before cheating, is 100 units, each seller's quota is 10, price is $2, and the cost of production is $1. Each seller will have a monopoly profit of $10. One seller decides to cheat, and increases his output from 10 to 15 units. As the market's output has risen to 105, price will fall — say to $1.80. By selling 15 units at $1.80, the cheater makes a profit of 80¢ per unit. His total profit is therefore $12, which is 20 percent higher than when he was adhering to the cartel. If several of the cartelists try this trick, the price will be driven down to the competitive price.

Despite the instability of cartels, nonenforcement of cartel agreements is unlikely to be an adequate remedy. By reducing the efficacy of price fixing by contract, it creates an incentive for the members of the cartel to consolidate into a single firm. The monopoly price can then be enforced without reliance on contracts.

The Sherman Act (1890) attempted to deal with the monopoly problem through criminal and civil sanctions for contracts and other combinations in restraint of trade, monopolization, and conspiracies and attempts to monopolize. Early decisions interpreted the act as forbidding cartels. Although the sanctions for violation originally were very weak, the act was reasonably effective in preventing cartelists from employing certain highly efficacious, but also highly visible, devices for eliminating cheating by cartel members. An example is the common sales agency, whereby all sales of the cartel's product are channeled through the agency, which sets a uniform price.[2]

§10.1   1. On the problems of enforcing cartels, see George J. Stigler, A Theory of Oligopoly, in The Organization of Industry 39 (1968); John S. McGee, Ocean Freight Rate Conferences and the American Merchant Marine, 27 U. Chi. L. Rev. 191 (1960).
2. See George J. Stigler, The Economic Effects of the Antitrust Laws, in The Organization of Industry 259 (1968).

But the Sherman Act had another effect that was inefficient. The output of a monopolized market is smaller than that of a competitive market. Upon formation of a cartel, therefore, much of the productive capacity of the market becomes excess and should be retired to economize on resources. But if the members are worried that the cartel may be short-lived, they will be reluctant to retire capacity lest they find themselves unable to expand output if and when the cartel collapses and price falls. The common sales agency and other "efficient" methods of cartelizing suppressed by the Sherman Act facilitate the withdrawal of excess capacity by increasing the stability and longevity of the cartel that employs them, and in this respect may be (why "may be"?) less wasteful of resources than the underground cartel, or price-fixing conspiracy, that has replaced it.

In the enforcement of the Sherman Act against cartels and conspiracies, emphasis has been placed on proving an agreement to fix prices — a legal issue — rather than on proving the effects of the sellers' conduct on price and output — the economic issue. An unintended consequence of this emphasis is that the cartels most likely to be discovered and prosecuted are those in which the price and output effects are small. They are the cartels with many members, so there is a better chance that one will become disgruntled and inform on the others; that depend on explicit and reiterated negotiation and agreement, which provide the essential evidence of violation; and that are likely to be riddled with cheating and collapse shortly amidst mutual recrimination — circumstances that create opportunities to obtain willing witnesses to offer evidence of agreement. The smoothly functioning cartel is less likely to generate evidence of actual agreement. What the law mainly punishes is the attempt to fix prices. The completed conspiracy often escapes attention.

Economic analysis can be used to identify the characteristics that indicate a market's predisposition to effective price fixing:

(1) The number of (major) sellers is one. The fewer the number, the lower the costs of coordinating their activities — a point that will be familiar from our discussion of transaction costs in Chapter 3.

(2) Another predisposing characteristic is the homogeneity of the product. The more homogeneous a product is, the more difficult it will be to cheat by altering product quality; the change will stand out.

(3) Another — but one especially difficult to measure — is the elasticity of demand with respect to price. Other things being equal, the less elastic demand is, the larger will be the profits that a monopoly price will generate and hence the greater will be the incentive to monopolize. (Intuitively, the less that quantity de-

manded will decline in response to price increases, the more freedom the monopolist has to raise price.)

(4) Another (and not sharply distinct — can you see why?) predisposing characteristic to cartelization, but again one difficult to measure, is the condition of entry. If entry can be effected rapidly
and entrants have no higher long-run costs than the members
of the cartel, the profits of cartelization will be small, and so
also the incentive to cartelize.

(5) The relative importance of price versus nonprice competition is
also important; fixing price could lead simply to a substitution
of nonprice competition that would wipe out the potential profits
of cartelization.

(6) Another factor is whether the market is growing, declining, or
steady over time. If demand is growing, cartelization will be difficult to police, because if a seller loses market share it may be
just from not doing so well as his competitors in attracting new
buyers to the market rather than from being underpriced. On
the other hand, the cartelists, rather than agree on price, may
agree on the rate of building new plants, and this should be easy
to police. If demand is steady or declining, a loss of market share
is more likely to be due (and attributed) to cheating on the cartel
price. A declining market is especially favorable to cartelization.
The risk of bankruptcy will be greater because fixed costs cannot
be reduced by cutting output; price competition will therefore
seem peculiarly destructive (see §12.8 *infra*), since, for reasons
explored in Chapter 14, a given dollar loss that produces bankruptcy is more costly than the same dollar loss that leaves the
firm with some profits. Moreover, entry is not a serious threat
in a declining market.

(7) Finally, the structure of the buying side of the market is important.
If there are many buyers of equal size, then cheating on the cartel
will require many transactions and the chance of detection by
the other members of the cartel will be great. But if there are
few (major) buyers, a member of the cartel may be able to cheat
just by luring one or two customers away from another member
of the cartel. Few transactions will be necessary, and this will
reduce the likelihood of detection. Also, the victim of the cheating
may find it difficult to tell whether he lost business because of
price cutting or random factors.

Economics can also indicate what type of evidence shows that a market
is being successfully cartelized, as distinct from whether it is merely
likely to be cartelized.

(1) One example is market-wide (why is this an important qualification?) price discrimination — a method, as we have seen, of exploiting monopoly power.

(2) Another example, well illustrated by the OPEC cartel,[3] is a decline over time in the market share of the largest firms in the market, which may indicate that they have been charging a monopoly price that has attracted new entrants who have bid business away from them by charging lower prices.

(3) A third type of evidence is evidence of industry-wide resale price maintenance, which, unless justifiable on grounds to be discussed shortly, may have been adopted to prevent cheating in the form of selling at a reduced markup to dealers.[4]

(4) Another kind of evidence consists of market shares that are too stable to be a product of normal competitive activity among the sellers.

(5) Another is regional price variations that cannot be explained by regional differences in cost or demand.

(6) Still another bit of evidence would be a price rise, coupled with a reduction in output, that cannot be explained by any other hypothesis than cartelization.

(7) Another is a (fairly) high elasticity of demand at the current market price, coupled with an absence of good substitutes for the product (i.e., comparable in both cost and value), suggesting that the high elasticity is the result of monopoly pricing; we shall come back to this point.

(8) Still another sort of evidence is a sudden and unexplained increase in the profit level in a market, followed by a gradual decline (why is that relevant?). The inference of monopolization would be reinforced if the initial profit spurt were greater for small firms than for large, since presumably only the large join the cartel (why?).

(9) Finally, it sometimes is possible to infer cartel pricing from a negative correlation between the number of firms in the market and the price level in the market. The theory of competition implies that price is determined by cost alone; the number of firms should be irrelevant. If instead price is a negative function of the number of firms, rising as the number falls and falling as the number rises, this implies collusion, because collusion is more effective (and hence leads to higher prices) the fewer the firms in the market.

Courts do not always have a clear understanding of what the economic objective of competition policy is; their touch seems less sure than in common law fields (can you think of a reason why?). Sometimes they

3. See Jack Hirshleifer, Price Theory and Applications 264-265 (3d ed. 1984); Robert S. Pindyck, Gains to Producers From the Cartelization of Exhaustible Resources, 60 Rev. Econ. & Stat. 238 (1978); Dermot Gately, A Ten-Year Retrospective: OPEC and the World Oil Market, 22 J. Econ. Lit. 1100 (1984).
4. If a dealer cuts his price, competitors of the dealer's supplier may be uncertain whether the price cut reflects a change in the retailer's operating costs or a price cut by the supplier; resale price maintenance eliminates this uncertainty.

seem to think that competition means rivalry; to an economist, it means the allocation of resources that is brought about when prices are not distorted by monopoly. Sometimes (as we shall see shortly when we consider resale price maintenance) they seem to think that price competition is more important than nonprice competition. And sometimes they seem to think that any interference with pricing is bad, thus confusing price levels with price dispersions. Suppose that in a market with many sellers, many buyers, and a homogeneous product, the product is sometimes sold at different prices on the same day because the market participants just are not aware of the full range of buy and sell offers. If the costs of information could be reduced by an agreement among sellers to pool offers (the kind of thing that formal exchanges — stock and commodity markets — do), producing a more uniform market price, efficiency would be promoted (why?). The dispersion of prices would be reduced, but the price level would not be raised; prices would not be distorted by monopoly. And yet this kind of agreement has sometimes been condemned on antitrust grounds.

The courts have often mishandled economic evidence in antitrust cases. For example, in the U.S. Steel monopoly case,[5] the Supreme Court, in ruling for the defendant, was impressed by the fact that U.S. Steel's market share had declined steadily after the combination of competing steel manufacturers to form the corporation (and that its competitors had not complained about its competitive tactics!). The Court failed to recognize monopoly behavior. The establishment of a monopoly price creates an incentive for new sellers to come into the market. The monopolist has three choices. He can stop charging a monopoly price, in order to discourage entry; he can do nothing; or he can reduce his output in an effort to offset the price effects of the new entrants' output. The first course of action utterly defeats the purpose of the monopoly. Under the second or third, the monopolist obtains some monopoly profits, at least temporarily, so we would expect him to follow either of these courses. Both result in a decline in his market share.[6] Which is better from the monopolist's standpoint (cf. §9.2 *supra*)?

In the second American Tobacco case,[7] the Supreme Court, in holding that the major cigarette manufacturers had conspired to eliminate competition, thought it ominous that the manufacturers had raised their prices during the depression of the 1930s despite the fact that it was a period of declining costs as well as demand. But we know from the preceding chapter that a profit-maximizing monopolist (or cartel) will reduce price in the face of a decline in costs and that a decline in demand will cause him either to reduce price (if marginal cost rises with output)

5. United States v. United States Steel Corp., 251 U.S. 417 (1920).
6. See George J. Stigler, The Dominant Firm and the Inverted Umbrella, in The Organization of Industry 108 (1968).
7. American Tobacco Co. v. United States, 328 U.S. 781 (1946).

or leave it unchanged (if marginal cost is constant). He will raise price only if marginal cost declines with output in the relevant region — which in the tobacco case would have implied, as we shall see in Chapter 12, that the cigarette industry was a natural monopoly; this is highly implausible. Another possibility is that a cigarette cartel was first formed in the depression, but there is no evidence of this. Another is that demand, as well as falling, was becoming less elastic. This would encourage the monopolist to raise price, and this effect might dominate his incentive to reduce price because demand was declining. But demands probably become more rather than less elastic during depressions, because people shop more carefully then. This hunch is supported by the competitive inroads made by the minor tobacco brands when the major tobacco companies made their price increase.

§10.2 Borderline Horizontal Agreements — Patent Agreements and the BMI-ASCAP Blanket Licenses

Patent agreements between competing firms raise perplexing questions. Such agreements can neither be condemned out of hand nor approved out of hand. We start with the first point. If two firms have "blocking" patents, meaning that neither patent can be used to create a commercially valuable product or process without infringing the other, the firms must be allowed to pool or cross-license the patents. And if a firm develops a patent the efficient use of which requires that it be licensed to competing firms (why might this be?), the firm can hardly be forbidden to license it. While in principle the firm can set a royalty rate that will protect it from the competition of its licensees (if it is also a producer of the patented product, and not merely the holder of the patent), in practice it may be necessary to fix a minimum price for the patented product; this should be allowed, too.

Suppose that the marginal cost to A, the patentee, of producing a patented widget is a constant $1 on a run of 100,000 widgets. A thinks B could produce another 10,000 widgets at a constant cost of 95¢, that B's costs would be very high at any higher quantity produced, and that at an output of 110,000 the market price of widgets would be $1.10. A therefore charges a royalty of 15¢ per widget to B so that B will lose money if it charges less than $1.10 for each widget it makes. But suppose it turns out that B can produce 20,000 widgets at a cost of only 85¢ per widget; and if it does produce this many, so that the total output of widgets (assuming that A as planned produces 100,000) will be 120,000, the market price will be only $1.01. B will have an incentive to produce the larger output, since after paying A the agreed royalty it will still make 1¢ on every widget sold. A, however, instead of making a profit of $11,500 (10¢ on each of the 100,000 widgets it produces, and 15¢ on the 10,000 widgets that B was expected to produce), will make only $4,000 (1¢ on each of its 100,000 widgets and 15¢ on each of B's 20,000). It is true that if A reduced its output to 90,000 widgets to maintain the market price at $1.10, its total income from the patent, $12,000, would be even greater than it had hoped when it licensed B — showing that it is always more profitable to license production to a more efficient producer than it is to produce oneself. But A might not notice that B was producing more than the expected number of widgets until price began to fall, and also A might have incurred costs, based on an expected output for himself of 100,000 widgets, that could not be fully avoided when output unexpectedly fell. Faced with such uncertainties, A, if forbidden to set a floor (i.e., $1.10) under B's price, may decide not to license the patent but instead to produce all the widgets itself, even though it is more efficient for B to be allowed to produce some of them.

Although some patents could not be developed without cooperation between competitors, when a patent is "thin" (meaning that it might very well be held invalid if challenged in court) licensing it provides a golden opportunity for firms to collude under the guise of lawful patent licensing. General Electric once licensed Westinghouse to produce light bulbs under the GE patent at a minimum price fixed in the license agreement. Some evidence that the GE patent may have been invalid is that General Electric charged Westinghouse the very low royalty rate of 2 percent — rising, however, to 15 percent if Westinghouse's share of the light bulb market rose above 15 percent of that market. Thus, Westinghouse had a disincentive to expand in competition with General Electric; if it was content with a small market share, it had to pay only a small royalty and would share in the monopoly profits created by a noncompetitive price structure. Nevertheless the Supreme Court upheld the arrangement.[1]

Another famous patent case that may have fooled the Supreme Court is the "cracking" case, also won by the defendants.[2] Several manufacturers of gasoline had patented processes for making gasoline by the inexpensive cracking method. They pooled their patents (which apparently were not blocking patents), thus eliminating competition among themselves. The Supreme Court, however, in an opinion by the ordinarily astute Justice Brandeis, thought this no problem because only 26 percent of the gasoline sold was produced by the cracking method and gasoline produced by other methods is physically indistinguishable — a perfect

§10.2   1. United States v. General Electric Co., 272 U.S. 476 (1926).
      2. Standard Oil Co. (Indiana) v. United States, 283 U.S. 163 (1931).

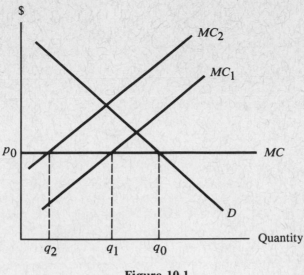

Figure 10.1

substitute. Figure 10.1 suggests that this analysis is incomplete. MC is the marginal cost of producing gasoline by the old method that cracking (partially) displaced, and MC_1 is the marginal cost to refiners if the holders of the cracking patents compete with each other in licensing its use to refiners. Under competition, cracking is the cheaper method up to quantity q_1, beyond which the conventional method will be used to satisfy the rest of the market demand (i.e., $q_0 - q_1$). But colluding patent holders will charge a higher price for use of the cracking method, thus raising refiners' marginal costs of using the method to somewhere above MC_1 — in Figure 10.1, to MC_2. As a result, less gasoline is produced by the cracking method. There is no change in the price of gasoline, because the conventional method is available to produce additional gasoline at a constant cost and hence price. But the total costs of producing gasoline are greater — by an amount measured by the difference between the areas under MC and MC_1 between q_2 and q_1. That difference is the social cost of the collusion among the patent holders.

Do not infer from this discussion that all cooperative agreements between competitors are monopolistic. The pooling of blocking patents, as we saw, is clearly not. And yet anytime there is cooperation among competitors, there is a danger of monopoly; the pool might charge a monopoly price. It seems, then, that there is sometimes a tradeoff between monopoly and efficiency. Another example is the method[3] by which the performing-rights organizations in the music field, ASCAP

3. Held not illegal per se in Broadcast Music, Inc. v. Columbia Broadcasting System, Inc., 441 U.S. 1 (1979).

and BMI, market rights to perform copyrighted musical compositions.
The composers (or other copyright holders) license the organization
to market their songs. The organization in turn grants a blanket license
to radio stations and other performing entities. The license allows the
station to use any song in the organization's repertoire (each organization has thousands of songs) without extra payment; the only fee is
the blanket-license fee itself, which is a percentage of the licensee's
revenues that is unrelated to how much or how little he uses his rights
under the license. The organization then distributes the revenues from
its fees among the composers, roughly in proportion to the frequency
with which each song is played.

Each of the performing-rights organizations is in effect an exclusive
sales agency for the composers in its "stable,"[4] and eliminates price
competition among them, just like the classic exclusive sales agency of
cartel lore. So maybe composers end up with higher incomes than if
they competed with each other (but see note 4). On the other hand,
the cost to the radio stations and other (intermediate) buyers of copyrighted music of dealing with composers individually would be prohibitive, so that the "cartel" blanket-license fee is probably much lower
than would be the corresponding charge for musical performing rights
in a purely "competitive" market. (This is a good illustration of the
fallacy of equating competition in the sense of efficient resource allocation with rivalry.) Moreover, the blanket license is an ingenious device
for minimizing the output effects of monopoly, because it allows each
licensee to play as much music as he wants without paying an additional
fee, so that he has no incentive to restrict his use below the competitive
level, as would the customer of an ordinary monopolist.[5] The device
is not perfect, however. The blanket-license fee may discourage some
radio stations from playing music — may even reduce the number of
radio stations. So if the fee contains a monopoly rent to composers, it
could have some of the substitution effects that are associated with monopoly.

How far should the idea of an efficient cartel be pushed? Suppose
competing firms form an exclusive sales agency, arguing that this will
(1) reduce buyer search costs, (2) increase the incentive to innovation,
and (3) reduce expected deadweight costs of bankruptcy? Are these
ridiculous arguments? If not, how should they be traded off against
the social costs of cartelization?

---

4. Except that the composer may if he wants deal directly with the station. Does this
right eliminate the possibility of cartel pricing and profits? Would it if there were a joint
sales agency among leading firms in a highly concentrated market rather than among
thousands of composers?
5. In other words, the marginal fee is zero. Is this also the marginal cost?

§10.3   Resale Price Maintenance

Manufacturers, when allowed by law to do so, will often set a resale price below which retailers are not permitted to sell their product. In the *Dr. Miles* case, the Supreme Court held that since the result is the same as if the retailers got together and agreed what price to charge, which would be illegal price fixing, resale price maintenance, too, is illegal per se.[1] This reasoning overlooks the possibility that resale price maintenance may have an additional effect, not present in the case of the dealer cartel: the provision of an optimum level of presale services for the manufacturer's product. Suppose there is a presale service that is valuable to the consumer, most efficiently provided by the retailer rather than by the manufacturer, and not feasibly priced separately from the manufacturer's product: A well-stocked showroom attended by courteous and uniformed salesmen would be an example.[2] The retailer who voluntarily provides this service may be undercut by a competing retailer who does not. The second retailer can take a free ride on the first — urging his customers to shop the first retailer and then come back to him for a bargain price made possible by his not bearing the expense of providing the elaborate presale services furnished by the first retailer. This is a good example of external benefits. By providing services to the consumer free of charge, the first retailer confers a benefit on competing retailers of the manufacturer's brand. A free rider is just a recipient of external benefits and to eliminate free riding just means to internalize external benefits and is prima facie efficient; we should recall from Chapter 3 that an important function of creating property rights is to internalize external benefits.

A manufacturer can prevent free riding on retailers who provide presale services by fixing a minimum retail price at a level that will generate enough revenues above the costs of barebones distribution to enable the retailer to provide the level of services desired by the manufacturer. Forbidden to compete in price but free to compete in service, each retailer will invest in presale services designed to lure the consumer away from rivals. This competition will continue until presale services have reached the level desired by the manufacturer and the monopoly profits that the retailers would have earned had they sold at the fixed price without offering any services have been completely squeezed out. This is one more example of the tendency discussed in the last chapter

---

§10.3   1. Dr. Miles Medical Co. v. John D. Park & Sons Co., 220 U.S. 373 (1911).

2. Why can't this service be sold separately? More generally, why is it difficult to sell information about a product separately from the product? And why is the argument limited to presale services? If it were feasible to sell presale services separately, would it be efficient to do so?

for potential monopoly profits to get transformed through nonprice competition into costs (here, of presale services).[3]

Although it is hard to see why the law would want to forbid a practice that serves to overcome the free-rider problems of lawful businessmen, it is not easy to show that economic welfare is actually enhanced by resale price maintenance. This can be seen in Figure 10.2, where $MC = p$ is the cost of barebones retail distribution and is therefore the retail price when no presale services are provided; p' is the minimum retail price fixed by the manufacturer and MC' the new cost of distribution, which includes the presale service that p' induces the retailers to offer; and D' is the new and higher demand curve that is created by the provision of the services.

The manufacturer is better off because he is selling more, and at the same price. (The price he charges the retailer is not, or at least need not be, affected by his fixing a resale price and thereby engendering the changes shown in the figure.) Some consumers are better off — including, by definition, all those who buy the product for the first time because of the services that are provided with it. But some other consumers are worse off — those who pay a higher price than they did before the presale services were provided yet do not obtain a corresponding benefit.

The benefits and costs are compared in the shaded areas in Figure 10.2. The shaded area between the demand curves is the benefit from resale price maintenance; the shaded area between the marginal cost curves is the cost. Although the benefit exceeds the cost, the figure could easily be redrawn to make the cost exceed the benefit, even while showing a higher demand at the higher price (why is that an essential feature?). The reason is that the benefit that a manufacturer confers on consumers by selling at a price that is below what they could be forced to pay under a system of perfect price discrimination — in other words, the consumer surplus — does not influence the manufacturer's decisions, because, by definition, he is not the recipient of the benefit. It is an external benefit, so he may take steps that reduce it, provided the steps increase his profits.

Should antitrust law worry about this point? Can you see why, if it

3. The "dealer services" theory of resale price maintenance prompts the following questions:
  (a) Does the theory presuppose that the manufacturer has monopoly power? If he does not, why couldn't retailers of competing manufacturers take a free ride on his dealers?
  (b) How might one distinguish empirically between resale price maintenance imposed by and for the benefit of the manufacturer and resale price maintenance that conceals a dealer-instigated cartel? What's wrong with simply asking whether the product is one normally sold with elaborate presale services?
  (c) Is there any analytical difference between resale price maintenance and either assigning exclusive territories to dealers or forbidding them to sell to or through other dealers?

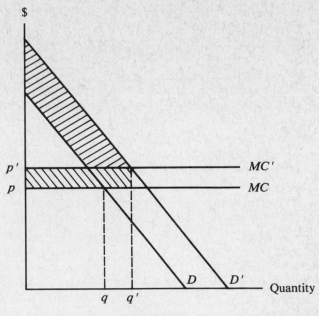

Figure 10.2

did, this would imply that a firm should be required to get the government's permission before increasing the quality of its product?

The effect of resale price maintenance in raising price but also raising quality (where quality includes presale services offered with a product) is sometimes described in terms of a tradeoff between price and nonprice competition, which is accurate, or between intrabrand and interbrand competition, which is not. Resale price maintenance does limit price competition among the retailers of the brand that the manufacturer has fixed the resale price of — intrabrand price competition — and in doing so promotes interbrand competition by making the manufacturer's brand more attractive relative to other brands. (Its increased attractiveness is measured by the distance between q and q' — can you see why?) But intrabrand competition is not reduced; it is simply changed from intrabrand price competition to intrabrand service competition. Resale price maintenance won't work for a manufacturer unless it induces his retailers to compete vigorously with one another — only in providing services rather than in cutting prices.

§10.4 Mergers to Monopoly and Oligopoly

The fact that a law that punished only cartelization could be evaded by consolidation of the cartel members into one firm provides economic

277

justification for the refusal of a majority of the Supreme Court in the *Northern Securities* case[1] to adopt Justice Holmes's position that the Sherman Act was inapplicable to mergers. But Holmes was right to be troubled about the implications of the law's reaching beyond cartels to mergers. The conditions of supply and demand in a market may be such that one firm can supply, at lower average cost than two or more firms, the entire output demanded; or one firm may have a superior management in whose hands the assets of all the other firms would be worth more than they now are. Either situation could lead to a monopoly through merger that might generate cost savings greater than the costs of the monopoly pricing that would result.[2] Unfortunately, it is exceedingly difficult to distinguish situations of this kind from the case of a merger to create a monopoly that involves few or no cost savings.

Despite their analytical interest, monopolies are rare. Oligopolies — markets in which a few firms account for most sales — are quite common and the question of their competitive significance is a controversial one. The 1950 amendments to section 7 of the Clayton Act, which have been interpreted to place stringent limit on mergers between competitors, are frequently defended as necessary to prevent more oligopoly. Although the number of firms in a market is relevant to a concern with cartels, because the fewer the firms the lower the costs of coordinating their policies, there are so many other factors relating to the propensity to cartelize that it is doubtful whether this point alone would justify a draconian antimerger law. It is, rather, the view of many economists that oligopoly leads to supracompetitive prices even when each firm's pricing decisions are independent that provides the law's intellectual basis. The reasoning is that on the one hand each firm will be reluctant to cut prices, knowing that its price cut will have so immediate and substantial an effect on the market shares of its rivals that they will quickly match the cut, thus wiping out the first firm's gains, while on the other hand if the firm raises its price its competitors will raise their prices too, knowing that all will make higher profits at the higher price.

But the interdependence theory has problems and, worse, may be otiose. It does not explain how oligopolists establish a price higher than the competitive price in the first place. If, as the theory posits, oligopolists are very wary of each other's reactions to any price change, a firm contemplating a price increase would worry that its competitors would delay in matching the increase, since by lagging behind him they would gain sales at his expense. Another problem is that the optimum pricing strategy of a firm that takes account of its rivals' reactions to its pricing moves is indeterminate. The firm must figure out not only how the competitor will react to a given price move but how the competi-

---

§10.4   1. Northern Securities Co. v. United States, 193 U.S. 197 (1904).
       2. What would be the effect of a decree forbidding merger in such a case?

tor will react to its reaction to the competitor's reaction, and so on *ad infinitum.*

An alternative approach is to view anticompetitive pricing in oligopolistic markets as a special form of collusion in which the fewness of the sellers minimizes the need for overt communication. The theory of oligopoly becomes a special case of the theory of cartels, though there is considerable doubt whether the law can do anything to prevent collusion so tacit that no contacts between the colluding firms are necessary to effectuate it.[3] It may, however, be able to prevent the emergence of an oligopoly by forbidding large horizontal mergers.

§10.5 Monopoly Power

We have thus far treated monopoly power as if it were unproblematic. If there is one firm in the market, it has monopoly power; if the firms in the market act as one through collusion, they jointly have monopoly power. But often it is unclear whether a firm (or a group of firms that may be pricing as one) has monopoly power, and it becomes important to antitrust law to be able to determine whether it does or not. Suppose two competing firms merge. The merger probably will be illegal if the resulting firm will have monopoly power, or even if a group of leading firms that includes the resulting firm will jointly have monopoly (oligopoly) power, but perhaps not otherwise. How can we tell whether it will have such power? And is it meaningful to speak of degrees of monopoly power?

Recall that the monopolist sells at the intersection — the point of equality — of marginal revenue and marginal cost. Assume marginal cost is constant over the relevant range of output and denote it by MC. Now we must find MR. We know that it is related to price (P) but is less than price if the seller faces a downward-sloping demand curve. If the seller is a competitive firm, which can sell all it produces at the market price without affecting that price, then $P = MR$; every additional unit sold increases the firm's revenues by the price of the unit. But if the demand curve is downward-sloping, the sale of an additional unit will yield less than P in additional revenue, because the sale, by adding to output, will cause P to fall. How far? This depends on the price elasticity of demand. Suppose the elasticity is 3 (actually -3, but we can ignore the minus sign). This implies that a 1 percent increase in output will lead to a $\frac{1}{3}$ of 1 percent decrease in price, implying a net increase in total revenues of $\frac{2}{3}$ of 1 percent. Generalizing from this

3. See, e.g., E.I. Du Pont de Nemours & Co. v. FTC, 729 F.2d 128 (2d Cir. 1984).

example, we can compute marginal revenue according to the formula, $MR = P(1 - 1/e)$, where e is the price elasticity of demand.[1] Since $MR = MC$, and since the competitive price would be equal to MC, we can (with a bit of rearranging) write the ratio of the monopoly to the competitive price, P/MC, as $e/e - 1$.[2] So the greater is the elasticity of demand, the smaller will be the ratio of the monopoly to the competitive price, and the less monopoly power will the firm have. (Why must e be greater than 1?) If e were infinite, meaning that the firm faced a perfectly horizontal demand curve (why would this make e infinite?), P would equal MC and the firm would have no monopoly power. If as in our example e is 3, then the monopoly price will be 50 percent greater than the competitive price; if 2, it will be twice the competitive price.

This formula is useful in showing that monopoly power (1) is variable rather than constant and (2) depends entirely on the elasticity of demand facing the firm at its profit-maximizing price. Another formula enables us to derive that elasticity (call it e_{df}) from the elasticity of demand facing the market of which the firm is a part (e_{dm}), the elasticity of supply of the other firms in the market (e_s), and the market share of the firm (S). This formula is $e_{df} = e_{dm}/S + e_s(1 - S)/S$. If a firm has 100 percent of the market, then the elasticity of demand facing the firm is, of course, the same as the elasticity of demand facing the market. But the smaller the firm's market share is, the higher will be the elasticity of demand facing it relative to the elasticity of demand facing the market.

This is a perfectly intuitive result. There may be no good substitutes for widgets, in which event the price of widgets might have to rise quite a bit before there was substantial substitution of other products; e_{dm} might therefore be only 2, so that if all the producers of widgets reduced their output by 2 percent, price would rise by only 1 percent. But a producer who sells only 10 percent of the widgets produced by the market cannot bring about a 1 percent price increase by reducing his own output by 2 percent; he must reduce the whole market's output by 2 percent, which means he must reduce his own output (which is only a tenth of the market's) by 20 percent. Hence e_{df} would be 20 even if the firm's competitors would not respond to his reduction in output by increasing their own. But of course they would, depending on the elasticity of supply (the responsiveness of quantity supplied to a small increase in price).

Suppose the competitors' elasticity of supply is 1, meaning that a 1 percent increase in price will lead them to increase their output by 1 percent. The larger their relative share of the market ($(1 - S)/S$), the

§10.5   1. For the derivation of the formulas in this section, see William M. Landes & Richard A. Posner, Market Power in Antitrust Cases, 94 Harv. L. Rev. 937, 983-986 (1981).

2. This assumes that MC is constant (a horizontal line). See id. at 941 for the significance of the assumption, which is adopted here to simplify exposition.

greater will be the effect of their added output in reducing the market price if a single firm reduces its own output in an effort to raise price. With the assumption that $e_s = 1$ and that the putative monopolist has only 10 percent of the market, it is easy to show that, after taking account of the supply response, e_{df} is not 20, but 29.

§10.6   Market Definition and Market Shares

The second formula in the last section indicates what the important things are in estimating monopoly power, or as it is sometimes called market power — the market elasticity of demand, the market share of the firm or firms whose monopoly power we are trying to measure, and the elasticity of supply of other firms. But this still leaves us with the task of estimating the market demand and supply elasticities. Although progress has been made in estimating these elasticities directly,[1] most antitrust cases continue to rely on extremely crude proxies, summed up in the concept of product and geographical market. If a product has no close substitutes in demand (meaning, nothing that seems to provide the consumer with the same services at roughly the same price), and sellers of other products cannot readily switch to making it, then the market elasticities of demand and supply are assumed to be low. From this it can be inferred that any firm with a substantial share of sales of this product has nontrivial market power — unless sellers of the identical product in other geographical areas could enter the (local or regional or national) market if price rose there slightly, in which event the market has been defined too narrowly and the relevant elasticities underestimated.

As one might expect, errors are frequent in attempting to define the market for antitrust purposes. A good example is the celebrated cellophane monopolization case, in which the Supreme Court held that cellophane was not a relevant market because there was a high cross-elasticity of demand between cellophane and other flexible packaging materials.[2] A monopolist, as we know, always sells in the elastic region of his demand schedule. And one reason that most demand schedules have an elastic region is that the higher the price of a product is, the more attractive substitute products become to the consumer. Hence it

§10.6   1. See, e.g., H.S. Houthakker & Lester D. Taylor, Consumer Demand in the United States: Analyses and Projections 166-167 (2d ed. 1970) (table 4.2); Robert Archibald & Robert Gillingham, A Decomposition of the Price and Income Elasticities of the Consumer Demand for Gasoline, 47 S. Econ. J. 1021 (1981); Eric A. Hanushek & John M. Quigley, What Is the Price Elasticity of Housing Demand?, 62 Rev. Econ. & Stat. 449 (1980).
   2. United States v. E.I. du Pont de Nemours & Co., 351 U.S. 377 (1956).

is not surprising to find a significant cross-elasticity of demand between a monopolized product and other products at the monopoly price-output level. The high cross-elasticity of demand for cellophane may have signified only that du Pont could not have increased the price of cellophane *further* without losing a great deal of business to substitute products, and this would be consistent with the existing price being the monopoly price. The Court's use of evidence of high cross-elasticity of demand would have made more sense if the case had involved a challenge to a consolidation of the producers of cellophane, where the issue would have been whether the consolidation would create or increase monopoly power. If the cross-elasticity of demand between cellophane and substitute packaging materials was high before the consolidation, the consolidated firm would have little power to raise price.[3]

Because of high costs of transportation relative to the value of a product, not all manufacturers of the product may be able to compete for the same customers; markets may, in other words, be geographically limited. The courts' tendency has been to include in the market those sellers who actually sell to the same group of customers and exclude those who do not. This is at once too many and too few. If the market is monopolized, the monopoly price will attract sellers from distant markets who could not have covered their transportation and other selling costs if the competitive price had been charged (the cellophane problem). If the market is not monopolized, there may be a group of distant sellers who at the moment do not ship into the market but who could and would do so if the price rose even slightly (i.e., there are good substitutes in production). Maybe the costs of the outside sellers in selling in this market would be 2 percent higher than those of the inside sellers, because of transportation expense. This would imply that if as a result of monopolization the market price rose by 2 percent, the outside sellers would begin to ship into the market and price could not rise any further. But even heavy freight costs may not give the proximate sellers monopoly power. Suppose that southeastern producers selling in the northeast incur extra transport costs equal to 6 percent of their total costs but that their nontransport costs are 4 percent below the costs of the northeastern sellers; the potential monopoly power of the northeastern sellers would be no greater than in our previous example.

If distant sellers make some local sales at the competitive price, how shall market shares be computed? Suppose that local sellers make and

---

3. The converse does not follow: If, in our hypothetical cellophane merger case, the cross-elasticity of demand between cellophane and various other packaging materials were low, we would not be entitled to conclude that demand for cellophane was price inelastic. The fact that a product has no close substitutes does not necessarily imply a willingness on the part of consumers to pay higher prices rather than do without. All that is necessary to assure that the demand for a product is price elastic is that consumers have alternative uses for their money to which they will turn in great number if the relative price of the product increases.

sell 90 of the 100 widgets sold in Illinois; an Indiana firm sells the other 10. However, the Indiana firm sells twice as many widgets elsewhere as it sells in Illinois; its total output thus is 30. Assuming that the current market price in Illinois is the competitive price (why is that relevant?), what is the Indiana firm's market share in Illinois — 10 percent (10/100) or 25 percent (30/(30 + 90))? The answer is 25 percent. Since the Indiana firm has overcome whatever barriers of transportation cost it faced because of its distance from Illinois consumers, it could divert the rest of its output to Illinois if price rose even slightly — and would. It must be making as much in Illinois as elsewhere; otherwise it would divert its sales from Illinois to elsewhere now. After a price increase in Illinois not matched elsewhere, it would be making more money in Illinois, so it would have every incentive to divert sales there. That possibility limits the monopoly power of the Illinois firms and is captured by including the Indiana seller's total sales — not just its Illinois sales — in the Illinois market.[4]

We have seen that in the absence of direct measurements of monopoly power, market share in a properly defined market is an indicator of monopoly power. Of course, without more, it is very difficult to draw a line and say, above this line a firm is a monopolist. We know, for example, that if the market elasticity of demand is 2, and the elasticity of supply is 0, a firm with 50 percent of the market would face an elasticity of demand of 4, and this would enable it to charge a price 33 percent above the competitive price — a lot. But if its share were only 20 percent, it could still charge a price 11 percent higher than the competitive price. Since, however, a higher market elasticity of demand, or a high elasticity of supply, could greatly reduce this figure, it is hard to base any conclusions on market share alone, even ignoring the substantial probability that if a firm has grown to a large size other than by recent (why this qualification?) mergers, it probably is more efficient than its competitors (why?), and its lower costs may outweigh the social costs resulting from its charging a monopoly price. Indeed, its monopoly price may be lower than the competitive price would be (show this graphically).

§10.7 Potential Competition

Potential competition has become an established concept in antitrust law — or rather two concepts: perceived potential competition and actual potential competition. Together they are a principal, perhaps the princi-

---

4. Evaluate the following proposition: Two products are in the same market if but only if their prices are closely correlated (positively). See George J. Stigler & Robert A. Sherwin, The Extent of the Market, 28 J. Law & Econ. 555 (1985).

pal, basis on which mergers are challenged today on antitrust grounds.

Perceived potential competition best captures the idea of "potential" competition. Firms that do not sell in a market but would do so if the market price were higher are potential competitors. Firms that will enter the market in the future even if the price does not rise —"actual potential competitors" in antitrust jargon — are better described simply as future competitors, and that usage will be used here.

We know that the higher the elasticity of demand facing a firm, the less market power it has; and we also know that if an increase in price will evoke new output from other firms, i.e., if the elasticity of supply is positive, then the firm elasticity of demand will be higher than it would otherwise be. This suggests, however, that there is no need for a separate doctrine of "potential" competition. All that is necessary is to define markets broadly enough so that they include firms that, although they do not currently sell in the market in question, would do so if price rose slightly. Suppose that aluminum and copper wire are good substitutes in production, because the same machines are used to produce both, but are poor substitutes in consumption. If the price of copper rose above the competitive level, producers of aluminum wire would switch to producing copper wire; and their ability to switch is approximated by their current output of aluminum wire (why?). Therefore the output of the aluminum wire market should be included in computing the market share of the parties to a merger between a producer of copper wire and a producer of aluminum wire.

But this is a case where the new entrant need not construct new facilities; what if he would have to? Since it takes time to construct production facilities, the threat of entry posed by such a firm is more likely to affect the long-run rather than the short-run elasticity of demand facing firms in the market; and since collusion is largely a short-run phenomenon (why?), maybe the elimination of such threats is not important enough to warrant antitrust concern, especially since it will be difficult to compute market shares for firms that do not yet have any productive capacity. Indeed, it will be quite difficult to identify which firms are likely to build productive capacity to enter the market if the market price rises above the competitive level.

Moreover, to apply the perceived potential competition doctrine to entrants who must build productive facilities in order to enter the market assumes that it is in the interest of colluding firms to set a price that deters entry even in the long run. This is called limit pricing, and it is by no means clear that it often, or ever, makes economic sense. Since the long-run costs of a new entrant are likely to be no higher than the costs of the firms already in the market, limit pricing implies pricing at or close to marginal cost — a questionable policy from a profit-maximization standpoint, especially since collusion is likely to collapse of its own weight within a fairly short time. The colluders' profit-maximizing strategy is likely to be one of pricing on the basis of the (higher) short-run elasticity of demand and hence ignoring any potential competitors who are unable, because they lack facilities to make the product in question, to enter the market immediately.

This still leaves the possibility of future competitors, whose entry might reduce price in the long run even if the perception of their potential entry had no short-run impact. But if collusion is unlikely to persist beyond the short run, why worry about the elimination through merger of a future competitor? As a prophylactic against future cartels? But since future competitive gains are worth less than present ones, how likely are they to outweigh whatever cost savings (which would be realized sooner) the merger enables?

§10.8 Predation

Our emphasis thus far has been on the acquisition of monopoly power by consolidation or other forms of cooperation among competitors. An important question is whether such power can be obtained or enlarged through the efforts of one firm. We may put aside the case where the firm obtains a monopoly or a large market share by superior efficiency or a government license and confine our attention to tactics that are thought to be abuses of the competitive process. One is predatory price discrimination: A firm sells below cost in some markets; after its competitors are driven out, it sets a monopoly price.[1] Confirmed instances of predatory price discrimination were rare even before the practice was clearly illegal. The reason is that the practice is very costly to the predator. He incurs a present and substantial loss for gains that not only are deferred but may be temporary since once the existing competitors are driven out of the market and a monopoly price is established, new competitors will be attracted to the market by that price; the tactic may have to be repeated.

If just the *threat* of predatory price discrimination were sufficient to bring competitors into line, it would be employed often since it costs little to make a threat (excluding legal punishment costs). But to be effective, a threat must be credible. A threat to sell below cost would ordinarily not be credible, since the victim of the threat would know that the threatener would be restrained by his self-interest from carrying it out, because it is so costly to sell below cost. The threat may be credible, however, where the threatener has a monopoly position in a

---

§10.8 1. If consumers will be hurt in the long run, why do they cooperate with the predator by buying from him when he sells below cost?

number of different markets while each of his competitors sells in only one of those markets. The monopolist may be able to convince each competitor that he will carry out a threat to sell below cost in particular markets in order to make his threats in other markets more credible. The cost of one or two episodes of below-cost selling may be small compared to the benefits he derives from having established his credibility.[2]

Assume, then, that predatory pricing might sometimes be attempted, and ought to be forbidden (does the second proposition follow from the first?). How can we operationalize the concept of below-cost selling? If a firm were operating at full capacity and selling at a competitive price (i.e., $P = MC$), then, curiously, *any* price reduction would be below cost. To say the firm is operating at full capacity is to say that it is operating in a region of rising marginal cost — otherwise it could have sold more at the competitive price. So if it expands its output, as it would have to do in order to take sales away from the target of its predatory designs, its marginal cost will rise, while its price — assumed to have been no higher than its marginal cost — would by definition have declined. And yet it would be a very odd rule that said that any price cut is presumptively predatory! (Why would a competitive firm ever cut price?)

Assume that the would-be predator already has some monopoly power, and is therefore selling above rather than at his marginal cost, and he decides to reduce price. So long as he does not cut price to below marginal cost at the new level of output brought about by the price cut, he is not selling below cost in this practical sense: His price cut could not drive out of business any but a less efficient competitor — a competitor with a higher marginal cost curve. The problem with making this observation the basis of a legal rule is that marginal cost is not a figure carried on a firm's books of account or readily derivable from the figures that are (a point noted in the discussion of contract damages in §4.8 *supra*). Although marginal costs are a function of variable rather than fixed costs — fixed costs are by definition unaffected by changes in output — marginal cost and variable cost are not synonyms.

Suppose the labor and materials and other variable costs of producing 100 widgets are $100, and would be $99 if 99 units were produced, so that the firm's marginal cost at an output of 100 is $1. But suppose further that if output is increased to 101 units, straining the firm's existing capacity, its total variable costs for its entire output will shoot up to $110, and its average variable cost will therefore be $1.09 ($110 ÷ 101). But its marginal cost will be $10. So if it dropped its price from $3 to $2 in order to create a demand for the higher output, it would be engaged in predatory pricing. Yet it would be difficult for a court to compute the firm's marginal cost. Although it has been suggested

2. For an analogy, see the analysis of expenditures on litigation in §21.8 *infra*.

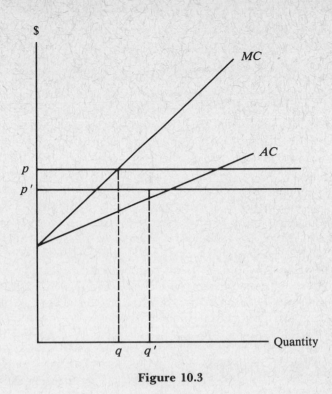

Figure 10.3

that average variable cost be used instead,[3] that cost in our example is as we have seen only $1.09. Its use as a proxy for marginal cost (which is $10) would lead to the incorrect conclusion that the price cut (to $2) was not predatory.

Figure 10.3 is a schematic representation of this problem. The firm is a competitive firm that wants to be a monopolist. It faces a rising marginal cost curve, implying a definite limit on the efficient size of the firm. The firm cuts price to p' and increases its output to q' (what determines q'?). At this point its marginal cost exceeds its price. But its average variable cost, which rises more slowly than marginal cost (because the high cost of the last unit of output is averaged in with the lower costs of the intramarginal units), is below its price, creating the misleading impression that the firm is not being predatory.

A further problem is that the calculation of variable cost and therefore of marginal cost is highly sensitive to the time period. In the very short run, most costs are fixed; in the very long run, virtually all (an exception

3. See Phillip Areeda & Donald F. Turner, Predatory Pricing and Related Practices Under Section 2 of the Sherman Act, 88 Harv. L. Rev. 697 (1975). The literature on predatory pricing is extensive. Some places to start are Frank H. Easterbrook, Predatory Strategies and Counterstrategies, 48 U. Chi. L. Rev. 263 (1981); Paul L. Joskow & Alvin K. Klevorick, A Framework for Analyzing Predatory Pricing Policy, 89 Yale L.J. 213 (1979).

would be the cost of incorporating a corporation) are variable. Rent, for example, is a fixed cost in the short run but is variable in the long run; if the firm's need for space changes, it will pay a different rent after the current lease expires. The same is true of insurance, executive salaries, pension benefits, property taxes, depreciation, advertising, and many other costs. In principle, the period within which to determine whether costs are fixed or variable should be the period of the alleged predatory pricing. If the price cut lasts a month, then the pertinent variable costs are those that vary in the course of a month, such as the hourly labor used in making the product and the raw materials consumed in its manufacture. The longer the price cut lasts, the larger the fraction of the firm's costs that are variable. If a firm were allowed to price indefinitely at its short-run variable cost, it would be able to drive out of the market a far more efficient firm, simply because the long-run variable costs of that firm — costs the firm would have to incur to stay in business — would be so much greater than even a less efficient firm's short-run variable costs. In our example, the predatory firm's average long-run variable costs might be not $1.09 but $2.20. Presumably, however, its long-run marginal cost would be much lower than $10, and probably only slightly more than $2.20.[4] To complete the symmetry notice that in the long run — the pertinent run when an alleged predatory price cut is persisted in for a long time — average variable costs merge with average total costs (fixed plus variable costs, all divided through by the firm's output). (Why?)

This discussion shows that average variable cost is a pretty good proxy for marginal cost in the long run (with qualifications discussed in Chapter 12). But would it ever make sense for a firm to engage in predatory pricing for a prolonged period? After all, that would lengthen the pay-back period when the predator, having destroyed his prey, raises his price to a monopoly level; and the monopoly profits made in that period would have to be discounted to present value in deciding whether below-cost selling (a current cost) will pay.

Here is another complication. Suppose a firm makes many different products, and some of the inputs — the time of its executives, for example — are the same for the different products. If the firm cuts the price of just one product, how should executive salaries be treated, in both the short and the long run, in deciding whether the price cut is predatory?

This question illustrates the difficult accounting problems that arise in predatory-pricing cases. Accountants, concerned as they properly are with minimizing the discretion of management in characterizing expenditures, do not always capture economic reality in their conventions. Take the case of advertising. Accountants require that advertising expendi-

---

4. Why? And why is long-run marginal cost invariably lower than short-run marginal cost?

tures be treated as current expenses. But since the effects of advertising often last for more than a year, they really are capital expenditures and ought to be depreciated over their useful life. When might it make a difference in a predatory-pricing case whether advertising expenditures were expensed, on the one hand, or capitalized and depreciated on the other?

§10.9   Foreclosure, Tie-Ins, Barriers to Entry

A number of other practices besides predatory pricing that are claimed to create monopoly power also have the property of imposing on the monopolist costs that are usually at least as high as those the intended victims must bear. Suppose a manufacturer were to buy up all of the retail outlets for the product of his industry in order to foreclose his competitors from access to the market. They would react by building their own outlets. This would involve costs to them, but no more (and probably less) than the cost to the would-be monopolist of purchasing a chain of retail outlets that would have a great deal of excess capacity after his rivals built their own outlets.

Foreclosure has often been considered an effective method of obtaining monopoly power for a firm that already has a monopoly in a related market. Suppose a firm has a patent for one product, say computers, and refuses to sell or lease its product unless the purchaser or lessee agrees to obtain its supplies of some other product, say floppy disks, from it. The firm thereby obtains a monopoly of disks (the tied product) used with its computers (the tying product). But it obtains no monopoly profits from the second monopoly. If it charges its computer lessees a price higher than the competitive price for the disks, they will treat this as an indirect increase in the computer rental; but if they are willing to pay a higher computer rental, it means that the computer company could have exploited their willingness directly — by charging a higher rental.

A possible advantage to a monopolist of imposing a tie-in, however, is that it may enable him to price discriminate effectively. If the computer company collects its monopoly revenues through the price that it fixes for each disk, in effect the computer rental rate varies from customer to customer according to the intensity of each customer's use, which may be a reasonable (but not infallible — why?) proxy for the elasticity of demand.[1] But so viewed, tying is not a method by which a firm can

---

§10.9   1. Could tying be used as a method of price discrimination in a case where the tying and tied products were used in fixed rather than variable proportions (e.g., a right and a left shoe) to produce the final product or service (a pair of shoes)?

use a monopoly in one market to obtain monopoly profits in a second market as well, nor is it likely in fact to foreclose access to the market to competing manufacturers of the tied product. Since the monopolist of the tying product cannot extract monopoly profits from the sale of the tied product, he has no interest in controlling its manufacture. His interest is only in having sales of the tied product funneled through him. Thus, tying agreements need not disturb the existing structure of the market for the tied product. (Might they still be objectionable?)

A subtler version of the foreclosure theory holds that foreclosure increases monopoly power indirectly by creating a barrier to entry. Narrowly conceived, a barrier to entry is a condition that makes the long-run costs of a new entrant into a market higher than the long-run costs of the existing firms in the market; a good example is a regulatory limitation on entry. The term is also used, however, as a synonym for heavy start-up costs. Thus, a market in which the capital or advertising expenditures necessary to obtain a foothold are large is frequently described as one in which there are barriers to entry, and it is in the latter sense of the term that foreclosure may create such a barrier.

If the existing firms in the market owned all of the retail outlets and were determined to deny them to new entrants, a new entrant would have to open his own retail outlets and this would increase his capital requirements. Or if floppy disks were tied to computer rentals a new entrant into the computer business would have to arrange to supply his customers with disks as well. But the capital costs of the existing firms are also higher as a result of vertical integration, so it is unclear what advantage these firms derive.[2] And so it is with advertising. A market in which firms advertise heavily may be difficult to enter without heavy advertising, but the entrant can take comfort in the fact that the firms in the market must incur heavy advertising costs themselves in order to maintain their positions.[3] Advertising is a bad example of a barrier to entry for two other reasons. The new entrant obtains a "free ride" on the advertising of the original firms in the market, which has created public acceptance for the product; and he has the option of advertising less and underpricing the existing firms, relying on the large retail chains to publicize the availability of a new low-price substitute.

If we ask not how large a new entrant's start-up costs would be but how large the ratio of start-up to operating costs — in other words, of fixed to variable costs — would be then we shall identify a real problem of entry. A high ratio of fixed to variable costs implies that the market may have room for only a few firms — maybe only one firm — of efficient

2. Might the new entrant, however, have to pay a higher interest rate for capital to establish a position in the market than firms already in the market have to pay for capital to replace their plants and other assets as they wear out? Might this depend on whether the new entrant was a new firm, or an established firm expanding into a new market?

3. Of course, this depends on how slowly the advertising depreciates.

size, making entry very risky (why?). This is the problem of natural monopoly, which is discussed in Chapter 12.

Another version of the foreclosure theory replaces the concept of a barrier to entry with that of a factor delaying entry. As mentioned earlier, the costs of entry are, within some range, a negative function of the time taken to enter (see §9.5 *supra*). And the optimal period for effecting entry is probably greater, the more complex the operations that must be coordinated for production to begin. Vertical integration might increase the complexity of entry and hence the time needed to effect it at costs no higher than those of the firms already in the market, because the new entrant would have to enter at two levels instead of one (retailing and manufacturing, in the earlier example).

§10.10   Boycotts; Herein of Monopsony

In the *Eastern States* case, a group of retail lumber dealers agreed not to buy lumber from any wholesaler who went into the retail lumber business in competition with a member of the retailer group.[1] But the agreement could deter the wholesalers from entering the retail lumber business only if the retailers had monopsony power vis-à-vis the wholesalers, an important term that will be explained with the aid of Figure 10.4. The figure depicts a firm's derived demand for some input (i.e., derived from the demand for the firm's final product). The supply price is assumed to be positively related to the amount of the input purchased, implying that the production of the input involves the use of scarce resources specialized to that production. The marginal cost to the firm of buying the input rises faster than the supply price (recall the discussion of this point in §10.7 *supra*) — that is, each increment in price raises the total costs of the input to the firm by a greater amount — because the price increase applies not merely to the incremental purchase but (assuming no price discrimination) to all previous purchases of the input. Thus, marginal cost is to supply price as marginal revenue is to sale price. The buyer's profits are maximized by limiting his purchases of the input to the level, q_2 in Figure 10.4, at which marginal cost equals marginal value. (Can you see why the derived-demand curve is a schedule of marginal value?) At this level, price is lower than if competition in the buying market led buyers to compete away the monopsony profits (measured by what?) generated at q_m, by bidding up price to p_c.

The attractiveness of monopsonizing depends on the positive slope

§10.10   1. Eastern States Retail Lumber Dealers' Assn. v. United States, 234 U.S. 600 (1914).

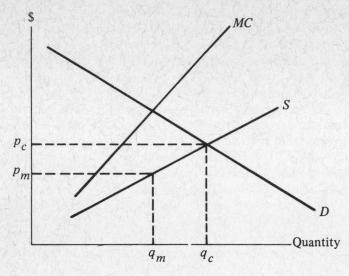

Figure 10.4

of the supply curve. If the curve were horizontal, limiting the quantity of the input that was bought would yield no monopsony profits (why?). Thus monopsony is a problem only where an input consumes resources that would be less valuable in other uses. Normally this condition is fulfilled only in the short run. Once a railroad track has been built, its value in alternative uses is severely limited, so a monopsonist of railroad services might be able to limit the price it paid for those services to a level at which the railroad could not recover its investment in track.[2] But the track would not be replaced; the steel, labor, and other inputs into its production would be shifted into markets where their costs could be recovered fully. A coal mine is another good example of a resource that can't be relocated without a tremendous loss of value.[3]

If the retail lumber dealers in the *Eastern States* case had monopsony power, why didn't they exercise it directly by reducing below competitive levels the amount of lumber that they bought from the wholesalers? Maybe the retailers found it easier to agree on cutting off competing wholesalers than on the optimal monopsony price of lumber. Another possibility is that the wholesalers were less efficient at retail distribution than the retailers and were attracted to the retail market only because the retailers were charging a cartel price. Then the boycott would in-

2. That investment is approximated in Figure 10.4 — assuming that the railroad uses no other specialized resources — by the triangular area bounded by the vertical axis, p_c, and the supply curve.
3. See Problem 5 at the end of Chapter 12.

crease the cartel's efficiency; monopsony pricing would not. And monopsony pricing would have only short-run effectiveness.[4]

§10.11 Antitrust Damages

Although equitable remedies, such as injunctions and divestiture, and criminal remedies (fines and imprisonment) are also used to enforce the federal antitrust laws, the antitrust damage remedy presents the most fascinating economic issues, and will be the focus of our analysis. An initial question is, when (if ever) should punitive damages be awarded as well as compensatory damages? The successful antitrust plaintiff is entitled to a tripling of his compensatory damages, so that two-thirds of every antitrust damage award represents punitive damages. We know from Chapter 7 that this would be sensible if there were a one-third chance of catching the antitrust violator. But, in fact, for antitrust violations committed in the open (mergers, for example) the probability is close to one, while for concealed violations (mainly price-fixing conspiracies) the probability, although lower than one, is not always one-third.

Turning to compensatory damages, we begin by asking how those damages should be computed, say in a suit (perhaps a class suit, see §21.8 *infra*) by consumers. Thinking back to Figure 9.7, should it be DW (the deadweight loss)? MP (the monopoly profits)? $DW + MP$? More?

DW is not enough. It measures only a part of the cost imposed by monopoly — the cost that is borne by those who stop buying the product when the price rises from the competitive to the monopoly level. It ignores the cost to those consumers who keep on buying the product but pay more. Their cost is MP, and the total social cost is therefore $MP + DW$. It is true that MP is not a net social cost, but just a transfer payment, at least if we ignore the tendency of monopoly profits to be transformed into costs of obtaining or defending monopoly. However, we want the monopolist, in deciding whether to monopolize, to compare the gain to him with the loss to everyone hurt by the monopoly — and that includes the consumers who continue to buy, as well as those deflected to (inferior) substitutes. And to make him do that we have to set damages equal to the total, not net, social costs of the monopoly.

Nor would it be enough to set damages equal to MP, on the theory that that would make monopoly profitless and therefore unattractive. Suppose the monopoly yielded some minor cost savings to the monopo-

4. Where have we encountered monopsony before in this book?

list. Then *MP* — at least if calculated according to the premonopoly
cost curve, i.e., according to what the consumers have lost rather than
what the monopolist has gained — would be less than the monopolist's
actual gain from monopoly, so he would not be deterred. And yet if
the cost savings were smaller than *DW,* we would want to deter him;
monopoly would not be cost justified.

The possibility of cost savings shows, however, that it would be unwise
to set damages (possibilities of concealment to one side) above the sum
of the monopoly profits and the deadweight loss. That would deter
monopolies that yielded cost savings greater than the deadweight loss —
assuming, realistically, that antitrust law does not excuse all such monopolies from liability.

What should damages be if a cartel is formed by firms that have
less than the whole market? We know from our formula for the firm
elasticity of demand that the cartel may still be able to charge a monopoly
price although not so high a one as if it controlled the entire market.
Suppose it succeeds in raising price by 10 percent. Naturally the firms
outside the cartel will benefit; they will be selling at the same price
(why?). And their consumers will lose. Should the cartelists therefore
be liable not only for their own monopoly profits but also those of
the innocent sellers (who themselves have violated no law)? They should
not. It is true that the customers of those sellers have suffered as a
result of the cartel. But if the cartel is to be charged with those losses
it should also be credited with the benefits (profits) it conferred on
the innocent sellers — and the two amounts are a wash. This is a straightforward application of the point about "economic" losses in Chapter
6: Losses offset by gains to others should not be figured in damages,
even though the losses were caused by the tort (cf. §6.7 *supra*).[1]

Often consumers do not buy directly from manufacturers but instead
from middlemen. Suppose a monopolist of shoes sells to 10 distributors
who in turn resell to 1,000 retailers who in turn resell to 1 million
consumers. It makes sense to permit the 10 distributors to sue the monopolist for the entire monopoly overcharge, even though they will in
all likelihood have passed on the bulk of the overcharge to the retailers
who in turn will have passed it on to the consumers. Depending on
the degree of passing on, the distributors' suit may yield them windfall
gains, yet the most important thing from an economic standpoint —
deterring monopoly — will have been accomplished more effectively
than if such suits are barred.[2] And maybe there won't be any windfall.

§10.11   1. What if the fringe firms have higher costs than the cartelists (as is likely —
why?)?
   2. The amount of passing on depends on the elasticity of demand. The more elastic
the demand, the smaller the fraction of the overcharge that will be passed on to the
next tier of distribution. Whether the distributor will be hurt by not being able to pass
on the entire cost to the next tier is a separate question, the answer to which depends

If the rule that there is no passing-on defense is well settled (as it is now), middlemen will charge lower prices in general. Their net costs of purchase from the manufacturer will be lower, because a middleman will have an expected gain from being able to sue if the price turns out to be an unlawful monopoly price. The lower prices charged by middlemen will compensate consumers for losing their own, less valuable right to sue. Their right is less valuable because, being at once more remote from the manufacturer and more numerous, consumers are less efficient antitrust enforcers and therefore are apt to gain less from an antitrust suit than middlemen are. If this is right, consumers have actually been made better off by the rejection of the passing-on defense!

Should competitors, as well as middlemen and (where there are no middlemen) consumers, be allowed to recover damages under the antitrust laws? At first glance the answer would seem to be no, if, as we have assumed throughout this chapter — and indeed as the courts increasingly *do* assume — the purpose of antitrust law is to promote the efficient allocation of resources. Monopoly creates inefficiency by driving a wedge between opportunity cost (= competitive price) and (monopoly) price; the welfare of competitors is neither here nor there. But sometimes a competitor is a more efficient antitrust enforcer than a consumer, because, like a middleman, he has more information and (depending, of course, on the precise damage rule) a greater stake in antitrust enforcement. Take predatory pricing. Consumers benefit in the short run; it is only after the predation succeeds and the monopolist jacks up his price that consumers begin to hurt. It is therefore unlikely that there

on whether the distributor owns any specialized resources used in the production of his output — for it is on those owners that the part of the cost that isn't passed on will come to rest. (What if there are no specialized resources?) The passing-on process is shown in Figure 10.5. The primed curve includes the overcharge, the nonprimed curve shows costs before the overcharge is imposed, and the vertical distance between the two represents the amount of the overcharge per unit of input bought.

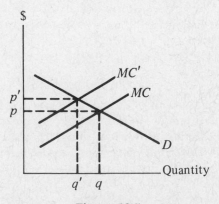

Figure 10.5

would be many consumer suits directed against predatory pricing. Of course one possibility for the law is to wait till the monopolist has succeeded and then let consumers sue. But maybe a better alternative is to allow the injured competitors, the victims of predation, to sue — but for what?

Although the injury that competitors suffer bears no necessary relation to the social costs of predation (which are the social costs of monopoly in the post-predation period, discounted to present value), there is an argument for allowing competitors to base their damages on that injury. If the immediate victims of predation, competitors, are made whole for the injury that predation causes them, the predator will not be able to intimidate them by the threat of predatory pricing. And we have said that predatory pricing is likely to be effective only when the predator can get his way, most of the time at least, by the threat rather than actuality of predatory pricing.

An important limitation on competitor damage actions is illustrated by the *Brunswick* case.[3] Firm A sued B for acquiring C, a competitor of A, and sought damages based on the injury that C had done to A as a result of being revitalized by B: But for the acquisition, C would have gone out of business, and A's output and profits would have been greater as a result. It was assumed that the acquisition had been illegal because it had created a danger (which had not however yet materialized) that B would finance predatory pricing by C. Nevertheless A was not permitted to get the damages it sought. Although those damages were caused by an illegal acquisition, they had the same economic significance as the harm to consumers from cartel pricing by firms that are not in the cartel: They were a harm offset elsewhere in the economic system. If B's acquisition of C enabled C to continue to compete with A without resorting to any improper tactics such as predatory pricing, then any loss to A must have been more than offset by the benefits of this competition to consumers; for it is only by making better (yet by assumption efficient — not below cost) offers to them that C could have wrested them away from A. There would be overdeterrence if B were made to pay A's damages. Compare §6.7 *supra*.

Suggested Readings

1. Roger D. Blair & David L. Kaserman, Antitrust Economics (1985).
2. Herbert Hovenkamp, Economics and Federal Antitrust Law (1985).
3. Louis Kaplow, Extension of Monopoly Power Through Leverage, 85 Colum. L. Rev. 515 (1985).

---

3. Brunswick Corp. v. Pueblo Bowl-O-Mat, Inc., 429 U.S. 477 (1977).

4. William M. Landes, Optimal Sanctions for Antitrust Violations, 50 U. Chi. L. Rev. 652 (1983).

5. ―――― & Richard A. Posner, Should Indirect Purchasers Have Standing to Sue Under the Antitrust Laws: An Economic Analysis of the Rule of *Illinois Brick,* 46 U. Chi. L. Rev. 602 (1979).

6. William H. Page, Antitrust Damages and Economic Efficiency: An Approach to Antitrust Injury, 47 U. Chi. L. Rev. 467 (1980).

7. Richard A. Posner, Antitrust Law: An Economic Perspective (1976).

8. George J. Stigler, The Organization of Industry, chs. 5-10, 21 (1968).

9. Economic Analysis and Antitrust Law (Terry Calvani & John Siegfried eds. 1979).

10. Antitrust and Economic Efficiency, 28 J. Law & Econ. 245 (1985).

Problems

1. The following are some leading antitrust cases decided by the Supreme Court. Read each decision. Then answer the following questions: Why did the defendant or defendants in fact adopt the challenged practice — to monopolize, or for some other purpose? To what extent does the decision of the Court rest on a judgment of the economic consequences of the challenged practice? Does the Court use economic analysis correctly?

United States v. Reading Co., 253 U.S. 26 (1920).

Chicago Board of Trade v. United States, 246 U.S. 231 (1918).

United States v. Container Corp. of America, 393 U.S. 333 (1969).

United States v. Sealy, Inc., 388 U.S. 350 (1967).

United States v. Continental Can Co., 378 U.S. 441 (1964).

Standard Fashion Co. v. Magrane-Houston Co., 258 U.S. 346 (1922).

United States v. Arnold, Schwinn & Co., 388 U.S. 365 (1967).

United States v. Singer Mfg. Co., 374 U.S. 174 (1963).

Sugar Institute, Inc. v. United States, 297 U.S. 553 (1936).

Arizona v. Maricopa County Medical Society, 457 U.S. 332 (1982).

United States v. United States Gypsum Co., 438 U.S. 422 (1978).

National Collegiate Athletic Association v. Board of Regents, 104 S. Ct. 2948 (1984).

2. Analyze the following proposition: Antitrust policy is profoundly antipathetic to the achievement of economically optimum amounts of (a) environmental protection and (b) consumer product information and safety.

CHAPTER 11

THE REGULATION OF THE EMPLOYMENT RELATION[1]

§11.1 The Special Treatment of Labor Monopolies

In the nineteenth century, the main question of antitrust policy was whether labor unions should be suppressed as unlawful combinations in restraint of trade. The classical economists thought not,[1] but neither did they believe that workers' combinations could be distinguished from combinations of employers to lower wages or of sellers to raise prices.[2] The main purpose of a union, most economists have long believed, is to limit the supply of labor so that the employer cannot use competition among laborers to control the price of labor. The common law was thus on solid economic ground when it refused to enforce agreements to join unions, enjoined picketing — an attempt to interfere with contractual relations between the picketed firm and its customers, workers, or other suppliers — and enforced yellow dog contracts (whereby workers agree not to join unions during the term of their employment). Regarding the last, the worker presumably would demand compensation for giving up his right to join a union — and if he was not compensated generously, this was not a social loss, since any compensation for not combining with other workers to create a labor monopoly is itself a form of monopoly gain.

Maybe, though, this picture of an efficient common law of labor relations rests on unrealistic assumptions about nineteenth-century Ameri-

---

1. On the principles of labor law, see Robert A. Gorman, Basic Text on Labor Law: Unionization and Collective Bargaining (1976); The Developing Labor Law (Charles J. Morris ed., 2d ed. 1983) (2 vols.).

§11.1   1. See, e.g., John Stuart Mill, Principles of Political Economy, bk. 5, ch. 10, §5 (1848).

2. See A.V. Dicey, Lectures on the Relation Between Law and Public Opinion in England During the Nineteenth Century 190-201 (2d ed. 1914).

can labor markets. Employers would have monopsony power if workers were ignorant of their alternative employment opportunities or had very high relocation costs, or if employers conspired to depress wages.[3] All three conditions may have been common in the nineteenth century, when there was much immigrant labor, the level of education was lower than today, the mobility of labor also was lower, firms had less competition, and the antitrust laws were not enforced against conspiracies to depress wages. Against all this are the facts (some noted in Chapter 8) that the great era of immigration to this country after the Civil War was a response to an acute labor shortage, that wages were always higher in America than in other countries, and that Americans have always been highly mobile. Moreover, even if labor monopsonies were a problem (and no doubt they were to some extent), labor monopolies are not much of a solution, at least from an economist's standpoint. The situation is one of bilateral monopoly, and with both sides trying to limit the supply of labor, though for different reasons, there is no assurance that the supply will reach the competitive level, although wages will be higher than if there is just monopoly.

This is shown graphically in Figure 11.1 (an elaboration of Figure 10.4 in the last chapter). S is the supply price of labor before a union is formed, and w_c is the competitive price for labor. The union, which is assumed to come first, raises the supply price to S' (a uniformly higher price is assumed for whatever quantity of labor is supplied). Without monopsony, the quantity of labor purchased will fall to q_{m1} and the wage will rise to w_{m1}. If the employer is a monopsonist, the supply will fall farther, to q_{m2}, and the wage will fall to w_{m2}. How will the bilateral monopoly solution compare to pure monopsony or pure monopoly? Does it make any difference whether the monopoly or the monopsony comes first?

Thus if we set aside labor monopsony, which is probably not a serious problem in this country today, we can say with some confidence (we shall consider a contrary suggestion later) that the effect of unionization is to reduce the supply of labor in the unionized sector. The higher wages obtained by the union will lead the employer to try to substitute cheaper for costlier labor (for instance, by relocating his business to a region of the country where unions are weak), capital for labor, and white-collar for blue-collar workers. Thus some workers benefit from unionization — those who are paid higher wages in the unionized industries and those newly employed by employers seeking substitutes for

3. Adam Smith thought such conspiracies common. See The Wealth of Nations 66-67 (Edwin Cannan ed. 1937 [1776]). And during the Pullman strike of 1894 the government invoked the Sherman Act against the organizers of the strike but not against the employers' conspiracy not to increase wages. See Almont Lindsey, The Pullman Strike, chs. 6-7, 14 (1942).

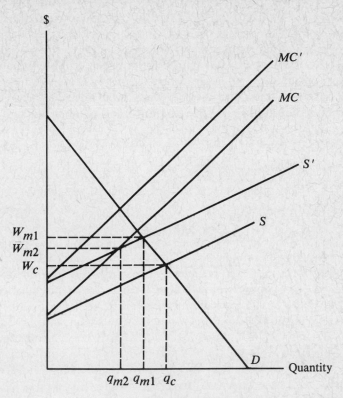

Figure 11.1

union labor. So do some shareholders: of firms whose competitors formerly paid lower wages than they did but are compelled as a result of unionization to pay the same wage. The losers are the consumers who buy from unionized industries (for those industries will pass along to their consumers a portion, at least, of their higher labor costs, cf. §10.10 *supra*), some stockholders and suppliers in those industries, and workers who cannot find employment because of the reduction in the demand for labor caused by union wage scales.[4]

As the classical economists might have predicted would happen, the Sherman Act was applied to labor union activities, notably, as already mentioned, in the Pullman strike of 1894.[5] Even after the Clayton Act in 1914 exempted labor from the antitrust laws, some state courts continued to enjoin strikes. But in the 1930s, public policy turned a sharp corner. The Norris-LaGuardia Act virtually eliminated the labor injunc-

4. Minority workers may be most adversely affected in this regard. See §§11.5, 11.7 *infra*.

5. See Lindsey, *supra* note 3, chs. 8, 12. See also Anderson v. Shipowners Association of the Pacific Coast, 272 U.S. 359 (1926).

tion and the Wagner Act of 1935 contained provisions that affirmatively encouraged the formation of unions. The passage of the Wagner Act led to a dramatic rise in union activity and wage rates in a number of industries.[6] Although the pro-union policy of the Wagner Act was trimmed some by the Taft-Hartley amendments of 1947, the National Labor Relations Act (as the Wagner Act, as amended by Taft-Hartley and subsequent statutes, is known) continues to embody a policy of encouraging unions.

§11.2   The Economic Logic of the National Labor Relations Act

If it is correct that unions are basically worker cartels and that the National Labor Relations Act basically encourages union formation, we have a fascinating counterpoint to the antitrust laws studied in the last chapter. The NLRA is a kind of reverse Sherman Act, designed to encourage cartelization of labor markets, whereas the Sherman Act (and the other antitrust laws) are designed to discourage cartelization of product markets. By studying how the NLRA does this, we shall deepen our insight into the economics of cartels and also see that the economic logic of the law is not always a logic of efficiency.

If public policy were neutral on unionization, efforts to organize a plant or other establishment would encounter classic free-rider problems. A worker who helped the union would be fired. Although the company would incur a cost by firing him, assuming he was a satisfactory worker (why is this a reasonable assumption?), the cost would probably be less than the benefit of signaling to the remaining employees that if anyone of them stepped forward to take the place of the fired employee as the union's organizer, he would be fired too. (Notice the analogy to rational predatory pricing, discussed in §10.7 *supra.*) If the workers hung together and struck in support of the fired employee, the balance of costs would be altered and the employer might back down. But the workers would encounter classic free-rider problems in agreeing to strike, given that the plant, by assumption, is not organized.

The National Labor Relations Act encourages union organizing efforts by forbidding the employer to fire or otherwise retaliate against union organizers and sympathizers. And the Norris-LaGuardia Act forbids yellow dog contracts, which would enable the employer to exploit the workers' free-rider incentives at little cost. Each worker would have an

---

6. On the effect of unionism on wage rates, see H. Gregg Lewis, Unionism and Relative Wages in the United States: An Empirical Inquiry (1963).

incentive to sign such a contract for a very modest consideration, knowing that if most workers signed, those who did not would be too few to be able to organize effectively.

If the organizing campaign succeeds to the point where 30 percent of the workers have signed cards authorizing the union to be their collective bargaining representative, the National Labor Relations Board, which administers the NLRA, will conduct an election for collective bargaining representative. If the union wins a majority of the votes cast, it will become the workers' exclusive bargaining representative. The employer will then be required to bargain with the union in good faith over the terms of an employment contract for all the workers in the collective bargaining unit; he will not be allowed to bargain separately with individual workers.

The representation election, the principle of exclusive representation, and the union shop[1] together constitute an ingenious set of devices (operating a little like the unitization of oil and gas fields, discussed in Chapter 3) for overcoming the free-rider problems that would otherwise plague the union as a large-numbers cartel. But for these devices, the rational strategy for the individual worker would be to hang back from joining the union or devoting any resources to promoting it. His hope would be that if the union got in as a result of the efforts of other workers, he would have the benefit of the union wage but would do better than the members of the union by not having to pay dues and by being able if he wanted to work more hours at a wage slightly below the union wage — just like the fringe firm in a cartelized market (see §10.1 *supra*). Another way in which the law prevents free riding — this time by the employer on the union's efforts — is to forbid the employer during the electoral campaign to offer higher wages or better working conditions to the workers.

A word about the electoral unit in representation elections, the bargaining unit as it is called. The Labor Board will certify any group of employees who are at once homogeneous in regard to the conditions of employment (wages, fringe benefits, work duties, etc.) and distinct from other employees of the firm. Often a single plant or facility may contain several different bargaining units each of which will negotiate separately with the employer. A hospital, for example, might have separate units of doctors, registered nurses, nurses' aides, and technical employees. Consistently with the law's policy of promoting worker cartels, the Board generally certifies the smallest rather than largest possible unit. Transaction costs among workers are lower the fewer the workers and the more harmonious their interests (why is the latter factor impor-

§11.2   1. A union shop — which the parties to a collective bargaining contract are allowed, other than in right to work states, to require — means that every worker in the collective bargaining unit must join the union or at least pay a portion of the union fees — an agency fee, it is called.

tant?), while the benefits of unionization are greater the smaller the unit is relative to the total employment of the firm. Suppose the unit consists of 10 workers in a plant of 100, and all workers earn the same amount. Then a 10 percent raise for the members of the unit will result in only a 1 percent increase in the employer's total wage bill. Of course, the unit must be important enough to the work of the firm to be able to make a credible threat to strike, but if the unit really is distinct, this condition can be satisfied even though the unit is small.[2]

If the union becomes the exclusive bargaining representative, the employer has as noted a duty to bargain in good faith with the union over the terms of a collective bargaining contract (a mass employment contract), but it has no duty to reach agreement. The only way the union can force the employer to come to terms is to threaten to call a strike if he does not.

The key to understanding the economics of strikes is the bilateral-monopoly character of the dealings between employer and union. In a product cartel, there is a reduction in output but not to zero. If, however, the customers banded together into a buyers' cartel, or if there were a single customer, it might respond to the sellers' cartel by threatening to stop buying from the cartel, in the hope that the threat of such a boycott would induce the cartel to back down. An employer is, in effect, the sole buyer of the labor services controlled by the union. If the union announces that it wants a higher price for those services, the employer can refuse, in effect threatening to buy nothing; and then the union, if it is to maintain credibility, must call the employer's bluff, and thus call the workers out on strike.

Since a strike will impose costs on both parties (unless the striking workers can be replaced at the same wage, a possibility discussed shortly) — forgone wages for the workers, and forgone profits for the employer — it might seem that the parties would always be better off negotiating a settlement. The problem, familiar from our discussion of predatory pricing in the last chapter, is that the terms of the settlement depend on the credibility of the parties' respective threats. The willingness of the employer to take an occasional strike, and of the union to call an occasional strike, may yield each party (ex ante) long-term benefits in enhanced credibility that exceed the short-term costs of the strike.

A strike will impose costs on the employer only if he cannot replace the striking workers. The National Labor Relations Act makes it easy to replace strikers in three ways, and hard in three ways. It makes it easy by

(1) withholding the protection of the Act from supervisory employees, thus making it feasible for the employer to use them as temporary replacements,

(2) allowing the employer to hire permanent replacements (the coun-

2. A contrary view is argued in Douglas L. Leslie, Bargaining Units, 70 Va. L. Rev. 353 (1984).

terpart in cartelized product markets to new sellers who come
into the market to replace the output that the cartelists have withdrawn from it) for the striking workers, and

(3) forbidding strikers to damage the employer's property (as by walking off the job without turning machinery off). Since by damaging
property the workers could impose very heavy costs on the employer at minimal costs to themselves (compared to the heavy
costs to workers of a protracted strike), allowing them to damage
property would greatly increase the monopoly power of unions.

The Act makes it hard for the employer to operate with replacement
workers by

(1) forbidding him to pay a higher wage than that of the striking
workers whom they replace,

(2) allowing the strikers to picket the plant, and

(3) forbidding him to sever the employment relationship with the
striking workers. He must reinstate the strikers when the strike
is over; if all the strikers' jobs have been filled by permanent
replacements, he must place the strikers at the head of the queue
to fill vacancies as they occur.

These three rules work together by allowing the strikers to identify the
replacement workers, by reminding the latter that when the strike ends
they may find themselves working side by side with the strikers — an
uncomfortable, sometimes a dangerous, proximity that deters many people from hiring on as replacements — and by preventing the employer
from paying a premium wage to compensate the replacements for this
additional cost of work. Incidentally, factors (2) and (3) also help to
prevent defections from the cartel; they discourage existing employees
from refusing to heed the strike call.

In sum, the Act does not go as far as it could go to promote cartelization of the labor supply, but it is not neutral; if the law were neutral,
unions would be less common and less effective than they are.

§11.3   Unions and Productivity

Thus far the assumption has been that all that unions do is try to raise
wages or — what amounts to the same thing, in economics — reduce
the costs of work by reducing the hours of work or by making the workplace cleaner, safer, or more attractive (at no reduction in wage: why
this qualification?). But unions do two other things that have led some
economists to speculate that unionization may enhance productivity,
perhaps completely offsetting its monopolistic effects.[1] Collective bar-

§11.3   1. See, e.g., Richard B. Freeman & James L. Medoff, What Do Unions Do?
(1984).

gaining contracts generally establish a grievance machinery for arbitrating workers' complaints and also give workers job security — not absolute security, for they can be laid off if the firm's demand for labor declines, but security against being fired other than for good cause (determined by means of the grievance machinery) and replaced by another worker. Without grievance machinery, it is argued, employers would not discover that their foremen were mistreating the workers until they noticed that job turnover was abnormal. And without job security, the argument continues, older workers would not share their experience with younger ones, fearing that the younger ones might replace them.

This theory does not explain, however, why, if grievance machinery and job security reduce costly turnover and enhance worker efficiency, employers do not adopt these devices without waiting for a union to come on the scene. If only one employer in an industry tumbled to their advantages, competition would force the others to follow suit. Probably the real reason that unions press for grievance machinery and job security is to make it harder for the employer to get rid of union supporters. The reason why collective bargaining contracts usually provide that if the employer must lay off workers because of a decline in his demand for labor he must lay them off in reverse order of seniority is similar: to prevent the employer from punishing union supporters by laying them off first. It may also enable the union to reward a class of workers — older workers — who are apt to be the strongest union supporters. Older workers have higher relocation costs than younger workers, both because of greater ties to the local area built up over many years and because their skills may have become specialized to the particular employer. This gives the employer some monopsony power over them and hence makes the union more valuable to them. In addition, they are more likely to obtain the full benefits of unionization than younger, more mobile workers who may quit shortly after the collective bargaining contract is signed.

§11.4   Employment at Will

One piece of evidence that job security is not really efficient is that outside of the unionized sector (which now employs less than 20 percent of the nation's labor force), and government employment (where tenure is a protection against politically motivated discharges — the "spoils system"), employment at will is the usual form of labor contract. The worker can quit when he wants; the employer can fire the employee when the employer wants. It might seem that this would leave the employee totally at the employer's mercy, but this is not true. If the employer gets a reputation for arbitrarily discharging employees he will have to pay new employees a premium. Since the employer thus cannot gain in the long run from a policy of arbitrary discharges — it is not effective predatory behavior — he might as well treat the employee fairly. But employment at will is currently under fire from the courts. A common law tort of unjust termination, sensibly applied to cases where a worker is fired for exercising a legal right — for example, giving truthful but damaging testimony against his employer in a suit by the government against the employer for tax evasion — is in some states turning into a *de facto* requirement of showing good cause for firing a worker, even though he is an employee at will. It is hard to see how workers in general can benefit from such a requirement. If the requirement were optimal it would be negotiated voluntarily; there do not seem to be the sort of information problems that might defeat transactions over workplace safety (see §8.2 *supra*, §11.6 *infra*). If such a requirement is not negotiated voluntarily, presumably this is because the cost to the employer of showing good cause for getting rid of an incompetent employee is greater than the benefit to the worker of being thus insured against an unjust discharge. The extra cost is a labor cost and will thus reduce the amount that the employer can pay in wages, in just the same way that increasing the employer's social security tax reduces (at least in the long run) the wage the employer will pay.

§11.5 Labor and Antitrust Law

Although the policy of the federal labor laws has been to place beyond the reach of the antitrust laws efforts to restrict the supply and raise the price of labor, a limited role for antitrust law in the labor field remains: that of preventing employers from using unions as agents in cartelizing or in other monopolistic practices in the employers' product markets. An extreme, and plainly unlawful, example would be a collective bargaining agreement between a union and a multi-employer bargaining unit representing the major sellers in the industry that fixed the prices at which the sellers had to sell their products. It might seem that a union would have no incentive to enter into such an agreement, since monopoly pricing of the industry's products would result in a reduction in the industry's output and hence in a reduction in its demand for inputs, including labor. The monopoly profits generated by monopoly prices could, however, be used to increase the wages of the remaining workers above the previous level, with perhaps enough left over to compensate the surplus workers for their costs of being discharged.

Sometimes it is unclear whether a restrictive provision in a labor agreement is intended simply to increase worker welfare or to create monopoly in the employers' product markets. Suppose a union representing plumbing construction workers enters into collective bargaining agreements with all of the plumbing subcontractors in an area whereby the subcontractors agree not to install any air conditioning units in which the internal pipe has been cut and threaded at the factory; their employees (the plumbing construction workers) will do all the cutting and threading. It has been argued that such an agreement should be viewed as creating a cartel among the subcontractors and hence as forbidden by the Sherman Act, since it enables the subcontractors to "secure greater profits if the union-demanded work is done by their companies rather than by a factory. . . ."[1]

The argument is questionable unless prefabrication enables the subcontractor to be bypassed altogether. The subcontractor provides an installation service using two inputs, labor and air conditioning equipment. He will combine them in the proportions that minimize his total costs. If internal pipe can be cut at a lower cost by the factory than by his own workers, and the cost saving is passed on to him in the form of a lower price, his total costs of installation will be minimized by buying the prefabricated air conditioners. His incentive will be unchanged if there is a cartel of subcontractors; a monopolist's (or cartel's) profits will rise if its costs decline.

The agreement of the subcontractors not to install prefabricated air conditioners is a device for increasing the subcontractors' demand for labor. Although it might seem that the subcontractor could compensate the union for the disemployment effect of the prefabricated air conditioner, that would depend on the size of the cost savings made possible by the prefabricated unit. Suppose it enables the subcontractor to dispense with two workers at a savings of $10,000 per job, but costs $9,500 more than the air conditioner fabricated on the job site. The savings of $500 may not be sufficient to compensate the workers for the costs of finding equally good jobs elsewhere.

§11.6 Minimum Wage and Related "Worker-Protective" Legislation

The federal minimum wage law reinforces the effect of unionization on wage rates by limiting the competition of nonunion labor. Suppose that in one part of the country unions are weak and wage rates therefore

---

§11.5 1. Douglas Leslie, Right to Control: A Study in Secondary Boycotts and Labor Antitrust, 89 Harv. L. Rev. 904, 909 (1976).

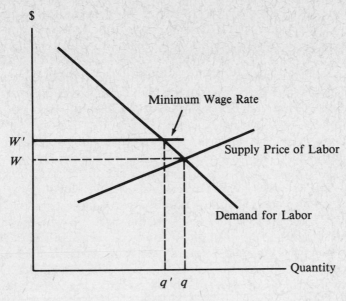

Figure 11.2

lower than elsewhere. Firms located in that area will have a competitive advantage that will enable them to grow at the expense of firms in unionized areas (for example, New England), and the result will be a reduced demand for labor in those areas. A minimum wage law counteracts this tendency by forcing up the wages of nonunion labor and so reducing the demand for that labor, as shown in Figure 11.2, where w is the competitive wage for nonunion labor and w' the minimum wage.

The unemployment effects of the minimum wage are substantial and are concentrated among marginal workers — middle-aged women, the young, and blacks, with the most severe effects being felt by black teenagers.[1] The fixing of a minimum wage has no effect on the demand for workers whose marginal productivity is high and who therefore receive a free-market wage above the minimum wage; the disemployed are those whose marginal productivity is lower, or perceived as lower,

§11.6 1. There is a vast empirical literature on the economic effects of the minimum wage law. See, e.g., Jere R. Behrman, Robin C. Sickles & Paul Taubman, The Impact of Minimum Wages on the Distribution of Earnings for Major Race-Sex Groups: A Dynamic Analysis, 73 Am. Econ. Rev. 766 (1983); Charles Brown, Curtis Gilroy & Andrew Kohen, The Effect of the Minimum Wage on Employment and Unemployment, 20 J. Econ. Lit. 487 (1982); Daniel S. Hamermesh, Minimum Wages and the Demand for Labor, 20 Econ. Inquiry 365 (1982); Peter Linneman, The Economic Impacts of Minimum Wage Laws: A New Look at an Old Question, 90 J. Pol. Econ. 443 (1982); Jacob Mincer, Unemployment Effects of Minimum Wages, 84 J. Pol. Econ. S587 (1976); Donald O. Parsons, Poverty and the Minimum Wage (1980); The Economics of Legal Minimum Wages (Simon Rottenberg ed. 1981).

than the minimum wage. To put it differently, the minimum wage, being well below the wage of unionized workers, does not raise *their* wages above the prevailing level and hence does not create unemployment among them. It raises the relative price, and hence reduces the attractiveness, of a substitute labor force consisting of marginal workers who but for the minimum wage would compensate employers for hiring them by accepting a lower wage than the more productive — but also more expensive — union workers.

Of course some workers are helped by the minimum wage — those who supply q hours of work in Figure 11.2. These are workers whose free-market wage is below, but whose marginal product is above, the minimum wage. (Were these workers underpaid before the minimum wage was put into effect? Are they still in a sense underpaid? Or should the entire area between w and the demand curve be viewed as merely the potential monopoly profits of the labor market depicted in the figure?) But because low-wage earners are often found in high-earning households, the minimum wage turns out not to be an efficient measure for combatting poverty even without regard to its adverse effects on marginal workers.

The analysis is more complicated when the minimum wage is applicable only in some occupations, and others are exempt (this is decreasingly true, however, in the United States). Then the minimum wage may reduce unemployment in the exempt sector and increase it in the covered sectors. Workers are attracted from the exempt to the covered sector, reducing the supply in the exempt sector and increasing it in the covered. Depending on the size of the wage difference between the sectors, workers might accept a prolonged period of unemployment in the covered sector as the price of finally landing a higher paid job there. One way of waiting for work to open up in the covered sector is to stay in school longer; so the minimum wage promotes college education. Does it also raise the crime rate because crime is an exempt sector? Could it conceivably lower the crime rate?

Much other legislation operates to increase the wage rates of selected subsets of workers. Restrictions found in building codes on the use of prefabricated materials increase the demand for labor, along the lines suggested in our discussion of prefabricated air conditioners. Child labor laws reduce the supply of labor and hence increase the wages of adult workers; this is not to say, however, that such laws are economically unjustifiable (see §5.4 *supra*). Laws "protecting" women workers have a similar effect and less justification (see §25.1 *infra*). Tariffs are frequently sought and obtained by unions as a method of offsetting the comparative advantage enjoyed by foreign firms that employ cheaper labor. Restrictive immigration laws prevent cheap foreign labor from coming to the United States to swell the labor supply and hence drive wages down.

The Occupational Safety and Health Act, which directs the establishment of minimum federal standards of worker safety and health, is a particularly ambitious example of worker protection legislation. Is it necessary? The employer has a selfish interest in providing the optimal (not necessarily the highest possible) level of worker health and safety. If an expected accident or illness cost of $1 can be eliminated for 99¢, eliminating it will reduce the employer's net wage bill by 1¢, since his employees presumably demanded compensation for the $1 expected cost. There may of course be disagreements among employers and workers (or their union representatives) over the relevant figures, but these can be ironed out in negotiations. Legislation prescribing the health and safety conditions of employment may raise the level of health and safety beyond the level desired by the employees and the employers, and then both groups will be harmed. If the legislation requires the employer to spend $1.05 to eliminate a health hazard that imposes an expected cost of only $1, the employer will reduce the wage rate by at least $1 (he no longer has to compensate the employee for the hazard) — and probably by $1.05 (why?).[2]

Maybe, though, this is all too pat, and ignores the costs of information about workplace safety. But, alternatively, maybe the real reason behind OSHA is to reduce the competition from nonunion labor. If the level of health and safety is generally lower in firms that pay nonunion wages — a plausible assumption, since the lower the worker's wage is, the lower will be the costs to him of being disabled — unions might press for legislation raising the level of health and safety in those firms to that prevailing in unionized firms. The nonunion employers might try to compensate for their added costs by reducing the wages paid their workers, but if those workers were already earning no more than the minimum wage, the employers would be unable to make a compensating wage reduction and their labor costs would rise relative to those of unionized firms. This hypothesis is supported indirectly by the Occupational Safety and Health Administration's preference for engineering changes designed to reduce workplace accidents over personal protection devices such as ear plugs and safety goggles. Even though the latter frequently are more efficient, the former increase the cost of capital and the latter the cost of labor.[3] The hypothesis is also supported by evidence that though OSHA undoubtedly increases employers' costs,

2. The analysis is not changed significantly if nominal wage rates are assumed to be inflexible downward because they are specified in collective bargaining contracts. The next time the union demands a $2 per hour wage increase by reason of inflation, increased productivity, or whatever, it will get only $1, to compensate the employer for having eliminated the health hazard.

3. See James C. Miller III, Is Organized Labor Rational in Supporting OSHA, 50 So. Econ. J. 881 (1984).

it seems not to have reduced the number of workplace injuries significantly.[4]

Maybe the two reasons we have given for OSHA are related: Workers in nonunion plants have less information about safety, because a union is an information gatherer for its members. Still another possible reason for the legislation is to correct inefficiencies resulting from governmental programs for the support of injured workers. Through the social security disability program (see §16.5 *infra*) plus a variety of special programs (for example, compensating workers disabled by black lung disease) the federal government defrays much of the cost incurred by workers injured as a result of unsafe or unhealthy work conditions. By shifting the costs of accident and illness from the workers and their employers to the federal taxpayer, these programs reduce the incentives of firms to maintain the optimal level of occupational safety and health. The limiting case is the worker whom the government compensates fully for any job-related illness or accident (is that realistic?). He would have no incentive to demand, or his employer to offer, a safe and healthy place to work.

Properly administered (an enormous qualification), OSHA might, therefore, simply raise the level of occupational safety and health to the level at which it would be but for the public subsidy of workers' injuries and illnesses. The problem, however, with using one government intervention in the marketplace (subsidizing workplace injuries and illnesses) to justify another (regulating workplace safety and health) is that it invites an indefinite and unwarranted expansion in government. A series of incremental steps each of which makes economic sense in light of the previous steps may, looked at as a whole, make no economic sense at all.

§11.7 Some Issues in Employment Discrimination on Grounds of Race, Sex, and Age

Racial discrimination in employment is a part of a larger issue — that of the causes and cures of racial discrimination — which is discussed in a later chapter (Chapter 27). Here we shall discuss one specialized topic in racial discrimination and also employment discrimination against women and the aged.

---

4. See Ann P. Bartel & Lacy Glenn Thomas, Direct and Indirect Effects of Regulation: A New Look at OSHA's Impact, 28 J. Law & Econ. 1 (1985); David P. McCaffrey, An Assessment of OSHA's Recent Effects on Injury Rates, 18 J. Human Resources 131 (1983); W. Kip Viscusi, The Impact of Occupational Safety and Health Regulation, 10 Bell J. Econ. 117 (1979); W. Kip Viscusi, Risk by Choice: Regulating Health and Safety in the Workplace, ch. 2 (1983).

1. Many unions long refused to admit black workers. Why? Economics suggests an answer. As we have seen, unions seek to raise the wage rate above the competitive level; and to the extent they succeed, an excess demand for union jobs is created. There are various ways in which this excess demand could be eliminated. One would be by auctioning off union membership. The successful bidders would be those willing to pay an entrance fee equal to the present value of the difference between the union wage scale and the wages in their next best employment. This would be the method of rationing used if unions were simply firms enjoying monopoly power over labor — firms that bought labor at the competitive wage and resold it to employers at a monopoly wage. But unions are not firms; they are representatives (however imperfect) of the workers, and they will not adopt a rationing method that would deny the union membership any net wage gains from membership. The problem with nonmonetary rationing methods, however, is that they induce applicants to expend real resources. If admission to the union is based on work skills, for example, applicants will incur real costs to obtain the requisite skills, and the competition in obtaining skills may result in eliminating the expected monopoly profits of union membership (cf. §§3.2, 9.3 *supra*). What makes criteria involving race or some other relatively immutable status (such as being the son of a union member) attractive is that they do not invite heavy expenditures on qualifying; the costs of changing one's race or parents are prohibitive.

2. The central economic question relating to employment discrimination against women is explaining the persistently higher average wage of men compared to women (women's wages per hour are on average about 60 percent of men's wages[1]). Irrational or exploitive discrimination is one possibility. Another is that male wages include a compensatory wage premium for the dirty, disagreeable, and strenuous jobs that men dominate presumably because their aversion to such work is less than women's. Another (these are not mutually exclusive possibilities, of course) is differences in investments in market-related human capital (earning capacity). If a woman allocates a substantial part of her working life to household production, including child care, she will obtain a substantially lower return on her market human capital than a man planning to devote much less time to household production, and she will therefore invest less in that human capital. Since earnings are in part a return on one's human capital investments (including education), women's earnings will be lower than men's.[2] In part this will show up in

§11.7   1. With certain adjustments the real percentage is estimated for 1974 at 66 percent, in Improvements in the Quality of Life: Estimates of Possibilities in the United States, 1974-1983, at 194 (Nestor E. Terleckyj ed. 1975).
    2. See Jacob Mincer & Haim Ofek, Interrupted Work Careers: Depreciation and Restoration of Human Capital, 17 J. Human Resources 3 (1982); Jacob Mincer & Solomon W. Polachek, Family Investments in Human Capital: Earnings of Women, 82 J. Pol. Econ. S76 (1974); Trends in Women's Work, Education, and Family Building, 3 J. Labor Econ. S1 (1985).

the choice of occupations: Women will be attracted to occupations that don't require much human capital. Of course the amount of time women are devoting to household production is declining for reasons explained in Chapter 5, so we can expect the wage gap to shrink if the economic model is correct.

Comparable worth refers to the movement, now being pressed in courts and legislatures, for raising the wage level of job classifications filled primarily by women (e.g., secretarial work) to that of predominantly male job classifications (e.g., truck driving).[3] The proposal is to determine the actual worth of the different jobs, and if the worth is the same equalize the wages (by raising the lower wage level) regardless of the market conditions. The effort to divorce worth from market value is troubling to an economist. If a truck driver is paid more than a secretary, even though the secretary works just as long hours and has as good an education, the economist's inclination will be to assume that the market is compensating a skill that is in shorter supply, or is offsetting a disamenity, rather than making arbitrary distinctions based on fast-vanishing stereotypes. The economist would therefore assume that if measurements of comparable worth failed to pick up the different worths of the two types of job, this was because of the crudeness of the measuring devices rather than the absence of real differences.

In any event, consider what the consequences will be if comparable worth is implemented. If wages in jobs now dominated by women are raised, the number of jobs available will shrink, as employers seek to substitute other, and now cheaper, inputs (e.g., word processors for typists), and as customers substitute other products for those made by firms whose wage bills and hence prices have risen because of comparable worth. At the same time, men will start competing more for those jobs, lured by the higher wages. So female employment in a job classification that had been (for whatever reason) congenial to women may (why not will?) drop. Some displaced women will find new employment in the predominantly male occupations such as truck driving — perhaps replacing men who have become secretaries! But these women may not be happier in their new jobs; after all, there is nothing to stop a woman today from becoming a truck driver if that is what she wants to be. Finally, under comparable worth the incentives of women to invest in human capital usable in the traditional men's jobs will drop as the relative wages in those jobs drop, so that in the end occupational sex segregation may not be greatly affected.

3. Federal law forbids public or private employers to force their em-

3. See June O'Neill, Comparable Worth (Urban Institute and U.S. Commn. on Civil Rights, unpublished, Jan. 29, 1985); June O'Neill & Hal Sider, The Pay Gap and Occupational Segregation: Implications for Comparable Worth (Urban Institute and U.S. Commn. on Civil Rights, unpublished, Dec. 29, 1984); Comparable Worth: Issue for the 80's (U.S. Commn. on Civil Rights 1984); Comparable Worth: An Analysis and Recommendations (U.S. Commn. on Civil Rights 1985).

ployees to retire before the age of 70, with the exception of a few job classifications such as airline pilot. The economist is naturally troubled by the government's intervening in the decision of a private employer to use age as a basis for terminating employment either on a retail or wholesale (mandatory retirement age) basis. The reply is that the use of age is arbitrary. Although this is true, it does not provide a good economic reason for government intervention in the employment market. The use of a single, readily determinable characteristic such as age as the basis for an employment decision economizes on the costs of information. True, there is diseconomy as well as economy: Sometimes a more competent older worker will be replaced by a less competent younger one. But that does not make the employer's use of age as a proxy for competence, crude as the proxy is, inefficient. The employer's objective is to minimize the sum of the costs of suboptimal retention decisions resulting from lack of individualized assessment of workers' abilities and the information costs of making such assessments.[4] If the sum is minimized by having a mandatory retirement age, the employer will have a mandatory retirement age; otherwise he will not. There is no externality calling for government intervention.

Suggested Readings

1. Thomas J. Campbell, Labor Law and Economics, forthcoming in Stan. L. Rev., vol. 37 (1986).
2. Richard A. Epstein, A Common Law for Labor Relations: A Critique of the New Deal Labor Legislation, 92 Yale L.J. 1357 (1983).
3. ———, In Defense of the Contract at Will, 51 U. Chi. L. Rev. 947 (1984).
4. Robert H. Lande & Richard O. Zerbe, Jr., Reducing Unions' Monopoly Power: Costs and Benefits, 28 J. Law & Econ. 297 (1985).
5. Edward P. Lazear, A Competitive Theory of Monopoly Unionism, 73 Am. Econ. Rev. 631 (1983).
6. Cotton M. Lindsay & Charles A. Shanor, *County of Washington v. Gunther*: Economic and Legal Considerations for Resolving Sex-Based Wage Discrimination Cases, 1 S. Ct. Econ. Rev. 185 (1982).
7. Mancur Olson, The Logic of Collective Action 66-97 (1965).
8. Richard A. Posner, Some Economics of Labor Law, 51 U. Chi. L. Rev. 988 (1984).
9. Albert Rees, The Economics of Trade Unions (2d rev. ed. 1977).
10. George J. Stigler, The Theory of Price, ch. 16 (3d ed. 1966).

---

4. This decisional problem is strikingly like that of deciding how much procedure to provide to litigants. See §21.1 *infra*.

11. Symposium: The Conceptual Foundations of Labor Law, 51 U. Chi. L. Rev. 947 (1984) (includes Suggested Readings 3 and 8).

Problems

1. A closed shop, outlawed by the Taft-Hartley Act, is created when the employer agrees with the union that he will hire only workers who are members of the union (in contrast to a union shop, where the workers have to join the union if and when it becomes the collective bargaining representative for their unit). What is the economic function of the closed shop?

2. Are unions likely to be more powerful in service industries or in manufacturing industries? In the public sector or in the private sector? More generally, what are the factors that predispose an industry to unionization? Cf. §10.2 *supra*.

3. What precisely does the leadership of a union try to maximize? The average hourly wage of its members? The average yearly wage? The total wages of workers employed in the unionized activity? What different effects might these various maximands have on the size of the union? Why might the union's leadership be concerned with the size of the union as well as with the incomes of its members? How does this explain featherbedding?

4. Wages have risen faster in nonunionized occupations, notably domestic service, than in unionized occupations. Does this indicate that unionization is ineffective in raising wages above competitive levels?

5. Can unions raise wages above competitive levels in the long run, if employers sell in competitive product markets? Or if all workers are unionized?

CHAPTER 12

PUBLIC UTILITY AND COMMON CARRIER REGULATION[1]

§12.1 Natural Monopoly

The situation where monopoly is inevitable because it is the cheapest way of organizing an industry is depicted in Figure 12.1. Observe that average costs (AC) are declining at the point where they intersect demand. Suppose there is one firm in the market, producing q units at an average cost of c. Obviously efficiency would be increased by carrying production to q', where demand and marginal cost would be equated. There are two ways to reach the larger output. One is for the existing firm to produce $q' - q$ more units. Another is for a new firm to enter the market and produce q_e units (equal to $q' - q$). At q', the existing firm's average cost would be c', but the new entrant would have to incur an average cost of c_e to produce q_e units, and c_e lies above c'. Thus it is cheaper for the existing firm to supply the additional units, not because the firm is more efficient in the sense that its cost curve lies below those of other firms — the cost schedules for the existing firm and the new entrant are identical in Figure 12.1 — but because one firm can supply the entire output demanded at a lower cost than could more than one firm. This is the condition known as natural monopoly.[1]

The condition arises when fixed costs are very large in relation to demand. If they can be spread over the entire output of the market, a

---

1. For good introductions to the legal subject matter of this and the next chapter, see Stephen G. Breyer, Regulation and Its Reform (1982); Ernest Gellhorn & Richard J. Pierce, Jr., Regulated Industries in a Nutshell (1982); Thomas D. Morgan, Economic Regulation of Business: Cases and Materials (2d ed. 1985).

§12.1 1. Must average costs actually be declining at the intersection with the demand curve? Or is it enough that two or more firms would have higher average costs than one?

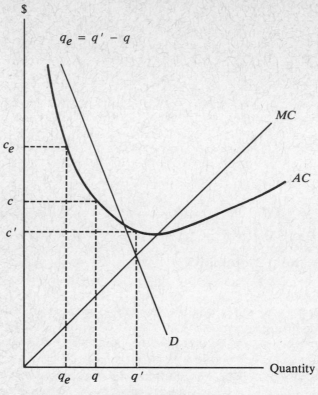

Figure 12.1

single firm supplying that output may have a lower average cost of production than two equally efficient firms, each of which would incur the same fixed costs but have to spread them over only one-half the output.[2] This is possible even if (as in Figure 12.1) marginal cost is increasing with output. To illustrate, suppose the fixed costs of producing some service are 10, and marginal cost increases as shown in Table 12.1 (from which Figure 12.1 is derived). If the market's output is 6 or less, one firm can supply that output at a lower total cost than could two or more firms (for example, at an output of 6, the total cost if there is one firm is 31, while the total cost if there were two firms, each producing 3 units, would be 32). Hence efficiency requires that only one firm serve this market unless the demand is for 7 or more units. A plausible example

2. Of course a large firm may be less efficient than a small one because of loss of control over subordinates, lack of innovative vigor, or other sources of diseconomies of scale. A natural monopolist is a firm that has *net* economies of scale over the whole range of its feasible output. This is an important qualification, raising the question just how important, empirically, natural monopoly is: perhaps not very, unless, as noted in the text below, the range of feasible output is quite small because market demand is quite small.

Table 12.1

Output	Fixed Costs	Total Costs Fixed & Variable	Marginal Cost	Average Total Cost
1	10	11	1	11.0
2	10	13	2	6.5
3	10	16	3	5.3
4	10	20	4	5.0
5	10	25	5	5.0
6	10	31	6	5.2
7	10	38	7	5.4
8	10	46	8	5.8

of natural monopoly is local electrical service; the market is limited in extent because of the cost of transporting electricity over long distances, while fixed costs (generating equipment, a city-wide grid of wires, etc.) are high. But if a market is small enough, almost any kind of firm can have a natural monopoly — a grocery store in a small village, for example — because every firm has some fixed costs, and they may dominate if output is low enough.

Natural monopoly presents three problems that have been thought to warrant public regulation. One is monopoly pricing. The firm that supplies a natural monopoly market has the same incentive as any other firm to maximize profit by restricting its output and a much better chance of achieving this goal since it need not incur the legal and administrative costs of collusion or corporate acquisition to do so. The antitrust laws are ineffectual in this situation (why?).

The second (and, superficially, inconsistent) problem is encouragement of inefficient entry, depicted in Figure 12.2. The monopolist sells quantity q at price p, as determined by the intersection of marginal cost and marginal revenue. A new entrant, seeing that he can supply a portion of the market, q_e, at an average cost (c_e) lower than the market price, has an incentive to enter. When he does so, the existing firm must either reduce price or curtail output, and if it follows the latter route, the average cost of production will be higher than necessary. (What will happen if instead it reduces price?) This is an example, is it not, of the tendency for economic rents to be converted into cost (see §§1.1, 3.2, 9.3 *supra*).

The third problem is the difficulty of devising an efficient price structure. At the point in Figures 12.1 and 12.2 where marginal cost intersects demand, the firm's average cost is greater than its marginal cost. In other words, the last unit of output costs less to produce than the average cost of all of the units produced. So if the firm sold its entire output at the cost of the last unit (marginal cost), its total revenue would be

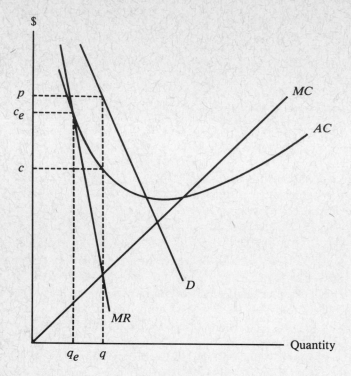

Figure 12.2

less than its total cost.[3] But if it therefore sells at a price equal to average cost, it will induce the marginal purchaser to switch to substitute products even though they cost more to produce than would carrying production of the first product to the point at which price just equals marginal cost. The marginal purchaser will be confronted with a (socially) false alternative.

The law's answer to the problem of natural monopoly is public utility and common carrier regulation. This type of regulation has three primary elements:

(1) profit control (the regulated firm's rates are not to exceed the level necessary to enable the firm to cover its cost of service, including a reasonable return on invested capital);

(2) entry control (a firm may not provide a regulated service without first obtaining a certificate of public convenience and necessity from the regulatory agency); and

(3) control over price structure (the firm may not discriminate in its rates).

3. Total cost is equal to average cost times quantity sold. If marginal cost is lower than average cost, then the product of marginal cost times quantity sold will be less than total cost.

The three controls, which are discussed in the following sections, relate to the three problems of natural monopoly sketched above; a major question is whether they solve them.

§12.2   Control of Profits and The Problem of Reasonable Return

There is a standard method by which public utility agencies attempt to limit the profits of regulated firms. The agency first selects a recent and presumably representative year of the company's operations and computes the total costs incurred by the firm that year in rendering the regulated service, less all capital costs including interest on long-term debt. The included costs are the company's test-year cost of service. To the cost of service the agency then adds a reasonable return on invested capital (long-term debt plus equity). The return component is determined by multiplying the company's rate base, which is an estimate of the value of the capital assets used by the company to render the regulated service, by the company's reasonable rate of return. The latter is a weighted average of the long-term interest rate plus the rate of return to the equity shareholders that the agency considers appropriate in light of the risk of the investment and the rate of return enjoyed by shareholders in comparable firms. The return component, when added to the cost of service, establishes the company's revenue requirements. The company submits to the agency a schedule of rates designed to generate just this amount of revenue, on the assumption that the quantity demanded of the firm's service will be the same as in the test year. When approved, these rates are the maximum the firm may charge.[1]

Determining the test-year cost of service is relatively straightforward, although some monopoly profits may get concealed in expense items such as managerial salaries and perquisites.[2] Determining the return component presents significant difficulties. The issue that has preoccupied courts and legal scholars is whether the rate base should be mea-

---

§12.2   1. There are two different procedures by which rates may be changed. First, the agency may initiate a proceeding, such as that described in the text, to review the firm's rates. Second, and more commonly, the firm may initiate a proceeding for permission to make a rate increase. This is ordinarily a more abbreviated proceeding. The burden of justifying an increase is on the firm. Incidentally, "public utility" and "common carrier" are largely interchangeable terms, although the latter is used principally of transportation and communications companies and sometimes connotes less pervasive regulation than described in the text.

The rates fixed are often minima as well as maxima. See §12.5 *infra*.

2. See §§12.3 and 27.3 *infra*.

sured by the depreciated original cost of the firm's capital assets or by their replacement cost. The issue is most important in periods of inflation, when the cost of replacing a long-lived capital asset may greatly exceed the asset's original cost, so that using replacement cost would entitle the utility to a higher rate-of-return allowance, resulting in higher rates.

An example will illustrate the nature of the problem and point us toward the economically correct solution. Suppose that a firm buys for $10,000 a machine that can produce 1,000 units per year and has a useful life of 20 years. Operating costs are $1 per unit and the annual cost of the capital used to purchase the machine is 5 percent. Average cost is therefore $2.[3] Demand for the firm's product increases and in the tenth year the firm decides to buy a second machine. But prices have risen. The identical machine now costs $15,000, and while operating costs are unchanged the cost of capital has increased to 6 percent. The average cost of production on the second machine is therefore $2.65. What should the firm's price be: $2.00, $2.325, or $2.65?

The answer given by economic analysis is $2.65. A lower price may induce the firm to make an incorrect investment decision. Suppose the price is $2.33. People who value the product at more than $2.33 but less than $2.65 will try to buy it. Faced with excess demand the firm may buy a third machine. When it then raises its price to cover the cost of production on that machine (which will also be, let us assume, $2.65), it will lose many of its new customers; it will have overexpanded.

If replacement (i.e., current) cost rather than original cost is the correct economic standard, why has the issue of original versus replacement cost been so controversial? There are three reasons.

First, replacement cost is not always the correct economic standard. If an industry's major capital assets (for example, railroad tracks, locomotives, and terminals) are not going to be fully replaced, because of declining demand for the industry's product, charging a price based on replacement costs will prevent full utilization of the existing capacity by driving consumers away. There is no point in confronting consumers with the cost of replacing assets that won't be replaced. The proper standard in such a case is the opportunity cost of the industry's existing assets; if, as in the railroad case, the assets are highly specialized (cannot readily be shifted to an alternative use), that cost may be much lower than the cost of replacing them (cf. §10.6 supra, §12.4 infra).

Second, where original cost is lower than replacement cost, the use of replacement cost to determine the firm's revenue requirements will cause the firm's revenues to exceed the costs shown on the firm's books, resulting in an apparent windfall for the firm's shareholders. But the

---

3. Depreciation is $10,000 ÷ 20, or $500 a year, which is equal to 50¢ a unit. The annual cost of capital, 5 percent of $10,000, is another 50¢ per unit, and operating costs are $1 per unit, making the average total cost $2 per unit.

windfall may be an illusion created by inflation,[4] and is in any event balanced by the losses to the shareholders and creditors of firms in other industries, such as railroads, where the value of specialized resources has plummeted because demand for the industry's output has declined rather than increased. Ex ante, there is no windfall.

Third, the legal issue of current versus replacement costs arises in a form that obscures the economic reality. The constitutional guarantee of just compensation for governmental takings has been held to entitle the shareholders of a public utility to a "fair" return on their investment. Two questions are relevant to deciding whether the use of original cost in determining a public utility's rate ceiling prevents the shareholders from earning a fair return. The first is, did the shareholders have notice of the standard to be applied when they invested? If they knew that the regulatory agency applied an original-cost standard, they can hardly charge confiscation; presumably, even with this feature, their investment in the regulated firm was more attractive than their alternative investment opportunities, or they would not have made the investment.[5] If they invested on the reasonable assumption that the agency would apply a replacement-cost standard, the argument of confiscation is more compelling.

The second question is whether the additional returns to the shareholders resulting from use of a replacement-cost standard are within the scope of the just-compensation guarantee. This may depend on whether or not they are characterized as windfalls. Either inquiry deflects attention from the question of the economic soundness of the original-cost standard.

Another major difficulty in determining the return component in the regulated firm's revenue requirements involves determining the cost of equity capital. But we postpone consideration of this problem to the chapter on capital market theory (see §15.4 *infra*).

§12.3 Some Other Problems Arising from the Attempt to Limit the Regulated Firm's Profits

The use of past rather than current costs means that the rates approved by the agency may be inappropriate to current conditions. If costs have

---

4. Or it may result from a change in underlying supply or demand conditions, unrelated to inflation, that has caused the real price of the good to increase. In the latter case, the "windfall" represents a form of economic rent. See §1.1 *supra*.

5. If the investors are bondholders, the regulated firm is presumably paying them a rate of interest sufficiently high to compensate them for the disadvantages that the original-cost standard may impose upon them. If they are stockholders, the rate of return on equity capital expected to be allowed by the agency presumably was, when they invested, sufficiently high to make the investment remunerative in spite of the agency's use of the original-cost standard.

risen since the test year, the rates will be too low to cover the firm's current costs, and the firm may not be able to catch up by filing for rate increases. If costs have declined, the current rates will be too high. If demand has increased, the rates may again be too high, since they are calculated by dividing the revenue requirements by the test-year output, and the average cost of a higher output will be lower if the firm is operating in a region of declining average costs. Observe also that the lag introduced by the use of a test year creates opportunities for a regulated firm to cheat: By reducing the quality of its output, it can reduce its current costs below its test-year costs and thereby increase its profits.

The popularity of the original-cost and test-year-of-service concepts is evidence of the eternal struggle in rate regulation between economic theory and feasibility. Both methods facilitate the use of the company's own books of account as the basic source of information for the rate-making process. Both lead to serious departures from efficient pricing.

In periods when inflation is slight and real input prices are steady or falling, public utility regulation appears to have little effect on price levels or profits, implying that it is a failure as a system for controlling monopoly.[1] In periods of sharp inflation, when regulatory lag works dramatically against the firm, profits may be depressed well below the competitive level, implying overcorrection. And mistakes involved in regulatory attempts to limit prices and profits do not cancel out. If rates are too high, consumers will be induced to purchase substitute products that in fact cost society more to produce. If rates are too low, consumers will be deflected from substitute products that cost society less to produce; again resources will be wasted.

Public utility regulation has interesting side effects:

1. To the extent it succeeds in its formal aim of placing public utility pricing on a cost-plus basis, it reduces the firm's incentive to minimize costs (see further on this point §14.14 *infra*). The penalty to the monopolist who fails to minimize costs is that his profits are lower than otherwise. The tendency of public utility regulation is to reduce that penalty. Regulatory lag may hold this tendency in check, however — showing that bureaucratic delay can be serendipitous!

2. The regulatory agency's success in monitoring the regulated firm's costs will inevitably be uneven. Since it is easier for the agency to police

§12.3 1. See George J. Stigler & Claire Friedland, What Can Regulators Regulate? The Case of Electricity, 5 J. Law & Econ. 1 (1962); Thomas Gale Moore, The Effectiveness of Regulation of Electric Utility Prices, 36 So. Econ. J. 365 (1970). Studies like these raise the question: Are we really better off trying to regulate natural monopolies than leaving them alone? For a negative answer, see Richard A. Posner, Natural Monopoly and Its Regulation, 21 Stan. L. Rev. 548 (1969). But cf. Robert A. Meyer & Hayne E. Leland, The Effectiveness of Price Regulation, 62 Rev. Econ. & Stat. 555 (1980), finding, contrary to Stigler-Friedland and Moore, that regulation of electrical rates has had some beneficial effects in some states.

salaries than perquisites, the management of a regulated firm may substitute the latter for the former. The substitution reduces value if a dollar spent on perquisites is worth less to the recipients than the same dollar given them in cash. (How is the analysis affected by the nontaxability of many perquisites?)

3. Similarly, if the cost of equity capital is not as effectively constrained as labor costs are — a plausible assumption given the difficulty of estimating the cost of equity capital — the regulated firm will have an incentive to use too much capital, relative to labor, in production.[2] It might, for example, engage in the form of predatory pricing, mentioned in Chapter 10, which consists of building a larger plant than the firm needs. The firm knows that once the plant is built, its capital costs will be fixed costs, which a court asked to decide whether the price of the plant's output is below cost may exclude. Even if the firm never succeeds in deterring or driving out a competing firm, it will be ahead of the game if the regulatory agency allows it to recoup all of its costs — and its capital costs at a monopoly profit.

The incentive of the regulated firm to substitute capital for labor may explain a famous bit of railroad lore: the reluctance of a railroad to short-haul itself.[3] Suppose the X railroad has a line from point A to point C, a distance of 800 miles, and a line from A to B, a distance of 400 miles; the Y railroad has a line from B to C, a distance of only 200 miles, so it is faster and cheaper to get from A to C through B (with the X and Y railroads providing joint service) rather than on the X railroad's longer single line. The X railroad is the only railroad serving A and controls the choice of the route. In the absence of regulation, X will choose the more efficient A-B-C route, even though this means "short-hauling" itself. X can capture all the monopoly returns from the traffic whichever way it is routed, and these returns will be greatest when it offers joint service with Y, because the shorter distance reduces total costs of service and increases the speed (hence value) of the service to shippers.[4] But under rate regulation the situation may be different. By short-hauling itself, the X railroad reduces its capital costs and will be unable to justify so high a rate for the shipment. If capital costs are regulated imperfectly, X may prefer the less efficient route that uses more of its own capital.

4. A regulatory agency will be less able to control a firm's profits if the firm has unregulated affiliates, to which the firm may be able to

2. See Harvey Averch & Leland L. Johnson, Behavior of the Firm Under Regulatory Constraint, 52 Am. Econ. Rev. 1052 (1962). But see Paul L. Joskow & Roger G. Noll, Regulation in Theory and Practice: An Overview, in Studies in Public Regulation 1, 10-14 (Gary Fromm ed. 1981).

3. See, e.g., Missouri-Kansas-Texas R.R. v. United States, 632 F.2d 392, 404-406 (5th Cir. 1980).

4. Can you think of a qualification of this sentence that might be necessary? Hint: See §3.7 *supra*.

allocate some of the profits of its regulated service; hence regulation creates incentives to expand into other markets even when such expansion is inefficient. This could be prevented by forbidding a regulated firm to operate in unregulated markets, but such a prohibition might prevent efficient expansion.

A strange halfway house between allowing and forbidding regulated firms to have unregulated affiliates has been created by an order issued by the Federal Communications Commission in the wake of the recent consent decree divesting AT&T of its operating telephone companies.[5] The order allows the divested companies to engage in what is now the unregulated, competitive business of selling telephones and other terminal equipment to the telephone subscribers, as well as to continue providing regulated local telephone service — but to engage in the unregulated business only through separate subsidiaries. And they really must be separate — they must have separate employees, facilities, and premises from their regulated affiliates. This requirement seems inconsistent with the main reason for allowing regulated firms to provide unregulated services — that they might be able to do it cheaper, by exploiting economies of joint operation, which the separate-subsidiary requirement prevents.

The requirement is defended as being necessary to prevent the hybrid regulated-unregulated firm from engaging in two distinct, and only superficially inconsistent, practices. The first is predatory pricing in the unregulated market. If the firm can reclassify some of its costs in that market to the regulated market, where they will be recoverable in the firm's cost of service, then even though it sells in the unregulated market at a social loss, it will have a private gain so long as its price is above the costs that it does not shift to its regulated market. And that gain can be made even larger by the firm's wresting market share from its unregulated competitors by underpricing them. This is another example of rational predatory pricing by a regulated firm, even without any recoupment by raising prices in the future. Query: Does the firm have to engage in predatory pricing to obtain this gain?

Second, the firm might try to pressure its regulated customers to buy their telephones and other terminal equipment from it rather than from its unregulated competitors, perhaps by giving better telephone service to users of its own equipment. In effect it would be using its regulated monopoly not to make its own unregulated equipment seem cheaper than it really was (predatory pricing) but to make the equipment of its unregulated competitors' equipment seem more costly than that equipment really is.

---

5. See FCC, Furnishing of Customer Premises Equipment, Enhanced Services and Cellular Communications Services by the Bell Operating Companies, 49 Fed. Reg. 1190 (Jan. 10, 1984), aff'd, Illinois Bell Tel. Co. v. FCC, 740 F.2d 465 (7th Cir. 1984).

§12.4   Incentive Regulation

Regulatory lag is an imperfect method of rewarding the efficient, and penalizing the inefficient, regulated monopolist. The costs of the regulated firm may be rising for reasons unrelated to its efficiency, such as inflation or a price increase in a key input, or falling for reasons unrelated to its efficiency, such as an increase in demand which enables it to spread its fixed costs further. Regulatory lag imposes windfall losses in the first case and creates windfall gains in the second.

One way of gearing the permitted level of profits more closely to the firm's performance would be to permit rate changes based on changes in an industry-wide cost index. Suppose there were 20 electric utilities, serving different areas but comparable in size and operating characteristics, and in one period the average per-kilowatt cost of these utilities rose by 1¢; under the index approach, each of these utilities would be permitted to raise its rates by (no more than) 1¢ in the next period. Utilities whose performance had been above average in the previous period would thereby earn an additional profit; below-average performers would be penalized.

The process would simulate that of competition, where firms that have lower costs earn supracompetitive profits in the short run. In the long run, as the more efficient firms expand production to close the gap between marginal cost and market price, the price level falls, and to continue obtaining supracompetitive profits the firms will have to find new ways of reducing cost. Similarly, under the index approach, the efforts of utilities to beat the average with superior cost controls would cause the average to fall (both directly and by inducing persistently below-average performers to change management), thus creating unrelenting pressure for continuing cost reductions.

This approach is to be distinguished from the automatic pass-throughs of fuel-input costs that became popular when fuel prices skyrocketed in the 1970s. The pass-through allows the regulated firm to add a dollar to its rates (without going through a formal rate proceeding) whenever an increase in fuel prices adds a dollar to its costs of service. The incentive to economize on the use of fuel, negotiate a better price, switch to a cheaper fuel, etc., is inadequate.[1]

It should be apparent by now that there are extremely difficult, maybe insoluble, problems in getting the regulated monopolist to perform efficiently without allowing him to have monopoly profits. Functionally, the problem is one of divided ownership: The property rights in the regulated firm's assets are in effect divided between the regulated firm

§12.4   1. A greater incentive to minimize fuel costs is created, though, by dollar-for-dollar than by percentage pass-through. Can you see why?

and the regulatory agency. As the problem of divided ownership is a recurrent one in areas regulated by common law, maybe there is a common law alternative to public utility regulation; we shall explore this possibility in the next chapter, where we compare common law and direct regulatory methods generally (see §13.7 *infra*).

§12.5 Regulation of Rate Structure and of Entry

The conjunction of profit control and entry regulation seems at first glance odd. The danger of inefficient entry is created by monopoly pricing. If monopoly pricing is eliminated, the danger disappears — the new entrant can gain a foothold in the monopolist's market only if his costs are lower than the monopolist's. Either the regulation of entry rests on a sophisticated awareness that control of the overall price level of regulated monopolists is often ineffectual, or, more plausibly, it has different purposes altogether. One may be to support the third major leg of public utility and common carrier regulation, which is control over price structure — how the firm's revenue requirements are translated into specific prices.

There is no entirely satisfactory answer to the question, raised earlier, of the optimal pricing of services when marginal cost is below average cost.[1] Pricing at average cost is unsatisfactory for reasons already discussed. It used to be thought that the best solution was to sell the service at (short run) marginal cost with the government making up the deficit resulting from the firm's inability to recover its total cost out of general tax revenues. But this solution has two serious drawbacks. First, by forcing up tax rates elsewhere in the economy, it causes the same kind of allocative distortions that it is supposed to cure (see §12.7 *infra*). Second, it encourages consumers to substitute services produced under conditions of declining average cost for services produced under conditions of increasing average cost, even when the former services are more costly to provide.

Suppose it costs no more to build and operate a bridge that can carry 1,000 cars a day than one that can carry 900. Estimated daily demand is 950 cars. The annual depreciation and operating costs of the bridge are $1 million. As long as fewer than 1,000 cars are carried, the marginal cost (i.e., the cost of increasing the output of the bridge by one more car journey) will be zero. But suppose the same number of cars could be carried (and at the same speed) by ferry at a total

§12.5   1. For illuminating discussions of the problem, see Ronald H. Coase, The Marginal Cost Controversy, 13 Economica (n.s.) 169 (1946); Ronald H. Coase, The Theory of Public Utility Pricing and Its Application, 1 Bell J. Econ. & Mgmt. Sci. 113 (1970).

annual cost of only $100,000, but marginal cost would be $5. There would be no demand for ferry service, provided the government built or paid for the bridge and charged a toll equal to marginal cost, i.e., charged nothing. Of course, if the government were all-seeing, and could resist consumer pressures, it would not build the bridge, because it would know there was a socially less costly method of providing the same service. But government is not all-seeing. And if the bridge had been built at a time when ferry service was not feasible, and later the question arose whether to replace the bridge, the government would be under great pressure from people who had grown accustomed to free bridge service to replace it.

One alternative to marginal-cost pricing is two-part pricing. The user of the bridge might be required to pay (1) an initial one-time fee so calculated that the sum of such fees defrayed the fixed costs of the bridge and (2) a toll, equal to marginal cost, payable every time he crossed the bridge. This method of pricing would enable both the fixed costs of the bridge to be covered and the marginal purchase to be made, but unfortunately it would not enable the marginal purchaser to obtain service — the purchaser who was willing to pay the marginal cost of his use of the bridge but not to contribute his proportionate share of fixed costs. Suppose the one-time charge is $10 and the toll (equal to marginal cost) is 2¢ (rather than zero, as in our previous example). Our marginal purchaser may be willing to pay a $1 one-time charge but no more, because he does not expect to use the bridge often. If he is denied service, the bridge company is worse off since he would have made *some* contribution to its fixed costs, and he of course is worse off too.

Another alternative is Ramsey pricing, which in its original form meant charging a higher price the less elastic the buyer's demand is. In contrast to two-part pricing, where the average price paid by each buyer declines the more he buys, this form of Ramsey pricing is uniform for each buyer but differs among buyers, with the less elastic demanders paying more and the more elastic demanders less. The best form of Ramsey pricing — if one ignores the formidable information costs entailed by efforts to measure elasticities and to prevent arbitrage — is the following. As in two-part pricing, every buyer pays an entry fee to cover fixed costs, but the fee varies inversely with the buyer's elasticity of demand — and the truly marginal buyer pays no entry fee. In addition to the entry fee every buyer pays the marginal cost of each unit that he buys. Given perfect information, output will be carried to the point where marginal cost intersects demand, yet without imposing a deficit on the regulated firm or a tax on nonusers of the regulated service.

Two-part and Ramsey pricing resemble but must be distinguished from price discrimination (see §9.4 *supra*). (Optimal Ramsey pricing, just described, resembles perfect price discrimination.) Under price discrimination, too, price varies with willingness to pay, and in the same direction (i.e., higher the less elastic the customer's demand is). Sometimes the resemblance is uncanny, as where the monopolist of a mimeograph machine requires users of his machine to buy ink from him. The price for buying or leasing the machine corresponds to the fixed charge in a system of two-part pricing; the price of the ink is the variable charge, and it is higher the more the customer uses the machine. But as the purpose of price discrimination is not to enable fixed costs to be recouped in a manner that permits marginal purchasers to be served, but to maximize the excess of revenues over costs, we can expect the average price to be higher under price discrimination than under two-part pricing, and output probably lower (why probably?). But like price discrimination, two-part (Ramsey) pricing can distort competition among buyers. Even when each buyer is assessed the same share of fixed costs, the average price will vary across buyers depending on the quantity purchased (the greater the quantity, the lower the average price), although there is no difference in the cost of serving different buyers. If they are in competition, one will have a competitive advantage unrelated to superior efficiency — although the fact that they are competitors will limit the price difference (why?).

Long before there were measured elasticities of demand, public utility and common carrier pricing sometimes approximated Ramsey pricing. An example is value of service ratemaking in the railroad industry before the coming of the truck.[2] Rail rates based on average cost would be roughly proportional to the weight of the shipment; rail rates based on Ramsey principles would, under certain conditions, be roughly proportional to the value of the shipment. Suppose the marginal cost of transporting each of two shipments by rail the same distance in the same time is $1 and the railroad is trying to figure out how to cover $3 in fixed costs while maximizing output. The value of one shipment (coal) is $10 and that of another (copper) is $100. If the railroad charges each shipper the same price, $2.50 (thus allocating half of the fixed costs to each), the coal shipper will perceive this as the equivalent of a 25 percent tax on his shipment and will cast about for alternative modes of transportation. If the railroad charges the coal shipper only $1 and the copper shipper $4, the tax on the former will be reduced to 10 percent, yet the tax on the latter will be only 4 percent.

This assumes that the copper shipper has no good transportation alternatives — as was true only in the early days of the railroads, before trucks. Shippers who benefited from value-of-service pricing — shippers of heavy, low-value goods — naturally resisted a readjustment of rates to reflect changing elasticities of demand for rail transport. Competing

2. See Sylvester Damus, Two-Part Tariffs and Optimum Taxation: The Case of Railway Rates, 71 Am. Econ. Rev. 65 (1981).

modes of transportation also resist adjustments to such changes for obvious reasons of self-interest that may nevertheless carry great weight with regulatory commissions, which respond to political pressures.

An example of the resulting misallocation is provided by the Supreme Court's ingot molds decision,[3] which upheld a ruling by the Interstate Commerce Commission forbidding railroads to cut price below average cost to attract business away from barge lines. At first glance rail-barge competition seems just like our bridge-ferry example. Railroads, like bridges, have heavy fixed costs (the rights of way, the track, rolling stock, etc.) and low marginal costs; barges, like ferries, have low fixed costs and high marginal costs. But this is not an argument for requiring the railroads to use average-cost pricing (unless the concern with competitive distortion in the purchasers' markets is considered overriding); it is an argument for requiring railroads to use Ramsey rather than marginal-cost pricing, resulting in low rates in competitive markets, where, as we know from Chapter 10, firm elasticity of demand will be high.

In fact there is a strong case for permitting railroads to charge even lower prices — prices equal to marginal cost. Recall the bridge example. The concern about a pricing system under which the users fail to pay the fixed costs of the bridge is that it creates false signals with respect to the efficient allocation of resources. Travelers use the bridge rather than the ferry, so it is assumed that resources should be shifted from ferry building to bridge building, but they prefer the bridge not because it really is cheaper but because they do not pay its full costs. The problem of false signals is not important with railroads. Railroads are a declining industry and a shift of some business from barge lines to railroads is not going to induce economically unjustified railroad expansion; it just will ensure maximum utilization of rail assets.

Regulatory suspicion of departures from average-cost pricing may be due to fear of predatory pricing, which may be a greater danger in unregulated than regulated markets (see §12.3 *supra*), and to the fact that in any event such departures are often triggered by the threat or actuality of competition — and hence are bound, whether predatory or not, to cause squawks by competitors and by those customers whose rates are raised. To explain, if a regulated firm serves two markets and faces competition in neither, and the volume and elasticity of demand for its service are the same in both markets and the marginal cost of serving customers in each is also the same, output will be maximized (without a deficit) by charging the same price in each market. This price will be equal to the firm's average total (i.e., fixed plus variable) costs; hence fixed costs will be allocated to the two markets equally. Suppose

3. American Commercial Lines v. Louisville & N.R.R., 392 U.S. 571 (1968). Since then, amendments to the Interstate Commerce Act, culminating in the passage of the Staggers Act in 1980, have given the railroads greater pricing flexibility.

a competitor appears in one of the markets. Competition will make the demand facing the regulated firm more elastic. The efficient response of the regulated firm, though it looks discriminatory, is to reduce its price in the competitive market and raise it in the monopoly market. For suppose the firm's fixed costs are $100, its marginal cost (= average variable, for let's assume for the moment that its marginal cost is constant) is $2, and the number of units demanded in each market is 50 (for a total of 100), making the total costs in the two markets $300 ($100 fixed plus $200 variable). So before the new entrant appears, the price per unit will be $3. Let the new entrant have fixed costs of only $40, and marginal cost of $2, so that it figures it can take the market away from the existing firm by charging a price slightly below $3, which will still yield it a substantial profit. The existing firm can retain this market by cutting its price in this market to $2 and raising its price in its monopoly market to $4 until the new entrant departs — as eventually he will (why?).[4] The effect will be to shift all of the fixed costs to the customers in the monopoly market. This may seem unfair both to them and to the new entrant. But if the regulated firm were forced to maintain a price of $3 in the competitive market, it would lose that market, so to remain in business it would have to raise the price in its monopoly market to $4 anyway. And the total social costs of serving both markets would rise from $300 to $340 (i.e., by the amount of the new entrant's fixed costs).

It makes no difference whether the different markets are different product markets or different geographical markets. The important thing is that there be costs that are common to both markets, such as corporate overhead, warehousing, and (in the case of the same product sold in different geographical markets) national advertising. So far as each market is concerned, these are fixed costs because they do not vary with changes in the output sold in that market. Of course they may be fixed only in the short run, so that if the firm abandoned one of the markets its common costs would indeed be lower after it had had time to adjust to its new situation. We have neglected so far the difference between

4. This analysis assumes
   (1) that $4 is not a high enough price to attract entry into the monopoly market,
   (2) that the quantity demanded in each market is unchanged by the price changes, and
   (3) as a function of (2), that there are no changes in marginal cost due to changes in output — although unless the firm's marginal cost curve is horizontal, changes in output will entail changes in marginal cost.

Obviously, (2), and therefore (3) as well, are unrealistic. The lower price in the market in which entry occurs will bring new customers into the market, so that the regulated firm will sell more, and its marginal costs may be affected. And the higher price in the monopoly market will drive some customers away, which means that a price of $4 may not enable the firm to recover all of its fixed costs. For example, if it sells only 40 units of output at the higher price, it will recover only $80 of its fixed costs, rather than the full $100. But these refinements in the analysis do not affect the essential points made in the text.

short run and long run marginal costs (we glanced at the difference in §10.7 *supra*). If the firm plans to remain in the market, its floor price should be long run rather than short run marginal cost, for the same reasons discussed in connection with the choice between original and replacement costs for computing the regulated firm's cost of capital (§12.2 *supra*). But if like some railroads the firm does not plan to replace its worn-out capital facilities, then price should be equal to short run marginal cost.

§12.6   Digression on Pay Television

An interesting variant of the bridge-ferry problem is presented by the controversy over whether pay television should be permitted,[1] now resolved after much struggle in favor of this service with only a few remaining restrictions. The economic argument against pay television is that since the marginal cost of broadcasting to another viewer is zero once the transmitter is in operation, viewers should be able to buy television programs at a zero price, as under the present system of predominantly free (to the viewer) television. But when marginal cost is zero, the problem of financing undertakings priced at marginal cost is, as we have seen, acute. The traditional solution of the television industry has been to sell television time to advertisers rather than to viewers. At first glance this seems an ideal solution, for it enables the costs of broadcasting to be defrayed without either a government subsidy or a departure from marginal cost pricing. But since television as an advertising and sales promotion medium has fairly good substitutes, and since a viewer's demand for the advertised product is uncorrelated with the pleasure he gets from the program, advertisers will not pay more than a few cents per viewer for television time. This makes it impossible to defray the costs of expensive programming unless an audience of tens of millions of people can be assembled. Advertisers will not support an opera broadcast that costs $400,000 to produce if it will draw a nationwide audience of only one million, for then it is paying 40¢ per viewer, and it could reach consumers at lower cost through other means. Yet a million viewers might be willing to pay 40¢ apiece to see the opera. Thus the absence of pay television would force them to substitute a less desired or more costly entertainment.

§12.6   1. For a lively debate on the issue, see Jora R. Minasian, Television Pricing and the Theory of Public Goods, 7 J. Law & Econ. 71 (1964); Paul A. Samuelson, Public Goods and Subscription TV: Correction of the Record, id. at 81; James M. Buchanan, Public Goods in Theory and Practice: A Note on the Minasian-Samuelson Debate, 10 J. Law & Econ. 193 (1967); Paul A. Samuelson, Pitfalls in the Analysis of Public Goods, id. at 199; Jora R. Minasian, Public Goods in Theory and Practice Revisited, id. at 205.

§12.7   Taxation by Regulation (Internal Subsidization or Cross-Subsidization)

In the ingot molds case, the inefficient rate structure subsidized a group of competitors. In other cases such rate structures subsidize particular classes of customers. Sometimes regulated firms actually provide service at prices below marginal cost; this was true of intercity railroad passenger service prior to Amtrak. But even prices above marginal cost may be too low. Suppose a firm has fixed costs of $500 and (constant) marginal cost of $1, and suppose that if it prices at average total cost it can sell 1,000 units at $1.50 per unit while if it uses a two-part price system, under which each customer contributes $10 to fixed costs but may then buy as many units as he wants for $1 per unit, it can sell 2,000 units. The two-part system favors the large purchaser; for example, the average price to a purchaser of 100 units is $1.10, whereas under average-cost pricing he would pay $1.50. But a buyer of only one unit is worse off. He pays $11 instead of $1.50. He would be far better off under average-cost pricing even though it would be inefficient because it would induce consumers willing to pay between $1 and $1.49 to substitute other products that cost society more than $1 to produce. The railroad industry again contains examples of this form of inefficient pricing. Agricultural commodities have long paid less than the share of fixed costs properly (that is, according to the intensity of their demand) allocable to them, owing to the persistence of value-of-service pricing into an era of vigorous truck competition. The result has been to increase the fixed-cost assessment against commodities, such as manufactured goods, for which there are now good substitute modes of transportation — with the result that shippers of such goods have largely abandoned rail transportation. Stated otherwise, the *persistence* of value-of-service pricing is a form of internal subsidization.

In both examples — pricing below marginal cost and failing to concentrate fixed costs on the customers willing to pay them — one group of customers is in effect taxed to defray a subsidy for the benefit of another. The taxation analogy brings out the essentially public nature of the income transfer brought about by the pricing scheme. An unregulated firm would not sell below marginal cost, except in the rare case of predatory price cutting. The railroads would have abandoned passenger service long before Amtrak if abandonments did not require the Interstate Commerce Commission's permission. Nor would an unregulated firm use average-cost pricing when it could increase its profits with some version of Ramsey pricing.

Internal subsidization is easy to condemn as inefficient, because it results in just the kind of inefficient substitutions that we identified in discussing the consequences of inaccurate profit controls. But if we assume for the moment that the object of the internal subsidy is a laudable one and then ask what alternative methods for providing the subsidy are available, we shall see that the condemnation is superficial. For example, if the money for the subsidy were obtained by increasing the federal income tax rate, this would be inefficient in the same sense that internal subsidization is inefficient, for just as internal subsidization makes the value of a product seem higher than it is by artificially depressing its prices, so income taxation makes leisure, and nonpecuniary income such as a housewife's imputed earnings, seem more valuable than they are by taxing their substitutes (see §§17.1, 17.6 *infra*).

Internal subsidization may be, however, an unnecessarily inefficient method of taxation. By requiring regulated firms to maintain high price-cost spreads in some markets in order to defray the cost of subsidizing service in other markets, it encourages inefficient entry. Suppose the regulated firm's average cost in the high price market is $2 but its price is $3 — not because its profits are not effectively controlled by the regulatory agency but because it is forced to sell the same $2 service in another market at a price of only $1. A firm that could serve the high price market at a cost of $2.50 would have an incentive to enter that market. To prevent the waste of resources that such entry (aptly called "cream skimming") would involve, as well as the collapse of the subsidy program, the regulatory agency must establish entry controls. These would be unnecessary were it not for internal subsidization — but could be eliminated, without doing away with internal subsidization, by substituting an explicit excise tax on the high price service with the proceeds earmarked for the support of the low price service. Entry would no longer have to be regulated, except that every firm entering the high price market would be subject to the excise tax. This would eliminate the inefficient advantage of the new entrant in our last example.

Internal subsidization requires regulatory control over exit as well as entry; otherwise the regulated firm would simply abandon those services that the agency wanted it to provide at unremunerative rates. A firm in an unregulated market doesn't abandon service unless its customers are unwilling to pay a price that covers the costs of the service. (Would an unregulated monopolist ever restrict output to the extent of abandoning an entire market?) The abandonment proceedings that have been such an agony for the railroad industry are explicable only on the assumption that the railroads are being forced to serve many shippers at rates lower than the railroad's opportunity costs. In interpreting the elastic standard of public convenience and necessity, which governs abandonment, the Interstate Commerce Commission has often forced railroads to continue serving shippers at unremunerative rates,[1] although in recent years, under prodding from Congress (reflecting the

§12.7   1. See, e.g., Southern Ry. v. North Carolina, 376 U.S. 93, 105 (1964).

railroads' increasingly parlous state), the Commission has become much more liberal in allowing abandonments.[2]

The proximate cause of the abandonment problem is the traditional regulatory prohibition of personal discrimination (charging a different price to different customers for the same service — same from the demand, not supply, side of the market), which is a potent method of taxation by regulation.[3] Since users of high-density facilities are cheaper to serve than users of low-density facilities, the former ought to be charged less for the "same" service, but the rule against personal discrimination forbids this. Suppose there are two railroad lines of equal length, which cost the same to maintain (why are we ignoring the cost of building the lines?) and which carry the same commodities. But there are 10 shippers located on one of the lines and only one on the other. If the railroad, to avoid personal discrimination, is forced to charge the same rates to all 11 shippers, then the shipper on the low-density line will pay a much smaller fraction of the total costs of the two lines than would be avoided if the railroad stopped serving him. The law now allows railroads to charge a surcharge on low-density lines. Allowing this surcharge reduces the amount of cross-subsidization — but also reduces the pressure for allowing abandonments.

Internal subsidization is often difficult to distinguish empirically from efficient pricing, especially in network services such as telephone. Telephone service is more valuable the more subscribers there are (a telephone system with one subscriber would have no value). Thus the addition of a new subscriber confers a benefit on existing subscribers. In order to get the right number of subscribers, the existing subscribers should be charged more and new subscribers less — perhaps less than marginal cost.[4] But if the telephone company does this, as by failing to charge a premium to subscribers located far from the nearest local exchange, it will appear to be subsidizing those subscribers out of revenues derived from other subscribers. This will make the latter services attractive to cream skimmers, who will be taking a free ride on the telephone common carrier. The resistance to this cream skimming will look like the defense of an internal subsidy but may in fact be the defense of an efficient pricing system, i.e., one that allows external benefits to be internalized.

Internal subsidization historically was quite important in the telephone industry in connection with long distance rates, which were very high, generating revenues used to make local service very cheap. The high

2. See, e.g., Illinois v. ICC, 722 F.2d 1341 (7th Cir. 1983). Question: From the standpoint of efficiency, should a railroad's overall profitability have any weight in deciding whether to allow abandonment of an unprofitable line?

3. See Richard C. Levin, Regulation, Barriers to Exit, and the Investment Behavior of Railroads, in Studies in Public Regulation 181 (Gary Fromm ed. 1981).

4. Narrowly defined, i.e., without regard to offsetting benefits to the other customers of the phone company.

long distance rates attracted new entry into the long distance market, forcing AT & T's rates in that market down; and with the divestiture of AT & T's long distance operations from its local operations, internal subsidization is in any event no longer possible. Since the divestiture, long distance rates have fallen and local rates have risen. What are the distributive effects of this deregulation? The poor are hurt by having to pay more for basic telephone service. Although they don't use much long distance service and hence don't benefit very much directly from lower long distance rates, they benefit indirectly — from the fall in the prices of products manufactured by firms that use long distance telephone service. They derive little benefit, however, from the lower long distance rates paid by individual as distinct from business users.

§12.8   Excessive Competition

The traditional rationale of public utility and common carrier regulation is the existence of natural monopoly, yet often and not inaptly the rationale is stated in terms of excessive competition. The linkage between natural monopoly and excessive competition is twofold.

First, the effort of a natural monopolist to recover its fixed costs by charging prices far above marginal cost in markets where it has no competition may make those markets attractive to competitors whose marginal cost may actually exceed that of the natural monopolist; the competition that ensues is excessive in a social sense.

Second, if firms have natural monopoly characteristics in the sense of having a high ratio of fixed to total costs, yet there is room for more than one such firm in the market, competition will be riskier than in normal markets, because a firm that has heavy fixed costs is more likely to go bankrupt if it encounters business adversities than a firm that does not have heavy fixed costs. Fixed costs by definition cannot be pared to alleviate the financial effects of an unexpected decline in demand for the firm's product (see further discussions of this point in §§14.2, 15.2 *infra*).

All this does not explain, however, why public utility and common carrier regulation is frequently found in markets that are not naturally monopolistic, including trucking, air transportation (until the recent deregulation of the airline industry), and natural gas production — markets that can and do efficiently support more, often many more, than one seller. The imposition of the same regulatory controls in competitive as in monopolistic markets is defended on the ground that without regulation to limit price cutting and new entry there would be excessive competition, resulting in bankruptcy and deterioration of service. But when businessmen in naturally competitive markets complain about excessive competition, what they usually mean is that they would be happier if their prices were higher than their average costs.

There is no more bizarre example of public utility regulation of a competitive market than the regulation by the Federal Energy Regulatory Commission (formerly the Federal Power Commission) of the production of natural gas. The Commission was established in the 1930s to regulate interstate sales of electricity and natural gas. Both the sale of electricity and the sale of natural gas by pipelines are plausible examples of markets with declining average costs, but in the 1950s the Supreme Court held that the Commission's mandate extended to the sale of gas by the producers to the (interstate) pipelines, as well as the resale of that gas by the pipelines. Not only is the production of gas naturally competitive, but it is extremely difficult to figure out the cost of producing gas, and this for two reasons.

First, much gas is produced jointly with oil, meaning that if the oil would be produced anyway the gas would cost nothing additional to produce — and vice versa. But obviously the cost of producing oil and gas is not zero. Economists have long illustrated the problem of joint production with the example of the beef and hides of cattle. (Where have we met a form of joint production before and how does it differ from the present example?) Each head of cattle produces some of both, and in more or less fixed proportions. Obviously, raising cattle is not costless, but it is not possible to speak separately of the cost of beef and the cost of hides. (How will their costs be allocated in a competitive market?)

The second problem is that an important but invisible cost of a mineral resource such as gas is the forgone opportunity to use it in the future (see §1.1 *supra*). If the resource is running out or is going to be more expensive to mine in the future, or if the future price is going to be higher than the current price (by more than the interest rate — why is that important?) because substitute minerals are being depleted more rapidly, the opportunity cost of mining now may exceed the direct mining costs. If that opportunity cost is ignored, price will be too low and the resource will be mined too quickly.

Faced with these problems, the Commission consistently underestimated the cost of natural gas and thus forced the price below market levels, giving producers an incentive not to produce and consumers an incentive to substitute natural gas for unregulated substitutes (such as oil) that were priced equal to their actual social costs. The result was a protracted shortage of natural gas marked by such absurdities as the importation of frozen natural gas from Algeria at prices much higher than the market price of natural gas would have been if the industry had not been regulated. The attentive reader will notice the analogy to the adoption market discussed in Chapter 5.

One thing the Commission tried to do to alleviate the problem was to allow gas from newly drilled wells to be priced higher than gas from old wells. The idea was that higher prices for gas from new wells would induce more drilling, whereas higher prices for gas from old wells would simply confer windfalls on the owners. The problem is that, with price an average of the new and the old gas price, the consumer is still confronted with false alternatives (as in §12.2 *supra*). Suppose the price of gas from new wells, a price equal to marginal cost, is $1 for some standard unit; the old-well price is 50¢; and equal quantities of gas are produced by new and by old wells, so that the average price is 75¢. Since most sales are of mixtures of old and new gas, 75¢ is what most purchasers will pay. So if unregulated oil costs 85¢ to produce the same heating value for the consumer, the consumer will think gas is cheaper. But it is not. It is more expensive. Any increments of demand must be met by increasing the output of gas, and that can only be done by drilling a new well at a cost of $1 per unit of gas produced by it.

§12.9   The Demand for Regulation

The deficiencies of public utility regulation viewed as a method of regulating profits, the degree to which it seems deliberately to maintain inefficient rate structures, and the frequency with which it has been imposed in naturally competitive industries and also used to discourage competition in industries that have some, but not pervasive, natural monopoly characteristics (railroads, for example) may lead one to wonder whether the actual purpose of public utility regulation is to respond to the economist's concern about the inefficient consequences of unregulated natural monopolies. Maybe instead regulation is a product, much like other products except supplied by the government, that is demanded by and supplied to effective political groups. Under this view there is no presumption that regulation is always designed to protect the general consumer interest in the efficient supply of regulated services. Particular consumers may demand a rate structure that, while inefficient overall, gives them benefits greater than the costs that it imposes on them in common with other consumers. Members of a competitive industry can benefit from the imposition of public utility controls since minimum rate regulation provides greater assurance of effective cartel pricing than does private agreement — while placing the cartel beyond the reach of the antitrust laws — and regulatory control of entry can remove one of the principal threats to the success of a cartel: the entry of new sellers attracted by the hope of monopoly profits. Coalitions between special-interest consumer groups (such as the shippers of certain commodities) and members of an industry may be especially effective in manipulating the regulatory process.

But there is a latent paradox here. In Part II we explained the common law as a system designed (on the whole) to promote efficiency. Here we use economic analysis to refute the view that another branch of law, public utility regulation, pursues efficiency with the same consistency, and to propose, indeed, that it often pursues a conflicting objective. An effort to explain the difference (further illustrated by the materials in the next chapter) is made in Chapter 19.

Suggested Readings

1. William J. Baumol & David F. Bradford, Optimal Departures from Marginal Cost Pricing, 60 Am. Econ. Rev. 265 (1970).

2. William J. Baumol, John C. Panzar, & Robert D. Willig, Contestable Markets and the Theory of Industry Structure, chs. 1, 12, 16 (1982).

3. Stephen G. Breyer, Regulation and Its Reform (1982).

4. Ann F. Friedlaender & Richard H. Spady, Freight Transport Regulation (1981).

5. Alfred E. Kahn, The Economics of Regulation: Principles and Institutions (1970) (2 vols.).

6. Theodore E. Keeler, Railroads, Freight, and Public Policy (1983).

7. Warren G. Lavey & Dennis W. Carlton, Economic Goals and Remedies of the AT&T Modified Final Judgment, 71 Geo. L.J. 1497 (1983).

8. Paul W. MacAvoy, Regulated Industries and the Economy (1979).

9. Richard A. Posner, Taxation by Regulation, 2 Bell J. Econ. & Mgmt. Sci. 22 (1971).

10. Richard Schmalensee, The Control of Natural Monopolies (1979).

11. Clifford Winston, Conceptual Developments in the Economics of Transportation: An Interpretive Survey, 23 J. Econ. Lit. 57 (1985).

12. Edward E. Zajac, Fairness or Efficiency: An Introduction to Public Utility Pricing (1978).

Problems

1. Among other rules governing public utilities that have not been discussed in this chapter, there is the rule that a public utility may not arbitrarily refuse to serve a customer, the rule that a public utility may not charge a price other than one contained in a published price list (tariff), and the rule that a public utility may not undertake the construction of additional plant without the permission of the regulatory agency. Can you explain the function of these rules? On the theory that the purpose of public utility regulation is to promote economic efficiency?

On the theory that its real purpose is to subsidize particular groups of customers? On the theory that its real purpose is to facilitate monopoly pricing by regulated firms?

2. Most hospitals in the United States today are voluntary (nonprofit) hospitals. These hospitals are widely believed to be mismanaged. They run huge deficits and, it is argued, are plagued by chronic excess capacity. In an effort to solve these problems, it has been proposed that hospitals be made public utilities subject to the usual public utility controls, in particular control over new construction (see problem 1 *supra*). What do you think of this proposal? Would nationalization of the hospital industry be better or worse from an economic standpoint? See Regulating Health Facilities Construction (Clark C. Havighurst ed. 1974); Clark C. Havighurst, Health Planning for Deregulation: Implementing the 1979 Amendments, 44 Law & Contemp. Prob. 33 (Winter 1981).

3. Can there be a problem of encouraging inefficient entry into a natural monopoly market if the monopolist employs multipart pricing? If he price discriminates?

4. A state law forbids the state's airport authority to charge unreasonable rates. At the only international airport in the state, the authority (which owns the airport) charges landing fees to each airline based on the relative amount of space in the airport used by the airline, the fees being so calculated as to return in the aggregate the total costs of operating the airport, including depreciation, except for the costs of the various concessions in the airport. In addition, the authority charges rental fees to parking lot, car rental, and other concessionaires, and these fees generate revenues substantially in excess of the costs of the concessions to the airport. Is the authority violating the state statute? See Indianapolis Airport Authority v. American Airlines, Inc., 733 F.2d 1262 (7th Cir. 1984).

5. The Staggers Act empowers the Interstate Commerce Commission to exempt from maximum rate regulation any commodity as to which there is no danger of the railroads' abusing their market power (if any). Suppose the price of U.S. coal sold for export is determined by a world market in coal, and the world market price is unaffected by the quantity of U.S. coal sold in it. Does it follow that if the railroads agreed not to compete among themselves in the rates they set for transporting coal to ports for sale in the export market, they would have no monopoly power over coal transportation, their rates being effectively constrained by the world market price for coal?[5] See Coal Exporters Assn. v. United States, 745 F.2d 76 (D.C. Cir. 1984).

6. Also under the Staggers Act, the Commission may not invalidate a rate for a railroad service as being unreasonably high so long as the revenues generated by the rate do not exceed 180 percent of the variable

5. Assume there is no intermodal competition (i.e., competition of nonrail carriers).

costs of the service. See 49 U.S.C. §10709. What is the economic rationale of this rule, and is the rule sensible?

7. In what circumstances if any should a natural monopolist be allowed to include advertising expenditures in its cost of service?

8. Responding to the sharp growth in federal expenditures under the Medicare program, Congress in the Deficit Reduction Act of 1984 imposed a 15-month freeze on the government's reimbursement of fees charged for physicians' services under Medicare and also on the amount of those fees. Explain the likely effects of these freezes on the demand for and supply of physicians' services, the incomes of physicians, the welfare of Medicare recipients, and the federal deficit.

CHAPTER 13

THE CHOICE BETWEEN REGULATION AND COMMON LAW

§13.1 The Theory of Optimal Regulation

Monopoly, pollution, fraud, mistake, mismanagement, and other un-happy by-products of the market are conventionally viewed as failures of the market's self-regulatory mechanisms and therefore as appropriate occasions for public regulation. But this way of looking at the matter is misleading. The failure is ordinarily a failure of the market *and* of the rules of the market prescribed by the common law. Pollution, for example, would not be considered a serious problem if the common law remedies, such as nuisance and trespass, were efficient methods of minimizing the costs of pollution. The choice is rarely between a free market and public regulation. It is between two methods of public con-trol — the common law system of privately enforced rights and the ad-ministrative system of direct public control — and should depend upon a weighing of their strengths and weaknesses in particular contexts.

The essential (and related) characteristics of the common law (exclud-ing the criminal law) method of regulating are two: (1) the method relies minimally on public officials (judges and other court personnel), and mainly on private citizens — victims and their lawyers; (2) incentives to obey are created by the threat of having to compensate victims for the harm done them by a violation of the rules. Direct or administrative regulation, in contrast, relies much more heavily on public officials (the staff of the regulatory agency) and tries to prevent injuries from occurring in the first place rather than to compensate victims of injuries. Under the common law of nuisance, the polluter may be compelled in a lawsuit to pay compensation to the people injured by the pollution; under the federal clean air and clean water acts, public agencies create and adminis-ter standards designed to prevent the emission of pollutants in harmful quantities.

From these simple distinctions one can infer where the common law method is likely to fall short in comparison to direct regulation. If the injury to each victim is too small to make a lawsuit a paying proposition, there is an argument for direct regulation, provided the total injury is substantial in relation to the cost of prevention. The argument is not airtight; as we shall see in Chapter 21, the class action is a device for aggregating small claims to make a single large lawsuit. Oddly, perhaps, the argument for direct regulation comes back into play when the injury is not very small but very large. An injurer may not have the resources to pay a very large damages judgment; and if not, his incentive to comply with the law will be reduced — in effect he is able to shift from himself to the victim the difference between the victim's actual cost and the maximum collectable judgment. It might seem, though, that provided the judgment would take away the whole of the injurer's wealth, it would provide incentive enough. But this is not true (cf. §7.2 *supra*). Suppose that B in the Hand Formula is $100, P is .001, and L is $1 million, so that $PL = \$1,000$, but the maximum judgment the (potential) defendant could pay would be $10,000. Then in deciding whether to spend B, he will be comparing an outlay of $100 with an expected judgment cost of only $10 ($10,000 $\times P$). He would have to be awfully risk averse to prefer the certain to the uncertain cost at these odds!

This analysis implies not that regulation should replace common law (mainly tort law) in any area but that it should supplement it in areas where tort law may not provide sufficient incentives to efficient conduct because the victim's damages are too small or too large. The analysis becomes more complicated, however, when we turn to other problems with common law regulation that may justify direct regulation. For example, the common law has a problem in dealing with fatal injuries that is related but not identical to its problem with very large injuries in general. It is related because a death is a particularly costly form of injury and may strain the injurer's resources. But in addition, as we saw in Chapter 6, it just is extremely difficult to place a dollar value on a human life. And although it might seem that this problem could not be avoided by shifting from common law to direct regulation of safety — that the regulators, in determining how strictly to regulate safety, would have to place at least an implicit value on a human life — this is not true. For example, the economic question raised by a proposal to force railroads to replace cross-buck crossing signs with flashing light signals is not the value that the traveler at a railroad crossing places on his life but the value that he places on a further reduction in an already small risk. We have a fair amount of information on how people value safety measures that reduce the risk of injury or death; the problem for the tort system is to extrapolate from these estimates to the value of the life itself. Although a method of doing this (or, more precisely, of avoiding having to do it) was suggested in Chapter 6, the tort system has not yet embraced the method.

If one thought that the tort system systematically underestimated damages in death cases, the role of direct regulation would again be one of supplementing rather than replacing the tort system — making it work better at the upper and lower ends of the injury distribution. But if one thought the tort system either systematically overestimated such damages or simply misestimated them most of the time, there would be an argument for preemptive regulation — unless one thought that the regulators would misestimate as badly as judges and juries do.

Another problem of common law regulation, touched on in Chapter 6, is that the causal relationship between a particular injurer (or even class of injurers) and a particular victim may be obscure. If we have a pretty good idea that a nuclear reactor accident will cause an increase of .01 percent in the number of cancers, but do not know which cancers will be caused by the accident, it will be difficult to bring the costs of the accident to bear on the owner of the nuclear reactor through the methods of the tort system. Air pollution raises this problem and another: that of uncertainty as to injurer. A given injury (lung disease, dirty laundry, stench, or whatever) from air pollution will usually be due to the combined emissions of numerous polluters, and it will be very difficult (often impossible) by common law methods to aggregate all the polluters in a single lawsuit or establish a causal linkage between a given polluter and the injury. (Do these problems argue for preemptive or supplementary direct regulation?)

The fact that the tort system or other methods of common law regulation may be radically imperfect in particular circumstances is an argument, but not necessarily a decisive one, for direct regulation — which itself may be radically imperfect. For one thing, it tends to be more costly than common law regulation, because it is continuous; the common law machinery is invoked only if someone actually is hurt. Notice the analogy to the question whether to reward rescuers (restitution) or punish those who fail to rescue (tort liability). See §6.9 *supra*. For another thing, direct regulation tends to be more politicized than common law, because it relies more heavily on the public sector and because judges, although public officials, are more protected from political reward and retribution than administrators are. Regulation is therefore less likely than the common law to be guided by a Hand Formula approach. A related point is that regulation involves serious information problems. If accident victims have nothing to gain from bringing an unsafe condition to the government's attention, the regulators may have difficulty finding out what exactly the problem is.

Regulation presumably will work best when it is possible by manipulating a few well-understood inputs into safety to bring about dramatic and plausibly cost-justified results. Punishing drunk driving is a good example. The external costs almost certainly exceed the benefits to the driver, and the difficulty of measuring the costs of fatal accidents argues for trying to prevent the accidents from occurring by forbidding the dangerous conduct before an accident results.

We shall illustrate some of these points with a more extensive, although necessarily highly incomplete, discussion of some specific examples of direct regulation, including a distinct form of regulation from direct administrative regulation — taxation (as a regulatory, not revenue raising, measure) — and close with a brief look at the possibility of using common law to control natural monopolies.

§13.2 Consumer Fraud Revisited

We noted in Chapter 4 that there are market forces working to give consumers information about the products that they buy but that these forces may not always work well and neither may the common law remedy for fraud (see §4.7 *supra*). That remedy could be improved. Defrauded consumers could be permitted to get their legal fees back, plus a penalty as an additional incentive to sue, in any successful action against the seller. Consumer class actions could be made easier to bring. The rights of firms that suffer sales losses as a result of misrepresentations in the sales materials of their competitors could be clarified.

These possibilities for improvement seem promising in light of the grave problems with the public remedies administered by the Federal Trade Commission. Originally consumers had virtually no incentive to invoke the Commission's enforcement machinery. The Commission could not award damages to a defrauded consumer. The threat of a complaint to the Commission would sometimes induce a seller to buy off an angry consumer, but once the Commission began proceedings the seller would have no further incentive to come to terms with the consumer; this must have limited consumers' interest in filing complaints with the FTC. (Recently the Commission has asserted a limited power to order restitution to defrauded consumers.[1]) Competitors of the seller did and do have an incentive to complain to the Commission, which can by issuing a cease and desist order bring to an end a practice that is diverting business from them. But since the Commission bears the entire expense of prosecution, the complaining seller has no incentive

---

§13.2 1. See, e.g., MacMillan, Inc., 96 F.T.C. 208, 304-306 (1980); but cf. Heater v. FTC, 503 F.2d 321 (9th Cir. 1974).

to avoid lodging essentially frivolous complaints designed to harass a competitor rather than to dispel consumer misinformation.

The combination of the consumer's lack of an adequate incentive to complain with the competitor's possession of too great an incentive creates an imbalance in the nature of the pressures that are brought to bear on the Commission. It hears less from defrauded consumers than from labor unions concerned about the effect of cheap Japanese imports on the sales of their members' employers, from furriers concerned about the competition of synthetic furs, from diamond merchants concerned about the competition of synthetic diamonds; given the nature of these inputs, it is not surprising that so much of the Commission's output of rules and decisions has been so tenuously, if at all, related to actual problems of consumer deception.[2]

In addition, the Commission lacks the weapons necessary to be effective against the fly-by-night operator, perhaps the major defrauder of consumers. He preys on people who are least likely to complain to the Commission, and anyway the Commission lacks sanctions appropriate to deal with firms that lack continuity of operation, that conceal their activities, or that are financially irresponsible.

The FTC's distinctive characteristics as an institution — its inability to punish, and the fact that it shoulders the responsibility and expense of prosecution — are sources of weakness in fighting consumer fraud, as is the fact that it is a federal agency with its operations highly centralized in Washington (most fraudulent selling is done by local sellers). The Commission could be made a more effective agency for fighting consumer fraud. It could be given the power to mete out penal sanctions, to assess the costs of prosecution against competitor complainants, and to grant autonomy to its local field offices. But observe that the effect of such changes would be to bring the administrative model of regulation closer to the common law model.

A distinct sanction that the Commission has been using in recent years deserves mention: corrective advertising. This means requiring a firm that has been found to have engaged in false advertising to make statements in future advertising that are designed to correct the misleading impression created by the false advertising. Corrective advertising is penal (meaning what, to an economist?), because the statements may cause consumers to switch their entire business to competitors, not just the part of the business that they would have given the competitors if there had been no false advertising. Here is an example. In 1976, the Commission required Johnson Products Company, which manufactures a well-known line of cosmetics for black people, to disclose clearly and conspicuously in all advertisements for Ultra Sheen hair relaxer the following statement:

2. See Richard A. Posner, Regulation of Advertising by the FTC (Am. Enterprise Institute 1973).

WARNING: Follow directions carefully to avoid skin and scalp irritation, hair breakage and eye injury.

Johnson was also required to display prominently on an information panel of the package or in a package insert a detailed warning that use of the hair relaxer might result in scalp and hair burns, hair loss, and eye injury.

It appears that the hair relaxers manufactured by other firms had similar hazards; but no orders were imposed on Johnson Products' competitors for more than a year and as a result Johnson lost considerable market share. The loss is easily understood when one considers that the consumer of hair relaxer had to choose between a product that continuously warned him of its danger and products that appeared safer since they contained no warning. A penal sanction with these effects is socially as well as privately costly; it punishes past deception at the cost of creating new deception.

§13.3   Mandated Disclosure[1]

Recent statutes such as the Truth in Lending Act, and recent initiatives of the Federal Trade Commission such as its rules requiring the posting of numerical octane ratings and disclosure of the tar and nicotine content of cigarette brands, embody a distinct approach to the problem of consumer product information: that of requiring sellers to provide information deemed valuable to consumers, rather than simply forbidding misleading representations. Mandated disclosure, as the new approach is sometimes called,[2] is different not only from corrective advertising but also from requiring affirmative disclosure where, in the absence of disclosure, the consumer would specifically assume the contrary (for example, that reprocessed oil was new oil); mandated disclosure may be ordered although sellers have not been accused of making misrepresentations.

As we saw in Chapter 4, there is some basis for concern that unregulated markets may not provide enough information about a product characteristic that is at once costly for the consumer to learn about and common to all brands of the product. The characteristic could be

§13.3   1. See Richard A. Posner, The Federal Trade Commission's Mandated-Disclosure Program: A Critical Analysis, in Business Disclosure: Government's Need to Know 331 (Harvey J. Goldschmid ed. 1979).

2. But it is not really new; it is the fundamental principle of securities regulation, which is discussed in §15.7 *infra*.

good or bad from a consumer standpoint — the low cholesterol content of margarine or the high cholesterol content of butter. An individual margarine producer may be reluctant to advertise the low cholesterol content of his product because his advertising will benefit his competitors, who have not helped defray its expense. (What if the production of margarine were monopolized?) And no butter producer has an incentive to advertise the high cholesterol content of butter.

The problem is not limited to brands that are identical with respect to the characteristic in question. Suppose that in a period before the hazards of cigarette smoking were generally known, one brand of cigarettes contained less tar and nicotine than the others. Before advertising this fact the producer would have to weigh the increase in his market share from convincing consumers that his brand was safer against the loss in his sales as a result of informing cigarette consumers of the hazards of smoking, thereby inducing some of them to substitute other products altogether.[3] The condition of entry is important in this analysis; the producer of the low tar and nicotine brand might as well advertise its tar-nicotine content if he can foresee the entry in the near future of new firms that will consider the low tar and nicotine content of their brands a sufficiently important marketing characteristic to warrant advertising it.

A less restrictive alternative to mandated disclosure is standardized disclosure. Let the government establish a standard say for octane ratings, but leave individual sellers free to decide whether or not to adopt it. If consumers value the information conveyed by the standard, some sellers will use it and consumers will draw adverse inferences about those who do not, thus creating competitive pressures for all sellers to adopt it.

Although there is a theoretical case for mandated, or at least standardized, disclosure of some consumer product information, the FTC's performance has left much to be desired. The Commission did require the cigarette companies to disclose the tar and nicotine content of their brands, but by the time (1970) it got around to doing this (after reversing its previous policy of *forbidding* the companies to disclose the tar and nicotine content of their cigarettes), the hazards of smoking were well-known and the market disincentive to advertise lower levels of tar and nicotine, discussed above, thus eliminated; it is not surprising that the disclosure requirement has apparently had little or no effect on the tar and nicotine content of cigarettes.

Another example of mandated disclosure is the FTC's rule requiring the disclosure of numerical octane ratings at the gasoline pump. The

3. Is the producer's market share relevant? Would it make a difference if cigarette production were monopolized?

Commission was concerned that people were buying unnecessarily high octane gasoline but it ignored the market incentives of gasoline producers to minimize octane content in order to reduce costs and the fact that the verbal octane ratings used by the companies — premium, subpremium, regular, and subregular — are functionally equivalent to the numerical ratings (each verbal category describes a narrow band of numerical octane ratings).

The Truth in Lending Act[4] requires uniform disclosure of credit terms and conditions — in particular, of the interest rate. Yet it is unclear that an explicit interest rate is necessary or even useful information to lower income people (the well-to-do and educated borrowers should be able to protect themselves).[5] The choice for the poor, realistically, is not among (1) buying on the installment plan, (2) borrowing from a bank and paying cash, or (3) not buying, and instead saving. It is among installment plans. And the purchaser can compare the burden of paying $20 a month for 40 months with that of paying $15 a month for 60 months (or $25 a month for 30 months) without being told what the annual percentage interest rates implied by these payment schedules are. Everyone knows what his personal discount rate is (which doesn't mean he could attach a number to it if asked).

In practice, mandated disclosure has often meant the government's prescribing the *form* of the disclosure, for, by the time the existence of a product characteristic is sufficiently demonstrable to justify the government's compelling disclosure of it, probably it is well-known to the consumer. There is, however, a theoretical argument for standardization that is unrelated to any concern that the market might not provide enough information. The benefits to a firm that tries to alter an existing standard are external; the costs will be concentrated on that firm. If for example a firm decided to adopt the metric system when all its competitors were using the English system of weights and measures, consumers would be likely to switch to its competitors, whose labels would be more familiar, hence convey information at lower cost to the consumer. So there is a role for government, and for trade associations (why not *just* for trade associations?), in standardizing consumer information — as well as railroad gauges, screw sizes, and other familiar examples. But the FTC's recent experience with standardization has not been a particularly happy one.

4. On which, see, e.g., William C. Whitford, The Function of Disclosure Regulation in Consumer Transactions, 1973 Wis. L. Rev. 400, 420.

5. For some corroborative evidence, see Thomas A. Durkin, Consumer Awareness of Credit Terms: Review and New Evidence, 48 J. Bus. 253 (1975); George G.C. Parker & Robert P. Shay, Some Factors Affecting Awareness of Annual Percentage Rates in Consumer Installment Credit Transactions, 29 J. Fin. 217, 223 (1974). On the general issue of consumer competence see Chr. Hjorth-Andersen, The Concept of Quality and the Efficiency of Markets for Consumer Products, 11 J. Consumer Research 708 (1984).

§13.4   Safety and Health

We saw at the beginning of this chapter that there is a respectable case for regulation of activities that can cause death. But the actual operation of safety and health regulation leaves much to be desired from an economist's standpoint. Consider first an example where there are lives on both sides of the social ledger. Laws that require drug companies to perform protracted and expensive tests before introducing a new drug delay the introduction of new drugs, resulting in the death of people who might have been saved by the earlier introduction of the drugs. Considering these and other factors, studies of new-drug regulation have found that the costs of the regulation exceed the benefits.[1] The general point is that where the cost of safety regulation is also safety, the case for regulation as an alternative to remitting the victims of dangerous products to their market and legal remedies is weakened.

A serious problem with the direct regulation of safety is that a regulation that focuses on a single input into safety may be ineffectual or even harmful. Automobile seatbelt requirements illustrate this point. They reduce the cost of fast driving to the driver and his passengers, and we would expect (by the Law of Demand) that drivers would respond by driving faster. But that will lead to higher accident rates, and while the costs to the driver and his passengers of each accident may be lower because of the protection afforded by the seat belt, the total accident costs to pedestrians should rise (there are more accidents, and pedestrians are not protected by seat belts). A study found that the seatbelt law had actually increased the total number and total costs of automobile accidents.[2]

§13.5   Pollution Revisited — Taxation as Regulation

The common law enforcement problem with respect to pollution is, in part anyway, the same as that with respect to consumer fraud: The

§13.4   1. See Sam Peltzman, The Benefits and Costs of New Drug Development, in Regulating New Drugs 113 (Richard L. Landau ed. 1973); Henry G. Grabowski, Drug Regulation and Innovation (Am. Enterprise Institute 1976); cf. Henry G. Grabowski, John M. Vernon & Lacy Glenn Thomas, Estimating the Effects of Regulation on Innovation: An International Comparative Analysis of the Pharmaceutical Industry, 21 J. Law & Econ. 133 (1978).

2. Sam Peltzman, The Effects of Automobile Safety Regulation, 83 J. Pol. Econ. 677 (1975). See also Auto Safety Regulation: The Cure or the Problem? (Henry G. Manne & Roger L. Miller eds. 1976); Clifford Winston & Fred Mannering, Consumer Demand for Automobile Safety, 74 Am. Econ. Rev. 316 (1984). Another study finds that people underestimate the safety benefits of seat belts; the authors attribute this to the difficulty of evaluating the benefits of reducing low-probability hazards. See Richard J. Arnould & Henry Grabowski, Auto Safety Regulation: An Analysis of Market Failure, 12 Bell J. Econ. 27 (1981). Does this finding suggest a distinct basis for safety regulation? Does it undermine the behavioral assumptions of the tort system?

individual injury may be too slight to justify the expense of litigation to the victim. Again improvements in the common law machinery are possible, but again the emphasis has been placed on direct regulation instead.

Among possible regulatory techniques, three will be discussed here. The first is for the legislature or an administrative agency to prescribe the specific measures that the polluter must take in order to avoid heavy legal sanctions (input control). For example, a municipality might be required to install a certain kind of sewage treatment plant, a steel mill to build its smokestacks four feet higher, automobile manufacturers to install a particular type of emission control device. This approach requires that the regulator have a tremendous amount of information about the costs and benefits of alternative methods of pollution control. A closely related point is that specification of the particular method of pollution control discourages the search for the most efficient method. In the deliberations before the legislature or agency leading to the formulation of the standard, the affected industry has an incentive to propose the cheapest pollution control method, regardless of its efficacy, and to deny the existence of any more costly devices (even if they are more efficient because of the amount of pollution eliminated). And once the specified measure is adopted, the industry has no incentive to develop better devices unless they happen also to be cheaper.

A second approach is to establish the level of pollution emissions deemed tolerable, to compel the polluters, under penalty of injunction or fine, not to exceed that level, but to leave the choice of method to the industry (output control). This appears to be a better approach than the first, but the appearance is deceptive. The polluting firm will be led to minimize the costs of complying with the emission standard, but the standard may be inefficient; it may permit too much, or too little, pollution from an economic standpoint. The solution to this problem would be to use cost-benefit analysis to set the standard. But this would require the agency to have as much information about the costs of complying with various standards as the firm has and would thus eliminate the principal efficiency associated with specifying the permitted level of emissions rather than the specific pollution control devices that the firm must use.

Although it is easy to see why the agency would prefer to fix an emission standard without regard to costs and benefits, it really is not feasible to banish such considerations. For when enforcement of the standard is attempted, the firm or industry will argue that the cost of compliance is prohibitive — meaning disproportionate to the benefits from reduced pollution. Such an argument cannot be ignored unless society wants to reduce pollution far below efficient levels. And more than efficiency is at stake. Even if abating pollution is not so costly that a plant can no longer operate economically, the limitation will raise the plant's costs; and the owner probably will respond by cutting output (as shown in Figure 3.2 in Chapter 3). This will lead to a reduction in employment, and possibly a resulting fall in workers' incomes. Of course the distributive effects will be the same whether or not the limitation on pollution is efficient. An efficient limitation may cause a plant to shut down; the full social costs of the plant (including pollution) may exceed the value of its output at any level of output. It is just that when regulation takes the form of specifying the particular pollution control technology, the distributive and efficiency effects are factored into the regulatory decision at an earlier stage.

The third approach, not yet employed in this country but a great favorite of economists, is to tax pollution. The tax rate for each pollutant would be set equal to the estimated social costs created by the resulting pollution, in the particular area affected; this distinguishes the tax from a fine intended to deter pollution in the usual manner of criminal sanctions (see §7.1 *supra*). A firm subject to a pollution tax would compare its tax costs with the costs of buying pollution control equipment or reducing its output or otherwise trying to reduce pollution. If a net tax saving would be possible through one of these measures, the firm would adopt it; otherwise it would pay the tax and continue to pollute.

This approach is somewhat similar to strict tort liability (input control in contrast resembles negligence liability — and rigid emission ceilings a penal sanction), except that it is publicly rather than privately enforced and there is no (explicit) defense of contributory negligence. The tax corresponds to the damages of the victims of pollution. The polluters are required to pay those "damages" whether or not there are methods of pollution control that would avert them at lower cost. This gives polluters an incentive to search for and to adopt cost-justified pollution preventives (including activity-level changes such as closing, reducing the output of, or relocating their plants — perhaps to foreign countries less concerned about pollution) but not to adopt any preventive that costs more than its benefit in reducing the social costs of pollution. Public determination of cost-justified pollution levels, which is implicit in the emission standard (and *a fortiori* the input control) approach (why?), is thereby avoided.

But the tax approach is very far from being a panacea:

1. It is likely to be counterproductive in those situations, which may be quite common, where the victim is the cheapest pollution avoider (by installing air conditioning, living farther from the factory, etc.). The polluter will spend on pollution control an amount equal at the margin to the estimated tax saving even though victims could have reduced pollution costs by the same amount at lower cost.[1]

§13.5 1. In principle, the victim of pollution could — and should — be taxed also; the analogy is to contributory negligence in a strict liability case. And it is not necessary actually to collect the tax on the pollutee; to complete the analogy to strict liability, the

2. Accidents usually are discrete events of relative infrequency. Their costs can be assessed in separate proceedings. But there are billions of emissions of pollutants every year, and it is totally infeasible to estimate the social cost of each one for the purpose of setting the correct tax rates. (To what extent do emission standards avoid this problem?) Obviously the social costs of different pollutants, and of the same pollutant in different parts of the country (or for that matter of a single state, county, or even city or town), are not uniform. Moreover, the social cost of pollution is not necessarily, or probably, a simple linear function of the amount of pollution. Suppose 10 firms each emit 100 units of pollution, and the aggregate social cost is $1,000. It might seem that the tax should be $1 per unit, and suppose that is the rate that is set. Then each firm will cast about for ways of reducing its tax liability, and suppose that at a cost of $10 each firm can reduce pollution from its plant by 15 percent but that the cost of reducing it any further would be prohibitive. The firms will incur this cost and there will be as a result 15 percent less pollution — but will that confer a $150 benefit (for a net of $50, after cost is taken into account)? Not necessarily. Maybe all the social cost comes from the first 50 units of pollution (5 percent), and the rest has no incremental cost (as might be the case if, for example, the first 50 units were enough to kill all the fish in a lake). Then the tax will have led the firms to incur abatement costs that have no social value, because the social cost of the pollution does not begin to decline till 95 percent is abated. Or maybe 90 percent of the social cost of the pollution comes from the last 5 percent of the pollution, so that if the pollution were reduced by only 5 percent the social cost of the remaining pollution would be only $100. In the first case certainly, and in the second case possibly, the firms will have been led by the tax to spend too much on pollution control. The correct tax would be one that was equal to the marginal rather than average social cost of the particular form of pollution and would thus vary with the level of pollution. But the information required to devise such a tax schedule would be formidable.

3. If we assume as in the previous examples that much pollution is cost-justified — that it would be prohibitively costly to have absolutely clean air and water — then a principal effect of pollution taxes will be not to reduce pollution but simply to increase the tax bills of polluting enterprises. The tax is in the nature of an excise tax since it is roughly proportional to output. Excise taxes are regressive. To assure the overall proportionality or progressivity of the tax system, the imposition of com-

---

tax liability of the victim need only be deducted from the polluter's to produce the economically correct amount of pollution control, as the inability of victims to obtain full compensation (the result of the deduction) will have the desired incentive effects. See William J. Baumol, On Taxation and the Control of Externalities, 62 Am. Econ. Rev. 307 (1972). The problem is measurement.

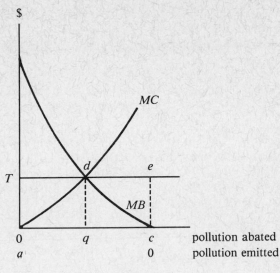

Figure 13.1

prehensive pollution taxes would require exemptions, rebates, or compensating changes elsewhere in the tax system. The fact that a pollution tax might well cost the firm more than direct controls, yet might not reduce pollution any more, is no doubt one reason why it is so unpopular!

The wealth effects of a pollution tax are shown in Figure 13.1. The amount of pollution that is abated is represented by the horizontal axis, dollars as usual by the vertical. The tax is set at a level calculated to induce the firm to emit the optimal amount of pollution — the amount at which the marginal social benefits (*MB*) from abating pollution equal the marginal costs of abatement. *MB* is assumed to fall to zero (cross the horizontal axis) at the point where zero pollution is emitted. Thus the point 0,*a* on the horizontal axis is the amount of pollution (i.e., 0) abated when no effort at abatement is made, and the amount of pollution emitted as a result (*a*), while *c*, 0 is the amount of abatement (*c*) at the zero pollution level (so *a* = *c*). At *q*, where the optimal amount of pollution is abated, the firm incurs a cost equal to the area, *dqa*, under *MC* between *a* and *q*, and in addition pays a tax, equal to the rectangle *decq*, on the unabated pollution. Under an emission standard that forced the firm to carry abatement to *q*, it would incur cost *dqa* but would pay no tax. Compare Figure 6.2 in Chapter 6, a parallel comparison of negligence and strict liability.

4. It might seem that a great social advantage of a tax system would be to spare the polluter the potentially astronomical costs of complying with excessively stringent emission standards; the tax would be the ceiling on the polluter's exposure. But in fact it is impossible to say *a priori* which system leads to a greater waste of resources if the regulation

355

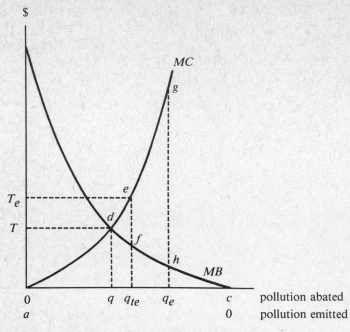

Figure 13.2

(whether tax or emission standard) is too strict. This is shown in Figures 13.2 and 13.3. T is again the optimal tax, and q the optimal abatement of pollution, whether induced by T or prescribed in an (optimal) emission standard. T_e and q_e are a proportionally equally more stringent tax and emission standard, respectively. In Figure 13.2, the tax induces the firm to carry abatement to point q_{te}, where marginal costs of abatement exceed marginal benefits, resulting in a waste of resources measured by the triangle *def*. The waste is smaller than that induced by the erroneous emission standard — the larger triangle *dgh*. But in Figure 13.3, the relation is reversed; the tax generates the larger waste. The intuition behind these results is that if marginal costs of abatement rise steeply in the region of the tax, the firm will prefer to pay the tax rather than abate the pollution; there will be a transfer payment but no social cost. But if the marginal costs of abatement rise more gently, the firm may prefer to carry abatement quite far, resulting in a substantial social cost.

Having said all this, it must be stressed that the tax approach has one great advantage over the other regulatory approaches: It does not require the agency to measure the costs of compliance with the pollution control criteria embodied in the tax rates (provided distributive effects are ignored); the agency need only estimate the benefits of reducing pollution. This makes it less likely that the tax will be set at the erroneous level than that an emission standard will be, in which event the problem

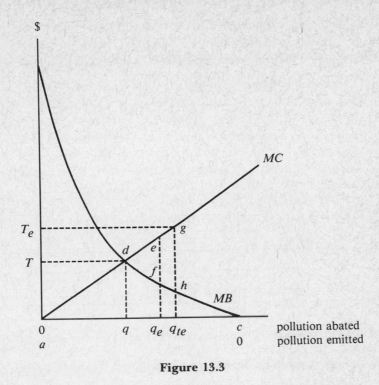

Figure 13.3

depicted in Figure 13.3 will be less likely to arise. To put this differently, emission standards require cost-benefit analysis; pollution taxes require only benefit analysis.

In areas involving safety and health, either cost-benefit analysis or benefit analysis requires monetizing risks to life and limb. But as should by now be clear, this does not require putting a price tag on lives or limbs. All it requires is knowledge of the amounts of money that people demand to run small risks — risks of the same general level as those that pollution and other regulated hazards create. The amount of money demanded for assuming the risk is the benefit of eliminating the risk.[2]

Even economists quite sympathetic to objections to trying to monetize

2. See §6.12 *supra* and, with specific reference to pollution, Albert L. Nichols, The Regulation of Airborne Benzene, in Incentives for Environmental Protection 145, 173-175 (Thomas C. Schelling ed. 1983). The extent to which the law requires or permits the use of cost-benefit analysis to guide administrative regulation of health and safety is a hotly controversial topic on which see, e.g., Paul M. Bangser, An Inherent Role for Cost-Benefit Analysis in Judicial Review of Agency Decisions: A New Perspective on OSHA Rulemaking, 10 Boston College Environmental Affairs L. Rev. 365 (1982); Benefit-Cost Analyses of Social Regulation: Case Studies From the Council on Wage and Price Stability (James C. Miller III & Bruce Yandle eds. 1979). And finally, on cost-benefit analysis in its original setting as a tool for evaluating public projects such as dams, see Arnold C. Harberger, Project Evaluation: Collected Papers (1972), especially ch. 2.

the benefits of abating pollution have been sharply critical of the Clean Air Act, the nation's most ambitious program of pollution control.[3] Among the economically weird aspects of the program, some of which however have fairly transparent political explanations, are:

(1) the more stringent regulation of new than of existing sources of air pollution,[4] which induces firms to delay the introduction of cleaner production technologies,

(2) the policy against allowing even slight degradation in the air quality of the nation's cleanest areas, even though the marginal social costs of pollution (particularly to health) are greater in dirty than in clean areas, and

(3) the insistence that all polluting sources reduce their emissions, without regard to the differing marginal costs of abatement across sources.

§13.6   Mandatory Container Deposits

The aesthetic pollution created by discarding beer and soft drink cans and bottles along highways and in parks is extremely difficult to control. The cost of picking up the litter is very high and the cost of apprehending litterers is also very high. Fines for littering are heavy in recognition of the low probability of apprehension, but they would have to be much heavier to have a significant deterrent effect — and we know from Chapter 7 that severe penalties are socially very costly. The device of the mandatory container deposit, adopted in a number of states, has seemed an alluring answer. The retailer is required to make his customers deposit a nickel or dime for every container they buy but he must return the deposit if the customer returns the container. The fact that, in principle, every cent of "tax" collected is to be returned to the taxpayer is a good illustration of the difference between using taxes to raise revenue and to regulate behavior. The mandatory deposit makes it costly for the consumer to litter, since he loses his deposit if he doesn't return the container, but it generates no revenue for anyone.

The basic problem with the scheme is that no effort is ever made to estimate the cost of litter and relate that to the level of the tax (deposit). This omission may be due to the fact that the proponents of the tax

3. See, e.g., Robert W. Crandall, Controlling Industrial Pollution: The Economics and Politics of Clean Air 57 (1983); Robert W. Crandall, Theodore E. Keeler & Lester B. Lave, The Cost of Automobile Safety and Emissions Regulation to the Consumer: Some Preliminary Results, 72 Am. Econ. Rev. 324 (1982).

4. In part this is due to the fact that the pollution control standards are more stringent for new than for existing sources (can you guess why?) and in part to the fact that the permit process for new sources is more effectively administered than existing sources are monitored.

regard it as costless because the customer has only to return the container to get his money back. But this reasoning ignores nonpecuniary costs. The customer incurs a storage and a time cost by returning rather than discarding his beverage containers. If the tax is set at a level lower than this cost, people will not return their containers and the only effect of the scheme will be to increase the bookkeeping costs of retailers (why won't their profits be any higher even if no customer returns containers and as a result the retailer never has to refund a container deposit?). If the deposit "tax" is set high enough to induce returns, it will impose a social cost measured by the time and other costs of those consumers who return the containers (cf. Figure 13.3 *supra*). If the aggregate social cost is less than that of the litter that is prevented, well and good; but if it is more, then regulation by mandatory deposit taxation is inefficient.

§13.7   Cable Television: Problems of Copyright and Local Monopoly

1. Cable television is a method of delivering television signals to the home by wire rather than by broadcasting them over the air from a transmitter. The cable system obtains its signals either from a master antenna that picks them up from nearby broadcast stations or from a microwave relay or satellite system that brings them in from a distant antenna that receives the signals of broadcast stations proximate to it. When it brings in a distant signal, the cable system increases the number of different signals available in the local market in which it operates. The local broadcast stations do not like this because they lose viewers to the new signal and with them advertising revenues. The people who own the copyrights on the programs carried on the distant signal do not like (free) importation either. True, by enlarging the audience for the program broadcast by the originating station, it increases the royalties that the owner of the copyright on the program can extract from the station, but this gain is offset by the loss of royalties from the station carrying the program in competition with the cable system. If the effects were perfectly offsetting, the copyright owner would be indifferent to the carriage of distant signals by cable systems. But such carriage makes it impossible for the copyright owner to offer exclusive rights to his program to a station competing with the cable system (which can carry the same program picked up from a distant broadcast station); and exclusive program rights command a premium, because they enable a station to differentiate its schedule from its competitors' schedules. Put differently, nonexclusive broadcast rights can create a congestion externality

(see §3.1 *supra* and especially the discussion of the right to exclusive use of one's name and picture in advertising, in 3.2 *supra*).

There are two methods of regulating distant signals: private property rights (copyright) and federal regulation of cable television operations (by the Federal Communications Commission). The FCC adopted limitations on importation; the Supreme Court held that importation was not a copyright infringement.[1] In so holding the Court reasoned that the construction of a cable television system is like the erection of a very tall antenna by an individual viewer. But the analogy does not illuminate the economic issue, which is the tradeoff between the social benefits in increased production of copyrighted works that is brought about by giving the copyright owner greater protection and the social costs imposed by raising the marginal cost of using copyrighted works (see §3.2 *supra*, and notice the analogy to the optimal pricing of a natural monopolist's output). The FCC's consideration of the economics of distant signals was biased by the fact that the suppliants before it included the local television stations as well as the copyright owners. Competition is not a common law tort, but a regulatory agency may and often does give sympathetic consideration to the interest of a firm in being free from competition. The major brunt of cable competition, it was believed, would be borne by independent stations, mostly those using the ultra-high-frequency bands of the electromagnetic spectrum. Since the Commission in its allocation and licensing policies had for many years assiduously nurtured the growth of UHF television, it was naturally inclined to sympathize with the complaints of the UHF independents about competition from cable television.[2]

2. A company wanting to provide cable television service must obtain a franchise from the municipal authorities. Its rates to subscribers may also be subject to regulation by state public utility commission.[3] Because the distribution by wire of television signals into the home resembles in its technical aspects local gas, water, and electric service — the standard examples of natural monopoly — it is not surprising to find wide support for regulation of subscriber rates. But there is an alternative approach, based on contract law.

To explain, any number of companies can build and operate a cable television system anywhere in the country. If there were no entry limita-

§13.7   1. Fortnightly Corp. v. United Artists Television, Inc., 392 U.S. 390 (1968). See also Teleprompter Corp. v. CBS, Inc., 415 U.S. 394 (1974).

2. Congress has amended the copyright law to extend copyright protection to distant signals. The amendment provides for compulsory licensing at royalty rates fixed in the law. Copyright Revision Act of 1976, 17 U.S.C. §111. The FCC's distant signal rules have been abrogated. Can you think of any economic reason for *compulsory* licensing? See generally Stanley M. Besen, Willard G. Manning, Jr. & Bridger M. Mitchell, Copyright Liability for Cable Television: Compulsory Licensing and the Coase Theorem, 21 J. Law & Econ. 67 (1978).

3. Both franchise regulation and rate regulation are constrained by federal regulations recently amended by the Cable Communications Policy Act of 1984.

tions, we would expect several companies to vie for the privilege of serving each community where there was a substantial demand for cable television. The company that offered the best package of price and service would sign up the most customers, and if local cable television service really is a natural monopoly, that company would have lower average costs than its competitors and would drive them from the market.

At this point the successful firm would have a monopoly. Would the subscribers therefore be at its mercy? Not if the promised level of price and service had been specified in a contract with each potential subscriber — and competition among rival aspirants to the local market should assure that potential subscribers would receive a binding contract. Nor would the process of determining which firm would prevail impose substantial costs in the form of duplicate facilities that turned out to be redundant. No firm would begin building its cable grid until after a period of solicitation, and if in that period a strong consumer preference for one firm was indicated the other firms would sell their subscriber contracts to it. If the period of solicitation revealed no strong preference for one firm, and each had subscribers scattered throughout the market, the firms presumably would exchange subscribers until each had a compact market area to serve.

Since contracting costs could be quite high (why?), a pure contract approach might not be satisfactory. But maybe a regulatory approach could be devised that preserved the essential elements of the contractual approach. The municipality, acting as the contracting agent of its residents, could solicit bids from competing applicants for the cable television franchise (or franchises). It would compare these bids and enter into a firm contract with the applicant that promised the best combination of low price and generous service. If it found it difficult to choose between different price-service packages, it might conduct a preference poll among the residents following a campaign by the applicants.

The modified contractual approach may seem quite like the existing system of cable franchising, for the franchisee is usually chosen from among several applicants. The difference is that under the present system the municipality ordinarily does not set as its goal obtaining the best possible contract for the subscribers. The approach, rather, is to extract concessions from the franchisee as the price of permitting it to charge a monopoly price. A typical cable franchise will provide that the franchisee must remit a percentage of its gross revenues to the municipality and also dedicate a certain number of channels, free of charge, for municipal services such as education. The residents gain something as taxpayers from the franchise, but they lose as consumers. They pay a monopoly subscription rate that is higher, because of the concessions, than it would be if the cable television company were an unfettered monopolist, let alone a company contractually obligated to provide service at a price equal to cost. This is illustrated in Figure 13.4, which compares the

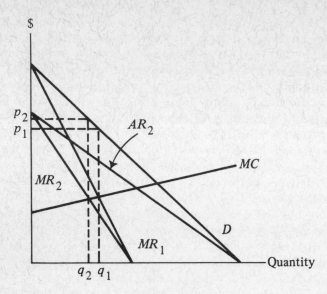

Figure 13.4

monopoly price with and without a gross receipts tax.[4] The example
points out the difference between taxation by regulation and consumer
welfare maximization by contract.[5]

If common law contracting (with perhaps some regulatory overlay)
is a possible answer to the regulation of cable television, why is it not
a possible answer to the regulation of other natural monopolies, and
hence an alternative to the elaborate regulatory system discussed in
the preceding chapter? In fact franchise regulation was the regulatory
system used in the early days of electrical distribution, street railways,
and telephone services, which are all grid-type services like cable television. It was a dismal failure, however, mainly it seems because the franchising authorities did not in fact represent the consumer interest and
hence failed to play the role of buyer in the conventional contract.

4. To understand the effect of the tax, bear in mind that from the seller's standpoint
the demand schedule is a schedule of average revenue — of price received rather than
price charged — at various levels of output. The effect of the tax is to alter the firm's
demand (average revenue) schedule, reducing it by a uniform percentage at every level
of output as shown in Figure 13.4. Its marginal revenue schedule is also altered, as shown
in the diagram, and the resulting profit-maximizing output is lower and price (including
tax) higher than before the tax was imposed.

Suppose the municipality in our example, instead of imposing a gross receipts tax,
charges a flat tax per unit of output. What would be the effect on the price and output
of a profit-maximizing monopolist? See §17.3 *infra*. Now suppose the municipality simply
auctions off the cable franchise to the highest lump sum bidder. What would be the
price and output effects? Would it make a difference whether the franchise was exclusive
or nonexclusive?

5. For criticism of the approach proposed above, stressing transaction costs, see Oliver
E. Williamson, Franchise Bidding for Natural Monopolies — In General and with Respect
to CATV, 7 Bell J. Econ. & Mgmt. Sci. 73 (1976).

In addition to this political problem, there is a purer economic problem that harks back to the discussion of landlord-tenant contracts in Chapter 3 (see §3.9 *supra*). The franchise has to have a fixed duration, for it is impossible to fix sensible terms (price, service, etc.) for the indefinite future. Suppose the optimal duration, having regard for the difficulty of providing sensibly for the distant future, is much shorter than the useful life of many of the assets of the franchisee (rights of way, etc.). At the end of the franchise term there will be a bilateral-monopoly problem of some gravity. The cost to the franchisee of removing the assets will be very high (in particular because they may have little or no value in other uses), but the cost to the franchisor of replacing the assets may also be very high. A simple solution would be to have the assets vest in the franchisor at the end of the term. But then, just as with tenant improvements that enure to the landlord at the end of the lease, the franchisee will underinvest. A better alternative, found in many cable television ordinances, is to establish at the time of franchising a formula for pricing the franchisee's assets at the end of the franchise term.[6]

Suggested Readings

1. Stephen G. Breyer, Regulation and Its Reform (1982).
2. Robert W. Crandall, Controlling Industrial Pollution (1983).
3. Richard Craswell, Interpreting Deceptive Advertising, Boston U.L. Rev. (forthcoming, 1986).
4. Sam Peltzman, An Evaluation of Consumer Protection Legislation: The 1962 Drug Amendments, 81 J. Pol. Econ. 1049 (1973).
5. Steven Shavell, A Model of the Optimal Use of Liability and Safety Regulation, 15 Rand J. Econ. 271 (1984).
6. _____, Liability for Harm Versus Regulation of Safety, 13 J. Leg. Stud. 357 (1984).
7. W. Kip Viscusi, Regulating Consumer Product Safety (Am. Enterprise Institute 1984).
8. Consumer Protection Regulation, 24 J. Law & Econ. 365 (1981).
9. Economic Analysis of Environmental Problems (Edwin S. Mills ed. 1975).
10. The Federal Trade Commission Since 1970: Economic Regulation and Bureaucratic Behavior (Kenneth W. Clarkson & Timothy J. Muris eds. 1981).
11. Incentives for Environmental Protection (Thomas C. Schelling ed. 1983).

---

6. Regulation is discussed further in §§15.8-15.9 *infra* (regulation of the securities markets and of banking).

Problems

1. Would a subsidy to a firm designed to defray the cost of reducing its emission of pollutants have the same allocative and distributive effects as a regulation requiring the reduction, without any compensation? Hint: What would be the effect of the subsidy on the industry's output?

2. There is much interest by economists in, and halting regulatory efforts toward, allowing a market to develop in licenses to pollute. Suppose each firm in a particular region were licensed to emit 10 units of pollution but were free to buy or sell units at freely negotiated prices. Then a firm that wanted to emit 14 units would be able to buy 4 units from a firm that was content to emit only 6. Compare the efficiency and distributive consequences of a scheme combining emission standards with marketable licenses to pollute with those of a pollution tax. Can you guess why environmentalists do not like marketable licenses to pollute?

3. If transaction costs between copyright holders and cable television companies were low, would the FCC's distant signal rules have had any effect on the output of copyrighted material? Would it have made a difference if many of the copyrights had been owned by television networks, each of which owns several television stations?

4. As noted in Chapter 3, the makers of home video recording equipment are not required to pay copyright royalties to the owners of copyrighted television programs, having been held not to be contributory infringers. The copyright owners have proposed that the federal government impose a tax on the sale of video recorders and video cassettes, and distribute the revenues from the tax to the copyright owners in proportion to their shares of the television audience, the shares to be recalculated periodically. Evaluate the economic properties of the proposed scheme in comparison to copyright liability.

5. Evaluate the following proposition: We have at hand an excellent example of a feasible and effective regulatory tax on harmful externalities to use as a model for a pollution tax — the excise tax on alcoholic beverages.

PART IV

THE LAW OF
BUSINESS ORGANIZATIONS
AND FINANCIAL MARKETS

CHAPTER 14

CORPORATIONS (WITH A GLANCE AT LENDING AND BANKRUPTCY)[1]

§14.1 The Nature of the Firm

Transaction costs — the costs involved in ordering economic activity through voluntary exchange — are a recurrent theme in this book. Here we use it to explain why so much economic activity is carried on by firms rather than by individuals.[1]

Contrast two methods of organizing production. In the first, the entrepreneur contracts with one person to supply the component parts, with another to assemble them, and with a third to sell the finished product. In the second, he hires them to perform these tasks as his employees under his direction. The first method of organizing production is the traditional domain of contract law, the second that of master-servant law. The essence of the first method is that the entrepreneur negotiates with each of the three producers an agreement specifying the price, quantity, quality, delivery date, credit terms, and guarantees of the contractor's performance. The essence of the second method is that the entrepreneur pays the producers a wage — a price not for a specific performance but for the right to direct their performance.

Neither method of organizing economic activity is costless, of course. The first method, contract, requires that the details of the supplier's performance be spelled out at the time of signing the contract. This may require protracted negotiations or elaborate bidding procedures, and should changed circumstances require modification of any term of the agreed-upon performance the agreement must be renegotiated.

---

1. See Victor Brudney & Marvin A. Chirelstein, Cases and Materials on Corporate Finance (2d ed. 1979); Harry G. Henn, Handbook of the Law of Corporations and Other Business Enterprises (2d ed. 1970).

§14.1 1. The explanation has its roots in another illustrious article by Ronald H. Coase, The Nature of the Firm, 4 Economica (n.s.) 386 (1937).

367

The second method, the firm, involves incentive, information, and communication costs.[2] Since the supplier (an employee or team of employees) is not paid directly for his output, he has less incentive to minimize his costs. And information about costs and value is obscured in the firm since the employees do not bid for the various resources that they use in production, a process that would indicate where those resources could be employed most valuably; in other words, the information impounded in prices is lost. Furthermore, since performance in the firm is directed by the employer's orders, machinery for minimizing failures of communication up and down the chain of command is necessary — machinery both costly and imperfect. In sum, the contract method of organizing economic activity encounters the problem of high transaction costs, the method of organizing economic activity through the firm the problem of loss of control. It is the control problem, or as it is sometimes called the problem of agency costs (the costs to the principal of obtaining faithful and effective performance by his agents), rather than the law of diminishing returns, that limits the efficient size of firms.[3] Diminishing returns limit merely how much of a single product a firm can produce efficiently.[4]

§14.2 Problems in Financing Business Ventures

The theory of the firm tells us why so much economic activity is organized in firms but not why most of those firms are corporations. A clue is that firms in which the inputs are primarily labor rather than capital often are partnerships or individual proprietorships rather than corporations. The corporation is primarily a method of solving problems encountered in raising substantial amounts of capital.[1]

How does the impecunious entrepreneur who has a promising idea for a new venture go about raising the necessary capital? Borrowing *all* of the needed capital is probably out of the question. If the riskless interest rate is 6 percent but the venture has a 50 percent chance of failing and having no assets out of which to repay the loan, the lender, if risk neutral, will charge an interest rate of 112 percent.[2] The high

2. Both methods involve potential bilateral-monopoly problems when performance over a protracted period of time is contemplated. Can you see why?

3. Intermediate between contract and firm is the principal-agent relationship — a fiduciary rather than arm's length relationship — when the agent is not an employee of the principal. See §4.6 *supra*.

4. Are "firm" and "vertical integration" (§10.7 *supra*) synonyms?

§14.2 1. Today, of course, there are also tax reasons for adopting the corporate form.

2. Suppose the loan is for $100 and is to be repaid at the end of a year. The lender must charge an interest rate that will yield an expected value of $106, given a 50 percent probability of repayment. Solving the equation $.5x = \$106$ for x yields $212 — i.e., $100 in principal plus $112 in interest.

interest charge, plus amortization, will impose a heavy fixed cost on the venture from the outset. This will increase the danger of failure (see §12.8 *supra*) — and in turn the interest rate.

These difficulties could in principle be overcome by careful and imaginative drafting of the loan agreement, but the transaction costs might be very high. An alternative is for the entrepreneur to admit a partner to the business who is entitled to receive a portion of the profits of the venture, if any, in exchange for contributing the necessary capital to it. The partner's compensation is determined automatically by the fortunes of the business. There is no need to compute an interest rate although this is implicit in the determination of the fraction of any future profits that he is to receive in exchange for his contribution. Most important, there are no fixed costs of debt to make the venture even riskier than it inherently is; the partner receives his profits only if and as earned.

But there are still problems. A partnership can be dissolved by, and is automatically dissolved on the death of, any partner. The impermanence of the arrangement may deter the commitment of large amounts of money to an enterprise in which it may be frozen for years. The partners may be able to negotiate around this hurdle but not without incurring transaction costs that may be high. Moreover, to the extent that they agree to limit the investing partner's right to dissolve the partnership and withdraw his money, the liquidity of his investment is reduced and (as we shall see later in this chapter) he may be placed at the mercy of the active partner. (Do you see an analogy to the problem of franchise regulation discussed in the preceding chapter?)

Further, since each partner is personally liable for the debts of the partnership, a prospective investor will want to figure out the likely extent of the enterprise's potential liability, or even to participate in the actual management of the firm to make sure it does not run up huge debts for which he would be liable. And still a risk of indefinite liability would remain. In principle, the enterprise could include in all of its contracts with customers and suppliers a clause limiting its liability to the assets of the enterprise (some business trusts do this). But the negotiation of such waivers would be costly. And it would be utterly impracticable to limit most tort liability in this way. Nor, as we shall see, is insurance a complete answer.

§14.3   The Corporation as a Standard Contract

The corporate form is the normal solution that the law and business practice have evolved to solve the problems discussed in the preceding section. The corporation's perpetual existence obviates the need for a special agreement limiting withdrawal or dissolution, although such an

agreement may turn out to be necessary for other reasons to be discussed. The shareholder's liability for corporate debts is limited to the
value of his shares (limited liability). Passive investment is further encouraged by (1) a complex of legal rights vis-à-vis management and any
controlling group of shareholders, and (2) the fact that equity interests
in a corporation are broken up into shares of relatively small value that
can be, and in the case of the larger corporations are, traded in organized
markets. The corporate form enables an investor to make small equity
investments, to reduce risk through diversification (see §15.1 *infra*), and
to liquidate his investment quickly and cheaply. Notice that without limited liability a shareholder would not even be allowed to sell his shares
without the other shareholders' consent, since if he sold them to someone
poorer than he, the risk to the other shareholders would be increased.

The alert reader will perceive, however, that limited liability is a means
not of eliminating the risks of entrepreneurial failure but of shifting
them from individual investors to the voluntary and involuntary creditors
of the corporation — it is they who bear the risk of corporate default.
Creditors must be paid to bear this risk.[1] Why might the investor want
to shift a part of the downside risk of business failure to the lender,
given that he must compensate him for bearing any added risk? The
answer is that the lender might be the superior risk bearer.

First, he may be in a better position to appraise the risk. Compare
the positions of the individual shareholder and of the bank that lends
the corporation its working capital. It may be cheaper for the bank to
appraise the risk of a default than it would be for the shareholder, who
may know little or nothing about the business in which he has invested
and may face high information costs of finding out.

Second, the shareholder is likely to be more risk averse than the
bank. Remember that we are talking about how to get individuals to
invest money in enterprises. Of course corporations can be shareholders
too, but the ultimate investors are individuals, and most individuals,
as has been noted many times in this book, are risk averse. A bank is
a corporation, and a corporation is likely to be less risk averse than
an individual (though not perfectly risk neutral, as we shall soon see)
because the shareholders can offset any risks incurred by the corporation
by holding a diversified portfolio of securities — provided there is limited

---

§14.3   1. To illustrate, suppose that in our previous example of a new venture with
a 50 percent chance of success the shareholders put up half the required capital and a
bank the other half, and the bank estimates that in the event of failure the assets of the
venture will be sufficient to repay 80 percent of the principal of the loan. The bank
therefore faces a 10 percent probability of loss and (if risk neutral) will demand 11.8
percent interest (based on the equation $.9x = \$106$). But suppose that if the shareholders
pledged their personal wealth to repay the loan in the event of business failure, the
bank would regard the loan as riskless and charge only 6 percent interest. The difference
between a 6 and an 11.8 percent interest rate is a measure of the compensation paid to
the bank by the investors in the new venture for assuming part of the risk of default.

liability. (Without limited liability, the shareholder, even if he held a diversified portfolio, would not be protected against the risk that he might be forced to give up all his wealth to make good the debts of one of the corporations whose shares he owns.) In any event, a large lender can eliminate or greatly reduce the risk of loss on a particular loan by holding a diversified portfolio of loans.[2]

It has been argued that limited liability enables a business to externalize the risk of failure.[3] But (with a limited exception noted later) there is no externality. The lender is fully compensated for the risk of default by the higher interest rate that the corporation must pay lenders by virtue of its having limited liability; and he is also free to insist as a condition of making the loan that the shareholders personally guarantee the corporation's debts, or insert in the loan agreement other provisions limiting the lender's risk. Any resulting reduction in the risk of default will of course reduce the interest rate.

The interest rate will reflect the risk of default as that risk is estimated when the loan agreement is signed, but thereafter the corporation may increase the risk of default, for example by obtaining additional loans not subordinated to the first loan or by transferring assets to its shareholders without full consideration. By doing these things the borrower unilaterally reduces the interest rate it is paying for the loan, a rate negotiated with reference to an anticipated level of risk that is lower than has come to pass. Anything that increases the borrower's debt-equity ratio will increase the likelihood of default, because debt charges are fixed costs to the firm and cannot be reduced if there are business adversities, such as a decline in demand for the firm's product, that lead to a reduction in its earnings.

But why would the firm deliberately increase the risk of defaulting? Any short run gains in reducing the firm's cost of debt will usually be outweighed by the long run loss of creditor confidence, resulting in much higher interest rates when the firm next wants to borrow. But the first lender might not discover the borrower's subsequent loans unless and until disaster struck (and it might not). Moreover, a firm that does not expect to remain in business for the indefinite future — that expects to be bankrupt and is trying to minimize the impact of bankruptcy on its shareholders — will discount, perhaps to zero, the loss of creditor confidence; and firms of this sort may account for a substantial fraction of actual defaults.

To protect himself against such dangers a lender might insist that the borrower agree to limit both its total indebtedness and the amount of dividends payable during the term of the loan, dividend being broadly

2. For a different approach to limited liability, see Frank H. Easterbrook & Daniel R. Fischel, Limited Liability and the Corporation, 52 U. Chi. L. Rev. 89 (1985).

3. See, e.g., Jonathan M. Landers, A Unified Approach to Parent, Subsidiary, and Affiliate Questions in Bankruptcy, 42 U. Chi. L. Rev. 589, 619-620 (1975).

defined for these purposes to include any transfer of corporate assets for less than full market value. Or the lender might insist on some minimum capitalization, impose other restrictions, require collateral — or forgo protection and demand a higher interest rate. But since the probability that the borrower would deliberately attempt to increase the riskiness of the loan would be difficult to quantify, the lender is unlikely to rely entirely on a higher interest rate — especially since the higher rate would increase the risk of default, by increasing the borrower's fixed costs.

One function of contract law, we discovered in Chapter 4, was to economize on transaction costs by supplying standard contract terms that the parties would otherwise have to adopt by express agreement; and it should be clear by now that the same is true with corporation law. For example, the rules of corporation law limiting the payment of dividends to the amount of earned surplus shown on the corporation's books give creditors some protection against attempts by corporate borrowers to increase the risk of default after the loan has been made — protection, we have seen, that in the absence of a legal rule creditors would probably write expressly into each loan contract. Similarly, by endowing every corporation with limited liability the law obviates the need for a lot of cumbersome express contracting on the scope of liability.

The contract analogy breaks down, however, in the case of involuntary extensions of credit, as when a pedestrian is struck by a moving van in circumstances making the moving company liable to him for a tort. Since the parties had no opportunity to transact in advance around the provisions of corporation law, the pedestrian will not be compensated for bearing the default risk created by the moving company's limited liability.

Even where the context is one of voluntary transacting, the costs of explicitly negotiating the extent of liability may be high in relation to the stakes involved. The slight probability that an employee will be seriously injured on the job, when multiplied by the further probability that the employer will lack sufficient assets to satisfy the employee's claim for workmen's compensation, may be too small to warrant inclusion of an express provision in the employment contract (e.g., an employer's bond) to cover that contingency. In this case too, whatever term is implied as a matter of corporate or bankruptcy law will control the parties' relations even if it is contrary to what the parties would have negotiated in a world of zero transaction costs. But there is a difference between this and the previous accident case: The wage rate can adjust to compensate the worker for the risk of nonpayment of any compensation claim that he may some day have against his employer. (But how likely is this to happen?)

§14.4 Corporate Debt — Bankruptcy and Reorganization

We have thus far taken for granted that corporations will have debt as well as equity — creditors as well as shareholders. To some extent this is indeed inevitable; a corporation cannot avoid the possibility of becoming an involuntary creditor as a result of a tort committed by an employee in the course of his employment. But this is the type of risk that can be guarded against fairly easily by insurance (though not completely, as we shall see). If corporate debt is not essential, it becomes unclear why limited liability is necessary. For if corporations just had equity capital, so that they couldn't default on loans, the only thing at risk unless the corporation committed a tort would be the stockholders' capital contributions.

There are several explanations for why corporations have debt as well as equity in their capital structures, though one is fallacious.

1. The fallacious one is that it increases the stockholders' rate of return, by making their investment a leveraged one; the fallacy is demonstrated in §15.2 *infra.*

2. A mixture of equity and debt capital enables the corporation to provide different risk-return packages to meet the varying preferences of investors (a term here used broadly to include lenders as well as shareholders). A corporation with just equity capital will provide an investment having a uniform expected risk and return for all the investors. As soon as the corporation borrows some money, however, the expected risk and return to the shareholders will rise; they will now have, as just noted, a leveraged investment. But even if the debt-equity ratio is very high, the creditors will have a less risky investment than would the shareholders in an all equity company, because creditors lose none of their investment until the shareholders' investment is completely wiped out. Secured creditors are in an even better position. All they have to worry about is the value of the specific assets earmarked to repay their loans; unless that value falls below the value of their loans, they don't have to worry even if the corporation goes broke. ("Liens pass unaffected through bankruptcy," as the lawyers say.) This means they save on the costs of monitoring the corporation's performance. But of course their expected return is less than that of unsecured creditors, who bear greater risk and monitoring costs, and is much less than that of the shareholders.[1]

§14.4 1. On the economics of secured financing see Douglas G. Baird & Thomas H. Jackson, Cases, Problems, and Materials on Security Interests in Personal Property 354-367 (1984). Professor Alan Schwartz has asked what corporations have to gain from issuing secured debt. See Security Interests and Bankruptcy Priorities: A Review of Current

A distinct group of creditors in terms of risk are the trade creditors (suppliers who do not demand payment in cash). Their position is less risky than that of other unsecured creditors (and sometimes that of secured creditors holding long-term debt) because their debt normally is outstanding for only a short time, so there is less danger of something unexpected happening to affect the riskiness of their investment.

Thus the corporate form with debt as well as equity capital allows a variety of investor preferences to be met simultaneously. Of course, the shareholder in an all equity corporation could always borrow money on his shares to obtain leverage; this would bring about a substitution of individual for corporate debt. But notice that this would cut somewhat against the grain of limited liability, since the shareholder's stake would no longer be limited to his equity investment. Presumably most shareholders would not consider this an attractive alternative to the present system, where lenders bear some of the risk of corporate default.

3. The large number of shareholders in the modern large corporation makes the problem of agency costs acute. No individual shareholder has much incentive to spend time and money on monitoring the performance of the people actually managing the company, since most of the benefit of his efforts will enure to the other shareholders. There is thus a classic free rider (external benefits) problem. One way to keep managers in line is to engage the services of people who will watch the managers. Boards of directors and auditors do this and so do holders of corporate debt, since by virtue of lending money to the corporation they obtain a stake in its success, though a smaller stake than the shareholders.

4. Still another way to keep managers in line is to maintain a nontrivial risk of bankruptcy; and this requires debt to do (why?). Bankruptcy will impose a heavy cost on managers because they will be blamed, and in a public and conspicuous way, for whatever mismanagement tipped the company over the brink. This would make little difference if the managers' jobs were unaffected. But bankruptcy will take control of the firm away from them and may cost them their jobs even if the firm is not liquidated. And they may find it difficult to find equivalent jobs, bearing as they do the stigma of association with a bankruptcy;

Theories, 10 J. Leg. Stud. 1 (1981), and The Continuing Puzzle of Secured Debt, 37 Vand. L. Rev. 1051 (1984). By giving a creditor security, the corporation reduces the interest rate that the creditor demands; but this also increases the risk borne by the other creditors (why?), so they will demand higher interest rates, and the corporation's overall debt cost will not be reduced. Cf. §15.2 *infra*. But look at the problem from the creditor side. If a creditor wants to make a long-term loan, security is a nice substitute for continuous monitoring of the debtor to make sure he doesn't deplete the assets available to pay back the loan. Very short-term lenders don't need either to have security or to do monitoring (see discussion in text below). Intermediate-term lenders presumably are specialists in monitoring. So, given a distribution of lender time preferences and (relatedly) of monitoring capabilities among lenders, secured debt may make economic sense.

and there may be no equivalent jobs, if they had developed human capital specific to the firm that had failed.[2]

5. Debt is a cheaper source of capital than equity because of the corporate income tax, which is in part an excise tax on equity capital (see §17.5 *infra*).

What exactly is corporate bankruptcy? At first glance the term seems an oxymoron. Since the shareholders can't be ruined by the collapse of the corporation — their loss is limited by what they invested — it might seem that they would not need bankruptcy. This is true but takes too narrow a view of the purposes of bankruptcy. Granted, an important function of *personal* bankruptcy is to encourage enterprise by risk-averse individuals, through the principle that bankruptcy discharges the bankrupt from his debts, or at least most of them. An individual would otherwise have to hazard his entire earning capacity on his business ventures, at least if the venture borrowed money (insurance could, as mentioned, take care of most involuntary debts). Thus limited liability is to corporate entrepreneurs what the right to declare personal bankruptcy is to individual entrepreneurs. But bankruptcy is a creditor's remedy as well as a debtor's right. The reason for having involuntary as well as voluntary bankruptcy is a transaction-cost problem that is created when there is a major default and many creditors.

Suppose the market for a corporation's only product collapses to the point where the market price is lower than the corporation's variable costs at any output, so that the only sensible thing to do is to shut down immediately and sell the corporation's assets for whatever salvage value they can command. If that value is less than the corporation's total debt, the shareholders will be indifferent to the opportunities from liquidation. Their rational course will be to abandon the company. The creditors will have an interest in liquidating the corporate assets for the highest possible value, but they may run afoul of externalities in trying to work out a plan of liquidation that will achieve this goal. What if a rental payment is due, and unless it is paid the assets of the company will have to be moved at great cost; which creditor will pay it? Each will have an incentive to hang back, hoping another will step forward. If there is enough money for the payment in the company's bank account, still one of the creditors may attach the account and take the money to satisfy his debt, leaving the other creditors to worry about the rent. Bankruptcy law takes care of this problem by giving a superpriority to one who lends the bankrupt money essential to preserve the value of the bankrupt's assets or provides other essential services.

Another possibility in a world without bankruptcy law is that creditors might try to work out side deals with the shareholders that would hurt other creditors. Here is an extreme example (a fraudulent conveyance).

2. See the further discussion of the corporation's capital structure in §15.2 *infra*.

Suppose the company has total debts of $1 million, of which $100,000 is owed to creditor A, and the total value of the company's assets is $200,000. Creditor A might offer to buy the assets from the company for $100,000, since he could resell them for $200,000 and recoup his loan that way. The shareholders would be happy because they would be recovering part of their investment, but the other creditors would be left out in the cold. The possibility of such deals would induce costly jockeying among creditors, and the uncertainty of creditors' positions in such a regime would result in higher interest rates to compensate for the greater risk that creditors would bear.

This type of problem would exist even if the firm simply repaid creditor A his debt in full before the other creditors (maybe because A was the first to reduce his claim to judgment) — granted A a preference, in the language of bankruptcy law. The effect on the other creditors would be to reduce their repayment prospects from 20 cents on the dollar ($200,000 divided by $1 million) to 11 cents on the dollar ($100,000 divided by $900,000) and to redouble the efforts of each of those creditors himself to get a preference. Each creditor in such a world will have an incentive to be first to get a judgment against the bankrupt, and the race is likely to drain the company of its assets too rapidly to maximize the value of those assets.

All of these problems can be solved, in principle, by transactions among the creditors; but if there are many creditors, the costs of these transactions may well be prohibitive. The alternative is bankruptcy, wherein a court-appointed neutral, the trustee in bankruptcy, sets aside any last minute preferences and administers the bankrupt's assets as the representative of all the (unsecured) creditors. Like a conventional trustee in a trust with multiple beneficiaries, the trustee in bankruptcy overcomes the difficulty that is created when multiple parties claim interests in the same assets. Analytically, the problem of bankruptcy, viewed from the creditors' standpoint, is the same as that of divided ownership of land (see §3.9 *supra*).

We have explained why involuntary bankruptcies, and voluntary bankruptcies by individuals engaged in business, are allowed, but not why voluntary nonbusiness bankruptcies (e.g., of consumers who go overboard buying goods on credit) and voluntary corporate bankruptcies are allowed. The former can perhaps be explained by reference to risk aversion; it provides a kind of insurance that is difficult to purchase in the market. The doubt intimated by the word *perhaps* has two sources. The first is the fact that a person cannot, when he borrows money, waive his right to seek discharge of the debt in bankruptcy. This is paternalistic. The second source is the reason why it is difficult to purchase insurance against defaulting on one's debts: It makes a default so attractive. One can buy and consume all sorts of nice things on debt and then default. This problem (a particularly serious form of the general moral hazard problem of insurance) could be solved only by distinguishing between voluntary and involuntary defaults and limiting the privilege of voluntary bankruptcy to the latter. But the distinction is very difficult to draw in practice. There is no sharp line between voluntary and involuntary defaults. The more debt one takes on, the more vulnerable one makes oneself to being unable to repay the debt because of an unforeseen change of circumstances, no matter how great one's good faith in intending to repay it.

The extensive amendments made to the bankruptcy statute in 1978 made it easier to declare personal bankruptcy; the result, an economist would predict, would be higher interest rates on personal loans. And to the extent that information costs prevent lenders from discriminating in their rates according to the probability that the borrower will be able to avoid his debts by declaring bankruptcy, the effect of liberal personal bankruptcy is to make prudent borrowers subsidize feckless ones — a curious basis on which to redistribute wealth!

The most interesting form of voluntary corporate bankruptcy is the corporate reorganization. Usually management is allowed to continue operating the corporation as debtor in possession; there is no trustee, and no steps are taken to liquidate the firm. But the corporation must come up within six months with a plan of reorganization, whereby the firm will continue in operation but with a different structure of ownership. The essence of such a plan is a proposal for converting the debt of the corporation into stock and other securities to be assigned to the creditors in payment of the corporation's debt to them, so that the creditors will become the corporation's owners (or principal owners, because often the original shareholders assign themselves some part of the stock). The creditors can object to the terms of the proposal; and then it is up to the bankruptcy court to determine what the true value of the corporation is and how it should be allocated in securities of the reorganized company among the creditors and, if it exceeds the value of their claims, to the original shareholders as well.

The essential point about reorganization is that it contemplates the continued operation of the firm rather than its liquidation. It might seem however that if the continued operation of the firm were economically feasible the creditors would have no interest in forcing it into bankruptcy in the first place.[3] But this is not correct. A firm can be at once insolvent and economically viable. If the demand for the firm's product (or products) has declined unexpectedly, the firm may find that its revenues do not cover its total costs, including fixed costs of debt. But they may exceed its variable costs, in which event it ought not be liqui-

3. Although the shareholders take the initiative in proposing a plan of reorganization, rarely do they file a petition for protection under Chapter 11 — as a proposal for reorganization is formally known — unless creditors are about to force the company into bankruptcy.

dated yet. And maybe in the long run the firm could continue in business indefinitely with a smaller plant. In that event it might not have to replace all of its debt when that debt was retired, its total costs would be lower, and its (lower) demand and (lower) supply curves might once again intersect. In short, the company may have a viable future, short or long, which it can get to it if it can just wipe out its current debt. One way of doing so is to convert that debt into equity capital, at which point the debt will cease being a fixed cost and thus cease preventing the company from meeting its other expenses. A bankruptcy reorganization does this. Since by hypothesis the company is to continue in operation, it is quite natural both to allow the present management rather than a trustee to manage the company during the period of reorganization and to vest the initiative to reorganize in that management. The management will have an incentive to "pull off" the reorganization and thus avoid liquidation (whether sale as a going concern or sale of the firm's assets for their salvage value). Liquidation would cost them their jobs, and they may have firm-specific human capital (i.e., skills that would be less productive in any other job), which by definition would go down the drain in a liquidation and which is almost impossible to insure. In any event, if they lose their jobs as a result of bankruptcy, they may, as we saw earlier, have difficulty convincing prospective employers that it was not their fault (indeed, it may very well have been their fault).

There is by the same token, however, a danger that the managers will attempt reorganization just to stave off the evil day of liquidation, even though prompt liquidation would be better for the creditors; courts cannot always distinguish viable from hopeless reorganization plans. Most reorganizations in fact end in liquidation — although this doesn't necessarily show that reorganization was a mistake. In our earlier example of a firm in a declining market, it might well be that its plant would never be replaced, as distinct from being replaced with a smaller plant, and yet the firm might be able to cover its variable costs until the plant wore out, in which event liquidation might be premature.

Another objection to reorganization is that whereas liquidation involves a market valuation of the corporation, reorganization involves a valuation by a court. Apparently these valuations are consistently over-optimistic, although it doesn't necessarily follow that creditors get securities in a reorganization that are worth less than the proceeds of a liquidation would be. Reorganization is no panacea; but to order the immediate liquidation of every firm that went broke would be a source of great social waste.

An alternative to the current system of reorganization would be to take the initiative away from the bankrupt firm and put it in the hands of a trustee. Whenever a firm went broke, a trustee would be appointed and would decide whether to liquidate the firm or make it over to the creditors (which is what happens in a reorganization, by virtue of the absolute priority rule examined in Problem 3 at the end of Chapter 15); he could of course retain the existing management pending liquidation or reorganization. It is difficult to know whether such a system would be superior to the present one. It would eliminate the incentives of the shareholders and managers of the bankrupt firm to attempt a hopeless reorganization merely to stave off a liquidation that would hurt them though help the creditors, and it would reduce the error-prone judicial role in reorganizations, but it would also impair the incentives of the shareholders and the managers to attempt a reorganization that might succeed, by terminating their control of the corporation earlier. Indeed, the overoptimistic valuations in reorganizations can perhaps be defended as giving shareholders and managers (who invariably are also shareholders) an incentive to attempt a reorganization rather than abandon the sinking ship to the creditors, since the higher the valuation is, the likelier are the shareholders to be awarded some of the stock in the reorganized firm.

§14.5   Piercing the Corporate Veil

Although limited liability serves an important function in making equity investments attractive to individuals, disregarding it — piercing the corporate veil, in the jargon of corporation law — may promote efficiency in two situations.

1. The first is illustrated by the taxi enterprise that incorporates each taxicab separately in order to limit its tort liability to accident victims. If this were a negotiated obligation, the creditor-victim would charge a higher interest rate to reflect the increased risk of a default; but it is not and cannot be.[1] The result of separate incorporation is therefore to externalize a cost of taxi service.

Yet piercing the veil may not be optimal even in this situation.[2] Permitting tort victims to reach the shareholders' assets would be a source of additional risk to the shareholders — and an increase in risk is a real cost to people who are risk averse. Although the company could insure itself against its torts, this would not be a completely satisfactory alternative to limited liability. The managers might fail to take out adequate insurance; the insurance company might for a variety of reasons refuse or be unable to pay a tort judgment against the insured (the insurance company might, for example, become insolvent); the particular

§14.5   1. Is this true with respect to *all* of the company's potential accident victims?

2. If the veil is pierced, unaffiliated one-cab corporations should be required to post a bond, to prevent their externalizing their accident costs, thereby obtaining an inefficient competitive advantage.

tort might be excluded from the coverage of the insurance policy. All this may sound pretty remote — until one replaces taxicab collisions by nuclear reactor accidents or asbestos-caused lung disease.

One alternative to piercing the corporate veil would be to require any corporation engaged in dangerous activity to post a bond equal to the highest reasonable estimate of the probable extent of its tort liability. Shareholders would be protected (in what sense?) and accident costs internalized. Another alternative would be in our taxi case to treat the assets of all of the affiliated taxicab corporations as a single pool for purposes of meeting tort victims' claims against any of the corporations. But there would be a problem in defining the appropriate boundaries of the pool: Should it include the assets of affiliated corporations in a different business, or of an affiliated corporation engaged in the taxi business but in another state?

2. The other and more important case in which piercing the corporate veil is warranted is where separate incorporation misleads creditors. If corporations are permitted to represent that they have greater assets to pay creditors than they actually have, the result will be to increase the costs that creditors must incur to ascertain the true credit worthiness of the corporations with which they deal.

Misrepresentation is in fact the dominant approach used by the courts in deciding whether to pierce the corporate veil. True, they often describe the criterion for piercing as whether the debtor corporation is merely an agent, alter ego, or instrumentality of the shareholder. But in applying the test the courts commonly ask whether the shareholder engaged in conduct, or made representations, likely to deceive the creditor into thinking that the debtor had more assets than it really had or that the shareholder was the real debtor. Some courts have explicitly adopted a misrepresentation rationale for determining whether to pierce the corporate veil.

Often a shareholder is a corporation rather than an individual, and it might seem that the policy of risk shifting that underlies the principle of limited liability would not apply in that case. If a parent corporation is made liable for its subsidiary's debts, the exposure of the parent's shareholders to liability, although greater than if the subsidiary enjoyed limited liability, is limited to their investment in the parent and can be further reduced by their holding a diversified portfolio of equities. It may be necessary to distinguish in this regard, however, between the publicly held corporation (many shareholders, regularly traded stock) and the close corporation (few shareholders, no market in the stock).

Suppose that Mr. A. Smith wants to invest in a mining venture but the entire Smith fortune (other than that which Smith plans to commit to the mining venture) is invested in a radio station owned by a corporation of which Smith is the sole stockholder. If he forms a new corporation to conduct the mining venture, and if the assets of affiliated corporations can be pooled to satisfy the claims of creditors of one of the affiliates, then Smith has hazarded his entire fortune on the outcome of the mining venture. In this case there is no difference between piercing the corporate veil to reach the assets of an affiliated corporation and piercing it to reach an individual shareholder's assets.

But where a large, publicly held corporation operates through wholly owned subsidiaries, it may seem artificial in the extreme to treat these as separate entities for purposes of deciding what assets shall be available to satisfy creditors' claims. The question of whether it is or not can be evaluated by dividing affiliated firms into two groups: firms in unrelated businesses and firms in closely related businesses. In the first group, maximization of the parent corporation's profits will require that the profits of each subsidiary be maximized separately; so the assets, costs, etc. of each subsidiary should be the same as they would be if they were separate firms. True, the common owner could take measures that concealed or distorted the relative profitability of his different enterprises, as by allocating capital among them at arbitrary interest rates. But it is not true that owners commonly adopt such measures, which are costly because they reduce the information available to the common owner about the efficiency with which his various corporations are being managed.[3]

Even when the activities of affiliated corporations are closely related — when for example they produce complementary goods — each corporation normally will be operated as a separate profit center in order to assure that the profits of the group will be maximized.[4] It is true that where there are substantial cost savings from common ownership, as in some cases where the affiliated corporations operate at successive stages in the production of a good (see §§10.7, 14.1 *supra*), the two corporations will be managed differently from separately owned corporations in the same line of business; their operations will be more closely integrated than would be those of independent corporations. But it would be perverse to penalize such a corporation for its superior efficiency by withdrawing from it the privilege of limited liability that its nonintegrated competitors enjoy. Moreover, in this case as well, the common owner has a strong incentive to avoid intercorporate transfers that, by distorting the profitability of each corporation, make it more difficult for the common owner to evaluate their performance. That is why the price at which one division of a vertically integrated firm will "sell" its output to another division is normally the market price for

3. The danger of abuse of the corporate form is therefore greatest in the case of the small business, where operation of the constituent corporations as separate profit centers is less necessary to assure efficient management — but where the individual investors' interest in the limited liability of corporate affiliates approaches the investor interest in preserving the limited liability of unaffiliated corporations. That is our A. Smith example.

4. Can you think of an exception? See §10.7 *supra*.

the good in question (less any savings in cost attributable to making an intrafirm transfer compared to a market transaction) rather than an arbitrary transfer price designed to increase the profits of one division at the expense of the other.

The important difference between a group of affiliates engaged in related businesses and one engaged in a number of unrelated businesses is not that the conduct of the corporations in the first group will differ from that of nonaffiliated corporations in the same business but that the creditor dealing with a group of affiliates in related businesses is more likely to be misled into thinking that he is dealing with a single corporation.[5] The misrepresentation principle, however, seems adequate to deal with these cases. Indeed, where there is no misrepresentation, a rule abrogating the limited liability of affiliated corporations would not reduce the risks of any class of creditors but would increase their information costs. Although the creditor of A Corporation would know that if A defaulted he could reach the assets of its affiliate B, he would also know that if B defaulted, B's creditors might have a claim on the assets of A that might cause A to default on the debt to him. So to know how high an interest rate to charge, he would have to investigate B's financial situation as well as A. And B might be in a completely unrelated business.

§14.6   The Separation of Ownership and Control in the Modern Corporation

Corporate law is widely believed to be tilted not only against the creditors of corporations but also against the shareholders themselves (are these beliefs consistent?). The latter contention is summarized in the idea of the separation between ownership (the shareholders) and control (the management) in the publicly held corporation. Much of the concern with this alleged separation is, however, based on a failure to distinguish between *firm* and *corporation* (see §14.1 *supra*). The firm is a method

---

5. Suppose, for example, that a bank holding company establishes a subsidiary to invest in real estate. The holding company gives the subsidiary a name confusingly similar to that of the holding company's banking subsidiary and the real estate corporation leases office space in the bank so that its offices appear to be bank offices. Unsophisticated creditors extend generous terms to the real estate subsidiary in the reasonable belief that they are dealing with the bank itself. In these circumstances it might be appropriate to estop (i.e., forbid) the bank holding company — or even the bank itself — to deny that it is the entity to which the creditors have extended credit. To protect the legal separateness of affiliated corporations could lead creditors as a class to invest a socially excessive amount of resources in determining the true corporate status of the entity to which they were asked to extend credit.

of organizing production; the corporation is a method, like a bond indenture, for attracting capital into the firm. The typical large business is both firm and corporation. The control of the firm resides in a management group that gives orders to the employees who actually buy the firm's inputs and make and sell its output. The management group consists of people who are experienced in the business and involved in it on a full-time, day-to-day basis. The typical shareholder (except in the closely held corporation or where one shareholder owns a very large percentage of the shares of the corporation) is not knowledgeable about the business of the firm, does not derive an important part of his livelihood from it, and neither expects nor has an incentive to participate in its management. He is a passive investor and, because of the liquidity of his interest, has only a casual and often a transitory relationship with the firm. His interest, like that of a creditor, is a financial rather than managerial interest.

It is no more anomalous that shareholders do not manage or control "their" corporation than that bondholders do not manage or control the corporations whose bonds they hold, or trust beneficiaries the trustee. All three groups have an investment interest. The difference lies in the greater vulnerability of the shareholder (as of the trust beneficiary) than of the bondholder to misfeasance and nonfeasance by corporate management. Since the bondholder has a fixed interest rate (and, for what it is worth, the cushion of the equity investment), his concern is not that the firm be well managed but that it not be so mismanaged that it defaults on its interest payments, or is unable to repay the principal when the bond matures, or makes these eventualities likelier than the bondholder thought when he negotiated the interest rate. In contrast, the shareholder's return is directly related both to how well the firm is managed and to how scrupulously the managers allot to the shareholders an appropriate portion of the firm's income — which is to say everything above the competitive return to the managers for performance of the managerial function.

The danger of mismanagement (negligence) is less serious than the danger that the managers will not deal fairly with the shareholders (disloyalty). Mismanagement is not in the managers' self-interest; it is in fact very much contrary to their self-interest, as it will lead eventually to the bankruptcy of the firm (and of the managers' future employment prospects), as a result of the competition of better managed rivals. Although managers thus have a strong incentive to manage the firm well or, if they are unable to manage it well themselves, to sell their offices to those who can,[1] their incentive to deal fairly with shareholders (meaning, maximizing the per-share value of the corporation's stock) is weaker.

§14.6   1. They are not permitted to do this directly; but there are indirect methods of sale, especially as part of a corporate acquisition. See §14.7 *infra*.

True, managers who do not deal fairly with the shareholders will have to pay a premium should they ever want to raise additional capital by a new issue of common stock; but the cost of the premium will not be borne (not primarily, anyway) by the managers; it will be borne by the original shareholders in the form of a dilution of their interest. There is thus enough of a potential conflict of interest between management and shareholders to lead us to predict that shareholders would normally insist upon the inclusion of protective features in the corporate charter.[2]

Corporation law reduces transaction costs by implying in every corporation charter the normal rights that a shareholder could be expected to insist on, of which the most important is the right to cast votes, equal to the number of shares he holds, for membership in the corporation's board of directors. The board does not manage the firm. Composed usually of representatives of management plus outsiders who, having full-time employment elsewhere, devote only sporadic attention to the corporation's affairs, normally the board ratifies the actions of management. The importance of the board lies in the fact that it, and through it the shareholders, can fire the existing managers and hire new ones who will be more attentive to the shareholders' interests.

The separation of ownership and control is a false issue. Separation is efficient, and indeed inescapable, given that for most shareholders the opportunity costs of active participation in the management of the firm would be prohibitively high. What is necessary in the interests of the shareholders is not participatory shareholder democracy but machinery for discouraging management from deflecting too much of the firm's net income from the shareholders to itself.

Naturally in a book on law we are interested in the legal machinery, but we should not overlook private incentives and arrangements that even in the absence of legal machinery would tend to keep managers in line. We have already mentioned the managers' interest in their reputation and how the practice of corporate debt tends to keep managers on their toes. Another very important device for aligning managers' self-interest with that of shareholders — a device increasingly used by U.S. business, as a matter of fact — is to make managerial compensation depend to a substantial extent on the performance of the firm as measured by the value of its shares.[3] Can you think of any limitation on the utility of this device?

2. There is a similar conflict of interest between the beneficiaries of a trust and the trustee (see §3.9 *supra*), and not surprisingly we find a similar set of protective features (fiduciary duties) in both contests. There is an important difference, however. The trustee is responsible for diversifying the investments of the beneficiary. The corporation is ordinarily a nondiversified enterprise; it is left to the shareholder, by buying shares in a number of corporations, to achieve the amount of diversification that he desires. But this gets us ahead of our story. See §15.5 *infra*.

3. See Symposium on Management Compensation and the Managerial Labor Market, 7 J. Accounting & Econ. 3 (1985).

Consider now the practice of paying dividends. At first glance it seems rather an odd practice given the structure of the tax laws. Dividends are taxable as ordinary income; if the same income is retained in the corporation, the value of the corporation's stock will be higher, and the shareholder can obtain the same cash he could get from receiving dividends by periodically selling some of his shares for capital gains taxable at a much lower rate. Paying dividends may be a way of depressing the real return paid the company's debt holders — hence the need pointed out earlier to limit the amount of dividends that the company is allowed to pay. Paying dividends also helps keep managers in line, both by forcing the corporation to return more often to the capital market to finance new ventures, as distinct from financing them out of retained earnings, and by making the risk of corporate failure greater (because the ratio of debt to equity will be higher if not all earnings are retained), just as having corporate debt in the first place does.[4]

§14.7   The Transfer of Corporate Control

If management is disregarding the shareholders' interests, the market price of the firm's common stock will fall. When this happens, alert investors will realize that the stock is underpriced — that the price would be higher if the firm were being managed with the object of maximizing the shareholder's return. They can exploit this knowledge in several ways:

1. Another corporation can try to persuade the current board of directors to cooperate in a merger of the two corporations that will give control to the acquiring firm. The acquiescence of the incumbent directors and managers of the acquired firm can be secured by promises of generous compensation in the form of lucrative consulting contracts, etc. The shareholders will have to vote on the proposed merger, however.

2. If the management and board of directors resist, the would-be acquirer can make an offer to buy a majority of the outstanding shares of the corporation from the existing shareholders at a price somewhere in between the current market price and the price to which the stock would rise under proper management and control. If the tender offer succeeds, the acquirer will have enough votes to elect his own board of directors, which will then replace the present management.

3. A corporate or individual investor can buy enough shares (a) to form a base from which to wage a campaign for the voting proxies of

4. See Frank H. Easterbrook, Two Agency-Cost Explanations of Dividends, 74 Am. Econ. Rev. 650 (1984).

the other shareholders and (b) to enable him to profit handsomely from the increase in the market price of the firm's common stock when the old board and management are overthrown.

Traditional scholars of corporation law place too much emphasis on corporate democracy (number 3) and not enough on the market in corporate control. The proxy fight waged by an individual who has not acquired a substantial ownership position most closely resembles the democratic political process but is the least feasible method of takeover, in part because of acute externalities: How can such an individual recoup the costs of the campaign with a profit commensurate with the risk of failure?

Unfortunately, the law places obstacles in the way of effective use of the tender offer, which in turn reduces the efficiency of the voluntary merger route as well (why?). For example, it forbids an investor bent on takeover to buy up a substantial portion of the target firm's shares without disclosing his purpose. Such disclosure tends to increase the price of the stock and thus to reduce the gain from takeover and therefore the incentive to attempt it; it externalizes much of the benefit created by the takeover bid.[1]

The antitrust laws as currently interpreted are a significant if diminishing obstacle to takeovers. Ordinarily a large corporation can be taken over only by another large corporation, and large corporate acquisitions are vulnerable to antitrust challenge. Today one often finds corporate management resisting a takeover on the ground that the resulting acquisition would violate the antitrust laws.

There would be another obstacle if proposals were adopted that would forbid a controlling shareholder, in selling his shares, to charge a premium for the control of the corporation that the sale bestows on the buyer. The underlying theory is that the controlling shareholder has fiduciary obligations to the minority shareholders. The theory has merit in the special case (discussed in a subsequent section) where there is a conflict of interest between majority and minority shareholders. But in the usual takeover situation, the minority shareholders will be more harmed than benefited by a rule that, by reducing the controlling shareholder's incentive to sell his control, retards the reallocation of the assets of the corporation to people who can use them more productively, to the benefit of all of the shareholders.

Another problem is the adoption by prospective takeover targets of devices for making takeovers more costly — for example, contracts guaranteeing seemingly extravagant severance pay for managers let go as a result of a takeover (the golden parachute, as it is called), and poison pills. The poison pill is a scheme whereby each shareholder receives

§14.7   1. See Gregg A. Jarrell & Michael Bradley, The Economic Effects of Federal and State Regulations of Cash Tender Offers, 23 J. Law & Econ. 371 (1980).

with each share a warrant that entitles him, should the corporation be acquired, to sell his shares to the acquiring firm at the price fixed in the warrant, which usually is several times the current market price of the share. If the tender offer is sufficiently generous, the poison pill causes no problem, because every shareholder will be happy to sell his shares (with the warrants attached) to the acquiring firm. But the optimal tender offer, from the offeror's standpoint, is one that does *not* attract all the shareholders; that would be too expensive; the goal is to set a price that will induce a bare majority of the shareholders to sell their shares. Having thus obtained control, the tender offeror will then offer to buy out the remaining shareholders (assuming he doesn't want to be bothered by minority shareholders) — but at a lower price, as they have nowhere else to go; the difference in price is the premium for control mentioned earlier. The two-tiered tender offer actually reduces the initial offering price, since shareholders will compete with one another to be in the first, and higher priced, tier, which receives the premium for control. The poison pill is (to mix the metaphor slightly) an effective antidote to two-tiered offers because it forces the acquiring corporation to buy out the second tier at a much higher price than the first, and thus it greatly reduces the expected gains of the offer.

The golden parachute is less clearly objectionable than the poison pill. A guarantee of high severance pay triggered by a takeover makes takeovers more costly, but also reduces the incentive of managers to resist takeovers; the effects may be offsetting.

Antitakeover devices such as the poison pill are defended as promoting equality among shareholders, causing tender offerors to sweeten their offers, and correcting undervaluations by the market. These defenses are implausible (the last especially, in view of the efficient market thesis explored in the next chapter). Their major effect is to discourage tender offers, and some studies have shown that when tender offers are defeated the shareholders of the target corporation — all of them — suffer losses.[2]

And yet the antitakeover devices require the approval of the corporation's board of directors — a board likely nowadays to have a majority of outside directors. Could they be acting against the corporation's interests? They could be. They have, after all, a conflict of interest, since if the corporation is taken over they are quite likely to lose their positions on the board, which pay handsome fees. Inside directors have even greater stakes in the continued independence of the company. More puzzling is why shareholders endorse antitakeover devices — for such

2. See, e.g., Frank H. Easterbrook & Gregg A. Jarrell, Do Targets Gain from Defeating Tender Offers?, 59 N.Y.U.L. Rev. 277 (1984). The evidence, however, is inconclusive. See Michael C. Jensen & Richard S. Ruback, The Market for Corporate Control: The Scientific Evidence, 11 J. Financial Econ. 5, 29–40 (1983).

devices often require, and often receive, the endorsement of a majority of the shareholders as well as of a majority of the board of directors.

If the studies that find that antitakeover devices hurt the shareholders are right, this suggests both that the market for corporate control is not working well and that its failure is a serious one. Must there not be a serious conflict of interest between managers and shareholders in many large corporations, if management often resists takeovers that would be in the shareholders' best interest? Unless something is done to improve the takeover market, there will continue to be an argument for doing even more, as a second best solution, to provide shareholders with effective legal protections against management, through proxy machinery, derivative suits, and other devices.

Some doubt is cast on this conclusion, however, by asking: What *should* be the posture of the management of a takeover target? Should it advise the shareholders to accept the first takeover offer made, or should it try to delay acceptance of the offer in the hope of stimulating a competition among takeover bidders in which the stock will be sold to the highest bidder?[3] It would be thought odd in an ordinary market to have a rule that required a seller to accept the first offer; and while no individual shareholder is required to accept a tender offer, he may lack the information that management has regarding the prospect for a higher offer if he turns down this one. The market for corporate control, however, is not an ordinary market, given the apparent conflict of interest between management and shareholders if managers have firm-specific human capital and feel their jobs jeopardized by the takeover bid. They may try to arrange an auction in the hope that by stalling they can defeat all takeover bids. Or they may simply hope that by reducing the gains to information about undervalued companies (which an auction does by preventing the initial bidder from having a clear shot at acquiring the target, and allowing subsequent bidders to take a free ride on the first one's investigation), the prospect of an auction will reduce the likelihood that a takeover bid will be made in the first place.

Evidence has recently been presented, however, that targets that resist tender offers yet are later acquired do better than targets that do not resist; if however they resist successfully, they do worse.[4] This evidence suggests that the conflict of interest problem may not be so serious after all. The expected gain from resistance may be positive, even though some fraction of resisters do too well, and are not acquired at all, rather than acquired at a higher premium — the purpose of the resistance, if the evidence has been correctly interpreted.

3. See Frank H. Easterbrook & Daniel R. Fischel, Auctions and Sunk Costs in Tender Offers, 35 Stan. L. Rev. 1 (1982).
4. See Gregg A. Jarrell, The Wealth Effects of Litigation by Targets: Do Interests Diverge in a Merge?, 28 J. Law. & Econ. 151 (1985).

§14.8   The Fiduciary Principle

The principal measure for directly assuring that the corporate managers serve as loyal agents of the shareholders is the fiduciary principle (see §4.6 *supra*), which imposes a duty of loyalty on the managers that is enforceable by a stockholders' derivative suit. This is a suit brought in the name of the corporation, but by a shareholder rather than by the corporation itself (which is to say, rather than by the corporate management), against the allegedly disloyal manager. The derivative suit can be used to enforce not only the duty of loyalty but also the duty of care. If an officer or other employee has squandered corporate assets in some feckless venture, he can be sued, and if the suit succeeds, he will be ordered to make good the corporation's losses. But there are serious problems in asking a court to second guess business decisions, and the law's response has been the business judgment rule, under which the courts defer broadly to a company's purely business judgments. Hence the principal importance of the derivative suit is in connection with disloyalty, which is to say conflicts of interest, such as seizing corporate opportunities for private gain. The derivative suit is a monument to the problem of agency costs; it would make no sense to allow a shareholder to bypass the corporate management in bringing a suit against an officer if one could be confident that management always acted in the shareholders' interest.

An important question is, what if the board of directors votes to dismiss a derivative suit? Should its decision be binding on the court, or should the court make an independent judgment as to whether the suit has merit? Such a judgment is a difficult one for a court to make, although not radically different from the judgments courts make when called on to decide whether to approve a settlement, for example in a class action suit (not that they do very well in evaluating such settlements; see §21.9 *infra*). But if the board of directors is dominated by management, the decision to dismiss may be infected by the same problem that led to the filing of the suit in the first place. Even if a majority of the board consists of outside directors, it is not obvious that the board should have the final say. Because they are outsiders, they may lack good information on the merits of the suit, being largely dependent on management for information about the company's affairs. A particularly feeble response to the problem is to confide the decision on whether to dismiss the suit to the outside directors, who unless they dominate the board may find themselves expelled from their lucrative directorships if they refuse to dismiss such suits. And maybe directors who get a reputation as hardliners don't get offered many directorships.

The question whether to give the board of directors the final say in derivative suits is related to the issue of antitakeover devices, discussed in the preceding section of this chapter. If those devices, which require approval by the board of directors, are contrary to the shareholders' best interests, this implies that the directors should not be allowed an unreviewable discretion to dismiss derivative suits, unless judicial oversight of the exercise of that discretion is completely incompetent.[1]

Should fiduciary obligations be waivable? Suppose a corporation has a choice between hiring a manager who promises to devote his entire efforts to the corporation for an annual salary of $250,000 and hiring the same manager for an annual salary of only $50,000 but allowing him to pursue certain business ventures on the side that might compete with the corporation. If the manager makes full disclosure of the conflict of interest and the directors hire him anyway, there is no breach of fiduciary duty, either in economics or in law; the parties are just cutting a different deal, in which the manager is a different kind of agent from a pure fiduciary, and receives a lower salary from his principal. Do you see an analogy to waiters receiving tips? How about policemen taking bribes?

§14.9   Corporate Squeeze-Outs and the Competition in Laxity

Not only has management a fiduciary duty to shareholders, but a shareholder majority has a fiduciary duty to the minority, leading to concern about the propriety of the corporate squeeze-out. Under Delaware corporation law the majority can force the minority to sell its shares to the corporation without having to show any business purpose for the action. Minority shareholders dissatisfied with the price offered by the majority for their shares are remitted to a judicial appraisal of the value of those shares, so that in effect the majority has a power of eminent domain with respect to the minority's shares.

Whether this coerced transfer ought to be allowed depends in part on whether there is any reasonable basis for a majority's wanting to squeeze out a minority. There is. A corporation's assets may be more valuable if the corporation's shares are held privately rather than registered under the securities laws and traded on one of the organized exchanges and therefore subject to extensive governmental and stock exchange regulations. Not only are these regulations costly to comply

§14.8   1. For a skeptical view of the efficacy of the derivative suit, bolstered by some empirical evidence, see Daniel R. Fischel & Michael J. Bradley, The Role of Liability Rules and the Derivative Suit in Corporate Law: A Theoretical and Empirical Analysis (forthcoming in Cornell Law Review).

with and a source of legal risks, but they make it difficult for a firm to operate in secrecy — which may prevent the firm from taking advantage of certain business opportunities. Moreover, going private produces a closer union of ownership and control, thus reducing agency costs. If a majority shareholder (or shareholders) therefore decides that his publicly traded corporation would be more valuable if it went private, he must persuade most of the other shareholders to surrender their shares. This might appear to be an easy negotiation since, by assumption, the corporation would be worth more private than public. But especially where the minority shareholders are numerous, there is a serious holdout problem of a sort that should be thoroughly familiar to the reader by now.

This is the economic rationale of the Delaware procedure. No showing of a justifiable business purpose for the squeeze-out would appear to be necessary; the appraisal remedy should assure that the "condemnees" receive the fair market value of their shares. The procedure would be fraudulent in an economic sense only if the Delaware courts refused to take their duty of appraisal seriously, which apparently is not the case.[1]

The concern with the squeeze-out is related to the prevailing notion that states compete to attract corporations by writing corporation charters that provide inadequate protections to creditors and to some or all shareholders, and that Delaware — the state of incorporation of some 40 percent of the companies listed on the New York Stock Exchange — has won the competition by the shocking laxity of its corporation law. There are perennial proposals to eliminate this competition by requiring the largest corporations to incorporate under a uniform federal corporation law. Yet minority shareholders themselves might be hurt by a provision that by giving them the power to block squeeze-outs could prevent corporations — and them as shareholders — from obtaining greater profits by going private.

Moreover, rational corporations would not incorporate in a state that provided no protection to creditors or shareholders. For if they did they would have to pay very high interest rates to creditors (or else have to agree in their loan agreements to elaborate protective provisions), and they would find it difficult to interest investors in their shares. Nor would a private corporation that wanted to go public but to offer only a minority of its outstanding shares to the investing public want to be governed by a squeeze-out provision that was unfair to minority

§14.9   1. An empirical study has found that squeeze-outs are not in fact exploitive of minority shareholders. See Harry DeAngelo, Linda DeAngelo & Edward M. Rice, Going Private: Minority Freezeouts and Stockholder Wealth, 27 J. Law & Econ. 367 (1984).

Should the going-concern value of the firm, as appraised, include the present value of the anticipated earnings increment from going private? Should the corporation reimburse the litigation expenses of the minority in the appraisal proceeding?

shareholders. Prospective shareholders would realize that, as minority shareholders in a corporation having a compact majority, they would be vulnerable to being squeezed out, and so they would not be willing to invest in a corporation that could expropriate their investment without compensation.[2]

A stronger conclusion is possible, is it not? Competition among states to attract corporations should result in optimal rules of corporate law.[3] A preemptive federal corporation law would carry no similar presumption of optimality (why not?).

§14.10   Insider Trading and the Problem of Entrepreneurial Reward

The most controversial application of fiduciary concepts is the rule that forbids insider trading — the practice by which a manager or other insider uses material information not yet disclosed to other shareholders or the outside world to make profits by trading in the firm's stock. The prohibition has been attacked on the ground that while in a sense a fraud on the other shareholders (who sell to the insider at a low price, or buy from him at a high price, only because he has failed to tell them what he knows), insider trading is an important incentive device.[1] This argument would be more forceful, however, applied to stock options, which create a genuine community of interest between management and the shareholders and make managerial compensation to a significant degree a function of the corporation's profitability. Insider trading does not reward efficient management as such. It rewards the possession of confidential information, whether favorable or unfavorable to the corporation's prospects. One can imagine cases where managers would have an incentive to take steps to accelerate the demise of their firm, possibly at significant social cost. Nor is the objection to insider trading met just by forbidding selling short on the basis of inside information. Managers would have an incentive to manipulate the disclosure of information about the firm in a manner calculated to produce sharp, if temporary, spurts in the price of the firm's stock. Their energies would be deflected from managing the firm so as to maximize its present worth to managing publicity about the firm so as to maximize the volatility of its stock.

---

2. Why would it be difficult to compensate them in advance for bearing this risk?

3. Is this proposition consistent with the criticism in §14.7 *supra* of the cumbersome procedures for corporate takeovers? With poison pills and other antitakeover devices?

§14.10   1. The classic exposition of this view is Henry G. Manne, Insider Trading and the Stock Market (1966).

Maybe this is not entirely a bad thing, though. A manager with firm-specific human capital may be risk averse, while the shareholders, holding diversified portfolios, may desire him to be risk neutral or even risk preferring. Allowing him to engage in insider trading encourages him to take risks, although the degree to which managers concentrate their financial investments in the stock of their corporation (and therefore underdiversify), and the lack of long-term employment contracts for managers, suggests that corporate managers are not in fact very risk averse.

Another objection to forbidding insider trading is that it reduces the efficiency of the stock market; the insider's decision to buy or sell provides information about the firm's prospects that permits the stock to be revalued accurately. But this advantage must be balanced against the loss of efficiency that is created when managers conceal information or disseminate misinformation, as they would have greater incentive to do if insider trading were permitted.

The costs of enforcing the rule against insider trading are high. Not only are concepts like insider and inside information slippery but devices for evasion of the rule abound. For example, insiders in different companies sometimes trade inside information about each other's companies. This loophole would be difficult to close — except by forbidding insiders and their families to trade in *any* corporate stock. There is the further problem that one can benefit from inside information by not making a trade that one would have made (to the benefit of one's trading partner) if not blessed with the information. The law cannot solve this problem.

These problems and the more fundamental one that insider trading is inherently easy to conceal may explain why corporations have made little effort on their own to ban the practice, leaving this function to public regulation instead. Otherwise their inaction would be powerful evidence that the practice was efficient. But if the probability of detection is so low that heavy penalties — which private companies are not allowed to impose (see §4.10 *supra*) — would be necessary to curtail the practice, it might not pay companies to try to curtail it.

§14.11 Managerial Discretion and the Corporation's Social Responsibilities

If there were no competition in product markets, no market for corporate control, no governance by directors and shareholders, and no law of fiduciary obligations, corporate managers would not be constrained to maximize corporate profits. They would maximize their own utility, presumably by skimming off the whole of the corporation's net income as salaries, or perhaps by liquidating the corporation and distributing its assets to themselves as bonuses. No one thinks that corporate managers are so unconstrained that they can behave in these ways, but some economists believe that in large, publicly held corporations managers are only weakly constrained, and do in fact choose maximands such as sales, or growth, or personal power that may bring them closer to personal utility maximizing than profit maximizing would bring them.[1] But are such maximands really distinct from profits? Suppose growth of corporate sales is what the managers wish to maximize.[2] To grow rapidly a firm must either generate large amounts of cash from current operations or obtain money from the capital markets. For either purpose it needs large profits (current or expected). Growth maximization thus blends insensibly into profit maximization. Now consider personal power as a maximand. The most powerful corporate executive is the one who controls a highly profitable enterprise. He is least likely to encounter criticism from shareholders, let alone a threat of a takeover. In addition, large profits generate capital (and enable additional capital to be obtained on favorable terms) that he can use for additional ventures. The debate over whether modern corporations are really profit maximizers may have little practical significance.

While some people criticize the modern corporation for not trying assiduously enough to maximize profits, others criticize it for making profit maximization its only goal. Corporations have long made charitable donations. Why, then, should they not devote a portion of their revenues to other social needs such as controlling pollution or training members of disadvantaged minorities?[3] But charitable donations are not a strong precedent; especially when they are made in the places where the corporation's plants or headquarters are located, they can

§14.11   1. See, e.g., William J. Baumol, Business Behavior, Value and Growth (rev. ed. 1967); Oliver E. Williamson, The Economics of Discretionary Behavior: Managerial Objectives in a Theory of the Firm (1967). Some studies have found, consistently with this position, that firms dominated or controlled by a single shareholder are consistently more profitable than firms with dispersed ownership (manager controlled), although only in cases where competition in the firm's product markets is weak. Other studies find no effect of owner control on firm performance. For illustrative recent studies on both sides of the question, see James L. Bothwell, Profitability, Risk, and the Separation of Ownership From Control, 28 J. Ind. Econ. 303 (1980); B.J. Campsey & R.F. DeMong, The Influence of Control on Financial Management: Further Evidence, 18 Rev. Bus. & Econ. Research 60 (1983); Robert L. Conn, Merger Pricing Policies by Owner-Controlled Versus Manager-Controlled Firms, 28 J. Indus. Econ. 427 (1980); Cynthia A. Glassman & Stephen A. Rhoades, Owner Vs. Manager Control Effects on Bank Performance, 62 Rev. Econ. & Stat. 263 (1980); Gerald P. Madden, The Separation of Ownership From Control and Investment Performance, 34 J. Econ. & Bus. 149 (1982); Sharon G. Levin & Stanford L. Levin, Ownership and Control of Large Industrial Firms: Some New Evidence, 18 Rev. Bus. & Econ. Research 37 (1983).

2. Why might they choose this maximand?

3. Compare the discussion of social investing by institutional investors in the next chapter (§15.7 infra).

usually be justified to shareholders as efficient advertising or public relations expenses.

There are economic reasons for questioning both the feasibility and appropriateness of major corporate commitments to social goals other than profit maximization. In competitive markets, a sustained commitment to any goal other than profitability will result in the firm's shrinking, quite possibly to nothing. The firm that channels profits into pollution control will not be able to recoup its losses by charging higher prices to its customers. The customers do not benefit as customers from such expenditures; more precisely, they benefit just as much from those expenditures if they purchase the lower-priced product of a competing firm that does not incur them. Thus the firm will have to defray the expenses of pollution control entirely out of its profits. But in a competitive market there are no corporate profits, in an economic sense, other than as a short-run consequence of uncertainty (the shareholders being the residual claimants of any excess of corporate revenues over costs). Accounting profits in a competitive market will, in the long run, tend to equality with the cost of attracting and retaining capital in the business. If these profits decline, the firm will, in all likelihood, eventually be forced out of business. True, if it has the usual upward-sloping marginal cost curve at its current output, it may be able to continue in business for a time by reducing its output — but not forever. At its lower output, it will not be able to pay the owners of whatever resources it uses in the production of its output as much as those owners could obtain elsewhere; monopsony is rarely a long-run game (see §10.9 *supra*). The only exception would be if the owners of these resources (who might be the firm's shareholders) were altruists who received utility from the firm's practice of social responsibility. How likely is that?

The prospects for social responsibility are only slightly brighter in monopolistic markets. If the firm has no rivals, it will be able to shift a part of the cost of pollution control equipment to its customers, but only a part. As shown in Figure 14.1, its profits will decline. To the outsider, the result is a reduction in monopoly profits (from *ABCD* to *EFGH*). To the shareholder, however, it is a loss. The price of a share of stock is equal to the present value of the anticipated future earnings of that share.[4] If the firm has a monopoly with a prospect of continued monopoly profits of a certain level, the share price will be higher than if a lower level of profits were expected. Suppose the firm decides to incur pollution control costs that had not been expected. Its anticipated future earnings are now lower, so the price of its shares will fall. This will be felt as a loss to the shareholder. In the usual case he will neither know nor care whether the corporation has monopoly profits. All he

---

4. Unless liquidation value is important. Another qualification that we need not worry about here, the volatility of the corporation's earnings, is discussed in §15.1 *infra*.

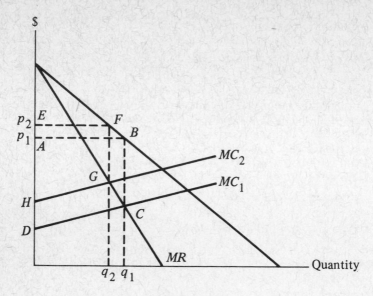

Figure 14.1

cares about is that the value of his holdings has declined. Managers will be reluctant to visit such consequences upon their shareholders.[5]

An additional consideration is that if there is competition to become a monopolist or to retain monopoly power, a monopolist may have no profits out of which to defray additional costs. The area *ABCD* in Figure 14.1 may represent not monopoly profits but the fixed costs of having obtained the monopoly, in which event any action that reduces that area will place the firm in danger of bankruptcy (see §9.3 *supra*).

Thus in neither a competitive nor a monopolistic market is it realistic to expect much voluntary effort to subordinate profit maximization to social responsibility. Is this regrettable? Maybe not. There are problems of:

(1) Suboptimization: The manager who tries both to produce for the market at lowest cost and to improve society is likely to do neither very well.

(2) Standards: How are managers to decide what is a politically or ethically correct stance?

5. Observe the tension between different social goals, here pollution abatement and competition. The more competitive a market is, the more difficult it will be to induce any seller to adopt costly pollution control equipment, for unless his rivals follow suit — and their incentive will be to hang back — he will be unable to recoup the costs of the equipment. Not only is a monopoly market less intractable to pollution control but the output of pollutants in such a market will normally be less. When a market is monopolized, production is reduced and with it the by-products of production such as pollution. But of course the production of substitute products will increase and may involve as much or more pollution (just as producing pollution control equipment creates pollution).

(3) Distributive justice: Is it proper that the costs of social responsibility be borne (mainly) by consumers in the form of higher product prices, a form of taxation that is usually regressive? [6] And

(4) Substitution: The exercise of social responsibility by the corporation reduces the ability of the shareholders to exercise social responsibility themselves, while profit maximization increases their wealth and with it the resources they can devote to political contributions, charitable gifts, and the like.

§14.12   Corporate Criminality

An important question about the social responsibility of corporations is whether the corporation should always obey the law or just do so when the expected punishment costs outweigh the expected benefits of violation. If expected punishment costs are set at the efficient level, the question answers itself; the corporation will violate the law only when it is efficient to do so. If those costs are set at too low a level, the corporation has an ethical dilemma. One resolution is for the corporation to proceed on the assumption that it is not its business to correct the shortcomings of the politico-legal system; its business is to maximize profits. Notice that if instead it takes the ethical approach, this will have the perverse result of concentrating corporate resources in the hands of the least ethical businessmen.

All this assumes that corporations should be liable for the crimes of their managers and other employees. This has sometimes been questioned. Recall that an important doctrine of strict liability in tort law is respondeat superior: the employer's liability, regardless of his personal fault, for torts committed by his employees within the scope of their employment. Employees usually are unable to pay substantial money judgments, and therefore tort liability has little effect on their incentives. If the employer is also liable, his incentives will be productively affected — he will take greater care in hiring, supervising, and where necessary firing employees. Since the criminal law does not rely primarily on monetary sanctions, since imposing criminal sanctions on the employer would duplicate tort sanctions, and particularly since criminal sanctions because they are so heavy can induce too much care, it is not surprising that the criminal law does not recognize respondeat superior.

The major exception, however, is the criminal liability of corporations.

6. This is because the poor spend (as distinct from saving) a larger fraction of their income than the rich. See §17.3 *infra.*

If a crime at least ostensibly in the corporation's behalf is committed or condoned at the directorial or managerial level of the corporation, the corporation is criminally liable, which means that the burden of the fine will be borne by the shareholders, who are analogous to employers of the people who did the actual deed. Since the corporation can only be fined, since corporations either are risk neutral or if risk averse at all are less so than individuals, and since corporate punishment carries with it little or no stigma (a corporation can act only through individuals, and there is a constant turnover of those individuals), corporate criminal punishment is less costly than individual punishment, so there is less danger of causing the shareholders to be too careful in hiring, supervising, and terminating directors (and through the board of directors, the managing employees).

Corporate criminal liability may have net benefits in these circumstances. Assume to begin with that the corporation's managers are perfect agents of the shareholders, so that any revenue obtained from criminal activity enures to the shareholders. Then if the shareholders bear no responsibility for a manager's crime they will have every incentive to hire managers willing to commit crimes on the corporation's behalf. Of course the shareholders will have to compensate the managers for the expected costs of criminal punishment, but given the limitations on the severity of criminal sanctions emphasized in Chapter 7, they may be able to do this and still have an expected gain from corporate criminal activity. Now assume that the managers are not perfect agents of the corporation — that in fact they use their corporate positions to facilitate criminal activity intended to enrich themselves. It is still the case that the corporation has supplied the facilities that they are using, and its owners should be given incentives to select and supervise managers more carefully.

The real puzzle about corporate criminal liability, it might seem, is why it has to be *criminal* liability. The entire rationale of the criminal law is that the optimal tort remedy is sometimes too large to be collectable, and how can that be a consideration with an entity that can only be subjected to monetary sanctions? But corporations are not infinitely solvent, and two of the fundamental techniques of criminal law are fully applicable even to an entity that cannot be punished other than by a nonstigmatizing fine — the use of public resources to raise the probability of punishment above what might be a very low level because of efforts taken to conceal criminal responsibility, and the punishment of preparatory activity in order to reduce the net expected gain from crime.

Since, however, corporate criminal punishment is purely monetary, it is not clear why the corporation should be entitled to the elaborate procedural safeguards of the criminal process. Those safeguards, as we shall see in Chapter 21, make economic sense only on the assumption that criminal punishments impose heavy costs rather than merely transferring money from the criminal to the state.

§14.13 The Closely Held Corporation

Our emphasis so far has been on the large, publicly held corporation. But much U.S. business is conducted in closely held corporations. The close corporation has few shareholders, most or even all of whom are active in management, and its securities are not publicly traded — and often are not saleable at all. The principal inducement to forming a close corporation, besides certain diminishing tax advantages, is to obtain perpetual existence and limited liability (though major creditors will often demand that the principals personally guarantee the corporation's debts).

Although many of the problems that we have considered in relation to publicly held corporations do not afflict the close corporation, it has economic problems of its own, above all the problem of bilateral monopoly. Suppose three people form a corporation to manufacture computer software and each receives one-third of the corporation's common stock. Should one of them later want to leave the business he probably could not sell his stock to anyone but his fellow shareholders (since any stranger who purchased would be afraid of being ganged up on by the other two); having him over a barrel, the other two might offer him very little for his stock. The solution is to enter into a buy-out agreement when the corporation is first formed. But now suppose the corporation needs more capital and thus wants to sell stock to a fourth person. The question will arise, whose interest shall be diluted to make way for this new shareholder? Each of the existing shareholders will naturally hang back from offering to dilute his own interest.

It might seem that these problems are easily solved by the principle of majority rule. But especially when there are very few electors, majority rule can be quite unstable. If two of the shareholders in our hypothetical close corporation try to gang up on the third, the third will have an incentive to try to pry loose one of the members of the ruling coalition. All this will make for high bargaining costs and also great initial uncertainty. A possible solution is to have a rule of unanimity for transactions that will alter the corporate structure, but of course this magnifies the bilateral-monopoly problem.

One thing the law can and generally does do is to allow the creators of close corporations to depart quite freely from the standard form contract that is the state's corporation law — to let the incorporators cut their own deal in a way that would not be feasible in a very large corporation, whose shareholders cannot be meaningfully consulted, in part because their stakes are too small to repay close study of the details of corporate governance. Another possibility recognized in the law is to allow a shareholder to petition for dissolution of the corporation if there is a deadlock that paralyzes corporate operations. Assuming that the assets of the corporation would be worth less upon dissolution, the prospect will increase the shareholders' incentive to negotiate their way out of their impasse. Of course, just as with divorce — which is an economic analog to the dissolution of a close corporation — it is very important that the grant of the petition be conditioned on proper compensation for the other shareholders. Otherwise the right to get dissolution would become a bargaining counter for whichever shareholder had the least to lose from dissolution.

Consider in this connection *In re Radom & Neidorff, Inc.*[1] Radom and his brother-in-law had a successful business in which the two were the only, and equal, shareholders. The brother-in-law died and his wife, Radom's sister, inherited his shares. Radom and his sister did not get along. Although the rules of the corporation required that both shareholders sign all checks, she refused to sign his salary check, on the ground that he was drawing excessive salary. Even though the corporation was profitable, the impasse between its shareholders prevented it from declaring dividends or even paying its debts. Radom petitioned for dissolution, but the court refused to grant it.

If the court had granted Radom's petition, the result would have been an effective expropriation of his sister's interest, as Radom, the active partner, could readily have continued the business under a new name. It would be like granting a unilateral divorce to a man whose wife had just finished putting him through medical school (see §5.3 *supra*). The court might have conditioned dissolution on Radom's paying his sister an equal share of the going-concern value of the corporation, rather than simply dividing its tangible assets with her. But maybe denying the petition served just as well; it put pressure (we do not know how effectively) on Radom to offer his sister a better price for her stock.

Does this analysis suggest a reason for the rule that a partnership dissolves on the death of any partner?

§14.14   Public Utility Regulation Revisited

In using terms like debt and equity in this chapter we have, as is usual in this book, been sticking closely to their legal meanings; and doing

§14.13   1. 307 N.Y. 1, 119 N.E.2d 563 (1954).

so can obscure interesting economic issues. Take the public utility, discussed in Chapter 12. Formally it is a conventional corporation with shareholders and bondholders. But to the extent that regulation succeeds in its formal aim of placing the utility's pricing on a cost-plus basis, it alters the real economic relationships within the firm. No longer is the stockholder the residual claimant. Changes in the fortunes of the company are registered in the price of its product or service rather than of its shares. The real equity holder is thus the consumer. This suggests the fundamental economic objection to cost-plus pricing. The consumer is in an even worse position than the stockholder to supervise management, since he has no voting power and cannot sell his shares; but in a system of cost-plus pricing, the consumer is the only person who has any economic incentive to supervise management, beyond the limited incentive that any long-term creditor has to keep tabs on the debtor. Of course there is no perfectly effective system of cost-plus pricing — and perhaps one reason there is not is that it would have fatal effects on incentives. But imperfect cost-plus pricing presumably has bad effects.

In a firm regulated as just described, should an unexpected capital loss (e.g., resulting from the abandonment of a half-built nuclear power plant) be chargeable to the rate payers in the form of higher rates or swallowed by the shareholders?

With the regulated firm we begin to move toward the world of noncorporate economic organizations — the union, the government agency, the joint venture, the charitable foundation. All can be analyzed within the general economic framework of this chapter but will receive little attention in this book (however, see §§18.4 and 23.3 *infra* for discussions of charitable foundations and administrative agencies, respectively).

Suggested Readings

1. Armen A. Alchian, The Basis of Some Recent Advances in the Theory of Management of the Firm, 14 J. Indus. Econ. 30 (1965).

2. Dennis W. Carlton & Daniel R. Fischel, The Regulation of Insider Trading, 35 Stan. L. Rev. 857 (1983).

3. Frank H. Easterbrook & Daniel R. Fischel, Corporate Control Transactions, 91 Yale L.J. 698 (1982).

4. David L. Engel, An Approach to Corporate Social Responsibility, 32 Stan. L. Rev. 1 (1979).

5. Daniel R. Fischel, The Corporate Governance Movement, 35 Vand. L. Rev. 1259 (1982).

6. Thomas H. Jackson, Bankruptcy, Non-Bankruptcy Entitlements, and the Creditors' Bargain, 91 Yale L.J. 857 (1982).

7. Michael C. Jensen & William H. Meckling, Theory of the Firm:

Managerial Behavior, Agency Costs and Ownership Structure, 3 J. Financial Econ. 305 (1976).

8. Saul Levmore, Monitors and Freeriders in Commercial and Corporate Settings, 92 Yale L.J. 49 (1982).

9. Richard A. Posner & Kenneth E. Scott, Economics of Corporation Law and Securities Regulation (1980).

10. Lawrence Shepard, Personal Failures and the Bankruptcy Reform Act of 1978, 27 J. Law & Econ. 419 (1984).

11. Michelle J. White, Bankruptcy Liquidation and Reorganization, in Handbook of Modern Finance, ch. 35 (Dennis E. Logue ed. 1984).

12. Symposium, The Economics of Bankruptcy Reform, 41 Law & Contemp. Prob. 1 (Autumn 1977).

13. Corporations and Private Property, 26 J. Law & Econ. 235 (1983).

Problems

1. Suppose that when the post office was still an executive department, you had been asked to design an appropriate organizational form for postal service. Would you propose a private corporation? A public corporation? Would either form be an advance over the executive department?

2. The Communications Satellite Corporation (Comsat) is a private corporation, but the President of the United States appoints several of the directors (a minority). Do you expect the firm to behave differently from other private corporations by virtue of these public directors?

3. Under German law, workers are entitled to elect some of the members of the counterpart (roughly speaking) to our board of directors. Would you consider this a worthwhile innovation in our corporate form? Cf. Detlev F. Vagts, Reforming the "Modern" Corporation: Perspectives From the German, 80 Harv. L. Rev. 23 (1966). Does your answer depend on what union leaders maximize (see problem 6)? Suppose workers were given shares of corporate stock: Would it make a difference whether it was stock of the company for which they worked or stock of some other company?

4. Discuss this proposition: Corporation law should be wholly permissive with respect to the allocation of power in the corporate charter between shareholders and directors.

5. How could a manager benefit from adoption of a corporate goal of sales maximization? Does your answer depend on whether the market for managers is competitive? Whether buyers in that market are well informed?

6. Would you expect the problem of managers' substituting their personal goals for organizational goals to be more acute in a university, labor union, or government regulatory agency than in a business firm? Can it be argued that the personal goals of the management of any

type of organization generally coincide with the goal of maximizing the present worth of the organization?

7. For purposes of applying the rule against insider trading, should "insider" include only corporate officers, their families, and people to whom they sell inside information, or should it include anyone who in fact possesses inside information? Why might the expanded definition be extremely costly, quite apart from administrative and enforcement costs?

8. The leveraged buy-out is a method of acquiring a corporation in which the purchaser borrows the money to make the purchase (in cash) from a bank or other lender and secures the loan with a pledge of the assets of the acquired firm. What is the effect on the risk borne by other creditors? What, if any, regulatory controls are indicated?

9. The Price-Anderson Act in effect places a limitation (of several hundred million dollars) on the tort liability of any manufacturer or owner of a nuclear reactor for the consequences of a reactor accident. What is the economic rationale of this limitation?

10. Would you expect racial discrimination to be more common in a publicly held or a close corporation? In a regulated or a nonregulated firm? Assume public policy is neutral on private discrimination. If stumped, see §27.3 *infra*.

CHAPTER 15

FINANCIAL MARKETS[1]

§15.1 Portfolio Design

This chapter takes a closer look at the market for corporate securities, particularly common stock; thus, our perspective shifts from the corporation itself to the shareholder and to the managers of investment portfolios — trustees, pension plans, banks, mutual funds, insurance companies, and individual investors.

A security has two dimensions: risk and expected return. The expected return is constructed by multiplying every possible return by the probability of its being the actual return, and then adding the results of the multiplication. Thus, if there is a 50 percent probability that a particular stock that sells for $10 today will be worth $12 one year from now, a 40 percent probability that it will be worth $15, and a 10 percent probability that it will be worth nothing, its expected return is $2 [(.5 × $2) + (.4 × $5) − (.1 × $10)].[1]

Although the expected return of a 100 percent chance of obtaining $10 is the same ($10) as the expected return of a 50 percent chance of obtaining $20 or a 1 percent chance of obtaining $1,000, we know that people are not indifferent to the various ways of combining uncertainty and outcomes to yield the same expected return. In choosing among securities that have identical expected returns, the risk-averse investor will always choose the one having the least uncertainty, unless the prices of the others fall, thereby increasing their expected returns, to compensate him for bearing greater risk.

---

1. See Robert C. Pozen, Financial Institutions: Cases, Materials and Problems in Investment Management (1978).

§15.1 1. The expected value is $12 [(.5 × $12) + (.4 × $15) + (.1 × $0)], and the current price is $10. To simplify analysis, it is assumed that no dividends will be paid. The expected return of a stock includes, of course, both appreciation and dividends.

The prevalence of risk aversion in investing is illustrated by the normally lower rate of return on bonds compared to the common stock of the same company. Suppose that the expected return (dividends plus appreciation) on a company's common stock is 10 percent. If investors were risk neutral — if they derived the same utility from identical expected returns however different in riskiness — they would demand 10 percent interest on the company's bonds as well. Although there is less risk to being a bondholder, since he has the cushion of the equity shareholders, who would have to be wiped out completely before he could lose his interest, this is offset in an expected-return sense by the fact that the bondholder cannot earn more than the interest rate specified in the bond. The difference between a company's bond interest rate and the (higher) expected return to owners of the common stock is simply the compensation to the stockholders for the extra risk that they bear.[2]

It follows that there should also be a systematic difference among the expected returns of common stocks that differ in their riskiness; but this point is subject to an important qualification. Suppose the expected per-share returns of two stocks (A and B) are the same, $2, but the expected return of A combines a 50 percent probability of no return and a 50 percent probability of a $4 return, while that of B combines a 50 percent probability of a −$6 return and a 50 percent probability of a $10 return. B is the riskier stock. But suppose there is a third stock (C) that, like B, has an expected return of $2 resulting from a combination of a 50 percent probability of a −$6 return and a 50 percent probability of a $10 return — only the fortunes of C and B are reciprocal, so that when B does well C does poorly and vice versa.[3] Then a *portfolio* composed of B and C will be less risky than one composed solely of A, even though A, considered in isolation, is less risky than either B or C. The investor will not insist on a risk premium for holding B and C in his portfolio. Their risks cancel; the portfolio itself is risk free.

This illustrates the fundamental point that portfolio design can alter the risk characteristics of securities considered individually. And in a world where the risks of different common stocks were negatively correlated, as in the preceding example, there would be few if any differential risk premiums among common stocks. Less obviously, this would also be true if the risks of common stocks, instead of being negatively correlated, were uncorrelated, i.e., random; for in a portfolio consisting of many different common stocks, the randomly distributed risks of the

2. But there is one risk that bondholders bear that shareholders do not (to the same extent). Can you guess what it is? If not, see §15.6 *infra*.
3. That is, there is a 50 percent probability that B will yield a −$6 return and C a $10 return, and a 50 percent probability that B will yield a $10 return and C a −$6 return.

securities in the portfolio would tend to cancel out, producing a riskless portfolio. By way of analogy, observe that while the risk of death faced by each individual in the country is nonnegligible, the country's death rate — the experience of the "portfolio" consisting of all individuals — is extremely stable. It is, in fact, much more stable than the stock market. This suggests that the risks of different common stocks are neither negatively correlated nor random but in fact have a strong positive correlation.

To the extent that the risk of one common stock is positively correlated with the risk of another — to the extent in other words that the stocks move together — a portfolio consisting of the two stocks will be as risky as the average of the two. And if in fact the risks of most stocks *are* positively correlated — as they plainly are, since otherwise the stock market as a whole (the market portfolio) would not fluctuate as dramatically as it does — it will be impossible to construct any portfolio that eliminates the risk associated with each component stock.

It is therefore necessary in portfolio design to distinguish between two components of risk. One is the component that is positively correlated with the risk of the whole flock of securities, the market. This risk cannot be eliminated simply by adding more and more securities. The other component is risk that is negatively correlated, or uncorrelated, with the risk of the market as a whole, and therefore can be diversified away. Diversification is an important goal of portfolio design because it allows one to get rid of a form of risk that is uncompensated (precisely because it can be eliminated at slight cost, through diversification) and so is a deadweight loss to the investor who is risk averse. But diversification does not eliminate all risk; some risk, as we have seen, is undiversifiable, and to bear that risk the investor (who we assume is risk averse) will insist on compensation. Because systematic risk — the risk component that is positively correlated with the risk of the market as a whole — is also compensated risk, the portfolio manager who wants to reduce it must be prepared to pay a price in the form of a lower expected return.[4]

Consider a security that rises on average 10 percent when the market rises 10 percent and falls 10 percent when the market falls 10 percent. Its systematic risk would be equal to that of the market. In the language of finance it would have a beta of 1, beta being the riskiness of the security in relation to that of the market as a whole. If the security rose 20 percent when the market rose 10 percent and fell 20 percent when the market fell 10 percent, its beta would be 2, and if it rose by only 5 percent when the market rose 10 percent and fell by 5 percent

---

4. Stocks that differ in systematic risk have been found empirically to differ in expected return, and the correlation between systematic risk and return has been found to be positive as expected. The evidence is summarized in James H. Lorie & Mary T. Hamilton, The Stock Market: Theories and Evidence, chs. 11-12 (1973).

when the market fell 10 percent, its beta would be .5.[5] Of course no
security moves in perfect lock step with the market. But we are not
interested in the portion of the stock's variance that is uncorrelated
with the movement of the market as a whole — that is diversifiable. While
a stock with a high beta will have a high expected return, a stock that
has a greater *overall* risk but a low beta — a stock that moves a lot but
not in step with the market as a whole — will have a low expected return.

Why do stocks differ in their riskiness, either systematic or random
(diversifiable)? Suppose a company has a high ratio of long-term debt
to equity in its capital structure. Then any decline in the firm's gross
revenues will hit the equity shareholders harder than if they did not
have a heavy fixed expense of debt service. The stock of such a firm
will tend to have a high beta because any development that affects adversely the business world (and hence stock market) as a whole, such
as an unanticipated fall in aggregate demand, will affect this company
even more adversely. Conversely, should the market as a whole rise
(because, say, of an increase in aggregate demand), this company will
tend to do better than firms having average amounts of debt, since
the costs of debt service are fixed. As an example now of diversifiable
risk, consider a company engaged in prospecting for uranium. Its fortunes will tend to rise and fall with its success or failure in locating
uranium deposits, an uncertain process but one unlikely to be systematically related to the movements of the stock market as a whole. It may
be a very risky stock but its beta may be no higher than average.

The foregoing analysis suggests that if we ignore the administrative
costs of diversification an investor's portfolio should be as widely diversified as possible in order to eliminate uncompensated risk. One measure
of a portfolio's diversification is its correlation with some broadly based
index of investment opportunities, such as Standard & Poor's 500 (S
& P 500). But because the movements of a portfolio consisting of only
32 (carefully selected) stocks would be 95 percent correlated with those
of the S & P 500, it is sometimes assumed that there is no point in
holding a larger portfolio, let alone one that would include 250 or 500
stocks. This is incorrect.[6] For example, although a portfolio consisting
of 50 stocks would have a correlation coefficient well above 90 percent,
its expected return would be a range of 4.5 percentage points on either
side of the expected return of the S & P 500, so that if one year the S
& P 500 rose by 10 percent, the 50 stock portfolio would be expected
to increase by anywhere between 5.5 and 14.5 percent. Even a portfolio

5. If the stock rose when the market fell, and vice versa — if in other words its beta
was negative — it would be highly prized by the risk-averse investor, since its inclusion
in the investor's portfolio would reduce the risk of the portfolio. This is stock C in the
example discussed earlier. But such examples are rare.

6. See James H. Lorie, Diversification: Old and New, J. Portfolio Management 25,
28 (Winter 1975).

consisting of 100 stocks would often differ by as much as 3 percent from the performance of the S & P 500; it takes a portfolio of 200 stocks to reduce this figure to 1 percent.[7] And even the S & P 500 is not completely diversified; it is a sample of only one type of asset traded on only one exchange.

A further implication of the analysis is that the portfolio manager, by his choice of the portfolio's beta (undiversifiable risk), will determine the investor's expected return. Thus he can vary that return without trying to pick winners. The best method of achieving the desired combination of risk and return is to adjust the proportions in which either relatively risk-free assets are included in the portfolio, or borrowed money is used to increase the portfolio's holdings. Consider as a reference point the hypothetical market portfolio consisting of all of the stocks traded on the stock market[8] weighted by the market value of each company whose stock is represented. The beta of the market portfolio is of course 1, and its expected return today probably about 12 percent.[9] Suppose the portfolio manager is willing to accept a lower return in exchange for less volatility, say half as much as that of the market as a whole. That is, he wants a portfolio that will have a beta of .5. How can he get this? He could simply cast out the riskier stocks in the market portfolio until the average beta of the stocks that remained was only .5. But in the process his portfolio would become less diversified, and as pointed out several times now risks avoidable by greater diversification are not compensated. The alternative is to add to the portfolio enough corporate or government bonds or other fixed-income securities, with their typically low betas, to pull the average beta of the portfolio down to .5. This has the advantage of not reducing the diversification of the common-stock component of the portfolio. It is a better strategy than replacing the common stocks in the portfolio with bonds having an average beta of .5, since the resulting portfolio would be badly underdiversified — it would, for example, be much more exposed to the risk of an unanticipated change in the inflation rate than a portfolio that included common stocks, whose earnings are not fixed in nominal dollar terms. A related point is that bonds added to a common-stock portfolio in order to reduce the portfolio's beta should be selected with a view toward maintaining the overall diversification

7. Ibid. These numbers depend on precisely how the sample is constructed. It may be possible to get better results using smaller samples.

8. There is, of course, more than one stock market. But since roughly two-thirds by value of all stocks publicly traded in the United States are listed on the New York Stock Exchange (NYSE), that exchange provides a pretty good proxy for the (United States) stock market as a whole; so we shall consider our hypothetical market portfolio to be limited to NYSE stocks.

9. Historically, the expected return to common stocks has been on average about 3 percentage points above the long-term corporate bond rate, which at this writing is roughly 9 percent.

of the portfolio. It would not do to hold a portfolio that consisted of $1 million in the shares of a market fund (i.e., a fund holding the market portfolio or some reasonable approximation thereto) and $1 million in the bonds of one company.

The investor who wants a higher expected return than that of the market as a whole can obtain it by borrowing money to buy additional securities for the portfolio. Suppose an investor of $500,000 of his own money borrows another $500,000, thus giving him $1 million in assets, which he invests in a fund holding the market portfolio; he pays 9 percent interest on the loan; and the expected return on the market portfolio is 12 percent. His expected rate of return, which is equal to the expected return of the portfolio (.12 × $1 million = $120,000) minus his interest costs (.09 × $500,000 = $45,000), divided by his personal investment, will be 15 percent ($120,000 − $45,000 = $75,000 divided by $500,000 = .15). This is higher than the market rate; but the beta of the portfolio is higher than the market's beta. If, for example, the market declined by 10 percent, the portfolio would be worth only $900,000 (we can ignore the interest cost of the borrowed money), and since the investor would still owe $500,000 to the lender his net assets would be only $400,000, 20 percent less than before the decline of the market. The portfolio's beta is thus 2. Although the investor could have gotten the same "play" by casting out the less risky stocks from the market portfolio until the average beta of the remaining stocks was 2, in doing so he would have been sacrificing diversification.[10]

§15.2 Diversification, Leverage, and the Debt-Equity Ratio

The analysis in the previous section is helpful in appraising the argument that the existence of conglomerate corporations — corporations whose divisions or subsidiaries operate in unrelated markets, thus seemingly condemning the corporation to diseconomies of underspecialization — is due to the fact that the conglomerate form overcomes certain inefficiencies in the financial structures of many firms. Conglomerates are highly diversified, and it has been argued that a highly diversified firm, by reducing risk to investors, enables capital to be acquired at lower cost than if the firm were not diversified. But this overlooks the fact that the individual shareholder whose portfolio consists of shares in

---

10. For a skeptical view of the standard finance model (the capital asset pricing model) presented in this section, see John G. Cragg & Burton G. Malkiel, Expectations and the Structure of Share Prices (1982).

firms that are not diversified but that operate in unrelated markets enjoys the same benefits of diversification that he would if those firms were consolidated into a single conglomerate. What is important to an investor is the diversification of his portfolio — not whether individual stocks are diversified.

A second point regarding financial structure is that many firms bought by conglomerate corporations have low debt-equity ratios and that the conglomerate, by increasing [this] ratio, can increase the return to the shareholders. This point is [............] first in the argument that the conglomerate's d [........................] the risks associated with high debt [................................] of shareholders' equity [..............................] ratio.[1]

Consider a hypotheti [.....................] stock outstanding, no [.....................] million a year. Since th [.....................] of its expected income [.....................] multiple of $3 millior [.....................] the multiple is 10. T [.....................] price of a share of st [.....................] $3, and the price-ear [.....................] million at 6 percent [.....................] f of the outstanding [.....................] s. The operating net [.....................] st expense of $900,0([.....................] 2.1 million, or $4.20 [.....................] om 1 million to 500,0([.....................] are of stock will be w [.....................] will be $21 million. [.....................] llion ($21 million equi [.....................] quity ratio has create [.....................] st be wrong. The ne [.....................] ginally because they ge [.....................] Noth- ing has happen [.....................] would a purchaser n[.....................]

He would [.....................] ion that the price-ear[.....................] the firm has. We know that the a[......] [.....................] ystematic risk to the shareholder (why systematic?). [.....................] investors are risk averse, the stock's price-earnings ratio will fan. [..]eed, since the productive value of the firm's assets is unaffected by how the firm chooses to arrange the components of its capital structure, we would

§15.2 1. As shown in Franco Modigliani & Merton H. Miller, The Cost of Capital, Corporation Finance, and the Theory of Finance, 48 Am. Econ. Rev. 261 (1958).

expect the firm's price-earnings ratio to fall to 7.14, the ratio at which the value of the firm is unchanged from before. There is no reason for the purchaser of a firm to pay a premium because its capital structure contains leverage, even if he prefers the high expected return of a high-risk investment. He can create his preferred debt-equity ratio by purchasing some of the stock with borrowed money. Or he can pair his purchase with investing in highly levered or otherwise highly risky firms.

The purity of the analysis is impaired by the differential tax treatment of interest and earnings. The government subsidizes the raising of capital through borrowing by permitting corporations to deduct the cost of borrowed capital, but not of equity, from their taxable income. In addition, when a firm's debt-equity ratio is very high, the risks both to the holders of debt and to the shareholders may become so great that the firm will be unable to attract either sort of investor. The amount of leverage in its capital structure is therefore not a matter of complete indifference to the shareholder (see also §14.4 *supra*); but it seems unlikely that this factor could explain many conglomerate mergers.[2]

§15.3   Why Do Corporations Buy Insurance?

If the stockholders of a corporation can diversify away the nonsystematic risk component of the corporation's expected earnings stream, why do we observe that most corporations, large as well as small, publicly held as well as closely held, carry insurance against losses as a result of tort suits, fire, theft by employees, and other adverse contingencies? Why are the shareholders of a publicly held corporation not adequately insured just by virture of holding diversified portfolios? Here are some possible answers:

1. Managers are risk averse and have too much of their wealth (including human capital) locked into the corporation to be able to diversify other than by insuring the corporation (why would personal wealth insurance not be a feasible alternative?). On this view, is the purchase of corporate insurance in the stockholders' interest, or is it another example of an agency cost?

2. The loading (administrative) cost of the insurance may be less than the expected deadweight cost of bankruptcy. In other words, the bankruptcy that insurance wards off, discounted by the probability of

---

2. An alternative explanation, based on the market for corporate control discussed in the last chapter, points out that conglomerate mergers did not become common until the tightening in the 1960s of the antitrust prohibitions against horizontal and vertical mergers. Do you get the point? Another alternative is that managers are risk averse and are not perfect agents of the shareholders. For more on conglomerates see §15.7 *infra*.

bankruptcy if the corporation is not insured, would cost more in real resources consumed (in legal fees, trustee's fees, and above all in lost production caused by the less efficient management of a firm that is operating under judicial control) than the amount by which the insurance premium exceeds the expected pay-out.

3. Insurance companies are specialists in monitoring the defense of certain claims. For example, if a corporation that does not carry liability insurance is sued under the doctrine of respondeat superior for an accident by one of its employees, it will have to go out and find a law firm to defend the tort action, and it will have to monitor the law firm's performance. All this will be difficult if the corporation does not have many tort claims against it. As a specialist in supervising the defense of tort claims, a liability insurance company may be able to arrange for the defense of such a claim at lower cost and with better prospects of success than the corporation itself could do. This analysis implies — and one observes — that corporations that encounter repetitive tort claims, such as railroads, frequently self-insure.

§15.4   Stock Picking and the Efficient-Market Hypothesis

In focusing on portfolio design and capital structure, we may seem to have lost sight of the most straightforward investment strategy — the purchase of undervalued, and sale of overvalued, securities — and, the same thing really (why?), the timing of market turns. But is this really an efficient strategy? To begin with, it is expensive. There are the research costs incurred in selecting specific securities to include in, or exclude from, the portfolio, the transaction costs incurred in buying and selling shares in accordance with the changing results of the securities analysis, and the sacrifice of diversification entailed by holding substantially less than the market portfolio (stock picking implies selectivity, diversification inclusiveness). For all these costs to be worthwhile stock picking must generate larger benefits, in the form of a higher expected return, than one could expect to receive from the market portfolio adjusted to impose the same level of systematic risk as the portfolio created by stock picking.[1]

It may seem virtually self-evident that a skilled investor, who conducts

---

§15.4   1. The qualification is vital: If the result of stock picking is to create a portfolio that has a beta higher than 1, the portfolio will have a higher expected return than the market portfolio. But this will be due not to the portfolio manager's skill as a stock picker but to the higher beta of his portfolio, which could have been achieved without any stock picking — simply by levering the market portfolio up to the same beta.

careful research into the conditions and prospects of particular companies and of the economy as a whole, will earn a higher return (always correcting for differences in systematic risk) than the investor who simply buys the market, blindly investing in the entire stock market list and never selling a stock when its prospects begin to sour. But since the value of a stock is a function of its anticipated earnings and therefore depends largely on events occurring in the future, it will often be impossible to determine whether a stock is undervalued at its current price without knowing what the future holds, and very few people are good at predicting the future. Although a stock may be undervalued because of some characteristic of the company (or of its competitors, suppliers, customers, political environment, etc.) that exists today but is not widely known or correctly understood, the problem here is that the underlying information is in the public domain,[2] meaning that it is equally available to all security analysts. The only way of making money from such information is to interpret it better than the other analysts. This is not a promising method of outperforming the market. It requires both that the analyst interpret publicly available information differently from the average opinion of the analyst community and that his deviant interpretations be correct substantially more often than they are incorrect (why substantially?).

Confirming these theoretical points, studies of the mutual fund industry have found that mutual funds, despite their extensive employment of security analysts and portfolio managers for the purpose of outperforming the market, fail to do so.[3] They do no better than the blind market portfolio. Although it has been argued that the proper comparison is not between all mutual funds and the market but between the most successful mutual funds and the market, the studies suggest that there are no consistently successful mutual funds. Some enjoy shorter or longer runs of success, but generally the degree of success observed is no greater than one would expect if luck, not skill, is indeed the only factor determining the fund's performance.

The studies support an even stronger conclusion: When brokerage costs and management fees are taken into account, the average mutual or common trust fund yields a lower net return than a broadly based market index such as the S & P 500.[4] This comparison was long derided

---

2. If it is not in the public domain — if it is insider information — and material, it cannot lawfully be used, at least by those most likely to be privy to it, in buying or selling stock (see §14.7 *supra*). Presumably the law has some deterrent effect.

3. The studies are summarized in James H. Lorie & Mary T. Hamilton, §15.1 *supra*, note 4, at ch. 4. See also R.A. Brealey, An Introduction to Risk and Return from Common Stocks, ch. 3 (2d ed. 1983). The empirical research has concentrated on mutual funds because they are required by federal law to report in detail on their performance; but all indications are that common trust funds, pension funds, and other institutional investors likewise fail to systematically outperform the market portfolio.

4. See, e.g., Michael C. Jensen, Risk, The Pricing of Capital Assets, and the Evaluation of Investment Portfolios, 42 J. Bus. 167 (1969).

on the ground that the S & P 500 is a hypothetical fund and hence has no administrative costs. Now that there are some real market-matching funds in operation (see §15.6 *infra*), it is possible to evaluate — and reject — this criticism. The administrative costs of a market fund turn out to be so low (on a $500 million portfolio, perhaps 10 percent of the costs of conventional management) that the expected return of a properly constructed market fund is only trivially different from that of the S & P 500.

§15.5 Monopoly Again

In Chapter 9 we noted the argument of some economists that monopoly impairs the incentive to reduce input costs and to innovate; as a distinguished English economist once put it, "the best of all monopoly profits is a quiet life."[1] Neither he nor later economists have laid a solid theoretical or empirical foundation for this proposition (see §9.3 *supra*); and here is a theoretical reason against it. As soon as a monopoly is anticipated, the price of the firm's common stock will increase as a method of discounting the expected monopoly profits until the ratio of expected earnings to market price is just equal to the normal rate of return of stocks in the firm's risk class. If thereafter the managers of the firm become indolent, the price of the stock will fall relative to other stocks — unless the indolence was anticipated! In that case, shareholders may not be disappointed — but the firm will be an attractive target for a takeover bid by someone who thinks he can increase the firm's monopoly profits by reducing its costs.

Capital market theory can help solve the problem of controlling regulated monopolists' profits. The problem is complicated by the difficulty of ascertaining the true cost of equity capital, a difficulty that is due in turn to the absence of a directly observable price. The present regulatory approach is a largely circular one of basing the permitted rate of return on the rates of return of other regulated companies. If the regulators were instead to begin by measuring the beta of the regulated firm's stock, they could fix a level of permitted earnings such that the expected return to the firm's investors was equal to that of investors in nonregulated firms of the same beta. This would be the true cost to the regulated firm of attracting equity capital without diluting the value of the shares held by existing shareholders. (Does it matter that regulation itself may have reduced the stock's volatility?)

§15.5 1. J.R. Hicks, Annual Survey of Economic Theory: The Theory of Monopoly, 3 Econometrica 1, 8 (1935).

Capital market theory might also be useful in deflecting regulatory agencies (and their critics) from what are largely spurious issues, such as the optimum debt-equity ratio. In the case of a regulated firm with a low ratio, it is often argued that if only the firm would increase the ratio, its cost of capital would decline — since the interest rate is lower than the return on common stock — and its prices could be reduced. But this is equivalent to arguing that regulated firms should be more highly leveraged. Since debt increases the volatility of equity, a firm that increased the proportion of debt in its capital structure would experience an increase in the cost of its equity capital. There is no reason to think that the overall cost of capital would be lower — or for that matter higher — with a higher debt-equity ratio (see §15.2 *supra*).

§15.6 Trust Investment Law and Market Funds

The basic principle of the extensive body of law on the trustee's duties in managing trust funds is that he must act prudently and cautiously with the primary purpose of preserving the principal of the trust. The assumption is that most trust beneficiaries are highly risk averse and therefore prefer to receive a lower expected return in exchange for taking fewer risks. The assumption is reasonable with regard to many, though not all, trusts. If the beneficiaries are a widow and minor children who have no other income, and limited earning power, and as a result of risky investments of the principal the trust income declines sharply, the position of the beneficiaries may become extremely awkward. Risky investments are more attractive to people who have regular salaries or other stable sources of basic income that protect their standard of living if the investments go sour — but of course some trust beneficiaries are in this position. The creator of a trust who desires the trustee to make risky investments can so provide by appropriate language in the trust instrument. The prudent man rule serves the now familiar common law function of reducing transaction costs by implying a provision in every instrument (unless there is language to the contrary) that most parties would otherwise incorporate by express language.

While the general principle underlying the prudent man rule makes economic sense, some of the traditional implementing rules, in particular that which applies the standard to individual investments rather than to the portfolio as a whole, do not. However well the portfolio performs, the trustee may be held accountable for the poor showing of one of the investments in the portfolio if he failed to verify the soundness of that investment before making it. This approach has three bad consequences:

1. Trustees are induced to spend time and money in investigating the prospects of individual securities even though the costs of search and execution involved in identifying and acquiring undervalued securities to buy and in continuously reviewing one's portfolio for overvalued securities to sell will, according to the economic analysis of stock picking, almost always exceed the benefits.

2. Trustees are deterred from investing in perfectly good securities merely because the company that issued them has poor earnings prospects. There is no presumption in economic theory that the stock prices of declining or even of bankrupt firms are typically overvalued. Those prices will be bid down to the point where the company's expected earnings (whatever they may be) will yield the investor a normal return on his investment for securities with the stock's volatility, which may be low.[1] Yet a trustee who knowingly bought the shares of a bankrupt firm might be considered to have acted imprudently.

3. The investment-by-investment application of the prudent man rule induces trustees to hold underdiversified portfolios. If the trustee is to investigate every stock that he buys and watch it closely after purchase, the number of different stocks that he can hold in the portfolio will be limited. The consequent underdiversification of the portfolio will expose the beneficiary of the trust to uncompensated risk that could have been diversified away at low cost. Inconsistently, the law requires trustees to diversify their portfolios; the cases do not specify the degree of diversification that is required.

One manifestation of the law's traditional preoccupation with care in the selection of individual investments is the concept, embodied in many state statutes and judicial decisions, that whole categories of investments are unlawful for a trustee unless expressly permitted to him in the trust instrument. For a long time trustees were not permitted to invest in common stocks. This naturally led them to invest heavily in bonds. What was overlooked was that a long-term bond exposes the owner to a risk that he would avoid if he invested in stock (or a short-term debt instrument): The risk that inflation will increase. A bond is perfectly good protection against the expected rate of inflation, for the interest rate fixed in the bond will include that rate as one component. But should the inflation rate unexpectedly increase during the term of the bond, the resulting reduction in the real (net of inflation) value of the bond will be borne entirely by the bondholder.[2] A risk-averse investor would not want to bear such a risk and does not have to.

§15.6   1. The firm may have a positive value even if its present earnings are zero or negative. Its assets may have salvage value, or it may have the prospect of earnings in the future.

2. The inflation will lead to an increase in the market rate of interest. See §6.13 *supra.* The price of the bond will be bid down until the interest it pays yields the market rate of interest on the price of the bond. Those who bought the bond when the market rate of interest was lower will therefore suffer a capital loss.

Even today the law in some states limits the authority of trustees to purchase shares in mutual funds. Yet where the assets of a trust are small it may be impossible to achieve reasonable diversification other than by purchasing shares in a mutual fund. The basis of the rule limiting the trustee's authority in this respect is the notion that by purchasing mutual fund shares the trustee abdicates to the mutual fund's managers his key responsibility of selecting the investments for the trust. This notion rests on the false premise that a trustee can by careful selection outperform the market by a margin greater than the expenses of trying to do so.

With the law so out of phase with economic reality, we would predict that the draftsmen of trust instruments would commonly include language waiving the limitations that are imposed by trust law in the absence of appropriate language. And indeed most current trust instruments waive the detailed limitations of trust law and vest broad discretion in the trustee — hence the paucity in recent years of reported litigation involving the investment duties of trustees.

Trust investment law has acquired a new importance as a result of the enactment of the Employees Retirement Income Security Act (ERISA), which both imposes the prudent man rule on pension fund managers and forbids the rule to be waived. And there are signs that modern capital markets theory is altering the traditional contours of trust investment law, leading to less emphasis on the evaluation of individual securities and more on the performance of the portfolio and on the duty to diversity. For example, the current regulations of the Department of Labor concerning the investment duties of ERISA fiduciaries define the statute's prudent man rule in a fashion thoroughly consistent with modern capital markets theory, stressing portfolio design and diversification and not requiring that the fiduciary watch each security in the portfolio. These regulations and other portents of legal receptivity to modern capital markets theory (another example of the law's responsiveness to economics) have emboldened a number of trustees to place significant portions of the funds entrusted to them in market funds. A typical market fund buys and holds a 200 to 500 stock portfolio designed to match the performance of the New York Stock Exchange (or perhaps some weighted average of domestic and foreign securities markets), performing no securities analysis and trading only insofar as necessary to maintain diversification, handle redemptions, and invest its shareholders' cash.

The market fund concept prompts the following questions: First, what if every investor adopted the passive strategy implied by the concept? Then the market would cease to be efficient (why?). But long before this happened, some investors would abandon the passive strategy to take advantage of the opportunities, which today are rare, for obtaining positive profits from securities analysis and active trading. How many active traders are necessary to keep the market efficient is a difficult question (need it be answered?). But observation of other markets, for example the housing market, where transactions are relatively infrequent and the products traded are heterogeneous (no two houses are as alike as two shares of the same class of the same company's stock), suggests that the stock market would remain efficient even if most investors were passive.

A second question about market funds concerns their implications for the effective working of the market for corporate control discussed in the last chapter and for corporate governance generally. If a majority of a corporation's shareholders were passive investors who never sold their shares when someone offered a high price for them — instead assuming that their holdings were always correctly valued at the current (and now higher) price — how would it ever be possible to take over a corporation through the tender offer route or even by a proxy fight? (What would a market fund do with the proxy materials it received?) Is this a serious potential problem? If it is, how could it be solved consistently with the basic assumptions of modern capital market theory?

§15.7   Social Investing by Trustees

Some corporations do things that seem immoral to influential segments of our society — such as doing business in the Republic of South Africa. The antagonists of such corporations sometimes urge investors not to buy or keep their stock. If the investor is an individual, his decision whether or not to heed this call is a purely personal one, raising no interesting issues of legal policy. But suppose the investor is the manager of a pension trust or university endowment and has the obligations of a trustee to the beneficiaries of the investment funds that he manages. Should he be permitted to practice "socially responsible" investing, as by casting out of his portfolio the securities of companies that do business in South Africa or that have records of sexual or racial discrimination, or in the case of a pension fund for city employees, by overinvesting (from the standpoint of normal investing principles) in the city's own securities?[1]

We shall ignore the ethical issues and consider only the economic consequences of social investing. First, the fund will incur administrative expenses, akin to those incurred by stock pickers, in identifying firms or government units whose securities will be excluded from or overincluded in the portfolio; this will lower the net return to the fund's benefi-

---

§15.7   1. For a recent and wide-ranging debate on the issue, see Disinvestment: Is It Legal? Is It Moral? Is It Productive? An Analysis of Politicizing Investment Decisions (Natl. Legal Center for the Public Interest 1985).

ciaries. Second, unless the favored and disfavored firms (or other entities) are a random draw from the universe of possible investments, and also constitute in the aggregate only a small fraction of all investment opportunities, social investing will result in underdiversification of the investor's portfolio. Since, as stressed throughout this chapter, an investor is not compensated for holding a less than optimally diversified portfolio, the expected return of the portfolio will not rise to compensate the beneficiaries for bearing greater risk.

Notice, however, that the theory of finance does not predict that adopting principles of social investing will result in a reduction in the expected return to the investor, except by the amount of the extra administrative costs that are incurred. The risk-adjusted return will be lower if there is underdiversification, but the return (before administrative expense), ignoring risk, will not be. It does not matter whether the favored or disfavored firms are more or less profitable than average; their stock prices will be bid up or down so that all represent an equally good investment, judged on an investment-by-investment rather than portfolio basis, to the risk-averse investor.

Since social investors are not likely to spend a lot of money on deciding which securities to cast out (or overinclude in) their portfolios, the principal economic consequence of social investing is underdiversification. This is only a minor problem if just a few corporations are proscribed, but a serious one if many are proscribed.[2] It may be a particularly serious problem in local-preference social investing. If cities in distressed areas of the country are finding it difficult to meet their obligations to contribute money to pension funds of city employees, the fund trustees may be pressured to help out the city by buying the city's securities. Yielding to the pressure may, however, cause significant underdiversification — too many of the pension fund's eggs in one very risky basket. But this is not a complete analysis. There is a tradeoff between underdiversification and what may be reduced pension contributions if the fund does not make a gesture of support to the city by buying more of the city's securities than financial theory indicates it should.

§15.8   The Regulation of the Securities Markets [1]

We have thus far treated the efficiency of the securities markets as a given. But the extensive regulation of these markets by the Securities

2. See Wayne H. Wagner, Allen Emkin, & Richard L. Dixon, South African Divestment: The Investment Issues, Financial Analysts J. (Nov.–Dec. 1984), at 14.

§15.8 1. For legal background, see Louis Loss, Fundamentals of Securities Regulation (1983).

and Exchange Commission is founded on the premise that without such regulation they would not function satisfactorily.

Securities regulation is rooted in part in a misconception about the great depression of the 1930s. It was natural to think that the 1929 stock market crash must have been the result of fraud, speculative fever, and other abuses and in turn a cause of the depression: *post hoc ergo propter hoc.* But a precipitous decline in stock prices is much more likely to result from the expectation of a decline in economic activity than to cause the decline.[2] This in turn suggests that the crash probably was not the result of abuses in the securities markets but was instead the anticipation of the depression. If this is right, one is entitled to be skeptical about aspects of securities regulation that are designed to prevent another 1929-type crash, such as the requirement that new issues of stock may be sold only by means of a prospectus which must be submitted to the SEC in advance for review to make sure it contains all the information (including adverse information) that the SEC deems material to investors.

Capital markets are competitive, and competitive markets generate without government prodding information about the products sold. Although as we know from Chapter 4 consumer product information is not always complete or accurate, it is plausible to expect the capital markets to generate abundant and, on the whole, accurate information about new issues in view of the presence of

  (1) sophisticated middlemen — the underwriters who market new issues — between issuer and purchaser;
  (2) sophisticated purchasers such as trust companies, mutual funds, and pension funds; and
  (3) the many financial analysts employed by brokerage firms and by independent investment advisory services.

Written in a forbidding legal and accounting jargon, prospectuses are of no direct value to the unsophisticated stock purchaser. Nor is it obvious that the disclosure requirements imposed by the SEC in fact increase the flow of information. By limiting selling efforts to the prospectus, and by taking a restrictive view of what may properly be included in a prospectus (for example, the SEC long was hostile to earnings projections), the SEC has limited the amount of information communicated by issuers.

In a famous study, George Stigler showed that before the registration system was initiated in 1933 purchasers of new issues fared, on average, no worse than purchasers of new issues today.[3] Although the details of the study are controversial, the basic conclusion — that the effect

2. But the crash may have contributed to its severity. See Robert J. Gordon & James A. Wilcox, Monetarist Interpretations of the Great Depression: An Evaluation and Critique, in The Great Depression Revisited 49, 80 (Karl Brunner ed. 1981).

3. George J. Stigler, Public Regulation of the Securities Market, 37 J. Bus. 117 (1964).

of regulation on new issues does not help investors — is now widely accepted by economists.[4]

Another major thrust of securities law is to reduce speculation in stock. Yet in stock trading as elsewhere, speculation serves the salutary purpose of enabling the rapid adjustment of prices to current values. The speculator is the eager searcher for undervalued and overvalued securities. The information that he uncovers diffuses rapidly throughout the market (the rapidity with which information spreads in the stock market is the principal reason why it is so hard to outperform the market consistently), enabling other traders to adjust swiftly to the changed conditions that he has discovered.[5]

The law discriminates against people who speculate on a downturn in the market. It does this for example by forbidding shares to be sold short at a price lower than the most recent price at which the share has traded. The legal attitude resembles the ancient practice of punishing a bearer of bad tidings. One who sells a stock short — agrees to deliver at the current market price, hoping the price of the stock will fall so that he can buy it when delivery is due for less than he has sold it — will lose money unless he has correctly predicted a decline in the price of the stock. But he cannot bring about that decline. The legal attitude toward short selling is especially odd in view of the concern with avoiding panics. To the extent that short selling is discouraged, market declines are likely to be more rather than less precipitous. Short sales are a signal that some traders believe the stock being sold short is overvalued. The signal facilitates prompt, continuous adjustment to the conditions depressing the stock's price.

Another effort to reduce speculation is the limitation on the purchase of stock on margin, in other words on the amount of leverage that may be employed in the purchase of stocks. The effort is unlikely to succeed. Leverage is just one way of increasing the risk and expected return of a purchase. An alternative that the margin limitation does not reach is to hold a portfolio of high-risk securities. A demand for such securities will lead corporations to increase the amount of leverage in their capital structures, as that will increase the beta of their stock. The result will be more risk than if margin were unregulated (why?).

Federal securities law is also a vehicle for giving the federal courts jurisdiction over outright securities frauds. The SEC's Rule 10b-5, which has been interpreted to create a right to sue for damages, forbids fraud in buying or selling securities and thus enables investors to litigate fraud claims in federal court. For this reason, and also because of the registra-

---

4. For a summary of the literature and additional evidence, see George J. Benston, Corporate Financial Disclosure in the UK and the USA (1976).

5. Speculators do not even earn (on average) high returns — society thus buys their valuable services cheap. See Lester G. Telser, Why There Are Organized Future Markets, 24 J. Law & Econ. 1, 4 n.3 (1981).

tion requirement, it is vital to know what counts as a security and what does not. Suppose an insurance company sells an annuity that guarantees the annuitant a minimum return on his investment, but whether he gets more depends on the performance of the securities portfolio in which the insurance company invests his contributions. Is the annuity a security? It is (the courts hold), because the investor's return is to a significant degree a function of the performance of what incontestably are securities.

Now suppose that the owner of a business that happens to be incorporated sells his business to another corporation. The buyer buys all the stock en route to merging the acquired firm into it. If the buyer thinks that the seller made misrepresentations in the sale, can he sue under Rule 10b-5 as the victim of a securities fraud? He can. This result makes little economic sense. Although again the buyer incontestably is buying securities, he is not in need of the protections that the securities laws extend to persons assumed to be passive investors, who do not have the stake or (often) the expertise that would motivate or make it easy for them to protect themselves at reasonable cost. But no one buys the whole of a business without careful investigation. Such a buyer needs no legal protections beyond those that the common law of fraud gives him.

Let us turn to problems of damages in securities fraud cases. Under conventional fraud principles a misrepresentation, to be actionable, must actually have been relied on by the allegedly defrauded person; otherwise the fraud is harmless. Suppose therefore that a misrepresentation in a prospectus for a new issue of stock leads brokers who read the prospectus to buy large amounts of the stock and to recommend that their customers do likewise. As a result the price rises. Suppose someone who has no knowledge of the prospectus — in fact no idea why the stock's price has risen — buys it at its higher price. Later the fraud is unmasked and the price falls. Should this someone be allowed to sue the issuer? The courts are coming around to the view that he should be; and this is the economically correct result. The fraud in effect is impounded in the market price, and the person who buys without knowledge of the prospectus is acting on false information to the same extent as those who buy with knowledge.

But now consider what the measure of damages should be. At first blush it might seem obvious: It should be the losses of those who bought at a price inflated by the false prospectus, after eliminating (by means of the capital pricing asset model sketched in §15.1 *supra*) other possible causes of the drop in the stock's price. But what about innocent people who profited from the fraud? Suppose that a person misled by the prospectus buys the stock as its price is rising but unloads it at a profit before the bubble bursts. Unless he is forced to disgorge his profit, the corporation that issued the misleading prospectus will be made to pay damages in excess of the harm caused to defrauded buyers. As there is no legal or practical basis for forcing restitution by those share-holders who were unjustly but innocently enriched by the fraud, there is a danger of overdeterrence (cf. §§6.7, 10.11 *supra* for discussions of similar problems in tort and antitrust law).

A stronger statement is possible, is it not? Often the profits from a stock fraud will be zero, at least as damages are usually measured in fraud cases. Suppose the managers of a corporation unjustifiably delay disclosing bad news about the corporation's prospects, in the vain hope that some miracle will restore those prospects. By doing this they stave off for two weeks a plunge in the price of the corporation's stock. People who buy the stock during this period will be hurt; but the sellers will be benefited, because if they had held on to the stock longer they would have suffered the loss that instead their buyers suffered. If the managers themselves had profited by selling their stock before the bad news hit the market, there would be no problem in forcing them to disgorge their gains (i.e., the losses they avoided). But suppose they didn't. Then what would be the basis for awarding damages based on the losses of some of the shareholders?

A pragmatic basis is the following. If the corporation is forced to pay the losses of those stockholders who were harmed by the delay in the release of the news, it will have an incentive to police its managers more carefully in the future. This is true even though the cost to the corporation will be borne by its shareholders, most or all of whom were innocent. Making them liable will affect the incentives of the board of directors they elect.

All this assumes that there is *some* social cost from the fraud, albeit not a cost equal to the losses of the shareholders who were hurt by the managers' concealment. Two kinds of social cost are possible, al-though difficult to quantify. First, the managers may have expended real resources in concealing the bad news. Second, and related, some investors will now have an incentive to expend more resources in trying to find out the truth about firms, since they have to overcome the disinfor-mation efforts of corporate managers. (Would investment in the stock market be made more risky, though?)[5]

§15.9   The Regulation of Banking

We conclude this chapter with a brief look at federal regulation of banks, which are, of course, an important source of capital. The basis of the

5. The regulation of futures markets (futures trading was discussed briefly in Chapter 4) also raises interesting economic issues. The articles in 4 J. Futures Mkts., no. 3 (Fall 1984), provide a good starting point for the reader wanting to explore them.

existing (but fast-disintegrating) system of federal banking regulation appears to be the decision in the wake of the 1930s depression to offer government insurance of bank deposits. The widespread bank failures of the period were thought, although perhaps erroneously, to have been an important cause of the severity of the business contraction.[1] A distinct reason for government deposit insurance is that in the event of a repetition of the widespread bank failures of the 1930s, private insurance might not be able to satisfy all depositors' claims.

Notice the parallel between deposit insurance and bankruptcy law. Because the depositor has a claim payable on demand, in the absence of deposit insurance a depositor would withdraw his deposit at the slightest sign that the bank might be in financial trouble. The efforts of all the depositors to do this at once would, however, break the bank, since a bank's assets are not totally liquid even if they greatly exceed its liabilities. A bank run is a classic example of a harmful externality; each depositor by attempting to withdraw his deposit will injure the other depositors but will not take the injury into account in deciding whether to withdraw.

The decision to insure bank deposits made some regulatory supervision of banks inevitable. Every insurer, public or private, has an interest in controlling (if feasible) the risk it insures against. One way to view the federal banking agencies is as surrogates for the depositors, insisting on the kinds of creditor protections that the depositors would demand were they not completely protected by insurance. Many banking regulations indeed resemble the kinds of protections on which private creditors often insist. Examples are the minimum capitalization requirements of insured banks and the limits on the riskiness of insured banks' loan portfolios. Minimum capitalization requirements reduce a creditor's risk by ensuring an adequate equity cushion of a prescribed size; limiting the risks that the borrower can impose on his assets prevents a borrower from unilaterally reducing the negotiated interest rate.[2]

Many banking regulations, however, go far beyond what a private creditor would insist upon in the interest of safety and seem (for this reason?) dubious. For example, requiring banks to lend money to the Federal Reserve System without interest (the reserves requirement) is both an unconventional and an inefficient (why?) method of reducing the riskiness of the bank's loan portfolio (federal securities are riskless). A better method would be to forbid banks to have any debt at all in their capital structure. While this seems a severe requirement, in fact

§15.9   1. Many economists believe that the bank failures were the result of a liquidity crisis brought about by the Federal Reserve Board's severely reducing the money supply, though many others disagree. The various points of view are well represented in The Great Depression Revisited (Karl Brunner ed. 1981).

2. The insurance premium for federal deposit insurance is based on the estimated probability of bank failure. If an insured bank increases the riskiness of its loans beyond the expected level, in effect it is being permitted to purchase deposit insurance at below-cost levels. See §14.3 *supra*.

it might be almost costless to the banks,[3] and it would increase the safety of bank deposits.

The Glass-Steagall Act forbids banks to engage in securities underwriting, thought to be a risky activity. The obvious solution to the problem of banks' diversifying into risky activities in an effort to increase the riskiness of the federal insurance guarantee (thus reducing the real cost of the insurance premium) is to require that they conduct those activities in separate corporations, for whose debts the parents would not be liable (in the absence of misrepresentation, see §14.5 *supra*, note 5) under the usual principles governing a parent corporation's liability for its subsidiaries' debts. The Bank Holding Company Act adopts this approach and has enabled the banks to circumvent many of the traditional limitations on diversification into nonbanking fields; but the Glass-Steagall Act still keeps the banks out of the securities underwriting business.

The suspicion naturally arises that the real purpose of the Act is not to protect the federal deposit insurance function but to protect securities underwriters from bank competition. Likewise the suspicion is strong that the reason for limitations on branch banking and interstate banking is not to protect banks from risks of competition that might be borne ultimately by the federal deposit insurance agency but to protect banks from competition, period. Statutes such as the Depository Institutions Deregulation Monetary Control Act of 1980 and the Depository Institutions Deregulation Act of 1982, however, have pried open the banking industry to much new competition, notably by enabling savings and loans associations to offer checking accounts in competition with the commercial banks. Not only did the former law give commercial banks a monopoly of checking accounts, but by forbidding banks to pay interest on such accounts they enabled the banks to exploit their monopsony power over depositors (what is the source of that power?).

Suggested Readings

1. William F. Baxter, Paul H. Cootner, & Kenneth E. Scott, Retail Banking in the Electronic Age: The Law and Economics of Electronic Funds Transfer (1977).

2. Fischer Black, Merton H. Miller, & Richard A. Posner, An Approach to the Regulation of Bank Holding Companies, 51 J. Bus. 379 (1978).

3. R.A. Brealey, An Introduction to Risk and Return from Common Stocks (2d ed. 1983).

3. See §15.2 *supra.* Why would it not be completely costless?

4. Thomas E. Copeland & J. Fred Weston, Financial Theory and Corporate Policy (2d ed. 1983).

5. John C. Cragg & Burton G. Malkiel, Expectations and the Structure of Share Prices (1982).

6. Frank H. Easterbrook & Daniel R. Fischel, Mandatory Disclosure and the Protection of Investors, 70 Va. L. Rev. 669 (1984).

7. _____, Optimal Penalties for Securities Offenses, 52 U. Chi. L. Rev. 611 (1985).

8. Daniel R. Fischel, Use of Modern Finance Theory In Securities Fraud Cases Involving Actively Traded Securities, 38 Bus. Lawyer 1 (1982).

9. _____ & Sanford J. Grossman, Customer Protection in Futures and Securities Markets, 4 J. Futures Mkts. 273 (1984).

10. Sanford J. Grossman & Oliver D. Hart, Corporate Finance, Structure and Managerial Incentives, in The Economics of Information and Uncertainty 107 (John J. McCall ed. 1982).

11. John H. Langbein & Richard A. Posner, Market Funds and Trust-Investment Law, Parts I and II, 1976 Am. Bar Foundation Research J. 1; 1977 id. at 1.

12. _____, Social Investing and the Law of Trusts, 79 Mich. L. Rev. 72 (1980).

13. James H. Lorie & Mary T. Hamilton, The Stock Market: Theories and Evidence (1973).

14. Susan M. Phillips & J. Richard Zecher, The SEC and the Public Interest (1981).

Problems

1. Appraise the following statements: "Because of its weighting, the S & P index portfolio [i.e., market portfolio] will always tend to do better [than conventional mutual funds] in a declining market but not as well in a rising one. Since the periods of rising prices tend to exceed the periods of falling prices, an index fund is a formula for a solid, consistent, long-term loser. Who needs that? Why is it prudent?"[4] "It would seem a matter of almost elementary prudence to reduce the stock portfolio's volatility at high levels of the market and to increase it at low levels."[5]

2. Should a trustee be permitted (in the absence of explicit language in the trust instrument) to invest in real estate equities? In real estate

4. Roger F. Murray, Investment Risk in Pension Funds: The Pension Benefit Guaranty Corporation View, in Evolving Concepts of Prudence: The Changing Responsibilities of the Investment Fiduciary in the Age of ERISA 37 (Financial Analysts Research Foundation 1976).

5. Id. at 40.

mortgages? Should he be permitted to operate a business with the trust funds, as opposed to mere passive investing?

3. The absolute priority rule of federal bankruptcy law is designed to assure that the claims of senior creditors are fully satisfied before junior creditors and shareholders are permitted to receive any money from the corporation. Suppose a corporation is undergoing reorganization in bankruptcy, having defaulted on its bonds, on which it now owes $100 in principal plus accrued interest. If the corporation is liquidated immediately, it will realize only $50 from the sale of its assets. But if it continues as a going concern, it can operate for one more year, at the end of which time its assets will have been all used up, with the following table of possible earnings from the year's operations:

Table 15.1

Earnings ($)	Probability
0	⅓
110	⅓
220	⅓

The expected earnings figure — the weighted average of all possible earnings outcomes — is $110. Assuming that a discount rate of 10 percent is appropriate for the level of risk associated with the corporation's possible outcomes, its present going-concern value is obtained by discounting the expected outcome of $110 at the end of one year by 10 percent, and thus it equals $110/1.10, which is $100. Would a plan of reorganization that gave the bondholders new bonds entitling them to receive a maximum of $110 out of the earnings available at the end of the year's operations, and the stockholders new common stock entitling them to any residue once the new bonds had been paid off, comply with the spirit of the absolute priority rule? Or should the bondholders be given the entire common stock of the corporation?

PART V

LAW AND THE DISTRIBUTION OF INCOME AND WEALTH

CHAPTER 16

INCOME INEQUALITIES, DISTRIBUTIVE JUSTICE, AND POVERTY

§16.1 The Measurement of Inequality

Money income is unevenly distributed. Economists have various ways of measuring this inequality. In Figure 16.1, percentage of income received, cumulated from lowest to highest, is expressed as a function of percentage of household units, cumulated from lowest to highest. If income were distributed evenly among all the household units in the country, the function would be the straight line labeled line of equality. At every point on that line, the fraction of income received by a given percentage of household units is exactly equal to that percentage: 20 percent of the units have 20 percent of the income, 55 percent of the units have 55 percent of the income, etc. The more bowed the actual distribution, the less equal it is. In 1982 the poorest 20 percent of the nation's families had less than 5 percent of the nation's family personal income and the wealthiest 5 percent had 16 percent.[1] The distribution of income changes slowly and appears to be quite similar for different countries in the same state of economic development, such as Sweden and the United States, even though the former is more socialistic.[2]

Statistics on income inequality do not provide clear-cut guidance for the formulation of social policy. For one thing, by taking a snapshot of incomes for one year, the statistics misleadingly compare people who are on different points of the life cycle (a distortion only partly corrected

§16.1 1. See U.S. Dept. of Commerce, Bureau of the Census, Money Income and Poverty Status of Families and Persons in the United States: 1982, at 11 (Current Population Reports, Consumer Income, series P-60, no. 140, July 1983) (table 4).
   2. See Robert M. Solow, Income Inequality Since the War, in Inequality and Poverty 50, 60 (Edward C. Budd ed. 1967).

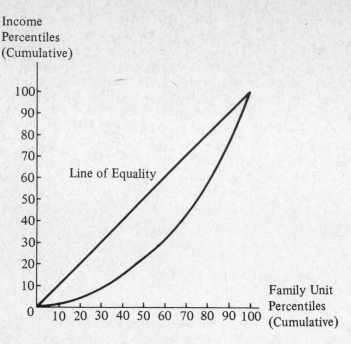

Figure 16.1

by not counting children, most of whom have zero income). For example, the statistics will place a young lawyer who has just joined a firm and a senior partner in the same firm in two different income classes, yet both may earn the same amounts in their lifetimes (in fact the young lawyer will probably earn more).

Furthermore, being limited to pecuniary income, the statistics on the distribution of incomes ignore many factors that are highly important to economic welfare — even quite narrowly defined — but difficult to quantify. Compare two households: In one both husband and wife work and each earns $10,000 per year; in the other only the husband works, and he earns $20,000. The pecuniary income of the households is the same, but the real income of the second household is greater. The wife stays home because her services in the home are worth more to the household than the income she would obtain from an outside job. If she is intelligent, energetic, and well educated, her alternative income may be quite high — as high as, or higher than, her husband's (see §5.1 *supra*). It is because the same qualities may make her an especially competent housewife and mother that her value at home may exceed her value in the market.

Even in paying jobs, an important part of the pay often is nonpecuniary. Teachers, for example, receive a big part of their income in the form of long vacations; pecuniary income figures understate their real income. The statistics not only leave out nonpecuniary income but count as income pecuniary receipts that actually are just cost reimbursement. We know, for example, that people in dangerous or unpleasant jobs will, other things being equal, receive higher wages than people whose jobs lack these undesirable characteristics; yet the real income of the two groups may be the same. Risk in the sense of economic uncertainty rather than danger is also important. Suppose that the income of a successful inventor is $200,000 a year and of an unsuccessful inventor zero and that the likelihood of an inventor's succeeding is one in ten (ignore the intermediate possibilities). The expected income of inventors is then $20,000 and is equal to that of civil servants certain to earn $20,000 every year. If a $20,000 ceiling were placed on the earnings of successful inventors, no one would choose a career in inventing; his expected income would be only $2,000. In fact 90 percent of the successful inventor's seemingly high income in our example is compensation for the risk of loss. (How would you factor risk preference and risk aversion into the analysis? Different personal discount rates?)

Now consider a simple distribution of four incomes: a 20-year-old carpenter, earning $15,000; a 20-year-old college student, earning nothing; a 30-year-old carpenter, earning $15,000, and a 30-year-old college graduate, an accountant, earning $20,000. The picture is one of substantial inequality, yet there may be none in actuality. The student's zero income represents an investment in education, which he recovers over his working life in a higher salary. The extra $5,000 he earns at age 30 compared to a carpenter who was working when the student was still in school may represent simply the repayment with interest of a part of the capital contribution in the form of tuition and forgone income that he or his family made when he was a student years earlier.[3]

Another important factor in gauging actual income equality is the distribution of economic benefits, pecuniary and nonpecuniary, excluded from most measurements of income. Federal and state government, and to a lesser extent other institutions (hospitals, foundations, etc.), provide a variety of benefits, such as education, police protection, health care, pensions, poor relief, and recreational facilities, without any direct charge. These benefits may have a differential impact on the welfare of different income groups. It is important not only to measure this impact but also to determine how the costs (primarily taxes) are distributed among income classes. If, for example, the burden of public education of poor children is borne primarily by poor families, no net transfer of wealth from wealthier classes in society may be accomplished by public education. But in fact the poor, although they pay higher

---

3. But to the extent the education was paid for by the state, the family, donors to the college, or anyone else besides the student, the "repayment" of capital is better described as the receipt of services from a gift than as a form of amortization. On the empirical importance of educational investment in explaining income differences, see Barry R. Chiswick, Income Inequality, pt. B (1974); Jacob Mincer, Schooling, Experience, and Earnings (1974).

taxes (mostly indirectly) than one might think, receive even more in transfers than they pay in taxes,[4] but perhaps only slightly more.[5]

For these reasons the proper interpretation of the inequality in money incomes revealed by Figure 16.1 is unclear. Inequality of real incomes may be greater than Figure 16.1 reveals, but it is probably smaller. An even more difficult estimation would be the inequality of income under genuine free-market conditions, i.e., without redistributive tax, spending, or regulatory policies.

§16.2   Is Inequality Inefficient?

Would the adoption of policies designed to move the society closer to equality increase economic welfare? The principle of diminishing marginal utility of money may tempt one to conclude that a transfer from a more to a less affluent person is likely to increase the sum of the two persons' utilities: A loss of a dollar hurts the millionaire less than the gain of a dollar pleases the pauper. Unquestionably this is true, but to generalize from this extreme example, and conclude that redistributing substantial wealth from higher- to lower-income people is bound to increase total utility, would be perilous even on the unrealistic premise that redistribution is costless. In Figure 16.2, utility is plotted on the vertical axis, money income on the horizontal. The curve on the left shows A's utility as a function of his money income. His present income is $70,000, and the area under the curve to the left of $70,000 is thus his total utility. The curve is negatively sloped, implying diminishing marginal utility: If A's income rose from $70,000 to $80,000, the increase in his utility (the area under the curve between these two figures) would be smaller than would be the increase in utility if his income had been $60,000 and had risen to $70,000. B's income is $30,000. His total utility is the area under the curve on the right-hand side of the diagram to the right of $30,000 on his scale.

If $10,000 of income is transferred from A to B, A's utility will decrease by the area under his marginal utility curve between $70,000 and $60,000 on his scale, while B's utility will increase by the area under his marginal utility curve between the same two points ($30,000 and $40,000 on his scale). The latter area, hatched in the diagram, is smaller than the area that measures the diminution in A's utility as a result of the transfer. The transfer has resulted in a fall in total utility. The reason is that while both A and B experience diminishing marginal utility, A gets more utility from a dollar than B in the relevant region.

4. See Richard A. Musgrave & Peggy B. Musgrave, Public Finance in Theory and Practice 264 (4th ed. 1984) (table 12-4).
5. See Benjamin I. Page, Who Gets What From Government 135-144 (1983).

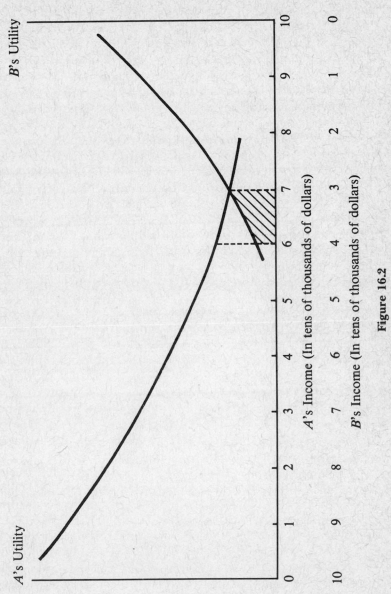

A's Utility

B's Utility

A's Income (In tens of thousands of dollars)

B's Income (In tens of thousands of dollars)

Figure 16.2

435

Since the shape and height of people's marginal utility curves are unknown, and probably unknowable, the possibility that wealthier people's marginal utility curves are on average higher than poorer people's cannot be negated. It has been suggested that the most plausible assumption, given this ignorance, is that marginal utility curves are the same across income groups; on this view equalizing incomes would probably increase total utility.[1] It seems at least as plausible, however, to assume that income and the marginal utility thereof are positively correlated — that the people who work hard to make money and succeed in making it are on average those who value money the most, having given up other things such as leisure to get it. And we have ignored the costs of redistributing income. If substantial, a question taken up later, they could equal or exceed any gains in total utility from the redistribution.[2]

Notice that an assumption that marginal utility of money income was uncorrelated with or negatively correlated with wealth, although it would show that aggregate happiness would be maximized by redistributing income from those with above average incomes to those with below average incomes (ignoring the costs of the redistribution), would not establish that the wealth of society would be increased. As a matter of fact, the wealth of society would be unchanged, or, more realistically, when the costs of redistribution are factored in, would be reduced by the redistribution, which therefore could not be defended on efficiency grounds if efficiency is defined as suggested in Chapter 1. Involuntary redistribution is a coerced transfer not justified by high market-transaction costs; it is, in efficiency terms, a form of theft.[3]

§16.3   The Contract Theory of Distributive Justice

The philosopher John Rawls has argued[1] that the distribution of income and wealth is just if there is no alternative distribution that would make the worst off people in society better off. The just distribution might be highly unequal, if, for example, the negative impact of a more equal

§16.2   1. See Abba Lerner, The Economics of Control 35-36 (1944).

2. These points are frequently neglected. For example, C. Edwin Baker, Utility and Rights: Two Justifications for State Action Increasing Equality, 84 Yale L.J. 39 (1974), after first admitting (see id. at 41-42 n.12) that Lerner's analysis, even if accepted, establishes only a probability that redistribution would increase total utility, drops the qualification, and asserts that taking from the rich to give to the poor will in fact increase total utility (id. at 45). The author's acknowledgment that the costs of redistribution must be subtracted from any gains (id. at 48 n.26) is also dropped, allowing him to conclude — without any further reference to the possible costs of redistribution — that it is an economically justified policy goal (id. at 55-56, 58).

3. An exception to this harsh proposition is discussed in §16.4 *infra*.

§16.3   1. In his celebrated book, A Theory of Justice (1971).

distribution on the incentive to work would be so substantial that the larger slice received by the worst off would be smaller in absolute size than the relatively smaller slice that they would receive under a less equal distribution.

To make the interests of the worst off paramount may appear to violate the principle to which virtually all modern economists subscribe that interpersonal comparisons of utility (happiness) are arbitrary. Rawls's justification is that it is plausible to suppose that, if one could somehow poll all of the people who have ever composed or will ever compose the society, in their "original positions" (that is, before they knew what their place in society would be), it would turn out that they preferred a set of arrangements that maximized the position of the worst off. This assumes that all people are risk averse, which is all right, but less plausibly that people are fantastically risk averse.

Compare two sets of social arrangements, X and Y. X leads to a distribution of income in which the average income of the poorest 10 percent of the people in the society is $10,000 a year and the average income of all of the people in the society is also $10,000. Y leads to a distribution of income in which the average income of the poorest 10 percent is $9,000 but the average income of all of the people in the society is $40,000. People in the original position, even if risk averse, are unlikely to choose X.[2] But all this shows is that the specific form of Rawls's principle of justice (maximin) is not established. His basic approach is not affected, and it ingeniously breaks the impasse that arose in the previous section when we tried to compare the utilities of people *after* life's lottery tickets had been drawn. An individual's utility may be reduced when his winning ticket is taken away from him and given to someone else even though the lottery was not conducted fairly. If A slices a cake and gives B the largest piece, B may be reluctant to give a portion of it to C, who received the smallest piece. But his reluctance is irrelevant to the question whether the method of slicing the cake was fair. Rawls's approach embodies the intuitively appealing principle of fairness that if one person slices the cake and the other gets first pick the division of the cake will be fair even if it is unequal.

---

2. Especially since Rawls assumes that no one in the original position is afflicted by envy, a form of interdependent negative utilities. If envy were assumed to be an important part of people's psychological makeup, the utility of a larger income in a society in which incomes were highly unequal might be less than that of a smaller income in a society in which incomes were equal.

Rawls is aware of the problem discussed in the text, but dismisses it, primarily on the ground that large increases in the welfare of the better off would almost certainly also increase the welfare of the worst off, at least when other safeguards incorporated into his principle of justice (such as open competition for positions) are taken into account. See Rawls, *supra* note 1, at 157-158. This ignores the possibility that substantial reductions in the welfare of the better off might lead to a trivial improvement in the welfare of the worst off, in which event a set of institutional arrangements that bore very heavily on the well-to-do might be required by his principle of justice.

Rawls asks us to do what we have done many times in this book: Imagine the content of a contract that cannot be made in the market because of high transaction costs. People in the original position know that the wealth of the society may be divided in many ways. If risk averse, they presumably want some protection against getting a very small slice (unless the cake is very large) or no slice at all. Rawls's principle, like the rule for dividing cakes (which it resembles), provides them with such protection.

Unfortunately, Rawls's theory of distributive justice has almost no operational content. Apart from the problem of determining how much risk aversion to assume, there is the problem of deciding who shall be counted as worst off, which Rawls recognizes but does not attempt to resolve.[3] If the worst off is a single person, some measures will be deemed unjust that would be just if the worst off were, for example, the poorest income decile. Whether the relevant universe is a single society or the world is also critical (why?), as is whether worst off is to be understood strictly in money income terms, with all the problems which that measure involves, or more broadly. There is also the problem that it is unclear what particular policies generate what outcomes. The result of all this is that Rawls's theory of justice seems quite compatible with on the one hand out-and-out socialism and on the other hand *laissez-faire* capitalism, depending on how much risk aversion people in the original position are assumed to have, how narrowly the group of worst off in whose interests all policies must operate is defined, and how effective one rates public institutions relative to the free market. Answering these questions "a great deal," "very," and "highly," respectively, leads to socialism; the opposite answers to capitalism.

§16.4 The Costs of Poverty and the Limitations of Private Charity

There are several good economic arguments, however, for governmental efforts to reduce the gross inequality (in a wealthy society) that we call poverty. The definition of poverty is elusive, its identification simpler. It is a relative concept: Poverty in Ethiopia and Bangladesh means something different from poverty in the United States. And within the same culture the concept changes over time. If one compares estimates from various periods in our history of the minimum income necessary to place a family of given size above the poverty level, one finds that the level has risen steadily, even after correction for the decline in the value

3. See id. at 98.

of the dollar due to inflation.[1] Even with a rising floor under what is considered a tolerable income, the incidence of poverty in the United States has declined markedly over the years.[2] Yet it is still significant.[3]

Poverty imposes costs on the nonpoor that warrant, on narrowly economic (i.e., wealth-maximizing) grounds and without regard to ethical or political considerations, incurring some costs to reduce it. For example, poverty in the midst of a generally wealthy society is likely to increase the incidence of crime. The forgone income of a legitimate alternative occupation is low for someone who has little earning capacity in legitimate occupations, while the proximity of wealth increases the expected return from crime.[4]

Probably the major cost of poverty, however, is the disutility it imposes on affluent altruists. We know from Chapter 5 that an increase in A's income will increase B's income as well if A's welfare enters into B's (positive interdependent utilities). Altruism is much stronger among family members than strangers,[5] but even a weak feeling of altruism may create an incentive for transferring income if there are great disparities of income. If A is extremely wealthy and B extremely poor, subtracting a dollar from A's income may as suggested earlier reduce A's utility by vastly less than adding a dollar to B's income would increase B's utility: Let us assume 100 times less. Then A would derive a net benefit from giving a dollar to B as long as he valued B's welfare, at the margin (meaning what?), any more than one-hundredth as much as he valued his own.

Although it might seem that since the affluent gain from reducing poverty the alleviation of poverty can be left to private charity, and

§16.4   1. See Oscar Ornati, The Poverty Bank and the Count of the Poor, in Inequality and Poverty 167 (Edward C. Budd ed. 1967).

2. Ibid.

3. In 1982, 15 percent of all U.S. residents were below the poverty line (the corresponding figure for 1959 is 18 percent), see U.S. Dept. of Commerce, Bureau of the Census, Characteristics of the Population Below the Poverty Level: 1982, at 7 (Current Population Reports, Consumer Income, series P-60, no. 144 (March 1984) (table 1)) — provided that noncash benefits are excluded. It has been estimated that if those benefits were included in figuring people's incomes, the number of people counted as poor might fall by as much as 42 percent (i.e., from 15 percent to 9 percent). See U.S. Dept. of Commerce, Bureau of the Census, Characteristics of Households and Persons Receiving Selected Noncash Benefits: 1982, at 5 (Current Population Reports, Consumer Income, series P-60, no. 143, Jan. 1984). See also Morton Paglin, Poverty and Transfers In-Kind: A Re-Evaluation of Poverty in the United States 61 (1980) (table 8).

4. See §7.2 *supra* and, for empirical support, Isaac Ehrlich, Participation in Illegitimate Activities: An Economic Analysis, in Essays in the Economics of Crime and Punishment 68, 94 (Gary S. Becker & William M. Landes eds. 1974). There is no necessary inconsistency in the fact that crime rates are frequently low in poor countries, even though inequality of wealth is often much greater in those countries than in wealthier ones. If wealth is highly concentrated, the costs of protecting it from criminals may be low. It is where wealth is more widely distributed that criminals are presented with an abundance of attractive targets.

5. Which is why the children of nonpoor parents are not counted among the poor!

that in any event altruism would not provide an argument for public intervention, the altruist faces a free-rider problem. A in our example will derive welfare from the increase in B's income whether or not A is the source of the increase. Naturally A would like to buy this increase in his welfare at the lowest possible price, so he will have an incentive to hang back in giving to charity in the hope that others will give. It might seem that regardless of what others give his contribution will add to the total amount of resources devoted to an end he values. But this is not certain. His contribution may lead others to cut back their contributions, since now a smaller contribution on their part will (in combination with A's contribution, which is new) buy the same reduction in poverty. So A will get less than a dollar benefit for every dollar he contributes, and this will lead to a lower contribution.[6]

Whenever there are free-rider problems, there is an economic argument for government intervention: Here an argument for forcing people to contribute to the alleviation of poverty so that they cannot take a free ride on private donations to charity. Of course the argument is not conclusive; the costs of the intervention must be considered. The disincentive effects of welfare programs can be very great. For example, the social security disability program has been found to create significant work disincentives, even though incapacity to work is a formal prerequisite to the receipt of disability benefits.[7] Welfare programs such as Aid For Dependent Children (AFDC) have been found to have surprisingly great negative effects on participation in the labor force — in the case of AFDC, participation by the mothers.[8] Overall it has been estimated that of every $1 transferred by government 23¢ is dissipated, when all social costs of the transfer are taken into account.[9] Another thing to be considered is the effect of government transfers on private charity. Government transfers are a substitute for private giving, so they should lead to a cutback in private giving — an effect compounded by the fact that the tax necessary to defray the cost of the transfer reduces the after-tax income available to the taxpayer for private giving. The total effect on private giving apparently is substantial.[10]

Notice also that the efficiency argument for public aid to the poor has a more limited reach than the more common, utilitarian argument. Go back to the example where B values his marginal dollar 100 times more than A values his own marginal dollar, and now assume that the

6. For some evidence of this, see reference in §17.8 *infra*, note 5.

7. See Howard P. Marvel, An Economic Analysis of the Operation of Social Security Disability Insurance, 18 J. Human Resources 393 (1982).

8. See studies summarized in Martin Anderson, Welfare: The Political Economy of Welfare Reform in the United States, ch. V (1978).

9. See Sheldon Danziger & Robert Haveman, How Income Transfer Programs Affect Work, Savings, and the Income Distribution: A Critical Review, 19 J. Econ. Lit. 975, 1020 (1981).

10. See Burton A. Abrams & Mark D. Schitz, The "Crowding-Out" Effect of Governmental Transfers on Private Charitable Contributions, 33 Pub. Choice 30 (1978); §17.8 *infra* (discussion of charitable deduction from federal income tax).

number is 10 rather than 100 and that A values B's welfare at one-twentieth his own. Then there is no free-rider argument for forcing A to transfer a dollar to B; but there would still be a utilitarian argument.

Another efficiency argument for poor relief is based on risk aversion. An affluent person who is risk averse will want to insure against the possibility of becoming poor sometime in the future, because of business reverses, poor health, changes in the labor market, or other misfortunes. Although some of the causes of poverty can be insured against in the private insurance market, comprehensive insurance against poverty is difficult to obtain, in part because of a serious moral-hazard problem: If it were really possible to insure against being poor, anyone who bought such insurance would have an incentive to engage in extremely risky economic behavior. Therefore social insurance becomes attractive. The tax contributions we make to fund poverty programs are crudely analogous to the premiums we pay for private insurance; the programs will be available to help us should we become poor.

Private charitable contributions do not assure adequate poverty insurance. The donor cannot be sure that the private charity will be willing and able to assist him, should he become poor, at anything like the level necessary to maximize his utility. For we must remember that the donors to private charities value the welfare of the poor at a much lower rate than the poor value (in a utility, not efficiency, sense) their own welfare.

Although there is an economic case for government assistance to the poor, it is not obvious that the government has to have an operating role. The economic problems that make private charity inadequate could be overcome by a program of government matching grants to charities. We already have an approximation to this in the charitable deduction from the income tax, discussed in the next chapter.

§16.5 Unrestricted Cash Transfers Versus Benefits in Kind

The causes and cures of poverty are not well understood. The simplest view is that poverty results from a lack of income and is most effectively treated by unrestricted cash payments to poor people. This approach (negative income tax) has growing support among scholars, but there are three economic points against it that may explain, in part anyway,[1] why it has not yet been adopted.

---

§16.5 1. The main reason may be, however, that a restricted, or earmarked, subsidy provides concentrated benefits to middle class groups (lawyers, social workers, construction workers, etc.) who may be politically influential, while unrestricted cash payments do not. See §19.3 *infra.*

1. Contrary to our earlier assumption, the affluent may not be concerned with the subjective utility of the poor but rather with the consumption pattern of the poor. They may want the poor to have decent housing, nutrition, and educational opportunities, even if the poor themselves would prefer other things, such as fine clothes, expensive cars, and lottery tickets. The affluent may hope that if the poor can be forced to buy some things rather than others, poverty will be reduced in the long run — that if, for example, a poor family is decently housed, fed, and educated, the next generation is less likely to be poor. Looking at things in this way, and especially if the affluent have better information than the poor, the affluent donor gets more bang for his buck — a greater alleviation of poverty when the future as well as the present is taken into account — by earmarking his contribution for particular uses by the poor recipient.

2. Some people are poor because they are incompetent at managing money; if so, unrestricted cash grants may be squandered, without alleviating poverty.

3. The unrestricted cash transfer involves a potentially serious incentive problem. If, for example, every family of four were guaranteed a minimum income of $5,000, the head of such a family would have no incentive to take a job even if it paid more than that. A job paying $110 a week would increase his gross income by only about $10 a week and his net income would actually decline. Working is expensive. The worker must pay for transportation, for work clothes, federal and state income tax, etc. — even if the work itself creates no disutility (as of course it may, especially if it is dirty, strenuous, or hazardous) so that there is no opportunity cost from forgoing the leisure of the unemployed state.

A graduated scale of cash transfers would preserve some work incentive. Suppose, for example, that for every dollar earned the government's contribution to family income would be reduced by only 50¢, even if the result was that a family's total income, earned as well as subsidized, exceeded the $5,000 guaranteed minimum income. But even a 50 percent marginal income tax rate, while better than 100 percent, is still very stiff and will have disincentive effects. A person who earned $5,000 a year would retain only $2,500, which after deduction of the costs of work would be chicken feed. And people not on welfare who were working for low wages might be induced to leave the work force. This would both increase the cost of the program and reduce the supply of labor in low paying jobs. Although the reduction in demand for such jobs would lead to an increase in the wages offered, and this would partly offset the disincentive effect by making work more remunerative, it would also increase the cost and hence price of the goods and services dependent on such labor, much like an excise tax. And excise taxes are, as we shall see in the next chapter, generally regressive.

The marginal income tax rate can be varied at will in order to mitigate the disincentive effects just discussed, but a substantial reduction in the rate would greatly increase the cost of the program. If the marginal tax rate were 25 percent, a family of four in which the head of the household earned $12,000 per year would still receive an annual income supplement from the government of $2,000; and he would have to earn $20,000 before he ceased being eligible for any supplement.[2]

Before condemning the "negative income tax" approach for its work-disincentive effects, however, notice that earmarked subsidies can have the same effects. If entitlement to a rent supplement, for example, is conditioned on one's income not going over a certain level, then income earned above that level will be taxed in effect by the amount of the rent supplement.

Work-disincentive effects to one side, the most serious problem with our present system, which is a system of earmarked subsidies and benefits in kind — public housing, rent supplements, food stamps, free legal and medical services, job training, etc. — is an informational one.[3] The willingness of a consumer, including a poor one, to pay the market price for one good in preference to another is evidence of the relative value of the goods to him. It does not matter how he came by the dollars he is using to express his preference. But when the price of a good is zero, it is very difficult to estimate the value of the good to the "buyer." Even if poverty officials had a general idea of how the poor ranked the various goods and services, this would enable only an average judgment, which, given the different needs of particular poor families, would lead to superfluity in many cases and insufficiency in many others. A less extensive program of cash transfers might yield greater net welfare to the poor while reducing the costs to the taxpayer. But of course the information problem does not cut only one way. As mentioned, many poor people must lack good information about how to get out of poverty. A program of unrestricted cash transfers might bring about a greater static reduction in poverty than a program of earmarked transfers but a smaller dynamic reduction.

The actual performance of our system of earmarked transfers leaves much to be desired. An example of particular interest to lawyers is the currently embattled program whereby the government, through the Legal Services Corporation, provides free legal assistance to the poor in civil matters. This method of helping the poor may actually prevent many poor people from achieving their most efficient pattern of consumption. Since governmental funds allocated to legal services for the poor are unavailable for other programs of poor relief, the cost to the

---

2. $5,000 − (.25 × $12,000) = $2,000; $5,000 − (.25 × $20,000) = 0.

3. See Ralph K. Winter, Jr., Poverty, Economic Equality, and the Equal Protection Clause, 1972 S. Ct. Rev. 41.

poor person of being entitled to $100 in legal services may be the benefit
he would have derived from receiving $100 of some other good or
service or in cash. Many poor people may be able to get along well
enough without a lawyer, either because they are fortunate enough not
to encounter legal problems or because they are clever enough to cope
with them unaided by a lawyer. But since the lawyer is free,[4] they will
use him unless the value of his services exceeds the (often slight) value
of their time in dealing with him. Faced with excess demand for his
time, the lawyer will try to limit his services to those whose needs for
legal service seem most acute; and since this requires a difficult judgment,
there are bound to be many cases where a poor person receives legal
services that cost $100 but are worth only $50 to him or fails to receive
legal services that would be much more valuable than their cost. The
waste involved in using a lawyer when the social cost exceeded the social
benefit would be avoided if poor people were given $100 cash instead
of a free lawyer. Problems of information and consumer competence
to one side, they would use the $100 to hire a lawyer rather than to
buy food, medicine, education, or housing only when the value of legal
services to them was at least $100, and they would also have the $100
to hire a lawyer when they really needed one.[5] (Is the availability of
legal insurance a relevant consideration?)

Further, legal services are typically although not invariably utilized
in a dispute — in the case of a poor person, with a landlord, spouse,
merchant, welfare agency, finance company, etc. The legal efforts made
on behalf of one of the parties to the dispute will increase the costs
to the other, who must either increase *his* legal efforts or abandon the
stakes in the dispute to the other party. These costs are typically marginal
costs — a function of output — so that, by a now-familiar analysis, they
will be passed on (in part at least) to the customers of the enterprise.
If most of those customers are other poor people, this means that the
costs generated by one poor tenant's or customer's or debtor's use of
a lawyer will be borne in large part by other poor people.[6] If the dispute
is with a government agency, the additional legal expense (or higher
grant level) of the agency will not be borne primarily by the poor unless
the agency is funded by means of a highly regressive tax. But they may
bear it indirectly. The increased cost of the program may result in a
reduction in the amount or coverage of the benefits provided by it.
The costs thereby imposed on a large number of poor may exceed
the benefits to those who employed lawyers in their dispute with the
agency.

4. Are his services entirely "free" to the client? Why not?
5. Legal assistance to a poor person charged with crime may present a special problem.
See §25.2 *infra*.
6. In the case of a lawyer hired to prosecute a divorce, this effect may be offset by
the fact that the spouse is also entitled to free legal service.

§16.6   Wealth Redistribution by Liability Rules: The Case of Housing Code Enforcement

Housing is a traditional service that the government assists the poor to obtain. Various methods of assistance are used. One is to hire contractors to build apartment houses for the government to own and operate, renting apartments to the poor at zero or nominal rentals. Another is to give poor people money that they are allowed to spend only for housing. This method of subsidy has the attractive feature, to an economist, that it preserves a private market in housing — it just gives the poor more effective demand for the housing supplied in that market. It is true that in the short run the effect may simply be to force up rental rates, and hence to make other renters poorer, and landlords richer, as a result of the subsidy. That is the standard short run response to a surge in demand, reflecting the fact that productive capacity is by definition fixed in the short run (see §21.12 *infra,* for a fuller explanation of this point). But in the long run the stock of housing will rise and the price will fall back toward (all the way toward?) its level before the subsidy. And public housing has even worse short run effects than these: In the short run — before the housing is actually built and rented — the poor obtain no benefit from public housing at all. A system of rent supplements or housing vouchers not only is more flexible but works more quickly to help the intended beneficiaries.[1]

Both public housing and rent supplements involve the taxing and spending branches of government rather than the courts. But there is a method of (purportedly) helping the poor to meet their housing needs that centrally involves the courts: the enforcement of housing codes. These codes specify minimum standards of housing — although whether in order to ensure a decent minimum level of safety and sanitation or to subsidize the building trades is a matter of debate. Legal scholarship has been imaginative in suggesting devices by which the violators of housing codes could be subjected to sanctions that would greatly reduce the incidence of violation. To deal with the problem of substandard housing by legal sanction has the additional attraction of enabling, or seeming to enable, a principal manifestation of poverty to be eliminated without any public expenditure.

The effects of housing code enforcement are depicted in Figure 16.3. D_1 is the market demand curve for low-income housing before enforcement. It slopes downward because not all tenants would leave if rentals rose as a result of an increase in the landlords' marginal costs. MC_1 is the landlords' pre-enforcement marginal cost curve and is positively

§16.6   1. For empirical analysis of the tradeoffs between public housing and rent supplements, see Edgar O. Olsen & David M. Barton, The Benefits and Costs of Public Housing in New York City, 20 J. Pub. Econ. 299 (1983).

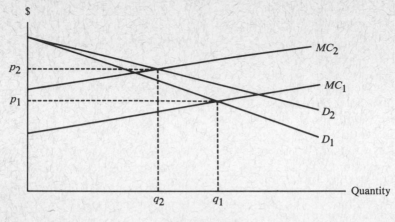

Figure 16.3

sloped to reflect the fact that the creation of low-income rental housing involves the use of some specialized resources — in particular, land — that would be worth less in any other use.

Enforcing the housing code has two main effects on the market depicted in Figure 16.3.[2] By improving the quality of the housing units it increases the demand for them. And by increasing the landlords' maintenance costs, which are marginal costs because they vary with the number of housing units provided, it shifts the marginal cost curve upward. The shift shown in Figure 16.3 is large relative to the shift in the demand curve, on the plausible assumption that if quantity demanded were highly responsive to an increase in the quality of the housing provided, the landlords would upgrade quality voluntarily and there would be no need to enforce a housing code. Both demand and supply in Figure 16.3 are depicted as being quite elastic, on the (again plausible) assumptions that slum dwellers lack the resources to pay substantially higher rentals and that slum rentals are already so depressed in relation to costs that a further reduction in those rentals would cause many landlords to withdraw from the low-income housing market (for example, by abandoning their property to the city).

Given these assumptions, housing code enforcement leads to a substantial reduction in the supply of low-income housing (from q_1 to q_2) coupled with a substantial rise in the price of the remaining supply (from p_1 to p_2). The quantity effect is actually understated (though by the same token the price effect is overstated) in Figure 16.3: Some of the higher-quality supply brought forth by housing code enforcement

2. A third effect is a reduction in the rent of land received by the landlords (assuming they are the owners of the land). The irony here is that these rentiers include a number of almost-poor people for whom ownership of slum property represents the first stage in the escape from poverty.

may be rented to the nonpoor.[3] These effects could be offset by rent supplements, but that would deprive the program of its politically attractive quality of entailing no public expenditures.[4]

Admittedly, the magnitude of the effects shown in Figure 16.3 depends on the (arbitrary) location of the curves. It has even been suggested that demand might be perfectly elastic in the relevant region (implying no price effect of housing code enforcement[5]) because the slightest increase would cause many tenants to double up.[6] But since doubling up is costly (it involves forgoing the value of the greater space and privacy of single family occupancy), tenants would surely be willing to pay something to avoid being forced to double up, the something being a somewhat higher rental. This implies a less than perfectly elastic demand. Empirical evidence suggests that Figure 16.3 provides a closer approximation to the actual conditions of the slum housing market than a model which assumes perfect elasticity of demand.[7]

The right given by unjust-eviction laws to a hearing before eviction can be analyzed the same way as housing code enforcement. The law increases the landlord's costs, leading to higher rentals and hence to a reduced housing supply for low-income tenants. Direct price effects aside, since the right to a hearing before eviction is less likely to be invoked by an affluent than by a poor tenant (the reason being that the former is less likely to default), the creation of such a right reduces the incentive of landlords to rent to poor people (cf. §4.7 *supra*).

The reader may be reminded of our analysis in Chapter 4 of the economic effects of outlawing efficient but sometimes oppressive methods of enforcing debts. Both analyses suggest that the use of liability rules or other legal sanctions to redistribute income from wealthy to poor is likely to miscarry. A rule of liability is like an excise tax: It induces a contraction in output and increase in price (see §17.3 *infra*).

3. Might a covert purpose of housing codes be to increase the supply of middle income housing at the expense of the poor? Cf. George J. Stigler, Director's Law of Public Income Redistribution, 13 J. Law & Econ. 1 (1970).

4. What would be the economic differences between coupling housing code enforcement with rent supplements and a program of rent supplements without code enforcement?

5. There would still be a quantity effect: show this graphically.

6. See Bruce Ackerman, Regulating Slum Housing Markets on Behalf of the Poor: Of Housing Codes, Housing Subsidies and Income Redistribution Policy, 80 Yale L.J. 1093 (1971), criticized in Neil K. Komesar, Return to Slumville: A Critique of the Ackerman Analysis of Housing Code Enforcement and the Poor, 82 Yale L.J. 1175 (1973).

One court has suggested that landlords might be forbidden, on a theory of retaliatory eviction, to abandon buildings as an alternative to code compliance if they were "able" to comply. Robinson v. Diamond Housing Corp., 463 F.2d 853, 869 (D.C. Cir. 1972). Would such a prohibition increase or decrease the long run supply of housing to the poor?

7. See Werner Z. Hirsch, Law and Economics: An Introductory Analysis 43-58 (1979); Werner Z. Hirsch, Effects of Habitability and Anti-Speedy Eviction Laws on Black and Aged Indigent Tenant Groups: An Economic Analysis, 3 Intl. Rev. Law & Econ. 121 (1983).

The party made liable, even if not poor himself (but that, as we have seen, is also possible), may be able to shift much of the liability cost to the poor through higher prices. The result may be a capricious redistribution of income and wealth within the class of poor people themselves and an overall reduction in their welfare.

§16.7   Open-Ended Benefits in Kind

To assist the poor with housing and nutrition and even education involves substantial but fairly predictable costs, as all of these are pretty standard commodities. But in the case of health, only the sky sets a potential limit on expenditures. Suppose that the poor were deemed entitled to any assistance they "needed" in a medical sense, regardless of cost. Then if a poor person had kidney failure, he would be entitled to dialysis treatment, which can be enormously expensive; or if he had heart disease he would be entitled to bypass surgery or even a heart transplant — perhaps even to the new mechanical heart. If he is denied any of these things then it can be argued that money is being allowed to decide who lives and who dies — an acceptable criterion from an efficiency standpoint, but one objectionable to many people.

Consider the requirement of federal law (the Education for All Handicapped Children Act) that every handicapped child receive a "free appropriate public education." The idea is to give the child at public expense the education necessary to maximize his learning, again regardless of cost. If the child has severe physical or medical handicaps, the cost may be astronomical. And the program is not limited to the needy. Although it can be argued that some measure of assistance to the educational needs of the handicapped is an efficient method of social insurance against a ghastly misfortune, and a method that involves minimal moral-hazard problems (why?), it is obvious that the optimal expenditure on educating handicapped children is nowhere near infinite, although infinite expenditures would be required to bring some of those children up to the level of the normal child.

Suggested Readings

1. Martin Anderson, Welfare: The Political Economy of Welfare Reform in the United States (1978).
2. Milton Friedman, Price Theory, ch. 12 (1976).
3. Harold M. Hochman, Contractarian Theories of Income Redistri-

bution, in Social Policy Evaluation: An Economic Perspective 211 (Elhanan Helpman, Assaf Razin & Efraim Sadka eds. 1983).

4. ——— & James D. Rodgers, Pareto Optimal Redistribution, 59 Am. Econ. Rev. 542 (1969).

5. Lars Osberg, Economic Inequality in the United States (1984).

6. Benjamin I. Page, Who Gets What From Government (1983).

7. Amartya K. Sen, Collective Choice and Social Welfare, ch. 9 (1970).

8. Henry C. Simons, Personal Income Taxation, ch. 1 (1938).

9. George J. Stigler, Director's Law of Public Income Redistribution, 13 J. Law & Econ. 1 (1970).

10. Ralph K. Winter, Jr., Poverty, Economic Equality, and the Equal Protection Clause, 1972 S. Ct. Rev. 41.

11. Economic Transfers in the United States (Marilyn Moon ed. 1984).

12. The Economics of Charity (Inst. of Econ. Affairs 1973).

Problems

1. If the principle of the diminishing marginal utility of money is accepted, does it follow that a corporation that obtains a monopoly and thereby increases its profits will become less concerned with minimizing its costs? To what extent is the principle applicable to organizations at all?

2. You are legislative assistant to a U.S. Senator. He asks you to advise him whether to vote for certain pending bills. He wants your views on the merits, not the politics, of the bills. Advise him. The bills are as follows:

(a) A bill to improve coal mine safety by requiring the installation of early warning devices against mine explosions and more frequent safety inspections of mines. The annual cost of these measures is estimated to be $500,000 and is to be defrayed by a special tax on the mining companies.

(b) A bill to provide an annual subsidy out of general tax revenues for railroad passenger service on routes of less than 80 miles, in the amount of $10 million per year.

3. Appraise the following passage:

[T]he Distribution of wealth . . . is a matter of human institutions only. . . . The rules by which it is determined are what the opinions and feelings of the ruling portion of the community make them, and are very different in different ages and countries; and might be still more different, if mankind so choose. [John Stuart Mill, Principles of Political Economy, bk. II, ch. I, §1, at 200 (W.J. Ashley ed. 1926).]

4. Is a food stamp program likely to increase the nourishment of poor people? Consider the following hypothetical example. A poor family, before the food stamp program, spent $700 a year on food. The family receives food stamps with a retail value of $500. Would you expect this to affect the family's eating habits more than a cash transfer of $500 would affect them? Might your answer be affected by what restrictions were placed on the use of the stamps (i.e., what specific foods could not be purchased with them)?

5. Contrast from an economic standpoint the following methods of increasing the employment of poor people: a government-subsidized job training program; a subsidy to employers of poor people; a negative income tax with a low marginal tax rate.

6. Is rent control, as in New York City, likely to help or hurt the poor as a whole? What would be the effect on the supply of housing if rent control were combined with strict enforcement of housing code provisions? Cf. Edgar O. Olsen, An Econometric Analysis of Rent Control, 80 J. Pol. Econ. 1081 (1972).

7. Professor Ackerman (§16.6 *supra,* note 6) asserts that it is uneconomical to build low income housing today without a government subsidy. If so, does this support his conclusion that strict enforcement of housing codes is unlikely to affect the supply of slum housing, except to cause abandonment of some marginal properties?

8. Javins v. First National Realty Corp., 428 F.2d 1071 (D.C. Cir. 1970), held that there is a warranty of habitability, measured by the standards set forth in the housing code of the District of Columbia, that is implied by operation of law in all leases. The suit was a landlord's suit for possession on the ground of nonpayment of rent. The court held that it was for the jury to determine what portion if any of the tenant's obligation to pay rent was suspended by the landlord's breach. In the course of its opinion the court stated (id. at 1079, footnotes omitted):

> The inequality in bargaining power between landlord and tenant has been well documented. Tenants have very little leverage to enforce demands for better housing. Various impediments to competition in the rental housing market, such as racial and class discrimination and standardized form leases, mean that landlords place tenants in a take it or leave it situation. The increasingly severe shortage of adequate housing further increases the landlord's bargaining power and escalates the need for maintaining and improving the existing stock.

What does the court mean by shortage? By bargaining power? Assuming that the quoted statement is accurate and coherent, would you expect the court's decision to make tenants in general better off, or worse off, than if no implied warranty of habitability were recognized? How about the particular tenants who brought the suit?

9. Discuss the following proposition: Policies designed to maximize the society's rate of economic growth are likeliest to satisfy Rawls's criterion of distributive justice.

10. Suppose Rawls's general theory of justice were thought satisfied by assuming that people in the original position would want to maximize their expected utility. Would the policies deducible from this assumption (assuming that specific policies could be deduced from it) be wealth maximizing? See Richard A. Posner, The Economics of Justice 99-101 (1981).

CHAPTER 17

TAXATION[1]

§17.1 Taxation and Efficiency

Taxation is sometimes used to change the allocation of resources (recall our discussion of pollution taxes) or the distribution of wealth, but mainly it is used to pay for public services. An efficient revenue tax would be one that required the user of a public service to pay the opportunity costs of his use. But this would be treating public services just like private goods, whereas they are public services precisely because it is judged infeasible or inexpedient to sell them. In the case of some public services, such as national defense, free-rider problems prevent the use of the market to provide the optimum amount of the service: The individual who refused to buy his share of the cost of our nuclear deterrent would receive the same protection from it as those who paid for it. In the case of other public services, such as education, the provision of the service by the government rests primarily on a judgment that unwillingness to pay the cost of the service should not disentitle the individual to use it.[1]

The heavy emphasis placed on distributive considerations in discussions of tax policy explains why the chapter on taxation appears in this part of the book. But efficiency considerations also weigh heavily. Taxing an activity creates an incentive for people engaged in it to substitute another activity that is taxed less heavily. Presumably, however, they were more productively employed in the first activity; otherwise the imposition of a tax would not have been necessary to induce them to

---

1. See Marvin A. Chirelstein, Federal Income Taxation (3d ed. 1982).

§17.1   1. Recall our discussion (§5.4 *supra*) of the potential conflict of interest between parents and children. Observe, however, that the government could require children to attend school, defray part or all of the costs of education for children whose parents lacked monetary means, and establish minimum educational standards — all without actually operating the schools.

switch to the second. Hence the tax has reduced the efficiency with which resources are being employed. The inefficiency might have been avoided or at least reduced, without revenue loss, had the tax been designed to minimize substitution effects; allocative efficiency in taxation is maximized by making the tax rate vary inversely with the elasticity of demand for the good or activity that is taxed.[2] Unfortunately, attempts to minimize allocative inefficiency may clash with the distributive goals of tax policy. A flat federal head tax on adults, for example, would have minimum efficiency effects (minimum, but not zero, because it would induce some people to emigrate), but it would be highly oppressive to poor people unless it were very low — in which event it would generate little revenue.

This chapter examines the distributive and efficiency consequences of several different forms of taxation. Death taxes are touched on in the next chapter, and problems of tax policy resulting from the federal structure of our governmental system are discussed in Chapter 26.

§17.2   Conscription[1]

Many taxes are implicit. The draft — conscription — is one. The economic objection to the military draft is that it gives the government an incentive to substitute excessive amounts of manpower for other defense inputs because the price of military manpower to the government is lower than the opportunity costs of the draftees' time. The objection is decisive (at least from an economic standpoint) in times of peace, when both the demand for and the dangers to military personnel are relatively small, thus limiting the amount of government expenditure necessary to obtain the desired personnel. But the expenditures necessary to man the armed forces in wartime on a purely volunteer basis would be very great. A substantial increase in tax rates (or in the rate of inflation, which is a form of taxation) would be required, with — as we are shortly to see — inefficient substitution effects. A wartime draft that is not anticipated (because the war was not anticipated) is unlikely to have similar substitution effects.[2] It is like a head tax.[3] The balance between the incentive that the draft gives the military to use too much

2. This is the tax counterpart to Ramsey pricing (see §12.5 *supra*) — in fact, Ramsey originally proposed his approach as a method of optimal taxation, not public utility pricing.
   §17.2   1. See The Military Draft: Selected Readings on Conscription (Martin Anderson ed. 1982), especially pt. IV and ch. 41.
   2. An anticipated draft would lead people to alter their educational and occupational choices depending on the pattern of exemptions from the draft.
   3. It could still be avoided — by emigration, self-mutilation, etc. — but these are very costly avoidance measures and so are resorted to infrequently.

manpower and the inefficient substitution effects of very high tax rates is uncertain, but probably the former inefficiency is relatively unimportant in conditions of all-out war when the military is not subject to a tight budget constraint and it may be optimal to assign virtually the whole physically fit young male population to the armed forces.[4]

§17.3 Excise Taxes

We begin our consideration of explicit taxes with a retail sales tax: For every widget sold the producer must remit 30 percent of the price to the government.[1] The widget industry is assumed to be competitive, meaning that before the tax was imposed the price of a widget was equal to its marginal cost. The effect of the tax is to shift the industry's demand schedule (viewed here as the schedule of average revenue to the industry rather than of average cost to the consumer) as shown in Figure 17.1. The industry's price will be determined by the intersection of the marginal cost schedule with the new average revenue schedule. That price is p_2 and is higher than p_1, the price before the tax was imposed. At the higher price the amount demanded by consumers, q_2, is less than the amount demanded before the tax was imposed. The higher price induces some consumers to shift to other products that now seem cheaper, although in fact they are either more costly to produce than, or inferior to, widgets — otherwise the substitution would have occurred before the tax pushed up the price. The tax has the same substitution effect as would monopoly pricing of widgets.

The magnitude of the effect depends on the price elasticity of demand. If demand is highly elastic, a relatively small increase in price induced by the tax will lead to a relatively large reduction in output. The revenue generated by the tax, being a function of sales, will also be smaller than if the tax had been levied on a product for which demand was less elastic. Thus the goals of minimizing the substitution effects of taxation and of maximizing the government's tax revenues both argue for taxing price-inelastic industries or activities the heaviest — the Ramsey principle.

But what of the distributive effects of the tax? The government revenue generated by the tax is represented in Figure 17.1 by the hatched

4. Evaluate eminent domain as a method of taxation, using the analysis developed above. How does it resemble conscription?

§17.3 1. For simplicity, we assume that the producer sells directly to the consumer. How would the analysis have to be modified if the tax were imposed on a retailer who purchased from the producer and resold to the consumer? We also assume that the product taxed is well defined. This important assumption is relaxed later.

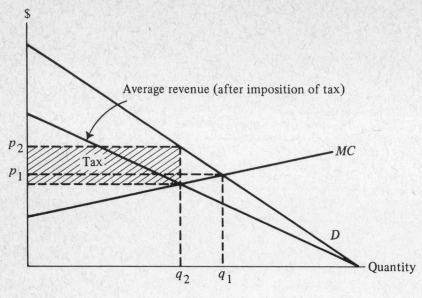

Figure 17.1

area. Notice that most of the tax, $q_2 \times (p_2 - p_1)$ is borne by the consumers of widgets.[2] Taxes on consumption tend to be regressive, that is, to take a larger fraction of the income of the nonwealthy than of the wealthy, because the nonwealthy consume a larger fraction of their income. True, the nature of the product — whether it is more likely to be bought by a wealthy than by a nonwealthy person — is also important. A tax on yachts would probably be progressive (subject to a qualification noted below). Products in heavy demand by the wealthy, however, are not necessarily (or generally) those for which demand is inelastic, so an efficient excise tax will often be regressive and a progressive excise tax often inefficient.

We said that "most" of the widget tax was shifted to consumers; the remainder comes out of the economic rents received by owners of factors of production used in making widgets. A tax that fell *entirely* on rents would have attractive features. By definition, there would be no substitution effects. Rents are a return over and above opportunity costs, that is, alternative returns, so a reduction in rents will not induce a shift of the resource to an alternative use. And a tax on rents certainly sounds progressive: Are not the recipients of rents invariably well-to-do? They are not. Notice that one effect of our widget tax is to reduce the output of the industry and so, presumably, its demand for inputs, including labor. If the workers laid off by the industry have equally

---

2. How else are consumers hurt by the tax?

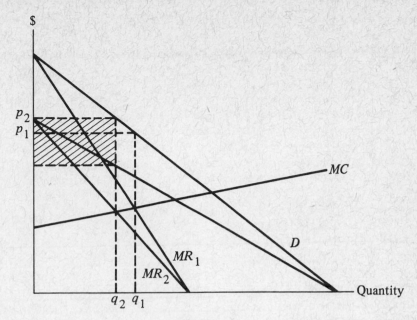

Figure 17.2

good job opportunities elsewhere and zero relocation costs, they will not be harmed by the tax. But if not, they will be harmed. They will lose rents that they earn from their present employment.[3]

If monopoly profits could be detected and measured, they could be taxed directly, and since they are rents the tax would have no substitution effects. An *excise* tax on monopolies, however, has essentially the same substitution and distributive effects as excise taxes on the goods of competitive sellers. As shown in Figure 17.2, the excise tax confronts the monopolist with a new demand (average revenue) schedule, which causes him to recompute his marginal revenue schedule. His new price, at the intersection of his marginal cost and new marginal revenue, is higher and output smaller. The tax (the hatched area in the diagram) is borne by consumers, the monopolist in the form of reduced monopoly profits, and owners of resources in inelastic supply used in the production of the product.

A final refinement in the economic analysis of excise taxes should be noted.[4] We have implicitly assumed that the tax is some fraction of

3. If we were discussing not an excise tax on widgets or yachts or some other minor part of the nation's productive activity but a general excise tax, i.e., a tax on goods sold, then the type of partial equilibrium analysis sketched in the text — an analysis in which the interactions between the taxed activity and the rest of the economy are ignored — would be inadequate. A much more complex type of analysis of tax incidence, employing a general equilibrium framework, would become necessary.

4. On which see Yoram Barzel, An Alternative Approach to the Analysis of Taxation, 84 J. Pol. Econ. 1177 (1976).

the price of the good (*ad valorem*). But a tax so computed will give the firm an incentive to reduce the quality (and hence price) of the good. For example, if the automobile excise tax is based on the retail price of the car with all options (air conditioning, stereo, etc.), and the options if bought separately are subject to no tax or a lower tax, the manufacturer will have an incentive to offer fewer options with the car. If, on the other hand, the tax is a flat tax (e.g., $100 per car), the manufacturer will have an incentive to increase quality — increments of quality being tax free. Which distortion seems more likely, and which form of excise tax would you therefore expect to be more common?

§17.4   Real Estate Taxes

Henry George's famous proposal to replace all taxes with a single tax on land was an attempt to limit taxation to pure rents.[1] The rent of land, however, is not great enough to meet all of a modern government's revenue demands. There is also a problem of measurement, arising from the fact that land is as likely to be used by the owner as to be rented to others. If I own a piece of land, build an apartment house on it, and rent the apartments, part of the rental I receive will consist of the rent of the land, but part will consist of revenue from the improvements on the property and this revenue may not include any economic rent at all. And if I own and occupy a house on my land, I will receive an imputed rent equal to the rent that I could have obtained by leasing the land. Another problem is that many landowners are not wealthy people. A heavy tax on the rent of land would impoverish many farmers, workmen, and retirees who had purchased land at a price that capitalized the expected rents. Suppose a farmer, using borrowed money, buys good farmland for $1,000 that yields an annual rent of $100, net of property taxes. A tax of $90 a year is later imposed on the property. His return will fall to $10. If he sells the land, he will recover only a small fraction of the money that he paid for it.

In practice, real estate taxes tax the rent of land but much else besides. Indeed, the improvements to land are usually taxed much more heavily than the land itself. One result is to give landowners an artificial incentive to avoid (or postpone) improving their land. More important, a tax on land improvements is essentially an excise tax. Consider an apartment house development. If the real estate tax is proportioned to the rent rolls, the owner will treat it in the same way that our widget manufacturer treated the sales tax: as reducing average revenue a uniform percentage

§17.4   1. See Henry George, Progress and Poverty (1879).

at all levels of output. To maximize return in these circumstances, he will raise price and reduce output. The burden of the tax will thus be shared between consumers — the people to whom apartments are rented — and a rentier — the owner of the land.

Real estate taxes also undermine the property rights system. Suppose I am a farmer in an area where more and more land is being developed for residential purposes. My land is worth only $100 as farmland but a developer offers me $200. I refuse because the land is worth more to me than to him — I am sentimentally attached to the land and do not want to move. At what value should the real estate tax assessor appraise the land? If he assesses it at the higher value he may force me to sell to the developer, since my farm income may be insufficient to pay a tax assessed on the basis of a use of the land that would yield a larger pecuniary income. From the assessor's standpoint this forced exchange is a good thing because it increases the tax base. But the land is more valuable to me than to the developer. The real estate tax has the same effect here as eminent domain, which also systematically extinguishes land values in excess of market price (see §3.6 *supra*).

§17.5   Corporate Income Taxation

The corporate income tax is in one aspect a crude device for taxing rents, here the rent that consists of the difference between a firm's total revenues and its total costs.[1] The trouble is that the tax in its current form does not permit a deduction for the cost of equity capital and so falls not only on profits in the economic sense, or other rents, but also (and probably mainly) on the cost of equity capital. The result is an incentive to substitute forms of capital, such as debt and human capital, the price of which to the firm is deductible; to substitute labor for capital inputs; and to substitute other forms of business organization for the corporate form. Also, since the cost of equity capital (as distinct from monopoly or other rents) is a marginal cost, part of the corporate income tax is passed along to consumers in the form of higher product prices, just like an (explicit) excise tax.[2]

Many intricate legal problems arise under the corporate income tax,

§17.5   1. The corporate income tax also serves to limit exploitation by taxpayers of the favorable treatment accorded capital gains. See §17.10 *infra*.

2. There is a large but inconclusive empirical literature on the incidence of the corporate income tax. An important study is Marian Krzyzaniak & Richard A. Musgrave, The Shifting of the Corporation Income Tax (1963). See also Richard A. Musgrave & Peggy B. Musgrave, Public Finance in Theory and Practice 411-419 (4th ed. 1984). The problem is the need to employ a general equilibrium approach. See §17.3 *supra*, note 3. Why is that needed here?

and often they have an economic dimension. Here is an example. If a corporation that has appreciated property liquidates, thereby transferring the property to the shareholders, and they later sell it, should the sale be treated as a sale by the corporation on which it must pay income tax or as a sale by the shareholders on which no corporate income tax is due? The latter is the approach of the Internal Revenue Code — and is objectionable on economic grounds as creating unnecessary transaction costs (the costs of a liquidation motivated by a desire to avoid corporate income tax). In some cases there may be even more serious misallocative results. Suppose a corporation has one plant, which is fully insured, and the plant burns down. The insurance proceeds minus the depreciated original cost of the plant would be treated as a taxable gain to the corporation even if it decided to liquidate. But suppose that instead the corporation buys or builds a new plant, using the full insurance proceeds for this purpose, and then sells the plant and distributes the proceeds of the sale to its shareholders, pursuant to a plan of complete liquidation adopted before the sale; there would be no corporate income tax.[3] The difference in tax treatment might induce a firm to build or buy a new plant even though it would be more efficient to liquidate without buying or rebuilding. (Why doesn't the Coase Theorem eliminate this inefficiency?)

Here is another problem. A business is sold for $1 million; should the buyer be allowed to treat the entire purchase price as a depreciable cost, or must the assets comprising the business be valued separately for purposes of determining that cost? The latter is the approach used; and if the assets are valued at less than the purchase price of the business, the difference is assigned to an intangible asset called goodwill or going-concern value and cannot be depreciated for tax purposes. Does this make economic sense?[4] If the firm's physical assets are valued by capitalizing the earnings that the firm is expected to generate with them, then since the purchase price will similarly be a capitalization of expected earnings, there will never be a residual. But if the physical assets are valued on the basis of what it would cost to replace them, there may well be a residual. Among the possible reasons for the discrepancy, two seem particularly important. First, there may be nonphysical assets, particularly human capital in various forms. Second, the firm may have some monopoly power, so that the price of its output is not bid down to marginal cost. In the second case, whether a tax deduction should be allowed depends, in principle, on the source of the monopoly power — but that would hardly be a feasible inquiry for the Internal Revenue Service to undertake in every sale of business. In the first case, the problem, in principle, is one of gauging the life of an unfamiliar

3. See Central Tablet Mfg. Co. v. United States, 417 U.S. 673, 690 (1974).
4. See Richard L. Doernberg & Thomas D. Hall, The Tax Treatment of Going-Concern Value, 52 Geo. Wash. L. Rev. 353 (1984).

(to the taxing authorities) kind of asset in order to determine the optimal period of depreciation. However, since under current law firms are allowed to depreciate physical assets for tax purposes much faster than the assets are actually expected to wear out, it would be arbitrary to worry about depreciating nonphysical assets at a faster rate than they wear out. When to all this is added the difficulty and cost of valuing assets by nonmarket methods, a strong argument can be made that the buyer should be permitted to depreciate the entire cost of acquiring the seller's business.

§17.6 Personal Income Taxation: Introduction

We may define an optimum tax as one that
  (1) has a large tax base, which facilitates the raising of the large amounts of revenues that modern governments demand;
  (2) taxes an activity the demand for which is highly inelastic, so that the substitution effects of the tax are minimal (the Ramsey criterion);
  (3) does not increase inequality[1] or offend equity;[2] and
  (4) is inexpensive to administer.
The taxation of personal income might seem to approximate this optimum. The tax base is large, the demand for income presumably is inelastic, income is a broad measure of welfare, and collection of the tax is facilitated by the fact that most people are employed by organizations. But in fact the second and third desiderata mentioned above cannot be attained with an income tax, because they depend on a definition of income so broad as to impose prohibitive administrative costs.

Even if it were feasible to tax all real income (including leisure), the income tax would not be an ideal tax. Income includes money that the recipient saves rather than spends. If such income is not taxed, the tax is not an income but a spending or consumption tax. The exclusion of saved income from taxation would violate the third criterion of optimal taxation by favoring wealthy people, who save a larger fraction of their income than the poor. But the taxation of income that is saved creates two economic problems.

The first, and lesser, derives from the potential conflict of interest between generations, mentioned in Chapter 5. Money that is saved is

---

§17.6   1. We postpone to §17.11 the question to what extent the tax system should attempt to reduce economic inequality.
  2. A tax on red haired people would offend equity; it probably would not increase inequality. Would it be efficient?

used to invest in activity that may not yield its full benefits until after the death of the investor, who has thus sacrificed his own consumption to increase that of future generations. A social obligation to save for future generations could conceivably be derived from the contract theory of distributive justice discussed in the last chapter: People in the original position, not knowing to what generation they belong, would want to make some provision to assure that all of the resources of society were not consumed by the first generation. But as a matter of fact there is no danger of the first generation's doing such a thing; it is too small, and too deficient in knowledge, to be able to consume more than a trivial fraction of the earth's resources. It is only in advanced modern societies that depletion of resources becomes a potential social problem. But precisely in those societies, the rate of accretion of new knowledge is so rapid that it is almost certain that the next generation will be wealthier than the present one; and why should we worry about reducing our own consumption so that they can consume even more? [3]

The more serious problem is that a tax on income that is saved reduces capital investment in general, not merely investment for the distant future. Machinery and most other capital assets wear out physically or become obsolete in a lot less time than a lifetime, and if savings are discouraged by taxation there will be a lot fewer such assets. Income taxation discourages saving, and thus investment, by taxing not only the income from savings but the income that goes into savings. Suppose I am in the 50 percent marginal income tax bracket and am trying to decide whether to consume $100 of my income or invest it in a bond that will mature at the end of one year and yield 5 percent interest (assume zero inflation). After tax I shall have $50 to either consume or invest. If I consume I will obtain a net benefit measured by the consumer surplus that the goods and services that I buy for $50 will generate, and let us assume that that figure is $2.50. I will pay no income tax on this benefit. But if instead I invest the bond, I will pay a 50 percent tax on the $2.50 in interest that the bond yields me. The services generated by consumption and the services generated by saving are thus burdened differently, which is inefficient. (Under what conditions will I nonetheless decide to save?)

It might seem, though, that to take care of this problem by replacing an income tax with a consumption tax with the same rates would simply create a bias in the opposite direction, by making my choice one between consuming a measly $50 and having $105 to spend at the end of the year. But this is not true. I have forgone the $2.50 in consumer surplus that I would have got from consuming the income that instead I invested;

3. Are there any market arrangements by which unborn generations can in effect buy from the present generation resources for their use? And what does the discussion in the text imply about the wisdom of corporate income taxation? The next chapter has a fuller discussion of intergenerational wealth allocation.

and should I try to recoup by spending my $5 in interest, I will have to pay the 50 percent consumption tax on it, as I will also have to do if I decide to consume the $100 this year.[4]

Notice, however, that the consumption tax rate would have to be higher than the income tax rate that it replaced (why?), at least initially (why this qualification?), in order to maintain the same level of government revenues. What would be the effect on incentives to work and to save?

§17.7   The Definition of Income

The exclusion of any real from taxable income reduces the tax base, creates incentives to substitute activities that yield the excluded form of income, and may, depending on the wealth of those who receive the excluded form of income, increase inequality. The broadest definition of income would be all pecuniary and nonpecuniary receipts, including not only leisure and (other) nonpecuniary income from household production but also gifts, bequests, and prizes.[1] If our paramount concern is with minimizing the substitution effects of personal income taxation, then the question of whether to treat gifts, bequests, and prizes as taxable income may turn on whether these are pure gratuities or actually compensation for work. Is a parent's gift to a child compensation for services performed or anticipated, or a pure expression of love (i.e., of interdependent positive utilities)?[2] If the former, it should be taxed lest children be induced to substitute household for market production because of the differential tax treatment of income from these alternative employments. If the latter, the failure to tax the gift not only would not cause a substitution away from market employment but would be a peculiarly costly form of taxation, since it would reduce the utility of two or more people (parents and child) in order to collect money from one. This analysis suggests an analytical basis for treating gifts that occur in the course of a business relationship as income, and (less strongly) other gifts not as income.[3]

4. The case for a spending or consumption tax is argued strongly in William D. Andrews, A Consumption-Type or Cash Flow Personal Income Tax, 87 Harv. L. Rev. 1113 (1974). Problems of implementation are discussed in Michael J. Graetz, Implementing a Progressive Consumption Tax, 92 Harv. L. Rev. 1575 (1979).

§17.7   1. It is sometimes argued that gifts should be excluded from taxable income because they are not part of the national income (why aren't they?). Why is that irrelevant?

2. Cf. §5.1 *supra.* Does it matter whether the gift is *inter vivos* (i.e., taking effect before the giver's death) or testamentary?

3. The distinction was rejected in Commissioner v. Duberstein, 363 U.S. 278 (1960), but was eventually restored by the enactment of §274(b) of the current Internal Revenue Code, which limits the deductibility of most business gifts to $25.

The present tax law distinguishes between prizes won in a contest (which are taxable) and other prizes (such as the Nobel Prize), which are not. The distinction is unsound. To fail to tax prizes in contests would induce people to substitute the entering of contests for other forms of productive activity.[4] But not taxing Nobel Prize winnings and other honors has a similar effect. The existence of these prizes affects research decisions by people in eligible occupations and even the choice of occupations. Although the elasticity of response to changes in the tax status (and hence in the net monetary benefits) of these prizes may well be slight, that is an argument for taxing them heavily rather than for exempting them from tax.[5]

Administrative costs preclude a comprehensive definition of income for tax purposes, but some of the necessary exclusions, notably that of leisure, may have significant substitution effects. The exclusion of leisure from income biases the choice of activities in favor of those that yield leisure instead of pecuniary income — activities such as teaching in which long, paid vacations[6] are an important part of the compensation for the job. A similar bias is introduced by the necessary exclusion of fame, prestige, comfort, excitement, and other intangible yields of activity, as well as the failure to exclude from taxable income that part of income which represents compensation for the dangers or disamenities (including risk in the economic sense) of some occupations. But many of the exclusions cannot be justified in terms of overwhelming measurement costs. Three examples are: services that are not sold in a market, the imputed rental of owner-occupied premises, and fringe benefits.

1. Often there is a choice between contracting for a service in the market and producing it in the household. An income tax law that counts only pecuniary receipts as income biases the choice in favor of household production. Probably the most important such bias created by the present income tax law arises from the failure to include the considerable real (but not pecuniary) income generated by housewives' services within the home. Suppose a woman could earn $10,000 outside the home, on which she would pay an income tax of $2,000, while if she stayed home her services would be worth only $9,000. The value of her work would be increased if she worked outside, but the effect of the incomplete definition of income in the tax law is to induce her to stay home.

There are of course serious difficulties in valuing nonmarket services; we pointed out earlier the error of equating the value of a housewife's services to the wages of a domestic servant (see §6.11 *supra*). But since those wages represent a minimum estimate of the value of most house-

4. In what sense is a lottery or contest productive activity?
5. Must we also consider the elasticity of response of the people who put up the money for such prizes to changes in the tax status of the prizes?
6. What does "paid vacation" mean to an economist?

wives' services, the inclusion of that amount as income imputed to every household in which the wife did not work outside the home would be a step in the right direction. The tax law has taken some halting steps to reduce the substitution effects caused by failing to tax housewives' imputed income by giving tax credits for modest expenditures on child care[7] and for some of the market earnings of the principal taxpayer's spouse. Because the credits are so modest and because tax credits are highly progressive compared to deductions, which are regressive (why the difference?), they have little effect on the incentives of the women who would be most productive in the market. The child care deduction is really quite weird; it encourages entry into the market of precisely those women who are most productively engaged in the household!

2. A man gives his two sons, A and B, $10,000 each. A puts his $10,000 in a savings bank that pays 5 percent annual interest, which he uses to pay the rent on the apartment that he leases. Because he is in the 20 percent federal income tax bracket, he pays $100 of the interest he receives each year to the government. B, who is in the same tax bracket as A, uses his $10,000 to purchase an apartment that has the same rental value as the apartment rented by A. B pays no income tax although he has put the same amount of money to the identical use as A. He is simply better off than A to the extent of $100 a year. This arbitrary difference in treatment creates an incentive (increased by the interest deduction) for people to own rather than rent their homes and for lawyers to create complex legal forms, such as the condominium, designed to enable rental properties to be recast as fee simple properties.[8]

There would of course be administrative difficulties in estimating the real but nonpecuniary rental income that people derive from owning their homes rather than renting them from other people. But even a crude estimate, biased downward, would reduce the incentive to substitute home ownership for rental. Observe that once this step were taken, the deductibility of home mortgage interest payments would cease to be objectionable, for the payments would then be an expense for the production of taxable income.[9]

An additional distortion in the tax treatment of owner-occupied homes is created by allowing the seller to escape having to pay any capital gains tax if he reinvests the proceeds in buying another home. The rationale for this provision — to avoid taxing purely nominal price rises caused by inflation — is unpersuasive, as we shall see when we discuss capital gains taxation.

7. See William D. Popkin, Household Services and Child Care in the Income Tax and Social Security Laws, 50 Ind. L.J. 238 (1975).

8. England once taxed imputed rental income. See Richard B. Goode, The Individual Income Tax 117-125 (rev. ed. 1976).

9. The deduction of expenses incurred in the production of income is discussed in the next section.

3. The exclusion of perquisites from taxable income gives executives an incentive to take part of their compensation in the form of a fancy office, a company car, etc., even if these things are worth less to them (excluding tax considerations) than their cash equivalent; the difference is pure waste. The exclusion of fringe benefits gives employees an incentive to take part of their compensation in life and health insurance, vacations, and pension benefits,[10] even if they would prefer — tax considerations aside — the cash equivalent. In many cases, the inclusion of the cash value of the benefits in taxable income would not impose substantial administrative expenses.

§17.8   Income Tax Deductions

The presumption should be (and is) against permitting the taxpayer to deduct expenses in figuring his taxable income, for an expenditure is generally not a reduction in welfare but the necessary step by which people transform money into an increase in welfare: A man is richer, not poorer, after he has exchanged cash for a new television set. Expenditures designed solely to produce income, however, are not of this character. They increase welfare only insofar as they generate income, so if the income is fully taxable the deduction of business expenses is necessary to avoid double taxation (why?). The principal problem with this deduction is that some business expenditures are simultaneously consumption expenditures. The restaurant meals and hotel lodging that I purchase on a business trip represent expenses that are normally indispensable to the production of the income that I obtain from the trip. At the same time, they represent consumption activities in which I would have engaged in some form had I not gone on the trip.

The law has dealt with the problem in a seemingly arbitrary manner by permitting the deduction of all living expenses (unless "lavish") incurred in overnight business trips, while forbidding as "personal" expenses the deduction of any expense for commuting to work and most other living expenses incurred in the place where one has one's office. Some distinction between local and out-of-town travel expenses, however, makes economic sense. Even if one didn't work, one would have to eat lunch; since the cost of having lunch is thus not avoidable by not working, it is not a cost of work. Commuting enables a worker to live in the place of his choice rather than next door to his place of work; it is therefore as much a personal as a business expense. There

10. Pensions are taxable. In what sense therefore is there a tax incentive to take income in the form of pension benefits rather than current salary?

is some personal consumption in out-of-town travel, of course, but its value is likely to be less than the full expense; and the difference is a pure business expense.

In principle, the difference, and not the entire expense, is what should be deductible from taxable income.[1] Suppose I take a three-day business trip to San Francisco, stay in a hotel that charges $100 a day, and eat meals costing me a total of $90. The full $390 should not be deductible; the saving in personal consumption expenditures made possible by the trip should be subtracted. The lodging component of the offset will usually be small, and for administrative convenience should probably be set at zero, since the marginal cost (cleaning, wear and tear, electricity, etc.) of spending one more night at home is usually trival. The meal offset will be larger, but it will be less than $90, because the cost of meals prepared at home is generally much less than the cost of restaurant meals. Granted, a $30 meal at a restaurant would be worth more to the diners than the $3 meal that they would have eaten at home; otherwise they would have stayed home. But since very few people eat frequently at expensive restaurants, the $90 that I spent on meals away from home in my hypothetical example probably yielded me a good deal less than $90 in value as measured by willingness to pay. Perhaps use of a compromise figure, such as 50 percent of the price of business meals, would be an appropriate way of implementing the suggested reform.[2]

The medical expense and casualty loss deductions in the tax code appear to be motivated by an effort to distinguish between expenditures that increase personal well-being and expenditures designed merely to restore the taxpayer to a former state of well-being.[3] The goal is presumably to equalize tax burdens among individuals who may have identical pecuniary incomes but different real incomes. One can sympathize with the goal but question both its feasibility and the specific means adopted to attain it. Consider the wage premium paid to people who have dangerous jobs. The premium does not increase their well-being compared with that of people who have safe jobs; it merely compensates them for the danger (what if they love danger?). But it would be infeasible to permit deduction of such wage premiums. Or consider two families of equal income, one more efficient at consumption than the other and so deriving a higher well-being from the same amount of money; again

§17.8 1. The government tried this approach long ago but gave it up because of its administrative complexity. The story is told in United States v. Correll, 389 U.S. 299, 301 n.6 (1967). See also Moss v. Commissioner of Internal Revenue, 758 F.2d 211 (7th Cir. 1985).

2. How should commuting expenses be treated under this approach?

3. The distinction is defended in William D. Andrews, Personal Deductions in an Ideal Income Tax, 86 Harv. L. Rev. 309 (1972), and Richard A. Epstein, The Consumption and Loss of Personal Property Under the Internal Revenue Code, 23 Stan. L. Rev. 454 (1971).

a deduction to equalize the after-tax well-being of the two families would be infeasible. In these and many other ways relative pecuniary income distorts relative well-being, and since most of these distortions cannot be corrected, it is doubtful whether an attempt to correct one or two of them contributes much to the goal of horizontal equity.

The specific deductions, moreover, are badly designed in terms of the goal. The measure of the medical deduction should be the cost of illness to the taxpayer rather than the cost of medical treatment. Some illnesses may be very costly but, either because of the state of the medical art or the taxpayer's financial situation, may not evoke substantial expenditures on treatment. And medical expenditures are sometimes incurred to increase well-being (for example, a face-lifting or nose-straightening operation) rather than to treat an illness or other deprivation of well-being; the examples suggest, moreover, how frequently tenuous is the distinction between increasing and restoring well-being. As for the casualty loss deduction, it at least is measured by the loss, rather than the reparative expenditure; but its effect is not so much to compensate people whose well-being has been impaired as to compensate people who have lacked the foresight to insure. The deduction also reduces the cost of self-insurance (why?), primarily to the benefit of wealthy taxpayers.

Part of the medical deduction, however, may be justifiable economically as a repair of human capital. Human capital, as we know, is as much an asset as a factory; it is purchased with inputs of time and money and yields pecuniary service over the (often very long) life of the asset. Since the income that it yields is taxable, the expenses of keeping it in good repair should be deductible — although, in principle, not all at once but over the period in which the expenses generate income. (Why, by the way, does efficiency require a temporal matching of income and expense for tax purposes?) This raises a narrow and a broad question. The narrow question is: Does this discussion suggest an economic argument for deducting the expense of some cosmetic surgery? The broad question is: Shouldn't the cost of human capital be amortizable over the working life of the owner and be deductible from his income? The law does not allow this, and there is a theoretical as well as practical reason why. Much of the cost of education, which is perhaps the major source of human capital (along with one's natural endowment of brains, energy, and character — an endowment that the owner does not pay for either), is not borne by the owner. And the principal cost — the earnings that are lost by going to school rather than working — is in effect written off at the time the investment is made, since taxable income is reduced by the full amount of the forgone earnings. There seems no need for an additional deduction.[4]

4. How would you treat the human capital that is created by on-the-job training? Does it matter whether it is firm-specific, or general, human capital? See Paul B. Stephan III, Federal Income Taxation and Human Capital, 70 Va. L. Rev. 1357 (1984).

Although many income tax deductions are questionable, to call them tax subsidies is a questionable usage. Deductions that are required by efficiency, notably deductions for business expenses, are not subsidies in any sense. But even where deductions have no economic (or perhaps other) rationale, but merely reflect the political muscle of the benefited class, to call them subsidies is implicitly to treat the government as the owner of all the personal income in the country. It is to say that by allowing deductions — or for that matter by setting the tax rate anywhere below 100 percent — the government is making a gift to the person whom it allows to keep some of the income that he earned through his own work or investment. Deductions not justified by Ramsey or other principles of optimal taxation are not on that account subsidies.

An important deduction, politically as well as economically, is the charitable deduction. It is politically important because it transfers from the government to the individual taxpayer some of the power to decide who shall be recipients of altruistic transfers, a decision that in most societies is made at the political level. It is economically important because it responds to the free-rider problem in charitable giving that was pointed out in Chapter 16. The charitable deduction may actually be more efficient than direct government charitable giving in inducing charitable expenditures. If as some empirical studies have found the price elasticity of charitable giving is greater than one, meaning that a 1 percent reduction in price leads to a more than 1 percent increase in the amount given, then the charitable deduction costs the Treasury less in lost revenue than charities gain in contributions.[5]

§17.9   The Special Treatment of Capital Gains

Federal law taxes earnings only when they are realized. Thus, if a corporation does not distribute all of its earnings to the shareholders in the form of dividends, the undistributed earnings are not taxed as personal income. This is proper. Retained earnings are not the property of the shareholder. Except in liquidation, they enrich him only insofar as they increase the value of his shares. It is the increment in that value that is income to him. When the stockholder sells his shares he must pay tax on the appreciation, including that part of the appreciation attributable to the retention of earnings. But this is not an adequate substitute for taxation of the appreciation as it occurs, since the postponement

5. See Martin Feldstein, A Contribution to the Theory of Tax Expenditures: The Case of Charitable Giving, in The Economics of Taxation 99 (Henry J. Aaron & Michael J. Boskin eds. 1980).
   What would be the two effects on charitable giving of reducing the top marginal income tax bracket from 50 to 35 percent?

of tax gives the taxpayer the interest on the amount he would have paid in tax had the appreciation been taxed when it occurred. The favorable tax treatment of appreciation is enhanced by taxing capital gains at a lower rate than ordinary income.

The favorable tax treatment of capital gains has had a number of inefficient consequences. The shareholder windfalls it causes may have been what led Congress to impose a corporate income tax, which as discussed earlier in this chapter is an inefficient tax. It may also explain the odd practice of corporations in sometimes buying up shares of their own stock in the open market (this is sometimes but not always also an anti-takeover device). The shareholder who sells his stock to the corporation pays only a capital gains tax; if instead of using its earnings to buy up shares the corporation had paid out the earnings in dividends, the same shareholder would have had to pay income tax on the same gain. It might seem that the corporation could bring about the same result just by retaining the earnings and using them in its business; the corporation would have more capital, and presumably its stock price would rise. But depending on the shareholders' confidence in management's ability to invest these earnings profitably, it might not rise by the full amount of the retained earnings. This presumably is the reason why closed-end mutual funds (where the shareholder has no right of redemption) usually sell at a discount from the market value of the stocks held by the funds.

But the special treatment of capital gains does give corporations an incentive to retain rather than distribute earnings; and by making corporations less dependent on new stock issues to finance expansion, and perhaps also by reducing the debt-equity ratio in corporations' capital structures, this reduces the discipline of the capital market. Also, people are induced to cling to property, even if it would be more valuable in other hands, by the desire to avoid a tax that grows larger every year as the property appreciates. And they are led to substitute activities that yield capital gains, such as real estate investment, for equally or more productive activities that yield ordinary income.

Given the corporate income tax, however, the taxation of capital gains at ordinary-income rates, indeed at any rate, would involve double taxation. And that might bias investment toward noncorporate modes of doing business — although the answer is not just to untax capital gains from selling corporate stock but also to untax corporate dividends.

There is an especially powerful economic objection to taxing capital gains that represent true capital increments. Compare two cases. In one, the price of a corporation's stock rises by the amount of the corporation's post-tax retained earnings. In the other, the price of the corporation's stock rises because the corporation has discovered that it owns unexpectedly valuable mineral resources. In the second case, the capital gain from the appreciation in the price of the stock results from the capitalization of future earnings, which will be taxed as they are received; in the first case, the appreciation results from the accumulation of past earnings. In both cases there is multiple taxation because of the corporate income tax, but in the second there actually is triple taxation: the tax on the capital gain, the corporate income tax when the earnings are received, and personal income tax on whatever part of the earnings are distributed as dividends.

Furthermore, it is one thing to want to tax unrealized appreciation in some cases (which cases?) in order to eliminate any vestige of favoritism for capital gains, and another to design a practical system for doing so. Where the capital asset is a share of stock, it is tempting simply to tax the retained earnings of the corporation as income to the shareholders, as well as the earnings that are paid out in dividends. But apart from the fundamental point that money over which the shareholders have no direct control is not really (or at least fully) their income, this would present formidable practical difficulties, especially in the case of corporate earnings that had to be allocated among different classes of securities.[1] The taxation of unrealized appreciation (e.g., of increments in the market value of the share of stock) would not present these problems (why not?) but would present other, equally serious problems. Taxpayers would find it difficult to predict their tax liability. Liquidity problems would frequently force taxpayers to sell securities or other property in order to pay taxes on unrealized appreciation. The provisions for averaging income from year to year would have to be expanded greatly (why?). The corporate income tax would have to be completely rethought (why?).

Finally, the essential advantage of being taxed on only realized appreciation, which is that the taxpayer is in effect permitted to compound interest tax free during the period of deferral, is, in a rough way anyway, balanced by the fact that much of the appreciation that is eventually taxed may be phantom appreciation caused by inflation. An example will illustrate the working of these two forces. Suppose the real interest rate for some class of moderately risky securities is 5 percent, the inflation rate is 3 percent, and the market rate of interest is therefore 8 percent. At the end of 10 years a bond that cost $10,000 and that accumulates interest (compounded annually) will be worth $21,589. If it is sold then and the capital gains tax rate is 25 percent, the tax will be $2,897. Net of inflation, the appreciation is only $6,289, and after tax only $3,392. If there were no inflation[2] the market interest rate would be 5 percent, the tax $1,572, and the bondholder's net appreciation after tax $4,717. This is more than in the case of inflation, indicating that

---

§17.9   1. For example, between holders of convertible debentures (i.e., bonds convertible into stock) and of common stock. (Why is there a problem?)
   2. Anticipated. Why this qualification?

some of the appreciation taxed in that case was indeed phantom appreciation caused by inflation.

By being able to postpone the tax, however, the bondholder was able to earn interest on income that he would otherwise have had to pay out in taxes. If he had received annual payments of $800 (8 percent of $10,000), on which he had paid an annual tax of 25 percent, his after-tax return would have been 6 percent, which compounded at the same rate would have amounted to $7,908 by the end of the period, compared with his actual after-tax return of $8,692 [.75 × ($21,589 − $10,000)]. The longer the tax is deferred, the larger will be the amount of taxation of phantom appreciation but, at the same time, the larger will be the amount of interest earned by the taxpayer as a result of being able to defer the payment of tax.

§17.10   The Progressive Principle

An income tax is proportional when everyone pays the same percentage of his income. Once the tax rate is made to increase with the taxpayer's income — is made progressive — a number of serious administrative problems arise. One is a timing problem. Under a proportional tax, the man who earns $10,000 one year and $100,000 the next pays the same total tax as the man who earns $55,000 both years. Under a progressive income tax system, the first man pays more tax than the second. Hence, a provision for tax averaging of incomes between years becomes necessary to avoid disincentive effects (what effects?).

The most common objection to progressive taxation — more precisely, to the high marginal tax brackets implied by progressive taxation (implied why?) — is that it causes an inefficient substitution of leisure for work, by increasing the price of work relative to that of leisure. But the substitution effect may be offset by an income effect. If leisure is a "superior good" — meaning that proportionately more of it is consumed as one's income rises — then the high marginal tax rate associated with progressive income taxation may reduce the value of leisure to the taxpayer, by reducing his real (i.e., after tax) income by more than it reduces the cost of leisure to him relative to work. (Of course, the income effect is increasingly less likely to equal or exceed the substitution effect as the marginal rate approaches 100 percent.) This point shows incidentally that increasing the personal exemption in the federal income tax reduces work incentives as well as being regressive. It is regressive because it reduces taxable income more for people in high marginal tax brackets than in low ones. It reduces work incentives because it increases the taxpayer's wealth without reducing the price of work relative to that of leisure, since the marginal tax rate is unaffected.

Income effects to one side, if total tax revenues are held constant some taxpayers' marginal tax rates will be lower under a progressive income tax than they would be under a proportional tax. The effect of those lower rates in increasing work incentives could be greater than the disincentive effect of higher marginal rates on other taxpayers. But assuming that generally the highest income taxpayers are society's most productive workers, the disincentive effect of the progressive tax would not be offset by the incentive effect of lower marginal rates for lower income taxpayers.

The progressive income tax reduces the amount of risk taking below the optimal level. Some high incomes consist largely of compensation for the risk of ending up with a very low income. Suppose one composer in 10 earns $100,000 a year from his composing and the other nine earn nothing. Although the average income of the group is very modest, its income is taxed at a much higher rate than it would be if each composer earned $10,000.

Among its other effects, discouraging risk taking perpetuates income inequalities between families. There probably is no more efficient way of creating income mobility, upward and therefore downward too, than by encouraging risk taking. The rich who take risks and lose end up much less rich; the poor who take risks and win end up taking their place. Maybe this is why extreme progressivity is not very popular among Americans of modest means.

Among the other social costs of a highly progressive income tax are the heavy legal and accounting expenditures on avoiding the tax. If the marginal tax rate were 90 percent for income in excess of $50,000,[1] someone with an income of $200,000 might be willing to spend up to $135,000 on measures to avoid having to pay any tax on his last $150,000 of income,[2] and the resources consumed as a result of this expenditure, like the costs incurred in monopolizing — a parallel case — would be unproductive. The analysis is complicated, however, by the income effect of steeply progressive taxation: The high earner will have less money

§17.10 1. Marginal income tax rates of 90 percent or more are found in some European countries, such as Sweden — and, between World War II and the early 1960s, in the United States. The marginal federal income tax rate in the United States was then 70 percent for many years and, even after it was lowered to 50 percent, "unearned" income (mainly interest and dividends) continued to be taxable at rates up to 70 percent; but recently this maximum was lowered to 50 percent too. At this writing there is much talk of a further reduction in the maximum rate, perhaps to as low as 35 percent. State and local income taxes, it should be noted, raise the effective maximum rate above 50 percent.

2. Is this conclusion invalidated by the fact that lawyers frequently can be hired on a contingent fee basis to obtain a reduction in the taxpayer's liability? And why might the taxpayer stop considerably short of $135,000?

to spend on avoiding taxes as long as the taxation system is at least partially effective. But this effect is offset to some extent by the fact that tax-avoidance expenses are tax deductible.[3]

The incentives that high marginal tax rates generate to find methods of tax avoidance may explain the number of ingenious loopholes by which taxpayers escape having to pay the maximum tax rate. These loopholes distort patterns of work and investment (can you think of some examples?). Although loopholes tend to defeat the purpose of progressive taxation in redistributing income from the more to the less wealthy, they do reduce the real incomes of the former. Not only do rich people's legal and accounting expenditures on tax avoidance reduce their real income but so do the inferior returns that much tax-sheltered income generates. Competition among wealthy taxpayers has driven the interest rate on tax-free state and municipal bonds well below the market rate (i.e., the interest rate on obligations of equivalent risk that do not enjoy a tax exemption). The individual who is induced by tax considerations to give a larger proportion of his income to charity than he would otherwise do derives less utility from the income so expended than he would have derived in the absence of high marginal income tax rates. Thus, real income inequality is reduced although redistribution from wealthy to poor may not be accomplished. But it is unclear what is gained by this unless there is much envy in society.

Even though a progressive income tax has serious drawbacks in comparison to a proportional income tax, one contrary consideration may be decisive. Most taxes other than income taxes are regressive; that is, they tax the poor proportionately more heavily than the rich.[4] If the tax system is to be proportional overall, income taxes should be progressive.[5] But should the overall incidence of the tax system be progressive or proportional? One effect of a progressive tax system is that it increases the political attractiveness of inflation as an instrument of policy, for inflation, by pushing more incomes (or whatever else is taxed on a progressive basis) into higher tax brackets, automatically increases governmental revenues by *more* than the increase in inflation (why?).

3. Should they be?

A further consideration is that a reduction in the marginal rates of high-income taxpayers will result in an increase in the marginal rates of lower-income taxpayers and hence an increase in the incentives of the latter to avoid taxation. But they have fewer opportunities for successful avoidance.

4. See Richard A. Musgrave & Peggy B. Musgrave, Public Finance in Theory and Practice 258 (4th ed. 1984).

5. Here it should be noted, however, that the more progressive the tax, the more regressive are its deductions. For example, if a taxpayer in the 20 percent bracket contributes $1,000 to charity, the cost to him is $800, so in effect an expenditure of $800 controls resources worth $1,000. If a taxpayer in the 50 percent marginal tax bracket donates $1,000 to charity, his donation controls the same amount of resources as the poorer taxpayer's but at a cost of only $500. For the same price that the poorer taxpayer must pay to control $1,000 in charitable resources — $800 — the richer taxpayer can "buy" control of the use of $1,600 in resources.

Inflation thus becomes a method by which government can increase its real income without raising the tax rate or otherwise altering the formal tax laws.[6]

It has also been argued that progressive taxation is peculiarly subject to abuse because it permits the electorate to shift the burden of taxation to a numerical minority, composed of people with high incomes.[7] But quite apart from our earlier point about risk taking, the practical ability of the poorer half to shift the burden of taxation to the wealthier half is limited by three factors.

(1) Those in the poorer half who expect to be in the wealthier half some day will be reluctant to support a steeply progressive income tax, especially since income taxation discriminates against the new rich;

(2) the poorer half may be reluctant to adopt a method of taxation that (at least at some level of progressivity) must impair incentives to work, since they benefit from the productivity of hardworking wealthy (or aspiring-to-be-wealthy) people;[8]

(3) simple voter majorities frequently do not determine public policy (see §19.3 *infra*).

A traditional justification for progressive taxation is the greater benefit that the wealthy are presumed to derive from government. Governmental protective services such as national defense and police and fire departments are arguably more valuable to the wealthy than to the nonwealthy: The wealthy man disabled by a criminal suffers a larger earnings loss than a poor man. But an increasing part of the federal, and also of state and local, budgets is devoted to services that benefit the poor. Here the benefits-received rationale breaks down. And under a proportional income tax, the absolute tax liability of a wealthy person would still be much higher than that of a poor person.

It should be clear from the last chapter that progressive taxation cannot be justified by reference to the principle of diminishing marginal utility of income. It is an open question whether it can be justified on the contract theory, as a measure designed to maximize the welfare of the worst off. They might conceivably be better off under a combination of proportional taxation (which might encourage greater productive activity than progressive taxation and would be cheaper to administer) and transfer payments to low-income groups.[9]

6. Property taxes are not progressive, but of course rise in inflationary periods because property values — the tax base — are rising. Yet if the only tax were a property tax, the effect of inflation on tax revenues would not make inflation an attractive policy for government officials desiring to expand the public sector. Explain.

7. Milton Friedman, Capitalism and Freedom 174-175 (1962).

8. Why do not the hardworking capture the entire social benefit of their work in the wages or other income they receive? (Hint: Distinguish between marginal and total product.)

9. Death and gift taxes are discussed in the next chapter.

Suggested Readings

1. Walter J. Blum & Harry Kalven, Jr., The Uneasy Case for Progressive Taxation (1953).
2. Geoffrey Brennan & James M. Buchanan, The Power to Tax: Analytical Foundations of a Fiscal Constitution (1980).
3. Arnold C. Harberger, Taxation and Welfare (1974).
4. Richard A. Musgrave & Peggy B. Musgrave, Public Finance in Theory and Practice, pts. 3-4 (4th ed. 1984).
5. Henry C. Simons, Personal Income Taxation (1938).
6. Paul B. Stephan III, Federal Income Taxation and Human Capital, 70 Va. L. Rev. 1357 (1984).
7. Edward A. Zelinsky, Efficiency and Income Taxes: The Rehabilitation of Tax Incentives, 64 Tex. L. Rev. (forthcoming 1986).
8. The Economics of Taxation (Henry J. Aaron & Michael J. Boskin eds. 1980).

Problems

1. Can you think of any economic reasons for or against the following tax rules:
   a. Income splitting by husband and wife.
   b. The treatment of a trust as a taxpaying unit.
   c. The nontaxability of compensatory damages in tort cases.
   d. The taxation of a wife's market income at the husband's marginal rate.
2. A company, we saw, may be able to shift an excise tax forward to consumers, backward to suppliers. Can a personal income tax ever be shifted? Suppose that a special surtax were levied on the income of accountants. Would accounting fees increase? Would it make a difference to your answer if accountants' incomes included some monopoly profits?
3. Discuss the following proposition: If death is treated as the realization of the decedent's capital gains, an important force for the stability of the stock market will be removed.
4. In Sanitary Farms Dairy, Inc., 25 T.C. 463, 467-68 (1955), the Tax Court held that the owner of a dairy company could deduct from his income tax more than $15,000 that he had expended on an African safari that he had taken with his wife. He had made movies during the safari that he later used extensively in advertising his dairy business. The court found that "the evidence shows that advertising of equal value to that here involved could not have been obtained for the same amount of money in any more normal way," and concluded: "No part of that cost is taxable . . . as personal travel and pleasure expense.

. . . They admittedly enjoyed hunting, but enjoyment of one's work does not make that work a mere personal hobby or the cost of a hunting trip income to the hunter." Is this result economically sound? Should the court have allowed no deduction? A partial deduction?

5. In what circumstances, if any, should the costs of legal service incidental to litigation be deductible from income tax?

6. In principle, is an income tax necessarily more efficient than an excise tax? See Milton Friedman, Price Theory, ch. 3 (1976).

7. Does risk aversion suggest that a tax credit for medical expenditures would be more desirable than a tax deduction designed to yield, in the aggregate, the same tax saving?

8. What do you think of the following method of assessing the value of real estate for purposes of real estate taxes? The owner would make his own assessment. He would file it in the local tax office. Anyone could buy his property at the value the owner had assessed it for, during the year that the filing was in effect. See Saul Levmore, Self-Assessed Valuation Systems for Tort and Other Law, 68 Va. L. Rev. 771 (1982).

9. Should a public utility be allowed to deduct charitable contributions? To treat them as a part of its cost of service for ratemaking purposes?

10. Redraw Figures 17.1 and 17.2 as flat rather than *ad valorem* excise taxes.

11. Liquor and cigarettes are popular subjects for excise taxation because their demand is thought to be highly inelastic. But is this really so? Both products often have deleterious effects on the health of their users. Suppose that the actual cost of buying a pint of whiskey or a carton of cigarettes is twice the purchase price when health costs are taken into account. How would this affect elasticity estimates for the two products? Cf. §10.5 *supra*. Has your answer any implications for tax policy? If the health costs are assumed to increase at a rising or declining, rather than constant, rate as quantity consumed increases?

CHAPTER 18

THE TRANSMISSION OF WEALTH AT DEATH

§18.1 Death (and Gift) Taxes

To many students of taxation the taxation of wealth at death seems substantially free from the substitution effects and regressiveness of so many other taxes. It is true that the measured distribution of wealth is far more uneven than that of income,[1] but it is true in part because social security is not capitalized in figuring people's wealth; if it were, the inequality in wealth would be much less.[2] Indeed, if both income and wealth were fully measured, the two distributions would be close to equal, because all income would be capitalized (mainly as human capital), while all services of capital would be treated as income (e.g., the imputed rental income from living in a house that one owns). But what is undeniable is that the amount of marketable assets at death varies widely across families. Even so, an estate tax (as distinct from an inheritance tax) is somewhat capricious, because it ignores the wealth of the people who are to share in the estate — they might all be poor cousins. Moreover, even if the estate tax has beautiful equity and efficiency properties, it is a lousy revenue tax because it yields only trivial revenue at current tax rates, while at higher rates it might yield even less revenue; for the evaluation of its substitution effects is more complex than is generally believed.

We must first consider why it is that people die having wealth rather than consuming it all during their lifetime. The answer that they do

§18.1 1. See Robert J. Lampman, Changes in the Concentration of Wealth, in Inequality and Poverty 80 (Edward C. Budd ed. 1967). Compare U.S. Dept. of Commerce, Bureau of the Census, Statistical Abstract of the United States 1984, at 481 (tables 794-795), with id. at 465 (table 765).

2. See Jeffrey G. Williamson & Peter H. Lindert, Long-Term Trends in American Wealth Inequality, in Modeling the Distribution and Intergenerational Transmission of Wealth 9 (James D. Smith ed. 1980). Furthermore, more and more workers have vested private (union or company) pension rights, which ought also be counted as wealth.

not know when they are going to die and so must retain wealth in case they live longer than they expect is superficial; by using one's wealth to purchase annuities (reverse insurance, which pays the annuitant a fixed or variable sum until he dies, with no accumulation), one can be assured of not leaving a significant estate at death.

People must want to accumulate estates for the sake of those who will benefit from their bequests. The bequest motive is a species of altruism, and an increase in the price of altruism will reduce the amount of it (more than proportionally, we saw in the last chapter). This implies that heavy death taxes reduce the incentive to save and increase the incentive to consume. But how bad a thing this is, given that all taxes have substitution effects, is hard to say. As noted in the last chapter, every generation is wealthier than the one before, and this appears to be due far more to increases in knowledge than to deferral of consumption by the previous generation. If there were no estate tax every person would choose for himself how much to try to save for the next generation. The estate tax leads him to save less. Although this is a distortion, maybe it is less costly than many other tax-induced distortions would be.

In fact the distortion may be quite slight, but not for reasons that suggest that the estate tax has much to commend it. Perhaps realizing that the next generation will be wealthier anyway, most people don't try to accumulate large estates; this inherently limits the revenue potential of estate taxes. Given an estate tax, those few who in its absence would accumulate large estates consume more and also give money during their lifetime to their heirs or other intended legatees, and minimize the resulting loss of control over the money by placing it in the hands of trustees under various restrictions. True, there is a gift tax, but it can be thwarted by making modest gifts of property that is expected to appreciate, or, a related technique, by making the gifts so far in advance of when the recipient will enjoy them (e.g., to one's grandchildren in trust until they are adults) that the natural operation of compound interest will make them grow into substantial sums — and the interest will be taxed at a lower rate than if the donor had retained the money until he died.

The gift tax can be escaped completely by making a gift of human capital, as by purchasing an expensive education for one's children. There are other ways to transfer wealth that escape gift taxation: A tax may deter father from giving junior a million dollars, but it will not prevent him from installing junior as executive vice president of his company. This form of gift, unlike a simple cash transfer, is not costless: Nepotism may reduce the company's productivity.

Because the estate tax raises so little revenue, the motives for it must be sought elsewhere than in notions of optimal taxation, or even in the power of interest groups to get the government to channel wealth toward them. There is of course the idea that the inheritance of a large amount of money confers an unfair advantage. But it is hard to see why it is more unfair than inheriting brains and energy. We are content to tax the income that one's genetic endowment yields; why not be content to tax the income on one's pecuniary endowment?

There is also the idea that estate taxation is necessary to prevent the creation over time of huge fortunes that might somehow result in political unrest. It is quite true that an enormous concentration of wealth was produced in England in part by tax-free inheritance, but the reason was the practice of primogeniture — of leaving virtually everything to the eldest son. When estates are divided among the heirs, even huge fortunes tend to be dissipated in a few generations. Primogeniture is common only where the major assets of estates are indivisible, so that leaving the assets to more than one child would result in diseconomies of divided ownership (see §3.9 *supra*). This is often true of farmland, the principal form of wealth throughout most of English history, but it is not true of most transferable assets today.

§18.2   The Problem of the "Dead Hand"

An apparent dilemma is presented by the frequent effort of testators to limit the uses to which the assets of their estate will be put. The problem of a "dead hand" controlling resource use by the living arises when death does not result in a clean transfer to living persons that permits them to do with the money as they please. Since one motivation for accumulating a substantial estate may be to project influence beyond death by establishing conditions (perhaps perpetual) on the use of the funds in the estate, a policy of disregarding a testator's conditions would in some instances have much the same effect on the incentive to accumulate as would a heavy estate tax. Yet if conditions, especially perpetual conditions, in a will were always obeyed, a frequent result would be that resources controlled by such conditions would be employed inefficiently. Unforeseen contingencies that materialized after the testator's death might require that the resources be redeployed in order to maximize efficiency. If the conditions in the will could not be altered, there would be no way to bring about the reallocation.

The character of the problem is illustrated by a controversy over a park donated to the city of Macon, Georgia, by Augustus Bacon, a United States senator from Georgia who died in the early years of this century. Senator Bacon's will, drawn during the era of segregationist legislation that followed the end of Reconstruction, stipulated that the park was to be used by white women and children only. In the 1960s, a suit was brought against the city charging that the enforcement of the racial condition violated the equal protection clause of the Fourteenth Amendment. The Supreme Court of the United States held the condition void,[1] whereupon the heirs of Senator Bacon, who were the residuary legatees under the will, brought suit to declare (1) the gift of the park void since the city could no longer comply with the racial condition of the gift and (2) the property theirs under the residuary clause of the will. They won.[2]

At first glance, the result may appear to vindicate the policy of enforcing testators' desires as revealed by the conditions in bequests. But on closer examination this becomes doubtful. It appears that Senator Bacon may have inserted the racial condition primarily to assure that the city would agree to administer the park. There was no indication that the dominant purpose of the gift was to foster racial segregation rather than to provide a recreational facility for the people of Macon. It seems likely that if Senator Bacon could be consulted on the matter, he would prefer that the park remain a park, albeit open to nonwhites, rather than that his distant heirs subdivide the property for residential or commercial use. This is especially plausible since the city could always repurchase the land from the heirs and continue to use it for a park — a park that would have to be open to nonwhites. In that event Senator Bacon's discriminatory intentions would not be respected and the only effect of the voiding of the charitable gift would be to confer windfall gains on the heirs, a result Bacon presumably did not want since he did not bequeath the property to them.

As the case suggests, the dilemma of whether to enforce the testator's intent or to modify the terms of the will in accordance with changed conditions since his death is often a false one. A policy of rigid adherence to the letter of the donative instrument is likely to frustrate both the donor's purposes and the efficient use of resources. In the Macon case itself no serious efficiency issue was involved since, as mentioned, if the land was more valuable as a park than in an alternative use the city could always purchase it back from the heirs. But suppose that Senator Bacon had given the city a tuberculosis sanatorium rather than a park. As the incidence of tuberculosis declined and advances in medical science rendered the sanatorium method of treating tuberculosis obsolete, the value of the donated facilities in their intended use would have diminished. Eventually it would have become clear that the facilities would be more valuable in another use. Unlike the case of the park, there would be no legal obstacle to continuing to enforce all of the conditions of the gift. Yet enforcement would in all likelihood be contrary to the purposes of the donor, who intended by his gift to contribute to the cure of disease, not to perpetuate useless facilities.

§18.2   1. Evans v. Newton, 382 U.S. 296 (1966).
2. Evans v. Abney, 396 U.S. 435 (1970).

The foregoing discussion may seem tantamount to denying the competence of a donor to balance the value of a perpetual gift against the cost in efficiency that such gifts frequently impose. But since no one can foresee the future, a rational donor knows that his intentions might eventually be thwarted by unpredictable circumstances and may therefore be presumed to accept implicitly a rule permitting modification of the terms of the bequest in the event that an unforeseen change frustrates his original intention. The presumption is not absolute. Some rational donors, mistrustful of judicial capacity intelligently to alter the terms of the bequest in light of changed conditions, might prefer to assume the risks involved in rigid adherence to the original terms. Even in such a case, there is an argument — how compelling a one will be left for the reader to decide — for disregarding the donor's stipulation against modification. The making of a gift at death is by definition a once-in-a-lifetime transaction — the somewhat inept choice of words only underscoring the unique character of the transaction. Information costs are uniquely high — one might say infinitely high; and maybe therefore anyone who tries rigidly to control the future shows he is behaving irrationally.

§18.3   The *Cy Pres* Doctrine

Where the continued enforcement of conditions in a charitable gift is no longer economically feasible, because of illegality (in the park example) or opportunity costs (in the sanatorium example), the court, rather than declaring the gift void and transferring the property to the residuary legatees (if any can be identified), will authorize the administrators of the charitable trust to apply the assets of the trust to a related (*cy pres*) purpose within the general scope of the donor's intent.

The *cy pres* doctrine is reasonably well designed to avoid frustration of the donor's intentions and could have been used in the Macon park case to justify disregarding the racial condition. True, the interest in efficiency, narrowly conceived, would be as well or better served by a rule providing that when enforcement of the conditions of a gift becomes either unlawful or uneconomical, the gift lapses and the property is transferred to the residuary legatees or (if they cannot be identified) the state, thus vesting the property in a living owner free to apply it to its most valuable use. The court might of course be mistaken in judging the charitable donation to be no longer economical but, if so, the charitable institution would presumably purchase the property from the new owner and continue to use it as before. But this approach may ultimately be an inefficient one because it would (1) reduce the incentive to accumulate wealth, by making it virtually impossible to create a perpetual charity with reasonably well-defined purposes, and (2) discourage the establishment of charitable trusts. If, however, the donor had specified in his will that under no conditions would he wish the terms of the gift altered — that in such a case he would prefer that the property go to the residuary legatees — there would be no economic justification for application of the *cy pres* doctrine.

§18.4   The Problem of Incentives of Charitable Foundations

Even where no unforeseen contingencies occur, perpetual charitable gifts raise an economic issue that echoes the concern with the separation of ownership and control in the modern business corporation. A charitable foundation that enjoys a substantial income, in perpetuity, from its original endowment is an institution that does not compete in any product market or in the capital markets and that has no stockholders. Its board of trustees is self-perpetuating and is accountable to no one (except itself) for the performance of the enterprise. (Although state attorneys general have legal authority over the administration of charitable trusts, it is largely formal.) At the same time, neither the trustees nor the staff have the kind of property right in the foundation's assets or income that would generate a strong incentive for them to maximize value. Neither the carrot nor the stick is in play.

The incentives to efficient management of foundation assets could be strengthened by a rule requiring charitable foundations to distribute every gift received, principal and interest, including the original endowment, within a specified period of years. The foundation would not be required to wind up its operations within the period; it could continue indefinitely. But it would have to receive new gifts from time to time in order to avoid exhausting all of its funds. Since donors are unlikely to give money to an enterprise known to be slack, the necessity of returning periodically to the market for charitable donations would give trustees and managers of charitable foundations an incentive they now lack to conduct a tight operation. Foundations — mostly religious and educational — that market their services or depend on continuing charitable support, and are therefore already subject to some competitive constraints, could be exempted from the exhaustion rule.

The objections to the suggested rule are that it is unnecessary — donors are already free to limit the duration of their charitable bequests — and that it might therefore (why therefore?) reduce the incentives to make charitable gifts. A counterargument is that many perpetual foundations were established at a time when the foundation was a novel institution; a person creating one at that time simply could not have foreseen the problem of inefficient and unresponsive management that might plague a perpetual foundation as a result of the peculiar set of constraints (or rather lack of constraints) under which they operate.

§18.5   Conditions in Private Trusts

The problems we have thus far been discussing in the context of charitable trusts also arise in that of private trusts and gifts. Suppose a man leaves money to his son in trust, the trust to fail however if the son does not marry a woman of the Jewish faith by the time he is 25 years old. The judicial approach in such cases is to refuse to enforce the condition if it is unreasonable. In the case just put it might make a difference whether the son was 18 or 24 at the time of the bequest and how large the Jewish population was in the place where he lived.

This approach may seem wholly devoid of an economic foundation, and admittedly the criterion of reasonableness is here an unilluminating one. Consider, however, the possibilities for modification that would exist if the gift were *inter vivos* rather than testamentary. As the deadline approached, the son might come to his father and persuade him that a diligent search had revealed no marriageable Jewish girl who would accept him. The father might be persuaded to grant an extension or otherwise relax the condition. But if he is dead, this kind of "recontracting" is impossible, and the presumption that the condition is a reasonable one fails. This argues for applying the *cy pres* approach in private as well as charitable trust cases unless the testator expressly rejects a power of judicial modification.

The point just made may also explain why, although the owner of an art collection is perfectly free to destroy it during his lifetime, a court might consider a condition in his will ordering its destruction to be unreasonable.[1] Perhaps no one knew of the condition and the outcry when it was discovered would have persuaded the testator to abrogate it — had he been alive to do so.

The *cy pres* rule as such is not applied in private trust cases; a trio of separate doctrines is applied in such cases. One — that of unreasonable conditions — has already been discussed. Another is the rule forbidding restraints on alienation: The owner of a fee simple interest may not be prevented by the grantor from transferring the property. If I

§18.5   1. See, e.g., Board of County Commissioners v. Scott, 88 Minn. 386, 93 N.W. 109 (1903).

sell you my automobile, I cannot extract from you an enforceable promise that you will not resell it, unless such a condition is necessary to protect a security interest I retain in the property (you may not have paid me in full). The rule against restraints of alienation is applicable to bequests. The merit of the rule, at least as applied to bequests at death, is that it prevents the inefficient use of resources that would frequently result from unforeseen contingencies; its now-familiar drawback is that it weakens the incentive to work hard in order to accumulate wealth.

The rule against restraints on alienation is inconsistent with the rule permitting perpetual restrictive covenants (see §3.7 *supra*), is it not? The *cy pres* doctrine represents a middle position between the approaches exemplified by the rule against restraints on alienation and the rule permitting perpetual restrictive covenants.

The common law Rule Against Perpetuities (modified by statute in some states) provides that no interest is valid unless it must vest within 21 years after lives in being when the interest was created. The rule is something of a misnomer. It does not limit the duration of a condition in a bequest, but rather limits the testator's power to earmark gifts for remote descendants.[2] The rule is, however, related to the other limitations on the "dead hand" that we have surveyed, since arrangements for the distant future are likely to result in an inefficient use of resources brought about by unforeseen contingencies.

§18.6   The Widow's Share

Another limitation on the power of a testator is the provision, found in the inheritance laws of all states, forbidding him to disinherit his widow completely. The limitation has an economic justification. The husband's wealth at death is likely to be a product, in part, of the wife's work even if she never had any pecuniary income (see §5.1 *supra*). By staying home, she enables money that would otherwise have gone to hire maids and nurses to be saved (or used to defray other expenses, thereby increasing the amount of money from the husband's income that can be saved) — and the husband's estate is simply the amount of savings in his name at his death. Without statutory protection against disinheritance, women could negotiate with their husbands for contractual protection (contracts to make bequests are enforceable). The statutory provision minimizes transaction costs.

The preceding analysis also demonstrates the economic basis for exempting from the estate tax on the husband's estate a part of the wife's

2. Today, tax avoidance is the usual motive for attempting such earmarking.

share of the estate. Some of the money she inherits from her husband represents an accumulation of her own (though usually imputed rather than pecuniary) earnings. Also, she is likely to be an older person, and should she die soon after her husband his estate would be subjected to estate taxation twice in a short period (so what?).

Suggested Readings

1. Lars Osberg, Economic Inequality in the United States 198-219 (1984).
2. Carl S. Shoup, Federal Estate and Gift Taxes (1966).
3. Gordon Tullock, Inheritance Justified, 14 J. Law & Econ. 465 (1971).
4. Richard E. Wagner, Inheritance and the State: Tax Principles for a Free and Prosperous Commonwealth (Am. Enterprise Institute 1977).
5. Modeling the Distribution and Intergenerational Transmission of Wealth (James D. Smith ed. 1980).

Problems

1. To what extent would the difficulties discussed in this chapter be reduced or eliminated if the present system of death and gift taxes were replaced by a cumulative gift-inheritance tax on recipients of gifts and bequests?
2. A man dies and in his will leaves $1 million in trust for his pet cat, with instructions that the income for the trust be used to enhance the cat's comfort and pleasure. From an economic standpoint, should the bequest be upheld?
3. Discuss the economic effects of forbidding people to disinherit their heirs.
4. Discuss: "Dead hand" problems are just another example of how high transaction costs can make a case for legal intervention in private arrangements.
5. What would be the effect on the number and size of gifts if gifts were taxed at the same rate as bequests?
6. Individuals, we know, have (positive) discount rates. Do nations? Suppose the government is considering whether to undertake a project that will not yield any benefits until the year 2050. In valuing the benefits should the government discount them to present value?
7. In §3.2 *supra*, mention was made of the right of a person to the exclusive use of his name or likeness in advertising. Apart from the effect on the incentive of people to invest in building up a valuable name and likeness, can you think of an economic reason for making the right inheritable?

PART VI

THE LEGAL PROCESS

CHAPTER 19

THE MARKET, THE ADVERSARY SYSTEM, AND THE LEGISLATIVE PROCESS AS METHODS OF RESOURCE ALLOCATION

§19.1 Legal and Market Allocation Compared

We have seen that the ultimate question for decision in many lawsuits is what allocation of resources would maximize efficiency. The market normally decides this question, but it is given to the legal system to decide in situations where the costs of a market determination would exceed those of a legal determination. The criteria of decision are often the same, but what of the decision-making processes? Here we find some surprising parallels, together with significant differences.

Like the market, the law (especially the common law) uses prices equal to opportunity costs to induce people to maximize efficiency. Where compensatory damages are the remedy for a breach of legal duty, the effect of liability is not to compel compliance with law but to compel the violator to pay a price equal to the opportunity costs of the violation. If that price is lower than the value he derives from the unlawful act, efficiency is maximized if he commits it, and the legal system in effect encourages him to do so; if higher, efficiency requires that he not commit the act and again the damage remedy provides the correct incentive. Like the market, the legal system confronts the individual with the costs of his act but leaves the decision whether to incur those costs to him. Although heavier sanctions — penalties — are sometimes imposed (see, e.g., §7.2 supra), normally this is done in circumstances where penalties are necessary to create the correct economic incentives. (How do injunctions fit the analysis?)

Again like the market, the legal process relies for its administration primarily on private individuals motivated by economic self-interest

491

rather than on altruists or officials. Through the lawyer that he hires, the victim of conduct that may be unlawful (inefficient)

(1) investigates the circumstances surrounding the allegedly unlawful act,

(2) organizes the information obtained by the investigation,

(3) decides whether to activate the machinery of legal allocation,

(4) feeds information in digestible form to that machinery,

(5) checks the accuracy of the information supplied by the defendant,

(6) presses if necessary for changes in the rules of allocation followed by the courts, and

(7) sees to the collection of the judgment.

The state is thereby enabled to dispense with a police force to protect people's common law rights, public attorneys to enforce them, and other bureaucratic personnel to operate the system. These functionaries would be less highly motivated than a private plaintiff, since their economic self-interest would be affected only indirectly by the outcomes of particular cases. The number of public employees involved in the protection of private rights of action is remarkably small considering the amount of activity regulated by the laws creating those rights, just as the number of public employees involved in the operation of the market is small relative to the activity organized by the market.

A closely related point is that the legal process, like the market, is competitive. The adversary system places the tribunal in the position of a consumer forced to decide between the similar goods of two fiercely determined salesmen. It is true that most cases are settled before trial, but those cases do not enter into the process by which legal rules are created and modified. The critical stage of the legal allocation process is dominated by the competition between plaintiff and defendant for the favor of the tribunal.

The Anglo-American adversarial process, however, is by no means universal. Many countries on the Continent and elsewhere use the "inquisitorial" system, whereby the judge takes the lead in gathering evidence and framing the issues, and the lawyers have a subordinate role — more than *kibitzers* but less than principals. The major economy of an inquisitorial system is that the amount of resources devoted to the adversary process is reduced, and this is a social saving to the extent that those resources offset each other rather than (just) increase the accuracy of the judicial determination (in this respect resembling expenditures on advertising). But against this must be set the fact that an inquisitorial system involves a very substantial shift of responsibility for law enforcement from the private to the public sector — as illustrated by the fact that the ratio of judges to lawyers is 10 times higher in Sweden and West Germany than in California.[1] This implies a loss of efficiency if,

§19.1   1. See Earl Johnson, Jr. & Ann Barthelmes Drew, This Nation Has Money for Everything — Except Its Courts, 17 Judges' J., no. 3 (Summer 1978), at 8, 10.

as generally assumed, the private sector is more efficient than the public.

The legal process also resembles the market in its impersonality — in economic terms, its subordination of distributive considerations. The invisible hand of the market has its counterpart in the aloof disinterest of the judge. The method by which judges are compensated and the rules of judicial ethics are designed to assure that the judge will have no financial or other interest in the outcome of a case before him, no responsibility with respect to the case other than to decide issues tendered by the parties, and no knowledge of the facts in the case other than what the competition of the parties conveys to him. Jurors are similarly constrained. The disappointed litigant will rarely have grounds for a personal animus against the tribunal, just as the consumer who does not find a product he wants at a price he is willing to pay will rarely have grounds for a personal animus against a seller.

Judicial impersonality is reinforced by the rules of evidence, which among other things (see §21.13 *infra*) exclude considerations that go not to the conduct of the parties but to their relative deservedness. The poor man may not advance poverty as a reason why he should be excused from liability or the wealthy man appeal to the judge's sense of class solidarity. Distributive factors cannot be entirely banished from the courtroom but are sufficiently muted to shift the focus of attention to allocative considerations. Likewise in the marketplace sellers have a strong incentive to ignore distributive considerations and thereby maximize efficiency, as we shall see in Chapter 27 when we discuss racial discrimination.

The allocative function of the legal system suggests a possible economic justification for government's defraying a portion of the costs of the system (judges' salaries, the cost of building and maintaining court houses, etc.). If the function of the legal system were solely to settle disputes, it would be appropriate to impose the entire costs of the system on the disputants. But that is not its only function. It establishes rules of conduct designed to shape future conduct, not only the present disputants' but also other people's. Since the social benefits of a litigation may exceed the private benefits to the litigants, the amount of litigation might (though this is hard to believe today) actually be too small if the litigants had to bear the total costs of the suit.[2] The government subsidy of litigation is modest. The main expenses — attorneys' fees — are borne entirely by the litigants.

The public good aspect of litigation is one reason, incidentally, why the provision of a court system is an appropriate function for government. It is true that we have private judges — the arbitrators who are used to settle many contract disputes (including most disputes arising out of collective bargaining contracts) — but, as one would expect since the state does not pay any part of the expense of arbitration, arbitrators

2. On the demand for and supply of legal rules see §20.2 *infra*.

rarely write opinions. The value of opinions enure chiefly to people other than the parties to the arbitration — people who would not contribute to the expenses of the arbitration as the taxpayer contributes to the support of the public courts. (Could the government therefore get out of the operating end of the judicial business, and merely subsidize arbitrators to write opinions? Can you think of any economic objections to this approach?)

The fundamental difference between law and the market as methods of allocating resources is that the market is a more efficient mechanism for valuing competing uses. In a market, people have to back up their value assertions with money, or some equivalent sacrifice of alternative opportunities. Willingness to pay imparts greater credibility to a claim of superior value than forensic energy does. The difficulties of judicially ascertaining preferences or relative values may explain the tendency of common law courts to avoid major allocative judgements. An example is the narrow approach that the courts take to deciding whether a plaintiff or defendant was negligent. They consider care; but except when deciding whether to subject a category of cases to strict liability, they do not consider whether the accident might have been avoided at a cost less than the expected accident cost by substituting another activity (see §6.5 *supra*).

Another consequence of the law's inability to measure preferences accurately is a tendency to suppress variances in value. Many people place a value on their homes that exceeds its market price. But a standard of subjective value in eminent domain cases, while the correct standard as a matter of economic principle, would be virtually impossible to administer because of the difficulty of proving (except by evidence of refusal to accept a bona fide offer just below the owner's valuation) that the house was worth more to the owner than the market price (see §3.6 *supra*).

It has been argued that a fundamental difference between legal and market transactions is that the transferor is not compensated in the former but is in the latter.[3] If A buys B's car, he must, of course, pay B for it. But if A smashes B's car in an accident in which neither party is at fault, A has been allowed in effect to use B's car as an input into driving, without having to pay B. The contrast, however, is overstated. There are many losers in the market, too. If I manufacture buggy whips, and the market for my product collapses when the automobile is invented, I will not be compensated for the loss of my business. That loss is efficient, but only because the gains outweigh the losses when summed across society — not because I obtain a share of the gains large enough to cover my losses. Indeed, the rejection, as in this example,

3. Jules L. Coleman, Efficiency, Utility, and Wealth Maximization, 8 Hofstra L. Rev. 509, 541-542 (1980).

of competition as a tort is a striking example of the common law's subordination of distributive to efficiency considerations.

And, on the other side, people often are compensated — in advance — for the losses that legal transactions impose on them. Suppose a negligence system is overall a cheaper system for controlling automobile accidents than a system of strict liability. Then the sum of my liability and accident insurance premiums should be lower under a negligence system. If I am injured in an accident in which neither party is at fault, I will be compensated under either system — by my accident insurer, under negligence, and by the injurer's liability insurer, under strict liability. But, by assumption, I will be compensated at lower cost to me under a negligence system.

§19.2 Judicial and Legislative Allocation Compared

While many of the legal rules discussed in previous chapters of this book seem designed to promote efficiency, many others, such as the minimum wage, auto safety legislation, the National Labor Relations Act, and restrictions on competition in banking — to name just a few — do not. The list of inefficient rules discussed in this book could be extended enormously, to cover much of the nation's statute law and administrative regulations.[1] Although the correlation is far from perfect, judge-made rules tend to be efficiency-promoting[2] while those made by legislatures tend to be efficiency-reducing.[3] How is this important difference in the character of judicial and legislative law to be explained?[4]

---

§19.2 1. See, e.g., William F. Baxter, NYSE Fixed Commission Rates: A Private Cartel Goes Public, 22 Stan. L. Rev. 675 (1970); Dennis A. Breen, The Monopoly Value of Household-Goods Operating Certificates, 20 J. Law & Econ. 153 (1977); Cabinet Task Force on Oil Import Control, The Oil Import Question (Govt. Printing Office 1970); George W. Hilton, The Consistency of the Interstate Commerce Act, 9 J. Law & Econ. 87 (1966); Richard A. Ippolito & Robert T. Masson, The Social Cost of Government Regulation of Milk, 21 J. Law & Econ. 33 (1978); William A. Jordan, Airline Regulation in America: Effects and Imperfections (1970); Joseph P. Kalt, The Economics and Politics of Oil Price Regulation: Federal Policy in the Post-Embargo Era (1981); Edmund W. Kitch, Marc Isaacson, & Daniel Kasper, The Regulation of Taxicabs in Chicago, 14 J. Law & Econ. 285 (1971); Paul W. MacAvoy, The Regulation-Induced Shortage of Natural Gas, 14 J. Law & Econ. 167 (1971); Lawrence Shepard, Licensing Restrictions and the Cost of Dental Care, 21 J. Law & Econ. 187 (1978); and, for a general (though dated) survey of the literature, William A. Jordan, Producer Protection, Prior Market Structure and the Effects of Government Regulation, 15 J. Law & Econ. 151 (1972).

2. Rules of the common law — not necessarily rules interpreting statutes.

3. Excluding legislative rules codifying common law principles (e.g., forbidding murder).

4. Administrative regulation is discussed in Chapter 23. On the reasons for the common law tendency toward efficiency see also §8.1 *supra* and §§19.7 and 21.4 *infra*.

One possible explanation lies in the differences in the procedures by which rules of law are formulated by judges as compared to legislators. A judge, especially of an appellate court, which is where most judge-made rules are made, is unlikely to decide a case on the basis of which of the parties is the "better" person. He knows the parties even less well than the trial judge; and as we have already discussed, considerations pertaining to the parties' relative deservingness (wealth, poverty, good breeding, etc.) are, so far as possible, suppressed. Moreover, a judgment based on such considerations would be difficult to rationalize in a judicial opinion, or, stated otherwise, to generalize in a rule. Finally, the methods of judicial compensation and the rules governing conflicts of interest exclude a choice among the competing activities based on the judge's narrowly economic self-interest. Almost by default the judge is compelled to view the parties as representatives of activities — owning land, growing tulips, walking on railroad tracks, driving cars. In these circumstances it is natural that he should ask which of the competing activities is more valuable in the economic sense.

The legislative process presents a marked contrast to the judicial. There is no rule against the admission of considerations relating to the deserts of the people affected by proposed legislation. The adversary system, with its comparison of concrete interfering activities that assures that questions of relative costs are always close to the surface of the controversy, is not employed. Also, the legislative tools for redistributing wealth are much more flexible and powerful than the judicial. Ordinarily, the only way a common law court can redistribute wealth is by means of (in effect) an excise tax on the activity involved in the suit (see §16.6 *supra*). If common law courts do not have effective tools for redistributing wealth — for, in other words, reslicing the economic pie among contending interest groups — it is to the benefit of all interest groups that courts, when they are enforcing common law principles rather than statutes, should concentrate on making the pie larger.[5]

§19.3   The Economic Theory of Legislation[1]

An institutional difference worthy of separate consideration is the greater reliance on the electoral process for the selection of legislators than

5. Why could not common law courts have evolved a concept of a minimum wage and used the concept to redistribute wealth?

§19.3   1. Proposed in George J. Stigler, The Theory of Economic Regulation, 2 Bell J. Econ. & Mgmt. Sci. 3 (1971). For extensions see Sam Peltzman, Toward a More General Theory of Regulation, 19 J. Law & Econ. 211 (1976); Gary S. Becker, A Theory of Competition Among Pressure Groups for Political Influence, 98 Q. J. Econ. 371 (1983); Gary S. Becker, Pressure Groups and Political Behavior, in Capitalism and Democracy: Schumpeter Revisited 120 (R.D. Coe & C.K. Wilbur eds. 1985). The last-cited paper is a particularly good summary of the theory.

for the selection of judges. That process creates a market for legislation in which legislators "sell" legislative protection to those who can help their electoral prospects with money or votes. This market is characterized by acute free-rider problems. Someone who is within the protective scope of some proposed piece of legislation will benefit from its enactment whether or not he makes any contribution, financial or otherwise, to obtaining its enactment. There is thus a close analogy to cartelization, an analogy reinforced by the fact that so much legislation seems designed to facilitate cartel pricing by the regulated firms. The analogy helps to explain why consumers fare badly in the legislative process: They are too numerous to organize an effective "cartel" in support of or in opposition to existing or proposed legislation.

While the factors that predispose an industry to cartelization (see §10.1 *supra*) thus are relevant to predicting who will succeed and who will fail in obtaining legislative protection, there are important differences between the ordinary cartel and the politically effective coalition. In particular, fewness of members is less critical in the legislative than in the market arena.

First, the fewer competitors there are in a market, the easier they will find it to organize a private cartel that is unlikely to be detected; hence their demand for legislative protection may be less than that of an otherwise similar but more numerous set of competitors.[2]

Second, since the antitrust laws do not, and could not constitutionally,[3] forbid competitors to collaborate in influencing legislative action (as distinct from setting price jointly), free-rider problems are more readily overcome in the legislative than in the market arena.

Third, to the extent that the number of firms seeking legislative assistance is positively correlated with the number of individuals employed by or otherwise economically dependent on the firms, or if individuals (for instance, the members of some profession or other occupational group) are seeking such assistance, large numbers, while complicating the free-rider problem, may have an offsetting effect by increasing the voting power of the group.

These factors may explain why monopolistic regulations are more common in areas like agriculture, labor, and the professions, where private cartelization would generally be infeasible because of the large numbers who would have to join any private cartel for it to be effective, than in highly concentrated industries such as steel and aluminum. Nevertheless, we would expect successful interest groups to be *relatively* small, and homogeneous, much as with effective bargaining units in a plant (see §11.2 *supra*). A small number of members reduces transaction

2. An important qualification, however, is that legislation can confer benefits beyond what a private cartel could obtain. For example, in a market of few sellers but easy entry, private cartelization might be unprofitable — while legislation that prevented new entry might be highly profitable — to those sellers.
3. See Eastern Railroad Presidents Conference v. Noerr Motor Freight, Inc., 365 U.S. 127 (1961).

costs, increases the cost of free riding (by making it less likely that there will be anything to take a free ride on — each member may be more essential to the group's success), increases the benefits of redistribution, and makes organized opposition less likely by reducing the cost per opponent. To grasp the last two points, notice that if a group of 10 takes $20 from 100 others, the cost per transferor is only 20¢ and the benefit per transferee is $2; if the size of the groups is reversed, the cost is $2 per transferor and the benefit is only 20¢ per transferee.

The reader may wonder why politically effective groups[4] should procure such seemingly inefficient methods of transferring wealth to themselves as limiting entry or price competition. A one-time lump-sum cash transfer to the industry, equal to the present value of the anticipated profits from a regulatory limitation of competition, would give the industry the benefits of reduced competition without its dead-weight cost in reduced output (see §9.2 *supra*). But this analysis ignores the question how the funds for the cash subsidy would be raised. The answer is taxation, which as we saw in Chapter 17 has the same kind of substitution effects as monopoly. In any event, the relative infrequency of explicit transfers probably has little to do with efficiency; rather, the implicit character of the transfer that is brought about by regulatory limits on competition raises the information costs of opposing the transfer.

All this makes interest groups sound pretty bad. But the real economic objection is not to interest groups but to the use of the political process to make economic decisions. Since the benefit of voting to the individual is negligible in any practical sense — vanishingly close to zero, in fact, in any but the most local election — it doesn't pay the average voter to invest much in learning about the different candidates or the policies they espouse, let alone in contributing to the cost of their campaigns.[5] Interest groups thus play an essential role in providing information to the electorate and in financing political campaigns. Unfortunately, for the structural reasons just discussed competition among interest groups cannot be depended on to yield either an efficient or an equitable set of laws.

Nevertheless it is apparent that many laws (most criminal laws, for example) are not the product of narrow interest groups. Although an interest group is less cohesive the larger it is, if the benefits sought by the group are great enough it may still be possible to overcome free-rider problems. But notice that once a public interest law is adopted, interest groups will form that have private interest in expanding its reach, quite possibly beyond the efficient limit. Corrections officers, po-

---

4. Need they always be groups of producers? See §12.7 *supra*.
5. Is it any wonder that only about half the eligible voting population actually bothers to vote? The wonder — to an economist — is why as many people vote as do; one would think that it would never pay to vote until the electorate was down to a hundred or fewer people.

licemen, and criminal defense lawyers have a pecuniary interest in the criminal justice system even though that system is not the product of narrow interest group pressures.

The role of interest groups is blunted in the court system (as strikingly evidenced by the early and steadfast rejection by the common law of the proposition that competition is a tort — a proposition that underlies much regulatory legislation), where the electoral process, though widely used at the state and local level, is less partisan, contentious, and expensive. Of course, by acting through elected officials interest groups can and do greatly influence judicial appointments; but once the judge takes office he is substantially insulated from interest group pressures — at the federal level almost wholly so.

Indeed, the traditional rules of adjudication make it difficult for interest groups even to be heard. The concept of "standing" limits the right to sue to a person or organization that can show that it will obtain a specific and tangible gain from the suit if it prevails. Traditionally this meant that trade associations and other organized groups could not maintain suit even though their members would benefit from a favorable outcome. The rules have been relaxed in recent years, so that now, if any member of the group would have standing, the group itself can maintain the suit. This relaxation is sometimes defended as giving consumer interests a better chance to be heard in the adjudicative arena. What do you think of this argument? Is an organized consumer group or public interest group likely to represent the generalized consumer or public interest — or to be just another interest group?

As suggested earlier, the best interest of most interest groups may be served by the courts' trying to maximize the wealth of society rather than trying to redistribute it. This will benefit some groups directly, and others indirectly by creating more resources for redistribution; few if any will benefit from the courts' trying to do redistribution themselves. So even in an interest group society, it may be that the courts in areas left to common law will not follow redistributive policies (although legislatures will), just as a socialist state might decide to retain a free market in most goods and services.

§19.4   The Regulation of Campaign Financing[1]

One way of limiting the influence of (some) interest groups on the legislative process is to limit the amount of money that may be spent in political

§19.4   1. See Sam Kazman, The Economics of the 1974 Federal Election Campaign Act Amendments, 25 Buff. L. Rev. 519 (1976). In Buckley v. Valeo, 424 U.S. 1 (1976), the Supreme Court invalidated on First Amendment grounds the Act's limitations on

campaigns. This is the approach taken in the Federal Election Campaign Act Amendments of 1974. The ceiling on contributions reduces the comparative advantage that a group able to overcome free-rider problems enjoys in making large contributions to politicians.[2] But there is a big loophole: The act permits the sort of nonpecuniary contributions that only an interest group can supply, for example union members' personal services, organized and contributed by the union.

The 1974 act may itself be an example of special interest legislation, the benefited group being the federal legislators themselves. The act favors incumbents in precisely the way in which a limitation on commercial advertising expenditures would favor producers of existing brands. A new product often requires heavy advertising to acquaint potential customers with its existence and advantages; the same is true of a fresh face in the political market. But probably the allocative (as distinct from the distributive) effects of limiting political advertising are less serious than would be the effects of limiting commercial advertising, not only because of the distortions created by interest group pressures (why are they not a factor in the economic marketplace?) but also because of the greater propensities for fraudulent political than for fraudulent commercial advertising (why greater?).

§19.5 Statutory Interpretation in a World of Interest Group Politics

The conventional view of statutory interpretation is that the court endeavors to discover and give effect to the intentions of the enacting legislature. This is consistent with viewing the legislative process as one dominated by deals among special interest groups; in this view legislative enactment is a bargained sale and the same methods used in the interpretation of ordinary contracts are appropriate. The process of discovering legislative intent, however, is more difficult than that of discovering the intent of an ordinary contract because of the plural nature of the enacting body. The statements of the individual legislators, even of legislative committees, cannot automatically be assumed to express the views of the "silent majority" that is necessary for enactment. Furthermore,

---

total campaign spending while upholding the limitations on the size of individual contributions. Evidently the principal effect of the Act as altered by judicial decisions has been to increase corporate contributions. See James B. Kau & Paul H. Rubin, Congressmen, Constituents, and Contributors: Determinants of Roll Call Voting in the House of Representatives, ch. 8 (1982).

2. What is the relevance of the provision for public subsidization of campaign expenditures? Can you think of an economic justification for such subsidization?

the proponents of interest group legislation may conceal the true objective of the legislation in order to increase the information costs of opponents. But to some extent this reticence is self-defeating. What is concealed from the public is likely to be concealed from the judges, leading them to construct a public interest rationale that may blunt the redistributive thrust of the legislation (but sometimes exaggerate it — when?).

Here are three other illustrations of how judges can go awry in interpreting legislation if they ignore the role of interest groups.

1. Judges will sometimes create a private damage remedy for violation of a regulatory statute if they think the statute would be enforced more effectively by allowing victims of violation to bring damage suits, as often it would be (see §22.1 *infra*). But this assumes that the statute was meant to be enforced with maximum effectiveness. Maybe the opponents of the statute were strong enough to force a compromise that limited the amount of enforcement. Judicial creation of a private damage remedy will undo the compromise.

2. Judges sometimes look at post-enactment legislative history to cast light on the meaning of a statute. This procedure is full of pitfalls. The balance of power in the legislature may have shifted since the statute was enacted; the post-enactment legislative history may be an effort to undo the deal struck by the earlier legislators.

3. Occasionally judges will use the policy embodied in one statute to cast light on the meaning of another, much as if the first statute were a judicial precedent. But to do this is to extend the scope of the deal cut in the first statute beyond its intended domain and to undermine the deal cut in the second statute. Only if both statutes were public interest statutes would it make sense to use the first as a reason for reading the second a particular way.

§19.6 The Relationship of the Independent Judiciary to Interest Group Politics

The considerable independence enjoyed by federal and to a lesser degree state judiciaries from the interest group pressures that play about legislators and other elected officials and the executive officers who serve at the pleasure of elected officials results not merely from the rules of judicial procedure[1] but also from the rules governing judicial tenure

§19.6 1. E.g., forbidding *ex parte* contacts, refusing to give standing to sue to interest groups as distinct from the individuals or firms actually injured by a claimed invasion of right, and excluding evidence unrelated to the legal merits of the claim (see §19.2 *supra*).

and compensation.[2] Yet how is the independence of the judiciary to be reconciled with an interest group view of the governmental process? One answer has already been suggested: It increases the probability that the judges will focus on trying to maximize the size of the economic pie, as even the interest groups may want them to do. Another answer, however, is that an independent judiciary facilitates the production of interest group legislation.

We know from Chapter 4 that in the case of private sales or contracts, unless performance is simultaneous on both sides of the bargain or desire for future business can be relied upon to assure faithful performance, the contracting parties will insist that there be a court or arbitrator — an independent third party — to turn to for enforcement of the contract. But there is no legal enforcement mechanism for applying sanctions to the legislature that fails to carry out its "bargain" with an interest group. If, for example, the airline industry obtains from Congress (as apparently it did in 1938) legislation designed to foster monopoly pricing while preventing the entry of new competitors that such pricing would ordinarily attract, the enacting Congress cannot prevent a subsequent Congress from amending the legislation in a way unfavorable to the airlines, or indeed from repealing it altogether (as finally occurred — but only after 40 years). It is true that congressional bad faith would reduce the present value of legislative protection to interest groups in the future, and hence the congressmen's future welfare. But for many individual congressmen, especially those who did not expect to remain in Congress for long, the benefits from repudiating a previous Congress's "deal" might outweigh the costs. Moreover, in any case where the initial vote on enacting the legislation was close, the defection from the winning coalition of only a few congressmen, as a result of retirement or defeat at the polls, might lead to a repeal in the next session of Congress; the newly elected congressmen would have no commitments to honor the "deals" of their predecessors.

The stability necessary to enable long-term legislative deals is supplied by (1) the procedural rules of the legislature and (2) the independent judiciary. The most significant procedural rule is the requirement that legislation (including amending or repealing legislation) must be enacted by a majority of the legislators voting. This requirement makes legislative enactment a difficult and time-consuming process because of the transaction costs involved in getting agreement among a large number of individuals. Once a statute is passed, it is unlikely, given the press of other legislative business, to soon be substantially altered or repealed.[3] The

2. Federal judges, for example, have lifetime tenure and their salaries cannot be reduced during their terms of office.

3. Other characteristics of the legislative process also create resistance to the speedy enactment of new laws: bicameralism, the committee system, filibusters, and the tradition of appointing committee chairmen on the basis of seniority. The use of seniority tends to channel chairmanships to holders of "safe" seats — legislators whose tenure can be expected to be long and who are therefore more likely to honor legislation.

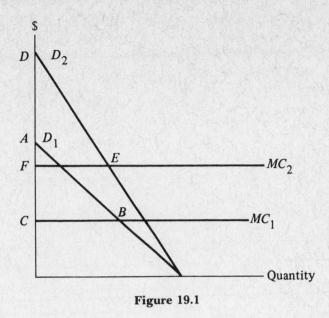

Figure 19.1

impediments to legislation endow legislation, once enacted, with a measure of durability, thereby increasing the value of and hence the demand for legislation.

But a second effect works in the opposite direction: By increasing negotiation costs and uncertainty and by deferring the benefits of the legislation, the impediments reduce the productivity of expenditure on obtaining legislation in the first place. Under plausible assumptions, however, the increase in the value of legislation will exceed the increase in its cost. This is shown in Figure 19.1. D_1 represents the demand curve for special interest legislation under the assumption that the benefits from the legislation will be limited to a single period (i.e., the term of the enacting legislature). The demand curve slopes downward because some groups will obtain greater benefits from protective legislation than others and therefore will be willing to pay a higher price to obtain it. MC_1 is the cost to the legislature of enacting such legislation. The net benefits of the legislation, which are presumably divided between the legislators and the interest groups, are thus the area ABC. If, however, the benefits of the legislation are obtainable over a longer period than the term of the enacting legislature, the demand curve becomes some vertical multiple of D_1 (such as D_2),[4] and the net benefits of the legislation are greater (DEF) than in the single period model even though the costs of enacting the legislation are also greater (MC_2).

Some legislation is ineffective without substantial annual appropria-

---

4. Why is the demand curve not simply D_1 times the number of periods in which the legislation is expected to remain in force?

tions by the legislature, either to pay a periodic subsidy or to defray the expenses of a public agency charged with enforcing the statute. Legislation incomplete in this sense at the time of enactment is much less valuable to its beneficiaries, who may have to "buy" the legislation anew every year. Hence we would expect interest group legislation typically to be cast in a form that avoids the necessity for substantial annual appropriations. Legislation setting up regulatory agencies that use power over rates and entry to redistribute wealth is an important example: The annual budgets of these agencies are very small in relation to the redistributions that they effect. And when direct subsidies are used their funding is often made independent of further legislative action by the device of the earmarked tax, as in the interstate highway and social security programs.

The problem of legislation that requires substantial annual appropriations to maintain its effectiveness is illustrated by the experience with Prohibition. The supporters of Prohibition were able to obtain a constitutional amendment — normally a particularly durable form of legislation. But prohibiting the sale of alcoholic beverages required a massive law enforcement effort that subsequent Congresses were unwilling to appropriate enough money for, with the result that the constitutional amendment was effectively nullified, and it was repealed in 1933 after having been in effect for only 13 years.

No legislation is completely self-enforcing. If the people subject to a law refuse to obey it, recourse to the courts is necessary. A judiciary that was subservient to the current membership of the legislature could effectively nullify, by interpretation, legislation enacted in a previous session of the legislature. Judges are less likely to do this if the terms of judicial tenure make them independent of the wishes of current legislators.

Since an independent judiciary is a source of costs as well as benefits to the legislature, we would expect the judiciary to be given less independence the shorter the expected duration of special interest legislation. This may be one reason (another is explored in §24.2 *infra*) why, as we move down the ladder from the federal to the state to the local government level, we find shorter terms for judges and greater reliance on election rather than appointment as the method of selecting them. The more confined or local is the jurisdiction of a legislature, the less scope it has for enacting protective legislation. There is more competition for residents among cities and towns than among states, and among states than among countries, because from the resident's standpoint different cities are better substitutes for one another than different states, and different states better substitutes than different countries. This limits the effectiveness of schemes of redistributing wealth from one group of residents to another at the state and local levels. If, therefore, interest groups will not seek durable compacts from state and local legislatures anyway, the political branches will be less willing to pay the price of an independent judiciary.

§19.7 What Do Judges Maximize?

We have assumed in the previous sections of this chapter that (1) when judges are the makers of the substantive law the rules of law will tend to be consistent with the dictates of efficiency and (2) when judges are applying statutes they will do so in accordance with the terms of the original "deal" between the enacting legislature and the beneficiaries of the legislation. This section sketches a theory of judicial incentives that tries to reconcile these assumptions.

The economist assumes that judges, like other people, seek to maximize a utility function that includes both monetary and nonmonetary elements (the latter including leisure, prestige, and power). But as we have seen, the rules of the judicial process have been designed both to prevent the judge from receiving a monetary payoff from deciding a particular case one way or the other and to minimize the influence of politically effective interest groups on his decisions. The effectiveness of these insulating rules is sometimes questioned. It is sometimes argued, for example, that the judge who owns land will decide in favor of land-owners, the judge who walks to work in favor of pedestrians, the judge who used to be corporate lawyer in favor of corporations. But where a particular outcome would promote the interests of a group to which the judge no longer belongs (our last example), the judge's self-interest is not advanced by selecting that outcome, although his previous experience may lead him to evaluate the merits of the case differently from judges of different backgrounds. And an increase in the judge's income from ruling in favor of a broad group, such as pedestrians or homeowners, to which he still belongs, will usually be so trivial as to be outweighed by the penalties, mild as they are (professional criticism, reversal by a higher court, etc.), for deciding a case in a way perceived to be unsound or biased. It is not surprising that attempts to link judicial policies and outcomes to the personal economic interests of the judges have foundered[1] and have pretty much been given up.

A somewhat more plausible case can be made that judges might slant their decisions in favor of powerful interest groups in order to increase their prospects of promotion to higher office, judicial or otherwise. This may be a factor in the behavior of some lower court judges, but their

§19.7 1. See Roscoe Pound, The Economic Interpretation and the Law of Torts, 53 Harv. L. Rev. 365 (1940).

behavior is held in check by appellate review; and state and federal supreme court judges (especially the latter) in general do not seek promotion. This is true even at the intermediate federal appellate level: Very few federal court of appeals judges leave office save by death or retirement.[2]

The principal explanation for judicial behavior must lie elsewhere than in pecuniary or political factors. One possibility that is consistent with the normal assumptions of economic analysis is that judges seek to impose their personal preferences and values on society. This may explain judges' sensitivity to being reversed by a higher court: The reversal wipes out the effect of the judge's decision both on the parties to the immediate case and on others, similarly situated, whose behavior might be influenced by the rule declared by the judge. As we shall see in the next chapter, the assumption that judges seek to impose their preferences on society may explain the role of precedent in judicial decisions; decision by precedent is a method of imparting durability to judicial rulings.

Decision according to the original tenor of legislation is explicable in similar terms. If judges did not decide questions of statutory interpretation so, the independence of the judiciary would cease to perform an essential function in the interest group system; legislatures would reduce the independence of the judiciary (that independence being, as we have seen, costly); and judges would lose some or all of the power and autonomy that judicial independence confers.[3]

The explanation for the other datum with which we began, the implicit economic content of the common law, seems straightforward with regard to those areas — contracts mainly, but also large stretches of property and torts — where transaction costs are low. In such areas, inefficient rules of law will be nullified by express agreement of the parties, while persistent judicial defiance of economic logic will simply induce contracting parties to substitute private arbitration for judicial resolution of contract disputes. In areas where there is no voluntary relationship between the disputants (for example, accidents between strangers, common law crimes), the courts are not subject to the same competitive constraints. But these are areas where there is a strong social consensus in favor of the use of the efficiency criterion; otherwise the criterion would long ago have given way to some distributive principle sought by a politically effective interest group. If courts refused to enforce the efficiency criterion in these areas — for instance, failed to punish the murderer or impose damages on the careless driver who had injured someone — the likely consequence would be legislative preemption of a major sphere

2. For statistics, see Richard A. Posner, The Federal Courts: Crisis and Reform 39 (1985).

3. Whether such a concern on the part of judges is plausible, given free-rider problems (what free-rider problems?), is discussed in §20.2 *infra*.

of judicial autonomy — the fashioning of common law rules and doctrines.[4]

Suggested Readings

1. James M. Buchanan & Gordon Tullock, The Calculus of Consent
(1962).

2. Gary S. Becker, Pressure Groups and Political Behavior, in Capitalism and Democracy: Schumpeter Revisited 120 (R.D. Coe & C.K. Wilbur
eds. 1985).

3. Anthony Downs, In Defense of Majority Voting, 69 J. Pol. Econ.
192 (1961).

4. Joseph P. Kalt & Mark A. Zupan, Capture and Ideology in the
Economic Theory of Politics, 74 Am. Econ. Rev. 279 (1984).

5. William M. Landes & Richard A. Posner, the Independent Judiciary
in an Interest-Group Perspective, 18 J. Law & Econ. 875 (1975).

6. Mancur Olson, Jr., The Logic of Collective Action (1965).

7. Richard A. Posner, Theories of Economic Regulation, 5 Bell J.
Econ. & Management Sci. 335 (1974).

8. George J. Stigler, The Citizen and the State: Essays on Regulation
(1975).

Problems

1. Should a federal judge be forbidden to serve as a director of a
diversified mutual fund? To own shares in the fund? If he does own
such shares, should he have to disqualify himself from cases involving
companies represented in the fund's portfolio?

2. How would judicial behavior be altered if judges' salaries were a
percentage of litigants' filing fees?

3. Should Congress be allowed to raise judges' salaries during their
terms in office?

---

4. A reason for the common law's tendency to efficiency that is unrelated to judicial
incentives is suggested in §21.4 *infra.*

CHAPTER 20

THE PROCESS OF LEGAL RULEMAKING

§20.1 The Body of Precedents as a Capital Stock

Most of the rules of the common law discussed in Part II of this book are judge made rather than statutory; and even in statutory fields, many of the specific rules of legal obligation are judicial glosses on broad statutory language. Judge-made rules are the outcome of the practice of decision according to precedent (*stare decisis*). When a case is decided, the decision is thereafter a precedent, i.e., a reason for deciding a similar case the same way. While a single precedent is a fragile thing — apt to be distinguished away, ignored, or rejected by a coequal or superior court or even by the same court on a later occasion — an accumulation of precedents dealing with the same question will often create a rule of law having virtually the force of an explicit statutory rule.

Viewed economically, the body of precedents in an area of law is a stock of capital goods — specifically, a stock of knowledge that yields services over many years to potential disputants, in the form of information about legal obligations. Capital goods depreciate; the value of the services that they yield declines over time. This can result either from the physical wearing out of the good or from obsolescence — a change in the environment that reduces the value of the services that the good yields. The former type of depreciation is unimportant in the case of information, the latter quite important; accident law developed to deal with collisions between horse-drawn wagons will be less valuable applied to automobile collisions.

The fact that a capital good depreciates does not mean, however, that the capital stock of which it is a part must grow smaller over time. That depends on the rate of replacement of the capital goods constituting the stock as they wear out. As old precedents obsolesce, eventually ceasing to be a part of the usable stock of precedents, new ones are added to the stock through litigation.

The depreciation rates of precedents constitute important data about the legal system, but it is only recently that an attempt has been made to measure those rates, using the number of citations to a decision in later cases as a proxy for the decision's precedential value.[1] Precedents depreciate more rapidly in a field where there is substantial statutory activity; a precedent based on the interpretation of statutory language is likely to become obsolete when that language is changed. And general legal capital depreciates more slowly than specific legal capital. The more general a rule, the less likely it is to be obsoleted by technical or statutory change (the rule of *Hadley v. Baxendale*[2] is a good illustration of this point). Hence we would expect and find that United States Supreme Court precedents depreciate more slowly than federal court of appeals precedents. The Supreme Court is far more selective in its choice of cases to review than the courts of appeals (indeed, unlike the Supreme Court, a federal court of appeals cannot decline to decide a case within its jurisdiction, although the court may, and nowadays often does, refuse to write an opinion, thereby depriving its decision of any significant weight as a precedent); and it is plausible to suppose that the Court would exercise its selection in favor of cases of greater generality (why?). The alternative theory that Supreme Court precedents depreciate more slowly because they are more authoritative, i.e., valuable, is economically unsound. The rate at which a good depreciates is not a function of its value (mainframe computers depreciate more rapidly than screwdrivers).

The low depreciation rate of precedents (generally 4-5 percent[3]) may explain why lawyers' incomes decline less rapidly with age than do those of most other professionals. A person's earnings represent, in significant part, a return on capital — the knowledge, based on education and experience, that he uses in his work. If this capital depreciates at a high rate, his earnings will fall rapidly when he ceases replacing it. As a person approaches retirement age, his incentive to invest in his human capital diminishes, because the period over which he can recover any such investment is so short. Thus in any occupation in which human capital depreciates at a high rate, earnings fall rapidly as retirement age approaches, while in an occupation where human capital depreciates slowly, earnings decline slowly with age. An important part of a lawyer's capital — his knowledge of precedents — depreciates very slowly.

§20.1   1. See William M. Landes & Richard A. Posner, Legal Precedent: A Theoretical and Empirical Analysis, 19 J. Law & Econ. 249 (1976).
2. 9 Ex. 341, 156 Eng. Rep. 144 (1854). See §4.11 *supra*.
3. See Landes & Posner, *supra* note 1, at 279. This is an annual rate.

§20.2   The Production of Precedents

The capital stock of precedents is the joint product of the lawyers and judges engaged in the argument and decision, respectively, of cases, mainly appellate cases. An odd feature of this production process is that the producers are not paid! Neither the judges nor the lawyers in *Hadley v. Baxendale* received any royalties or other compensation for a precedent that has guided the decision of thousands of cases and, even more important, has structured the commercial relations of millions of buyers and sellers. But before concluding that the production of precedents is suboptimal, we must consider the character of precedents as a by-product of the litigation process. A great deal of factory smoke is produced although there is no market for it, because of the demand for goods whose production yields smoke as a by-product. So it is with precedents and litigation.

Settlement out of court is cheaper than litigation. So only if each disputant expects to do better in the litigation than the other disputant expects him to do are the parties likely to fail to agree on settlement terms that make them both consider themselves better off compared with how they anticipate faring in litigation. Uncertainty is a necessary condition of such a divergence of estimates. It can be either factual or legal but only legal uncertainty is relevant here. If it is great, there will be much litigation, including much appellate litigation. But since litigation, especially at the appellate level, generates precedents, the upsurge in litigation will lead to a reduction in legal uncertainty. Hence the amount of litigation will fall in the next period. Thus, even though there is no market for precedents as such, the production of precedents will rise when their social value rises — when there is little uncertainty and therefore little litigation.

This assumes, of course, that judges are interested in producing precedents, but such an assumption is a natural extension of the model of judicial behavior sketched in the last chapter. A precedent projects a judge's influence more effectively than a decision that will have no effect in guiding future behavior. This also suggests why judges follow as well as make precedent, and therefore why lawyers argue cases on the basis of precedent. If the current generation of judges doesn't follow precedent, the next generation is less likely to follow the precedents of the current generation. The reason is not retribution; that would not make economic sense here. The reason is that if the current generation's judges don't follow precedent, the next generation's judges are less likely to be criticized for not following their predecessors' precedents. The costs in professional criticism for failing to follow precedent will therefore be less. Those costs are modest, but because the rules

of judicial tenure and compensation so diminish the usual incentives
that operate on people, judges are likely to be influenced by what in
most walks of life is the weak force of professional criticism.

True, there is a free-rider problem. The judge who disregards a precedent in his desire to establish his own contrary precedent may impair
only trivially the practice of decision according to precedent; the private
costs of this action may be smaller than the private gains. But the structure of appellate review keeps the free-rider problem in check. The
judge who disregards precedent will be reversed by a higher court that
has no interest in letting *him* impair the practice of decision according
to precedent in order to magnify his own influence. In each jurisdiction
there is a supreme court whose decisions are not subject to further
review. And within a single court the free-rider problem is diminished.
If the justices of the Supreme Court disregard precedent in their decisions, they know they are reducing the probability that their own decisions will be given weight as precedent by future justices.

Another factor pushing judges to follow precedent is the impact of
disregarding precedent on the volume of litigation. That volume will
rise, because of the resulting reduction in legal certainty, and will create
pressure to add new judges (thereby diluting the influence of the existing
judges), or to make each judge work harder, or to substitute arbitral
and administrative tribunals for courts.

§20.3 Statutory Production and the Choice Between General and Special Rules

The production of statutes may seem a straightforward process compared with the production of precedents as a by-product of litigation.
But then why has so much law remained judge made rather than statutory? In fact, the costs of statutory production of rules are high. The
enactment of a statute requires the agreement of a majority of the legislators, and we know from Chapter 3 that transaction costs are high when
there are several hundred parties to the transaction. As noted there,
the number of links necessary to connect up each member of an n-
person set with every other member is given by the formula $n(n -
1)/2$, or equivalently $(n^2-n)/2$. Thus, the necessary number of links
grows exponentially with the size of the set. This also means that a
legislature's productive capacity is difficult to expand. Indeed, adding
legislators may reduce that capacity by increasing the transaction costs
of enactment. But reducing the number of legislators, although it might
by reducing the costs of each enactment increase the number of statutes

that the legislature could produce, would impair the representative function of the legislators.[1] And maybe we don't want to make it too easy to legislate (see §24.2 *infra*).

The costs of legislative enactment imply that statutes will often be ambiguous. After all, one way to reduce the cost of agreement is to agree on less — to leave difficult issues for future resolution by the courts. This implies in turn that if courts adopt a policy of narrow interpretation of legislation (strict construction), they will reduce the effective output of the legislature. The costs of legislative enactment also imply that statutory rules will more often be broad than narrow (why?). Courts have more of a choice between making broad and narrow rules.

Let us consider more systematically the tradeoffs between broad (general) and narrow (specific) rules — between, for example, forbidding unreasonably fast driving and forbidding driving in excess of a specified speed limit. To control behavior through a set of detailed rules rather than through a general standard involves costs both in particularizing the standard initially and in revising the rules to keep them abreast of changing conditions; as we have noted, a specific rule will obsolesce more rapidly than a general standard. The costs of governance by specific rules are particularly high for bodies like the Supreme Court or Congress, where every rule is very costly to promulgate. But often the benefits of particularization outweigh the costs. These benefits are obtained at three levels: in guiding the courts themselves, in guiding the behavior of the people subject to the rule, and in guiding the behavior of the parties to actual disputes. We postpone discussion of the last of these benefits to the chapter on procedure, but discuss the first two here.

1. One can imagine the common law having a single decisional standard — some version of the Hand Formula — that would be applied anew in every case. A serious problem, however, would be the information costs to judges and juries of finding the efficient outcome for every dispute. The existence of specific rules limits the scope and hence cost of the judicial inquiry; in economic terms, the search for a local maximum is substituted for the more elusive quest for a global maximum.

2. If a law is unclear, prospective violators will discount the punishment cost of the violation not only by the probability that they will be caught (see §7.2 *supra*) but also by the additional probability, significantly less than one, that the rule will be held applicable to the conduct in which they engaged. Thus the deterrent effect of the law will be reduced. Also, the vagueness of the rule will create a risk that legitimate conduct will be found to violate it. This will further reduce the deterrent effect

§20.3   1. The limited capacity of legislatures may help explain the enormous growth in administrative agencies during this century. An additional explanation is suggested in Chapter 23.

of the law, since that effect depends on the difference between the expected punishment cost of unlawful and of lawful conduct.[2]

It will also deter some legitimate activities, as stressed in Chapter 7, an effect particularly significant when the legitimate activity deterred by the vague prohibition is more valuable socially than privately. Then even a slight increase in its costs (due to the threat of punishment) may greatly reduce the private demand for the activity, and in doing so may impose substantial social costs. This point may explain why the Supreme Court has held that overbroad criminal statutes are constitutionally impermissible when the conduct regulated by the statute is closely related to the expression of ideas.[3] The social value of ideas often exceeds their private value (as we shall see in Chapter 28) because of the absence of an effective system of property rights in ideas.

The above analysis also suggests why less vagueness is tolerated in criminal than in civil statutes generally. Since, as we know from Chapter 7, criminal sanctions are more costly than civil, the social costs of punishing legitimate conduct as a result of the vagueness of the legal rule are greater. Also relevant here is the fact that criminal penalties cannot be insured against (why not?). Even a small probability of punishing criminally a lawful activity may induce the risk averse to forgo the activity, although its value may be substantial.[4]

The more precise a rule is, however, the more likely it is to open up loopholes — to permit by implication conduct that the rule was intended to forbid (why?). The loophole effect can be minimized by making the rule deliberately overinclusive — for example, establishing a speed limit that is lower than the optimal speed in normal driving conditions. The costs of overinclusion are lower the milder the sanction and the lower the costs of transacting around the rule. One is therefore not surprised to observe (1) greater use of strict liability in tort and contract than in criminal settings and (2) many rather arbitrary rules in those property and commercial law settings where the rules can be transacted around at low cost; these are settings where the lawyer's precept that often it is more important that the law be settled than that it be settled right can be given an economic meaning.[5]

2. For example, if the expected punishment cost for people who steal is 10, but people who don't steal face an expected punishment cost of 3 because of the vagueness of the theft statute, the effective expected punishment cost for theft is only 7. This effect of vague rules is similar to that of legal error, discussed in §21.2 *infra,* and that of overinclusiveness, discussed in §7.2 *supra.*

3. See, e.g., Thornhill v. State of Alabama, 310 U.S. 88, 97-98 (1940); Smith v. California, 361 U.S. 147 (1959).

4. Can you see the analogy to the tax effect of imposing a duty to rescue? See §6.9 *supra.*

5. For further discussion of general versus specific rules see §§21.5 and 22.2 *infra.*

§20.4 Stare Decisis

The discussion in the preceding section suggests an important reason besides judicial self-interest why decision according to precedent is preferred to deciding every case afresh on the basis of first principles. The latter approach would be the equivalent of decision according to a broad standard; it would have the drawbacks discussed in the preceding section plus the procedural costs associated with great uncertainty that are discussed in the next chapter. This implies that the more comprehensive and particularized a nation's statutory code is, the less emphasis we can expect to find placed on *stare decisis*; casual observation of Continental practice supports this prediction. We would also expect, and we find, that *stare decisis* is less rigidly adhered to the more rapidly the society is changing. Change makes many precedents irrelevant and some erroneous. In both cases there is rapid depreciation, but in the first the precedent simply is no longer used and in the second it must be overruled. A rigid rule of adherence to precedent would substantially reduce the efficiency of legal rules in ordering social behavior.[1]

A system of decision according to precedent has another economizing property: It reduces the costs of litigation by enabling the parties to a case, and the tribunal also, to use information that has been generated (often at considerable expense) in previous cases. If it has been held in 20 cases that an electric crossing signal is a required (cost justified) precaution at busy railroad crossings, the marginal gain in knowledge of the relevant costs and values from incurring the expense of a trial in the twenty-first case may be smaller than that expense. A rule of the common law emerges when its factual premises have been so validated by repeated testing in litigation that additional expenditures on proof and argument would exceed the value of the additional knowledge produced. The faster the relevant social and economic conditions are changing, however, the greater will be the value of the additional knowledge, and hence the less valuable will be adherence to precedent. The authority and information aspects of decision according to precedent thus converge in suggesting that the practice will be consistently followed only in highly stable societies.

Suggested Readings

1. Isaac Ehrlich & Richard A. Posner, An Economic Analysis of Legal Rulemaking, 3 J. Leg. Stud. 257 (1974).

§20.4 1. Notice the analogy here to the issue of rigid adherence to the definition of property rights on a first-in-time, first-in-right basis, discussed in §3.4 *supra*.

2. William M. Landes & Richard A. Posner, Legal Precedent: A Theoretical and Empirical Analysis, 19 J. Law & Econ. 249 (1976).

Problems

1. Why is it incorrect to expect the volume of litigation in a field
of law to grow as a simple function of the activities (number of divorces,
crimes, automobile accidents, etc.) giving rise to the litigation?

2. Why might one expect the British Parliament to play a greater
role in the production of rules of law relative to the British courts than
the U.S. Congress does relative to the federal courts?

3. Discuss the pros and cons of prospective overruling of prior decisions in light of the analysis in this chapter.

4. Does this chapter suggest a possible economic theory of the constitutional principle of equal protection of the laws?

CHAPTER 21

CIVIL AND CRIMINAL PROCEDURE[1]

§21.1 The Economic Goals of Procedure; Herein of Due Process

The objective of a procedural system, viewed economically, is to minimize the sum of two types of cost. The first is the cost of erroneous judicial decisions. Suppose the expected cost of a particular type of accident is $100 and the cost to the potential injurer of avoiding it is $90 (the cost of avoidance by the victim, we will assume, is greater than $100). If the potential injurer is subject to either a negligence or a strict liability standard, he will avoid the accident — assuming the standard is administered accurately. But suppose that in 15 percent of the cases in which an accident occurs, the injurer can expect to avoid liability because of erroneous factual determinations by the procedural system. Then the expected cost of the accident to the injurer will fall to $85, and since this is less than the cost of avoidance to him ($90), the accident will not be prevented. The result will be a net social loss of $10 — or will it?

We must not ignore the cost of operating the procedural system. Suppose that to reduce the rate of erroneous failures to impose liability from 15 percent to below 10 percent would require an additional expenditure of $20 per accident on the procedural system. Then efficiency tells us to tolerate the 15 percent probability of error. The cost of error ($10) is less than the cost necessary to eliminate the error cost ($20), and the economic objective is to minimize the sum of the error and direct costs of the procedural system.[1]

1. See Richard H. Field, Benjamin Kaplan, & Kevin M. Clermont, Materials for a Basic Course in Civil Procedure (4th ed. 1978); Charles Alan Wright, Law of Federal Courts, chs. 10-11 (4th ed. 1983).

§21.1 1. What if the purpose of the substantive rule in question is not to improve efficiency? In what sense could we still speak of the goal of procedure as being the minimization of the sum of error and direct costs?

This type of cost comparison is implicit in the Supreme Court's decision in *Mathews v. Eldridge*,[2] which held that in deciding how much process is due to someone complaining that the government has deprived him of his property, the courts should consider the value of the property, the probability of erroneous deprivation because the particular procedural safeguard sought was omitted, and the cost of the safeguard. In Hand Formula terms, due process is denied when $B < PL$, where B is the cost of the procedural safeguard, P is the probability of error if the safeguard is denied, and L is the magnitude of the property loss if the error materializes.

Of course, as with the Hand Formula itself, it is rarely possible (or at least efforts are not made) to quantify the terms. But the formula is valuable even when used qualitatively rather than quantitatively. Suppose, for example, that the issue is whether the owner of an apparently abandoned car should be notified, and given an opportunity for a hearing, *before* the car is towed away and sold for scrap. The chance that the car wasn't really abandoned, but broke down or was stolen, is not trivial, and the cost of a hearing is modest relative to the value of the car; so maybe, as most courts have held, the owner should be entitled to the hearing. But suppose we are speaking not of abandoned but of illegally parked cars. Since the cars are not about to be destroyed, the deprivation (L) is much less than in the case of the abandoned car. The probability of error is also much lower, because ordinarily the determination of whether a car is illegally parked is cut and dried. And the cost of a predeprivation hearing is very high; if the owner has to be notified before the car is towed, he'll remove it before it can be towed away, and the deterrent effect of towing will be eliminated. So courts hold that due process does not require a predeprivation hearing in the case of illegally parked cars.

§21.2   The Costs of Error in Civil Cases

Figure 21.1, formalizing slightly the point made at the outset of this chapter, depicts the effects of erroneous judicial determinations. D represents the value of a unit of safety equipment in accident costs avoided as a function of the quantity of equipment purchased; another name for D is the marginal product of safety equipment. C represents the

    2. 424 U.S. 319 (1976). See also Sutton v. City of Milwaukee, 672 F.2d 644, 645 (7th Cir. 1982); and, for criticism of the Supreme Court's approach, Jerry L. Mashaw, The Supreme Court's Due Process Calculus for Administrative Adjudication in *Mathews v. Eldridge*: Three Factors in Search of a Theory of Value, 44 U. Chi. L. Rev. 28, 47-49 (1976).

cost of the equipment. Value is maximized by purchasing the amount of safety equipment indicated by the intersection of D and C — that is, q. If the industry is fully liable for the cost of accidents, then D becomes the industry's demand for safety equipment and the optimum quantity is purchased. But if through error in the legal system the industry can expect to be liable for only p percent of the costs of the accidents it inflicts, its demand for safety equipment will fall to D' (equal to $p \times D$) and it will purchase only q_1 amount of safety equipment, resulting in a social loss of L. The effect of error on the industry's behavior is the same as that of a tax on gross receipts (see §17.3 *supra*).

But the analysis is incomplete in two important respects. First, whatever causes errors in favor of the industry in some cases (lying witnesses, for example) will probably also cause errors in favor of accident victims in others, and this will tend to shift D' to the right. But it is likely that, on balance, D' will lie below D. All errors in favor of the industry move D' downward, whereas only some errors against the industry move it upward. An error that simply inflates the industry's liability in cases where it has been negligent or otherwise culpable (the accident victim convinces the court that his damages are greater than they really are) will tend to make safety equipment more valuable to the industry and thus raise D'. But if the error results in liability when additional safety equipment would not have reduced the industry's liability (the accident may not have occurred at all, or may have been caused by someone other than a member of the industry), the industry will have no incentive to purchase additional safety equipment, and D' will not increase.

Second, the social cost of a reduction in the industry's incentive to

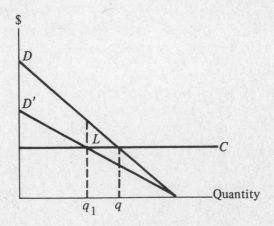

Figure 21.1

avoid accidents is likely to be partially offset by the increased incentive of victims to avoid accidents. The effect of a downward shift of D' is to increase the expected uncompensated accident cost to victims and therefore their incentive to prevent accidents. Although victim avoidance in these cases will be less efficient than avoidance by the injurers (why?), there will be some offset.

Legal error may alter substantive rules *de facto*. To illustrate, recall that the impossibility doctrine of contract law seeks to shift certain losses entirely from promisor to promisee (see §4.5 *infra*). The possibility of legal error creates some probability that the promisor will in fact be stuck with the loss. This means that the doctrine is (viewed ex ante) really one of loss sharing rather than complete loss shifting. Indeed, if decisions applying the doctrine were made randomly, the doctrine would be one of 50-50 loss sharing, for parties that signed contracts to which the doctrine might be applied would end up bearing 50 percent of their losses because of contingencies within the scope of the doctrine. Error blurs the dichotomous character of legal outcomes.

The analysis of error costs has many interesting applications to problems of civil procedure. The preponderance-of-the-evidence standard that governs civil cases directs the trier of facts to find in favor of the party (usually though not always the plaintiff) who has the burden of proof if that party's version of the disputed facts is more probably true than the other party's version. This implies that of cases decided erroneously, about half will be lost by deserving defendants and about half lost by deserving plaintiffs. Whether this is the efficient result depends on whether the costs of each type of error are about the same. The principle of diminishing marginal utility of income implies that the loss to the deserving plaintiff who loses is probably on average slightly smaller than the loss to the deserving defendant who loses (can you see why?).[1] Maybe this explains why the defendant is given the benefit of a tie. Another reason is that an error in a plaintiff's favor involves a cost not incurred when the error goes the other way — the cost of actually collecting a legal judgment.

The preponderance standard is not always followed literally. If, for example, the only evidence the victim of a bus accident had linking the accident to the defendant bus company was that the defendant operated 80 percent of the buses on the route where the accident occurred, the victim could not win without additional evidence of the defendant's liability. This result makes some economic sense. If bus accident cases are decided on such a scanty record, the rate of error will be at least 20 percent (why at least?). An error of this magnitude is likely to be quite costly to society, in particular because one consequence will be that the defendant's competitors on the route will bear zero liability,

----

§21.2.   1. Compare the discussion of adverse possession in §3.10 *supra*.

resulting in an increase in their market share and accident rate. The error costs may justify the adoption of procedures that create incentives to produce additional evidence. If the plaintiff is not allowed to get damages without producing more evidence, he will introduce more evidence in those cases where the defendant is in fact liable, and abandon the other cases, and the error rate will fall.

But the defendant would in any event have a strong incentive to introduce evidence in cases where he was in fact not liable. So a rule that requires the plaintiff to introduce evidence beyond just the defendant's market share is an appropriate economizing measure only if it is cheaper for the plaintiff to put in additional evidence than for the defendant to do so.

§21.3   Proof Beyond a Reasonable Doubt

The requirement in criminal cases of proof beyond a reasonable doubt implicitly weights an erroneous conviction more heavily than an erroneous acquittal. This is consistent with the economic analysis of the criminal sanction presented in Chapter 7. We saw there that even when the only criminal sanction is a fine, the full cost of the sanction to the convicted defendant will not show up elsewhere in the social books as a benefit. And when there is no fine, the only benefit of a criminal conviction is its deterrent effect. The deterrent effect of convicting the innocent is not only not positive (why not?), but negative; it reduces the net expected punishment costs of the guilty. So the net social cost of convicting an innocent person may be even more than the cost to him of the sanction imposed. But the net social cost of acquitting a guilty person is limited to the increase in the total social costs of crime resulting from having thus reduced the probability of punishing criminal activity; and the acquittal of one guilty person will not lead to a significant increase in crime. The requirement of proof of guilt beyond a reasonable doubt is thus founded on the reasonable assumption that it takes several erroneous acquittals to impose a social cost equal to that of one erroneous conviction for the same offense. In the civil setting the effects of erroneous imposition of liability and erroneous exoneration from liability are symmetrical: a reduction in the deterrent effect of the legal rule in question. That is why the errors are weighted (approximately) equally.

This analysis does *not* imply, however, that many guilty people are acquitted. In fact it is possible that fewer guilty defendants are acquitted than liable civil defendants are exonerated; the reason is explored in §21.8 *infra*.

§21.4 An Economic Formula for Deciding Whether to Grant a Preliminary Injunction

The standard of proof in criminal cases is an example of weighting errors by their costs. Another example is the formula based on *Mathews v. Eldridge* for deciding whether someone has been denied due process of law. Still another is the following formula for deciding whether to grant or deny a preliminary injunction: grant it if but only if $P(H_p) >$ $(1 - P)H_d$, where P is the probability that the plaintiff will prevail in the full trial on the merits (and therefore $1 - P$ is the probability that the defendant will prevail), H_p is the irreparable harm that the plaintiff will suffer if a preliminary injunction is not granted to maintain the status quo pending the trial, and H_d is the irreparable harm the defendant will suffer if the preliminary injunction is granted.

The problem for the judge asked to grant a preliminary injunction is that he is being asked to rule in a hurry, on the basis of incomplete information. The risk of an error is high. The judge can minimize the expected error costs by comparing the weighted error costs (the two sides of the inequality) of the parties. An example will illustrate the nature of the comparison. Suppose that the plaintiff has a 60 percent chance of being proved right after a full trial. Then the risk of error in denying his motion for a preliminary injunction is 60 percent. Conversely the risk of error if the judge grants the injunction is 40 percent. But further suppose that if the injunction is denied, the plaintiff will suffer an irreparable harm (the only kind that we should be interested in in this setting — why?) of $50, while if the injunction is granted the defendant will incur an irreparable harm of $100. Then the expected cost of error is greater for the defendant than for the plaintiff ($40 versus $30) and the injunction should be denied. The courts in fact use an approach that is an approximation to the formula presented above.[1]

§21.5 The Decision Whether to Settle or Go to Trial; Herein of Rules of Civil Procedure and the Evolution of Common Law Rules

That cases are ever litigated rather than settled might appear to violate the principle that when transaction costs are low, parties will voluntarily

---

§21.4 1. See Roland Machinery Co. v. Dresser Industries, Inc., 749 F.2d 380, 387-388 (7th Cir. 1984); John Leubsdorf, The Standard for Preliminary Injunctions, 91 Harv. L. Rev. 525 (1978). The formula can be rearranged in a way that may make it more

transact if a mutually beneficial transaction is possible. In fact the vast majority of legal disputes are settled without going to trial; one study found that only 2 percent of automobile accident claims are actually tried.[1] This is as economic theory would predict but we have still to explain the small fraction that go to trial.

As with any contract, a necessary condition for negotiations to succeed is that there be a price at which both parties would conclude that agreement would increase their welfare. Hence settlement negotiations will fail, and litigation ensue, only if the minimum price that the plaintiff is willing to accept in compromise of his claim is greater than the maximum price the defendant is willing to pay in satisfaction of that claim. For example, if the plaintiff won't settle for less than $10,000 and the defendant won't settle for more than $9,000, settlement negotiations will fail.

Although the existence of an area of overlap between the parties' minimum terms or reservation prices — a settlement range, as we shall call it — is a necessary condition for a settlement, it is not a sufficient condition. Settlement negotiations are a classic example of bilateral monopoly. The plaintiff can settle only with the defendant and the defendant only with the plaintiff, and each party is eager to engross as much as possible as the surplus that settlement will generate over litigation. Indeed, the larger the settlement range, the more the parties will stand to gain from hard bargaining and the likelier (it may seem) the parties are to end up litigating because they cannot agree how to divide the available surplus. But there are offsetting factors: A larger range will by definition contain more points that are mutually beneficial; and the larger the range, the less it will cost the parties to determine that a settlement is in the best interests of both.

Each party's best settlement offer will depend on how he expects to fare in litigation. Under the American system, where the winning party's litigation costs are not reimbursed by the loser, the plaintiff's net expected gain from litigating is the judgment if he wins discounted by his estimate of the probability that he will win, minus his litigation costs. The defendant's expected loss is the judgment if he loses discounted by his estimate of the probability of losing (or, stated otherwise, of the plaintiff's winning), plus his litigation costs. If the plaintiff's expected gain from litigating is $10,000, he will not settle for less than $10,000 (unless he is risk averse, a complication we postpone); and if the defendant expects to lose only $9,000 if the case is litigated, he will not

---

intuitive for some readers: $P/1 - P > H_d/H_p$. In words, the preliminary injunction should be granted if but only if the ratio of the plaintiff's to the defendant's chances of winning exceeds the ratio of the defendant's to the plaintiff's irreparable harm.

§21.5   1. See H. Laurence Ross, Settled Out of Court: The Social Process of Insurance Claims Adjustments 179, 216 (1970). See also Patricia Munch Danzon & Lee A. Lillard, Settlement Out of Court: The Disposition of Medical Malpractice Claims, 12 J. Leg. Stud. 345, 365 (1983) (fewer than 10 percent litigated).

settle for more than $9,000. Moreover, the best settlement offer will be adjusted upward by the plaintiff and downward by the defendant to reflect the costs of settlement. If those costs are, say, $500 for each party, then the plaintiff's best offer will be $10,500 and the defendant's $8,500.

The condition for litigation to occur is summarized in inequality (1). J is the size of the judgment if the plaintiff wins. P_p is the probability of the plaintiff's winning as estimated by the plaintiff, and P_d is the defendant's estimate of that probability. C and S are the costs to each party of litigation and of settlement, respectively. This is a very simple model because it assumes that both parties are risk neutral and that the stakes in the case, the costs of litigation, and the costs of settlement are the same for both parties;[2] we shall relax some of these assumptions later.

The condition for litigation,

$$P_p J - C + S > P_d J + C - S, \tag{1}$$

can be rewritten as

$$(P_p - P_d)J > 2(C - S). \tag{2}$$

If the parties agree on the probability that the plaintiff will win in the event of litigation, the left-hand side of (2) will be zero and the case will be settled, because litigation is more costly than settlement; *a fortiori* it will be settled if one party is more pessimistic than the other so that $P_p - P_d$ is negative. In general, then, litigation will occur only if both parties are optimistic about the outcome of the litigation.

A numerical example may help fix the point. Suppose that J is $10,000, C $1,000, S $100, P_p .9 and P_d .6. That is, the plaintiff thinks he has a 90 percent chance of winning $10,000 but the defendant thinks plaintiff has only a 60 percent chance — a divergence of estimates reflecting uncertainty about the probable outcome. Plugging these values into inequality (2), we find that litigation will occur, because the left-hand side of (2) is $3,000 and the right-hand side only $1,800. In terms of inequality (1), the plaintiff's minimum settlement price is $8,100 and the defendant's maximum offer only $6,900, so there is no settlement that will make both parties consider themselves better off than if they litigate.

Inequality (2) brings out the important point that, other things being equal, the higher the stakes in a case the more likely the case is to be litigated (i.e., the more likely is the inequality to be satisfied). The intuitive explanation is that when the stakes are small the potential gains

2. It also assumes a dichotomous outcome from litigating (either some fixed J or nothing) and that the costs of litigating and of settling are exogenous (i.e., unaffected by other terms in the formula). The latter assumption is relaxed in §21.8 *infra*.

from litigating as perceived by the parties are also small and tend to be dominated by the higher costs of litigation relative to settlement. But two partially offsetting considerations are that (1) larger cases attract better lawyers, who will be more skillful at predicting the outcome of litigation, and thus of shrinking $P_p - P_d$; (2) larger stakes increase risk by expanding the variance in possible outcomes of litigation. The riskier litigation is, the more will risk-averse parties want to settle.

Let us change some of the assumptions of the model. Suppose:

1. The stakes in the case are not the same to both parties — maybe the parties have different rates at which they discount a future to a present value, which will cause their J's to diverge. The critical question is how they diverge. Inequality (1) implies that if the plaintiff's J is smaller than the defendant's, litigation is less likely than if they are the same size, while it is more likely if the defendant's J is smaller than the plaintiff's.

2. The parties are not risk neutral. If both are risk averse, the likelihood of litigation will be reduced (why?). If the parties differ in their risk preferences, the analysis is similar to that of a difference in the stakes.

3. The parties' costs of litigation and settlement really aren't fixed, but vary with the stakes — or more realistically still, they contain both a fixed and a variable component. There is a minimum expenditure on litigating or settling a case, represented by C and S in inequalities (1) and (2); and probably it is about the same for both parties in most cases. But beyond that, parties will spend more on litigation the more they have to gain — litigation is an investment as well as an expense. So probably the greater J is, the more each party will spend on the litigation, because every increment in p_p (for the plaintiff) or p_d (for the defendant) brought about by an additional expenditure on litigation will confer a larger expected gain the larger J is. Presumably, however, this variable component of the expenditure on litigation rises less rapidly than J; for example, it might rise as the square root of J.

We could refine the model to incorporate this subtler version of the determinants of litigation expense, but the qualitative implications of the model would be unchanged. Later we shall consider the complications that are introduced if there is strategic behavior — that is, if each party, in deciding how much to spend on litigation, tries to take account of the other party's expenditures on litigation.

How do rules of procedure affect the settlement rate? We begin with pretrial discovery. A full exchange of the information in the possession of the parties is likely to facilitate settlement by enabling each party to form a more accurate, and generally therefore a more convergent, estimate of the likely outcome of the case; and pretrial discovery enables each party to compel his opponent to disclose relevant information in his possession. One may wonder why compulsion is necessary, since the exchange of information is a normal incident of bargaining. But such an exchange is less likely in a settlement negotiation than in an ordinary commercial transaction. If a commercial negotiation fails, the parties go their separate ways; if a settlement negotiation fails, the parties proceed to a trial at which surprise has strategic value. Each party has an incentive to withhold information at the settlement negotiation, knowing that if negotiations fail, the information will be more valuable at trial if the opponent has had no opportunity to prepare a rebuttal to it.

Although pretrial discovery in general is likely to increase the settlement rate, the effect of particular discovery provisions is less certain. Consider Rule 35 of the Federal Rules of Civil Procedure, which authorizes a party to compel his opponent to be examined by a physician designated by the party, if the opponent's health or fitness is in issue. (Rule 35 is most often invoked by defendants in personal injury actions.) Suppose the plaintiff is less seriously injured than the defendant would have believed had he not been able to compel an examination by his physician. Then the defendant will not be willing to make so large a settlement offer as he would have been willing to make before the examination, when he exaggerated the extent of the plaintiff's injuries; but the plaintiff's minimum settlement offer is unaffected since the examination presumably discloses no new information to him concerning the extent of his injuries. Thus the likelihood of a settlement is — or may be (why "may be"?) — reduced. But in cases where the Rule 35 examination convinces the defendant that plaintiff's injuries were more serious than he (the defendant) had believed, Rule 35 increases the likelihood of settlement (why?).

A well-known study of judicial administration argues that allowing a winning plaintiff interest on the judgment from the date of accident (or other event giving rise to his claim) does not affect the settlement rate even if the plaintiff has a higher discount rate than the defendant.[3] In fact the addition of prejudgment interest will reduce the likelihood of a settlement whatever the discount rates. Suppose that before the addition of interest, and ignoring litigation and settlement costs, the expected value to the plaintiff from litigating was $120 and the expected loss to the defendant $100 (this was the example used in the cited study). If interest is added, say at 6 percent for one year, the expected gain to the plaintiff will increase to $127.20 and the expected loss to the defendant to $106. The difference is larger than without interest — $21.20 instead of $20 — and this will increase the likelihood of litigation. In terms of inequality (2), the effect of interest is to make J larger. This result holds even if the parties have different discount rates.[4]

3. Hans Zeisel, Harry Kalven, Jr., & Bernard Buchholz, Delay in the Court 133-136 (1959).

4. Assume that before the addition of interest the stakes are $10,000; the plaintiff's subjective probability of prevailing is 80 percent; his discount rate is 15 percent a year,

As prejudgment interest increases the likelihood of litigation by increasing the stakes, so delay would seem to reduce the likelihood of litigation by reducing the stakes, assuming that the parties have positive discount rates (why is this assumption necessary?). But this conclusion must be qualified in three respects:

(1) If the defendant's discount rate is higher than the plaintiff's, delay may reduce the likelihood of a settlement by causing the defendant's maximum settlement offer to shrink faster than the gap between the offers.

(2) Delay increases uncertainty as to outcome (why?), which as we have seen can be expected to reduce the chances of a settlement.

(3) If all the costs of the litigation can be deferred to trial, those costs will shrink (through discounting) at the same rate as the stakes, and hence the ratio of the parties' best settlement offers will be unchanged.

But not all of those costs can be deferred to trial; when there is a trial queue, it usually doesn't begin until the parties announce themselves ready for trial, implying completion of pretrial preparations. And even if all of the costs could be deferred to trial, the settlement range would be narrowed even though the ratio of the offers was the same (why?); and this would probably reduce the likelihood of settlement, for reasons discussed earlier.

Could the fact that litigation probably is more likely the larger the stakes are help to explain the apparent tendency of the common law to develop efficient rules of conduct?[5] An inefficient rule, by definition, imposes larger costs on society than an efficient one. This might seem to create incentives to litigate inefficient rules more, until the courts make them efficient. But this depends in part on how the costs are distributed. If a rule is inefficient but its costs are spread very widely

---

with an expected delay of 2 years; the defendant's subjective probability of winning is 60 percent (i.e., he thinks the plaintiff has a 40 percent chance of winning); and his discount rate is 10 percent. Then the plaintiff's minimum settlement offer (ignoring litigation and settlement costs) will be $6,049 and the defendant's maximum offer will be $3,306, a difference of $2,743. If we now increase the judgment by 12 percent (two years' interest), the three figures become $6,775, $3,702, and $3,073, respectively. If we reverse the parties' discount rates, then the plaintiff's minimum offer, the defendant's maximum offer, and the difference, before imposition of interest, are $6,611, $3,024, and $3,587 respectively; after interest, the respective figures are $7,405, $3,387, and $4,017.

Now reverse the plaintiff's and the defendant's best offers in our original example, so that the plaintiff's minimum offer is $100 and the defendant's maximum $120. Would our conclusions with respect to the effect of adding prejudgment interest hold, or would they be reversed? Why is the altered example not realistic, however?

5. A much discussed issue on which see, e.g., Paul H. Rubin, Why Is the Common Law Efficient?, 6 J. Leg. Stud. 51 (1977); George L. Priest, The Common Law Process and the Selection of Efficient Rules, 6 J. Leg. Stud. 65 (1977); William M. Landes & Richard A. Posner, Adjudication as a Private Good, 8 J. Leg. Stud. 235, 259-284 (1979); Jack Hirshleifer, Evolutionary Models in Economics and Law, 4 Research in Law & Econ. 167 (1982).

throughout society, no one may have a large enough stake to try to change the rule by litigating. But suppose the costs are concentrated, and compare two rules, one of which leads to twice as many accidents as the other with no offsetting reduction in the cost of safety measures. The inefficient rule will lead to more litigation than the efficient rule, and thus give the courts more opportunity to reexamine it. Suppose that, just by chance, the courts in the course of this reexamination hit on the efficient result. The number of accidents will fall; the rate of litigation will fall; and the courts will be less likely to reexamine the rule in the future. Thus, over time, there will be a tendency for less efficient rules to be weeded out and replaced by efficient ones, because efficient rules are less likely to be reexamined and hence less likely, once adopted, to be discarded in the future.

But the analysis ignores the role of precedent. If the rule is inefficient, but *stare decisis* matters to the court, the effect of frequent litigation under the rule may be merely to solidify the rule. And if *stare decisis* competes with other judicial values, it becomes essential to specify those values. If they are pro-efficiency values, the march toward efficiency will be accelerated, since inefficient rules will automatically be brought back again and again to the courts for reexamination. But if they are anti-efficiency values, the effect of more frequent litigation of inefficient than of efficient rules will be to accelerate the march of the law away from efficiency.

§21.6   Liability Rules Revisited

A complete analysis of the choice among alternative liability rules requires consideration of the procedural costs of each alternative, a point that can be illustrated by asking whether efficiency would be served by replacing negligence liability by strict liability (see §6.5 *supra*). Assume to begin with that the number of accidents would be unchanged. Nevertheless, adoption of strict liability would lead to an increase in the number of injury *claims*, because the scope of liability would be greater. So if the fraction of claims that went to trial remained the same as under a negligence standard, and if each trial was as costly under the new standard as under the old, the aggregate costs of tort litigation would rise.

Both ifs, however, are questionable. Since strict liability eliminates a major issue in tort litigation, that of the care exercised by each party, the amount of uncertainty involved in predicting the outcome of litigation if the claim is not settled would be reduced; and a reduction in uncertainty concerning the outcome of litigation should reduce the fraction of claims that go to trial. Simplification of issues might also lead to a reduction in the cost of each trial, although this is uncertain. The elimination of the negligence issue would tend to increase the value of the plaintiff's claim and this might (though it need not) lead him to spend more money on his case rather than less; the defendant, however, might spend less.[1] Even if the cost of trial were lower under strict liability, by narrowing the gap between the costs of litigation and those of settlement this would make litigation relatively more attractive than under the negligence standard, resulting in a larger fraction of claims tried.[2]

Thus far we have assumed that a change from strict liability to negligence would not affect the number of accidents; but it might. Of particular relevance here, a rule of strict liability is more definite than one of negligence and hence is likely to be administered with fewer errors. Legal error both reduces the efficiency of the liability system directly and, by increasing the number of accidents, increases the number of claims and hence the administrative expense of a liability system.

§21.7 Plea Bargaining and the Reform of Criminal Procedure

The counterpart in criminal procedure to settlement negotiations in civil procedure, plea bargaining is criticized both as denying the defendant's right to the procedural safeguards of a trial and as leading to reduced sentences. Neither criticism is persuasive to an economist. If a settlement did not make both parties to a criminal case better off than if they went to trial, one or the other would invoke his right to a trial. Hence plea bargaining as such should not result, on average, in either heavier sentences or lighter sentences than a system in which everyone had a trial.

But suppose plea bargaining is, for whatever reason, undesirable. What should be done about it? Should the number of judges be increased so that more cases could be tried? Increasing the number of judges might not affect the amount of plea bargaining. Plea bargaining takes place because negotiation is a cheaper way of resolving controversies than litigation. Its incidence is therefore determined by the relative costs of negotiation and of litigation and by the amount of uncertainty over the outcome of litigation — factors not greatly affected by the number of judges (uncertainty might actually be greater with more judges). Although more judges might enable speedier trials (but see §21.10 *infra*),

§21.6 1. The determinants of litigation expenditures are complex. See §21.8 *infra*.
2. Although settlement costs may also be lower if prediction of the outcome of litigation is easier (why?), a proportionately equal reduction in both litigation and settlement costs would result in a reduction in the absolute difference between them.

and speedier trials might affect the stakes to the defendant (and prosecutor?[1]) and thereby the terms of the bargain, this should not affect the *amount* of bargaining.

Intuitively it might seem that the provision of counsel to indigent defendants would reduce the proportion of bargained pleas, but the intuition is contrary to economic theory. Although the defendant who has no lawyer will have very poor prospects if he elects to go to trial, this just means he will accept a longer bargained sentence than if he has the assistance of counsel. If anything, providing counsel for the indigent should facilitate plea bargaining, since a defense lawyer is more likely than an uncounseled defendant to make an accurate estimate of the probable outcome of a trial.

If plea bargaining were forbidden and there were no increase in the number of judges — if, in other words, the demand for criminal trials increased several-fold with no increase in the supply (unless judges stopped trying civil cases) — the result would be an enormous increase in the waiting period for criminal trials. The expected punishment cost of people free on bail would fall precipitously and that of people imprisoned until trial would increase (unless they could successfully argue that their constitutional right to a speedy trial had been infringed by the delay). Since litigation is more costly than plea bargaining, there would be some increase in the legal expenses of criminal activity, but most of these expense are now borne by the government and by *pro bono* private lawyers (which means, in part at least, by their paying clients) rather than by the accused criminals themselves. Although the average sentence should not be affected by whether it is negotiated or imposed after trial, the variance in sentencing would increase since a trial is likely to result either in acquittal or in a stiffer sentence than the bargained sentence would have been (why?). This would introduce additional risk into the expected cost of punishment.

The length of time it takes to bring federal criminal defendants to trial has been greatly shortened as a result of the Speedy Trial Act, although with great disruption of the civil trial calendars of federal judges. Is the disruption worthwhile? The standard "line" on speedy trial is that delay in bringing a criminal defendant to trial is hard on the defendant by subjecting him to protracted uncertainty about his fate, and hard on society by reducing the expected cost of punishment for anyone with a positive discount rate. But both of these assertions can't be true for the same defendant; delay will make things either worse or better for him. Each assertion may be true, however, of a different group of defendants — those who are let out on bail and those forced to stay in jail awaiting trial, respectively. Speedier trials increase the

§21.7   1. What assumptions are being made about the prosecutor's incentives? See §22.3 *infra.*

punishment costs of the first group and reduce those of the second. And for those defendants in the latter group (denied bail) who are guilty of crime but are either acquitted at trial or receive a sentence shorter than the period of their pretrial imprisonment, that imprisonment *is* their punishment, and any measure that reduces its length reduces the effective punishment cost — and speedy trial does that.

This analysis implies that although a more liberal bail policy, by postponing the beginning of punishment, would reduce the expected punishment cost of people accused of crime who are now denied bail, this effect would be at least partially offset by the provision of a speedier trial, which could accelerate the imposition of punishment for those admitted to bail. The net effect on the average expected punishment cost of combining more liberal bail with speedier trials is thus ambiguous. In contrast, an increase in pretrial incarceration, as advocated by proponents of preventive detention, would unambiguously increase the expected punishment cost of criminal activity. But those who advocate preventive detention also advocate speedier trials, which would reduce the effect of preventive detention in increasing punishment costs.

The new federal criminal code, enacted in 1984, both introduces preventive detention and, when it is fully implemented, will curtail the sentencing discretion of federal judges. Although the new criminal code is generally (and rightly) regarded as "hard line," the curtailment of sentencing discretion may actually reduce the deterrent and preventive effects of criminal punishment. Broad sentencing discretion enables the judge to practice a form of price discrimination that consists of deciding what penalty is optimal given the particular characteristics of the defendant. If the defendant seems to belong to a class of people who are easily deterrable, a light sentence may suffice to deter him, and those like him, in the future; if he is a hardened and inveterate criminal, a heavy sentence may be necessary for this purpose. If these sentences are averaged together and the same sentence given to each defendant, there will be less deterrence; the heavier sentence will be wasted on the easily deterrable, and the lighter sentence will underdeter the hardened criminals. Of course this problem can be remedied by "averaging up"; but the extra costs of lengthy imprisonment of the easily deterrable are wasted from a social standpoint.

To evaluate proposed procedural changes such as preventive detention merely in terms of the effect on punishment takes, of course, too narrow a view. We want the optimal punishment rather than the maximum punishment. In particular, if it is correct that the social costs of convicting an innocent person are much higher than those of acquitting a guilty person (see §21.3 *supra*), then we must be concerned about policies that increase the probability of convicting an innocent person. Preventive detention does this, if conviction is defined realistically to mean any commitment to prison. Preventive detention involves jailing a person on the basis of a skimpier hearing than is required to convict in a full-scale criminal trial; therefore the probability of imprisoning an innocent person is increased. This cost must be compared with the benefits in deterrence and prevention of crime by accelerating the punishment of the guilty.[2] The economic formula derived from *Mathews v. Eldridge* provides a useful framework for this analysis (see §21.1 *supra*).

§21.8 Expenditures on Litigation

If settlement negotiations fail, there is a trial for which each party purchases legal services and other litigation inputs. A party optimizes his litigation expenditures by spending up to the point where a dollar spent increases the expected value of the litigation to him (by increasing his chances of winning) by just a dollar. But every expenditure decision by one party affects the expenditure decision of the other, by altering the probability and hence expected value of an outcome favorable to the other, much as every price or output change by an oligopolist alters his rivals' optimum price and output (see §10.4 *supra*). If each party, in deciding how much to spend on the lawsuit, therefore takes account of the effect of his expenditures on the other party's, then, as in the oligopoly case, there will be no equilibrium level of expenditures — no level at which neither party has an incentive to make any further change in his expenditures.

Since these expenditures are largely offsetting, parties to litigation often find it mutually advantageous to agree not to incur a particular litigation expense (for example, by stipulating to a fact so that it doesn't have to be established by testimony). But offsetting expenditures on litigation are not necessarily wasteful from a social standpoint. They increase the probability of a correct decision by giving the tribunal more information. Even without being able to model precisely the reaction functions of each party to the expenditure decisions of the other, we are on pretty firm ground in suggesting (in accordance with §21.5 *supra*) that the parties will tend to spend more on a litigation the greater the stakes. The expected benefit of an expenditure on litigation derives from its effect in increasing the probability of a favorable outcome and is therefore magnified by any increase in the value (or cost) of the outcome. Hence we would expect bigger cases to be decided correctly a

2. Is preventive detention consistent with the model of criminal punishment developed in Chapter 7?

higher proportion of the time than smaller cases: An erroneous conviction *or* acquittal is less likely in a capital murder case than in a speeding case.

Many procedural rules can be viewed as being designed to increase the productivity of the parties' litigation expenditures. An example is the rule that permits the judge to take judicial notice of obviously true facts so that the party having the burden of proof need not establish the fact by evidence. The effect of this rule on the party's litigation expenditures is shown in Figure 21.2. D is the average value to the party of various quantities of evidence and S the average (equal to marginal) cost of that evidence. A rule of procedure (such as judicial notice) that reduces the cost of evidence without reducing its value shifts S downward, to S_1, leading the litigant to expand his purchase of evidence from q to q_1. Whether his total expenditure (price times quantity) will increase depends, however, on the price elasticity of demand in the region of the demand curve between q and q_1. If the elasticity is less than one, total expenditures will increase; if it is equal to one, they will be the same; and if it is greater than one, they will decrease.

It is often thought that wealthy individuals or large firms might try to overwhelm their litigation opponents by heavy spending. Our discussion of predatory pricing (see §10.7 *supra*) is relevant to an appraisal of this concern. If a party anticipates a succession of similar lawsuits, it may be rational for him in the first suit to make a threat to overwhelm his opponent, and to carry out that threat by spending heavily on the litigation, in order to enhance the credibility of threats against subsequent opponents. And knowing that it may be rational for the party to carry out the threat, the opponent may yield.

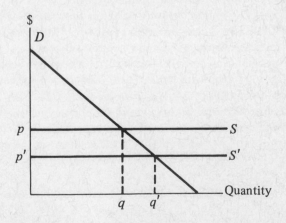

Figure 21.2

§21.9   Access to Legal Remedies — Contingent Fees, Class Actions, and Indemnity of Legal Fees

The principal input into litigation is lawyers' time. The purchase of this input is essential to vindicating even a meritorious claim, but the input is costly. Since the economic aim is to minimize the sum of direct costs and error costs, there is on the face of it nothing inefficient about the fact that a person having a valid claim may not be able to afford to hire a lawyer to press it; this just means (one might think) that the direct costs of the litigation would exceed the benefits in correcting errors. But there are problems with this simple view that have called forth some interesting private and social institutions.

Suppose a plaintiff has a claim of $100,000 and a 50 percent probability of vindicating it if he has a good lawyer. The expected value of the claim is $50,000 and would justify him in expending up to that amount in lawyer's fees to protect the asset. (He is assumed in this example to be risk neutral.) But suppose the claim is his only asset. Ordinarily this would be no problem; one can borrow a substantial sum against an asset as collateral. But it is not always possible to borrow against a legal claim. Banks and other lending institutions may be risk averse (because of government regulation of financial institutions, discussed in §15.9 *supra*) or may find it costly to estimate the likelihood that the claim can be established in court. These factors may make the interest rate prohibitively high. And many legal claims (for example, a personal injury claim arising from an accident) are by law not assignable — in order to prevent the fomenting of litigation — and so are worthless as collateral. (Can you think of an economic reason for this rule?)

The solution to this liquidity problem is the contingent fee contract. The lawyer lends his services against a share of the claim. Risk is reduced because the lawyer specializing in contingent fee matters can pool many claims and thereby minimize the variance of the returns. Specialization also enables him to estimate risks more precisely than could a conventional lender; and there are economies in having the same person or firm assess the risk and insure it.

It has been argued that contingent fees are often exorbitant. But it is easy to be misled here. A contingent fee must be higher than a fee for the same legal services paid as they are performed. The contingent fee compensates the lawyer not only for the legal services he renders but for the loan of those services. The implicit interest rate on such a loan is high because the risk of default (the loss of the case, which cancels the debt of the client to the lawyer) is much higher than that of conventional loans, and the total amount of interest is large not only because the interest rate is high but because the loan may be outstanding for many years — and with no periodic part payment, a device for reducing the risk of the ordinary lender.

But if what the lawyer is doing is making a risky loan of his services, why should the contingent fee not be the opportunity cost of those services with interest, rather than a fraction of the judgment or settlement? There are three related economic answers:

(1) The optimal expenditure on legal services is a function of the stakes. The larger the stakes, the more the defendant will spend to ward off a judgment and the more, therefore, the plaintiff's lawyer will have to spend in time and effort to win. So the cost of his services will be proportional to the stakes and therefore can be expressed as a percentage of them.

(2) Making the lawyer's fee vary with the success of his effort is a way of giving him an incentive to do a good job. This is the same rationale for proportioning salvage awards (see §6.9 *supra*) to the value of what is saved.

(3) More risk is shifted from the plaintiff to his lawyer. Since the lawyer does better when the plaintiff wins big, and worse when he wins small, the variance in the plaintiff's expected benefit from suit after deduction of attorney fees is reduced.[1]

A problem with the contingent fee is that in any situation of joint ownership (and a contingent fee contract makes the lawyer in effect a cotenant of the property represented by the plaintiff's claim), each owner, as we know from Chapter 3, may lack an adequate incentive to exploit the right, because part of the benefit of his efforts to do so would accrue to another person. Suppose the plaintiff's lawyer is offered a settlement of $100,000; if he goes to trial, there is a 90 percent chance that the plaintiff will win $150,000, but it will cost the lawyer $25,000 worth of his time to try the case; the parties are risk averse; and the contingent fee is 30 percent. If the plaintiff agrees to the settlement, he will net $70,000 and the lawyer $30,000. If the case goes to trial, the net expected gain to the plaintiff rises to $94,500 [.9 × ($150,000 − $45,000)],[2] but the lawyer's net expected gain falls to $15,500 [($45,000 × .9) − $25,000)]. So there is a conflict of interest between the parties, due solely to the fact that the lawyer does not obtain the whole benefit of a trial (the expected net benefit of trial is ($50,000 × .9) − $25,000, and is thus positive).

Is this a reason for banning or regulating contingent fees? Surely

---

§21.9   1. For example, if the expected judgment range is $0 to $100,000, with every point in the range an equally likely income, the contingent fee is 25 percent, and the flat fee equivalent would be $12,500 (why this figure?), the range of net expected outcomes to the plaintiff is −$12,500 to $87,500 under the flat fee approach and $0 to $75,000 under the contingent fee approach.

2. $45,000 is the lawyer's 30 percent fee on a $150,000 judgment.

not for banning them (although most countries do). But given the poor information of many consumers in the legal services market (how often in a lifetime does a person find himself shopping for a tort lawyer?), there is an argument for regulation. How good a one need not be assessed here, althoug⸜ it is interesting to note that a judge can on his own motion revise the terms of a contingent fee contract if it seems unfair to the client. The specific problem of the lawyer's having an excessive incentive to settle rather than litigate could be solved by making the contingent fee percentage higher if the case goes to trial, but contingent fee retainer agreements rarely provide this (suggesting what?). They do, however, usually give the lawyer a higher percentage if there is an appeal (why?).

Very small claims would create no problem for the legal system if it were not for the fixed component in the costs of litigation, discussed in §21.5 *supra*. Without that component, people just would invest less when the stakes were less. If, however, the fixed cost can be spread over many claims, it may be possible to vindicate more claims, with a resulting reduction in the error costs of the legal system and without incurring prohibitive direct costs. There have long been techniques for aggregating a number of small claims into one large enough to justify the costs of suit — or, stated otherwise, for realizing economies of scale in litigation. A department store performs this function with respect to the claims of its customers against the manufacturers whose products the store sells. The customer who buys defective merchandise may not have enough at stake to sue the manufacturer but he will not hesitate to complain to the department store, which will replace the merchandise or refund the customer's money and, if several customers complain, will pool these complaints and present them to the manufacturer. If the latter is unwilling to reimburse the store for its costs in responding to the customers' complaints, the store will be able to make a credible threat to sue the manufacturer.

The modern class action generalizes this technique. Suppose the manufacturers of toothbrushes have conspired to charge a monopoly price. Millions of consumers are harmed; the aggregate cost may be substantial; and yet the injury to each consumer may be only a few cents. If all of these claims are aggregated in a class action, the stakes in the action will be large enough to defray the costs of suit.[3]

The class action device may seem, however, of limited utility in the very case where it is most needed — where the individual claim is very small. The defendant can be compelled to pay a judgment equal to the costs of his violation — but to whom? The costs of identifying the

---

3. If the manufacturer does not sell directly to the consumer, the consumer will not be allowed to sue, in a class action or otherwise; the middlemen will have the only right to sue. But this is an economical alternative to the consumer class action for reasons discussed in §10.10 *supra*.

members of the class and giving each one his individual damages (a few cents, in our example) may exceed the judgment. True, the most important point from an economic standpoint is that the violator be confronted with the costs of his violation — this achieves the allocative purpose of the suit — not that he pay them to his victims. And our earlier emphasis on the importance of compensating the injured party in order to motivate him to operate the legal machinery and prevent him from taking excessive precautions (see §6.4 *supra*) is inapplicable here; the stakes are too small to induce any victim to bear any of the burden of obtaining legal redress. The problem is that the costs of actually effecting compensation to the members of a numerous class may be extremely high, and in some cases may exceed the benefits in deterrence yielded by the action.

Moreover, the absence of a real client impairs the incentive of the lawyer for the class to press the suit to a successful conclusion. His earnings from the suit are determined by the legal fee he receives rather than by the size of the judgment. No one has an economic stake in the size of the judgment except the defendant, who has an interest in minimizing it. The lawyer for the class will be tempted to offer to settle with the defendant for a small judgment and a large legal fee, and such an offer will be attractive to the defendant, provided the sum of the two figures is less than the defendant's net expected loss from going to trial. Although the judge must approve the settlement, the lawyers largely control his access to the information — about the merits of the claim, the amount of work done by the lawyer for the class, the likely damages if the case goes to trial, etc. — that is vital to determining the reasonableness of the settlement.[4]

The English and Continental practice of requiring the losing party to a lawsuit to reimburse the winning party's attorney's fees (indemnity) might appear to provide an alternative to the class action as a method of vindicating meritorious small claims. No matter how small the claim, the claimant will not be deterred from pursuing his legal remedies by the cost of litigation since his litigation expenses will be reimbursed if he wins. But there are several problems.

1. The indemnity is never complete, because the plaintiff's time and bother (which may be considerable in relation to the value of the claim, if it is small) are not compensated (could they be?).

2. Unless the plaintiff is certain to prevail, his expected cost of litigation may still exceed the expected benefit to him. If his claim is for $1, the probability of his winning is 90 percent, and his litigation expenses are $100, the expected benefit from litigating will be only 90¢ and the expected cost $20 (assuming his opponent's litigation costs

4. For empirical evidence that the problem discussed in the text is a real one, see Andrew Rosenfield, An Empirical Test of Class-Action Settlement, 5 J. Leg. Stud. 113 (1976).

are also $100, so that if the plaintiff loses he will owe a total of $200 in attorney's fees). So he will not sue.

3. Indemnity lacks the economies-of-scale feature of the class action. Suppose there are 1,000 identical claims for $1 each, the cost of litigating each one is $100, and the probability of prevailing on the claims is 100 percent. If all 1,000 claimants sue — as they may, since each has a net expected gain of $1 from suit — $100,000 will be spent to vindicate those claims. If the claims had been aggregated in a class action, the expenses of suit might have been only a small fraction of this figure. (Why is the example unrealistic, and why doesn't this matter?

It would be error to conclude, however, that if the class action were not a feasible alternative, indemnity would result in a socially excessive amount of litigation because $100,000 would be spent litigating claims worth only $1,000. The feasibility of such suits would in all likelihood have deterred the defendant from committing the wrongful act in the first place. This is an important benefit of indemnity (and also shows the pitfalls of comparing the cost of litigating a claim with the value just of that claim). But a class action would be more efficient.

The most debated question about indemnity is its effect on the litigation rate, with its advocates touting indemnity as the answer to the caseload crisis. With indemnity, the condition for litigation, inequality (1) in §21.5 *supra*, becomes

$$P_p(J + C) - C - (1 - P_p)C + S > P_d(J + C) + C - (1 - P_d)C - S. \quad (3)$$

The gain to the plaintiff if he wins at trial (and loss to the defendant if he loses at trial) now includes the plaintiff's litigation expenses (C) as well as the damages awarded (J); but the plaintiff's expected gain must be reduced by the defendant's litigation expense (also C) discounted by the plaintiff's subjective probability of loss, $1 - P_p$. A similar adjustment is necessary for the defendant's expected loss from litigation.

Inequality (3) can be rewritten

$$(P_p - P_d)J > 2[(P_d + 1 - P_p)C - S]. \quad (4)$$

The difference between this formulation and inequality (2) (the parallel condition for litigation without indemnity) is the right-hand side. It will be larger or smaller in inequality (4) than in inequality (2) depending on whether $P_d + 1 - P_p$ is larger or smaller than 1. If it is smaller than 1, the right-hand side of (4) will be smaller than the right-hand side of (2), thus making litigation more likely under an indemnity system. And it will be larger than 1 only if P_d is larger than P_p — that is, only if the defendant rates the plaintiff's chance of prevailing higher than the plaintiff himself does. But in these circumstances (mutual pessimism) the case will be settled anyway. So for purposes of assessing the effect of indemnity on the likelihood of litigation, we can confine our attention to the class of cases in which P_p exceeds P_d — and in all such cases indemnity makes litigation *more* likely than it would be without indemnity by making the right-hand side of (4) smaller than that of (2). (Can you give an intuitive explanation for this result?)

But the analysis is incomplete.

1. By increasing the variance of the possible outcomes of litigation, indemnity discourages litigation by the risk averse. Without indemnity, the plaintiff receives $J - C$ if he wins the suit and pays C if he loses; the range of outcomes is thus from $J - C$ to $-C$. With indemnity the range is broader, from J to $-2C$. The analysis for the defendant is similar. But just how important is risk aversion in litigation? In corporate litigation (e.g., most breach of contract suits), probably not very (why?). Even in personal litigation (e.g., most tort suits) its importance may be small, as the plaintiff's risk may be buffered by a contingent fee contract (how completely?) and the defendant may be a corporation or insured (or both).

2. The cost to a party of exaggerating the probability of his prevailing is greater under an indemnity system (why?). Hence indemnity should result in a greater convergence of the parties' estimates of the probable outcome of the litigation, thereby reducing the litigation rate. This suggests, incidentally, a possible reason why indemnity is the rule in England but has never caught on in the otherwise basically similar U.S. legal system. The rigid adherence to *stare decisis* by English judges, the greater clarity of English statutes, which is due to the fact that Parliament is a more disciplined body than the U.S. legislature (it is effectively unicameral, and controlled by the executive — the Cabinet), the abolition of the civil jury in England, and the greater simplicity of English law due to the absence of states and of a justiciable constitution, make litigation outcomes more predictable in England than in the United States. This in turn makes a mistaken prediction as to outcome more culpable in England, in the sense of more easily avoidable, with the result that penalizing such mistakes is more likely to reduce their incidence than under a system like ours where much mistaken prediction is inevitable because of the uncertainty of litigation. As a judicial process approaches randomness, penalizing mistaken predictions becomes tantamount to making people liable for their unavoidable accidents — a liability with limited economizing properties. The detailed statutory codes, professional judiciary, and absence of juries that characterize the Continental legal systems may explain why indemnity is the rule on the Continent as well as in England.

3. A related point is that even under American law a prevailing party can obtain indemnity of his legal fees if the other party's claim (or defense) turns out to be utterly groundless (frivolous). Perhaps most non-frivolous but losing claims and defenses in our system are the result of unavoidable mistake in an economic sense. It might seem that no penalty would be necessary even in the frivolous case since the cost of

turning down a settlement offer and then losing at trial is borne by the person who makes the mistake. But this is not entirely so. The other side bears litigation costs, too, and as we know the taxpayer also bears some of them; these costs are external to the loser.

Although it is unclear whether on balance indemnity raises, lowers, or does not change the litigation rate, it has other effects that must be considered in any total evaluation. If, as we have assumed, the rate of legal error is indeed a negative function of the parties' litigation expenditures, then indemnity should reduce the error rate by inducing additional expenditures on litigation. For indemnity encourages the optimistic litigant to spend heavily on the litigation because he expects that his costs will ultimately be borne by his opponent. But this also means that while in one sense indemnity internalizes an external cost, in another sense it creates one! (Explain.)

Indemnity should further reduce legal error by encouraging the meritorious small claim and, conversely, by discouraging the nuisance claim — a frivolous claim presented only in the hope that the defendant can be induced to settle for at least a nominal sum.[5] Without indemnity, the net expected cost of litigating a claim that both parties believe to be wholly frivolous is C to both the plaintiff and the defendant. But with indemnity the net expected cost of litigating such a claim rises to $2C$ to the plaintiff and falls to zero to the defendant (can you see why?). Indemnity could have quite dramatic effects in increasing the number of meritorious claims if for example the rule of liability was strict liability, it did not pay prospective defendants to reduce their liability exposure by reducing their activity levels, and many of the potential claims were for very small amounts of money. With indemnity, there would be many more claims, since prospective defendants would, by assumption, not be deterred from engaging in the conduct that gave rise to such claims by the prospect of having to pay.

To summarize, probably indemnity raises the direct costs of litigation but reduces the error costs. The net effect on efficiency is unclear.

§21.10   Rule 68[1] and One-Way Indemnity

Rule 68 of the Federal Rules of Civil Procedure is receiving increasing attention as a device for encouraging settlement at a time when the

---

5. When is it rational to make a nuisance claim? When is it rational for the nuisance claimant to actually sue on his claim?

§21.10   1. Analyzed from an economic standpoint in George L. Priest, Regulating the Content and Volume of Litigation: An Economic Analysis, 1 S. Ct. Econ. Rev. 163 (1982), and Geoffrey P. Miller, An Economic Analysis of Rule 68, 15 J. Leg. Stud. 93 (1986).

federal courts (the state courts as well) are drowning in litigation. The rule provides that if the defendant makes a settlement offer before trial, and the plaintiff turns it down and then does worse at trial, the plaintiff must pay his own costs of suit, although as the prevailing party he normally would be entitled to insist that the defendant pay both parties' costs. In the absence of statute the costs to which the rule refers are the rather minor items that even under the American rule the loser usually has to reimburse the winner for, including court fees, copying costs, and (some) witness fees, but excluding the big item — attorney's fees. Recently the rule has been held to cover attorney's fees when such fees are provided for by statute, at least if the statute treats such fees as costs. Many statutes, including the federal civil rights statutes, entitle the prevailing party (often just the prevailing plaintiff) to an award of reasonable attorney's fees, to be paid for by the other party as part of the winner's costs. The prevailing plaintiff in a case governed by such a statute would be denied an award of attorney's fees if the defendant had made an offer of judgment and the plaintiff had turned it down and then did worse at trial.

Does Rule 68 increase the settlement rate? Probably not. The rule makes litigation more costly to the plaintiff, since even if he wins he may have to pay his own costs (sometimes including his attorney's fees), and therefore he will demand less in settlement of the case. But by the same token, the defendant, who now has less to lose from litigation, will offer less. So the settlement range will not be larger. But the rule has an indirect effect that may encourage settlement. It increases the defendant's incentive to make a realistic offer, i.e., one close to the plaintiff's expected gain from trial, since if the offer is not realistic and is declined, and the case goes to trial and the plaintiff wins, the defendant will benefit from having made a settlement offer only if the plaintiff does worse at trial than he would have done by accepting the offer.

In some cases the defendant will find it impossible to make a Rule 68 offer that will beat the judgment at trial if the case goes to trial and the plaintiff wins. Suppose for example that the plaintiff thinks he has a 50 percent chance of losing and a 50 percent chance of winning $100,000 and therefore will not accept a settlement offer of less than $50,000 (we can ignore the expense of litigation and settlement in this example). There are no intermediate possibilities; if the case goes to trial the plaintiff will win either $100,000 or nothing. The defendant thinks the plaintiff has only a 40 percent chance of winning and therefore will offer no more than $40,000. This may be a good offer because the defendant's estimate of the plaintiff's chances is better than the plaintiff's, yet there is no way the defendant can obtain a Rule 68 benefit from the offer. If the plaintiff loses, Rule 68 is inoperative (for then he has to pay his costs anyway, as the losing party); if he wins, he will win $100,000, which is more than the defendant's offer.

The main effect of Rule 68 is to transfer wealth from defendants to plaintiffs — but maybe not by much even when the rule applies to attorney's fees. The plaintiff would not turn down a Rule 68 offer unless he expected to do better at trial, and if he did worse than expected it would mean he had made a mistake in turning down the offer. So (to repeat an earlier point) the rule would only penalize the plaintiff for a mistake — and he should (ex ante) welcome the penalty: It will make him more careful in his own interest! But this ignores risk aversion. The decision to accept or reject the settlement offer has more downside risk when Rule 68 is in play, especially when the rule applies to attorney's fees as well as conventional costs. But as noted earlier, Rule 68 increases the defendant's incentive to make a realistic settlement offer, and the offer will be more generous, the greater the benefits that Rule 68 confers on the defendant if the plaintiff declines the offer and then does worse at trial. So maybe the rule is only slightly disadvantageous to plaintiffs.[2]

What by the way are the effects of statutes that give just a prevailing plaintiff a right of reimbursement? Under such a regime, inequality (3) becomes

$$P_p(J + C) - C + S > P_d(J + C) + C - S, \tag{5}$$

which can in turn be rewritten as

$$(P_p - P_d)J > 2(P_d/2 + 1 - P_p/2)C - S). \tag{6}$$

In all cases where $P_p > P_d$, the situation of mutual optimism that ordinarily is necessary for litigation to occur, a comparison with inequality (4), the parallel condition for the English rule, shows that litigation is less likely. This is because the negative number on the right-hand side, $P_d - P_p$, is cut in half. But a comparison with inequality (2) shows that litigation is more likely than under the American rule. Can you think of an intuitive reason for this result? (Hint: order the three rules according to the stakes.) This conclusion is contrary to the conventional view that one-way indemnity foments litigation more than any other rule. It should be noted, however, that while the English rule discourages nuisance claims, indemnity in favor just of plaintiffs encourages them.

§21.11   Res Judicata and Collateral Estoppel

The refusal of courts to permit the same claim to be relitigated between the same parties (res judicata) may seem surprising. Having lost once,

2. Would it make sense to amend the rule so that the plaintiff as well as the defendant could make a settlement offer, having the same effect as the defendant's offer?

the party will presumably be reluctant to try again; the loss is evidence of the likely outcome of his second suit. But why should he be forbidden to try, any more than an advertiser should be forbidden to repeat an advertising campaign that failed when first tried a few months previously? The answer is that the cost of relitigation is positive, while the benefit in reducing error costs is in general zero since there is no way of determining which outcomes in a series of inconsistent outcomes (A sues B and loses; A sues B again and wins; B now sues A to recover A's judgment against B and wins; etc.) are the correct ones. Wherever the chain is broken, there is no reason for thinking the last decision more probably correct than a prior inconsistent decision — assuming the stakes are the same or similar in the different actions and (a related point) that the first tribunal is on the same approximate plane of competence as the subsequent tribunals (e.g., not a traffic court). Both assumptions are necessary in order to make it unlikely that the error costs in a second litigation would be lower than those in the first.

Res judicata also forbids a plaintiff to "split" his claim. Suppose a plaintiff has both a tort and a contract cause of action against a defendant, growing out of the same incident. He will not be allowed to sue on one cause of action first, and then on the other. Although they are different causes of action they will be regarded as a single claim, in recognition of the economies obtainable by combining the two theories of liability in a single suit.

Incidentally, would it be necessary (or as necessary) to have a doctrine of res judicata if the English rule on indemnifying attorney's fees were in force? If all costs of litigation were internalized?

An interesting question is, when can a judgment be used to bar relitigation of the same issues in a subsequent litigation (collateral estoppel), not necessarily with the same party? Suppose A sues B and wins, and then sues C, and some issue decided in A's favor in his suit against B (maybe whether a product sold by both B and C is defectively designed) is also in issue in A's suit against C. To permit A to use the prior judgment to bar relitigation of this issue would create a serious risk of legal error. The prospect of being able to use a prior judgment to foreclose an issue in a subsequent suit might lead A to invest excessive resources in prevailing on that issue in his suit against B. He might for example pick as his first defendant (B) someone whose stake in the correct determination of the issue was too small to warrant investing significant resources in having it decided in his favor, while A would spend a great deal, anticipating benefits in subsequent litigation.[1]

Now reverse the facts: B wins A's suit against him and tries to use the judgment to foreclose a key issue in E's similar suit against him.

---

§21.11 1. Would it be relevant whether and at what cost C and other potential defendants could intervene in A's suit against B?

The problem discussed above is a bit less acute since B presumably did not choose who sued him first. But there is still a danger that he might expend disproportionate resources on the trial of an issue, anticipating benefits from being able to use the judgment in subsequent litigation.

Cases such as these have given the courts little difficulty.[2] But now suppose that, A having sued B and won, E brings a similar suit against B and seeks to use A's judgment to bar B from relitigating any common questions.[3] This is called offensive collateral estoppel. Unless there is collusion between A and E, we need not fear that A will invest excessively in the prosecution of his suit against B because he anticipates using that judgment against other defendants; he does not. The danger of applying collateral estoppel in this case is rather that B may invest excessively in defending himself against A's suit since the consequence of losing that suit may be much greater liability in subsequent suits. Of course if B, having invested excessively in the first suit, still loses that suit, that is pretty good evidence that A's claim was good; and why therefore should E have to prove its essential elements all over again? But if E is allowed to use A's judgment in this way, B will have, as we have said, a great incentive to invest disproportionately in the defense of A's suit, and this will increase the danger of an erroneous judgment in B's favor in that suit.

Now consider defensive collateral estoppel. A, who has similar claims against F, G, and H, sues G first and loses. Should F and H be permitted to use G's judgment to bar A's claims against them? Presumably A chose his strongest case to bring first (why?); if he loses it, this implies that the remaining cases are also without merit. But now appears the mirror image of the problem just discussed in connection with offensive collateral estoppel. A may pour resources into that first suit knowing that a loss there will be a disaster. B's stakes are much less. This asymmetry may allow A to win a case he does not deserve to win. We increase the probability of such a result if we allow a judgment in B's favor, when there is one, to be used against A by subsequent defendants.

Since the two types of collateral estoppel seem symmetrical, at least from an economic standpoint, it comes as a surprise that the courts are more hospitable to defensive than offensive collateral estoppel.[4]

2. Although for a reason different from the one suggested in the text: that the party sought to be collaterally estopped from litigating an issue (C in the first example, E in the second) never had his day in court.

3. So B has had his day in court on the issue — in A's suit against him.

4. Does the analysis also suggest an objection to *stare decisis* in some types of case? (cf. §22.3 *infra*.) Why is the objection less forceful?

§21.12 Court Delay and the Caseload Crisis

The law's delay has been a lament of popular literature since Shakespeare's time, but much of the traditional criticism of this delay is superficial. The inverse relationship between cost and time (see §10.8 *supra*) implies that eliminating the entire interval between the commencement and the decision of a lawsuit would be inefficient. Also, court delay is a "figurative" as distinct from a "literal" queue. Waiting in line for a table at a restaurant is a literal queue; it imposes an opportunity cost measured by the value of the customer's time while waiting. There is no such cost with court delay, as the litigants are free to go about their business while waiting for trial. There are, however, other costs of undue court delay (what are they?).

Excessive court delay is not, as is sometimes suggested, the inevitable consequence of the fact that the demand for litigation is large and the amount of judge time limited. The demand for lobsters is also large and the capacity to expand production to meet new increments of demand also limited. People queue up to buy litigation but not to buy lobsters because judicial time is not rationed by price and lobsters are. If the demand for lobsters increased faster than the supply, the price would rise until demand and supply were equated. An appropriately graduated system of surcharges for people desiring to have their cases heard promptly would have the same effect on litigation. If the prices necessary to clear the market (eliminate the queue) were very high, it would be a signal that an investment of resources in hiring more judges would probably be cost justified. The prices might not be high. Only a small fraction of litigants might have enough interest in an early trial to pay a surcharge. That would be a signal not to add judges.

Although the demand for court services, both state and federal, has been growing very rapidly since about 1960, no effort has been made to use the price system to moderate the demand and guide the supply response. The main response to the growth in demand has been to add judges and supporting judicial personnel. Such a response is unlikely to have a significant effect on court delay other than in the very short run. By increasing the quality of legal redress, at least to those who value prompt justice, an expansion in the number of judges will induce some people to use the courts who previously had been deterred by the delay. The analogy is to the construction of a new freeway to relieve traffic congestion. The new freeway may induce people who formerly used other methods of transportation because of the cost of congestion to substitute driving, until the freeway is as congested as the roads it replaced. In both examples, by increasing supply in a way that reduces the quality-adjusted price, the government simultaneously increases demand.

Figure 21.3 depicts the effects of an unanticipated increase in demand in a private market. In the short run, when supply is fixed, the increase in demand (from D_1 to D_2) causes a sharp rise in price, from p_0 to p_1. In the long run, however, when producers can expand capacity to meet the new demand (which is why the long-run supply curve, S_2, lies below the short-run supply curve, S_1), price falls from p_1 to p_2. It does not fall all the way back to p_0, because the efforts of producers to bid away inputs they need from other industries cause the prices of those inputs to rise. In other words, the long-run elasticity of supply is not infinite (a horizontal line to the right of the intersection between p_0 and q_0), because some of the inputs used to make the product in question are inherently scarce in relation to the demand for them.

Transposing this model to the judicial context, we would expect a surge of unexpected demand for judicial services to be met in the short run by an increase in the price of those services, as by raising filing fees. This was not done. In the federal courts, for example, filing fees have actually fallen in real (i.e., inflation-adjusted) terms since 1960.

Suppose the government had placed a ceiling on price at p_0 in the market depicted in Figure 21.3. There would be excess demand, and producers would have to choose who would be allowed to buy their product at p_0 (or how much each could buy). The counterpart in the judicial setting would be to let some people who wanted to file suits file them but turn the rest away. This was not done either. For example, minimum-amount-in-controversy requirements (e.g., the court will not take jurisdiction of a suit unless the stakes are more than $10,000) were not raised in the federal courts. On the contrary, they were abolished in most classes of case, and drastically cut by inflation in the rest. If

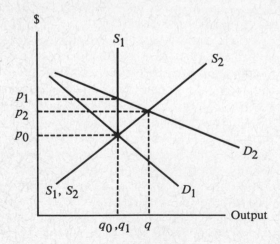

Figure 21.3

sellers confronting excess demand refuse to pick and choose among customers or limit the quantity each customer may buy, the only thing that is left is to make customers wait. If 1,000 people want to buy a product at price p_0, and annual production is only 500, the 1,000 customers can still all be supplied if supply is spread out over two years. (In polygymous societies, the average age of marriage is much higher for men than for women; can you see the analogy?) Delay is in fact the standard judicial response in the short run to an unanticipated (or unprovided for) surge in demand.

For the long run, responding to a surge in demand by adding judges and other court personnel without increasing the price of judicial services would make sense if the supply of court services were infinitely elastic in the long run, and this might seem to be the proper model. If an industry is composed of many firms of equal size and therefore, presumably, of equal costs (why?), new increments of demand for the industry's product will be met by the creation of similar new firms, perhaps at little increase in the industry's average costs in the long run. This would be a real-world approximation to infinitely elastic long-run supply. It might seem that each judge in a judicial system is like one of these small firms, so that new increments in demand for the system's services can be met by adding judges at no increase in average cost. But this ignores the fact that as the number of judges grows, especially at the appellate level, where judges sit in panels rather than by themselves, the transaction costs of judicial decision making grow. This growth can be contained to some extent by making the judicial system more hierarchical. Hierarchy is how business firms and other institutions overcome the transaction cost problem that would exist if decisions were made by negotiation among numerous equals. The creation of an intermediate appellate court in most states (and the federal system) between trial court and supreme court was a previous generation's adaptation to the problem of caseload growth. But lengthening the judicial hierarchy imposes delay by creating a new stage of appeal in a case.

What would be a better demand response to the caseload problem: higher minimum-amount-in-controversy requirements or higher filing fees? The economist prefers the latter. The minimum-amount-in-controversy approach is the equivalent of an infinite filing fee for cases below the minimum and a zero filing fee for cases above it. This is not an optimal mechanism for sorting cases among different judicial systems. In contrast, a fixed filing fee would operate as a proportionally declining tax on lawsuits. A fee of $1,000, for example, would constitute a 100 percent tax on a case in which the stakes were $1,000, and a 1 percent tax in a case in which the stakes were $100,000. If the fee is set equal to the cost of the lawsuit to the judicial system (including not only the direct costs but also the costs of causing other cases to be backed up), it would confront the litigant (presumably the plaintiff, but the defendant could be required to reimburse the plaintiff if the plaintiff won) with the full social cost of using the system. A minimum-amount-in-controversy requirement does not do this.

Both requirements can be criticized as favoring the wealthy. But the criticism is incomplete, even if stakes and wealth have a strong positive correlation. Since the parties will spend more on litigation the higher the stakes in the case are, and since higher expenditures on litigation will in general reduce error costs, the entire society, rich and poor alike, has an interest in allocating the highest-quality judicial resources to the biggest cases, leaving the smaller cases to be tried in lower-quality tribunals.

Another criticism is that a system of fully compensatory filing fees would eliminate the subsidy to litigation, briefly touched on in the last chapter, that results from not charging litigants the costs of the judicial system itself, a subsidy that may be justified by the external benefits that litigation confers by creating rules of conduct for the society. Minimum-amount-in-controversy requirements preserve the subsidy, for if a case meets the requirement, the litigants do not have to contribute to the costs of the judicial system. But the subsidy approach could be preserved in a system of filing fees simply by subtracting the optimal subsidy from a fee calculated to return the full cost of the lawsuit to the judicial system. Moreover, concern with court congestion and delay suggests that the existing subsidy for litigation is too large. Indeed, the optimal subsidy may today be negative, in which event perhaps the government should be defraying some of the costs of settlement, not litigation (and in fact there has been some recent movement in this direction).

With fully compensatory filing fees, it would be possible to consider abolishing the requirement of standing — which means, basically, that to maintain a suit a plaintiff must have suffered an actual injury that the suit will ameliorate, or compensate him for, if he wins. If litigants had to pay the full costs of using the legal system, including all congestion costs, the judiciary would no longer have to worry about a litigant's stake in the case. The litigant would compare the benefit to him of suing with the full social costs of suing, and if the former exceeded the latter would sue, as we would want him to do in that situation. Rules of standing thus resemble minimum-amount-in-controversy requirements; from an economic standpoint both are inferior to realistic filing fees as ways of rationing access to the courts.

Filing fees might seem unusable when litigants are indigent, as many litigants (particularly criminal defendants and prisoners) are. But this is incorrect. Even if the filing fee is not paid by the litigant himself, whoever does pay it will have an incentive, absent under the present system, to compare the full social costs of the suit with the benefits to the litigant.

§21.13 Jurors and Arbitrators

Court queues are almost always greatest for parties seeking civil jury trials. This makes economic sense. These cases are more costly to try than nonjury cases, both because of jury fees (which, as we shall see, understate the true social costs of the jury) and because a case normally takes longer to try to a jury than to a judge (why?). Parties are therefore "charged" more for jury trials by being made to wait in line longer.

The origins of the jury are apparently political. But its political function, discussed briefly in a subsequent chapter (see §24.1 *infra*), is limited largely to criminal cases and to other cases to which the government is a party. The United States is now the only country in which a jury is regularly used in private cases, and it may be doubted whether the added costs of jury trial are offset by a reduction, if any, in factfinding errors. Still the jury offers a rich field for economic analysis.[1]

Once the decision was made to entrust factfinding to laymen it was inevitable that several laymen rather than one would be used for this purpose. To have people of varied backgrounds and points of view deliberating together is necessary to offset the greater expertise of the professional judge, for whom the jury is a substitute in finding facts and applying the law to them; the error costs of entrusting judgment to a single layman would be enormous. This suggests the essential tradeoffs in designing an economically optimal jury system. Enlarging the jury reduces error costs by increasing the variety of experience and ability that will be involved in the factfinding process — for example, by making it more likely that the jury will include at least one perceptive and articulate juror who can focus the jury's deliberations. But at the same time it increases the direct costs of the jury by increasing the number of people who have to be paid, the amount of time they will spend deliberating, and the probability of a hung jury and hence of a retrial. Also, like any form of diversification, increasing the size of the jury (provided selection is random or nearly so) reduces the risk of extreme outcomes. (If you were a tort defendant, would you prefer a 6-person or a 12-person jury?)

Another variable besides the number of jurors is the required majority for a verdict. A rule of unanimity will be more costly than one of simple majority. It takes longer to negotiate a unanimous verdict — the agreement of more parties is needed — and increases the likelihood of a hung jury. But the quality of the deliberations may be increased, and hence

§21.13 1. See Alvin K. Klevorick & Michael Rothschild, A Model of the Jury Decision Process, 8 J. Leg. Stud. 141 (1979); Alvin K. Klevorick, Jury Size and Composition: An Economic Approach, in The Economics of Public Services (Martin S. Feldstein & Robert P. Inman eds. 1977); Donald L. Martin, The Economics of Jury Conscription, 80 J. Pol. Econ. 680 (1972).

error costs reduced, by requiring that everyone be convinced of the correctness of the outcome preferred by some. Stated differently, requiring unanimity increases the effective size of the jury compared to majority rule.

The use of conscription to obtain jurors seems at first glance highly inefficient. It leads to an understatement of the social costs of the jury and hence to overuse of juries. But it would be difficult to obtain juries of people with diverse backgrounds — juries presumably more efficient as factfinders — without the use of compulsion. A fee set at a level that would just fill the number of jury slots would produce juries composed mainly of people of low economic status. A fee set high enough to attract upper-income people would create excess demand for jury positions (why?). And if the courts rationed the excess demand by using some criterion of fitness — education, occupation, or whatever — the jury would lose its random-sample character, which is a positive factor in its ability to make correct factual determinations.

Jurors are not the only laymen used to adjudicate legal disputes. Most commercial arbitrators are nonlawyers (most labor arbitrators, however, are lawyers), and, by definition, none is a publicly employed judge. The difference between arbitrators and jurors is that the former are chosen for their expertise in the area in dispute, and the latter for their lack of expertise! The difference can be explained, though. There is a tradeoff between expertise and impartiality. The more a person knows about some area of life, the less the arguments and evidence of two disputants will influence his resolution of the dispute; the increment to his knowledge is less. The expert, then, is more powerful. If two disputants choose (usually in advance of the dispute) to submit their dispute to an expert, there is no reason not to respect their choice. But judges and juries exercise the coercive power of government. That power is buffered by insisting that they do not know so much about the dispute that they are unlikely to listen attentively to the submissions of the disputants, and diffused by having more than one juror.[2]

§21.14   Appeals

The losing party in a lawsuit can appeal to a higher court. The appeal serves two social purposes: to reduce the costs of legal error (is this consistent with the earlier discussion of res judicata and collateral estop-

2. See further, on the economics of arbitration, Orley Ashenfelter, Evidence on U.S. Experience with Dispute Resolution Systems (Industrial Relations Section, Princeton University, Working Paper No. 185, March 1985); William M. Landes & Richard A. Posner, Adjudication as a Private Good, 8 J. Leg. Stud. 235, 236-259 (1979).

pel?); and to enable uniform rules of law to be created and maintained. As it usually is no part of the losing party's desire to improve the law, it may seem that there would be too few appeals from a social standpoint, even with the modest subsidy of the appellate (as of the trial) process that consists of not charging the parties for any part of the judges' salaries and related expenses. But there is a natural equilibrating mechanism. If there are too few appeals in period one, the appellate courts' production of precedents will fall, making it difficult for people to settle their disputes (because they cannot agree on how the disputes are likely to be resolved in court), resulting in more litigation and hence more appeals in period two.

Appellate courts give plenary review to pure issues of law; that is, they do not give any deference to the trial judge's view on such issues. If they did, the law would vary from trial judge to trial judge and it would be impossible (or at least very difficult) for people to know what the law was. But appellate courts do defer quite broadly to the trial judge's (or jury's) findings of fact. Since facts are different from case to case anyway, uniformity of factfinding is less important; moreover, the trier of fact has lower information costs in making factual determinations than the appellate judges, who do not see the witnesses.

Appellate courts do not reverse for harmless errors. Such an error is by definition unlikely to lead to a different result if the case is retried. The expected benefit of reversal in such a case is low in relation to the cost of the further proceedings in the trial court that will ensue if the judgment is reversed.

Perhaps the most interesting question about appealability is, when may the trial court's ruling be appealed? When it is entered or not till the end of the proceeding in the trial court? The federal system, like virtually all of the states and most foreign countries as well, has adopted a strong presumption in favor of postponing review to the end of the proceeding in the trial court. This is the final judgment rule. But it is riddled with exceptions, to some extent unavoidably, as can be seen by considering the pros and cons of the rule.

There are two benefits to allowing immediate appeals of intermediate (interlocutory) rulings. The first is to avoid delay in determining the correctness of the ruling. The second is that an immediate determination of correctness may head off lengthy proceedings in the trial court; this will be true for example if the district court erroneously denied a motion to dismiss the complaint.

But corresponding to these two benefits are two costs. The first is that the proceeding as a whole may be delayed by frequent interruptions for appeals from interlocutory orders. The second is that postponing appellate review may head off unnecessary appellate proceedings, for many of the orders that trial judges issue in the course of a proceeding are moot by the time the proceeding is ended. Suppose, for example, that a judge rules adversely to the plaintiff time and time again (on questions of admissibility of evidence, for example), yet in the end the plaintiff prevails anyway. In a system that freely allowed interlocutory appeals he might have appealed every one of those rulings at the time they were made, but if interlocutory appeals are not allowed all of the rulings will be mooted by the final judgment.

There is an additional economy from postponing appeal till the end of the case. Instead of having to consider 10 appeals in the same case, the court of appeals has to consider only one appeal with (perhaps) 10 issues, and to the extent the issues are related to each other — for example by being based on the same facts — the one appeal may be less time consuming for the judges, even though it has many issues, than 10 single-issue appeals in the same case would have been.

Notice that a regime of interlocutory appeals economizes on the time of the trial courts at the expense of the appellate courts, while a final judgment rule does the reverse. Under the former, the trial judge stops work on a case as soon as a ruling is appealed, and if he is lucky the first (or a subsequent) interlocutory appeal will end the case; but the courts of appeals may be inundated with appeals. Under the latter regime the trial judge may be forced to carry lengthy proceedings through to the end only to discover that some order he made early on was erroneous and that he must redo the whole proceeding. The court of appeals, however, has the comfort of knowing that a single case in the trial court can produce no more than one appeal.

It is inevitable, at least in retrospect, that the federal system would have placed greater weight on economizing on the time of appellate judges than on that of trial judges. The reason lies in the pyramidal structure of a judicial system combined with the geographic extent of the federal judicial system. As we have seen, the number of appellate judges in a unitary system cannot be expanded indefinitely without adding new tiers of appellate courts, since a vital task of the appellate process — maintaining a reasonable uniformity and consistency of law — cannot be performed effectively if there is more than a handful of judges. If the appellate workload is such that more than a few judges are needed to handle it, they must break up into smaller panels, but then there is a problem of coordinating the panels. Eventually the only answer is another tier of appellate review. The federal system has a three-tiered system, although access to the third tier, the Supreme Court, is limited. But if interlocutory appeals were freely allowed, three tiers would not be enough; they are not enough in New York State, which has long allowed such appeals with unusual liberality.

Multiple appellate tiers are workable in New York because the first tier (the Appellate Term of the Supreme Court) is usually found in the same building with the trial judges, so interlocutory appeals can be handled with dispatch. It is very hard to imagine such a system on a national scale. Many cities in the United States have only one or two federal district judges, and even if interlocutory appeals were freely allowed there would not be enough work to keep a panel of appellate judges fully occupied in such cities. The appellate judges would have to ride circuit, or the lawyers would have to present their interlocutory appeals in other cities than where the trial was taking place; considerable delays would be introduced in either case. The problem would have been completely insoluble in the conditions of transportation that prevailed in the first century of the federal courts. It is not surprising that the final judgment rule was adopted from the first.

Nevertheless, in many cases the balance of costs and benefits inclines strongly in favor of an immediate appeal, and the federal judicial system would be unduly rigid if no provision were made for these cases. For example, delay in getting an interlocutory order reviewed might be very costly where the order was a preliminary injunction forcing the defendant to shut down his business or was a ruling on a potentially dispositive issue which if decided the other way would head off a year long trial. So it is not surprising that a statute allows interlocutory orders granting or denying injunctions to be appealed immediately,[1] and that a judge-made doctrine, the collateral order doctrine, allows orders not winding up the whole litigation to be appealed immediately if they involve separate issues from the merits of the litigation and an immediate appeal is necessary to prevent irreparable harm to the appellant. Suppose the trial court refuses to make the defendant post a bond to assure that if he loses the case he will be able to reimburse certain expenses of the plaintiff to which the latter would be entitled. If the order is not immediately appealable and later the plaintiff wins and the defendant turns out not to be good for the money, the plaintiff will be out of luck. So the costs of forgoing an immediate appeal could be great. And since the issue of the bond is completely separate from the merits, there will be no judicial diseconomy from having to hear separate appeals on the bond and on the merits.

§21.15   Choice of Law

Suppose a resident of State A, while driving in State B, injures a resident of B, who sues. Which state's law should be used to decide the rights of the parties — A's or B's? Both states have an interest in the outcome of the suit. At the simplest level, A will benefit if its resident wins,

§21.14   1.   28 U.S.C. §1292(a)(1).

because he will have more money, and B will benefit if its resident wins. These benefits are offsetting and can be ignored. But A also has an interest in its resident's being able to drive in State B without undue restrictions and B an interest in protecting its resident from being injured by a negligent driver. In other words, both states have an allocative as well as a distributive interest in the dispute. And here it becomes significant that the accident occurred in B. Presumably B's rules are tailored to driving conditions — the state of the roads, weather, etc. — in B. Since B thus has (subject to a qualification to be noted shortly) a comparative regulatory advantage in regard to accidents which occur in B, there is an economic argument for the traditional common law rule that the law of the place where the tort occurred is the law that will be applied in a suit, wherever brought, to redress that tort.

This rule, however, has given way in most states to a more complex analysis of the respective "interests" of the states affected by the suit. The issue ought not to be interests; it ought to be which state's law makes the best "fit" with the circumstances of the dispute. Suppose the issue is which state's statute of limitations shall apply. If the purpose of the statute of limitations is to reduce the error costs associated with the use of stale evidence, there is a strong argument for applying the statute of the state where the case is tried because that statute presumably reflects the competence of the courts of that state to deal with stale evidence. But if the purpose of the statute is just to enable people to plan their activities with greater certainty, there is an argument for applying the statute of limitations of the injurer's state, because it is the injurer who is subjected to the uncertainty. Or suppose the issue in a breach of contract suit between residents of different states is the capacity of the promisor to make a binding promise (must he be 21 or is 18 old enough?); the rules of the promisor's state of residence governing capacity would seem to have the comparative advantage in resolving the dispute, since those rules presumably are based on the capacities of that state's residents.

Exquisite difficulties are presented by a case where two residents of state A are involved in a collision in state B. The tort rules of B will be better adapted to location-specific factors such as the state of the roads and climate conditions, but the tort rules of A will be better adapted to person-specific factors such as ability to take care. (Why was this not a problem in the case we started with?)

Suggested Readings

1. Lucian Arye Bebchuk, Litigation and Settlement Under Imperfect Information, 15 Rand J. Econ. 404 (1984).
2. Donald N. Dewees, J. Robert S. Prichard, & Michael J. Trebilcock,

An Economic Analysis of Cost and Fee Rules for Class Actions, 10 J. Leg. Stud. 155 (1981).

3. Patricia Munch Danzon, Contingent Fees for Personal Injury Litigation, 14 Bell J. Econ. 213 (1983).

4. _____ & Lee A. Lillard, Settlement Out of Court: The Disposition of Medical Malpractice Claims, 12 J. Leg. Stud. 345 (1983).

5. Frank H. Easterbrook, Criminal Procedure as a Market System, 12 J. Leg. Stud. 289 (1983).

6. William M. Landes, An Economic Analysis of the Courts, 14 J. Law & Econ. 61 (1971).

7. _____, The Bail System: An Economic Approach, 2 J. Leg. Stud. 79 (1973).

8. John Leubsdorf, The Contingency Factor in Attorney Fee Awards, 90 Yale L.J. 473 (1981).

9. Geoffrey P. Miller, An Economic Analysis of Rule 68, 15 J. Leg. Stud. 93 (1986).

10. Richard A. Posner, An Economic Approach to Legal Procedure and Judicial Administration, 2 J. Leg. Stud. 399 (1973).

11. _____, The Federal Courts: Crisis and Reform, pts. I-II (1985).

12. Kenneth E. Scott, Standing in the Supreme Court — A Functional Analysis, 86 Harv. L. Rev. 645, 670-683 (1973).

13. Steven Shavell, Suit, Settlement, and Trial: A Theoretical Analysis Under Alternative Methods for the Allocation of Legal Costs, 11 J. Leg. Stud. 55 (1982).

14. Note, An Analysis of Settlement, 22 Stan. L. Rev. 67 (1969).

Problems

1. Can you think of an economic rationale for the replacement of notice pleading by issue pleading as in the Federal Rules of Civil Procedure?

2. Should a party to a lawsuit be able to compel the attendance of a witness?

3. In Clauss v. Danker, 264 F. Supp. 246 (S.D.N.Y. 1967), a tort action, the plaintiff sought discovery of the particulars of the defendant's liability insurance policy, even though those particulars would not be admissible as evidence in the trial of the case. The court said it would be desirable that such discovery be permitted, primarily in order to facilitate settlement, but held that under the existing Federal Rules of Civil Procedure discovery of insurance coverage could not be ordered. In 1970 the rules were amended to permit such discovery. The advisory committee noted: "Disclosure of insurance coverage will enable counsel for both sides to make the same realistic appraisal of the case, so that settlement and litigation strategy are based on knowledge and not specu-

lation. It will conduce to settlement and avoid protracted litigation in some cases, though in others it may have an opposite effect."

Is the change in the rules likely to increase or reduce the frequency of settlement? How, if at all, does the analysis differ from that of Rule 35 in §21.5 *supra*?

4. Compare the costs of reducing crime by (a) lowering the prosecutor's burden of proof and (b) making criminal prohibitions more specific.

5. What would be the consequences if, instead of requiring the defendant to post bail, the state were required to pay the defendant the costs he incurred by remaining in jail pending trial?

6. Would it be a good idea, from an economic standpoint, to compensate the defendant who is acquitted of a criminal charge? What would be the appropriate measure of compensation? What implications, if any, would compensation have for the appropriate standard of proof in a criminal case?

7. In a suit for treble damages under the antitrust laws, should the plaintiff be required to establish the defendant's liability beyond a reasonable doubt?

8. Here are some questions about indemnifying the winning party's attorney's fees:

   a. The plaintiff is limited to a reasonable attorney's fee, even if he actually incurred a greater fee. Can you see why this rule is necessary to prevent strategic behavior?

   b. Suppose the winning party was represented by a public interest law firm. Should the attorney's fees be based on the actual costs incurred by the firm, or on what lawyers of equal competence would have charged for the services rendered by the firm? See Blum v. Stenson, 465 U.S. 886 (1984).

   c. Should a risk multiplier ever be allowed? Suppose the plaintiff had only a 20 percent chance of winning, and if he had lost, his lawyer would have gotten nothing because the lawyer had agreed to take the case for a contingent fee. If the plaintiff wins, should the lawyer's fee be multiplied by five in order to compensate him for the risk he bore? See Laffey v. Northwest Airlines, Inc., 746 F.2d 4 (D.C. Cir. 1984); McKinnon v. City of Berwyn, 750 F.2d 1383 (7th Cir. 1984).

9. Suppose one of several beneficiaries of a trust hires a lawyer to sue the trustee. If as a result of the suit the assets of the trust are increased, the law will allow the lawyer to claim a portion of his fee from the other beneficiaries. Does this make economic sense? See Saul Levmore, Explaining Restitution, 71 Va. L. Rev. 1 (1985).

10. The rules of evidence (hearsay, best evidence, etc.) are primarily designed to keep from the jury evidence believed either to have slight probative weight or to be unduly prejudicial. What do these terms mean to an economist, and what would be an optimal set of such rules? See

Note, The Theoretical Foundation of the Hearsay Rules, 93 Harv. L. Rev. 1786 (1980); Thomas Gibbons & Allan C. Hutchinson, The Practice and Theory of Evidence Law — A Note, 2 Intl. Rev. Law & Econ. 119 (1982).

11. To obtain a preliminary injunction, a plaintiff must, as we have seen, show that he will suffer irreparable harm if the injunction is denied. From an economic standpoint, which if any of the following types of arguably irreparable harm should be a basis for a preliminary injunction in a damage suit?

a. The defendant may become insolvent before the end of the trial.

b. The plaintiff may declare bankruptcy before the end of the trial as a result of the defendant's alleged wrongdoing.

c. Damages will be difficult to calculate.

12. Should a judgment be given collateral estoppel effect if it was not appealed?

13. Would you expect a clause providing for the arbitration of disputes arising under the contract to be more common in standard-form contracts or in individually negotiated contracts?

CHAPTER 22

LAW ENFORCEMENT

§22.1 Public Versus Private Law Enforcement: The Tradeoffs

In common law fields such as torts, contracts, and property the enforcement of law — the process by which violations are investigated and a legal sanction applied to the violator — is, like its formulation, entrusted mainly to private persons: the litigants, their lawyers, and various specialists in proof or investigation whom they hire. But a good deal of the responsibility for law enforcement has been entrusted, either concurrently with private enforcement or exclusively, to public agencies; and this chapter examines some of the properties of public in comparison to private enforcement.

Why have public enforcement at all? Gary Becker and George Stigler have proposed that law enforcement be wholly privatized.[1] Under their proposal, private individuals and law firms would investigate violations, apprehend violators (including criminal offenders), and conduct legal proceedings to redress violations, including criminal prosecutions. A private enforcer would be entitled, if successful, to retain the full proceeds of the suit — for example, the fine paid by the convicted offender. If the offender was judgment proof, the state would pay the enforcer a bounty.

This proposal would solve the problem of the class action discussed in the last chapter. And, radical as it may seem, it would really be just a return to an earlier way of enforcing law. Criminal (as well as virtually all other) law enforcement in primitive and ancient societies is almost entirely private.[2] And for centuries the enforcement of the criminal and

§22.1 1. See Gary S. Becker & George J. Stigler, Law Enforcement, Malfeasance, and Compensation of Enforcers, 3 J. Leg. Stud. 1 (1974).

2. See Richard A. Posner, The Economics of Justice, chs. 5, 7-8 (1981); Alan F. Westin, Privacy in Western History: From the Age of Pericles to the American Republic (Report to the Association of the Bar of the City of New York, Special Comm. on Science and Law, Feb. 15, 1965).

regulatory laws of England followed the pattern suggested by Becker and Stigler. Parliament and municipal authorities (as well as private firms and individuals) paid bounties for the apprehension and conviction of offenders. In the case of offenses punished by fines, the fine was divided between the Crown and the enforcer. There were no public prosecutors, and the police were public in name only.[3]

Private enforcement, however, imposes certain costs that public enforcement avoids, which may explain the actual mixture of public and private enforcement in the legal system today. Suppose the fine for some offense is substantially below the optimal level and the probability of apprehension and conviction substantially above it, and the fine (f) is raised in an effort to move closer to the optimum. Only if the probability of apprehension and conviction (p) declines will the increase in the fine enable expenditures on law enforcement to be reduced without any diminution in deterrence. But under private enforcement p will rise. Although the increase in the fine will at first reduce the number of offenses by increasing the expected cost of an offense, it will also increase the returns to enforcers from apprehending an offender, and the latter effect may lead to an increase in the absolute number of apprehensions. If so, clearly the result will be an increase in p, for p is simply the ratio of the number of apprehensions to the number of offenders. But even if the increase in the fine has so great a deterrent effect that it results in fewer apprehensions, the return per apprehension will be higher, and competition will lead the firms in the enforcement industry to spend greater resources than before per apprehension. Hence the probability of apprehension (p) should rise, which will interfere with the legislature's purposes in increasing the fine (to save resources by reducing p).

This problem (overenforcement) would not arise if the optimum probability of apprehension and conviction were one, for in that case the optimum fine would be equal to the social costs of illegal activity, and if those costs rose the optimum fine would rise by the same amount. This would be (properly) perceived by enforcers as an upward shift in the demand curve facing them, and would have the effect of increasing the resources devoted to crime prevention, as in the case of an ordinary product the demand for which increases. But where the probability of apprehension and conviction is less than one, the optimum fine is higher than the social costs of the illegal activity, not as a signal that additional

---

3. See 2 Leon Radzinowicz, A History of English Criminal Law and Its Administration From 1750 (1948). Police were paid only nominal salaries by the state, and they looked to bounties, fines, and the like for their principal compensation; in effect they were licensed private enforcers.

resources should be devoted to preventing the activity but as a means of minimizing those resources. In the case of public enforcement the fine need not be taken as a signal to invest greater resources in crime prevention, since the public enforcer is not constrained to act as a private profit maximizer.

Could private enforcement be driven down to the desired level by imposing an excise tax on enforcers? The tax (on what exactly?) would shift the demand curve as perceived by the enforcers to the left without reducing f and thereby impairing the deterrent effect of the law. But the tax would drive a wedge between what offenders paid and what enforcers received, creating attractive opportunities for bribery and corruption, for both the apprehended offender and the enforcer would be better off if they negotiated a private transfer payment that was less than the statutory fine but greater than the fine minus the tax. A major criticism of public enforcement advanced by Becker and Stigler, that it creates incentives for bribery and corruption because the gain to the enforcer from enforcement is generally less than the offender's potential penalty, might no longer be a strong argument for private enforcement.

When imprisonment and other nonmonetary sanctions are introduced, the state must offer bounties to enforcers if there is to be adequate incentive for private enforcement. Assuming that the optimum system continues to involve a combination of severe penalties with low probabilities of apprehension and conviction, a bounty that is the exact monetary equivalent of the costs of the penalty to the offender will induce excessive enforcement, as enforcers pour resources into apprehending and convicting offenders and thereby raise p above its (low) optimum level. If, however, the bounties are set below f so as to reduce enforcement, there will be a gap between the cost of punishment to the offender and the gain to the enforcer, and opportunities for bribery and other corruption will be introduced. Still, the problem may be less severe than it would be under a system of fines only. Even though the bounties are smaller than the cost of punishment to the offender, they may exceed his ability to pay since it is the limitations on offenders' resources that require reliance on nonpecuniary penalties in the first place.

It might appear that private enforcement would increase the number of innocent people convicted of offenses. The private enforcer is paid per offender convicted, regardless of the actual guilt or innocence of the accused. There are several ways in which the enforcer can increase his "catch," and hence his income, by augmenting the supply of "offenders."

(1) He can fabricate an offense.
(2) He can prosecute an innocent person for an offense that actually occurred.
(3) He can encourage an individual to commit an offense that he

would not have committed without encouragement, and then prosecute him for the offense; this is entrapment.[4]

(4) Knowing that someone is about to attempt the commission of a crime, the enforcer can wait until the crime has been committed and then prosecute him, rather than apprehend him in the attempt stage and prosecute him for a criminal attempt. The incentive for waiting is to obtain greater compensation, since the penalty for the completed crime will be heavier than the penalty for the attempt.

But these abuses also arise under public enforcement — indeed, the rules against entrapment, knowing suppression by the prosecution of evidence favorable to the accused, etc., were developed to prevent the commission of these practices by public enforcers — and there is no basis for expecting them to be more widespread under a system of private enforcement. Although the private enforcer is compensated on an explicitly piecework basis, and the public enforcer is not, the other side of the coin in that the private enforcer may be more sensitive to the costs of the unsuccessful prosecution. This may lead him to screen out the innocent more carefully than the public enforcer would, because resources devoted to prosecuting the innocent are likely to be less productive than those devoted to prosecuting the guilty. And a private enforcer may derive less (no?) return from harassing the innocent with unfounded prosecutions than the public enforcer (why?).[5]

§22.2 Public Versus Private Enforcement: Positive Implications

The analysis in the preceding section helps explain several features of the legal system:

4. But private, not public. See §7.3 *supra*. An interesting variant of entrapment is the operation of schools for criminals by private enforcers in eighteenth-century England. Such schools could be rational from the standpoint of both teachers and students. The student would learn skills that would reduce the probability of his apprehension for any particular offense that he might commit. This reduction in the expected punishment cost of crime would increase the amount of criminal activity, i.e., the stock of offenders. Thus, from the private enforcers' standpoint, the operation of the school would resemble the stocking of a pond by fishermen (what would be the difference?).

5. Two questions:

(a) Is erroneously failing to prosecute and convict more likely under private than under public enforcement?

(b) Are *inadvertent* errors likely to be more or less frequent under private as compared to public enforcement? Assume that a given fraction of all enforcement proceedings, either public or private, results in the conviction of an innocent person; and consider whether there are likely to be more enforcement proceedings under private than under public enforcement, and, if so, whether it follows that the aggregate error costs will be higher under the former system.

1. With few exceptions, there is a public monopoly — more precisely a series of public monopolies — of criminal law enforcement. True, the same act is often both a crime and a tort, and then private enforcement is possible in principle. But if the offender is judgment proof, as most criminal offenders are, the tort remedy is ineffectual and the public enforcer has a *de facto* monopoly. In contrast, in areas of the law such as contracts and torts (excluding those torts that are also crimes), the main burden of enforcement falls on the private sector.

The relevant difference between crimes, on the one hand, and torts and breaches of contract, on the other, is that with very small resources devoted to apprehension, the probability of apprehension tends to be much less than one in the former case and to approach one in the second (it is one, in the case of breaches of contract). The victim of a breach of contract knows who the promisor is; the victim of an automobile accident usually knows the identity of the other driver;[1] but the victim of a burglary rarely knows the burglar's identity. If p is assumed equal to one in the average tort or contract case, the problem of socially excessive private enforcement cannot arise, as we have seen — provided that property rights in enforcement are *not* assigned on a first-come first-served basis, but are reserved to the victim of the tort or breach of contract. If for example the marginal harm inflicted by some tort were $9 and the marginal costs of apprehension and conviction $1, and hence $f = \$10$, the enforcer who was the first to stake his claim would receive a rent of $9. The opportunity to obtain such rents would induce expenditures on enforcement in excess of $1. Exclusive victim rights eliminate this source of waste. (What other economic advantage do they have?)

2. The cost of enforcement may be so high relative to the value of the claim that the legal claims "market" would not work if the principle that the victim had the exclusive right to the claim were adhered to strictly. A good example is a price-fixing conspiracy that imposes a small cost on each of a large number of buyers. The class action and the middleman suit are devices already discussed for overcoming this problem. In effect the property rights normally possessed by the victims of an alleged violation are reassigned to the lawyer for the class or to the middleman.

3. The budgets of public enforcement agencies tend to be small relative to the potential gains from enforcement as they would be appraised by a private, profit-maximizing enforcer. For example, the Internal Revenue Service is operating at a budgetary level where the marginal cost of enforcement is far below the marginal return, measured (as a private

§22.2 1. Although partly as a result of criminal and other regulatory statutes involving licensing of drivers, registration of vehicles, and punishment for leaving the scene of an accident — an example of public enforcement that is designed to strengthen private enforcement.

enforcer would measure it) by the additional tax revenue that additional expenditures on enforcement would generate. The assumption of a budget constraint would be unrealistic as applied to a private enforcer, for assuming reasonably well-functioning capital markets he would be able to finance any enforcement activities in which the expected return exceeded the expected costs. But for Congress to appropriate additional funds to an agency such as the IRS that could use the funds to increase the net yield of enforcement could produce overenforcement. The public agency's budget constraint is thus like a tax on private enforcement designed to reduce the level of private enforcement to the socially optimal level.

4. A public monopoly of enforcement enables the public enforcer in effect to nullify particular laws, or particular applications of law, simply by declining to prosecute violators. This power appears to be exercised frequently. Such nullification would not be a feature of private enforcement; all laws would be enforced that yielded a positive expected net return. Is this good or bad?

The analysis of rulemaking in Chapter 20 implies that rules of law will almost always be overinclusive; the costs of precisely tailoring a rule to the conduct intended to be forbidden are prohibitive because of the inherent limitations of foresight and ambiguities of language. But if enforced to the letter, an overinclusive rule could impose very heavy social costs; it would be just like punishing an innocent person in order to reduce the probability of acquitting a guilty one. Discretionary nonenforcement is a technique by which the costs of overinclusion can be reduced without a corresponding increase in underinclusion (loopholes). The police overlook minor infractions of the traffic code; building inspectors ignore violations of building code provisions that, if enforced, would prevent the construction of new buildings in urban areas; air traffic controllers permit the airlines to violate excessively stringent safety regulations involving the spacing of aircraft when landing and taking off from airports.

The existence of a public monopoly of enforcement in a particular area of the law is a necessary rather than sufficient condition of discretionary nonenforcement. A public agency could in principle enforce all of the laws entrusted to its administration. But in practice it cannot, given the budget constraint mentioned earlier. And while conceivably it might concentrate its resources on precisely those areas of conduct that had been brought inadvertently within the scope of the statutory prohibition, this seems unlikely. Capriciousness is not the central tendency of public enforcement (see §§22.3, 23.3 *infra*).

5. Blackmail is the sale of exclusive rights to information to the person who would be incriminated by its disclosure, and at first glance appears to be an efficient method of private enforcement of the law (the moral as well as the positive law). The value of the information to the black-

mailed person is equal to the cost of the punishment that he will incur if the information is disclosed and he is punished as a result. So he will be willing to pay up to that amount to the blackmailer for the exclusive rights to the information. The "fine" may be identical to what he would have had to pay had he been apprehended and convicted for the crime that the blackmailer has discovered[2] but paid to the blackmailer rather than to the state. Why then is blackmail a crime?

The decision to forbid blackmail follows directly from the decision to rely on a public monopoly of law enforcement in some areas of enforcement, notably criminal law. If blackmail were lawful, the public monopoly of enforcement would be undermined and overenforcement could result. An alternative, and only superficially inconsistent, possibility is that the blackmailer will subvert the statutory punishment scheme by accepting from the offender a payment less, often much less, than the specified fine for the offense. This problem would be eliminated if the blackmailer, as an alternative to transacting with the offender, were permitted to "sell" him to the state for the statutory fine. But this solution simply converts the blackmailer into a pure private enforcer; it does not solve the overenforcement problem.

Consistently with the foregoing analysis, practices indistinguishable from blackmail, although not called by that name, are permitted in areas of conduct where the law is enforced privately rather than publicly because the overenforcement problem is not serious. No (serious) objections are raised to a person's collecting information about his or her spouse's adulterous activities, and threatening to disclose that information in a divorce proceeding or other forum, in order to extract maximum compensation for the offending spouse's breach of the marital obligations. But a third party is not permitted to blackmail the offending spouse; that would undermine the assignment of the exclusive right to enforce such contracts to the victim of the breach. Consistently, too, blackmail is forbidden in areas where there are no legal prohibitions at all — where the information would humilitate, but not incriminate, the blackmailer's victim. The social decision not to regulate a particular activity is a judgment that the expenditure of resources on trying to discover and punish it would be socially wasted.

6. Blackmail and bribery are similar practices from the standpoint of the analysis of private enforcement. The blackmailer and the bribed official both receive payment in exchange for not enforcing the law. One would expect, therefore, that in areas where there is a public monopoly of enforcement, bribery, like blackmail, would be prohibited, while in areas where there is no public monopoly it would be permitted. And so one observes: The settlement out of court of a tort or contract or private antitrust case is a form of perfectly lawful bribery, although the

---

2. But it probably will be much lower. Give two economic reasons why.

term is not used in these situations (except by economists!) because of its pejorative connotation.

§22.3 Choice of Cases By the Public Agency

The process by which a law enforcement agency decides where to concentrate its resources is of great interest in view of the monopoly position in law enforcement that public agencies so frequently occupy. The process is explored here on the assumption that the agency acts as a rational maximizer, comparing the expected returns and expected costs of alternative uses of its resources. This assumption may seem inconsistent with the fact that public law enforcement bodies are a part of the political process, a domain in which value maximization is not the ruling criterion. But there is no inconsistency. Political considerations may affect the weights that the agency uses in determining the return from winning a particular type of case: It may assign a higher weight to punishing defection from a cartel than to punishing membership in one. But once these weights are assigned and goals thus determined, the agency will try (although probably not as hard as a private firm — why not?) to use its resources as effectively as possible in achieving its goals.

Agencies are criticized for devoting disproportionate resources to trivial cases. Economic analysis suggests that this criticism is superficial. The importance of the case — the stakes to the agency of a successful outcome — is only one criterion of the efficient allocation of agency resources. Let us see why.

The expected utility of a case to the agency is the gain to it if it wins discounted by the probability that it will win. To simplify the analysis, assume that the agency is interested in just two cases, A and B, and the decision it must make is how to allocate a fixed budget between them. A is the more important case. If the agency wins it, the agency's utility will increase by 100 units; a victory in B is worth only 50 units; a loss in either case is worth zero. Since the probability of a successful outcome, and hence the expected utility, is in both cases a function in part of how much the agency spends on prosecution, it might seem that the agency should devote all or most of its resources to trying to win A. But this would be correct only if the agency's outlays were the only factor affecting the probability of the outcome in either case, and they are not. The defendant's outlays are critical, as is the relative effectiveness of the agency's and the defendant's outlays in influencing the outcome.

If the case is very important to the defendant, he may spend a large amount on its defense. The more he spends, the less effective the agency's outlays on the litigation will be, unless it increases those outlays in order to neutralize the defendant's expenditures (see §21.8 *supra*). In either event the expected utility of the case to the agency, net of its costs of prosecution, will be smaller. Thus, other things being equal, the agency will prefer to invest resources in a case that is relatively unimportant to the defendant. Of course if the stakes to plaintiff and defendant were always the same, the reduction in cost to the agency from bringing a case that was unimportant to the defendant would be offset by the reduction in the agency's expected utility because of the unimportance of the outcome to it. But a case may be important to the agency but not to the defendant because, although the monetary stakes — which usually are all the defendant cares about — are small, the case, if won by the agency, will be a useful precedent, increasing the effectiveness of the agency's litigation outlays in future cases and deterring some future violations altogether. Yet the case may seem trivial to observers who ignore its precedent-setting significance.

Suppose that starting from an initial allocation of equal resources to cases A and B, the agency can increase the probability of prevailing in A from 60 to 65 percent by spending $1,000 more on A and $1,000 less on B and that this will reduce the probability of its prevailing in B from 80 to 70 percent. Suppose further that the agency can increase the probability of prevailing in B from 80 to 95 percent by spending $1,000 more on B and $1,000 less on A and that this will reduce the probability of its prevailing in A from 60 to 55 percent. The expected utility generated by the agency's initial allocation was $(100 \times .60) + (50 \times .80)$, or 100. The agency's expected utility after reallocating $1,000 from B to A would be $(100 \times .65) + (50 \times .70)$, or 100. But its expected utility after reallocating $1,000 from A to B — from the big case to the small one — would be $(100 \times .55) + (50 \times .95)$, or 102.5, which is greater than under the alternative allocations.

So far we have assumed that the number of cases brought by the agency is a given, but of course it is not. As an agency brings more and more cases of a particular type, its total expected utility will rise but at a diminishing rate. It becomes more difficult to find cases that are easy to win. The probability of success therefore declines. The higher the rate at which the probability of success declines with the number of cases brought, the fewer cases will be brought. Probably the rate of decline will be higher in classes of relatively important cases than in classes of relatively unimportant cases. The universe of minor violations is ordinarily larger than the universe of major ones; one does not "run out" so soon of cases that are easy to win. This is another reason for expecting small cases to dominate the agency's workload.

Theory suggests, and there is some empirical evidence, that in areas of private law, plaintiffs win about 50 percent of the cases that are tried.[1] This is because parties are likelier to agree on the probable outcome of a one-sided case than a more evenly balanced case. But most public agencies have much higher than 50 percent win rates. The reason is that agencies unlike private enforcers operate under a budget constraint. An agency with a tight budget constraint may not bring *any* hard cases. (This is true of most criminal enforcement today.) Therefore, although most of its cases will be settled, its trials will still be selected from a population of one-sided cases.

The fact that agencies behave like rational maximizers (given whatever distributive weights the legislature assigns to the agency's enforcement outcomes) suggests an economic reason for the public provision of counsel to indigent criminal defendants. A prosecuting agency's success may well depend on its winning as many cases (weighted by their importance) as possible, as cheaply as possible. Since it may be cheaper to convict a defendant who is not represented by counsel than one who is, even if the former is innocent and the latter guilty, prosecutors might have an incentive to prosecute innocent people who were indigents. The result would be to impose socially unproductive punishment costs, reduce the deterrent effect of criminal punishment, and deflect prosecutorial resources from areas where they could be employed more productively from the standpoint of society. The right to counsel can thus be defended as a method of imparting correct incentives to prosecutors.[2]

Suggested Readings

1. Gary S. Becker & George J. Stigler, Law Enforcement, Malfeasance, and Compensation of Enforcers, 3 J. Leg. Stud. (1974).
2. William M. Landes & Richard A. Posner, The Private Enforcement of Law, 4 J. Leg. Stud. 1 (1975).
3. Richard A. Posner, The Behavior of Administrative Agencies, 1 J. Leg. Stud. 305-323 (1972).

Problems

1. How should Congress and the Internal Revenue Service determine the proper level of investment in the enforcement of the federal tax laws? Suppose it is estimated that, last year, taxpayers evaded the payment of $10 billion in taxes. Should the government spend up to $10 billion to collect these taxes? Suppose the IRS has no idea how much

§22.3   1. See George L. Priest & Benjamin Klein, The Selection of Disputes for Litigation, 13 J. Leg. Stud. 1 (1984).
2. Another possible economic justification of the right is considered in §25.2 *infra*.

evasion there is in the aggregate but knows that for every additional dollar it spends on enforcement it collects $300 in additional revenue. Is this sufficient reason for spending more money on enforcement? What if the IRS increases its expenditures until an additional dollar brings in only 75¢ in additional revenue? Is this conclusive evidence that the service is now spending too much?

2. The Internal Revenue Service offers informers a reward of up to 10 percent of the unpaid taxes collected. Is this too much or too little? Would 100 percent be an appropriate reward? Could a figure higher than 100 percent be defended?

CHAPTER 23

THE ADMINISTRATIVE PROCESS[1]

§23.1 The Delegation Rationale

The independent regulatory agency (ICC, FCC, FTC, NLRB, etc.) is an interesting combination of legislative, litigative, and enforcement functions. The original rationale for the creation of such agencies was to relieve Congress of some of the burdens of legislating. Congress could not deal efficiently with the numerous, highly technical, rapidly changing problems of a complex modern industry such as railroading; through delegation to agencies, such problems could be taken out of politics. This is unconvincing. The regulatory function could just as well have been delegated to the courts, whose traditional role is precisely to formulate and apply rules regulating activities that often are complex, using the criterion of efficiency. One can argue that the case method constrains the rulemaking effectiveness of courts, but since the agencies have with rare exceptions relied exclusively on the case method as their legislative technique the argument provides little basis for preferring agencies to courts. Certainly the agencies have proved more susceptible to political influence than courts. Their more specialized jurisdiction subjects them to closer scrutiny by congressional appropriation subcommittees, through which the political influences that play on Congress are transmitted to the agency, and to closer attention by the industries that the agency regulates. The political independence of the administrative agencies is also less than that of judges because their members serve for limited terms and turnover is in fact rapid.

Maybe the real purpose of delegation is not to improve the technical functioning of the legislative process but precisely to assure a more sympathetic enforcement of policies not motivated by efficiency goals than could be expected from the courts. Borrowing from the analysis

1. See Robert L. Rabin, Perspectives on the Administrative Process (1979).

of the independent judiciary in Chapter 20, we can describe the administrative agencies as a form of "dependent" judiciary designed to promote the operation of interest group politics rather than allocative efficiency. This approach suggests three propositions about administrative regulation that have some empirical support.

1. Administrative agencies will be established most frequently when the probability of *de facto* judicial nullification of legislation is high (for example, during the New Deal, when the courts were hostile to federal economic regulation). The power of courts to nullify legislation, especially by adverse factfinding in enforcement proceedings, can be curtailed by consigning the factfinding function to an administrative agency, which will tend to be more subservient to the legislature.

2. The legislature will, however, preserve some judicial review of administrative determinations in order to assure that the agency, in its eagerness to serve the current legislature, will not stray too far from the terms of the legislative "deal" made in establishing the regulatory program that the agency administers.

3. But since judicial review cannot be expected to be wholly effective, we expect — and find — that administrative adjudication is far less consistent over time than judicial. (A related point is that precedent plays a smaller role in administrative than in judicial decision making.) This follows directly from the relatively dependent character of administrative judging.

§23.2   Combination of Functions

A heralded innovation in the administrative process was the administrative agency's looseness of structure. The agency would be able to issue rules, bring cases, decide cases, conduct studies, propose legislation, and so on. The combination of functions was thought a source of strength — a tribute to vertical integration bestowed by people who often condemned it in other contexts. In practice, the most significant combination has probably been that of prosecution and adjudication.

If we think of the production of administrative decisions as a sequence of activities — investigation, pleading, trial, judgment, and appeal — we shall see that the combination of the issuance of the complaint and the decision of the appeal in the same body indeed corresponds to vertical integration in business. The economic justification for vertical integration in the business context is that it permits cost savings through the substitution of command for contract as a method of coordinating production (see §10.8 *supra*). A parallel argument is possible in the administrative context.

The essence of the coordination problem in making steel is to assure that the iron maker produces and delivers to the steel maker the right amount of iron, of the right quality, and at the right time, *right* meaning in accordance with the steel maker's specifications. If the companies are separately owned, these specifications will either be written into a contract between the companies or left to ad hoc negotiation. If the companies are jointly owned, coordination will be achieved in a different manner — the managers of the enterprise will tell the iron maker how much to produce, of what quality, etc.

The administrative agency problem is similar. Issuing a complaint that has little or no chance of being upheld after trial and appeal is normally a waste of everyone's time and money; it corresponds to the production of unwanted iron. If prosecution is not controlled by the agency, the agency will communicate to the prosecutor its "demand" for complaints indirectly, through rules or opinions setting forth the doctrines that the agency accepts and the evidentiary requirements that it imposes. Such communication serves the same function as the specifications in a buyer's contract with a seller. The alternative method of coordination is for the tribunal to control the issuance of complaints. Then it can veto complaints that it has reason to doubt it would sustain, and it can command the preparation of complaints that it deems meritorious and important.

It is not clear *a priori* which method of coordination is more efficient in the administrative context, any more than the optimum amount of vertical integration is clear *a priori* in most industrial contexts. One can argue that communication through rules and decisions is apt to be more efficient than internal direction because it forces the agency to articulate policies and priorities — to plan in advance rather than react to proposals for complaint submitted by the agency's staff. On the other side it can be argued that to formalize the agency's relationship to the complaint issuance process in this fashion deprives the agency of valuable flexibility and control.

Coordination is only one element to consider in a benefit-cost analysis of combination versus separation of functions. Another is bias, which in this context means that the agency weights the costs of an erroneous decision to dismiss a complaint more heavily than the costs of an erroneous decision to enter a remedial order against the defendant. The limiting case is where the agency gives a weight of zero to the costs incurred by the innocent punished. Then it would (if free to do so) adopt procedures that assured the conviction of all defendants. These procedures would minimize the social costs imposed when violators escape punishment and would do so at minimum administrative cost, since the evidentiary burdens on the prosecution would be slight and the procedural rights of the defendant nil.[1]

§23.2   1. Does this conclusion depend on whether the agency seeks to maximize (a) number of convictions weighted by severity or (b) deterrence?

Should one expect less bias in an agency in which the functions of prosecution and adjudication are separated (such as the National Labor Relations Board, whose General Counsel has complete control of prosecution and is not appointed by and cannot be removed by the board)? Probably not. An administrative agency such as the Labor Board or the Federal Trade Commission differs crucially from a court in being charged with the accomplishment of some substantive regulatory end (preventing unfair labor practices or deception of consumers or growth of monopoly) rather than just with the resolution of disputes. The Trade Commission's goals would not be changed if the issuance of complaints in matters tried before it were delegated to an independent body, just as the goal of the Labor Board (primarily, the elimination of unfair labor practices) was not changed by the vesting of the prosecutorial function in an independent general counsel. And in relation to the agency's goals, the entry of a punitive or remedial order has inherently a different weight from the dismissal of the complaint. The entry of the order furthers the agency's goal; the dismissal does not, in any sense likely to be perceived by those who judge the agency's work. Imagine that one year the Trade Commission (or the Labor Board) dismissed all of the complaints brought before it, perhaps because the economic conditions that had given rise to the statutes enforced by the agency had wholly changed. The agency would be inviting its liquidation by Congress. Such prospects must deter. Courts, with their diversified portfolio of cases, do not have similar inhibitions against dismissing many or most complaints brought under a particular statute.

The desire to control agency bias lies behind the provisions of the Administrative Procedure Act relating to administrative adjudication and to judicial review of agency action. Judicial review owes much of its effectiveness to the requirement that in adjudicative cases a trial record must be compiled before an independent hearing examiner (administrative law judge), who normally issues a written decision. This system of protections does not guarantee that biased adjudication will be detected and corrected by a reviewing court but it does reduce the gains to the agency from bias. The agency cannot always escape detection, and if it develops a bad reputation with reviewing courts the results can be very serious, since the agency's activities can be hamstrung by hostile courts.

When the agency is responsible for actually issuing the complaint, as well as adjudicating, another weight is added to the scales and further biases adjudication. The agency that dismisses many of its own complaints is subject to the criticism that by bringing unmeritorious cases it displayed bad judgment and squandered scarce resources. But whether the increment in bias is substantial given the safeguards of the Administrative Procedure Act may be doubted.[2] So if coordination costs are

2. For empirical evidence that it is not substantial, see Richard A. Posner, The Behavior of Administrative Agencies, 1 J. Leg. Stud. 305, 323-344 (1972).

significantly reduced by combining prosecution and adjudication there is a case for combination — but no one knows whether they are or not.

The danger of agency bias may, incidentally, be responsible for the refusal of legislatures to give agencies strong remedial powers. The normal administrative remedy is the cease and desist order, in essence an injunction, and the absence of other remedies is, as we have seen (see §13.2 *supra*), a source of weakness. If agencies could impose sanctions that inflicted heavy costs on defendants, the social costs of biased agency adjudication would of course be much greater than they are.

§23.3   The Behavior of Administrative Agencies

Our analysis suggests that the administrative process may well be efficient in achieving its goals, whether or not these goals have anything to do with efficiency or any other broadly based conception of the public interest. There is not much evidence for the competing view that the failure of the agencies to effectuate public interest goals is due to accidents of their behavior that could and someday will be remedied by the appointment of better people to the agencies.

The last chapter discussed one bit of alleged such evidence already — the fact that the agencies bring a lot of seemingly trivial cases. Others are that agency personnel are frequently paid lower salaries than their counterparts in the private sector and — a related point — that they frequently leave the agency for better paying jobs with the industry regulated by the agency. The inferences frequently drawn from these data are that agency personnel are inferior, that they are subtly corrupted in the performance of their duties for the agency by the prospect of employment by the regulated industry, and that the turnover of agency personnel is excessive. In fact the evidence is equally consistent with the inferences that

(1) agency personnel are hired by industry because the specialized training and experience acquired while working for the agency increase their productivity in the regulated industry compared to alternative employments,[1] and

(2) agencies are able to attract competent people at salaries lower than private employers would have to pay precisely because the training and experience imparted by the agency increase the lifetime earning power of the employee — an investment of human capital that he pays for in the form of temporarily lower wages.

Under this view, the hiring of the agency's employees by the regulated industry carries no implication of a reward for past favors, and the rela-

§23.3   1. See Ross D. Eckert, The Life Cycle of Regulatory Commissioners, 24 J. Law & Econ. 113 (1981).

tively low wages paid by the agency carry no implication that its employees are substandard.[2]

Among the mechanisms by which an agency and its staff are prevented
from using resources wastefully, there is first the ambition of the agency
members. Their aspirations for higher office or well-paying private employment are enhanced if they earn a reputation for efficiency. A second
factor is the legislative appropriations process. The competition of agencies for appropriations corresponds, though only approximately, to the
competition of business firms for capital. The inefficient firm fares poorly
in the capital markets; the inefficient agency (with much less certainty,
however) loses appropriations to its more efficient rival.

Since the output of an agency is not sold in a market and is therefore
difficult to evaluate, and since the incentives of congressmen are complex, the discipline of the appropriations process is surely much weaker
than that of the capital markets.[3] And the absence of product-market
competition removes another important pressure to minimize costs.
Also, political considerations affect hiring and therefore competence.
It is almost impossible to fire government employees below the highest
levels.[4] For all these reasons the average agency is less well managed
than the average business firm, but the difference may be less dramatic
than many think.

§23.4   Judicial Review of Agency Action

The analysis presented in this chapter has a number of implications
for judicial review of administrative agencies' decisions. Some have been
mentioned already; here are some others. The *Chenery* doctrine,[1] which
forbids a reviewing court to uphold administrative action on a rationale
different from that of the agency (typically a rationale advanced by the
agency's lawyers in defending its decision in the reviewing court), can
be understood as a recognition of the political character of administrative
adjudication. If the agency could be thought engaged simply in a search
for truth, then it would be appropriate for the reviewing court to uphold
the agency's decision on any ground that made sense to the court; presumably the agency would embrace that ground. But if the real springs

2. Is the agency necessarily harmed by the fact that former employees often represent
litigants before the agency? Why not?

3. Even though the agency, unlike the business firm, has to return to its capital market
every year. An agency has no retained earnings.

4. Are the effects all bad? Why not?

§23.4   1. See SEC v. Chenery Corp., 318 U.S. 80, 94 (1943).

of agency decision-making are political, then it will be difficult for the court to predict whether the agency would adopt the suggested ground. Of course the *Chenery* doctrine would also make sense if agencies dealt with such difficult subject matter that courts could not tell whether a proposed rationale was right. Sometimes they do, but the doctrine is applied regardless of how technical or complex the issue is.

The analysis in this chapter, however, undermines the principle that reviewing courts should give great deference to the agency's interpretation of the statutes it administers. The statute sets the terms of the political compromise; to allow the agency to change the meaning of the statute through interpretation is to allow it to undo what may have been a carefully crafted deal.

A recurrent question is whether judicial review of agency action should be in a district (trial) court initially, with a right of review in the court of appeals, or whether the aggrieved party should go directly to the court of appeals. In economic terms the question is whether the cost of an extra layer of judicial review (the district court) is less than the benefit in reduced legal error costs. This turns out to involve complex tradeoffs. If the rate of appeal from the district court is more than zero but less than 100 percent, as of course it will be, having two tiers of review will increase the total number of court cases but reduce the number of court of appeals cases. Suppose there are 100 administrative decisions, review is sought in 50, and if the district courts have an initial review jurisdiction 20 percent of their review decisions will be appealed to the courts of appeals. Then in a two-tier system there will be a total of 60 cases, 50 in the district courts and 10 in the courts of appeals, and in the one-tier system only 50 cases — but all in the courts of appeals. If court of appeals review is more costly to the judicial system, for reasons suggested earlier, then the two-tier system may be more efficient even if the additional tier has little effect in reducing the number and hence costs of legal errors. Moreover, the two-tier system may reduce the total number of judicial review proceedings (why?).

Notice that the higher the appeal rate is, the less efficient will the two-tier system be, especially since a high appeal rate may connote a high error rate at the district court level. The lower the appeal rate is, and also the less complete the agency record (which may require factfinding by the courts, a function in which district courts have a comparative advantage over appellate courts), the more efficient will the two-tier system be.

Suggested Readings

1. Richard A. Posner, The Behavior of Administrative Agencies, 1 J. Leg. Studies 305, 323-344 (1972).

2. _____, Theories of Economic Regulation, 5 Bell J. Econ. & Mgmt. Sci. 335 (1974).

3. George J. Stigler, The Theory of Economic Regulation, 2 Bell J. Econ. & Mgmt. Sci. 3 (1971).

Problem

The question of delay in administrative proceedings presents an interesting example of the conflict between the view that administrative agencies are created to serve the public interest but frequently fail to do so because of bad policies or personnel and the view that the agencies are in fact designed to promote the interests of effective political groups — which they do more or less efficiently. Is delay always inefficient? Can you think of cases where delay helps or hurts particular interest groups affected by administrative action? Cf. §12.3 *supra*.

PART VII

THE CONSTITUTION AND THE FEDERAL SYSTEM

CHAPTER 24

THE NATURE AND FUNCTIONS OF THE CONSTITUTION[1]

§24.1 The Economics of Constitutionalism: An Introduction

The U.S. Constitution differs from an ordinary statute in (1) its costs of enactment (including amendment) and, less distinctly, (2) its subject matter. The principle that constitutional provisions are to be interpreted more flexibly than statutes reflects the greater costs of changing the Constitution than of changing a statute. Flexible interpretation imparts generality to the constitutional language and hence, by the analysis in Chapter 20, durability.

The distinctive subject matter of the Constitution is found in its provisions allocating the powers of government between the states on the one hand and the federal government on the other and, within the latter, among the executive, legislative, and judicial branches of government. As we shall see in the next section, the nature of these provisions requires that it be very costly to change them. The same is not true, however, of all of the constitutional provisions that create personal rights (for example, freedom of religion). Some of these differ from statutory rights not in their fundamental character but only in the fact that, being constitutional, they are more costly to abrogate. Others buttress the allocation of powers in the first set of provisions discussed, and it makes sense to establish similar barriers to retracting them.

Certain rather enigmatic constitutional provisions — mainly those guaranteeing equal protection of the laws and due process of law — have been interpreted to give the courts authority to invalidate legislation as unreasonable whether or not it violates the allocation of governmental

1. See Gerald Gunther, Constitutional Law: Cases and Materials (10th ed. 1980).

powers in the Constitution or invades specific personal rights. The analysis of interest group politics in Chapter 19 suggests that this assertion of judicial power may rest on a misconception of the nature of the political system.

Lawyers naturally are most interested in those parts of the Constitution that create justiciable rights, but some of the nonjusticiable parts are equally interesting from an economic standpoint. For example, it is noteworthy that the Constitution establishes a representative government, which is a compromise with pure democracy. Policies are not voted on directly by the people; elected representatives make policy. Costs of information would make it impossible for the people to make intelligent policy choices; the representative principle enables specialization in policy formation.

It is not inherent in the nature of government, though, that the representatives should be popularly elected. In the original Constitution only the members of the House of Representatives were elected by the people directly; and the electorate was limited to white male owners of property. The malapportionment of the state legislatures created substantial disparities in actual voting power among individuals, until it was declared unconstitutional in the early 1960s. The argument for universal suffrage is threefold:

(1) the disfranchisement of any group will invite efforts (which are socially costly, yet yield no social gain) to redistribute wealth from them to other, electorally powerful groups;

(2) elections yield information, valuable to policy makers, about preferences and aversions (in an age of scientific polling this argument is less important than it used to be); and

(3) the larger the electorate, the more difficult it is to form coalitions for redistributive ends (this is related to the first argument).

Only the second argument explains why those having the vote would ever dilute their own power by enlarging the franchise, unless the excluded group was likely to use force if not peacefully awarded a share of political power. But maybe the franchise is expanded whenever the dominant group in the community believes that the currently disfranchised prefers its candidates to those of rival groups.

§24.2 The Separation of Powers

The Constitution seeks to prevent the centralization of governmental power, both by dividing political power between the states on the one hand and the federal government on the other hand and by splitting the federal government's powers among three independent branches —

executive, legislative, and judicial — and, in the case of the legislative power, also within the branch (the legislative power is divided among the House of Representatives, the Senate, and the President with his veto power). The purpose of the separation of powers, stated in economic terms, is to prevent the monopolization of the coercive power of the state, a form of monopoly potentially far more costly than any discussed heretofore in this book.

The point made in Chapter 10 that the costs of collusion to the colluders rise with the number of people whose agreement is necessary to make the collusion effective applies to political as well as to commercial conspiracies. The application of governmental force under the system envisaged in the Constitution requires the concurrence of the legislative branch, to enact the coercive measure; the executive branch, to bring an enforcement action (does this suggest another reason for a public monopoly of law enforcement in some areas?); and the judicial branch, to apply a sanction for noncompliance. Three is not a large number of conspirators, but only one of the three — the executive — is unitary even in principle.

An important aspect of the separation of powers (at least historically) is the requirement that randomly selected private citizens (i.e., jurors) concur in the imposition of a criminal sanction or the award of civil damages, unless the defendant waives his right to trial by jury. Finally, the sharing of the national governmental power with numerous quasi-sovereigns (the states) enormously complicates efforts to achieve a monopoly of political power.

The separation of powers might have been ineffective (though English experience suggests otherwise) if the Constitution had also authorized one of the branches of government — the Congress — to combine them if it wished. The procedure for combining them must be made more costly than the procedure for enacting a statute. This is the economic rationale for judicial review of the constitutionality of federal statutes, conducted by judges insulated by life tenure from legislative or executive retribution.

The fact that the framers of the Constitution deliberately separated the major branches of government raises a question about the legitimacy of the administrative process discussed in the last chapter. The process is defended as enhancing efficiency, but the (alleged) enhancement is achieved by combining executive, legislative, and judicial powers in one body. This seems the type of efficiency that the constitutional framers thought on balance inefficient because of the danger it created of excessive centralization of political power. True, the right of the parties to an agency proceeding to get judicial review of the agency's decision limits administrative power. (By the same token, the measures that have been adopted, notably in the Administrative Procedure Act, to make the right of judicial review of agency action a meaningful one reduce the efficiency of the administrative process.) But judicial review provides no check on the exercise of legislative power by an administrative agency through rulemaking under a broad delegation of power from Congress — a practice designed to circumvent a deliberately cumbersome system of legislative enactment.

Even more ominous, however, than the "independent" administrative agencies, whose members are appointed for fixed terms of office and hence enjoy some independence from executive control, are the many administrative agencies within the executive branch, such as the Environmental Protection Agency and the National Highway and Traffic Safety Administration. The independent agencies are a fourth branch of government, and to the extent they are independent of the other branches, they actually enhance the separation of powers. But the executive agencies obliterate the separation of powers, by empowering the executive to exercise judicial and legislative as well as executive powers.

The framers didn't worry much about placing checks on the judicial branch itself. They assumed it was naturally weak and dependent on the other branches. Even though Congress is forbidden to lower the salaries of federal judges during their incumbency, the judiciary cannot operate without congressional appropriations and cannot enforce its judgments without the cooperation of the executive branch. Moreover, since the federal courts, whatever political role they were intended to play in maintaining the separation of powers, are courts, they cannot make policy except in the context of deciding justiciable cases. This makes it difficult for the judges to establish a coherent agenda for policy making. Also, as noted in Part VI, judges have some incentive to adhere to precedent; this limits the pace at which they can fashion new policies.

Despite these constraints on the federal judicial power, the elastic language and obscure history of many constitutional provisions give the judges great scope to translate their policy preferences into constitutional law. The principle of judicial self-restraint teaches that judges should hesitate to use their power to limit the other branches of government — and can be defended by reference to the economic concept of risk aversion. Because the judiciary represents a potentially enormous concentration of political power — a majority of the nine Supreme Court justices can alter major public policies at a stroke — a restrained exercise of this power would stabilize public policy.

It should be emphasized that separation of powers is not just a centrifugal force. Before the Constitution was adopted, Congress was all-powerful at the federal level; there were no independent executive and judicial branches. The high transaction costs of legislative bodies makes them inefficient decision makers. The creation of hierarchical executive and judicial branches to perform important governmental functions may make government on balance more rather than less efficient.

§24.3   The Protection of Rights

Many of the rights protected by the Constitution are related to the antimonopoly purpose of the separation of powers, discussed above; they limit the power of government to intimidate opponents. Even the just-compensation clause of the Fifth Amendment can be interpreted in this light (how?). But this is not true of all constitutional rights. Although the protection of political speech in the First Amendment is plainly related to the maintenance of decentralized government (why?), the same cannot be said for freedom of religion (in matters purely spiritual) or freedom to publish sexually candid books that have no political content. These freedoms are ends — aspects of people's utility — rather than means toward preventing the monopolization of political power.

The nonpolitical rights in the Constitution (some of them are in it, though, only by judicial interpretation) are more plausibly regarded as a particularly durable form of legislative protection obtained by particularly effective interest groups (a term used here with no pejorative connotation). This view has implications for a number of constitutional questions; two are discussed here, and one is the subject of the next section.

1. It is sometimes suggested that the protection of freedom of speech and of the press by the First Amendment should be limited to political expression, on the theory that the only function of the First Amendment that is related to the central purpose of the Constitution is to protect the electoral process by which members of Congress and the President are selected. The much broader view of the scope of the First Amendment that the Supreme Court has adopted in recent years (discussed in Chapter 28), however, is consistent with viewing the First Amendment as also being a form of protective legislation on behalf of an interest group consisting of intellectuals, publishers, journalists, pamphleteers, and others who derive pecuniary and nonpecuniary income from publication and advocacy.

2. It is sometimes asked whether it isn't a perversion of constitutional principle to invoke a constitutional provision on behalf of a majority rather than a minority group, as in cases challenging reverse discrimination (for example, preferring blacks to whites; see §27.6 *infra*) or discrimination against women, or cases challenging schemes of legislative malapportionment adopted by popular referendum. But since a large group will often be politically less effective than a small one because of the higher costs of collective action to the large group (see §19.3 *supra*), the large group may be more rather than less needful of constitutional protection against the legislature.

A third economic perspective on constitutional rights sees them as designed to prevent certain particularly harsh and costly forms of wealth redistribution. To take away a person's property without compensation, or make him a slave, or prevent him from practicing his religion are some illustrations of redistributions that are likely to be extremely costly. By putting them beyond the power of the legislature to accomplish, the Constitution reduces the risks that political power over the distribution of wealth (broadly defined) creates. As a risk-reducing device this resembles the principle of judicial self-restraint; are these consistent devices?

§24.4 Rationality Review

There is a long-standing debate over whether the Supreme Court should use the due process and equal protection clauses of the Fourteenth Amendment to strike down state legislation that, even though it does not infringe a specific constitutional right such as freedom of speech, is unreasonable as judged by some general criterion of social welfare or public interest. Economic analysis suggests that the assertion of such a power by the Supreme Court would change fundamentally the nature of the democratic political process — an objective that cannot reasonably be attributed to the framers of the Constitution or consistently attained by the Court. We saw in Chapter 19 that there is no presumption that legislation is enacted in order to promote the public interest. A characteristic product of a democratic — perhaps of any — legislative process is the unprincipled redistribution of wealth in favor of politically effective interest groups. The public interest need not enter the process except as window dressing to increase the information costs of opposition or repeal. Justice Hugo Black, a former senator, who seems to have had a more clear-sighted conception than any other justice of the interest group character of the legislative process,[1] also — and as a necessary corollary — rejected the notion that legislation that did not invade any of the interests specifically singled out for protection in the Constitution must still be found reasonable in order to be upheld.[2]

It has been suggested that the Supreme Court should invalidate under the equal protection clause any statute in which the method chosen of achieving the declared purpose of the statute is not reasonably related

§24.4 1. See his opinion for the court in Eastern Railroad Presidents Conference v. Noerr Motor Freight, Inc., 365 U.S. 127 (1961).

2. See Ferguson v. Skrupa, 372 U.S. 726, 729 (1963). Would there be a need for any constitutional rights against state legislation besides the right of rationality review?

to that purpose.[3] A statute requiring barbers to have medical training, ostensibly to improve the public health, would thus be invalid. But if the state revised the statute to declare that its purpose was to increase the income of barbers, the revised statute would be upheld. This proposal would reduce the information costs of opposition to special interest legislation, but its effectiveness in thereby reducing the amount of such legislation would depend on the importance of those costs in the passage of such legislation and (a related point) on the ability of legislators to devise plausible preambles. Even if the proposal were effective, it would still be open to the objection that it assumes, without basis in the language or history of the relevant constitutional provisions, that the Constitution is designed to correct free-rider problems in the legislative process even when they do not lead to an invasion of any protected rights or undermine the separation of powers. The proposal hearkens back to an era in which the Court did review legislation for its substantive rationality. That era is discussed in the first section of the next chapter.

Is it possible that the proposal is superfluous? See §19.5 *supra*.

Suggested Reading

Richard A. Posner, The Federal Courts: Crisis and Reform, chs. 7, 9 (1985).

---

3. Gerald Gunther, The Supreme Court 1971 Term — Foreword: In Search of Evolving Doctrine on a Changing Court: A Model for a Newer Equal Protection, 86 Harv. L. Rev. 1, 20-21, 23 (1972).

CHAPTER 25

ECONOMIC DUE PROCESS

§25.1 Liberty of Contract as a Constitutional Principle

For a period of 50 years ending in the late 1930s, liberty of contract was a key component of due process under the Fifth and Fourteenth Amendments to the Constitution as interpreted by the Supreme Court, and it was the ground on which the Court invalidated, although fitfully,[1] a number of state and federal statutes regulating economic activity.[2] Classical economic theory was thereby elevated to the status of constitutional principle, for the idea that voluntary transactions almost always promote welfare, and regulations that inhibit such transactions almost always reduce it, is a staple of classical theory. The Court upheld the constitutionality of the antitrust laws and laws subjecting monopolists to maximum rate controls, but these laws are commonly thought to be necessary to preserve, or simulate the results of, free markets.

Although long viewed simply as grotesque distortions of constitutional principle, the liberty of contract decisions recently have attracted some staunch advocates as part of a growing revival of interest in classical economic principles.[3] And although there are grave difficulties in reconciling their position with the philosophy of judicial self-restraint or the interest group theory (and reality) of government, the same can be said about the modern emphasis in constitutional law on personal liberties.

§25.1 1. See David P. Currie, The Constitution in the Supreme Court: The Protection of Economic Interests, 1889-1910, 52 U. Chi. L. Rev. 324 (1985).

2. See Robert G. McCloskey, Economic Due Process and the Supreme Court: An Exhumation and Reburial, 1962 S. Ct. Rev. 34.

3. See, e.g., Michael Conant, Antimonopoly Tradition Under the Ninth and Fourteenth Amendments: *Slaughter-House Cases* Re-Examined, 31 Emory L.J. 785 (1982); Richard A. Epstein, Taxation, Regulation, and Confiscation, 20 Osgoode Hall L.J. 433 (1982); Richard A. Epstein, Not Deference, But Doctrine: The Eminent Domain Clause, 1982 S. Ct. Rev. 351; Richard A. Epstein, Toward a Revitalization of the Contract Clause, 51 U. Chi. L. Rev. 703 (1984); Bernard H. Siegan, Economic Liberties and the Constitution (1980).

589

The arguments for giving greater protection to personal than to economic liberties are superficial. Thus, while it is said that there was no source for a doctrine of liberty of contract in the text or history of the relevant constitutional provisions, the same criticism can be (and has been) made of the Court's decisions in a wide variety of other constitutional areas. It is also said that economic questions are more difficult for courts to decide than questions involving the rights of criminal defendants, political dissidents, or members of racial minorities — yet in fact less is known about those questions than about conventional economic problems. It is said that economic rights are less important than other rights; even if this is so (a question to which we return in §28.4 *infra*), it does not follow that the Court should give them no protection at all. It is said that the Court's mistake in the liberty of contract cases was to be out of step with dominant public opinion. But this was true only toward the end of the era, and is the reason why the era ended when it did. Moreover, the criticism can easily be turned into a compliment to the Court for its steadfastness in the face of contrary popular opinion. It is also said that the victims of economic controls are businessmen well able to protect themselves without the Court's help, unlike the powerless minorities typically involved in a noneconomic constitutional case. Yet as we are about to see, the brunt of the economic legislation challenged during the liberty of contract era was often borne by politically unorganized groups such as consumers. Nor is it correct that racial and religious minorities are unable to compete effectively in the political arena.

Almost as a detail — but an important one in view of the subject matter of this book — it is commonly believed that the liberty of contract decisions reflected a weak grasp of economics. An early criticism based on this view is found in Justice Brandeis's dissenting opinion in *New State Ice Co. v. Liebmann*.[4] The case involved the constitutionality of a state statute that required anyone who wanted to manufacture and sell ice to obtain a certificate of public convenience and necessity and that provided that a certificate would be denied if existing service was adequate. New State, which had such a certificate, sought to enjoin Liebmann, who did not, from entering the ice business in New State's territory. Liebmann's defense was that the statute was unconstitutional. The Court invalidated the statute for reasons with which most economists would concur:

> Stated succinctly, a private corporation here seeks to prevent a competitor from entering the business of making and selling ice. . . . There is no question now before us of any regulation by the state to protect the consuming public either with respect to conditions of manufacture and distribution or

4. 285 U.S. 262 (1932).

to insure purity of products or to prevent extortion. The control here asserted does not protect against monopoly, but tends to foster it. The aim is not to encourage competition, but to prevent it; not to regulate the business, but to preclude persons from engaging in it. . . . It is not the case of a natural monopoly, or of an enterprise in its nature dependent upon the grant of public privileges. The particular requirement before us was evidently not imposed to prevent a practical monopoly of the business, since its tendency is quite to the contrary.

The Court likened the certification provision to an attempt of one shoe-maker, under state authority, "to prevent another shoemaker from making or selling shoes because shoemakers already in that occupation can make and sell all the shoes that are needed."

Justice Brandeis's economic argument begins with the proposition that the ice business may be "one which lends itself peculiarly to monopoly"; "the business is conducted in local plants with a market narrowly limited in area" because of the weight and perishability of the product. But the fact that a firm has only a local market area does not preclude competition. Brandeis's opinion reveals, moreover, that prior to the passage of the challenged statute there was competition in the ice business in many localities in the state. He argues that "even in those localities the prices of ice were ordinarily uniform," but since, as he stresses elsewhere in his opinion, the product is uniform, one would expect competitive sellers to charge the same price.

The test of natural monopoly is the size of the market in relation to the conditions of supply (see §12.1 *supra*). But on the critical issue of the supply conditions in the ice business, Justice Brandeis's opinion is obscure and contradictory. Brandeis remarks on "the relative ease and cheapness with which an ice plant may be constructed" and on the fact that increased production of ice has not "had the effect of greatly increasing the size of plants in the ice business." These remarks suggest that competitive provision of ice is no more costly than monopolistic. But he also states that "ice plants have a determinate capacity, and inflexible fixed charges and operating costs," which implies production under conditions of declining average cost.

No doubt the real purpose of the statute was to foster cartelization of the Oklahoma ice industry. As Brandeis himself curiously emphasizes,

Trade journals and reports of association meetings of ice manufacturers bear ample witness to the hostility of the industry to such competition, and to its unremitting efforts, through trade associations, informal agreements, combination of delivery systems, and in particular through the consolidation of plants, to protect markets and prices against competition of any character.

He also notes: "the ice industry as a whole in Oklahoma has acquiesced in and accepted the Act and the status which it creates."

In viewing the case as one in which Liebmann's economic rights were pitted against the interests of the poor people of Oklahoma who could not afford refrigerators, Justice Brandeis got it backwards. The right he would have vindicated was the interest of New State Ice and other established ice companies to be free from competition. The people actually wronged by the statute were the poor, who were compelled to pay more for ice; the well-to-do, as Brandeis pointed out, were more likely to have refrigerators.

If the ice business were a natural monopoly, the Brandeis position might be economically defensible, since (as we saw in an earlier chapter) the effort of a natural monopolist to maximize his profits by establishing a monopoly price could lead to a wasteful duplication of facilities. Not only is the premise false, however, but it appears from the latter part of Brandeis's opinion that the natural monopoly language of the earlier part is a makeweight and that he was prepared to embrace the sweeping proposition that ruinous competition is a common phenomenon of economic markets and was a major factor behind the great depression of the 1930s. The case was decided in 1931, and although the Oklahoma statute predated the depression, Brandeis discusses extensively, and with apparent approval, the proposition that the philosophy embodied in the Oklahoma limitation on entry into the ice business might be a remedy of general application to the current economic crisis.

The view of the great depression as rooted in the excesses of competition and curable by reducing competition is discredited (cf. §15.9 *supra*). Of course, when demand declined during the depression much of the existing industrial capacity, geared as it was to supplying a larger demand, became temporarily excess. But limiting competition would not have increased purchasing power and therefore demand; it would just have impaired the efficiency of economic activity at its reduced level. Nonetheless the cartel remedy for depressions was tried in the early New Deal statutes, such as the National Industrial Recovery Act, which authorized industries to fix minimum prices. Soon the pendulum of opinion swung the other way and it was argued that monopoly rather than competition had been responsible for the depression, or at least for its severity, but the argument is no more convincing than its predecessor. A monopolist will reduce his price more slowly than a competitive firm when the volume of demand declines.[5] But then prices must fall faster in other markets, for the relatively high price that the consumer continues to pay for the monopolized product reduces the amount of money that he can spend on competitively produced products, thereby accelerating the decline in the demand for and (assuming rising marginal

_____

5. See §10.1 *supra*; Richard D. Reimer, A Comment on Oligopoly Pricing Practices and Economic Theory, 38 J. Bus. 210 (1965).

costs[6]) price of such products. The effect of monopoly on aggregate consumer purchasing power is unlikely to be significant.

Some of the statutes upheld by the Supreme Court in the period when it was guided by liberty of contract notions also were attempts to suppress competition under the guise of promoting the general welfare. In *Muller v. Oregon*,[7] for example, the Court upheld a state statute fixing a maximum work day of 10 hours for women employed in laundries. Unless the state also had a minimum wage law and the wages of women employed in laundries were not significantly higher than the minimum, the statute probably had little effect. Forced to reduce the work day, the employer would compensate by reducing the daily wage. If the employer were prevented from reducing the daily wage, he would treat the statute as having increased the cost of his labor (he gets less output for the same wage) and, under a now-familiar analysis, would adapt by buying a smaller quantity of labor, raising prices, or doing both things. The reduction in employment would harm any workers he laid off who did not have equally good alternative employment opportunities; the increase in prices would harm consumers, and by reducing his output would lead him to further reduce his labor inputs.[8]

Since the Court's repudiation of liberty of contract, it has frequently upheld statutes designed to foster monopoly, such as a state statute that, on grounds of public health, forbade opticians to replace eyeglass frames without a prescription signed by an optometrist or an ophthalmologist[9]— although the statute could have had no purpose other than to increase the incomes of optometrists and ophthalmologists at the expense of opticians and consumers.

§25.2   Economic Due Process Revived: The Poor as a Constitutionally Protected Class

In *Griffin v. Illinois*,[1] the Supreme Court held that requiring a criminal defendant to buy the transcript of his trial as a condition of getting

---

6. Why is this assumption necessary?

7. 208 U.S. 412 (1908).

8. There is evidence that such laws reduced female employment — especially employment of immigrant women (why?). See Elisabeth M. Landes, The Effect of State Maximum Hours Laws on the Employment of Women in 1920, 88 J. Pol. Econ. 476 (1980). Cf. §11.6 *supra*.

9. See Williamson v. Lee Optical Co., 348 U.S. 438 (1955). For an extreme example of the Court's tolerance see Kotch v. Board of River Port Pilot Commrs., 330 U.S. 552 (1947).

§25.2   1. 351 U.S. 12 (1956).

appellate review of issues dependent on the trial record discriminated against those who could not afford the payment. The Court could have reached the same result by holding that due process in criminal proceedings requires that the defendant have a right to appeal (as the Court was many years later to hold) and that the right implies an opportunity, if necessary at the state's expense, for a meaningful appellate review of the conduct of the trial. But if, as the *Griffin* opinion seems to hold, a poor defendant is entitled to a free transcript simply in order to neutralize an advantage over him that the affluent defendant would otherwise enjoy, new vistas of constitutional obligation are opened up. If the state must neutralize the advantages conferred by the possession of money in this area, why not in others? It has in fact been argued that *Griffin* was the first in a series of cases that can best be explained on the theory that government is required, as a matter of constitutional principle, to satisfy people's "minimum just wants" regardless of ability to pay.[2] Another in the series is said to be the *Harper* decision, which invalidated the poll tax.[3]

The argument amounts to saying that government is required to provide certain benefits in kind, and is based on John Rawls's theory of justice, discussed in Chapter 16. His theory implies that society should establish a floor beneath the worst off, but it does not specify the particular form that the floor should take — whether unrestricted cash transfers or specific benefits in kind[4] — and the latter is often an inefficient method of helping poor people (see §16.5 *supra*). But the granting of minimum procedural safeguards to indigent criminal defendants may be an appropriate in-kind method of poor relief. This conclusion, which implies a narrow interpretation of *Griffin* that assimilates it to the cases guaranteeing counsel for indigent criminal defendants, recognizes that the individual who (perhaps through no fault of his own) is destitute still has a valuable property right: his freedom of action. If the government can take it away arbitrarily — which is one way of characterizing a criminal proceeding in which only the government has counsel or in which the defendant cannot effectively appeal his conviction — the value of that property right is diminished.[5]

The *Harper* decision, however, seems unrelated. Because the benefit-cost ratio of voting to the individual is so low anyway, even a moderate poll tax might deter many poor people from voting. It would thus have

2. Frank I. Michelman, On Protecting the Poor Through the Fourteenth Amendment, 83 Harv. L. Rev. 7 (1969), criticized in Ralph K. Winter, Jr., Poverty, Economic Equality, and the Equal Protection Clause, 1972 S. Ct. Rev. 41.

3. Harper v. Virginia Bd. of Elections, 383 U.S. 663 (1966).

4. See John Rawls, A Theory of Justice 275 (1971).

5. An alternative economic rationale of the right to counsel was suggested in §22.3 *supra*.

Why wouldn't it be better to give everyone a guaranteed minimum income and let him buy legal insurance?

the same practical effect as forbidding the poor to vote, which would be inconsistent with principles of universal suffrage that may, as we saw in the last chapter, have an economic justification.

The furthest development to date of the implications of the *Griffin* decision is the invalidation by several state courts, beginning with the Supreme Court of California in *Serrano v. Priest*, [6] of the practice of financing public education out of local property taxes. Under such a system of financing, the amount of money per pupil spent for public education in each school district is a function in part of the value of property in the district. It might seem that since wealthier districts as a rule contain more valuable properties, the children of wealthier parents receive a more expensive education than the children of poorer parents — which could be both inefficient and inequitable. The purpose of public education is to invest in human capital, and the optimal investment depends on the child's brains rather than wealth (see §5.4 *supra*). Also, to invest most in the human capital (earning capacity) of children who already have above average wealth would increase income inequalities. But the correlation between the real estate tax base and the income of the families who use the public schools need not be positive. In New York City, for example, there are many wealthy people and much valuable real estate. But since the wealthy people do not send their children to public schools and much of the property tax is levied on commercial rather than residential property, the effect of financing the public schools out of property taxes is to redistribute income to the poor. If expenditures per pupil were equalized on a statewide basis, New York City would be classified as a wealthy district and its expenditures per pupil would be reduced, although many of these pupils are poor. The primary beneficiaries of equalization would be rural inhabitants.

Equalization also would weaken the public school system by reducing the incentive of wealthy communities to tax themselves heavily to pay for high-quality public education, and some poor people would be hurt. Virtually no community is completely homogeneous. *Some* of its residents will be poor, and they will enjoy a high-quality education paid for by their wealthy neighbors (especially if the poor have larger families). This effect will become especially pronounced if current government policies of dispersing public housing into suburban areas make any headway. Indeed, one reason why suburbs resist such dispersion is that it would require them to bestow the costly public education that their residents demand for their own children on children whose parents are not able to pay a proportionate share of the costs.[7]

6. 5 Cal. 3d 584, 487 P.2d 1241 (1971). The U.S. Supreme Court has declined to follow *Serrano*. See San Antonio Independent School Dist. v. Rodriguez, 411 U.S. 1 (1973). For economic analysis, see Robert P. Inman & Daniel L. Rubinfeld, The Judicial Pursuit of Local Fiscal Equity, 92 Harv. L. Rev. 1662 (1979).

7. For further discussion of the constitutional rights of poor people see next section and also §28.4 *infra*. See also discussion of exclusionary zoning in §3.8 *supra*.

§25.3   The Due Process Rights of Consumers and Public Employees

The judicial reawakening of interest in economic rights is further illustrated by two lines of cases that at first glance seem conventional in their insistence on purely procedural safeguards (see §21.1 *supra*). In *Fuentes v. Shevin*,[1] the Supreme Court invalidated state statutes authorizing, upon the posting of a security bond, the replevy (repossession), without prior notice or hearing, of property that the person seeking replevin claims is rightfully his. The plaintiffs were sellers under installment sales contracts, the defendants buyers who allegedly had defaulted. The Court reasoned that since the buyers had a right to the possession of the goods sold under the contract, the goods were their property within the meaning of the due process clause of the Fourteenth Amendment of which they could not be deprived by state action without notice and an opportunity for a hearing in advance.

The basic premise of the Court's decision — that a person's "right to enjoy what is his, free of governmental interference," is a right worthy of judicial solicitude[2] — is congenial to economic analysis, but the Court's conclusion is not. The Court did not question that repossession is an appropriate remedy for defaulting on an installment sales contract (see §4.13 *supra*). The issue was how best to prevent the remedy from being invoked as a method of harassment when there is no actual default. From the standpoint of economics, the best method is to create a disincentive to replevy groundlessly. The statutes in issue did this, by requiring the sellers to post bonds. Although the replevin procedure, like the procedure for obtaining a preliminary restraining order, is summary initially, a final decision may not be made without a hearing. If it appears at the hearing that the property was wrongfully replevied, the seller must return it and make good the buyer's damages, if any; the seller is also out of pocket the cost of the bond. Thus he has nothing to gain and money to lose from invoking the remedy groundlessly. Since the requirement that the seller post a bond should both discourage frivolous invocations of the remedy and protect the buyer when mistakes are made, buyers have little to gain from also having a right to a prior hearing.

The Court noted the seller's economic incentive to avoid invoking the remedy groundlessly but held that such an incentive is no substitute for the judgment of a neutral official. The preference for authority over self-interest as a regulator of human conduct is curious to an economist,

§25.3   1. 407 U.S. 67 (1972).
2. Id. at 81. An even more extravagant paean to property rights appears in Lynch v. Household Finance Corp., 405 U.S. 538, 552 (1972).

who would also think it odd that the Court should draw so sharp a distinction between the particular thing replevied and its economic equivalent. By their requirement that the seller post a bond and justify the replevin at a subsequent hearing, the statutes protected the value of the buyers' interests if not the continuous possession of the specific good. In the case of the common consumer products involved in these cases, the good and its market value are interchangeable. The effect of *Fuentes* is to increase the cost of the installment sales contract — a dubious blessing to consumers.

The next line of cases, which also proceeds from the unexceptionable premise that the Constitution forbids government to deprive a person of property without due process of law, holds that teachers and other public employees with tenure contracts — contracts that forbid arbitrary discharge — have a property right in their jobs so that if they are fired without a hearing their constitutional rights have been violated. The use of the term "property right" in these cases is not conventional. Tenure is a contract right, not a property right. The opposite of tenure is not an employment contract but employment at will — employment with no contractually guaranteed and legally enforceable safeguards against termination (see §11.4 *supra*). In any event, it is odd that courts should think these employees in need of federal constitutional protections. If a public employee who has tenure is fired, he can sue the state under state contract law. And if the state does not give a fired public employee decent legal remedies for breach of the tenure term of the employment contract, then wages for public employees will be higher than they would be if there were such remedies. If the remedies would cost less than the wage premium that must be paid to compensate for their absence, the state will have an incentive to create such remedies. If they would cost more, the employee himself would prefer (ex ante) not to have them. And since the right that is enforced in a suit under the Fifth or Fourteenth Amendments to enforce a tenure contract is a product of that contract, and since remedies for breach can be viewed as an implied term of the contract, it is not clear what property right the employee has been deprived of if he receives the remedies to which he is contractually entitled, even if they do not include a hearing that meets federal due process standards.

Suggested Readings

1. Robert E. Scott, Constitutional Regulation of Provisional Creditor Remedies: The Cost of Procedural Due Process, 61 Va. L. Rev. 807 (1975).
2. Bernard H. Siegan, Economic Liberties and the Constitution (1980).

3. Ralph K. Winter, Jr., Poverty, Economic Equality, and the Equal Protection Clause, 1972 S. Ct. Rev. 41.

Problems

1. Does the Supreme Court use the same economic premises in the decision of antitrust cases as in the decision of the modern economic rights cases, such as *Fuentes v. Shevin*?

2. Assume it has been convincingly demonstrated that the federal minimum wage law, at present levels, significantly reduces the employment opportunities of poor people (see §11.6 *supra*). Should the law therefore be invalidated as a violation of equal protection?

3. If a negative income tax were adopted, would — or should — the Supreme Court reexamine the question of the constitutional right to a transcript in a criminal case, or any other questions involving the constitutional rights of the poor?

CHAPTER 26

THE ECONOMICS OF FEDERALISM[1]

§26.1 The Allocation of Responsibilities Between Federal and State Governments

The government of the United States is superimposed upon the governments of the 50 states, and a recurrent question is whether to vest this or that governmental responsibility at the federal or state level. Viewed economically, the choice involves a tradeoff among three factors:

1. *The monopoly power of government.* The federal government has more monopoly power than any state government. It is relatively easy for most people to relocate from one state to another but very difficult to relocate to a different country. If a state government tries to use its taxing or regulatory powers to transfer wealth from one group of citizens to another, the victims may well decide to move to another state.[1] But the redistribution would have to be enormous before many people would try to make a go of it in another country — especially since the United States is the wealthiest large nation in the world.

Although monopoly achieved is apt to be more harmful at the federal than at the state level, it is harder to achieve at the federal level. The larger and more heterogeneous the polity, the greater are the transaction costs of organizing a dominant coalition. Hence the expected costs of monopoly may be no greater at the federal than at the state level once the greater probability of monopoly at the state level is taken into ac-

---

1. On the constitutional law of state taxation, the principal topic covered in this chapter, see Jerome R. Hellerstein & Walter Hellerstein, State and Local Taxation: Cases and Materials, ch. 6 (4th ed. 1978), and Walter Hellerstein, Constitutional Limitations on State Tax Exportation, 1982 Am. Bar Foundation Research J. 1; on the jurisdiction of the federal courts, also discussed in this chapter, see David P. Currie, Federal Jurisdiction in a Nutshell (2d ed. 1981).

§26.1 1. That is, they will "vote with their feet." With exit as a method of popular control of government, compare voice. Can you figure out what these terms mean? What their counterparts are in corporation law?

count. Of course if the expected costs are the same but most people are risk averse, the expected *disutility* of monopoly may be greater at the federal level. This may be why the separation of powers, which makes it harder to achieve political monopoly, is more elaborate at the federal level than in any state.

2. *Diseconomies of scale and diversity of approaches.* If all government in the United States were federal, the bureaucracy of government would be immense and unwieldy, and the scope of experimentation with divergent approaches to problems of public policy would be curtailed. In principle, any organization can avoid problems of giantism and monolithicity by adopting a decentralized form of organization, as many business firms do by constituting different branches of the firm as separate profit centers (cf. §9.3 *supra*). But this is not so easy in practice (why?); and since we have state governments already, it may make more sense to assign them functions in which diversity or small scale is desirable than to decentralize the federal government.

3. *Externalities.* If either the benefits or costs of an activity within a state accrue to nonresidents (the externality may be the state government, itself, as we shall see), the incentives of the state government will be distorted. One might think the Coase Theorem would apply, especially if only two or three states are involved: If pollution from State A dirties the air in State B, why don't A and B negotiate the cost-minimizing solution? Obstacles are:

(1) the bilateral monopoly setting;
(2) the difficulty of executing a legal judgment against a recalcitrant state;
(3) the lack of strong incentives at any governmental level to minimize costs;
(4) and the difficulty of deciding how to allocate a payment to a state among its citizens.

Here, then, are some elements in an economic theory of federalism. The remaining sections in this chapter look at specific applications of the theory, beginning with the division of jurisdiction between the state and federal courts.

§26.2 Federal Courts

The allocation of judicial power between the state and federal courts is illuminated by the foregoing analysis. For example, although the federal courts' diversity jurisdiction (which allows suits between citizens of different states to be maintained in federal courts even if the basis of the suit is state law) is traditionally justified by reference to presumed hostility to nonresidents, there is an economic explanation for at least a part of the jurisdiction that is unrelated to xenophobia. Suppose a resident of State A has a collision with a resident of State B in B, and the resident of B sues the resident of A in a state court in B. If the plaintiff wins, the benefits accrue to B; if the defendant wins, the benefits accrue to A; so the court may tilt toward the plaintiff.

Such a tilt is less likely if the parties have a preexisting relationship. Suppose the suit arises out of a contract between a resident of A and a resident of B. If courts in B are known to favor residents, either the contract will require that any disputes under the contract be resolved other than in a lawsuit in B or the resident of B will have to compensate the resident of A in the contract price or some other term for bearing the added risk of litigation in B. B's courts will gain nothing in the long run from tilting in favor of residents.

The Federal Tort Claims Act allows people injured by torts committed by federal employees to sue the United States — but only in federal court. The economic rationale for confining these suits to federal court is similar to that for the diversity jurisdiction. If a postal van runs down a resident of State A, and he can sue the Postal Service in a state court of A, that court may lean in his favor, knowing that if the plaintiff loses, the costs to the Postal Service will be spread throughout the United States rather than concentrated in A.

Much of federal criminal law (which is enforced exclusively in federal courts) is explicable as a response to the problem of interstate externalities. Suppose a criminal gang operates in many states. Each state will have some incentive to bring the gang to justice, but less than it would have if the full costs of the gang's activities were borne within the state. Of course, if each state does some investigating, the aggregate resources expended on investigation may be as great as if a single entity were responsible for the investigation. But the resources will not be as efficiently employed, because it will be costly to coordinate the activities of the different states.

Here is a different kind of externality that justifies a federal role in criminal law enforcement. A person defrauds a bank whose deposits are insured by the Federal Deposit Insurance Corporation. Some of the costs of the fraud may be borne by stockholders and others within the state, but most of the costs will be borne by the federal government. (Does this depend on how deposit insurance rates are set?)

Some federal criminal jurisdiction is explicable by reference to the point made in the preceding section of this chapter that monopolies of political power are more easily achieved at the state than at the federal level. Federal criminal prosecutions of corrupt local government officials exploit the relative incorruptibility of federal officials — stemming from the greater costs of corrupting a federal agency (what are they?) — in order to reduce corruption at the local level.

Much federal civil law, as well, reflects a concern with externalities at the state level. Labor law, for example, has been thoroughly federalized. National policy (still) favors the creation of labor unions, which we know seek to raise wages above competitive levels. Such a policy would be extremely difficult to effectuate at the state level, since it would cause employers to relocate to states that did not have a policy of encouraging unionization.

§26.3   State Taxation: Excise Taxes

Each state has an economic incentive to impose taxes whose burden will fall, so far as possible, on residents of other states. Such an incentive is undesirable. It not only deflects the state from the search for taxing methods that maximize efficiency and distributive criteria for the nation as a whole; it also leads to socially excessive government expenditures, by enabling the state to externalize the costs of its public services. States may also use taxation not to raise revenue but to protect the state's producers or other sellers from the competition of nonresidents. Such a tax will harm resident consumers as well as nonresident sellers of the out-of-state goods that are taxed — and indeed the loss to the resident consumers will usually exceed the gain to the resident sellers.[1] But since special interests frequently obtain legislation that reduces efficiency, we should not be surprised to find that with states as with nations, taxes that discriminate against importers are sometimes imposed. Such a tax distorts the optimum geographical distribution of enterprise. Production that could be carried on more efficiently in State A will be carried on in B instead if B's tax on imports from A exceeds the cost advantage of producers in A. Thus we have two separate things to watch out for: a state tax that exports the costs of state government, and a state tax that protects local producers from the competition of out-of-state producers.

Two qualifications should be noted, however. First, a tax that discriminates in favor of out-of-state firms will cause the same distortion of comparative geographical advantages as a tax that discriminates against them. Second, there is no discrimination, whether against nonresident consumers or nonresident producers, if the difference in tax burdens

---

§26.3   1. The tax raises the price of the imported good relative to that of the local good, and so induces consumers to substitute the latter. The substitution benefits the local seller while harming the consumer. But not all consumers make the substitution. Some continue to buy the imported good at the higher price, and their loss is not captured by a resident seller. The analysis is similar to that of monopoly: consumers lose more than the monopolist gains (see §9.3 *supra*).

reflects a difference in the benefits or services provided by the state to the different taxpaying groups.

The Supreme Court has adequate formal authority under the commerce clause and the privileges and immunities clause of the original Constitution, and the due process and equal protection clauses of the Fourteenth Amendment, to prevent states from imposing taxes that have either or both of the uneconomical features just identified (taxing nonresident consumers or excluding nonresident producers). It has exercised this authority to forbid clearly extraterritorial taxes, and tariffs on goods imported from other states, but it has often failed to prevent states from reimposing such taxes and tariffs under names that conceal the true economic effect.

If Montana imposed a tax on the sale of coal in Illinois, the invalidity of the tax would be clear; yet a tax on the extraction of coal from mines in Montana (a severance tax) is clearly valid. The dichotomous treatment makes no economic sense. If the demand for Montana coal is relatively inelastic, and if the ultimate consumers of this coal are mainly nonresidents, then the tax, assuming it is proportional to the output produced, will be paid mostly by nonresidents in the form of higher prices for coal, as shown in Figure 26.1.[2]

One could argue that the severance tax is in fact a royalty, to which the state, as the original owner of the natural resources found within its boundaries, should be entitled.[3] It is true, as we shall see when we discuss interbasin water transfers, that efficiency is promoted by vesting the state with ownership of natural resources in which private individuals or firms have not yet obtained property rights; that initial vesting is the first step to creating markets in the resources. But if the state either retains ownership of all of the rights to a resource or sells them all to a single purchaser, the result — if there are no good substitutes, as assumed in our coal example — will be monopoly. Monopoly is not inherent in state ownership of its natural resources, because the state can disperse the rights sufficiently broadly to assure competition.[4] But a severance tax, imposed on a resource that lacks good substitutes produced in other states, is monopolistic. The tax drives price above the competitive level and output below it and generates supracompetitive revenues (albeit received by the state rather than by the rights holders).

Not every excise tax "monopolizes," in the sense of creating the misal-

2. The example ignores the fact that there are intermediate sellers between the producer and the consumer. Does this make a difference? Observe also that the example assumes a flat tax (for example, $2 a ton). Would it make a difference if the tax were in the form of a percentage of coal revenues? Cf. §17.3 *supra*.

3. A factual problem with the argument should be noted: Except in Texas and Alaska, the original and present owner of most natural resources is the federal government, rather than states.

4. Is this a possible reason why actual diversion is required to establish a property right in water? See §3.1 *supra*.

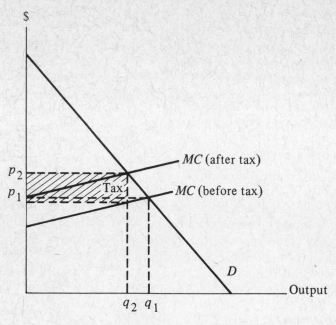

p_2

p_1

Tax

MC (after tax)

MC (before tax)

D

Output

q_2 q_1

Figure 26.1

locative effects associated with monopoly. If there were good substitutes for Montana coal, so that the demand schedule in Figure 26.1 were horizontal, the excise tax would merely reduce the output of that coal and the value of Montana coal fields, leading to a compensating increase in output and land values elsewhere. It would be a tax on economic rent (see Figure 26.2). It would be a responsible form of taxation (as well as an efficient one), provided the owners of Montana coal fields were Montanans, because then residents of the state imposing the tax would be the real and not merely nominal taxpayers.[5]

An intermediate case is one where, although demand for the resource taxed is inelastic because there are no good substitutes elsewhere, there is a substantial market within the state, so that the major burden of the tax falls on residents. One could still object that the tax was monopolistic in its effects, but the objection would not be forceful. Virtually all taxes have allocative effects (see, e.g., §17.3 *supra*). The revenues of modern government cannot begin to be raised by taxes on economic rent alone. As long as the incidence of the tax is local, there is no special objection; for there are then the usual political checks on the level of the tax.

If a state imposed a tax designed to exploit a locational monopoly —

5. Redraw Figure 26.2 to show the effect if the tax were a percentage of gross receipts rather than a flat tax per unit produced, assuming the coal fields are owned by Montanans.

604

say Louisiana levied a heavy toll on all ships using the part of the Mississippi River wholly within the state — the element of extraterritoriality
(interstate externality) would be unmistakable, and the tax would be
struck down. Yet the severance tax, in cases such as our Montana coal
example, has the same economic character. The only difference, which
is economically irrelevant, is that the state's monopoly is founded on
control of a scarce natural resource rather than a strategic location.
The vice of the tax in both cases is to shift the burden of taxation to
people who have no control over the size of the tax because they can't
vote in the taxing jurisdiction. By weakening the incentives to economize
on government spending, this increases the misallocative effects of taxation.

The Supreme Court has been more critical of state import taxes —
that is, of excluding nonresident producers as distinct from burdening
nonresident consumers. Early decisions held that a state could not levy
its general sales tax on sales made to its residents by out-of-state sellers.
If you wonder how the uniform levy of a sales tax could discriminate
against such sellers, consider two states, one that raises revenue primarily
by a sales tax (State A), the other by a property tax (B). Since the value
of commercial property is normally based on its capitalized earnings,
the net income from sales to residents of State A by a firm located in
State B will be capitalized in the property tax paid by the firm to B.
The firm thus pays B a tax on its sales in A. Its competitors in State
A pay simply sales tax. If the firm in B is also subject to State A's
sales tax, it will pay more tax than its competitors in A while receiving
no greater government services (why not?). This tax differential, unrelated to any difference in costs, discriminates against the out-of-state
seller, although the effect may be reduced by the fact that State A's

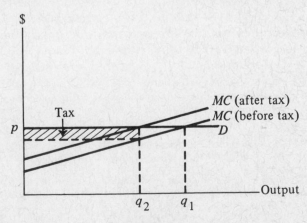

Figure 26.2

sales tax reduces the value of the firm's property and hence the amount of tax it pays to B.[6]

The Court has, however, upheld a clearly evasive device known as a compensating use tax. This is a tax, equal to sales tax, on goods that residents of the taxing state buy but do not pay sales tax on. The residents of State A in our example who purchased from the firm in B would have to pay A a tax equal to the sales tax they would have paid if they had bought the same goods from a seller in A. The Court has also permitted states to compel the out-of-state seller to collect the compensating use tax, which completes the functional identity of the two taxes.

Perhaps the reason why the Court failed to "see through" severance and compensating use taxes — the former taxing nonresident consumers, the latter excluding nonresident producers — is that until recent years it phrased the question as whether the state had placed a tax "on" interstate commerce. The petroleum as it comes out of the ground and the good after it has been received by the resident purchaser are reassuringly present, in a physical sense, within the boundaries of the state. But it is irrelevant from an economic standpoint whether a tax is "on" interstate commerce or where the nominal subject of the tax is physically located. The economic issues are how much of the tax is ultimately borne by nonresidents and whether the effect of the tax is to increase, without justification based on higher costs of governmental services, the prices of imported compared to domestic goods.

In some instances, emphasis on whether a tax is "on" interstate commerce has given unjustified tax breaks to out-of-state sellers, thereby creating an opposite but equally inappropriate incentive to substitute interstate for intrastate goods and services. Suppose a firm located in a state that relies primarily on a sales tax to raise revenues makes most of its sales to residents of other states that rely primarily on property taxes to raise revenues. If the firm's domiciliary state is forbidden to apply its sales tax to the firm's interstate sales, because those sales are in interstate commerce, the firm will pay lower taxes than competitors who mostly make intrastate sales, although it receives no fewer governmental services than they.

---

6. But not eliminated. Suppose that the sales tax in State A is 3¢ on the dollar, the out-of-state seller's normal profit is 10¢ on the dollar, and State B's property tax is equivalent to 30 percent of the seller's normal profit and hence is also 3¢. If State A's sales tax is not imposed, the out-of-state seller obtains net profits of 7¢ on the dollar. If it is imposed the seller's profit before imposition of the property tax is only 7¢. The property tax is 30 percent of this amount, or 2.1¢, so the seller's total tax burden is 5.1¢, leaving a profit of only 4.9¢. Thus if sellers in State A are subject only to sales tax, the imposition of that tax on the out-of-state seller gives them a competitive advantage unrelated to efficiency, for we are assuming that the out-of-state seller receives no greater governmental services although his taxes are more than 40 percent greater than the local sellers. It is also plain, however, that the out-of-state seller's additional tax burden (2.1¢) is less than the sum of the two taxes to which he is subject.

The Supreme Court in recent years has moved away from the question-begging approach of asking whether the tax is "on" interstate or local commerce. It has begun to recognize the economic issues. But believing itself institutionally incapable of resolving the difficult issues of tax incidence that disputes over the constitutionality of state taxes raise, it continues to tolerate what appear to be clearly objectionable taxes, such as Montana's 30 percent severance tax on coal.[7]

The essential economic point — that the consumption of governmental services is not necessarily related to the destination of a firm's goods — implies that our two criteria of suspect state taxes may conflict in particular cases. The criteria are whether the tax falls primarily on nonresidents and whether it distorts comparative geographical advantage. In the example of a sales tax on a firm that sells mainly into other states, the first criterion would imply a policy of prohibiting taxation of the firm's interstate sales by the domiciliary state, since the burden of the tax would fall primarily on nonresidents. But the second criterion would lead us to approve such a tax so that the taxes paid by an interstate firm will not be lower than those paid by a local firm because of a difference in their status rather than in the amount of governmental services they receive.

Can the criteria be reconciled? One approach might be (1) to permit all states to impose a general sales tax applied indiscriminately to interstate and intrastate sales by sellers in the state but (2) to forbid taxes on particular products that are primarily export goods when products of equivalent importance sold primarily in the local market are not taxed as heavily. Under this approach, severance taxes would be dubious[8] and the last vestige of justification for compensating use taxes would be removed since the out-of-state seller would be subject to sales tax in his state of residence even on his out-of-state sales.

§26.4 State Taxation: Real Estate and Corporate Income Taxes

The Supreme Court has tended to treat real estate taxes as inherently local. They would be if they were taxes solely on the rent of land and all land were locally owned. But because the rent of land just isn't that great (see §17.4 *supra*), a state that taxes a railroad's real estate, for example, is more likely to proportion its tax to the railroad's revenues than to the rent of land. The railroad will treat such a tax as an excise

7. See Commonwealth Edison Co. v. Montana, 453 U.S. 609 (1981).
8. If it is true that they are mostly export taxes.

tax and shift as much of it as possible to the railroad's customers, most of whom will be nonresidents. (What factors will determine whether the railroad can do this?) To the extent that the tax is on rents, the burden will again be borne primarily by nonresidents — the railroad's shareholders.[1] Real estate taxes on the property of firms that are owned by and do business mainly with nonresidents should be subject to careful scrutiny like severance taxes, yet perhaps because the physical characteristics of land place it so firmly within state boundaries, the Court has not critically scrutinized real estate taxes on railroads and similar commercial properties.

Similar dangers inhere in state corporate income taxes. The burden of such a tax is normally shared between consumers and shareholders (see §17.5 *supra*), most of whom, in the case of a corporation doing business in several states, will not be residents of either state. The temptation of each state to impose a heavy corporate income tax on the multistate corporation is therefore great. It might appear that so long as each state has a uniform tax rate for all the corporations that do business in the state, local as well as multistate, there is no danger of discrimination. The problem, a classic joint-cost problem (see §12.5 *supra*), is that it is usually impossible to assign a particular part of a multistate firm's income to a particular state. If a firm has its manufacturing plant in one state, its sales force in another, and its corporate headquarters in a third, its costs and revenues, and hence income, are the joint product of the activities in each of the three states. Since there is no rational means of apportioning such a firm's income among the different states in which it operates, it is not surprising that the Supreme Court has allowed states to choose, within broad limits, whatever formula for apportionment attributes the largest possible share to the taxing state. But if a state in which a railroad has a lot of track but runs relatively few cars apportions the railroad's income by track mileage, while a state in which the railroad has relatively little track but runs a great many cars apportions the railroad's income according to cars, the railroad's combined income tax bill will be larger than that of any pair of similar but local firms one of which is located in the first state and the other in the second. The effort of both states to export their tax burdens will result in the multistate firm's being compelled to pay a higher tax than if it operated in only one state, even though the firm does not require greater governmental services. The result is to create an inefficient incentive to do business in as few states as possible.

Suppose, as is common nowadays, that a state calculates the income tax due from a multistate corporation doing business in the state as follows. To determine the corporation's taxable income in the state,

§26.4 1. This assumes that the land was owned by the railroad before the tax was anticipated. What difference does this make?

the state multiplies the corporation's total income by the average of the following three ratios: the ratio of the corporation's in-state payroll expense to its total payroll expense, the ratio of the value of its in-state property to the value of all its property, and the ratio of its in-state sales revenues to its total sales revenues. Is this one tax or three? Is the incidence of the tax simply the average incidence of a payroll tax, a property tax, and a sales tax?

§26.5   Due Process Limitations on Personal Jurisdiction

A company in New York sells widgets to a buyer in Oklahoma. The sale is negotiated in New York and the widgets are shipped from there, but the seller does have a small sales office and some warehouse facilities in Oklahoma. If a dispute arises under the contract, should the buyer be allowed to sue the seller in Oklahoma or must he go to New York to sue?

To allow the buyer to sue in Oklahoma will impose additional costs on the seller, not just in travel but in the increased risk of losing the case if it is tried in a less friendly forum. But if the buyer must sue in New York, then a similar cost increment is imposed on him. One possible approach, which is used in deciding which of two or more courts with jurisdiction over a dispute should be the actual site of trial, is just to compare the costs, and require that the suit be brought in the state where the total costs of both parties will be minimized. The problem with this approach (which goes by the name of *forum non conveniens*) is that it gives the plaintiff a potentially very large choice of states to sue in — for who knows where the parties' joint litigation costs would really be minimized? The solution that the courts have adopted is to require that the state chosen by the plaintiff have conferred at least some benefit on the defendant, so that the defendant cannot complain too bitterly if he is forced as a quid pro quo to defend himself in a forum that is not ideal from his standpoint. This condition would be satisfied in our hypothetical case, where the defendant has some tangible presence in Oklahoma.

But now consider this case. A New York car dealer sells a car to a New Yorker who is injured, allegedly because of a defect in the car, while on a trip to Oklahoma. Can the buyer sue the dealer in Oklahoma? He cannot.[1] There is a sense in which the dealer benefits from the fact that Oklahoma has roads, just as a telephone company in New York

§26.5   1. See World-Wide Volkswagen Corp. v. Woodson, 444 U.S. 286 (1980).

benefits from the fact that there are telephones in Oklahoma, but the benefit is exceedingly tenuous.

§26.6   Interbasin Water Transfers[1]

Since water is a surplus commodity in many states and a deficit commodity in others, there would appear to be promising opportunities for increasing the overall value of the resource by transferring water from the surplus to the deficit regions. The cost of transporting water over large distances is substantial; but the major obstacles to interregional transfers are legal and institutional factors deriving from the structure of the federal system.

If the out-of-state purchaser could obtain the quantity of water he needed by purchasing individual appropriative rights owned by residents of the state or states having a water surplus, no special problem would be presented, since a state may not forbid the sale of an appropriative right to an out-of-state purchaser. But the heavy transaction costs involved in the purchase of even a single appropriative right (see §3.10 *supra*) would make the costs of attempting to aggregate a large number of such rights by individual purchase prohibitive.

An alternative is the purchase of unappropriated waters, which are found in large quantities in some states, especially in the Pacific Northwest. Unfortunately, no one can convey clear title to such waters. Recall from Chapter 3 that it is only by the act of appropriation that a property right is created. A nonresident could attempt an appropriation but he would be met by the argument that the rents of unappropriated waters belong to the residents of the state within which they are located. And more than rents are involved. Unappropriated waters are not necessarily unused waters. There are many economically valuable but nonappropriative uses of water, such as recreation and the dilution of pollutants, that a major transfer to another water basin might impair.[2]

The problem could be overcome by the payment of appropriate compensation by the out-of-state user to the state of origin. But the allocation of the compensation among affected residents would pose substantial administrative difficulties, quite apart from the absence, prior to appropriation, of a recognized owner. And any title conveyed by the state

§26.6   1. See Charles J. Meyers & Richard A. Posner, Market Transfers of Water Rights: Toward an Improved Market in Water Resources, pt. 4 (National Water Commission report, July 1, 1971, published by the National Technical Information Service); Stephen F. Williams, Free Trade in Water Resources: Sporhase v. Nebraska ex rel. Douglas, 2 S. Ct. Econ. Rev. 89 (1983).

2. Does this suggest another criticism of the appropriative-rights system in water law, besides that discussed in §3.4 *supra*?

would be clouded by the extensive but unquantified interests of the federal government and of other states. The United States has rights — the extent of which has never been determined — to use the waters of the rivers on the extensive federal public domain in the western states (Indian reservations, national parks and forests, military bases, etc.). It also has ill-defined but extensive interests in the waters of all navigable rivers by virtue of its navigational servitude. A substantial interbasin diversion would therefore require the approval of the federal government, and probably only Congress could give this approval. It would also require the approval of the other states in the river basin, since the diversion of a substantial quantity of water from one point in a river system can affect recreational, environmental, and other valuable economic interests up and down the river system. A definition of each state's interests would require an apportionment by the Supreme Court, by interstate compact, or by Congress.

§26.7   The Exportation of Poverty

The cost of the governmental services that the nonworking poor consume is higher than the tax revenues that they contribute to the support of those services: They are a deficit item in the public finance of the state. If in addition they have little political power, there will be strong support for attempting to "export" them. A cheap method of doing this is to establish a level of welfare benefits so low that the beneficiaries are induced to migrate to states that grant higher benefits. A similar problem plagued the English administration of poor relief from its beginnings and led to prohibitions against paupers' leaving their original parish. The traditional solution of our states, a milder version of the English practice, was to require that an individual reside in the state for a period of time, usually one year, before he could receive welfare benefits. Despite this rule many indigents from low welfare benefit states such as Mississippi migrated to high welfare benefit states such as New York, scraping by with the help of relatives or friends during the one-year waiting period. But no doubt others were discouraged.

In *Shapiro v. Thompson*,[1] the Supreme Court invalidated residence requirements on the ground that they inhibit interstate travel. But migration that is induced by the prospect of receiving larger welfare payments than available in the migrant's state of origin distorts rather than promotes the efficient geographical distribution of population. Society is not better off if indigents move from Mississippi to New York because

§26.7   1. 394 U.S. 618 (1969).

New York has more generous poor relief. It is worse off; indigents can be supported decently at lower cost in Mississippi than in New York. It is not even clear that indigents as a group are made better off by such migration, although individual indigents are. Free migration encourages the low welfare benefit states in their policy of inducing emigration by inadequate public assistance. Its effect in the high welfare benefit states is more complex. On the one hand, the increase in the number of its indigent residents may augment the political influence of the poor of the state, resulting in still higher levels of support. On the other hand, each increase attracts new welfare recipients from other states and eventually the state must realize that it is allowing itself to be used by the low welfare benefit states to relieve them of the burden of supporting the poor of those states. Once the high welfare benefit state stops increasing its welfare budget, the average welfare benefits of its residents will decrease, for indigents will continue to arrive, drawn by a level of support that, while static, and in average terms declining (the pie is not growing but it is being divided into more pieces), is still higher than in their own states.

The basic problem, both in English poor relief and in ours, is regional organization, which creates socially unproductive incentives: the incentive of states to shift the cost of welfare to other states, the incentive of the poor to migrate to areas where welfare benefits are more generous. A residence requirement is a crude and only partially effective method of dealing with this problem: crude, because it may often discourage the migration of a poor family that is attracted by superior employment opportunities in the high welfare benefit state but requires modest public assistance during the first few weeks or months of residence in a new state;[2] only partially effective, because the requirement invites fraud and because, as noted earlier, an indigent family may be able to scrape by for a year without public assistance. By undermining the regional approach to welfare administration, the *Shapiro* decision may have hastened the national solution[3] that seems essential to overcome the locational inefficiencies that traditional decentralized welfare schemes create.

Suggested Readings

1. Walter Hellerstein, Constitutional Limitations on State Tax Exportation, 1982 Am. Bar Foundation Research J. 1, 27-42.

2. Could such a poor person borrow the necessary assistance? Observe also that the residence requirement discourages indigents in high welfare benefit states from seeking employment in other areas (why?).
3. Is an appropriate national solution a uniform level of benefits regardless of location? Why should a cost of living differential *not* be included?

2. ———, State and Local Taxation of Natural Resources in the Federal System: Legal, Economic, and Political Perspectives, chs. 4-6 (1985).

3. Saul Levmore, Interstate Exploitation and Judicial Intervention, 69 Va. L. Rev. 563 (1983).

4. Charles E. McLure, Jr., Incidence Analysis and the Supreme Court: An Examination of Four Cases From the 1980 Term, 1 S. Ct. Econ. Rev. 69 (1982).

5. Richard A. Posner, The Federal Courts: Crisis and Reform, ch. 6 (1985).

6. Susan Rose-Ackerman, Does Federalism Matter? Political Choice in a Federal Republic, 89 J. Pol. Econ. 152 (1981).

7. Stephen F. Williams, Severance Taxes and Federalism: The Role of the Supreme Court in Preserving a National Common Market for Energy Supplies, 53 U. Colo. L. Rev. 281 (1982).

8. The Economics of Federalism (Bhajan S. Grewal, Geoffrey Brennon & Russell L. Mathews eds. 1980).

9. Fiscal Federalism and the Taxation of Natural Resources (Charles E. McLure, Jr. & Peter Mieszkowski eds. 1983).

10. Regulation, Federalism, and Interstate Commerce (A. Daniel Tarlock ed. 1981).

11. The State Corporation Income Tax: Issues in Worldwide Unitary Combination (Charles E. McLure, Jr., ed. 1984).

Problems

1. Why should Montana, in our severance tax example, be restrained from taxing nonresidents? Do not nonresident consumers of coal benefit from the services that Montana renders to the coal producers located in the state?

2. Can economic theory help you to devise a formula for apportioning a firm's movable property (for example, an airline's aircraft) among the states for state tax purposes?

3. Should states be permitted to impose corporate income taxes at all? Suppose states that impose such taxes were required to adopt a uniform formula for apportioning corporate income among the states. Which would be a better formula: percentage of corporate revenues derived from sales to residents of the taxing state or percentage of employees within the taxing state? Would percentage of the corporation's tangible property located in the state be better?

4. In Baldwin v. G.A.F. Seelig, Inc., 294 U.S. 511 (1935), the Supreme Court held that a New York State law fixing a minimum price for milk sold in the state could not constitutionally be applied to milk produced in Vermont and imported into New York. The Court's strong condemnation of New York's attempt to subject such milk to its minimum price

law has been criticized as follows: "New York's interest was not simple economic bias against out-of-state competitors; it dealt primarily with local economic well-being and health." Gerald Gunther & Noel T. Dowling, Cases and Materials on Constitutional Law 651 (8th ed. 1970).[4] Can "economic bias against out-of-state competitors" be differentiated from "local economic well-being"? Is the criticism tantamount to asserting that states should be permitted to impose some tariffs?

5. Why do some states have higher welfare allowances than others? Is it because the taxpayers in those states attach a greater value to reducing poverty? If so, can it still be argued that efficiency is reduced rather than increased if the poor gravitate to these states?

6. Under the market participant doctrine, a state is allowed to discriminate against nonresident sellers if it is actually participating in the market, for example as a buyer, rather than regulating a private market. Thus a state could have a rule that it would buy paper clips only from resident sellers even though it couldn't require private purchasers of paper clips to adopt such a policy. Would this doctrine make good economic sense if states had the same economic incentives as private persons? If a state wanted to transfer wealth from nonresidents to residents? Could there by any such transfer if the market for the product in question were national rather than state or local? See W. C. M. Window Co. v. Bernardi, 730 F.2d 486 (7th Cir. 1984).

7. Under current interpretations of federal antitrust law, state agencies are immune from liability, but not municipalities and other local agencies unless acting under direction of the state government. Is this pattern consistent with the economics of federalism? Would the opposite pattern perhaps be more consistent? See Frank H. Easterbrook, Antitrust and the Economics of Federalism, 26 J. Law & Econ. 23 (1983).

---

4. Subsequent editions of this leading casebook have deleted the materials on state taxation.

CHAPTER 27

RACIAL DISCRIMINATION

§27.1 The Taste for Discrimination

Some people do not like to associate with the members of racial, religious, or ethnic groups different from their own and will pay a price to indulge their taste. Thus, although there are pecuniary gains to trade between blacks and whites — to blacks working for whites (or vice versa), whites selling houses to blacks, and so forth — much as there are pecuniary gains to trade among nations, by increasing the contact between members of the two races such trade imposes nonpecuniary, but real, costs on those members of either race who dislike association with members of the other race. These costs are analogous to transportation costs in international trade, which also reduce the amount of trading.

There is nothing inefficient about this, but the wealth effects can be dramatic. Assume that whites do not like to associate with blacks but that blacks are indifferent to the racial identity of those with whom they associate. The incomes of many whites will be lower than they would be if they did not have such a taste.[1] They forgo advantageous exchanges: For example, they may refuse to sell their houses to blacks who are willing to pay higher prices than white purchasers. But the racial preference of the whites will also reduce the incomes of the blacks, by preventing them from making advantageous exchanges with whites; and the reduction in the blacks' incomes will be proportionately greater than the reduction in the whites' incomes. Because blacks are only a small part of the economy, the number of advantageous exchanges that blacks can make with whites is greater than the number of advantageous transactions that whites can make with blacks. The white sector is so large as to be virtually self-sufficient; the black sector is much smaller and more dependent on trade with the white.

§27.1   1. Some whites — those who are not prejudiced — will have higher incomes than they would if other whites were not prejudiced (why?).

615

The international trade analogy can help clarify the point. The United States constitutes so large an aggregation of skills, resources, and population that it could survive a substantial reduction of its foreign trade in relative comfort. Switzerland could not. Its markets are too small and its resources too limited to permit it to achieve economies of scale and of specialization without trading with other countries. The position of the black minority in the United States is similar to that of Switzerland in the world economy.

Although discrimination is perfectly consistent with competition, just as a reduction in international trade due to higher costs of transportation would be no evidence that international markets were not competitive, there are economic forces at work in competitive markets that tend to minimize discrimination. In a market of many sellers the intensity of the prejudice against blacks will vary considerably. Some sellers will have only a mild prejudice against them. These sellers will not forgo as many advantageous transactions with blacks as their more prejudiced competitors (unless the law interferes). Their costs will therefore be lower, and this will enable them to increase their share of the market. The least prejudiced sellers will come to dominate the market in much the same way as people who are least afraid of heights come to dominate occupations that require working at heights: They demand a smaller premium.

The tendency for the market to be dominated by firms with the least prejudice against blacks is weaker under monopoly. The single seller in the market will be, on average, as prejudiced as the average, not as the least prejudiced, member of the community. True, any monopolies that are freely transferable (such as patents) are likely to come into the hands of the least prejudiced. A monopoly that requires association with blacks is less valuable to a prejudiced owner; he suffers either a reduction in his pecuniary income by forgoing advantageous transactions with blacks or a nonpecuniary cost by making such transactions. Therefore the less prejudiced will tend to purchase monopolies from the more prejudice. But not all monopolies are freely transferable.

If the monopoly is regulated, the market forces working against discrimination are weakened further. One way to evade a profit ceiling is by substituting nonpecuniary for pecuniary income, since the former is very difficult for a regulatory agency to control; and one type of nonpecuniary income is freedom from associating with the people against whom one is prejudiced.[2]

Labor unions with monopoly power may reduce the effectiveness of competition in minimizing discrimination. A monopolistic union, by in-

---

2. For some evidence on this point, see Armen A. Alchian & Reuben A. Kessel, Competition, Monopoly, and the Pursuit of Money, in Aspects of Labor Economics 157 (Natl. Bur. of Econ. Research 1962).

creasing wages above the competitive level, creates excess demand for the jobs in which these wages are paid. If the union controls the jobs, it will have to allocate them somehow. It could auction off vacancies as they occur or permit members to sell their union membership, or it could adopt nonprice criteria, such as nepotism or, as unions once did, membership in the white race. The members of the union took a part of their monopoly profits in the form of freedom from a type of association they found distasteful.[3]

Thus government policy, which is responsible for profit controls on monopolists and for strong labor unions, may increase discrimination above the level that would exist in an unregulated market.[4] The effect is even greater when the government enacts and enforces laws that require discrimination, as was long the practice in the southern states. Although such laws would not be enacted unless there was a strong antipathy in the community to associating with blacks, it does not follow that they add nothing to private feeling. Some whites may have relatively little taste for discrimination and might therefore not be willing to bear the expense of maintaining separate public rest rooms, schools, and other facilities in their community.

§27.2 School Segregation

In *Brown v. Board of Education*,[1] the Supreme Court invalidated state laws requiring or permitting racial segregation of public schools. The Court held that segregated education was inherently unequal because it instilled a sense of inferiority in black children. The analysis in the preceding section suggests an economic as distinct from a psychological basis for rejecting the notion of separate but equal. Segregation reduces the opportunities for valuable associations between races and these associations would be especially valuable to the blacks because of the dominant position of the whites in the society. The Court had recognized this point in *Sweatt v. Painter*,[2] which held that blacks could not be ex-

---

3. An alternative explanation suggested earlier is that race is an inexpensive method of rationing access and thereby increasing the net gains from monopolizing the labor supply. See §11.7 *supra*. Either explanation has the same consequences for the welfare of the excluded blacks.

4. These are not the only government policies that have an adverse effect on racial minorities. Another example is the minimum wage. See §11.6 *supra*; Harold Demsetz, Minorities in the Market Place, 43 N.C.L. Rev. 271 (1965). Does the analysis in this section suggest an economic reason why the disemployment effects of the minimum wage might be concentrated on the members of a minority that is discriminated against rather than members of the majority?

§27.2 1. 347 U.S. 483 (1954).

2. 339 U.S. 629 (1950).

cluded from state law schools. The Court pointed out that black students
in a segregated law school would have no opportunity to develop valuable professional contacts with the students most likely to occupy important positions in the bench and bar after graduation. It rejected the
argument that this disadvantage was offset by the disadvantage to white
students of being barred from association with black law students, noting
that the blacks' weak position in the profession made such associations
less valuable to white students.

If our earlier analysis is correct, the laws invalidated in *Brown* that
forbade local school districts to operate integrated schools made discrimination greater than it would have been in the absence of such laws —
but perhaps not much greater. While the federal courts, the Department
of Justice, and other agencies were eventually able to compel the southern states to stop enforcing their segregation laws, many whites were
willing to pay the additional costs necessary to perpetuate school segregation. They sent their children to segregated private schools or moved
to school districts containing few black residents. The Supreme Court
had made discrimination more costly but since the white population
valued school discrimination highly, the effect of the Court's action on
the amount of discrimination was for many years small (it may still be
small). Further, since the white population controlled the public finance
of the states, it could deflect the force of the Court's action, in part at
least, by reducing appropriations for public education and by subsidizing
private education through tuition grants and tax credits. These measures
made it cheaper for parents to shift their children to segregated private
schools.

The Court could have exploited the value that the whites attached
to school segregation by requiring, as a condition of maintaining segregated schools, that the southern states devote much larger sums to the
education of blacks than had been their practice. Blacks conceivably
might have been better off under such an arrangement even if the *Brown*
decision had received prompt and wholehearted compliance. Imagine
a community composed of 200 blacks and 800 whites, where the average
income of the blacks is $5,000 and of the whites $10,000. Assume that
the elimination of segregated education would increase the pecuniary
and nonpecuniary income of the blacks by an average of $2,000 (ignore
the lag between changed educational conditions and better employment). The black community would therefore gain $400,000 from deseg-
regation. But suppose the whites in the community would be willing
to pay an average of $1,000 apiece not to integrate the schools. They
would therefore be willing to spend $800,000 on better education for
the blacks as the price of continued segregation, and let us assume
that every dollar so spent would benefit blacks by one dollar. Then
this expenditure would increase the blacks' incomes by $400,000 more
than integration would increase it.

The *Brown* decision has been criticized on the ground that it denied freedom of association to whites at the same time that it promoted freedom of association of blacks, and that there is no neutral principle by which to choose between the associational preference of whites and blacks.[3] But economic analysis suggests an important distinction: Because blacks are an economic minority, the costs to them of the whites' prejudice are proportionately much greater than the costs to the whites.

§27.3   The Requirement of State Action

The Fourteenth Amendment, which was enacted primarily for the benefit of racial minorities, provides that no *state* shall deny anyone the equal protection of its laws or deprive anyone of life, liberty, or property without due process of law. Economic analysis can help clarify the issues involved in distinguishing state from private action.

Three levels of state involvement in discrimination can be distinguished: a law or other official action that orders discrimination; discrimination by a public enterprise; state involvement in private enterprises that practice discrimination but not in the decision of the enterprise to discriminate. Both the first and second levels of state involvement were involved in the *Brown* case but they were not distinguished.

The first aspect of the Court's decision is the invalidation of laws requiring all public schools in a state to be segregated. Such laws may be presumed to enact the prejudices of the more prejudiced half of the population and thus to produce greater discrimination than if the decision to segregate were left to individual public school districts. The second aspect of the decision is the invalidation of state laws permitting local school districts to segregate at their option. When the decision to segregate is left to each local school district, it is not so obvious that the result will be a different amount of discrimination from what there would be if all education were private; but probably there will be more. A public school system is a nontransferable monopoly (private education, because it costs the consumer as distinct from the taxpayer more than public education, is not a good enough substitute for the latter to deprive a public school district of all its monopoly power), and we saw earlier that nontransferable monopolies may be expected to discriminate more, on average, than competitive firms or freely transferable monopolies. Since most governmental services are in the nature of nontransferable monopolies, this point has general application to public agencies.

3. Herbert Wechsler, Toward Neutral Principles of Constitutional Law, 73 Harv. L. Rev. 1 (1959).

The analysis is different when the decision to discriminate is made by a private individual or firm, even though the state is involved to some extent in the private activity. The question should be whether the state's involvement makes discrimination more likely. Where that involvement takes the form of public utility or common carrier regulation, then, as we saw earlier, the likelihood that the firm will discriminate is greater, and so its discrimination could be viewed as state action under the Fourteenth Amendment. But where the state's involvement does not make discrimination more likely, there is no basis for attributing the decision to discriminate to the state. The state maintains an extensive system of land title recordation and is otherwise deeply involved in the regulation of land use, but the state's involvement does not increase the probability that a white homeowner will refuse to sell his house to a black buyer because of distaste for association with blacks.

The foregoing analysis suggests not a narrower but a different definition of state action from what the courts have employed. It would support a prohibition under the Fourteenth Amendment of racial discrimination by trade unions, for the governmental policies that have fostered the growth of monopolistic unions have thereby increased the likelihood that they would practice racial discrimination. It would not forbid discrimination by the private concessionaire in a public office building[1] unless the public authority had encouraged the concessionaire to discriminate.

An interesting question is presented when the state involvement takes the form of legal enforcement of a private decision to discriminate. May racial covenants be enforced?[2] May the city of Macon as trustee of the park donated by Senator Bacon comply with the racial condition in the gift?[3] Does the equal protection clause forbid recourse to civil and criminal trespass remedies by shopkeepers who do not want black customers? It is hard to believe that without property rights there would be less discrimination. There might be more, especially in communities where the taste for discrimination was widespread, since without legally protected property rights more economic activity would be directed either by political decision or by threat of violence.

It is true but trivial that if the state enforced all private decisions except those to discriminate, the cost of discrimination would be higher and the incidence lower. A more interesting point is that in the restrictive covenant and charitable gift cases the effect of enforcing a racial condition would be to create more discrimination than the members of society today want. To return to the international trade analogy, it is a little as if nations had agreed in the nineteenth century that they would never

§27.3   1. But see Burton v. Wilmington Parking Authority, 365 U.S. 715 (1961).
2. Shelley v. Kraemer, 334 U.S. 1 (1948).
3. See Evans v. Newton, 382 U.S. 296 (1966); §18.2 supra.

permit international trade to be conducted other than in sailing ships. This is an application of the broader concern discussed in Chapter 18 that a perpetual condition in a deed or gift may cause resources to be employed inefficiently if an unforeseen contingency, in this case a decline in the taste for discrimination, materializes. But it is fortuitous whether the result of a perpetual condition is more discrimination than contemporaries want or less. If there were a secular increase rather than decline in racial discrimination, enforcing racially motivated deed or gift restrictions (such as a provision in a foundation charter declaring the purpose of the foundation to be to promote racial integration) might produce less discrimination than contemporaries wanted.

§27.4 Antidiscrimination Laws

Federal laws forbidding private discrimination in the sale and rental of real estate, in employment, and in restaurants, hotels, and other places of public accommodation are sought to be justified first as necessary to eliminate the effects of centuries of discriminatory legislation and second as promoting interstate commerce. The second justification strikes many people as contrived, yet makes economic sense. Discrimination reduces transactions between blacks and whites and many of the transactions that are prevented would be in interstate commerce, even narrowly defined. The first justification is plausible but indefinite. *Any* deprivation from which black people suffer today could be due in part to past discrimination resulting from discriminatory laws or other governmental policies. If black children on average perform less well than whites even in northern schools, it may be due to the fact that the return to education for black people has traditionally been low because of particularly severe employment discrimination against educated blacks, which may have been influenced by the discriminatory governmental policies of the southern states from which many northern blacks originated. This kind of argument provides the strongest justification for reverse discrimination, which is discussed in the next section of this chapter.

Economic analysis helps explain the variance in compliance with antidiscrimination laws. If the interracial associations brought about by such a law are slight, the cost of association even to prejudiced people will be low and they will not be willing to incur heavy costs in the form of punishment for, or legal expenses of, resisting compliance in order to indulge their taste. It is not surprising that there has been general compliance with laws forbidding people to refuse on racial grounds to sell real estate, although few resources have been allocated to enforcing these laws. Unless the seller plans to stay in the neighborhood, his association with a black purchaser is limited to negotiating the sale (and a broker does that anyway). Similarly, the association between a hotel owner and staff on the one hand and the guests of the hotel on the other are impersonal except where the establishment is very small — and for this reason small establishments were exempted from the public accommodations law — so again it is not surprising that widespread compliance was rapidly and easily achieved. School integration is different. Not only is the association among school children intimate and prolonged but to the extent that black children, for whatever reason, on average perform worse in school than white children, integration may involve costs to whites over and above the nonpecuniary costs imposed by an undesired association.

Laws forbidding discrimination in employment involve interesting questions of proof, of statutory purpose, of remedy, and of efficacy. A firm may have no black employees, even if it is located in an area with a large black population, for reasons unrelated to discrimination by either the management of the firm or the white workers. There may be no blacks with the requisite training or aptitude, or blacks may not like the type of work, or they may simply be unaware of job openings at the firm. If an employer is forced to hire unqualified blacks, pay them a premium to induce them to do a type of work that they do not like, or advertise in the black community openings for jobs in which very few blacks are interested, the firm incurs costs greater than the benefits to the blacks who are hired. The unqualified black employee imposes productivity losses that he does not recoup in higher wages. The premium paid to the black employee who does not like to work in this type of job is a cost to the firm but not a benefit to the black employee; it just offsets the nonpecuniary cost of the job to him. Advertising job openings in the black community may not confer a benefit commensurate with its costs if the advertising fails to generate a significant flow of qualified applicants. Since most of the additional costs probably will be passed on to the firm's customers, these methods of improving the welfare of black people are regressive as well as inefficient.

Laws forbidding job discrimination are costly even when they are applied to employers who in fact discriminate. The employer may have to pay a higher wage to those white workers who have both a taste for discrimination and attractive alternative employment opportunities in firms that do not have black employees. If they lack such opportunities, the elimination of discrimination may impose no pecuniary costs — by hypothesis the workers have no choice but to accept association with blacks — but it will impose nonpecuniary costs in the form of an association distasteful to the whites. And the costs are unlikely to be offset by the gains of black workers for whom jobs in the firm are superior to their alternative job opportunities or by the economic advantages that increased trading with blacks brings to the firm and hence to its customers; if there were such offsetting gains, the blacks would probably have been hired without legal pressure (why?).

Regarding the appropriate remedy in a job discrimination case in which a violation has been found, economic analysis suggests that the employer should be required to pay the damages of any person he has discriminated against (perhaps doubled or trebled to facilitate enforcement in cases where damages are small). This will both compensate and deter and seems preferable to an injunctive remedy requiring the employer to hire a specified number or percentage of blacks. The injunction will force him to lay off white workers or, what amounts to the same thing, to favor black over white job applicants until the quota fixed in the decree is attained. By imposing costs on white employees who may be untainted by discrimination in order to improve the condition of black workers, such an injunction operates as a capricious and regressive tax on the white working class.[1]

The analysis is more complicated if the employees share responsibility with the employer for the discrimination. The employees may have barred blacks from their union. Or the employer may have discriminated only because of his workers' taste for discrimination — he himself being free from it. (Indeed, from an economic standpoint, who is more likely to harbor discriminatory feelings — the white employer or the white employee? What is the appropriate remedy in a case in which employee responsibility for the discrimination is proved?)

Suppose an employer pays white workers more than black workers in the same job classification. Should the measure of damages be the difference between the two wage rates? What if any weight should be given to the possibility that if the employer had had to pay the same wages to whites and blacks, he would have employed fewer workers of both races? Should the employer be allowed to defend by showing that part of the wage difference is a return to the white workers' greater investment in education? If only a few employers in a labor market discriminate, can it be argued that no difference in wages between black and white workers could be due to discrimination, whatever the employer's taste?

Thus far we have assumed that whatever their other effects, laws forbidding discrimination (however defined) will improve the net welfare of the victims of discrimination. But this need not always be true. For example, a study of state fair employment laws found that, while the laws indeed increased the demand for black workers, the provisions of the laws requiring that blacks be paid as much as whites caused disemployment of blacks, and the two effects cancelled each other out.[2]

§27.4 1. Under what conditions might the tax be minimal and even zero?
2. See William M. Landes, The Economics of Fair Employment Laws, 76 J. Pol. Econ. 507 (1968).

§27.5 Reverse Discrimination

It is often urged that blacks should be given preferential treatment —
for example, that law schools should set lower admission standards for
blacks than for whites even if the admission criteria provide unbiased
estimates of black academic performance. Is such reverse discrimination
a fundamentally different animal from the old-fashioned discrimination
against blacks? To answer this question will require us to go behind
the assumption heretofore employed that discrimination is simply a result of taste and inquire more closely into its causes.

Racial discrimination has a number of possible causes. Sheer malevo-
lence and irrationality are factors in many cases. Discrimination is sometimes anticompetitive — this appears to have been a factor in the
internment during World War II of California's Japanese residents —
and sometimes exploitive, as in slavery; race enters as a convenient
factor identifying the members of the competing or exploited group.
A neglected factor, however, is the costs of information.[1] To the extent
that race or some attribute similarly difficult to conceal (sex, accent,
etc.) is positively correlated with the possession of undesired characteristics, or negatively correlated with desired characteristics, it is rational
for people to use the attribute as a proxy for the underlying characteristic
with which it is correlated. If experience has taught me (perhaps
incorrectly)[2] that most Mycenaeans have a strong garlic breath, I can
economize on information costs by declining to join a club that accepts
Mycenaeans as members. Although I might thereby be forgoing valuable
associations with Mycenaeans who do not have a strong garlic breath,
this opportunity cost may be smaller than the information cost that
more extensive sampling of Mycenaeans would entail. Discrimination
so motivated has the same basic character (its distributive effects may
of course be different) as a decision to stop buying Brand X toothpaste
because of an unhappy experience with a previous purchase of it, albeit
the next experience with the brand might have been better.

The fact that some racial discrimination is efficient does not mean
that it is or should be lawful. On utilitarian grounds it may well be
unjust, even if efficient (explain). The information-costs theory of racism
does suggest, however, that the balancing approach sometimes used
in constitutional cases (see §28.2 *infra*) might, if honestly followed in
racial cases, result in upholding some racial discrimination on efficiency

---

§27.5 1. On the information-costs theory of discrimination see, e.g., Edmund S.
Phelps, The Statistical Theory of Racism and Sexism, 62 Am. Econ. Rev. 659 (1972).
    2. Because of the difficulty of establishing property rights in information, people may
have inadequate incentives to investigate even the average characteristics of the groups
with which they deal. What are the policy implications of this proposition if accepted?

grounds (depending, however, on the weight placed on the distributive costs of discrimination).

An alternative to balancing is to argue that what is forbidden by the Fourteenth Amendment and other antidiscrimination measures is precisely the use of race as a proxy for underlying personal characteristics. This principle has the many appealing characteristics of a simple rule (see §20.3 *supra*), compared with a rule merely forbidding unreasonable discrimination. But a possible corollary of the suggested principle is that reverse discrimination is unconstitutional, because it is based on the use of race as a proxy for underlying personal characteristics. The rationale for preferential admissions of blacks to law school is not that blackness *per se* is a desirable characteristic but that it is a proxy for characteristics relevant to the educational process or to performance in the legal profession — characteristics such as a background of deprivation, empathy for the disadvantaged, etc. Blackness is used as the criterion for preference in order to economize on search costs. The result, it can be argued, is to confer capricious benefits on middle class blacks in much the same way that discrimination against blacks based on the characteristics of many poor blacks has imposed capricious burdens on the middle class blacks who lack these characteristics.

Suggested Readings

1. Gary S. Becker, The Economics of Discrimination (2d ed. 1971).
2. Discrimination in Labor Markets (Orley Ashenfelter & Albert Rees eds. 1974).
3. Richard A. Posner, The Economics of Justice, chs. 12-14 (1981).
4. Thomas Sowell, Civil Rights: Rhetoric or Reality? (1984).

Problems

1. This chapter has suggested a neutral principle for forbidding discrimination. Is it an economic principle? Can one argue that discrimination is inefficient? In economic terms, are the costs of interracial associations, given prejudice, any different from the crop damage caused by the interaction of railroading and farming?

2. Suppose a number of blacks bought homes on land contracts and later defaulted on the contracts. They claim that they should not be held liable for the default because they were forced to pay higher prices than white purchasers of similar property, as a result of discrimination against blacks. The developers reply that the blacks should be grateful that they were willing to sell them such desirable property. What light

can economic analysis shed on the issues in such a litigation? Would the welfare of blacks as a whole be increased or reduced if the developers lost?

3. Can it be argued that racially restrictive covenants might increase efficiency?

4. Suppose that a law school that found that its black graduates had lower lifetime professional earnings than whites because of racial discrimination decided therefore to impose higher admission requirements on blacks than on whites. Could this policy be defended as enhancing efficiency? If so, would that make it a good policy?

5. Black males have a shorter life expectancy than white males. Discuss the allocative and distributive effects of rules forbidding life insurance companies to vary premium rates on the basis of the race of the insured.

6. Compare two forms of reverse discrimination: In one the employer sets a quota for black employees and hires only blacks until the quota is reached; in the other he hires without discrimination but he gives his black employees greater seniority than his white employees, so that when and if economic conditions require layoffs fewer blacks than whites will be laid off. Consider whether it makes a difference whether the employer is public or private, whether there is or is not a union, and whether the policy of granting superseniority to blacks is adopted before or after any whites affected by it are hired. Which combination of attributes produces the most inefficient discrimination, which the least inefficient?

CHAPTER 28

THE MARKETPLACE OF IDEAS AND THE PRIMACY OF POLITICAL OVER ECONOMIC RIGHTS

§28.1   The Economic Basis of Freedom of Speech

Ideas are a useful good produced in enormous quantity in a highly competitive market. The marketplace of ideas of which Holmes wrote is a fact, not merely a figure of speech.[1] This marketplace determines the "truth" of ideas, other than of purely deductive propositions such as the Pythagorean theorem. When we say that an idea (the earth revolves around the sun) is correct, we mean that all or most of the knowledgeable consumers have accepted ("bought") it. Even in science — the traditional domain of objective validity — ideas are discarded not because they are demonstrated to be false but because competing ideas give better answers to the questions with which the scientists of the day are most concerned.[2]

If competition among ideas is the method by which truth is established, the suppression of an idea on the ground that it is false is irrational, barring some market failure. An idea is false only if rejected in the marketplace, and if it is rejected, there is no occasion to suppress it. To declare an idea true when the competing ideas have been suppressed would be like declaring a brand of beer to be the most popular brand when the sale of the other brands had been suppressed.

But this does not explain why constitutional protection has been thought necessary for this particular marketplace and not for others. Two possible explanations are congenial to economic thinking. The first is that regulation of the marketplace of ideas creates a danger of subvert-

---

§28.1   1. Abrams v. United States, 250 U.S. 616, 630 (1919) (dissenting opinion).
2. See Thomas S. Kuhn, The Structure of Scientific Revolutions (2d ed. 1970).

ing the democratic process, thus conducing to that most dangerous of monopolies — the monopoly of government power (see §24.2 *supra*). The second and broader explanation (the first is limited to political speech) emphasizes the fragility of markets in information. For reasons explored early in this book (see §3.2 *supra*), it is not feasible to create property rights in pure ideas. Hence they are likely to be underproduced. The problem is particularly serious if popular ideas are a good substitute in the marketplace — as in fact they are — for valuable but unpopular ideas. Then any costs that government imposes on unpopular ideas may cause massive substitution away from them. Indeed, the conjunction of "valuable" and "unpopular" suggests that there is a class of ideas the benefits of which are almost entirely external. So there is an economic reason to worry about "chilling" the exercise of freedom of expression.

§28.2   The Scope of the Protected Activity: Incitement, Threats, Defamation, Obscenity

Not all statements communicate ideas in a sense to which the concept of marketplace is relevant; and some statements, whether true or false, have another attribute — dangerousness — that may justify public regulation if the market in ideas fails (in the economic sense of market failure) to regulate them. For example, if I say "I am going for a walk now," or "I am going to rob a bank," or "I am organizing an armed insurrection," I am not appealing to the marketplace of ideas but merely stating an intention, and my statement may be evidence of an attempt to commit a crime that may have nothing to do with ideas, a crime such as robbery. To punish the attempt does not impede the marketplace in ideas. Statements of intention are not intended to compete with other views, as a statement that the world is flat is intended to compete with other views; and there is no risk of underproduction, because there is no investment in producing the idea behind the statement (cf. §4.6 *supra*).

Now suppose I say, "armed insurrection tomorrow would be a good thing," or (if I am a producer of widgets) "the industry would be better off if the price of widgets were 10 percent higher," or "I intend to vote for X." These statements express genuine ideas, because they make a bid to displace competing ideas in the marketplace of ideas. The problem is that the first two may also be invitations to commit illegal acts (treason and price fixing, respectively). As invitations, they would seem punishable on the same principle that makes attempts and conspiracies punishable. But punishment will have the collateral effect of suppressing an idea.

An economic formula to deal with these mixed cases of idea and incitement was proposed by Judge Learned Hand (of course) in *United States v. Dennis.*[1] The courts, he wrote, must in each case "ask whether the gravity of the 'evil' [i.e., if the instigation succeeds], discounted by its improbability, justifies such invasion of free speech as is necessary to avoid the danger."[2] This is equivalent to Hand's negligence formula $(B < PL)$ if B is defined as the cost of the reduction in the stock of ideas as a result of the government's action, P as the probability that the crimes urged by the speaker will come to pass, and L as the social cost if they do come to pass. If B is less than PL, it is efficient for the government to take steps against the speaker. Query: Should there also be a discount for remoteness in the sense of futurity as distinct from unlikelihood, by analogy to discounting future lost earnings to present value in personal-injury cases (see §6.11 *supra*)?

The application of the *Dennis* formula depends on just what steps the government means to take. If it proposes to punish the speaker criminally, B will be substantial and will therefore require a substantial PL to offset it. But if the government just proposes to monitor the speaker's activity, so that it can take action if and when the danger of a criminal violation becomes imminent, B will be less (because the deterrence of free speech will be less), and therefore a lesser PL than in the first case will suffice to outweigh it and justify the government's action.

The formula, impossible though it is to quantify, is helpful in explaining why, for example, the advocacy of very great evils — genocide or revolution or whatever — is more likely to be tolerated than urging a lynching, which is a lesser evil, or even committing the trivial "evil" created by a blaring soundtruck. If the circumstances make the probability that genocidal advocacy will succeed remote, the discounted cost of the utterance may be smaller than that of a threat to lynch. In the case of the soundtruck, while the harms caused by its blare (L in the formula) are small, so is the cost in forgone benefits, since the speaker can propagate his message by less offensive means. The soundtruck case, like other cases involving restrictions on the time, place, and manner, rather than the substance, of the speech, is analytically similar to our case of the government's merely investigating, rather than punishing, the speaker. Notice that both the soundtruck and the incitement to crime impose external costs, a traditional rationale of regulation.

The *Dennis* formula may seem paternalistic and therefore not truly efficient. Suppose a group is trying to persuade people that a violent revolution would make them better off, and the circumstances make the probability of success sufficiently high to trigger the test even though no *immediate* revolutionary action is being urged. Since there is time

---

§28.2   1. 183 F.2d 201 (2d Cir. 1950), *aff'd,* 341 U.S. 494 (1951).
2. Id. at 212. He meant "discounted by its probability."

for competing groups to persuade the people that a revolution would not make them better off, why interfere with the market in ideas? One answer is that, given the interval for counterpersuasion, P is really quite small, so that the formula would not justify repression. The case for repression is stronger where, as in the usual incitement case, the interval between speech and action is too short to permit competing views to be presented; in such a case punishing speech is like punishing monopoly — there is a similar kind of market failure. In the soundtruck case, too, the market in ideas cannot be relied upon to protect the victims of the harm (this is a general characteristic of time, place, and manner restrictions), because, as we have seen, the costs are external to the marketplace of ideas. A second soundtruck would make matters worse rather than better.

There is a similar economic argument for suppressing the advocacy of violent revolution even in the distant future. Although such advocacy may contain ideas (e.g., that capitalists make greater profits than they should, or that the gap between rich and poor is widening), it is also an invitation to engage in activities that are contrary to the criminal law. The invitation might be attractive even if the marketplace of ideas convincingly showed up the falsity of the advocate's ideas. Suppose the speaker urges the poor to rise up and take away the money of the rich because the rich are exploiting them. Even if counteradvocacy shows convincingly that the rich are not exploiting the poor, it is still the case that the poor might decide to rise up and despoil the rich, as invited to do by the speaker. To the extent that advocacy depends on the truth of certain ideas, the marketplace of ideas may weaken the advocacy by exposing the falsity of those ideas, but that merely reduces P in our free speech Hand formula — not necessarily to zero.

The discussion has thus far assumed that there is a sharp line between a statement of intention and an idea. But consider the class of statements of intention known as threats. I say that I will blow your head off if you don't hand over your wallet. The threat communicates genuine information about my intentions — but only in a sense; for it is in the nature of most threats that the threatener doesn't want to carry out the threat except to maintain credibility. Therefore if threats are effectively suppressed, the substantive evils threatened will (usually) be suppressed as well. Also, the investment in making the threat has no social product; so we want to discourage, not protect, it. But now take the case where I threaten to do something completely lawful, like turn you over to the police, unless you pay me for my silence. Why should a statement of intention to do a lawful act be punishable? But again the key is that the intention is conditional. I don't want to turn you in; I want your money. So if blackmail is unlawful (see §22.2 *supra*), solicitations used in committing blackmail should also be unlawful. It is a detail whether the solicitation takes the form of a carrot (I offer you my silence for money) or a stick (if you don't pay me, I'll turn you in).

Damaging statements about individuals are an important part of the marketplace of ideas and can in principle be validated in the same way as other ideas — by competition. But they are special in several respects (fit them into Hand's free speech formula). They inflict costs that are both concentrated (why is that relevant?) and at least crudely measurable; the falsity of the defamation may be readily demonstrable, implying that a legal determination of truth may be a pretty good substitute for market determination; and (a related point) competition may not be an effective remedy — how do I compete with *Time* magazine if it libels me? Perhaps, therefore, producers and sellers of ideas, as of other goods, should be liable for injuries to reputations. But in an effort to prevent defamation suits from unduly curtailing freedom of speech and (especially) of the press too much, the Supreme Court has laid down strict limitations beyond which the states may not go without violating the First Amendment in giving redress against defamation. In particular, they may not allow a public figure (usually though not always a politician or public official) to recover damages without showing that the defendant either knew the defamation was false or was reckless in failing to determine whether it was false. People who are not public figures have somewhat broader rights of suit. The distinction makes economic sense. A public figure has a better chance of getting the media to carry his reply to the defamer than a nonpublic figure has, and a reply is less costly than a defamation suit to the values of the First Amendment, as it preserves the marketplace of ideas without regulation. Also, information about public figures has on average greater social value than information about private ones. (Why? And why is this relevant?)

The requirement of showing actual knowledge of (or reckless indifference to) the falsity of the defamation is defensible on the not implausible assumption that the publication of criticisms of public figures has benefits not fully captured by the publisher. The effect of the requirement is to excuse the injurer (the publisher) from liability for negligence, and we have seen other cases where this was done because the defendant had conferred an external benefit by the negligent act (see, e.g., §6.4 *supra*). If a reporter gets a scoop, his newspaper will capture in higher sales revenues only a part of the value that the public attaches to the news, because the item will be carried in all competing papers with only a slight time lag. Therefore if the reporter and the newspaper that employs him are faced with the prospect of large damages, they may be reluctant to publish the item even though the total social benefits (but not their private benefits), as measured by the willingness of all newspaper readers to pay to read the item, may exceed those damages. One way of encouraging the newspaper to publish the item is to reduce the costs of publication; and this is done by making it unnecessary for the newspaper to conduct as thorough an investigation of the truth of the item as it would have to do if it were strictly liable or liable for negligence in publishing a false defamation.

An objection to this approach is that it forces the victims of defamation to subsidize the production of ideas. This might not be so bad if it were easy to ensure against the consequences of being defamed; then the incidence of the subsidy would be dispersed throughout the entire insurance pool. The present form of the subsidy has the curious effect of discouraging people from becoming public figures. An alternative approach would be to subsidize the media directly but allow the victims of defamation to retain their full common law rights. Another possible approach would be to recognize more extensive property rights in news. The *Associated Press* decision,[3] which held that a news service could enjoin the unauthorized publication of its dispatches by a rival service, would be a helpful precedent in this regard had it not been eroded by later decisions.[4]

In the cases both of dangerous speech and of defamation (and even more clearly in soundtruck and other noise cases), there is a harmful externality, which furnishes a conventional economic argument for regulation: The speaker incites his listeners to hurt others or the newspaper titillates its readers by accusing someone of scandalous behavior. Pornography, too, creates an externality — when it is publicly displayed to an unwilling audience, as it is on theater marquees in London. Suppressing the public display of pornography eliminates the nuisance at a minimal cost, measured by the reduction in the effectiveness of advertising pornography by nonpornographic means. This is a good illustration of time, place, and manner restrictions on free expression, which, as noted earlier, are treated more permissively than outright suppression.

There is a further point to bear in mind: Suppression not only reduces the audience by more than does a restriction on the time, place, or manner of display, but also reduces the incentive to create the work of art or literature in the first place. The marketplace of ideas has, in other words, both a creative and a communicative dimension. This should be evident from our much earlier discussions of patents and copyrights (see §§3.2, 10.2, 13.7 *supra*); patent and copyright protection increases the incentive to create ideas but reduces the rapidity of their dissemination (why?). If government regulates the places where sexually explicit art can be seen, this reduces the audience for and hence the incentive to create the art in the first place, but only to a minor degree (depending on the precise nature of the regulation). If it punishes as

---

3. International News Service v. Associated Press, 248 U.S. 215 (1918).
4. See Edmund W. Kitch & Harvey S. Perlman, Legal Regulation of the Competitive Process 34-37 (2d ed. 1977).

a criminal anyone who creates such art, then it enormously reduces the incentive to create it.

This discussion implies that if obscenity is defined as that form of sexually explicit depiction or narration that is so offensive as to be punishable, a lesser degree of offensiveness would justify time, place, or manner restrictions, such as placing sexually explicit books in special rooms of libraries, with access by children restricted; or banning sexually explicit movies from television on the theory that parents can't effectively prevent their children from watching anything that is shown on television. In *Dennis* terms, L is lower but so is B. Notice the analogy to the economic argument mentioned earlier for allowing the government to investigate speech not dangerous enough to be punishable.

All this leaves unexplained, however, the prohibition against selling pornography to adults, in circumstances where it is unlikely to be displayed to people who would be offended by it. Is this not a typical victimless crime? But putting aside all questions of the possible effects of pornography on the family or on sex crimes, would it not be basis enough for prohibition that people who were not consumers of pornography were greatly distressed to know that it was available for purchase in their community? Or is this not a genuine externality?

Whether it is or is not, the law seems on firm economic ground in giving less protection to sexually explicit art and literature than to political and scientific ideas. Art and literature that is sexually explicit in the extreme form that the legal concept of obscenity denotes has good substitutes: slightly less explicit art and literature. The social costs of suppression are therefore lower than in the case of political and scientific ideas: A false idea is not a good substitute for a true idea that is suppressed.

§28.3   The Regulation of Broadcasting

One of the exceptions to freedom of speech deserves special attention because it is an explicit application of economic theory. This is the principle, illustrated by the Supreme Court's *Red Lion* decision,[1] that the government may regulate the content of broadcasting because of the physical limitations of the electromagnetic spectrum. The regulation is not so intrusive an interference with the marketplace of ideas as punishing the expression of particular ideas would be, but it does reduce the

§28.3   1. Red Lion Broadcasting Co. v. Federal Communications Commission, 395 U.S. 367 (1969). See also National Broadcasting Co. v. United States, 319 U.S. 190, 226 (1943).

broadcaster's freedom to decide what ideas to broadcast and his incentive to air controversial matter (why?). A similar regulation applied to newspapers has been held to violate the First Amendment.[2]

The difference, the Court has reasoned, is that broadcasters, unlike newspaper owners, have monopoly power. Since two broadcasters could not broadcast on the same frequency in the same area without creating intolerable interference, an FCC license to use a particular frequency in a particular area confers a monopoly of that frequency that has no counterpart in other media of expression.

This is economic nonsense. While it is true that only one frequency can be used in the same place at the same time, the result need not be monopoly, since different frequencies are, within a range, perfect substitutes for one another. The Federal Communications Commission generally licenses more than one television station in each market. Most markets have at least three or four stations and a few have nine to eleven. This is invariably more than the number of newspapers in the same market. And these are just over-the-air stations; there are now a large number of independent cable television channels.

The fact that the electromagnetic spectrum is limited certainly does not distinguish it from other resources. The inputs used in the alternative methods of communicating ideas are also limited. The range of frequencies at which electromagnetic waves can be propagated is vast, its use in broadcasting limited only by opportunity costs and by government policy. If other uses of the spectrum, such as mobile communication, were valued less highly, the number of channels available for television broadcasting could be increased substantially. The viewer would also receive more television signals if the FCC adopted a different policy for the allocation of television frequencies. Instead of seeking to promote local stations, the FCC could license only stations that would broadcast to a large regional market. By careful engineering of a system of regional broadcasting the FCC could eliminate the many dead spaces, necessary to prevent interference between stations in adjacent markets, that reduce the number of different signals viewers receive. The scarcity of television channels differs from the scarcity of other natural resources only in the fact that it is to a significant extent the product of deliberate governmental policies.

Newspapers suffer from more acute scarcities that, in conjunction with the pressure of substitute competition, have brought about a degree of local monopoly much greater than in broadcasting. The shrinkage of demand for newspapers, a shrinkage due to the rise of television, has accentuated the natural monopoly conditions of newspaper production; for as we know, these conditions are more important the smaller the demand for the market's product (see §13.1 *supra*). Many of the

2. See Miami Herald Publishing Co. v. Tornillo, 418 U.S. 241 (1974).

costs of a newspaper are fixed: in particular the cost of researching and writing the articles and features and the cost of composing and setting type for them and for the advertisements. The marginal cost — the cost of printing another newspaper — is small. So unless there is a big demand, there is unlikely to be room for more than one newspaper per community.

Suppose a broadcaster did have an effective monopoly of the market in which he operated. What impact on the dissemination of news and opinion might we expect? He might limit the amount of time he broadcasts, and this would reduce the distribution of ideas to the people in the market. But the fairness doctrine is not calculated to increase the broadcaster's output of ideas. On the contrary, it penalizes him for presenting controversial ideas by requiring him to present all sides of a controversy, and it thus induces the substitution of uncontroversial ideas.

Might the monopoly broadcaster distort the news, and suppress opinions he disagrees with, in an effort to convert viewers to his own views? Any broadcaster could do this; the significance of monopoly is that the cost to the broadcaster is less than in a competitive market and the harm to viewers greater. The cost to him is less because his viewers have no good substitutes and because his control of their source of information will make it hard for them to discover that they are being deceived. The cost to them is greater than in the competitive case because there the partiality of one broadcaster would not deny them access to other views. Two replies, both incomplete, are possible. The first is that the monopoly broadcaster's profits will be less if he intrudes his personal preferences into the decision of what to broadcast. The second is that the management of a large publicly held corporation will have difficulty finding issues on which a partisan stand would not alienate large numbers of shareholders.[3]

Another possibility is that the monopoly broadcaster will alter the mixture of broadcast ideas merely as a by-product of trying to maximize his pecuniary income. For we know from Chapter 9 that a monopolist may produce a different quality of good from a competitive firm (see §9.3 *supra*). But the monopoly broadcaster might easily produce a higher rather than lower quality of broadcast output. Suppose there are two television stations in a given market, each owned by a different firm, each competing vigorously with the other. Probably each will try to attract as large an audience as possible in order to maximize advertising revenue. Hence the stations can be expected to broadcast pretty similar stuff, just as the two major parties in a two-party political system are usually both centrist. A single owner of both stations might, however, carry sharply different fare on the two stations in order to maximize the stations' total audience.

3. When can a *competitive* broadcaster indulge his personal preferences in programming?

§28.4 False Advertising and the Relationship Between Political and Economic Rights

A discussion of one other exception to the right of free speech will help clarify a fundamental puzzle of constitutional law and social thought generally. The First Amendment has been held not to forbid the government to regulate the communication of information and ideas in connection with the sale of goods or services. If the seller of a drug advertises that it can cure arthritis, the Federal Trade Commission can enjoin the claim if it is shown to be probably false. If the same claim were made in a book, it would be clear that the First Amendment forbade the commission to enjoin it, at least if the author were not the seller of the drug.[1] The different treatment of the two cases is curious. Since the claims are identical, the difference cannot be that advertising claims are either obviously true or obviously false; clearly, they often are neither. Nor can the presence of a commercial motive in one case but not in the other be the distinguishing factor. The author of a book on health will have a strong incentive to make false claims if he believes they will increase his income from the book, unless he thinks exposure would harm him more — but the risk of exposure is the same for the seller of the drug. Political candidates have an incentive to make false claims if they think such claims will bring them closer to power, and so it is with professors and academic reputation.

Although commercial speech may be less important than political speech because the latter but not the former is an essential bulwark against the potentially very great social costs of a monopoly of political power, this cannot explain the different treatment of noncommercial nonpolitical speech (chiefly artistic expression), which is accorded almost complete protection under the First Amendment,[2] from that of commercial speech. The difference is related to a larger dichotomy, between the protection of competition in goods and the protection of competition in ideas, that is characteristic of modern thinking.[3] The classical liberals believed in both economic and intellectual freedom. The modern Supreme Court's preference for the latter freedom may reflect the special importance of political rights to lawyers, judges, and constitutional scholars — people with a strong interest (in both senses of the word) in the public and political arenas of action. Economic rights are as important to a larger, if less articulate, part of the population. And we know that

§28.4   1. Cf. Rodale Press, Inc. v. Federal Trade Commission, 407 F.2d 1252 (D.C. Cir. 1968).

2. With the exception of obscenity.

3. See Aaron Director, The Parity of the Economic Market Place, 7 J. Law & Econ. 1 (1964); Ronald H. Coase, The Market for Goods and the Market for Ideas, 64 Am. Econ. Rev. Papers & Proceedings 384 (1974); Ronald H. Coase, Advertising and Free Speech, 6 J. Leg. Stud. 1 (1977).

the government frequently infringes these rights. Legislation may limit choice of occupation, transfer wealth from consumers to shareholders, and prevent people from obtaining services that they want and for which they are willing to pay.

The Supreme Court has begun to close the gap between the treatment of commercial and noncommercial speech under the First Amendment, notably in its decision invalidating a statute that forbade druggists to advertise the prices they charge for prescription drugs.[4] The Court thought the restriction unreasonable and also especially onerous to the poor. The decision has opened up new vistas of constitutional law. Now every false advertising case before the Federal Trade Commission, like every defamation case, raises a potential First Amendment question,[5] although one apt to be resolved in the Commission's favor.

But have we overlooked a fundamental difference between free speech and free trade — that the former is necessary to prevent what we noted earlier was the most dangerous form of monopoly and the latter is not? Perhaps, though, economic and political freedom are not so neatly separable. Political dissent requires financial resources. In a society in which government controlled all economic activity — in which paper was rationed, printing was licensed, and the state, directly or indirectly, was the principal employer — it would be extremely difficult to organize and finance political activity in opposition to the government. In the heyday of Senator Joseph McCarthy, people believed to be sympathetic to communism were barred from government employment, even in nonsensitive jobs. These people did not starve. They found jobs in the private sector and today some of them are again active in politics. The costs of dissent would have been greater had the government been the only employer so that the consequences of holding unpopular views might be denial of all opportunity to obtain a livelihood.

Political and economic rights converge in another sense. The trend in constitutional adjudication is toward recognition of the special claims to constitutional protection of groups other than the traditional racial, religious, and political minorities, notably poor people and women. Their interests, however, are frequently identical to the broader public interest in economic liberty. The invalidation of restrictions on women's occupational choices would promote efficiency as well as women's rights. The abrogation of laws restricting economic freedom would often benefit the poor more than other groups.[6]

4. Virginia State Bd. of Pharmacy v. Virginia Citizens Consumer Council, 425 U.S. 748 (1976). For evidence that such statutes raise prices, see Lee Benham, The Effect of Advertising on the Price of Eyeglasses, 15 J. Law & Econ. 337 (1972). For subsequent freedom of commercial speech cases, see Bolger v. Youngs Drug Products Corp., 463 U.S. 60 (1983), and decisions cited there.

5. As in Encyclopaedia Britannica, Inc. v. FTC, 605 F.2d 964, 972-973 (7th Cir. 1979).

6. There is still an argument for regulating false advertising of goods and services more stringently than false political or pernicious cultural expression: The expected error costs of regulation are lower.

Suggested Readings

1. Ronald H. Coase, The Market for Goods and the Market for Ideas, 64 Am. Econ. Rev. Papers & Proceedings 384 (1974).
2. ———, Advertising and Free Speech, 6 J. Leg. Stud. 1 (1977).
3. Aaron Director, The Parity of the Economic Market Place, 7 J. Law & Econ. 1 (1964).
4. Bruce M. Owen, Economics and Freedom of Expression: Media Structure and the First Amendment (1975).

Problems

1. If the economic analysis of freedom of speech were accepted, would blackmail be a protected activity?
2. Blockbusting is the practice by which real estate brokers allegedly attempt to frighten white homeowners into selling their homes at distress prices, by telling them that the neighborhood is becoming black. Should the practice be protected by the First Amendment? Should it make a difference whether the information that the broker tells the homeowner is true?
3. Many courts have held that a funeral parlor in a residential neighborhood is a nuisance. See Comment, 20 Syracuse L. Rev. 45 (1968). Is this an appropriate application (or extension) of the economic theory of nuisance (see §3.6 *supra*)? Suppose it could be shown that the introduction of a pornographic bookstore in a community reduced property values. Should the bookstore be deemed a nuisance?
4. In terms of the economic analysis presented in this chapter, should a law forbidding all cigarette advertising on radio and television be held to violate the First Amendment? Cf. Capital Broadcasting Co. v. Mitchell, 333 F. Supp. 582 (D.D.C. 1971), *aff'd,* 405 U.S. 1000 (1972).
5. Is there an economic argument for regulating obscenity more restrictively on television or radio than in the print media?

CHAPTER 29

THE FOURTH AMENDMENT[1]

§29.1 The Right of Privacy Revisited

The Fourth Amendment guarantees the right of people to be secure in their persons, homes, papers, and effects against unreasonable searches and seizures, and also forbids general warrants (i.e., warrants that do not describe with particularity the person or thing to be seized or searched). At its narrowest, the amendment might be thought just to protect people from trespasses to person or property by federal (and ever since the amendment has been held applicable to the states under the due process clause of the Fourteenth Amendment, state) officers. This would be protection of privacy in an important although limited sense. If the police come into your house and interrupt what you are doing to search through it, there is an invasion of privacy in much the same sense as an unwanted telephone solicitation is an invasion of privacy, even if the police do not obtain any information about you. If the police tap your phone, there is an invasion of privacy in a quite different sense, one touched on however in Chapter 3 (see §3.2 *supra*). There is no interruption — no breaking in on your solitude or concentration — but there is an invasion of privacy as secrecy. Although Chapter 3 questioned whether privacy in this sense is worth protecting unless trade secrets are involved, there is an argument for at least limited secrecy of telephonic communications. Without it, people will incur costs to switch to more secure but less efficient methods of communication. This is no loss — it is a gain — if the communications are illegal; but if they are legal, there is a loss, and this provides an economic argument for the *Katz* decision,[1] which held that wiretapping was a form of seizure within the meaning of the Fourth Amendment and hence unlawful if

1. See Wayne R. LaFave, Search and Seizure: A Treatise on the Fourth Amendment (1978) (3 vols.).
   §29.1 1. Katz v. United States, 389 U.S. 347 (1967).

unreasonable (which means, as we are about to see, if the costs exceed the benefits).

The fact that searches and seizures (including arrests) impose social costs is not, of course, an argument for banning them. But it is an argument for regulating them, so that the police do not conduct searches when the social costs exceed the social benefits. We can use the Hand Formula to frame the inquiry. A search (or seizure) is reasonable if the cost of the search in impaired privacy (B) is less than the probability (P) that without the search the target of the search cannot be convicted, multiplied by the social loss (L) of not convicting him. P has two components: the probability that the search will turn up something of value to the police (probable cause); and the probability that that something is essential to conviction. The value of the search is therefore less if the same evidence could be obtained without a search (so presumably at a lower B). The more intrusive the search, the more essential the evidence sought must be (P) or the graver the crime being investigated must be (L) in order to justify the higher B imposed.

The courts seem generally if imperfectly aware of these factors. A minimally intrusive search (i.e., low B) — a stop-and-frisk or pat-down — is permissible on a lower P than a search of the home or an arrest. If a search is necessary to prevent the imminent repetition of a crime, which is one of the things that can make L large, a lesser showing of probable cause will suffice. The intrusiveness of the search and the two components of P are routinely considered and the existence of alternatives to searches sometimes. But the gravity of the crime usually is not considered, although logically it should be. In particular most courts seem unaware that a higher L will justify a lower P; the more serious the crime, the less probable cause the police should be required to demonstrate in order to justify a search of a given intrusiveness (B).

§29.2 Remedies

There are three common remedies against violations of the Fourth Amendment. One is preventive: the requirement that where feasible the police get a warrant from a judge or magistrate. Actually the Fourth Amendment does not in so many words require a warrant in any case. It just forbids general warrants. When the amendment was passed it was the practice of custom officers and other government agents to get search warrants in the hope that the warrant would immunize the agent against a suit for trespass by the person whose property was to be searched or seized. Not until the 1940s did the Supreme Court decide that the warrant was a protection for the target of the search. The significance of the warrant is that the determination of probable cause is made, or more realistically reviewed, by the magistrate, who is not part of the police and therefore presumably looks more impartially at the evidence that has induced the police to decide to search.

The Court has come full circle in recent years by holding that if the police executing the warrant rely in good faith on the apparent validity of the warrant, they are immune from being held liable in damages to the target if the warrant was for some reason invalid. The problem with this approach is that the determination of probable cause is made in an ex parte proceeding by a magistrate, rather than by judge and jury in a damage suit, as is done when there is no warrant. The damage remedy is closer to a market approach, the magistrate to a bureaucratic approach, to preventing unlawful searches (cf. §25.2 *supra*).

The most important remedy against unlawful searches is still the exclusionary rule, which provides that evidence and leads to evidence turned up by an unlawful search may not be used in evidence in a criminal trial against the target. The rule is highly controversial — and rightly so. It is a classic example of overdeterrence. The cost to society of doing without the evidence may greatly exceed the social costs of the search. Suppose that B, the cost to the defendant of the search in terms of damage to property or seizure of lawful private communications is $1,000; P, the probability that he could not be convicted without this search, was 1 percent at the time of the search; and L, the social cost (in reduced deterrence and prevention of crime) of not convicting him is $50,000. The search will therefore be illegal under the Hand Formula. But suppose the evidence obtained in the search is essential to conviction. This is not inconsistent with P having been very low at the time of the search. It may have been low because the police had no good reason to think the search would be productive — it was a shot in the dark — rather than because there were alternative methods, less invasive of privacy, of obtaining essential evidence. So even though the social cost of the search is only $1,000, the exclusionary rule will impose a punishment cost of $50,000 on the society. This ignores the cost to the defendant of being punished, but it is right to ignore it since it will have been taken into account in the decision that the social cost of not punishing him is $50,000.

The excessive costs of the exclusionary rule are recognized in some cases. For example, if the police arrest a man illegally, they are not barred from putting him on trial, even though they are barred from using any evidence seized from him as a result of the arrest. The cost of not being able to try him at all would on average be greater than the cost of having to forgo the use of some evidence — although of course when the evidence is essential to conviction, the two costs converge.

The alternative to the exclusionary rule is the tort suit for an unconstitutional search or seizure. Section 1 of the Civil Rights Act of 1871[1] provides a highly effective vehicle for tort suits to enforce federal constitutional rights against state officers, and similar suits can be brought directly under the Fourth Amendment against federal officers. From an economic standpoint the tort suit is preferable to the exclusionary rule, since it allows the sanction to be scaled to the actual social costs of the invasion of privacy caused by the illegal search.

An important issue in such suits is the defendant's immunity, if any, from damage liability. We have already seen one example of the policeman's good faith immunity. Another and more general example would be if he had reasonably but incorrectly believed that the search was legal. Under ordinary tort principles this would not be a defense, on the theory that liability has the salutary effect of giving people an incentive to find out what the law is. But, perhaps, since police officers are unlikely to be able to capture the full social benefit of zealous work, neither should they have to pay the full social costs of being too zealous.[2] Even if they were fully liable, however, their employer could restore the previous incentives by indemnifying them for tort liability, as in fact is commonly done.

Should such an immunity be imputed to the employer, the state or local police department, if it is the defendant? Logically, no, the department being in a much better position that the individual officer to internalize the benefits of vigorous police work. But the question does not arise under existing law, which does not allow the plaintiff to hold the employer liable in a civil rights suit on the basis of respondeat superior. Does *that* make economic sense?

Suggested Readings

1. Richard A. Posner, The Economics of Justice 311-322 (1981).
2. ———, Rethinking the Fourth Amendment, 1981 S. Ct. Rev. 49.
3. ———, Excessive Sanctions for Governmental Misconduct in Criminal Cases, 57 Wash. L. Rev. 635 (1982).

Problem

In a civil rights damage suit for illegal search and seizure, brought by a person who was convicted on the basis of the fruits of the search, should the cost of the criminal punishment to him be part of his legally recoverable damages, or just the time and inconvenience costs and any property damage or personal injury or fear incident to the search itself?

§29.2   1. 42 U.S.C. §1983.
2. See Jerry L. Mashaw, Civil Liability of Government Officers: Property Rights and Official Accountability, 42 Law & Contemp. Prob., Winter 1978, at 8, 26-27.

TABLE OF CASES

643

Author Index

Abrams, Burton A., 440n
Ackerman, Bruce A., 52n, 447n, 450
Alchian, Armen A., 41n, 262n, 401, 616n
Altree, Lillian R., 57n
Anderson, Martin, 440n, 448
Anderson, Terry L., 33n
Andrews, William D., 463n, 467n
Archibald, Robert, 281n
Areeda, Phillip, 287n
Aristotle, 243-44
Arnould, Richard J., 351n
Ashenfelter, Orley, 550n
Averch, Harvey, 325n

Bailey, Martin J., 183n
Baird, Douglas G., 373n
Baker, C. Edwin, 23n, 436n
Baker, Nancy C., 139n
Bangser, Paul M., 357n
Bartel, Ann P., 312n
Barton, David M., 445n
Barton, John H., 123
Barzel, Yoram, 457n
Baumol, William J., 340, 354n, 394n
Baxter, William F., 57n, 75, 426, 495n
Beales, Howard, 100n
Bebchuk, Lucian Arye, 554
Beccaria, Cesare, 20n
Becker, Gary S., 3n, 16n, 20, 138n, 144,
    145, 225, 244, 496n, 507, 559-561, 568,
    625
Behrman, Jere R., 309n
Belli, Melvin M., 198
Benham, Lee, 637n
Benston, George J., 422n
Bentham, Jeremy, 20n
Besen, Stanley M., 360n
Bishop, William, 65n, 117n, 244
Black, Donald J., 24n
Black, Fischer, 426
Black, Hugo, 586
Blackstone, William, 30n, 145, 211n
Blair, Roger D., 296
Block, Michael K., 212n

Blum, Walter J., 476
Blume, Lawrence, 50n
Bothwell, James L., 394n
Bradford, David F., 340
Bradley, Michael, 386n, 390n
Brams, Marvin, 146
Brandeis, Louis D., 272, 590-592
Brealey, R. A., 414n, 426
Breen, Dennis A., 495n
Brennan, Geoffrey, 476
Breyer, Stephen G., 317n, 340, 363
Brown, Charles, 309n
Bruce, Christopher J., 188n, 190n
Brudney, Victor, 367n
Buchanan, James M., 24n, 224n, 333n, 476,
    507
Buchholz, Bernard, 526n

Calabresi, Guido, 19-20, 62n, 75, 186n,
    197
Caldwell, Bruce J., 17
Campbell, Thomas J., 315
Campsey, B. J., 394n
Carlton, Dennis W., 113n, 340, 401
Cheung, Steven N. S., 64n
Chirelstein, Marvin A., 367n, 453n
Chiswick, Barry R., 433n
Clark, Homer H., Jr., 127n
Clawson, Marion, 75
Clermont, Kevin M., 517n
Coase, Ronald H., 3n, 7n, 19-20, 39n, 44n,
    75, 244, 261n, 328n, 367n, 636n, 638
Coleman, Jules L., 17, 26, 229n, 494n
Combs, E. Raedene, 135n
Conant, Michael, 589n
Conard, Alfred F., 187n
Conley, Bryan C., 184n
Conn, Robert L., 394n
Cooter, Robert, 214n, 226
Cootner, Paul H., 426
Copeland, Thomas E., 427
Cragg, John G., 410n, 427
Crandall, Robert W., 358n, 363
Craswell, Richard, 100n, 363

647

SUBJECT INDEX